Examples of Citations Within the Text of a Manuscript

Single author/single citation

❑ List the author's last name followed by the date of publication.

Smith (1998) examined the effects of delayed reinforcement.

At least one experiment examining the effects of delayed reinforcement (Smith, 1998) demonstrated . . .

❑ You may also include the date as a part of the sentence.

Watson published his APA presidential address in 1913 and started a debate regarding . . .

Single author/multiple citations

❑ List the author's last name followed by the dates of the individual citations.

Smith's research (1996, 1998, 1999) demonstrates that . . .

Recent research on this topic (Smith, 1996, 1998, 1999) . . .

Two or more authors/single citation

❑ If there are two authors, list both names followed by the date of publication. Use an ampersand (&) when the citation is within the parentheses.

Allumbaugh and Hoyt (1999) examined the effectiveness of . . .

In a recent review of grief therapies (Allumbaugh & Hoyt, 1999) . . .

❑ If there are three to five names, list all the names in the first citation. On subsequent citations, list the last name of the first author followed with et al. and the date.

First citation:

Gutek, Bhappu, Liao-Trouth, and Cherry (1999) examined . . .

Recent research examining service relationships (Gutek, Bhappu, Liao-Trouth, & Cherry, 1999) . . .

Subsequent citations:

Many researchers believe that the Gutek et al. (1999) study indicated . . .

Several tests of this construct exist (Gutek et al., 1999).

❑ If there are six or more names, list only the first name followed by et al. and the date for all citations.

Multiple citations

❑ If you include several citations from different authors in the same parentheses, list the citations alphabetically by the authors' names. Separate the citations with a semicolon.

Several studies (Allen, 1980, 1981, 1985; Babcock & Wilcox, 1993; Collins & Zager, 1972) . . .

Translated work

❑ If the original work was translated into English, list the author's name, the date of the original publication, and the date of the translated publication.

Freud (1913/1952) developed the theory of screen memory.

Corporate author

❑ List the name of the organization followed by the date of publication.

Sleep disorders are a common symptom of depression (American Psychiatric Association, 1994).

Newspaper or magazine article with no author

❑ List a short version of the title followed by the date of publication.

The popular press often sensationalizes psychological research (IQ tests measure nothing, 1999).

General notes regarding citations in text

❑ Do not include an author's first name unless there are two authors with the same last name.

Jones (1999) concluded that unconscious transference does not occur. Several authors, most notably David Ross (2000) and Robert Ross (2002), found substantive errors in Jones' methodology and data analysis techniques.

BEHAVIORAL RESEARCH DESIGN AND ANALYSIS

David J. Pittenger

The University of Tennessee at Chattanooga

Boston   Burr Ridge, IL   Dubuque, IA   Madison, WI   New York
San Francisco   St. Louis   Bangkok   Bogotá   Caracas   Kuala Lumpur
Lisbon   London   Madrid   Mexico City   Milan   Montreal   New Delhi
Santiago   Seoul   Singapore   Sydney   Taipei   Toronto

McGraw-Hill Higher Education

*A Division of The **McGraw-Hill** Companies*

BEHAVIORAL RESEARCH DESIGN AND ANALYSIS

Published by McGraw-Hill, a business unit of The McGraw-Hill Companies, Inc., 1221 Avenue of the Americas, New York, NY 10020. Copyright © 2003 by The McGraw-Hill Companies, Inc. All rights reserved. No part of this publication may be reproduced or distributed in any form or by any means, or stored in a database or retrieval system, without the prior written consent of The McGraw-Hill Companies, Inc., including, but not limited to, in any network or other electronic storage or transmission, or broadcast for distance learning.

Some ancillaries, including electronic and print components, may not be available to customers outside the United States.

This book is printed on acid-free paper.

1 2 3 4 5 6 7 8 9 0 DOC/DOC 0 9 8 7 6 5 4 3 2

ISBN   0-07-233310-3

Vice president and editor-in-chief: *Thalia Dorwick*
Publisher: *Ken King*
Project manager: *Christine Walker*
Production supervisor: *Enboge Chong*
Senior media technology producer: *Sean Crowley*
Design manager: *Laurie Entringer*
Cover photo: *Christie Chung*
Associate supplement producer: *Kate Boylan*
Compositor: *Interactive Composition Corporation*
Typeface: *10/12 Times Roman*
Printer: *R. R. Donnelley/Crawfordsville, IN*
On the cover: Christie Chung, PhD student from Claremont Graduate University, presents a poster of her research on memory at the Western Psychological Association 2002 convention.

Library of Congress Cataloging-in-Publication Data

Pittenger, David J.
    Behavioral research design and analysis / David J. Pittenger.-- 1st ed.
      p. cm.
    Includes bibliographical references and index.
    ISBN 0-07-233310-3 (alk. paper)
     1. Psychology--Research--Methodology. I. Title.
    BF76.5 .P58 2003
    150'.7'2--dc21

                            2002010355

www.mhhe.com

ABOUT THE AUTHOR

David J. Pittenger is Professor and Head of the Department of Psychology at The University of Tennessee at Chattanooga. He is a Fellow of the American Psychological Association and an active member of the Society for the Teaching of Psychology. His primary research interests and publications focus on the partial reinforcement extinction effect, psychometric properties of personality inventories, the coping strategies of caregivers, and ethical issues related to the behavioral sciences. David received his undergraduate degree in psychology from The College of Wooster, and his MS and PhD degrees from Texas A & M University and The University of Georgia, respectively. Before moving to Chattanooga, David chaired the Department of Psychology at Marietta College, in southeastern Ohio. In 1988, he received the Early-Career Teaching Award from the Society for the Teaching of Psychology, and in 1998 became a McCoy Teaching Fellow at Marietta College. David is also a coauthor of *Fundamentals of Behavioral Statistics* and *Statistics Tutor*.

To my wife, Denise, who has, by example, taught me to enjoy the moment and to worry less about the future, which I cannot control.

CONTENTS

Chapter 7   Creating and Using Tests, Surveys, and Objective Measures   181

Chapter 8   Correlation Statistics: Their Use and Interpretation   212

Chapter 9   Research Design I: Between-Subjects Designs   243

PREFACE

The pursuit of knowledge requires no justification.

—David J. Pittenger

PHILOSOPHY FOR WRITING THIS BOOK

For those of us who teach research methods, one of the most gratifying experiences is watching students develop a passion for conducting research. These students discover that they can convert their natural curiosity about behavior into testable hypotheses. Moreover, they learn that studying research methodology is not arcane and irrelevant. Indeed, they come to appreciate the fundamental value and importance of empirical research. Because the vitality of psychology depends upon the passion to learn more about behavior, I believe that a course in research methods is one of the most important courses that any student can take. Therefore, I attempted to write a textbook that would be attractive to students and share with them my enthusiasm for psychological research. To reach my goal I strove to incorporate several features in my book.

STYLE

I wanted to write a textbook using an editorial style that is inviting for the reader. Therefore, I gladly adopted the role as the active narrator in order to make the textbook as engaging and interesting as possible. Although there is a clear conversational style to the text, there is no lack of rigor. Throughout the text, I provide comprehensive accounts of psychologists' best ideas and research methods.

EXAMPLES

Another strategy that I took was the selection of familiar and contemporary examples. I based many of my examples on well-known phenomena in psychology and on current research that examines interesting phenomena. Specifically, I selected research conducted on topics including sexism, the spread of HIV, and the effectiveness of psychotherapy. My goal in selecting these examples was to illustrate important topics covered in the chapter and to show how researchers use research tools to answer complex and important questions.

ASSUMPTIONS

Those familiar with parametric statistics know that they come with many mathematical strings attached. If the researcher cannot ensure that the data and the design of the data collection methods meet these basic assumptions, then the inferences derived from the statistical analysis may be suspect. In some cases, the statistic is extremely robust to violations of its assumptions. Other statistics fail to withstand even minor deviations from the requirements. As I began to write this book, I soon realized that I must establish my foundation assumptions and let the reader beware.

The first assumption is that the student using this book will have completed at least a general introduction to statistics course. Consequently, the book does not introduce the reader to every statistical concept, especially the more basic concepts such as measures of central tendency, measures of dispersion, or standard scores. Nonetheless, many students seem to forget much after completing the final exam of their statistics course. This unfortunate phenomenon may reflect that a single course in statistics is not sufficient to develop in students a sufficiently stalwart schema to ensure more efficient and durable encoding and retrieval of material. Therefore, this text does review critical statistical concepts as they relate to specific methodological techniques.

The second assumption for writing the book is that the faculty teaching the course work within the liberal arts branch of their college or university. This assumption is dear to me as I believe that the liberal arts perspective and philosophy of education remains the best preparation for the next generation of educated citizens. Following this assumption allowed me to incorporate discussions that extend beyond the scope of data collection and analysis. I attempted to incorporate discussion from history and philosophy where they supplement my goals. Consequently, my review of research ethics incorporates a discussion of Jeremy Bentham, John Stuart Mill, and Immanuel Kant. One cannot have a reasonable debate of ethical issues without first acknowledging the perspectives that these great thinkers provided.

A text should challenge students beyond their current ability. If education is not to extend the grasp of our students, then what is an education for? Thus, while I labored to write as clearly as I could, I also labored to ensure that I challenged students to extend beyond the bounds of their comfort and present to them the tools needed to understand contemporary behavioral research. In doing so, I hope that the instructor recognizes that he or she is not bound to teach every chapter or every topic in each chapter. Instead, I assume that both student and instructor will recognize that the book is a resource from which to draw information.

INTEGRATION OF RESEARCH METHODS AND STATISTICAL CONCEPTS

After teaching a "traditional" research methods course for several years, I found that many of my students started the course with only a vague notion of how the statistics they had studied in the prerequisite statistics course related to research design. Over time, I found myself teaching concepts related to statistical analysis along with traditional concepts related to research methods. Indeed, a careful review of statistical techniques requires discussion of research methodology. Similarly, discussions of research design require a review of statistical principles.

Therefore, I decided to write *Behavioral Research Design and Analysis* to present my experiences teaching this important course. In writing the book, I wanted to ensure that students receive a comprehensive and detailed review of the best techniques for studying behavior. Consequently, each chapter provides a comprehensive review of research methods and the statistical concepts that support them. The review of the statistical principles, while comprehensive, is conceptual and nontechnical. Students who have completed a course in statistics will find these sections to be a useful review of important topics. Students who have not studied statistics will find these sections a suitable and readable introduction to these topics.

For example, the review of sampling procedures examines the different methods researchers use to create representative samples and demonstrates how the central limit theorem allows one to make valid inferences using sample statistics. Other topics receive attention throughout the book. One of these themes is statistical power. Because of the importance of this concept, reviews of statistical power occur in many parts of the book. The goal is to show students that they can control power by adjusting sample size and by gaining control over specific types of variance—increasing variance due to the independent variable and decreasing variance due to random or sampling error.

ORDER OF CHAPTERS

I arranged the sequence of chapters to match the steps in conducting research. Consequently, the first few chapters present the history of research in psychology and an overview of various research methods. Subsequent chapters review such topics as bibliographic research, the ethics of research, and methods for generating samples. The next set of chapters reviews how to create reliable and valid measurement instruments. Thus, there are separate chapters on creating tests and using correlation statistics to evaluate the reliability and validity of any measurement. The lessons learned in these chapters set the stage for all types of psychological research. The subsequent chapters examine the issues and steps common to all single-factor and multifactor studies, as well as single-subject and nonexperimental methods. The final chapter reviews how to prepare a paper that follows the editorial guidelines of the American Psychological Association. Instructors will find that they can rearrange the order of the chapters without a loss of continuity, however.

PEDAGOGY

Each chapter uses multiple methods to present the material, including clearly written text, familiar and interesting examples, and visual illustrations to help the reader understand complex and abstract concepts. The specific pedagogical features include:

- **Active Learning:** Each chapter includes case studies and critical thinking exercises. The goal of these exercises is to help the reader apply critical concepts to a research scenario. For example, the student may read an abstract that describes how a researcher collected the data. Following the abstract are a series of questions to determine whether the reader can recognize the type of research design used to collect the data and whether there was any confounding of the independent variables. Other exercises ask the reader to consider how one could use a specific experimental design to solve a research problem.
- **Achievement Checks:** Each chapter contains several achievement checks, which consist of a series of questions that require the reader to apply the material to objective problems. These questions require more than rote memorization because they ask the reader to apply the material.
- **Multiple Presentations of Concepts:** Throughout the book, the reader will find a combination of text, pictures, and examples to illustrate various concepts.
- **Glossary:** Each chapter contains definitions of important terms.
- **Statistical Tables:** The first appendix contains a comprehensive list of commonly used statistical tables.

ACKNOWLEDGMENTS

Although I am the author of the book, I cannot claim that what you will read is my work alone. Many people have had a hand in helping me write this text. These people have earned my deepest admiration and continued thanks.

I am grateful to my editor, Ken King, who has guided me through the jungle better known as the publishing world. Many reviewers read and commented on preliminary drafts of this book. The job of a reviewer is to scold the author for making mistakes and to offer praise only when deserved. The reviewers did their job well. Their comments were often humbling because I had failed to describe something as clearly and accurately as possible. Similarly, their comments flattered me when they found parts of the book that they liked. Consequently, the book you are about to read very much reflects their supportive criticism. By listing their names here, I offer them my sincere thanks.

Gordon A. Allen
Miami University

Phillip J. Best
Miami University

Dorothee Dietrich
Hamline University

Catherine Evans
Drake University

Gerald L. Frincke
California State University, Sacramento

Jeanette M. Gassaway
Michigan State University

Robert Hamm
Virginia Commonwealth University

William D. Hopkins
Berry College

Dena Hulbert
Chapman University

Pamela S. Hunt
College of William and Mary

Lene Arnett Jensen
Catholic University of America

Mark A. Krause
University of Texas

Sharon E. Lovell
James Madison University

Shana Pack
Kentucky Wesleyan College

Blaine F. Peden
University of Wisconsin—Eau Claire

Flip Phillips
Skidmore College

Rhonda Reid
University of Wyoming

Laura Thompson
New Mexico State University

Theresa K. Vescio
Penn State University

Alexander von Eye
Michigan State University

Jacqueline R. Wall
University of Indianapolis

Heidi A. Wayment
Northern Arizona University

Jeffrey N. Weatherly
University of North Dakota

Toni G. Wegner
University of Virginia

Countless professionals working at McGraw-Hill also deserve my sincere thanks. Specifically, I want to thank the production staff of McGraw-Hill (Christine Walker, Laurie Entringer, and Enboge Chong) who helped me convert my manuscript into its final form.

1 PSYCHOLOGY, THE SCIENCE OF BEHAVIOR

The whole of science is nothing more than a refinement of everyday thinking.

—Albert Einstein

INTRODUCTION

Hello. I am David Pittenger, the author of your textbook. I know it is strange to have the author speak directly to you. In most cases, authors are the passive narrators who tell you about the unfolding events in the book and rarely emerge from the shadows to reveal their character. Although I will soon adopt that role, I would like to take some time to tell you about myself.

I fell in love with psychology in high school when I took a general psychology course. When I entered college I decided to be a psychology major. More specifically, I wanted to be a clinical psychologist. I imagined that I would sit in my office, listen to clients tell me their problems, and then dispense helpful advice. All I needed to do was learn how to do therapy; or so I thought.

During my first term at college, I took three courses: a freshman orientation seminar, an introduction to philosophy, and an introduction to psychology. From the first day, the psychology instructor emphasized that psychology is a science and that we would learn how psychologists use the scientific method to understand human behavior. What a shock! I had taken biology, chemistry, and physics in high school. These were sciences—how could anyone confuse psychology with a science? What really startled me was when the instructor told us about the major. After the introductory course, we would have to take a course in statistics and then another course in research methods. Then, in our senior year we would have to conduct a scientific study related to psychology. Math was never my favorite subject, and I had planned to dodge college-level mathematics as artfully as I could.

I began to doubt my decision to major in psychology. Was all this science stuff really for me? Was I in the right major? I wanted to help people. Why did I have to suffer through courses in statistics and research methods? Then something interesting happened.

My philosophy course surveyed great ideas in western thought. During the middle of the semester, I realized that my philosophy instructor talked about the same topics as my psychology instructor. For example, in my philosophy course we read sections from Wittgenstein's essay on the meaning of words. In the psychology course, we learned how psychologists study children's language development. I recognized then that psychologists study many of the same questions that have confronted the great thinkers throughout history.

When I began graduate school, I still wanted to be a clinical psychologist and hoped to learn how the science of psychology guided therapists to new and effective treatments. By then I was not surprised to learn that my coursework included statistics and research methods. Even the courses in clinical psychology emphasized how psychologists use research to determine the effectiveness of different therapies.

When I finished my master's degree, I worked in a residential psychiatric hospital as a counselor. I was a member of a treatment team and offered group and individual therapy under the direction of the ward's psychiatrist. Although I enjoyed my job, I noticed that something was missing. How did we know that our therapy worked? Our clients got better; but did their improvement reflect our efforts, or did they just get better? Other questions nagged at me. Why, for example, do people continue to do something that they agreed was self-destructive? Why was a specific treatment useful for one client but not another? When I shared my questions with a former professor, his response was, "David, you are asking questions like an experimental psychologist. You want to understand what causes behavior. Go back to graduate school and follow your interests." I did. I returned to graduate school where I studied the foundations of psychology—learning, memory, and the physiological basis of behavior, and I am now a professor of psychology teaching the courses that I once dreaded.

RATIONALE FOR THIS COURSE

What are some of the lessons that you can learn from this account of my career? First, you should never make predictions, especially about the future. I would have never believed that I would become a professor of psychology and teach courses in statistics and research methods. Life offers countless unexpected opportunities. The best way to capitalize on these opportunities is to be well prepared. As I look back, I feel fortunate that my college required me to take many different courses and to develop many intellectual skills. Therefore, I hope that you do not see this course as a dreaded experience that you have to get out of the way and will come to see that much of what you learn in this course is relevant for any career you wish to pursue.

A second lesson is that statistics and research methods are the foundation of psychology. Chances are that you recently completed an introductory psychology course in which you learned about the biological basis of behavior, learning and memory, child development, personality, social psychology, and abnormal behavior. What you learned came from research. Although there are many ways to study the human condition, most psychologists prefer the perspective provided by the scientific method. Statistics and research methods are the most commonly required courses in undergraduate and graduate psychology degree programs. Therefore, to understand psychology you will need to study its main tool, the scientific method.

THE ROLE OF SCIENCE IN EVERYDAY LIFE

H. G. Wells, the 19th century author, predicted that, "Statistical thinking will one day be as necessary for effective citizenship as the ability to read and write." I believe that this prediction has come true.

Although you may not plan to become a researcher, obtain an advanced degree in psychology, or follow a career in the social sciences, you will still confront questions that have their answers in scientific research. Consider the following questions.

- What effect does child care have on child development?
- What are the best ways to prevent drug abuse?
- Are treatment programs for drug and alcohol abuse effective?

- Will a specific test accurately predict how well a person will do on a job?
- Will this new drug cure multiple sclerosis?
- What is the best way to present new information to a large group of people?

These are clear and direct questions that anyone could ask. Will you send your children to day care? If you do, what will you look for in the program? As a parent, what should you do to discourage your children from using illegal drugs? If you have a management position, should you use personality tests to predict who will be a good employee? Although you may not be a professional psychologist, you may have to confront these questions.

Many disciplines rely on the scientific method and the results of empirical research. For example, in a landmark legal case (*Daubert v. Merrell Dow Pharmaceuticals, Inc.,* 1993) the Supreme Court ruled that judges, not the jury, must determine the merits and scientific validity of testimony given by expert witnesses. In response to the court's decision, the Federal Judicial Center wrote the book *Reference Manual on Scientific Evidence* (1994) to help judges and lawyers understand the principles of research methods and statistics. As the authors of the book noted,

> no longer can judges . . . rely on their common sense and experience in evaluating the testimony of many experts. . . . The challenge the justice system faces is to adapt its process to enable the participants to deal with this kind of evidence fairly and efficiently and to render informed decisions. (p. 1)

THE FAR SIDE   By GARY LARSON

Math phobic's nightmare

FIGURE 1.1
Many people dread mathematics and statistics, as illustrated in this cartoon. There is little to fear, however. Statistics and research methods are important topics that you can master. (*THE FAR SIDE © 1990 FARWORKS, INC. Used by permission. All rights reserved.*)

As Wells predicted, the knowledge of the scientific method is now a vital part of our government and judicial system and therefore our everyday lives.

There may also be cases where you will have to collect and analyze data. Many psychology majors want to work in some form of counseling or social service agency. Clinical psychology and counseling are extremely dependent upon the scientific method. Giving a psychological test and interviewing a client are forms of data collection. A psychological test is a specialized statistical tool. To understand the results of the test, you will need to understand basic statistical principles.

Many clinical psychologists must also conduct outcomes assessment research to evaluate the effectiveness of the treatment they provide (Ogles, Lambert, & Masters, 1996). Insurance companies, for example, want to be sure that psychotherapy is cost effective. Therefore, mental health agencies routinely collect data to demonstrate the effectiveness of their therapies. Given the importance of outcomes assessment techniques, these agencies are always looking for employees who can help collect and interpret useful data.

If you fear statistics and research methods, you are not alone (see Figure 1.1). Many people seem to detest mathematics and statistics because they do not understand the relevance or importance of these topics. Nothing could be farther from the truth. As you will learn in this course, understanding statistics and learning how to conduct scientific research is an invaluable skill that you will be able to use the rest of your life.

BRIEF HISTORY OF THE SCIENCE OF PSYCHOLOGY

Before we take a step forward to examine how we incorporate science within psychology, we should first take a step back and review the history of science. Why study the history of science? The best answer, I believe, is that the past is prologue. To understand where we are, we need to understand where we have been.

Psychology is a young science. Many historians set the start of experimental psychology in 1879 when the German philosophy professor, Wilhelm Wundt (1832–1920), created his psychology laboratory in Leipzig, Germany. Although psychology is a young discipline, it has a long past. As the famous German psychologist, Hermann Ebbinghaus (1850–1909) noted, "psychology has a long past, but only a short history." (1910, p. 9)

Ebbinghaus's observation seems to be a paradox; how can a science with a short history have a long past? The answer is that psychology has been the focus of much discussion, speculation, and debate for centuries. We know that the Greek philosophers wrote extensively about many familiar topics including learning, language, memory, and dreams. Although many writers and great thinkers wrote about how they thought the mind works, none conducted anything that we would call an experiment. The problem is that the mental events are difficult to observe and measure. Consequently, many philosophers believed that we cannot observe or measure mental events the same way that we observe or measure physical objects.

The Greek philosophers had a profound effect on the generations of scholars who followed them. For many centuries, students and scholars believed that the writings of Aristotle, Galen, and Plato were infallible. By the 16th and 17th centuries, however, some people began to question the authority of the Greek philosophers as having the final word. This questioning of authority started the scientific revolution.

The scientific revolution was just that, a revolution. Seventeenth century scientists decided that there was more to learn about nature than was contained in the books of the ancient philosophers. One of the more articulate spokespersons for the new scientific revolution was Francis Bacon.

Francis Bacon

Francis Bacon (1561–1626) was not a scientist. For the majority of his life, he participated in British politics. He was interested, however, in the developments of empirical science and became one of its more effective proponents. In 1620 he published a book on the scientific method titled *Novum Organum* ("the new instrument"). Bacon saw the scientific method as a better way to answer questions. Like many of his contemporaries, Bacon distrusted the wholesale belief in everything that the ancient philosophers had to say. He (Bacon, 1620/1994) wrote,

> For the ancients . . . out of a few examples and particulars, with the addition of common notions and perhaps some portion of the most popular received opinions, they flew to the most general conclusions or principles of the sciences . . . through intermediate propositions, they extracted and proved inferior conclusions. (p. 127)

In essence, Bacon accused the earlier philosophers of making hasty generalizations that have little or no merit. He also argued that to comprehend the physical world, we must use the scientific method to ask and answer questions. Perhaps Bacon's most important contribution to the history of science was his discussion of human tendencies, or biases, that often cause us to make irrational decisions or ignore important information.

According to Bacon, there are four human tendencies he called idols, which hinder our ability to think clearly. The four idols are The Idols of the Tribe, The Idols of the Cave, The Idols of the Marketplace, and The Idols of the Theatre. Bacon's observations were insightful for the time and are as accurate now as they were in 1620. We use research methods, statistics, and critical analysis to overcome the obstacles created by each of the idols.

Idols of the Tribe

The first source of bias Bacon described is what he called the **Idols of the Tribe.** Bacon recognized that we too often depend on our intuitions and common sense to reach conclusions. To quote Bacon (1620/1994),

> The *Idols of the Tribe* lie deep in human nature itself and . . . it is wrongly asserted that the human sense is the measure of all things. It is rather the case that all our perceptions . . . are reflections of man [*sic*][1] not of the universe, and the human understanding is like an uneven mirror that cannot reflect truly the rays from objects, but distorts and corrupts the nature of things by mingling its own nature with it. (p. 56)

---

[1]Bacon's use of the term "man" is sexist by contemporary editorial standards. Men *and* women have minds and can think. Current editorial style guides, such as the one prepared by the American Psychological Association, tell authors to use gender neutral terms such as "people."

Bacon recognized that many people have a tendency to believe that what they see and how they interpret events is accurate, and that their common sense is well informed and infallible. Thus, we selectively perceive events around us, trust our first impressions, and then uncritically use those impressions to make decisions. One example of the Idols of the Tribe is the **self-fulfilling prophecy.**

The self-fulfilling prophecy describes the fact that when we believe something is true, we have a tendency to act in ways that causes what we expected to come true (Baron, Graziano, & Stangor, 1991). In most cases, we are unaware of how our attitudes affect our behavior. Moreover, when we believe something to be true, we tend to remember events that agree with our beliefs and forget or ignore events that disagree with our beliefs. At the heart of the problem is that our preconceived ideas have considerable influence on how we interpret and react to different situations.

Many psychologists (e.g., Nisbett & Ross, 1980; Rosnow & Rosenthal, 1997) have examined the shortcoming of human decision making. The consensus among researchers is that humans tend to rely too much on intuition and common sense to make decisions. An example is the **gambler's fallacy.** If I toss a coin three times in a row and get heads each time, most people believe that the fourth toss of the coin *must* be tails. Some people will argue, "It makes *good common sense* that you cannot have four heads tossed in a row!" However, the probability that I will get heads on the next toss is constant—50%. Many people make the error because they trust their intuition and preconceived beliefs about probability; that is a sure way to loose a lot of money at the gambling tables.

In summary, the Idols of the Tribe refer to the human tendency to depend too much on common sense and that we have a tendency to make consistent errors in logical reasoning.

Idols of the Cave

The **Idols of the Cave** describe the effects of culture, common practice, and education. According to Bacon, our life experiences shape how we look at things. Although our experiences are valuable, there are important limitations. As Bacon (1620/1994) described them,

> The *Idols of the Cave* arise from the individual's particular nature, both of mind and body, and come also from education, habits and by chance. Though there are many different kinds, I cite those which call for the greatest caution, and which do most to pollute clear understanding. (p. 61)

The problem with personal experience is that it is personal. Consider you, the reader and me, the author. As I write this book, I am a 40-something white male. I grew up on a small farm in rural northeastern Ohio. Chances are that your background and mine are much different. Who is to say which of us has a more valid worldview? Each of us experienced different important events in our lives. These events shape our beliefs and perceptions and affect how we perceive things. Although these beliefs and perceptions make us unique, we need to recognize their effect on our decision making and reasoning.

Karl Popper (1902–1994), a famous philosopher, provided an interesting example of depending too much on personal experience. Early in his career, Popper worked with the psychotherapist, Alfred Adler, who had developed a comprehensive theory of personality development based on his clinical experiences. Popper (1963) described the following episode:

> Once . . . I reported to him [Adler] a case which to me did not seem particularly Adlerian, but he found no difficulty in analyzing in terms of his theory of inferiority feelings, although he had not even seen the child. Slightly shocked, I asked him how he could be so sure. "Because of my

thousand fold experience," he replied; whereupon I could not help saying: "And with this new case, I suppose, your experience has become thousand-and-one fold." (p. 35)

Popper went on to describe the philosophical problems he had with Adler's comment. The problem relevant to our discussion is Adler's use of personal experience. That Adler was a professional psychoanalyst does not mean that his experiences are automatically valid. A moment's thought will reveal the limitation of personal experience. Adler was a therapist and treated people suffering various psychological problems. His patients were hardly representative of the general population, and, therefore, not the foundation for a comprehensive theory of personality development that describes all people.

The Idols of the Cave refer to the fact that we too often depend upon our personal experiences to determine why things happen as they do. As we will soon see, we must do more than merely rely upon personal experience to develop scientific explanations.

Idols of the Market-place

The next bias that Bacon examined is our use of language. Bacon described this as the **Idols of the Market-place.** Turning to Bacon (1620/1994) we read,

> "The *Idols of the Market-place* [*sic*] are the most troublesome of all; these are idols that have crept into the understanding through the alliance of words and names." (p. 64)

Bacon recognized that our use of words shape how we think about things. Consider an example related to day care for children. Scarr, Phillips, and McCartney (1990) noted that during the 1950s and 1960s developmental psychologists who studied the effect of child care examined the effects of *maternal absence* or *maternal deprivation.* Clearly, these emotionally charged phrases create a negative bias against women who choose to pursue a career while their children are infants and toddlers. Why use these phrases as if the mother deprived her children of food and water? What about the father's absence? If children suffer *maternal deprivation,* why don't they suffer *paternal deprivation* as well? Could it be that fathers are guilt free because societal norms allow men to work outside the home? Furthermore, the words *absence* and *deprivation* evoke images of children warehoused in dangerous day-care centers. Scarr and her colleagues argued that these terms grew out of "fantasies about child development . . . mother-infant attachment . . . and the role of early experience for later development" (p. 255). These terms fell out of favor during the 1970s when the rights of women to pursue a career became popular. Researchers then began to examine the benefits of day care.

Idols of the Theatre

The last of Bacon's idols represents the effects of our education. Here we find Bacon (1620/1994) complaining that many of the things we learn may mislead us.

> The *Idols of the Theatre,* on the other hand, are not innate, nor are they secretly insulated into the understanding, but are imposed and received entirely from the fictitious tales in theories, and from wrong-headed laws of demonstration. (p. 66)

The **Idols of the Theatre** represent any explanation that people accept as true without question. In many cases, we accept certain explanations because we learned them from someone we trust or see as an authority figure. There are countless examples of such theories. A classic example is the belief that the earth is the center of the universe. Until the 17th century, many people believed that the sun revolved around the earth, and to say otherwise was blasphemy.

An example from psychology of the consequence of the Idols of the Theatre is John Garcia's research on taste aversion. Garcia (1980) described the difficulty he experienced when he attempted to publish the results of an experiment he conducted. His experiments on taste aversion revealed that several well-established principles of classical conditioning were not accurate. Unfortunately, many psychologists did not accept Garcia's conclusions because the results contradicted the prevailing theories of classical conditioning. Garcia found it difficult to publish his papers in scholarly journals, and many reviewers ridiculed his work. In retrospect, Garcia's research has had a monumental effect on our understanding of classical conditioning principles.

The defining characteristic of the Idols of the Theatre is our acceptance of the truth of a statement without criticism. This problem arises whenever we passively accept something as true simply because others tell us that it is true. As you will learn, the best defense against the Idols of the Theatre is to think critically about what someone is asking you to believe.

Bacon's legacy

Bacon's primary legacy is that he clearly identified the obstacles to critical thinking as they apply to science even today. Although the scientific method has been around for 400 years, the effects of his idols remain. Each of us can fall prey to the idols. Studying Bacon will help you understand why researchers use specific tactics when conducting their research. Researchers use research methods and statistics to overcome many forms of bias. By studying Bacon, you will learn that you can never become complacent with your knowledge. The lesson we can learn from Bacon is that the Idols of the Tribe, Cave, Market-place, and Theatre are always present, and we guard against these biases whenever we attempt to study and explain the behavior of people. Take some time to review Table 1.1 and think of examples of Bacon's idols.

Gustav T. Fechner

On October 22, 1850, Gustav T. Fechner (1801–1887) invented experimental psychology by discovering a way to measure mental events. The common feature for all science is

TABLE 1.1
Review of Bacon's idols

Idols of the Tribe	Biases due to overreliance on common sense and the tendency to make errors in logical reasoning.
Idols of the Cave	Biases due to dependence on personal experience to explain why things occur the way they do.
Idols of the Market-place	Biases due to how we use specific words to describe things.
Idols of the Theatre	Biases due to uncritical acceptance of explanations that people in authority tell us are true.

measurement. Measurement is nothing more than objectively assigning numbers to observations. All sciences have specific methods for measuring the phenomena that they study. However, before October 22, 1850, psychologists had no objective method for measuring mental events.

Fechner studied physics and human perception. In his research, he observed that there was not a one-to-one relation between the intensity of a stimulus and our perception of the stimulus. For example, imagine that I ask you to hold out your hand and close your eyes. If I put a pencil on your hand, you will notice its weight. Now imagine that I put this textbook on your hand. You will feel the weight of the book. What if I then place the same pencil on top of the book? You will probably not be able to detect the additional weight. Why are you able to feel the weight of the pencil in one situation but not the other? Fechner reasoned that by studying the relation between changes in the intensity of a stimulus (a physical event) and changes in a person's perception (a mental event) he could study how the mind works. He then proceeded to conduct a series of famous experiments that we now recognize as the start of psychophysics.

Fechner's experiments may not sound like the most exciting thing that you learned today. Nevertheless, his work is very important because it caused people to recognize that it is possible to study mental events using empirical techniques. Soon after Fechner published his work, other researchers began to study psychological processes. For instance, upon reading Fechner's book, Hermann Ebbinghaus began to conduct his famous research on memory. It did not take long until the science of psychology became common practice.

John B. Watson

John B. Watson (1878–1958) is another important person in the history of psychology. In 1913, Watson wrote an influential paper titled "Psychology as the behaviorist views it." The paper began with the proclamation "Psychology as the behaviorist views it is a purely objective experimental branch of natural science. Its theoretical goal is the prediction and control of behavior" (p. 158). This statement seems obvious to most of us now. The chances are that one of the opening sentences in your introductory psychology textbook said much the same thing. The historical relevance of Watson's paper is that he wrote his paper at a critical moment in the history of psychology, and his comments about the purpose of psychology did much to shape how psychologists now study psychological processes (Murray, 1983).

At the start of the 20th century, psychology was a young science, and psychologists were searching for the best methods to conduct scientific research. At the time, many psychologists used a procedure known as **introspection.** Introspection means to examine or look within. Whenever you think about your thinking and mental events, you are using a form of introspection. Try this "experiment" in introspection. What reactions do you have when you read the word "mother"? Your report represents the result of your introspection.

Although introspection can be revealing, it has several shortcomings. Take a moment to think of a few. The most troubling question is, *How do we know that the self-report is accurate?* When I ask you to introspect about something, will you report everything that occurs to you? Is it possible that thinking of your mother evokes a painful memory that you do not want to share? How complete is your report? Although you may report things of which you are aware, could there be reactions that you did not recognize as important and worthy to share with others? Is it possible that there are unconscious mental processes that you do not directly experience?

Psychologists' use of introspection troubled Watson because there is no way to verify the accuracy of an introspective report. The problem with introspection is that only one person can *experience or observe* your mental events—you. In science, researchers want to examine phenomena that others can see when they use the same procedures.

There are other problems with introspection. To what extent does your introspection influence the mental events you wish to study? Does thinking about your thinking affect your thinking? Are you confused? Try another thought experiment. Can you read and introspect about the process of reading at the same time? If you are like me, reading for content while introspecting is impossible. As soon as I start examining the process of reading, I am no longer reading. When I read for content, I cannot introspect.

What are some other problems with introspection? Can you ask an infant to introspect? Can children ages 7 or 8 provide objective observations of their mental events? What about a person with depression or schizophrenia; will their introspections be accurate? If introspection requires objective and knowledgeable self-analysis, then we cannot use introspection to study children, people with severe psychological disorders, or animals.

Watson (1913) rejected introspection as a research tool and recommended that psychologists study behavior exclusively. He believed that by focusing on behavior, psychologists could engage in the objective study of all living creatures. For Watson, if you can observe the behavior then you can conduct scientific research.

Watson's legacy

Watson's legacy to psychology is that he focused our attention on behavior. Most contemporary psychologists subscribe to **methodological behaviorism,** a philosophical stance evolving from Watson's beliefs. Methodological behaviorism suggests that psychologists should study overt and observable behaviors as the primary focus of their research. Psychologists use observable behaviors to make inferences about the emotional, cognitive, and other mental processes that occur within a person.

As you will learn in this and other psychology courses, behavior is the focal point of psychological research. A developmental psychologist examining the memory of infants will conduct experiments that examine the infants' behavior. A social psychologist examining altruism examines behavior. A clinical psychologist who studies depression also examines behavior. Following Fechner's and Watson's lead, we use the observable behavior of individuals to make inferences about various mental or cognitive events.

ACHIEVEMENT CHECK
(1) Describe an area of psychology that you find most interesting. How does the scientific method help researchers better understand this area of psychology?
(2) Psychology is not the only discipline that examines human behavior. The authors of many great novels write about the human condition and use their stories to describe why people behave as they do. Describe the difference in perspective between a psychologist and the author of a novel.
(3) Many people believe that professional athletes have moments when they are "in the zone," during which their performance is greatly enhanced. There are also times when the athlete will be "in a slump." By contrast, statisticians argue that these phases do not exist and are

nothing more than random events. Which of Bacon's four idols best describes the belief that athletes are in the zone or in a slump?

(4) You want to buy a new car. A friend of yours, an auto mechanic, says, "Stay away from that car, my shop is always filled with them. I plan to send my kids through college on the work that model makes for me." How does this example relate to Bacon's Idols of the Cave?

(5) Imagine that Gustav Fechner and John Watson are alive and meet for a conversation. In what ways would they agree that psychology is a science?

(6) Describe the meaning of introspection and why Watson objected to its use in psychology.

(7) Jean Piaget was a famous psychologist who studied the cognitive and intellectual development of children. For much of his research, he asked children of different ages to solve logical problems. Can we consider Piaget to have followed the perspective of methodological behaviorism?

WHAT IS SCIENCE?

Science is a way of thinking and explaining the world around us. Science consists of the methods for collecting, analyzing, and drawing conclusions from data. We call this process the scientific method. Much of the scientific method evolved to overcome and protect us from the idols that Bacon (1620/1994) described in *Novum Organum*.

Research methods and statistics are complementary techniques that we use to acquire information and reach reasonable conclusions. When we speak of research methods, we refer to procedures for collecting information. When we speak of statistics, we refer to procedures for organizing, summarizing, and making inferences from the data. Before proceeding, however, we should look more closely at the assumptions of any science and the fundamental characteristics of scientific research.

Assumptions of All Sciences

All sciences make the same basic assumptions about their subject matter. Psychologists, like other scientists, take these assumptions to be true and use them to justify their use of the scientific method to study behavior.

Behavior is determined

Our first assumption is, perhaps, the most important. Psychologists believe that there are specific causes for each of our behaviors. The name for this perspective is **determinism.** A determinist believes that everything that happens has a cause or set of causes. As you study more psychology, you will learn that almost all psychologists are determinists of one form or another.

Sigmund Freud (1856–1939), for example, was a psychical determinist because he believed that human behavior reflected a series of unconscious drives and motivations. He believed that there are no accidents of behavior—everything we do reveals something about our character and unconscious drives. By contrast, B. F. Skinner (1904–1990) was an environmental determinist because he believed that an individual's interaction with the environment produces changes in behavior. Other psychologists are biological determinists because they believe that biological processes control many behaviors. Finally, some psychologists are sociocultural determinists because they believe that cultural traditions, customs, and regulations control people's lives. When you study different areas of psychology, such as child development, social behavior, abnormal behavior, or psychophysiology, you will find that psychologists in each area conduct research to find the things that determine behavior. Regardless of their perspective, each type of determinist believes that by observing behavior and the surrounding conditions we can infer the causes of the behavior.

Some people object to determinism and suggest that human behavior is subject to **free will.** The principle of free will states that a person's soul or mind controls how he or she acts. Many religious faiths and philosophical schools of thought teach that humans are special because we have a spirit and self-awareness that guides us through life. These religions also teach us that we have the freedom to choose between the good and virtuous or the evil and sinister.

There is quite a contrast between determinism and free will. Belief in determinism holds that we can explain observable behaviors by looking for and examining material causes. By contrast, belief in free will holds that each person is unique and that we cannot use the scientific method to understand human behavior.

It is not helpful to cast determinism and free will as an either-or decision that you have to make. If you are willing to accept that people share some basic characteristics, then you will find that the scientific method does a good job of finding the causes of those behaviors.

Science does not have all the answers to important questions. Science, religion, philosophy, literature, and the arts are ways of knowing and experiencing our world. Each answers a unique set of questions using a different perspective. As Gould (1999) noted, science and religion are two ways of knowing, both equally important and both answer different questions. The perspective of science allows us to understand how things work. For psychology, we try to discover why we do the things we do. The perspective of religion allows us to examine our values and discover how we should behave. For many people, science and religion are not competing forces, but are methods for answering different important questions.

We can measure the critical variables

The second assumption that we will consider is the belief that we can directly or indirectly observe the important causes of behavior. All sciences rest on a foundation of measurement. Fechner's insights allowed psychology to become a science because he realized that we could use a person's behavior to make inferences about mental events. Physicists, chemists, and other scientists routinely use observable events to make inferences about the existence of things that they cannot directly observe. For example, no one has seen gravity, only its effects. Nevertheless, physicists can use the motion of the planets and stars to infer that there is gravity and to describe its effects. Psychologists follow the same logic. We study behavior events to make inferences about mental events that we cannot directly observe.

WHAT IS SCIENTIFIC RESEARCH?

Thus far, our review of research has been broad. In the following section I will examine the specific characteristics that make research scientific.

Empirical Analysis

Empirical analysis means to use observation and experimentation to learn. In the sciences, we use our ability to observe events as the foundation of knowledge. In other words, everything that we know within a scientific discipline comes from direct experience. Contrast this method with other ways of knowing.

Mathematicians, for example, do not use empirical analysis. They discover new ideas using deduction and formal proofs. Here is an example of the difference between the empirical method of knowing and the mathematical way of knowing. Imagine that you have 10 quarters in your hand and toss them in the air. What is the probability of obtaining 0, 1, 2, 3, . . . or 10 heads? There are two ways of finding the answer.

The first method is empirical. You would toss the 10 coins, count the heads, and then repeat these steps several thousand times until you had enough samples to make a relatively accurate conclusion about the probability of each outcome. You will eventually come to the correct answer, if you were willing to spend the hours of drudgery tossing and counting coins.

The second method uses deductive logic and analytical techniques. If you know enough about probability theory and your way around mathematical proofs, you can derive an equation that gives you the correct answer. There is nothing wrong with either method, although most people find the mathematical solution more convenient, less time consuming, and less prone to error.

There are many times, however, when the analytic method does not work and the empirical method is the only alternative. We can use mathematics to solve the coin problem because we know several critical things to be true, such as each coin has a 50% chance of landing heads. From these facts, we can derive additional truths.

The deductive method works well when we have the necessary information before us to solve a problem. In many cases we do not have this information. Consequently, we must go about gathering data so that we can answer the question. In other words, the empirical and deductive methods have their strengths and weaknesses.

The following is an example that illustrates the potential weakness of sole reliance on deductive logic.

1. All psychologists are human.
2. <u>David Pittenger is a psychologist.</u>
3. Therefore, David Pittenger is a human.

Although extremely simple, this example illustrates a categorical syllogism that contains two premises (Statements 1 and 2) and a conclusion (Statement 3). In deductive logic, if we accept the premises and use the appropriate rules of logic, then the conclusion is true. Now consider the deduction.

1. All unicorns are purple.
2. <u>Annie is a unicorn.</u>
3. Therefore, Annie is purple.

The conclusion about Annie's color is logically consistent if we accept the premises. This example illustrates a potential problem with finding answers by deductive logic or pure reason. If we accept the premises of an argument, then we must accept the truth of logically consistent conclusions. In the example of the unicorn, the conclusion is valid although it has no bearing in truth—unless you can find a living purple unicorn. Bacon, and many others, recognized that deductive logic can lead to erroneous conclusions based on a false or unproven premise. Consequently, scientists attempt to verify the truth of premises through empirical analysis. In other words, if we can obtain observable evidence that unicorns exist and are purple, then we can conclude that Annie is purple.

Another characteristic of empirical analysis is measurement. As I noted previously, measurement is a defining characteristic of any science. Without measurement, there can be no science.

Measurement is converting observation into numbers. There are different types of measurement. In some cases, we use our primary senses to collect information; we watch, we listen, we touch, we smell, and we taste. In other cases, we use tools to do the measurement for us.

Public Verification

Public verification is another important feature of empirical research. Using the empirical method means that we rely on our senses. Using public verification means that we measure things in such a way that others can experience the same thing. Therefore, public verification implies that anyone who uses the same procedure should be able to observe the same general outcome. Watson (1913) emphasized this requirement of science when he called for all psychologists to drop introspection and adopt the study of behavior. Studying your mind is fine, but you are the only one who can directly experience your thoughts. Therefore, your mental events are not subject to public verification. Your behavior and actions are, however, something that we can observe. We can videotape you as you talk with a friend or a stranger. Using the videotape, anyone can observe your gestures, facial expressions, and listen to what you say in the conversation. We can also attach sensors to your body and monitor your heart rate, the sweat on your palms, and the electrical activity of your brain. We can give you a personality test as a way to measure how you perceive yourself. In each case, we have collected public information that others verify.

Public verification also means that anyone with the appropriate equipment can repeat an experiment. This facet of public verification is extremely important. Our ability to repeat experiments gives us greater confidence in the generality of the results. The more times we can repeat an experiment and obtain similar results, the more likely we are to agree that the effect is real and not a fluke.

Systematic Observation

Systematic observation refers to the way we go about collecting information. Whenever we collect data, we want to make our observations under various conditions and attempt to rule out alternative explanations. Imagine that a psychotherapist claims that a new form of therapy helps depressed people. Although this claim sounds great, we need to determine its truth. We can do this using systematic observation. For example, we should determine if the treatment produces better results than no treatment or a placebo treatment. To do this study, we would have depressed people receive no treatment, a placebo treatment, and the new therapy. In this example, the systematic observation means that we measure changes in people's depression under different treatment conditions.

Another way that we can use systematic observation is to compare the new therapy to current psychotherapies. For this type of research, we want to determine whether the therapy is in some way better than other forms of therapy. Yet another way to use systematic observation is to determine if the therapy works better with some people than others. Thus, we would conduct studies comparing the differences among men and women; children, adults, and the elderly; or people who are or are not taking antidepressant medication.

The goal of systematic observation is to examine the phenomenon under as many relevant situations as possible. We continue to repeat the experiments to determine which conditions produce the effect and determine whether other factors affect the phenomenon. Unfortunately, many people do not recognize the importance and necessity of systematic observation, and tend to accept testimonials without question. Can you explain why a testimonial is an example of the Idols of the Cave and the Idols of the Theatre?

Testimonials are not a form of systematic observation, although many people treat them as such. Watch an infomercial on the television and you will hear many testimonials given by legions of happy customers. The typical testimonial goes something like, "My life was really going nowhere fast until I enrolled in Research Methods. Now I'm 'the king of the world!' " Testimonials are nothing more than an example of Bacon's Idols of the Theatre. When people make a claim like this, we are supposed to believe what they say. Testimonials are also an example of the Idols of the Cave because they reflect personal experience. Researchers shy away from testimonial claims because they are neither systematic nor objective. Can you explain why?

Control of the Environment

In all forms of research, we attempt **control of environment** in some way. We do this to ensure that the conditions of our observation are consistent. Researchers have the greatest level of control when they conduct research in a laboratory setting because they can control many or all of the environmental conditions. This control over the environment helps us determine which factors affect the subject's behavior.

There are, however, many cases when the researcher cannot directly control the environment. For example, in field studies, the researcher collects data in the natural environment of the subject. Even for this research, the researcher will attempt to ensure that the environment is the same each time he or she collects the data.

Rational Explanation

A **rational explanation** refers to the two basic assumptions of science that behavior is determined and follows a lawful pattern. Rational explanations of behavior, therefore, include two essential components. The first component is that the explanation refers only to causes that one can observe or confirm through public verification. The second component is that the explanation makes a clear and logical link between the cause and effect.

Some people offer explanations that are not rational and, therefore, are not scientific explanations. We call these **pseudoexplanations** because they sound like sophisticated explanations when they are not. Two common names for pseudoexplanations are the **nominal fallacy** and the **circular** or **tautological explanation.** Understand and recognize pseudoexplanations for what they are, another example of Bacon's Idols of the Tribe. As you will see, pseudoexplanations tend to appeal to our want for a common sense explanation. Unfortunately, the explanations are attractive and often taken at face value without careful examination.

Pseudoexplanations are typically circular. In other words, the explanation uses the phenomenon to define itself. Here is an example from the history of psychology to illustrate a circular or tautological explanation. A typical early definition of a reinforcer was, *a stimulus, produced by a behavior, that increases the probability that the individual will repeat the behavior.* Figure 1.2 demonstrates why this explanation is circular. In the diagram, there is no independent definition of the reinforcer. The definition uses the effect of reinforcement to define the property of reinforcement. Why is this technique a problem? Consider the following exchange.

Question: "What is a reinforcer?"
Answer: "A reinforcer is anything that increases the probability of a behavior."
Question: "How do we know that something is a reinforcer?"
Answer: "Because it increased the probability of a behavior."
Question: "Why did the probability of the behavior increase?"
Answer: "Because we used a reinforcer."

Figure 1.2 illustrates the circular nature of the definition of reinforcement. The problem with this cycle is that we have no way of defining the reinforcer without referring to the behavior it affects. In other words, this type of definition tells us nothing about why a reinforcer works. Using the definition of reinforcement does not allow us to predict what things will be effective reinforcement. Furthermore, the definition says nothing about why some things are good reinforcers and other things are not good reinforcers. Finally, the definition does not explain why a reinforcer will increase the probability of reinforcement. These are important problems.

Fortunately, David Premack (1959, 1965) developed what we now call the Premack principle. Premack discovered that high-frequency behaviors can reinforce low-frequency behaviors. The advantage of Premack's definition of reinforcement is that it breaks the circular definition. Using this definition, we can predict what will and will not serve as a successful reinforcer.

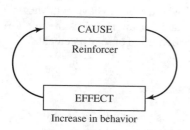

FIGURE 1.2
A pseudoexplanation. In a circular definition the effect defines the cause, and there is no independent definition of the cause.

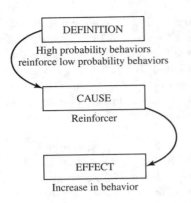

FIGURE 1.3

An explanation without a tautology. The cause can be defined independent of its influence on the effect.

Figure 1.3 illustrates how Premack's theory broke the tautology. His theory defines the cause independent of the effect. Specifically, Premack's theory states that any high-frequency voluntary behavior will reinforce a low-frequency voluntary behavior. In other words, the definition of the cause is independent of the effect. This is an important step because we can now predict what will and will not be a reinforcer. According to this definition of reinforcement, we can take several behaviors and categorically predict which will and will not be reinforcers.

Consider this example. "For Alex, playing video games is a high-frequency behavior and studying math is a low-frequency behavior. Therefore, playing video games will serve as a reinforcer for studying math." We can then verify the truth of the statement with an empirical test by allowing Alex to play video games only if he spends more time studying math. When we ask why there was an increase in the time spent studying math (the effect), we can say that the reinforcement caused the change. When we ask how we know that the video game is a reinforcer, we then say that it is a high-frequency behavior.

Another feature of a rational explanation is that a researcher can empirically test and determine whether the explanation is correct. What if I told you that there is a special energy force the affects the brains of some people and causes them to be schizophrenic? The first question you should ask for is the empirical evidence. What if I told you that no known apparatus can detect the radiation? There is no way to verify the existence of the radiation, so you should conclude that I have offered a pseudoexplanation.

When we can objectively define the cause, then we can objectively and systematically test the accuracy of specific predictions of hypotheses. Once Premack discovered a way to objectively define reinforcement, other researchers were able to verify the accuracy of his theory of reinforcement. Indeed, many researchers have tested the accuracy of the Premack principle. Some researchers have verified Premack's predictions, whereas others have not (Mazur, 1998). Using the results of these experiments, Timberlake and Allison (1974) were able to refine Premack's definition and offer a more comprehensive definition of reinforcement.

Parsimonious Explanation

In addition to being rational, we strive to make explanations parsimonious. **Parsimony** refers to simplicity. An explanation is parsimonious if it makes relatively few assumptions, does not refer to unobservable causes, and refers to specific causes. This requirement is also know as **Occam's razor.**

Consider an example from the history of psychology. For a long time, psychologists who followed Freud believed that schizophrenia resulted from severe conflict within a person's unconscious. According to this perspective, schizophrenia developed in response to psychological abnormalities in the person's development. Many psychologists now believe that much of schizophrenia reflects imbalances in various neurotransmitters in the brain.

The biological account of schizophrenia is more parsimonious than Freud's because of the number of assumptions and unobservable constructs that each theory uses. Freud's theory depends on a large number of interpsychic processes (e.g., id, ego, and superego) as well as a host of other conditions such as the "schizophrenicgenic mother." Psychologists cannot measure these constructs objectively. By contrast, the biological theory is relatively parsimonious because its states that schizophrenia results from imbalances in specific neurotransmitters. Researchers can measure these neurotransmitters and regulate them with medication. Furthermore, regulation of these neurotransmitters corresponds with changes in a person's schizophrenic symptoms.

There are several points that I should make clear about parsimonious explanations. Simplicity does not automatically make a theory correct. Our knowledge of schizophrenia has not evolved to the point where we are ready to pronounce the biological theory correct merely because it is more parsimonious than the Freudian theory. Rather, the advantage of the biological theory is that it makes specific predictions that researchers can directly test. Its value to science is its ability to generate many ideas for specific research projects.

Tentative Explanations

Whenever a researcher presents the results of a study, the explanation of the results is **tentative.** No single study can account for all the potential explanations of the results. You can think of an individual study as a small step in a long journey. Although each step may take us closer to our goal, it may also take us in the wrong direction.

Consider the biological theory of schizophrenia. Although the theory is useful, it is not complete. Researchers recognize that schizophrenia is a complex set of behaviors that requires careful analysis. Although the neurotransmitter theory is useful, psychologists who study schizophrenia continue to look for additional explanations of this disorder.

As you read more about psychology, you will learn that researchers are continually revising their explanations for why things work the way they do. The change occurs because each study adds new information. Some of the new information confirms what we already know and we continue to use the theory to explain the phenomenon we study. Some of the new information, however, may indicate that the theory cannot account for specific events and must be revised or replaced.

Therefore, to avoid the Idols of the Theatre that Bacon (1620/1994) described, psychologists recognize that explanations of behavior are as good as the data they have collected. Researchers recognize that as new data are collected, they may have to revise their explanations or develop new explanations.

Now that we have reviewed the general tenants of experimental psychology, we can look at a practical application of research methods in psychology. The following example illustrates the errors that people can make when they do not use the scientific method to examine a problem. In addition, the example shows how the scientific method can resolve a serious controversy.

RESEARCH IN ACTION: THE CASE OF FACILITATED COMMUNICATION

Autism is a distressing condition. Children with autism are withdrawn and do not show normal signs of social or cognitive development. Raising an autistic child is challenging because the child requires exceptional patience and much attention. Although there are many treatments for autism, these programs are time consuming and expensive.

Several years ago, a new procedure called facilitated communication became popular among people who treat autism. The theory behind facilitated communication is that people who have autism have unique mental barriers blocking their normal communication (Biklen, 1990). According to Biklen, a person with autism can communicate with the help of a trained facilitator. The person with autism uses a keyboard to type messages. The facilitator helps by holding the autistic person's hand or arm. Biklen believed that the physical contact of the facilitation helps the autistic person focus his or her thoughts and express them through the keyboard. Although the facilitator holds the client's hand or arm, they claim that they do not influence what the child types.

Facilitated communication quickly became a popular treatment for people with autism. Many therapists attended seminars where they learned to become certified facilitators. Several schools and residential facilities incorporated facilitated communication into the treatment programs for their clients. Those who used facilitated communication often gave vivid and emotional testimonials of how facilitated communication was a godsend. Parents discovered that after many agonizing years they could finally communicate with their children. Teachers discovered that their autistic students were bright and talented people. By all accounts, facilitated communication appeared to break through the barriers of autism and liberate the person within.

Although facilitated communication appeared to be a phenomenal treatment for autism, several researchers were skeptical (e.g., Hudson, Melita, & Arnold, 1993; Montee, Miltenberger, & Wittrock, 1995; Moore, Donovan, & Hudson, 1993; Wheeler, Jacobson, Paglieri, & Schwartz, 1993). These skeptics began to ask critical questions regarding the claims about facilitated communication and suggested the need for controlled experiments to determine whether facilitated communication worked.

Why is skepticism important in science? Sometimes skeptics seem to be more of a nuisance than anything. Skeptics seem to ask questions for the sake of asking questions and dismiss what seems to be a good thing. Despite these characterizations, skepticism is essential in science as it helps to ensure that we are not tricked into believing in something that is not true.

Why was it important to test the claims of facilitated communication especially if the children seemed to benefit from the treatment and the parents and teachers thought that the treatment worked? How would you go about determining whether facilitated communication allowed the child to communicate through the facilitator? How would you show that it was not the facilitator typing the child's responses?

Facilitated communication appeared to work and showed that people with autism were bright individuals and could interact with others. The problem is that perception can be deceiving. Just because people with autism appeared to communicate does not mean that the treatment worked as advertised. The skeptics argued that facilitated communication needed to be tested under controlled conditions to rule out alternative explanations. Anytime that we find that a treatment works, we need to ensure that the improvement results from the unique characteristics of the treatment and not other conditions.

Montee et al. (1995) conducted an experiment in which the facilitator and the autistic person sat at a table. On the table was a large T-shaped screen that kept the facilitator and the autistic person from seeing what the other saw. The researcher showed both people pictures and asked the persons with autism to type what they had seen. The facilitator then helped with the typing as they normally would. As an example, the researcher might show both people a photograph of a cat. We would expect that the autistic person would indicate that he or she had seen a cat or at least an animal. The real test came when each person saw a different photograph. For example, the facilitator may see a picture of a car and the person with autism may see a picture of a hamburger. Remember that the facilitator did not see the same picture that the autistic person saw and visa versa. The results of this test are critical. If the person with autism indicated that he or she saw a hamburger, a sandwich, food, or lunch, we would have evidence that the facilitated communication worked. However, if the person said that they saw a car, we must conclude that the person doing the typing was the facilitator, not the person with autism.

The results of these experiments were clear; the person doing the typing was the facilitator, not the person with autism. When the researcher presented different pictures, the response always corresponded with what the facilitator saw, not what the client saw. Montee et al. (1995) replicated the findings of many other studies that examined the validity of facilitated communication. These experiments used different pairs of facilitators and clients, different pictures, and different techniques for presenting the pictures. The results were the same, however. There was no convincing evidence that facilitated communication worked to help people with autism. Consequently, facilitated communication has lost favor among professionals in the field.

One of the most important lessons to be learned from this example is the importance of skepticism and empirical research. We cannot always take the results we receive at face value. At first glance, facilitated communication seemed to be a great intervention, and many people were quick to adopt the new treatment as a way of solving a long-standing problem. What would have happened if no one intervened and questioned the value of facilitated communication? How much money would people have paid for a treatment that did not work? How long would people with autism be deprived of treatment programs that do work? Empirical skepticism determined the limitations of facilitated communication.

ACHIEVEMENT CHECK

(8) Use the example of facilitated communication to explain why we cannot depend upon testimonials to evaluate an empirical claim.

(9) Using the example of facilitated communication, show how researchers used (a) empirical analysis, (b) public verification, (c) systematic observation, and (d) control of the environment to question the validity of facilitated communication.

Use the following scenario to answer questions 10 and 11: Imagine that your friend believes that he has psychic powers. He claims that he can often guess what another person is thinking. Two of your other friends agree and claim that there have been several times when your friend has shown his psychic abilities. Given this information, respond to the following questions:

(10) Why would you want to use empirical methods to confirm your friend's psychic abilities? Why not rely upon the testimonials of your friends who are being honest when they say that your friend is psychic?

(11) Your friend agrees to a test. You create a list of randomly selected common words. As you concentrate on the word, your friend tries to read your mind. He failed the test and was unable to guess any of the words. To explain the failure, he says, "Well you see, it only works when there is no doubt of my ability. You doubt my ability and that creates negative energy that blocks my ability to read minds." Based on what you read in this chapter, comment on your friend's reaction.

(12) According to the text, what are the essential elements of scientific research? Describe how psychologists incorporate these in their research.

(13) Contentment is a mental phenomenon that we cannot directly observe; yet it is a common experience. Describe how a psychologist might measure contentment and make it an observable phenomenon.

(14) A therapist claims that he has developed a new therapy to treat aggressive children. You find several children who received the new therapy, but still start fights with other children. The therapist states that the therapy only works when the child really wants to change his or her behavior. Comment on the therapist's reaction.

(15) Why is public verification especially important for the science of psychology?

(16) In an interview, a reporter asked a government official to explain why an accused computer hacker had broken into the government's high security computers. The official replied, "The accused has an antisocial personality." Comment on the value of this response.

(17) Would psychology exist as a science if there were no measurement? Defend your answer.

CHAPTER SUMMARY

This chapter introduced you to research methods by briefly examining the history of science within psychology and by offering an overview of the meaning of scientific research. The goal of this chapter was to illustrate that studying research methods is an important component of any student's education, especially students in the behavioral sciences.

Empirical science and research methods are a part of contemporary psychology. Psychologists use the scientific method to conduct basic research to understand various behavioral phenomena. Research methods also have many practical applications. Many people, regardless of their career, need to understand the foundations of science and research methods.

Francis Bacon was an early advocate of empirical science. He believed that the scientific method would overcome several human tendencies that are obstacles to a better understanding of our world. He called these tendencies idols and identified four specific idols. The four idols are: 1. Idols of the Tribe (common modes of thought that lead to irrational conclusions), 2. Idols of the Cave (overreliance on personal experiences), 3. Idols of the Market-place (biases in beliefs based on the meaning and use of words), and 4. Idols of the Theatre (biased thought based on tradition, habit, or deference to authority).

We credit Gustav T. Fechner as the first experimental psychologist because on October 22, 1850, he recognized that researchers could indirectly observe or make inferences about mental events by observing reactions to physical stimuli.

John Watson's contribution to psychology was his insistence that behavior is the subject matter of all psychology and that introspection is not a useful procedure for science. Although most psychologists rejected several of Watson's extreme views, they do agree that the objective study of behavior allows them to understand behavioral and cognitive phenomena. Therefore, most psychologists are methodological behaviorists.

Psychologists believe that they can use the scientific method to study behavioral and cognitive phenomena. They base this belief on three assumptions: 1. the behavior they study is determined by specific causes, 2. there is a lawful or regular relation between specific causes and specific behaviors, and 3. they can objectively observe the relevant causes and reactions.

Scientific research, regardless of the discipline, has several general characteristics: 1. Empirical analysis is the process of learning through observation and experimentation and through quantifying observations. 2. Public verification requires that we conduct research that can be repeated by others and specifically that the variables we examine can be observed by everyone. 3. The systematic observation criterion requires us to make our observations under various conditions or settings. 4. Control of environment refers to our ability to conduct our research under consistent conditions.

When researchers explain various phenomena, they attempt to make their explanations rational, parsimonious, and tentative. The rational explanation means the terms are clearly defined and can be independently assessed and defined. The explanations are also parsimonious, which means they are specific, make few assumptions, and generate many testable ideas. Pseudoexplanations, by contrast, are circular in definition and cannot be directly or objectively assessed. Finally, explanations are tentative. Researchers recognize that their explanations must be revised in the face of additional research.

In the last section of the chapter, we examined the case of facilitated communication. This example illustrates what can happen if we casually and uncritically accept claims about human behavior. The example also illustrates how empirical research can demonstrate the value of a therapy.

CHAPTER GLOSSARY FOR REVIEW

Control of Environment   A feature of empirical research. The researcher attempts to observe the phenomenon under identical conditions. The term also implies that the researcher reduces the effects of distracting or nuisance conditions that will add confusion to the data.

Determinism   A philosophical stance that states that natural events and human behavior are the result of an orderly sequence of preceding events that can be predicted using fundamental scientific laws.

Empirical Analysis   Using observation and research methods to find the answer to questions.

Free Will   A philosophical stance that human behavior is independent of external causes and that humans are free to choose how they will act.

Gambler's Fallacy   An example of the Idols of the Tribe. The fallacy is a belief that random events follow a predetermined pattern. For example, many people believe that for six tosses of a fair coin, the pattern THHTHT is more likely than TTTHHH; both are equally likely.

Idols of the Cave   Bacon's phrase to describe the tendency to use one's personal experience as the foundation for truth or the measure of all things.

Idols of the Market-place   Bacon's phrase to describe how our use of words shape our perception of and reaction to things.

Idols of the Theatre   Bacon's phrase to describe the tendency to accept a theory or statement as fact and fail to question its accuracy or generality.

Idols of the Tribe   Bacon's concept to describe common errors in humans' thinking. These errors of thought are present, to varying extents, in all people and include overreliance on common sense and logical errors of reasoning.

Introspection   A process by which one attempts to analyze his or her conscious experiences.

Measurement   The process of converting observations to numbers using a set of rules.

Methodological Behaviorism   The belief that psychologists should study observable behaviors to conduct scientific research in psychology. By observing the conditions under which behavior occurs, one can then infer the causes of the behavior or the presence of mental processes that cannot be directly observed.

Nominal Fallacy   An example of a pseudoexplanation that makes the erroneous assumption that naming a phenomenon is the same as explaining the phenomenon.

Occam's Razor   A version of parsimony that requires that we do not create more distinctions among things than is necessary.

Parsimonious Explanation   A requirement in science that we offer explanations that make the fewest assumptions and require reference to few or no unobservable phenomenon.

Pseudoexplanations   An explanation of a phenomenon that does not really explain the phenomenon.

Public Verification   The requirement that the subject matter of any empirical research must be observable to any person who uses the same procedures and equipment to examine the phenomenon.

Rational Explanation   Offering a description or explanation of a phenomenon that follows the rules of logic.

Self-fulfilling Prophecy   An example of the Idols of the Tribe. People will act in ways that bring about the result they expected.

Systematic Observation   A process where the researcher varies the conditions under which he or she studies the phenomenon.

Tautological Explanation   A form of pseudoexplanation that uses circular definitions. In a circular definition the explanation uses the phenomenon to be described to define its cause.

Tentative Explanation   The recognition that all descriptions and explanations that arise from empirical research may be incomplete or inaccurate. Additional research may force us to revise our beliefs.

Testimonial   A statement that a person makes about the truth of a fact or a claim based on personal experience.

2 THE FOUNDATIONS OF RESEARCH

CHAPTER OUTLINE

- ✦ Introduction
- ✦ The Hypothesis in Research
- ✦ Types of Hypotheses
- ✦ Measurement
- ✦ Reliability of Measurement
- ✦ Validity of Measurement
- ✦ Determining Validity
- ✦ Populations and Samples

Science knows only one commandment—contribute to science.

—Bertold Brecht

INTRODUCTION

Psychologists look for patterns of behavior and then try to explain them. You may recall reading about the famous child psychologist, Jean Piaget (1896–1980). Piaget spent his career studying the cognitive development of children. He observed that children between the ages of 2 and 7 years (the preoperational period) think differently than children 13 and older (the formal operations period). After much careful systematic empirical observation, Piaget concluded that there are interesting similarities within these age groups and important differences among these groups. He then used these data to develop an innovative theory that revolutionized the study of child development.

This chapter will introduce you to many of the basic concepts that form the foundation of the material presented in this book. We will begin by examining the research **hypothesis.** The hypothesis is important in all research because it determines the type of data that the researcher will collect, the research methods used to collect the data, and the statistical procedures used to analyze the data. In addition to studying different types of research hypotheses, we will examine how researchers collect data to verify or confirm the hypothesis. Finally, we will turn our attention to gathering data from the population and review how samples of data allow us to make inferences about the population.

THE HYPOTHESIS IN RESEARCH

What is a hypothesis? If you are like most people, you will say, "A hypothesis is an educated guess." Although it is technically correct, that definition misses the true purpose and role of the hypothesis in research. Therefore, set that definition aside for one that offers a bit more information.

Highlight the following sentence—it is important. *A hypothesis is a prediction about the relation among two or more variables based on a theory or on previous research.* I realize your definition was shorter and easier to remember, but mine offers a better description of how researchers use a hypothesis.

Hypotheses Come from Theory or Previous Research

The common definition of a hypothesis says that it is an "educated guess." Where did this education come from? Is a hypothesis a guess such as, "Guess a number between 1 and 10?" Most research hypotheses do not come out of thin air, nor are they wild guesses. There are two general sources for the hypothesis, previous research and theories.

In chapter 1 I noted that replication serves an important role in all research. The more we repeat an experiment, especially under different conditions, and obtain similar results, the greater confidence we have in the finding. Consider the effects of positive reinforcement on behavior. Whether the research examined humans or nonhumans, adults or children, or people with profound emotional and behavioral disorders, the results come out the same: People repeat behaviors that produce positive reinforcement. Therefore, if you want to study positive reinforcement, then you will use the results of previous research to frame the hypothesis for your study. When you write a hypothesis you are saying, "If the results of previous research are consistent, then when I conduct my study, I should obtain similar results."

In many cases, we can deduce or derive a hypothesis from a theory. What is a theory? A **theory** is a broad set of general statements and claims that allows us to explain and predict various events. Here is an example of a simple theory from which we can derive several hypotheses: *Aggression and violence are learned behaviors.* This theory explains why people behave violently. Using this simple theory, we can also create several hypotheses. For example:

- Children who watch television programs with aggressive themes will be more aggressive than children who watch television programs with nonaggressive themes.
- Children whose parents use punishment (e.g., spanking) will be more aggressive than children whose parents use other parenting techniques.
- Children taught to use conflict resolution techniques will be less likely to be aggressive.

You can easily add your hypotheses to this list by using the theory to make predictions about the link between learning and aggression. Therefore, our ability to confirm or refute each hypothesis will help us evaluate the overall accuracy of the theory.

Figure 2.1 represents the interrelation between previous research, theory, and the research hypothesis. The figure also illustrates that the results of a study serve as the foundation for additional research as well as a test of the theory. As a generality, research hypotheses designed to test the predictions of a theory represent **confirmatory research** because the researcher plans to use the data to evaluate the validity of a theory.

One of the many virtues of a hypothesis is that it helps protect us from the Idols of the Theatre, the uncritical acceptance of theories. Bacon (1620/1994) warned us not to accept a theory merely because it sounds correct, is popular, often repeated, or presented by an authority. Rather, we should determine if we can empirically verify the hypotheses derived from the theory. Most researchers will support a theory as long as it generates interesting

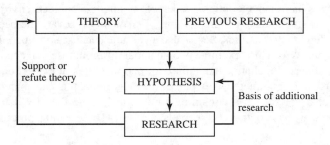

FIGURE 2.1
A diagram of the role of theory, hypothesis, and research. The individual research hypothesis is the product of theory, previous research, or both. For confirmatory research, the data derived from a study can influence a theory as well as serve as the guide for additional research. For exploratory research, the results of a study may inspire additional research.

and empirically testable hypotheses. Researchers begin to doubt a theory when the data do not confirm its predictions or when someone offers a different theory that accounts for the same phenomenon as well as new and unexpected findings.

Not all research is confirmatory, however. Much research in psychology and the other sciences is **exploratory research.** Exploratory research need not be guided by theory, merely the want to investigate an interesting phenomenon. Bacon (1620/1994) advocated the collection of empirical data from many diverse sources and suggested that data collection should be free of preconceived notions in order to avoid the Idols of the Cave, the willingness to depend on personal experience to understand things. Systematic observation forces us to expand our experiences by collecting much data under widely different conditions.

Many psychologists share Bacon's perspective on exploratory research. For example, in 1949, Skinner wrote a paper in which he asked the question "Are theories necessary?" His answer was "No!" Skinner argued that empirical research is valuable whether or not the researcher wants to confirm a theory. As an example, most people are familiar with Pavlov's (1927) research on the conditioned reflex. What many people forget is that Pavlov used classical conditioning to test his theories of how the brain worked. (The title of one of his more influential texts was *Conditioned Reflexes: An Investigation of the Physiological Activity of the Cerebral Cortex.*) Although we now know that Pavlov's theories of the brain are not accurate, his data are still useful and illuminating. Researchers who study classical conditioning still refer to Pavlov's data as illustrations of various conditioning phenomena.

The importance of exploratory research is one that must be emphasized—the goal of any science is to examine and better understand the relation among variables. Conducting research allows us to accumulate knowledge that, in turn, helps us develop new and important insights into the interesting questions that we ask.

Hypotheses Direct Our Observations

When we prepare a hypothesis, we focus our attention on the type of information that we will study. Specifically, the hypothesis identifies the variables that we will examine and the data we will collect.

A **variable** is any characteristic of a person, nonhuman subject, environment, or research condition that can have different values. Personality is a variable because different people have different personalities. Sex is also a variable because some people are men and others are women. We can also examine people under different research conditions. We can vary the heat of the room, change the number of people sitting at a desk, or adjust the difficulty of the task to be completed. Any part of the experiment that can change is a variable. The opposite of a variable is a **constant,** a numerical value that, by definition, cannot change. A minute always contains 60 seconds, $\pi = 3.1416\ldots$, and a pint of water weighs 16 ounces.

An empirical hypothesis will generally state the relation between two or more variables. Consider the hypotheses listed on page 29 and illustrated in Figure 2.2. In each case, the hypothesis states that changes in one variable correspond with changes in another variable. On the left side of the illustration is the variable that we believe allows us to predict or account for the second variable. In these examples, we want to find the variables that allow us to explain or predict levels of aggression.

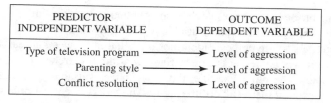

PREDICTOR INDEPENDENT VARIABLE	OUTCOME DEPENDENT VARIABLE
Type of television program ⟶	Level of aggression
Parenting style ⟶	Level of aggression
Conflict resolution ⟶	Level of aggression

FIGURE 2.2
The relation between variables described in a hypothesis.

In most research, there are two types of variables, the dependent variable and the independent variable. The **dependent variable** is the focus of the study and is the condition that the researcher wants to explain, describe, and predict. As an example, the first hypothesis in Figure 2.2 states that some children are more aggressive because they watch more violent television programs than children who are not aggressive.

The other variable in the hypothesis is the **independent variable.** In the hypothesis, we use the independent variable to explain, describe, and predict the dependent variable. As you will soon learn, different types of research have different types of independent variables.

In some cases, the researcher can control or manipulate the levels of the independent variable. We call these **manipulated independent variables** because the researcher can manipulate or control the variable and because the status of the variable is independent of, or not affected by, other variables in the study. For example, we might conduct an experiment where the researcher has children watch several hours of violent-theme cartoons and the other children watch several hours of nonviolent cartoons. Because the researcher controlled what type of cartoon the children saw, we would call the variable a manipulated independent variable.

Another type independent variable is the **subject variable.** The subject variable is a condition that the researcher cannot manipulate or control, but may use as an independent variable. As a rule, if a condition exists for a person before the start of the research, it is most likely a subject variable. Personality, sex, intelligence, height, weight, and age are examples of subject variables. When people participate in a research project, they bring unique characteristics to the study. Although researchers cannot change a subject variable, they can still use it to describe and predict the dependent variable.

Consider the content of television programs that children watch. We could treat this variable—content of programs—as either a manipulated independent variable or a subject variable. How would we know whether television programming is a manipulated independent or subject variable? The answer to that question comes from examining the control that the researcher has over the variable.

First, imagine that a researcher can control the television programs that the children watch. The researcher can have some children watch violent shows and others watch nonviolent shows. Because the researcher has direct control over the child's television experiences, the variable is a manipulated independent variable.

Now imagine a researcher who has no control over what the children watch. The researcher can, however, monitor what each child watches. Some children may choose to watch programs with violence whereas other children may select programs that have a nonviolent content. Because the researcher cannot control what the children watch, but can record their viewing preferences, the variable is a subject variable.

In summary, a good hypothesis identifies the relation between at least two variables. One of these variables is the dependent variable that the researcher hopes to explain, describe, and predict. The other variable, the independent variable, is the one that the researcher uses to explain the results of the study. The independent variable will be either a manipulated variable or a subject variable.

Hypotheses Describe the Relation Among Variables

Finding the orderly relation among variables is the goal of any science. Thus, one of the most important components of a hypothesis is that it describes the relation that we expect to observe between the variables. When we prepare a hypothesis, we use different verb phrases to describe the relation between the independent and dependent variables. For example, we can state that when one variable increases, the other variable will also increase: *Children who watch more violence on television will be more likely to act aggressively*. We can also predict that an increase in one variable will lead to a decrease in the other variable: *Children who learn conflict resolution skills will be less likely to act aggressively*. The purpose of all research, regardless of its form or type, is to find and describe a relation among variables. Therefore, you will learn about many research methods and statistical techniques that allow us to describe the relation between the variables.

Hypotheses Refer to Populations

Most hypotheses are general statements about the relation among variables in a population. The hypothesis, *Children who watch television programs with aggressive themes will be more aggressive than children who watch television programs with nonaggressive themes,* implies that the relation between aggression and television programming is a universal statement applying to all children. Stated from a different perspective, if this hypothesis is correct, we will observe the relation between aggression and television programming for any sample of children.

Populations and samples are familiar terms. We often talk about the population of the United States or the population of a city. Similarly, we often hear the word "sample" in day-to-day language. When I walk through the grocery store, I often see a salesperson offering me a sample of a convenience food. The company marketing the food hopes that my experience with the bite-sized sample will compel me to buy their product. For the most part, the conventional use of these terms is similar to their technical uses. There are, however, several points that we need to make clear.

Technically, a **population** is a group of people or things that share one or more characteristics. In some cases, the definition of a population will be broad and inclusive. A social psychologist, for example, may believe that altruism is a general characteristic of all people. Therefore, he or she hopes that the results of an experiment on altruism will generalize to all people. In other cases the population will be much more specific, as when psychologists study children within a specific age range (e.g., infants less than 6 month of age), or people diagnosed with a specific psychological condition (e.g., depression with psychotic features).

A **sample** refers to a subset of the population. In most cases, when researchers speak of samples they mean a group of individuals or things that represents the population. If we assume that the sample is representative of the population, then we can assume that conclusions based on the sample will generalize to the population.

Researchers define the population using empirical characteristics. In other words, researchers use publicly verifiable characteristics to define a member of a population. The definition of a population can also be general (e.g., all children) or specific (e.g., 8- to 12-year-olds). As a generality, the more specifically we can define the population of interest, the better our ability to describe and explain the behavior we wish to study.

TYPES OF HYPOTHESES

We now need to examine different types of hypotheses. The difference among the hypotheses has to do with the predictions that the researcher wants to make. In some cases, the researcher will examine the correlation between two variables; in other cases the researcher will determine if there is a meaningful difference between two groups. The type of hypothesis that a researcher uses determines the research methods that he or she will use as well as the types of conclusions the data allow. For our purposes, there are four types of hypothesis: 1. estimation of population characteristics, 2. correlation among variables, 3. differences among two or more populations, and 4. cause and effect.

Estimation of Population Characteristics

This hypothesis is the simplest of the four. Its goal is to estimate the characteristics, or parameters, of the population using the information from a sample. There are special terms we use whenever we estimate population parameters. These terms include **data, descriptive statistics,** and **parameters.** Populations are generally too large to use for our research. Therefore, we use a representative sample of the population to estimate the population parameters.

In all research, we collect data. For our purposes, the data will always be numerical and derived from objective and empirical techniques. Regardless, of the type of data collected, we assume that the data reflect the variables of interest.

Once we collect the data, we need to calculate descriptive statistics. A descriptive statistic is a number that is the result of a specific mathematical operation and that allows us to organize, summarize, and describe the data. In addition to describing the sample, we can use descriptive statistics to estimate the value of population parameters. A parameter, therefore, is a number that summarizes and describes a characteristic of a population.

As a quick summary, statistics are numbers based on direct observation and measurement and refer to the sample. Parameters are values that refer to the population. In most cases, we use statistics to estimate parameters. If the sample is representative of the population, then we can infer that what is true of the sample is also true of the population.

A common practice in research is to represent statistics using Roman letters (e.g., A, B, C, D . . .) and to represent parameters using Greek letters (e.g., α, β, χ, δ . . .). By convention, we use the letter M to represent the sample mean and the letter μ (*mu*) to represent the population mean. Another convention is to treat parameters as constants and statistics as variables. Statistics are variables because each time we take a sample from the population, we will select different individuals. Therefore, the data and statistics will vary from sample-to-sample. We assume, however, that the population parameter, at the time of the study, is constant.

What would a descriptive hypothesis look like? The general form for the estimation of population parameters is, *How much time does the typical 2- to 6-year-old child spend a day watching television.* In this hypothesis, we want to know the relation between a subject variable (the age group of the children) and the dependent variable (time spent watching television). Another way that we can say the same thing is to write $M \approx \mu$. This expression states that the sample mean estimates the value of the population mean. Remember that although a sample may represent the population, it is always an estimate. Our statistics are, at best, approximations, or estimates, of the corresponding population parameter.

Correlation Between Two Variables

Another useful hypothesis is to state that there is a correlation between two variables. A correlation between variables means that something links them together, and that high or low levels of one variable correspond with high or low levels of the other variable.

There is, for example, a correlation between years of education and annual income. If we collect a sample of people and ask them to tell us their level of education (high school, college, . . .) and their annual income, we will find that there is a positive correlation between education and income. People with less than a high school education tend to make the lowest annual income. By contrast, people with greater levels of education tend to earn more money.

When we hypothesize about correlations, we can predict that there will be a positive, a negative, or no correlation between the two variables. A **positive correlation** means that an increase in one variable corresponds with an increase in the other variable. The correlation between years of education and income represents a positive correlation—an increase in years of education corresponds with an increase in annual income.

By contrast, a **negative correlation** means that increases in one variable correspond with decreases in the other variable. What is your prediction about the correlation between one's golf score and time spent practicing? There is a negative correlation between the two variables. Remember that in golf, the lower the score the better. Now compare me to Tiger Woods. I play golf about once every two years. My score for an 18-hole round is usually much greater than 100. Tiger Woods, by contrast, consistently shoots an 18-hole round in the 60s. The difference is practice. Those of us who rarely play golf show our lack of practice with exceptionally high scores. People who practice the game with fervent dedication have lower scores. Therefore, more practice predicts lower scores, a negative correlation. Figure 2.3 presents three graphs that represent (a) a positive correlation, (b) no correlation, and (c) a negative correlation.

When there is **no correlation,** there is no systematic relation between the two variables. There is no correlation, for example, between shoe size and intelligence. People with small feet are just as likely to be bright as people with big feet. Similarly, dull-witted people are equally likely to have small or large feet.

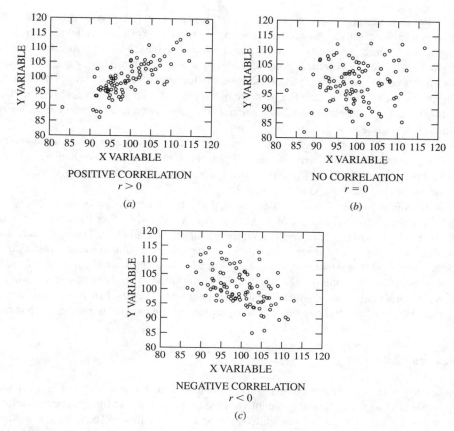

FIGURE 2.3
Three correlations: (a) a positive correlation, (b) no correlation, and (c) a negative correlation. The letter r represents the correlation for a sample. The Greek letter ρ (*rho*) represents the correlation for the population.

When we speak of a correlation between populations, we often use the parameter ρ (*rho*) to express the size of the correlation between the two variables. When we predict that there is a positive correlation between the variables, we write $\rho > 0$. When we predict that there is a negative correlation between the variables, we write $\rho < 0$. If there is no correlation, we write $\rho = 0$.

Difference Among Two or More Populations

There are many cases when we want to know if members of separate populations are different on average from each other. The independent variable may be either a manipulated independent variable or a subject variable that we use to classify the individuals as a member of separate populations. The second variable is a common dependent variable that we measure for all participants in the study. Once we have the data, we determine if there are meaningful differences among the groups. Here are two examples of this type of hypothesis.

In the first example, we use a manipulated independent variable to differentiate the groups of individuals in the research. If we were examining the effects of television violence on aggressive behavior, we might have some children watch a television show that includes many acts of violence. Another group of children would watch a television show that includes no violence. After the children watched the television show, we would observe the children and look for evidence of aggressive behavior. In this case, the content of the show is a manipulated independent variable because the researcher could control whether the children in the study watched one type of show or another.

In the second example, we use a subject variable to distinguish the individuals. For example, we may want to determine whether boys are more aggressive than girls. In this example the sex of the child, boy versus girl, is a subject variable because it is a condition that the researcher cannot control.

In both examples, we want to determine if the typical behavior of members of one group is different from members of another group. As with the other hypotheses, we use sample statistics to make inferences about the population parameters. Therefore, when we compare two groups, we compare the difference between the sample means. If the difference between the sample means is sufficiently large, we then infer that the population means are different from each other. As an example, if you wanted to predict that the mean of one group is greater than another, you would use the statement $\mu_1 > \mu_2$. In this example, μ_1 represents the mean of the first population and μ_2 represents the mean of the second population.

Cause and Effect

The last hypothesis is the most demanding hypothesis to test. For this hypothesis, we want to prove that changes in the independent variable cause changes in the dependent variable. Discussions of cause and effect can quickly become complicated and have been the subject of considerable philosophical analysis and debate. For our purposes, we will examine John Stuart Mill's (1806–1873) criterion for determining cause and effect.

Mill (1843/1986) argued that one must show three things to infer a cause and effect relationship. First, the cause must precede the effect in time. This requirement recognizes that time moves in one direction, from the past to the future. Consequently, events that occur in the past can influence future events, and it is impossible for events in the future to influence events in the past.

The second criterion for showing cause and effect is to show a correlation between two events. If we believe that the independent variable causes the dependent variable, then we should observe a consistent relation between the two variables. We can demonstrate the relation between the independent and dependent variables by examining the correlation between the two variables or by comparing the differences among group means. The difference between the groups is evidence that the independent variable is correlated with the dependent variable.

Although the first two criteria are necessary to show causation, they are not sufficient to prove cause and effect. To prove cause and effect, according to Mill (1843/1986), we need to rule out or exclude all other explanations. This third criterion is difficult to achieve because it is often difficult to account for all possible explanations except for the one implied in the hypothesis.

TABLE 2.1
Features of the four general hypotheses used in empirical research

Type of hypothesis	Purpose of research	Example of mathematical hypothesis	Example of written hypothesis
Estimate parameter	Use sample statistics to estimate population parameters	$M \approx \mu$	What is the average score of fifth grade students taking a reading comprehension test?
Correlation between variables	Measure two variables to determine their correlation	$\rho > 0$ or $\rho < 0$	There is a positive correlation between time spent studying and exam grade.
Difference among populations	Comparison of two representative groups to determine if they are different	$\mu_1 > \mu_2$ or $\mu_1 < \mu_2$	Men, on average, are taller than women.
Cause and effect	Determine if the independent variable causes differences in the dependent variable	$IV \rightarrow DV$	High levels of dopamine cause schizophrenia.

In chapter 3, we will survey some of the research techniques we can use to test cause and effect hypotheses. Recognize now that all the other hypotheses describe the population parameter and the general relation between the two variables; they do not allow us to infer cause and effect.

When we conduct research to examine cause and effect, we still examine the correlation between the variables and compare the differences among groups. Therefore, we will still determine whether $\mu_1 > \mu_2$. If we find that this statement is correct and the experiment meets the criteria for determining cause and effect, we can then infer that the independent variable caused the dependent variable, or $IV \rightarrow DV$. The arrow ($\rightarrow$) indicates that changes in the independent variable caused changes in the dependent variable.

Table 2.1 presents a summary of the four types of hypotheses. Be sure that you understand the similarities and differences among the four.

ACHIEVEMENT CHECK

(1) Describe the differences between a theory and a hypothesis.
(2) Consider each of the following statements and determine whether they meet the criteria for a hypothesis.
　(a) It is not good to spank children.
　(b) Students should spend more time studying and less time playing video games.
　(c) Intelligence is an inherited trait.
　(d) To avoid cognitive dissonance, people will change their attitudes to match their behavior.
　(e) People in an ambiguous situation will be more likely to conform with other members of a group.
　(f) People with low self-esteem will not be as likely to volunteer for extra credit projects.
(3) Jackie is interested in students' perception of their faculty. Her college uses a standard faculty evaluation form that asks students a series of questions regarding their performance in the course and their evaluation of the instructor's effectiveness. Jackie

asks the dean if there is a relation between the students' expected course grade and instructor evaluations.

    (a) Rewrite Jackie's question as a hypothesis.

    (b) What is the independent variable?

    (c) Is the independent variable a subject or a manipulated independent variable?

    (d) What is the dependent variable?

(4) Tim wants to replicate a finding first reported by Chase and Simon (1973). First, Tim finds 30 good chess players and another 30 people who rarely play the game. For the study, he shows the participants 10 photographs of chess pieces on a chessboard. For half the pictures, the chess pieces are randomly arranged on the board. The other pictures represent the chess pieces as they would appear midway through a game. Tim shows each participant a photograph for 30 seconds. After a 10-second pause, Tim then asks the participant to recreate the arrangement of the chess pieces on a chessboard. Tim then records the accuracy of the reconstruction.

    (a) What hypothesis or hypotheses do you believe that Tim can test with this research? State these in your words.

    (b) What are the independent variables?

    (c) For each independent variable, determine whether it is a manipulated independent variable or subject variable.

    (d) What is the dependent variable?

(5) Carlos administers two tests to 500 adults (250 men and 250 women). The first test is a standard measure of empathy. The second test is a measure of the personality construct, self-monitoring.

    (a) What hypothesis or hypotheses do you believe that Carlos can test with this research? State these in your words.

    (b) What are the independent variables?

    (c) For each independent variable, determine whether it is a manipulated independent variable or subject variable.

    (d) What is the dependent variable?

(6) Rebbecca conducted a study that examined how people react to different types of feedback. Sixty people volunteered to participate in the study. During the first part of the study, Rebbecca asked all the participants to solve a series of logical problems. Rebbecca told a random half of the participants, *You must be really smart; you did much better than average on this test.* She told the other participants, *You must have tried hard; you did much better than average on this test.* Rebbecca than gave all the participants another set of problems that contained items that could not be solved. She timed how long the participants spent on the impossible-to-solve items.

    (a) What hypothesis do you believe that Rebbecca tested with this research? State the hypothesis in your words.

    (b) What is the independent variable?

    (c) Is the independent variable a subject or a manipulated independent variable?

    (d) What is the dependent variable?

MEASUREMENT

At the heart of all science is measurement. Measurement allows researchers to do many things. First, it is a special form of empirical observation. Measurement allows us to record and quantify our observations in an objective and consistent manner. Therefore, measurement is a means to an end that allows us to answer the question, *What do we have?*

Second, measurement, when done correctly, is objective. Many people dismiss psychology as an "inexact science." This statement implies that psychology is not as good or as important as other sciences such as physics or chemistry. This attitude misses the point because objectivity, not the precision of measurement, is a defining characteristic of science. Although we strive for precision and accuracy in all measurement, our first goal is objectivity. When done correctly, measurement reduces sources of bias from our observations. This characteristic of measurement allows us to address Bacon's Idols of the Market-place, the effect that words have on our understanding of different phenomena. When we objectively define our variables, other researchers can choose to accept or reject our definition.

Third, researchers can repeat their measurements. As you recall, one criterion of all science is that we use public verification. A good measurement technique ensures that any competent person can observe the same phenomenon that another researcher has observed. Can you see how public verification protects us from the Idols of the Theatre? If any person can verify a theory, we do not have to rely on an authority to tell us what is true or false; we have the opportunity to collect the data and evaluate the results for ourselves. In this section, I will introduce you to some of the basic concepts that represent the foundation of all measurement. As you move through different chapters, we will explore special measurement issues related to the various types of research.

All forms of measurement share four essential features:

(*a*)   operational definitions,
(*b*)   measurement scale,
(*c*)   reliability, and
(*d*)   validity.

We will examine each of these features in some detail.

Operational Definition

Measurement is the process of assigning numbers to objects, situations, or observations using a rule. The **operational definition** is the rule we use to convert our observations into numbers.

Consider the following questions.

1. What is the distance between Cleveland and New York?
2. How many people voted in the last presidential election?
3. What is the appearance of a light with a primary wavelength of 684 nm?
4. How large is the working memory?
5. How proficient is Martha at algebra and plane geometry?
6. How depressed is the client seeking therapy from a psychotherapist?

What does each of the questions have in common? First, each question refers to a specific construct. In the order of the questions, the constructs are

1. distance,
2. frequency,
3. appearance,
4. capacity,

5. proficiency, and

6. severity.

Second, we can answer each question using some form of measurement that allows the researcher to collect data that answers each question. To perform the measurement, we will have to define the variable and develop an appropriate measurement technique. Operational definitions define variables by stating the objective and empirical procedures for our measurement. Consequently, creating an operational definition is a critical step in any research.

Operational definitions are different from dictionary definitions, which tend to be descriptive and imprecise. For example, a dictionary definition of "anxiety" may be, *A state of apprehension or psychic tension.* Can you see the problem with this definition? What are the observable characteristics and features of anxiety? "Apprehension" and "psychic tension" are private emotions that other people cannot directly observe. An operational definition, by contrast, refers directly to observable events open to public verification. We then use these observations to infer or describe the construct. We can examine the list of questions to create an operational definition of a construct.

Take the question about the distance between Cleveland and New York. We need a clear operational definition of distance. What, specifically, do we mean by distance? How should we measure the distance? Should we draw an imaginary straight line between the city halls of the two cities and count the number of miles? Would the mode of transportation (plane, train, boat, or automobile) affect our measurement? One could measure the length of the interstate highways connecting the two cities as a measure of distance. Once we decide upon the route we want to measure, what **metric** will we use? Should we record the distance in miles, kilometers, or time spent traveling? The point that you need to recognize is that an operational definition depends on the type of information the researcher needs to collect and how he or she will use that information.

Measuring distance is relatively straightforward. By contrast, how do we measure a variable that we cannot directly observe? We cannot directly observe many psychological variables. The capacity of working memory, proficiency for mathematics, and severity of depression are cognitive and emotional events that we cannot directly observe in other people. Yet, we want to use these variables to explain and predict behavior. How can we use variables that are not directly observable to explain behavior? The answer to the dilemma is that we use observable behaviors to infer the presence of events that we cannot directly see.

As you may recall from chapter 1, Fechner may have been the first experimental psychologist. Fechner's great insight was that we can use a person's behavior to make inferences about their mental events. In psychology, we use **intervening variables** to describe the variables that we cannot directly observe. We also use intervening variables to explain various phenomena. Consider the concept of anxiety as an example. Figure 2.4 presents an illustration of how we might use anxiety in a hypothesis and how we might operationally define anxiety.

The illustration in Figure 2.4 consists of two parts. On the right side are observable events that are open to public verification. A researcher can create a pending threat by asking a person to give a speech on an unfamiliar topic to a group of strangers. We can also measure or directly observe many reactions. With the proper physiological recording equipment, we can objectively measure the person's physiological reactions to the pending threat. Similarly, we can watch the person to see how he or she acts in this situation, and

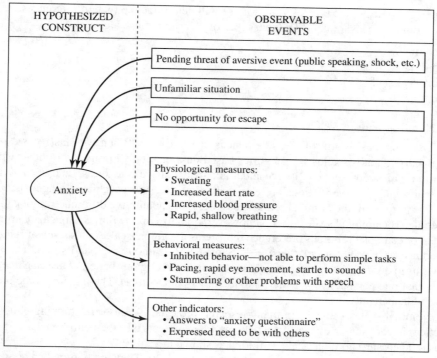

| HYPOTHESIZED CONSTRUCT | OBSERVABLE EVENTS |

FIGURE 2.4

Depiction of the relation between a hypothetical construct, or intervening variable
(anxiety), and various observable conditions and reactions. We use the hypothesized
construct to help explain the link among variables. We use the observable reactions
of the person to infer the presence and magnitude of the intervening construct.

then infer whether the person is anxious. In addition, we can design questionnaires or psychological tests to indicate the person's level of anxiety.

On the left side of Figure 2.4 is the hypothesized construct. We use the hypothesized
construct, or intervening variable, to help explain the link between one set of variables
with another. For example, we may note a positive correlation between the pending
threat and specific physiological events. From this correlation, we infer that the person
is anxious.

Measurement Scale

Most people do not give much thought to the meaning of numbers. The general attitude
seems to be that numbers are numbers regardless of their use. However, there are different
classes, or types, of numbers. More accurately, when we measure things, we can use numbers in different ways. Furthermore, it is important to recognize the differences among the
types of measurement scales. Researchers and statisticians often speak of four types of
measurement scale. Each scale has unique features and presents information in a special

manner. In addition, the type of scale we use will determine the type of inferences we can make from our measurement. The four types of measurement scales are:

(a) nominal,
(b) ordinal,
(c) interval, and
(d) ratio.

Nominal scale

The most basic form of measurement is classification. When we classify, we place things into mutually exclusive categories based on a qualitative property. In other words, **nominal scales** represent qualitative and mutually exclusive categories. Examples of nominal scales include sex, religious preference, marital status, or psychiatric diagnosis.

The purpose of the nominal scale is to indicate the qualitative difference among things or people. The nominal scale does not, however, organize or rate things using a quantitative scale. For example, religious preference represents a nominal scale. In a survey of religious preferences, we might use: Atheist = 1, Baptist = 2, Catholic = 3, and so on. The scale allows us to differentiate among people regarding their religious beliefs. The scale does not imply that one perspective is better than the other perspectives. The list orders the preferences alphabetically.

Nominal scales show up in many research projects. If you were studying child-care practices in your state, you may want to know where parents take their children during work. You could create a nominal scale definition as shown in Table 2.2.

In this example, you created three types of child care. They are nominal categories to the extent that you do not wish to imply that one type of day care is better than another, only that the three types are different. Your goal will be to estimate the number of parents who select one of these options for their child or children.

Ordinal scale

With the **ordinal scale,** the numbers refer to a quantitative scale that uses ranks. In other words, whenever you rank something from highest to lowest, you are using an ordinal scale. In a horse race, for example, we rank the horse's order of finish as 1st, 2nd, 3rd, 4th, 5th, . . . last. Movie critics use the number of stars to rate the quality of movies. A five-star rating usually means that the critic enjoyed the film and recommends it without reservation. By contrast, a one-star rating means that someone should burn all copies of the movie. Recognize that ordinal scales are not precise. In a horse race, a horse can win by a nose or 14 lengths.

The critical feature of the ordinal scale is that the scale does not represent consistent differences between the numbers of the scale. Therefore, all we can assume is that $1 < 2$ and that $2 < 3$. We can make no assumption about the size of the differences among the

TABLE 2.2
Example of operational definitions for nominal scale

Type of care	Home care	Relative or friend	Unlicensed day care
Definition of category	Child stays with an unemployed parent.	Child stays with an unpaid relative or friend.	Parent purchases child care from an unlicensed provider.

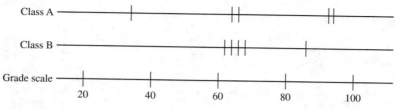

FIGURE 2.5
An ordinal scale. The vertical lines (|) represent the students' scores.

numbers. For example, look at Figure 2.5. Imagine that two classes took the same exam. The vertical lines (|) represent the scores of individual students. In each class, one student can brag that he or she earned the highest score. Does this mean that both students did equally well? As you can see, the best score in Class A is in the 90s, whereas the highest score in Class B is in the 80s. Also, look at the difference between the 1st and 2nd scores in the two classes. In Class A, the difference between the two highest scores is slight. In Class B, the difference between the two highest scores is large.

The ordinal scale lacks the precision and accuracy found in other forms of measurement. There are many times, however, when the ordinal scale is the best quality scale that the researcher can use or find.

Interval and ratio scales

The interval and ratio scales represent the most comprehensive type of measurement. These scales are quantitative because there is a one-to-one correspondence between the construct and the measurement scale. In addition, the difference among the numbers along the scale represents equal units. There is, however, an important difference between the scales.

The primary difference between interval and ratio scales is the meaning of the zero (0) on the scale. For the **interval scale,** the 0 is an arbitrary point selected for the sake of convenience. For the **ratio scale,** the 0 represents the absence of the construct. We can use scores on a math test as an example of the difference between an **arbitrary 0** and an **absolute 0.**

Figure 2.6 may help illustrate the difference between an interval and a ratio scale. As you can see there are two scales, one representing an individual math test and the other representing mathematical knowledge. The scale for the math test covers a small range of math skills. In this example, the test measures skills related to basic algebra. By contrast, the math knowledge scale has a true 0 meaning that the individual knows nothing about math, such as the meaning of numbers, the ability to count, or any of the basic math skills. The mathematics scale ranges from no knowledge of math to knowledge of complex mathematics beyond calculus.

Imagine that a student scored a 0 on the math test. What does the score represent? Can we assume that the student knows nothing about math? No, we cannot make that assumption. Because the test measures only a small portion of all math skills, we cannot infer that a 0 means that the student knows nothing about math. Therefore, the 0 on the math test is an arbitrary number relative to the broader construct, knowledge of math. What about two students who take the math test, one who scores an 80 and another who scores a 40? Does the student with the 80 know twice as much math as the student with the 40? Although $80 = 2 \times 40$, we cannot conclude that the student with the higher score knows twice as much math. If you look at the math knowledge scale, the difference between the two grades

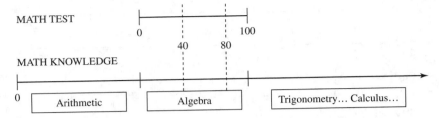

FIGURE 2.6
The difference between interval and ratio scales. The lower scale represents the full range of math knowledge. A 0 for the Math Knowledge scale means absolutely no knowledge of any mathematical concepts. By contrast, a score of 0 on a Math Test does not mean that the person has no math knowledge, only that they did not earn any points. Similarly, a score of 80 on the math test does not mean that the student knows twice as much math as the student scoring 40.

TABLE 2.3
Characteristics and examples of the four measurement scales

Scale	Characteristics	Examples	Mathematical operations
Nominal	Unordered and mutually exclusive categories; qualitative differences among groups	• Sex: male vs. female • Psychiatric diagnosis • Religious preference • Political party	$=$ vs. $\neq$ Number on observations in each group $f(x)$
Ordinal	Ranking or ordering of measurements	• Rank in class • Level on a personality dimension (high vs. low self-esteem) • Rank of quality: (1 = poor, 10 = excellent)	$<$ vs. $>$
Interval	Order, equal intervals, and arbitrary zero	• Temperature in Celsius • Scores on most psychological tests: Intelligence, personality, and depression	$A - B$ vs. $B - C$
Ratio	Order, equal intervals, and absolute zero	• Height, weight, age, speed • Time to complete a task • Number of problems solved	$\dfrac{A}{B}$ vs. $\dfrac{B}{C}$

is minor relative to the amount of math both students know. Therefore, we would conclude that scores on the math test represent an interval scale for measuring math aptitude.

Examples of ratio scales include grams of food consumed, time spent on a task, and numbers of problems solved. As a guideline, ask yourself what the 0 on the scale means. If it indicates the absence of the construct being measured, then the 0 represents an absolute 0. Consider an example. If we find that a rat consumed 0 grams of food, we can assume that it ate nothing. In addition, eating 20 grams of food is twice as much as eating 10 grams. The same is true of time on task. If a child spends 0 seconds on a task, we can assume that the child did not work on the task. In addition, 10 minutes on task is twice as long as 5 minutes on task. Table 2.3 summarizes the attributes and differences among the four scales.

RELIABILITY OF MEASUREMENT

Reliability refers to the consistency of measurement. A reliable test will produce similar results each time we measure the same thing. As you might guess, all researchers strive to develop and use the most reliable measurement devices available. Tests that have poor reliability are of little value to the researcher as they can lead to the downfall of a research project.

Unfortunately, no test is perfectly reliable because **measurement error** affects all measurement techniques. For our purposes, measurement errors are random events that increase or decrease an individual score each time we use a test. Measurement error is not the same thing as bias. Measurement error is a random variable that changes each time we use the test. In contrast, **bias error** is a constant present each time we use the test. A reliable test can be biased. A bathroom scale, for example, may reliably report your weight although it consistently adds five pounds to your true weight.

The classical theory of test reliability states that any test score is the sum of the true score plus the effects of measurement error. We can write this statement as:

$$\text{Test Score} = \text{True Score} \pm \text{Measurement Error}$$

The $\pm$ symbol in the equation indicates that measurement error can add to and remove from the true score of the construct that we want to measure. For example, imagine that you administer an intelligence test to a student who has a true intelligence quotient (IQ) of 110. Due to measurement error, each time you administer the test, you will get different results.

Table 2.4 illustrates the effects of measurement error and the difference between two tests, one with higher reliability and one with lower reliability. As you can see for both tests, measurement error raises and lowers the observed test score. Although measurement error affects both tests, the variability among the test scores is smaller for the test with higher reliability. The relation between reliability and measurement error is simple—the greater the reliability of a test, the less the measurement error.

Many things contribute to measurement error. I could easily fill this book with examples of these errors. For the sake of brevity, Table 2.5 lists the general classes of measurement error and several examples of each. As a researcher, your job is to determine what factors could affect the reliability of your measurement device and then design procedures to

TABLE 2.4

Illustration of reliability. A person completes two intelligence tests on five occasions. For both tests, there is random error. The random error is smaller for the test with the higher reliability.

Testing	Test with higher reliability	Test with lower reliability
1	$107 = 110 - 3$	$118 = 110 + 8$
2	$112 = 110 + 2$	$105 = 110 - 5$
3	$111 = 110 + 1$	$107 = 110 - 3$
4	$109 = 110 - 1$	$111 = 110 + 1$
5	$109 = 110 - 1$	$109 = 110 - 1$
	110	110

TABLE 2.5
Sources of error that reduce the reliability of a measurement technique

Source of error	Examples
Instrument error	• The equipment stops working. • Questions on a test are poorly worded. • The measurement scale is not precise.
Participant variability	• The participant becomes fatigued or bored. • The participant does not understand the instructions. • The participant is unwilling to cooperate. • The participant cannot respond to some items.
Researcher variability	• The researcher makes errors recording the data. • The researcher does not follow procedures consistently.
Environmental variability	• Distractions in the environment such as sounds or the subject's discomfort. • Inconsistent measurement conditions for different participants.

reduce the error. For example, if you believe that environmental distractions will corrupt the data, you will need to conduct your research in a setting where the testing conditions are consistent from subject to subject.

One of the more common methods to improve the reliability of the data is to increase the number of measurements. Carpenters have an old saying, *Measure twice, cut once.* Nothing is more frustrating than cutting a board and then finding that it is too short. To be careful, a good carpenter will double-check the necessary measurements to have greater confidence before cutting a board or drilling a hole. Trust me; I've made enough goofs to learn this lesson the hard way. The same is true for research. As you can see in Table 2.4, an individual measurement may be a bit off the mark, but the average of several measurements will tend to hit the target.

VALIDITY OF MEASUREMENT

Validity refers to degree to which a test or research method accurately measures the construct of interest. If we say that a test is valid, we imply that the instrument allows us to quantify the specific construct with minimal bias. If we say that a test is not valid, we imply that the test measures things unrelated to the construct we want to measure.

Figure 2.7 represents the difference between reliability and validity. The picture represents three targets with arrows. The targets represent what we want to measure and the arrows represent the measurements we make. When the arrows are scattered across the target, as is the case for the left target, we say that the test is neither reliable nor valid.

High reliability is not a guarantee of validity, however. As you can see in the middle picture, all the arrows hit the same point on the target, but each is well off the bull's eye. In this example, the results are consistent, but biased away from the construct. Using this visual example, you should conclude that reliability is necessary but not sufficient for validity.

The right target represents a condition where the measurements are reliable and valid. All the arrows are close to the bull's eye (validity) and close to each other (reliability).

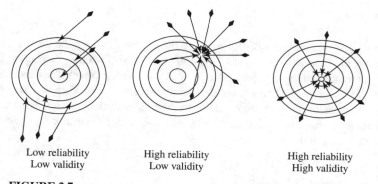

Low reliability   High reliability   High reliability
Low validity   Low validity   High validity

FIGURE 2.7
The relation between reliability and validity. The arrows represent separate measurements.

DETERMINING VALIDITY

Validity is difficult to quantify because there is no single measure or indicator of validity. In the broadest sense of the term, validity is a value judgment based on empirical evidence and the interpretations we want to make from the data. As Kaplan (1964) noted, validity refers to what we can accomplish using the data. Stated from a different perspective, no data are invalid until we interpret them.

The definition of validity is fuzzy and vague because validity refers to the interpretation of the test score, not the test. Imagine that I gave you a test that examined your knowledge of rules of grammar. The test may contain questions about your knowledge of gerunds, dangling modifiers, relative pronouns, infinitives, subordinate conjunctions, participles, and active voice. Assuming that the test is reliable, what inferences can we draw from your score? Would it be appropriate to assume that you recognize all these terms and the associated rules of grammar? Depending on your score, such an interpretation may be correct. Can we use the test score to determine if you are a creative writer? Probably not, regardless of your score. Good creative writing may be independent of knowledge of the formal rules of grammar. Thus, the same test score can be valid or invalid depending on how we interpret the score.

Generally, researchers use several criteria to determine the validity of a test. As you just learned, the reliability of a test is one criterion for validity. Researchers also consider additional criteria to determine the validity of a measurement device. These criteria are:

(a) face validity,
(b) content validity,
(c) predictive/concurrent validity, and
(d) construct validity.

Face Validity

Face validity asks, *Does the test appear authentic to the person taking the test?* In many situations, face validity is an important consideration. If the people taking the test do not believe that the procedure is valid, they may not respond honestly.

Content Validity

As the name implies, **content validity** refers to the degree to which the measurement technique samples the behaviors relevant to the construct. If you want to determine a person's proficiency at mathematics, you will ask them to solve math problems, not recite Lincoln's Gettysburg Address. In most cases, we determine the content validity of a test by having experts on the subject review the test. Therefore, you might ask several professors of mathematics whether a math test adequately assesses the student's ability to understand and apply specific mathematical concepts.

Predictive/Concurrent Validity

One of the important components of any good test is that it allows us to predict other behaviors. In some cases, we hope that measurements that we take now will allow us to predict events. If a test allows us to make these predictions, then we say that the test has **predictive validity. Concurrent validity** means that a test score correlates with other relevant behaviors that the person currently can perform.

Construct Validity

Look again at Figure 2.4. You can think of this picture as the model for **construct validity.** Because most of the things we measure in psychology are intervening variables, we need to use behavioral indicators to define them. According to Figure 2.4, the threat of an aversive event, such as receiving an electrical shock, produces anxiety. In turn, increases in anxiety produce increases in heart rate. If we accept this definition of anxiety, and we can demonstrate that heart rate increases during periods of threat, we can assume that increases in heart rate represent anxiety.

POPULATIONS AND SAMPLES

Previously, I noted that hypotheses refer to the relation between variables and the population. Our research, however, uses data, gathered from a sample, to answer the questions implied in the hypothesis. Although chapter 6 provides a detailed discussion of populations and samples, we do need to review how we can use data, based on samples, to make inferences about the population. Therefore, we need to examine the relation between target populations, sampling populations, and samples.

The research hypothesis refers to variables in the population. Because most populations are extremely large, it is impractical or impossible to truly sample from the population. Consequently, most researchers use a **sampling population.** The sampling population is a subset of the target population to which the researcher has easy access. For most psychological research, the sampling population consists of people who live and work near the researcher. The sample is, therefore, a representative subset of individuals drawn from the sampling population.

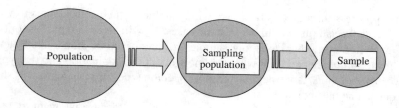

FIGURE 2.8
Relation between population, sampling population, and the sample.

For example, assume that you want to study altruism. Your population may be all adults. Chances are that you will use students from your college for the research. Therefore, students at your college represent the sampling population. The students who participate in your experiment represent the sample. Figure 2.8 represents the relation among populations, sampling populations, and samples.

The logic of a sampling is deceptively simple. First, take a representative sample from the sampling population. The representative sample will be a manageable size and share the same characteristics as the sampling population. Next, conduct the study and collect the data. Once you have analyzed the data, you can generalize from the sample to the sampling population. If your sampling population is representative of the population you can then assume that what is true of the sample will be true of the population.

This description of using samples to generalize about the population sounds simple and straightforward. Unfortunately, this advice is the same as saying that to build a house you buy a lot of building materials and follow the blueprints. Although technically correct, the instructions gloss over many important points.

The fundamental question that we need to ask is, *How do we know that the sample is representative of the population?* We can answer that question by examining two interrelated characteristics of samples. The first characteristic of a sample is its size. The second characteristic is its ability to represent the population.

How large should the sample be? We will revisit this question several times throughout this book. Research requires time, money, and energy, and each member of the sample requires these resources. Therefore, to control costs and not spend a lifetime on a single project, we want to keep the sample to a reasonable size. At the same time, the sample has to be large enough to represent the population. If the population contains much diversity, then the sample may have to be large to reflect that diversity. A large sample, however, is not a guarantee that the sample will accurately reflect the population. This leads us to the second characteristic of a sample, its ability to represent the population.

Many popular magazines publish the results of surveys of their readers. Sometimes the editors will tout that more than 20,000 readers responded to the survey published in a previous issue. Do these results provide a good and useful source of information? Can we consider the data to be representative of the population or even the sampled population? After a moment's consideration, you should say, "No!" There are many problems with these data. First, only people who read the magazine had the opportunity to respond. Second, although 20,000 is a big number, it is not an automatic protection against bias. The people who responded may represent a minority of the readership.

As we progress through this book, we will examine methods researchers use to determine how large the sample should be. In some cases, we will be able to use one or two people for our research. In other cases, our sample will number in the hundreds. Determining the size of the sample depends on what we know about the population and the type of behavior we are studying. As we begin to explore specific types of research, I will show you ways to determine the size of the sample.

To be useful, samples must represent the population. Because we want to generalize about the population, we need to ensure that the sample is an accurate model of the population. The **representativeness of a sample** is the consequence of the procedure the researcher uses to collect the data, not of the sample. In other words, we determine whether the sample is representative by examining the methods used to collect the data.

One of the most common sampling techniques is **simple random sampling.** Simple random sampling means that each member of the sampling population has an equal probability of being selected. Therefore, if the sample is sufficiently large, the laws of probability ensure that the sample will reflect the population. Failure to use simple random sampling can produce questionable results. Consider the following example. Hyde and DeLamater (1998) presented the results of two surveys of men's and women's sexual behavior. The first method was simple random probability sampling. The second method was **convenience sampling.**

For convenience sampling, the researcher uses members of the population that are easy (convenient) to use in the research. A convenience sample is not a random sample because some people in the population have no chance of being selected.

Figure 2.9 presents the results of the two studies that examined the frequency of sexual relations among adults. Hyde and DeLamater (1998) noted that the convenience sampling represents data collected from clients of a clinic for the treatment of sexual dysfunctions and their

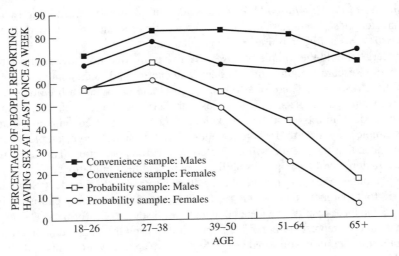

FIGURE 2.9
The difference in data produced by a convenience sample and a probability sample. Data presented in Hyde and DeLamater (1998).

friends. These people may not represent the typical person in the population. The other set of data represents research conducted by researchers who used random sampling of the population.

We cannot trust the results of the convenience sample because the sample (people attending the clinics) is not representative of the population. By contrast, we have greater confidence in the results of the probability sample, as the results are more likely to represent the target population.

Role of Random Sampling in Research

Many students are surprised to learn that few research studies in psychology use random sampling. There seems to be a general impression that all research *must* use random sampling to be valid. In some cases, this assumption is correct. In other cases, we may not need to use random sampling to conduct valid research. Our choice of whether to use random sampling depends on the type of research we conduct and the goals of the research.

When random sampling is essential

Random sampling from the target population is essential when we want to estimate, with as much precision as possible, specific characteristics of the population. Political polling is an example of research where random sampling is imperative. To predict who will win an election, or which policy issues are most important among registered voters, a pollster will take great pains to ensure that he or she collects a random sample from the target population. The random sample will allow the researcher to predict, for example, that "Strickland will receive 57 percent of the votes whereas Hollister will receive 43 percent, ±3 percentage points." If the pollster used true random sampling of likely voters, then he or she can predict that Strickland will receive between 54 and 60 percent of the vote.

There are also many cases in psychology where we want to ensure that we have a representative sample from the target population. For example, imagine that you created a new test of depression. What scores on your test indicate normal moods; what scores represent depression? To answer these questions you need to randomly sample from a population of depressed adults and from another population of depression-free adults. The data for the two groups will help you find which scores represent "normal" moods and which scores represent depression.

When random sampling is not essential

Many psychologists conduct research that examines the relation among variables. For example, what is the relation between positive reinforcement and behavior? People tend to repeat behaviors that produce positive reinforcement. Notice that I made a generalization about a population (all people) that did not estimate specific values. All I did was state that there is a lawful relation between two variables. For this type of research, we describe the *qualitative* relation between two variables; we do not estimate the *quantitative* values of any characteristics of the population.

When we conduct research that examines the qualitative relation among variables, we examine the general characteristics of the population. Using the current example, we assume that all people will repeat behaviors that lead to positive reinforcement, although the size of the effect may vary from person to person.

Most psychologists conduct their research using people they can easily find. They may use children in local day-care facilities or schools. They may advertise in the local newspaper for volunteers to participate in their research. They will use students enrolled in their psychology courses.

We are taking a risk in making such a generalization from a nonrandom sample. The students at your college or university may be radically different from students at other colleges. Children raised in the northeast portion of the country may be much different from children raised in the deep south. People who respond to newspaper advertisements may be different from the typical person. Thus, significant cultural or geographic factors may bias the data. Although this is a legitimate concern, we must remember that researchers strive to replicate important findings. If a researcher discovers an interesting finding, then other researchers, from different parts of the country, will attempt to replicate those findings.

A good example of this replication comes from the study of obedience to authority. During the late 1960s, Milgram (1974) conducted a series of experiments designed to study the degree to which people would follow orders and give what appeared to be a powerful electrical shock to another person. Milgram repeated his experiments many times to ensure that his results were consistent. He used volunteers living in New Haven as well as other cities in Connecticut. Each time he conducted the study, he got similar results. Other researchers (Brief, Buttram, Elliott, Reizenstein, & McCline, 1995; Meeus & Raaijmakers, 1995), using different procedures and different sampling populations, have also examined obedience. The results of these studies support Milgram's original findings.

RESEARCH IN ACTION: MEASURING SEXISM

Do some people believe that women cannot be effective leaders? Schimmelpfenig and Sibicky (1997) asked this question in a study they conducted. They noted that although a substantial number of women have entered the work force, only a few have been promoted to leadership roles. In addition, the authors noted that the dominant stereotype of a good leader continues to represent a masculine stereotype. Therefore, they decided to determine how people who have sexist attitudes would evaluate the leadership skills of women.

A technical issue that Schimmelpfenig and Sibicky (1997) had to overcome was how to measure sexism. They found a test called the Modern Sexism Scale (Swim, Aikin, Hall, & Hunter, 1995) that contained a series of statements including, *Discrimination against women is no longer a problem in the United States,* and *It is easy to understand the anger of the women's groups in America.* For each question, the person responded on a scale ranging from 1, which indicated *Strongly Disagree,* to 7, which indicated *Strongly Agree.* The researchers had 73 men and 83 women from their college complete the survey. Based on the Modern Sexism Scale, the researchers divided the people into two groups: High Sexism and Low Sexism.

Four weeks later, Schimmelpfenig and Sibicky (1997) asked the same people to complete another task. The cover story was that the college's administration wanted to choose a recipient for the college's annual leadership award (a real award at the college). The researchers led the people to believe that the description came from *Who's Who In American Leadership.* In addition, the researchers led half of the people to believe that the leader was

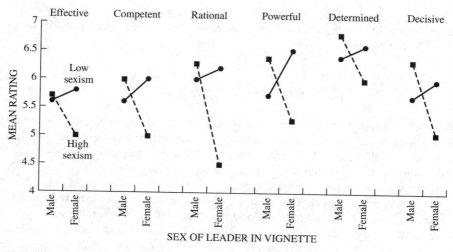

FIGURE 2.10

Interaction between level of sexism and attitudes toward leader based on leader's sex. From Schimmelpfenig and Sibicky, 1997. Used with permission of the authors.

a man. The other people read the same description of a woman as leader. All the participants in the study then rated the person for the following qualities: effective, competent, rational, powerful, determined, and decisive.

Figure 2.10 presents the results from Schimmelpfenig and Sibicky's (1997) study. The horizontal axis of the graph represents the various leadership qualities the participants rated. The vertical scale represents the average score the groups of participants gave the male and female leaders. Look at the effective construct at the left of the graph. Is there evidence that sexism influenced a person's rating of the leader? Participants who were not sexist (low sexism) rated the male and female leaders the same (the differences between the means are trivial). By contrast, people who were sexist (high sexism) gave the woman lower marks. This pattern of results repeats across the six leadership characteristics. Consequently, these data appear to offer tentative evidence that people who score high on the Modern Sexism Scale are more likely to evaluate men and women's leadership behavior differently, even when it is the same behavior.

ACHIEVEMENT CHECK. Use the Schimmelpfenig and Sibicky (1997) study to answer the following questions.

(7) What is the population and sampling population for this research?

(8) Is random sampling a critical issue for this research?

(9) Can you identify the independent and dependent variables in this study?

(10) Are the independent variables manipulated or subject variables?

(11) Which scale of measurement best represents: (a) The raw score on the Modern Sexism Scale and (b) the score on the sex of the leader in the vignette?

(12) Schimmelpfenig and Sibicky used an elaborate cover story for the second part of the study. How does the cover story relate to face validity?

(13) Why is sexism an intervening variable?

(14) What is the operational definition of sexism in this study?

(15) How do the results of this study help verify that the Modern Sexism Scale does assess sexism?

CHAPTER SUMMARY

In this chapter we reviewed the foundations of all empirical research. In any scientific research project, the researcher will state a hypothesis, determine how he or she will measure the relevant variables, and then collect the necessary data. The "Research in Action" section demonstrated how we combine these elements in a study.

As we reviewed in this chapter, a hypothesis is more than an educated guess. The hypothesis is a statement that directs the course of the research by describing the variables to be examined, how the data are to be collected, and the relation between the variable. Some researchers develop hypotheses from specific theories in the hope of confirming the utility of the theory. In other cases, the researcher conducts exploratory research to learn more or explore interesting topics.

Most hypotheses refer to dependent and independent variables. Dependent variables refer to the focus of the study—the variable that the researcher hopes to be able to describe, predict, and explain. The independent variable is the variable that the researcher hopes will allow him or her to describe, predict, and explain the dependent variable. The independent variable may be a characteristic of the participant. Characteristics such as sex, intelligence, and personality are examples of subject variables because they are conditions that the researcher cannot manipulate. A manipulated independent variable is a type of independent variables that the researcher can control or manipulate.

There are four types of hypothesis including descriptive hypotheses, correlation hypotheses, differences among populations, and cause and effect.

For the descriptive hypothesis, the researcher hopes to collect data that will allow him or her to estimate or infer characteristics of a population. A developmental psychologist may want, for example, to describe the cognitive problems that children of a specific age can solve.

When a researcher poses a correlation hypothesis, he or she predicts that changes in one variable correspond to changes in another variable. An example of a correlation hypothesis is the prediction that there is a positive correlation between the personality variables, extroversion, and assertiveness.

The third type of hypothesis allows the researcher to predict that members of one group are different from another group. This type of hypothesis allows us to compare two or more groups. Examples of the hypothesis are, *Smokers are more anxious than nonsmokers* and *Children who attend day care are more cooperative than children who do not attend day care.*

The final hypothesis refers to cause and effect. To show cause and effect, one must show that (a) the cause precedes the effect, (b) that there is a correlation between the two variables, and (c) that all other explanations have been accounted for.

All research depends upon measurement. In this chapter we examined the foundations of measurement, which include operational definitions, measurement scales, reliability, and validity.

Operational definitions allow us to link observable behaviors to inferred constructs. Depression, for example, is a construct that cannot be directly observed. We can operationally define depression by identifying the behaviors that we believe indicate this condition.

When we operationally define a construct, we refer to a measurement scale. The measurement scale can be nominal (putting observations into categories), ordinal (ranking the construct from lower to higher), interval (a scale with a consistent scale, but no absolute 0), and ratio (a scale with a consistent scale and an absolute 0).

Reliability refers to the consistency of measurement. A reliable measure is one that provides consistent answers. Reliability is not the same thing as validity, however. To consider a test valid, we must show that data produced by the test allow us to make useful predictions.

In the last section of the chapter, we reviewed populations, sampling populations, and samples. Researchers use samples to evaluate hypotheses. The hypothesis, however, refers to the population. Therefore, researchers hope that what is true of the sample will also be true of the population.

Random sampling is not frequently used in behavioral research because it is difficult to gain access to the entire population. Researchers examine the qualitative relation among variables. In addition, researchers will attempt to replicate interesting findings. The more we can replicate a finding, the more confident we are in the findings.

In the "Research in Action" section, we saw how researchers can use a psychological test to measure a complex construct (sexism) and then use that test to compare differences among groups of people.

CHAPTER GLOSSARY FOR REVIEW

Absolute 0   A zero point on the scale that represents the absence of the construct.

Arbitrary 0   A zero point on the scale selected for convenience. The 0 does not represent the absence of the construct.

Bias Error   A consistent error in measurement that reduces the validity of the test.

Confirmatory Research   Conducting research to determine the relative merits of a theory by testing hypotheses derived from the theory.

Constant   A measurable characteristic that does not change or take on different values.

Construct Validity   The ability of a test to measure the variable or construct it was designed to measure.

Content Validity   The degree to which a test appears to be valid to experts familiar with the variables being measured.

Convenience Sampling   A sampling technique where the researcher uses only those members of the population most easily obtained or incorporated into the research.

Data   The information we collect in research that is a product of measurement.

Dependent Variable   The variable in the research that the researcher wants to explain, describe, and predict.

Descriptive Statistic or Statistic   A number that allows us to organize, summarize, and describe the data. Statistics refer only to samples.

Exploratory Research   Conducting research to examine the relation among variables and to understand a particular phenomenon.

Face Validity   The degree to which a test appears to be valid to the people taking the test.

Hypothesis   Any statement or prediction that describes the relation among two or more variables based on theory or previous research.

Independent Variable   The variable that the researcher uses to explain, describe, and predict the dependent variable.

Interval Scale   A quantitative measurement scale that uses an arbitrary 0 and consistent differences between values.

Intervening Variable   A hypothetical variable created within a theory and used to explain the link between two or more observable behaviors.

Manipulated Independent Variable   An independent variable that the researcher can directly control or manipulate in an experiment. The researcher can assign individuals to different levels of the independent variable. Other variables in the study do not affect the independent variable.

Measurement Error   Errors in measurement due to random and unpredictable events that reduce the accuracy and reliability of the test.

Metric   Refers to a standard of measurement, or the specific scale, used to make measurements.

Negative Correlation   The description of a systematic relation between two variables—as one increases the other decreases.

No Correlation   There is no linear relation between the two variables.

Nominal Scale   A qualitative measurement scale that places individuals or observations into mutually exclusive categories.

Operational Definition   A rule used to define a specific construct empirically and objectively and to determine how the researcher will measure the construct.

Ordinal Scale   A quantitative measurement scale that ranks the observations for a particular characteristic. The difference among the numbers need not be equal.

Parameter   A number that summarizes or describes a characteristic of a population. Parameters refer only to populations and are estimated by statistics.

Population   A group of people or things that share one or more publicly verifiable characteristics.

Positive Correlation   The description of a systematic relation between two variables—as one increases the other increases.

Predictive/Concurrent Validity   The ability of a test to accurately estimate current behavior or predict future behaviors.

Ratio Scale   A quantitative measure measurement scale that uses an absolute 0.

Reliability   The degree to which a test produces consistent measurements of the same thing.

Representativeness of a Sample   A condition that occurs when the sample data mirror the corresponding parameters of a population. The representativeness of a sample is the product of the sampling procedures used to create the sample.

Sample   A group of people or things, drawn from the population, which represents the population from which it was drawn.

Sampling Population   A subset of the population from which the researcher draws the sample. The researcher assumes that the sampled population represents the target population.

Simple Random Sampling   A method for creating samples. There is an equal chance that the researcher will select any member of the population.

Subject Variable   A variable that represents some preexisting characteristic of the individual in the research. The researcher cannot control the subject variable, but may use it to describe or predict the dependent variable.

Theory   A broad statement about the general causes of a phenomenon. Theories are more expansive than hypotheses and are often the source of specific hypotheses.

Validity   The degree to which a test measures what it is supposed to measure.

Variable   Any measurable characteristic that can have different values.

3 SURVEY OF EMPIRICAL METHODS

CHAPTER OUTLINE

✦ Introduction

✦ Internal and External Validity

✦ Survey of Empirical Methods

✦ Intact Groups Designs and Quasi-Experimental Studies

✦ Surveys

✦ Correlational Studies

✦ Single-Participant Research Methods

✦ Meta-Analysis

There are only a handful of ways to do a study properly but a thousand ways to do it wrong.

—D. L. Sackett

INTRODUCTION

In many ways, conducting research is a creative process much like painting a picture. Using many brushes, colors, and painting techniques, the artist creates a unique piece of art. Each piece creates its own technical challenges that the artist must solve. The same is true of a researcher who must decide which research technique will produce the best data that answers the research question.

Many students seem to think that learning research methods should be like reading a cookbook. If you want to make chicken soup, find a recipe and follow the directions. If you want to conduct an experiment, find the appropriate chapter and follow the steps. As I hope you will learn, good research does not follow preset formulas. There is no such thing as the "single factor experiment recipe" nor are there five easy steps to conducting a research project. Each research project presents unique technical challenges that the researcher must solve. Selecting from a range of techniques, researchers create a **research design** that allows them to find the answer to empirical questions. Therefore, a research design is a plan for collecting data using empirical techniques. As you will learn in this chapter, there are many research techniques, each with notable merits and limitations.

As the quotation at the start of this chapter suggests, the research design requires careful planning. As Sackett recognized, there are a lot of ways to do a study poorly, but only a few ways to do research well. Therefore, in this chapter I will help you learn how researchers take an interesting hypothesis and develop a research design that produces clear and useful data.

In chapter 2, we reviewed the concept of validity as it relates to measurement. As you learned, a test is valid if it measures what we want it to measure. Specifically, a test is valid if it allows us to make specific interpretations or conclusions. We can extend this definition of validity to empirical research. Specifically, we can ask if the data support specific conclusions. Just as a test or measurement device measures some constructs, but not others, some research designs allow us to answer some questions but not others. When we evaluate the validity of a research project, we examine two forms of validity, internal validity and external validity.

INTERNAL AND EXTERNAL VALIDITY

Researchers collect data to make interpretations, or inferences, about the relation among variables. As you will learn, the interpretative process is one of the more critical steps in the research process because the data do not speak for themselves. Unfortunately, many people use phrases such as "*Research shows . . .*" or "*The research proves. . . .*"

The problem with these phrases is that research does not speak. Research is a verb that describes the work that researchers perform, specifically the act of seeking information.

Once the researchers have the data, they must interpret them. Because research requires interpretation, no data are valid or invalid until someone interprets the data. Consequently, I want to impress upon you that the *researcher* tells us how he or she *interpreted* the data. Thus, I prefer the phrase *"Researchers tell us . . ."* or *"The researchers concluded that . . . ."* As you will see, this is an important distinction when reviewing internal and external validity.

Here is an overly simplified example. What is the average Scholastic Assessment Test (SAT) score at Mythical College? Two possible answers are, *"The average SAT score of all Mythical College students is 1067"* and *"This average score indicates that students at Mythical College are better prepared for college than the typical student."* Are these statements valid? The first statement is a straightforward answer to the question. Within the scope of the question, the answer is valid because the mean represents the typical SAT score of students at the college.

Is the second response acceptable? Although the data are the same, I doubt that you would agree with the interpretation. To verify the validity of that statement we must first obtain the answers to several additional questions. Is an average score of 1067 better than averages for other colleges? Is the SAT test really a measure of students' preparation for college? Finally, what do we mean by *the typical student?* Is the typical student anyone who graduates from high school, only students who attend college, or only students who complete college? Some statements about the data are valid whereas others are not.

In chapter 2, I reviewed the concept of measurement validity and argued that it is a process of interpretation of test scores. When we say that a test is valid, we really mean that the interpretation of the test score is valid. The same is true for interpreting the results of an experiment. We use validity to describe our interpretation of the data, not the data specifically. When researchers talk about the validity of their interpretations, they discuss two general forms of validity, internal validity and external validity.

Internal Validity

Internal validity refers to the cause and effect relation between the independent variable and the dependent variable. You should recall from chapter 2 that we can examine the hypothesis IV → DV only under certain circumstances. Saying that an experiment is internally valid means that there is no doubt that changes in the independent variable, which the experimenter controlled, caused changes in the dependent variable. By contrast, if factors other than the independent variable caused changes in the dependent variable, then we cannot conclude that the study is internally valid because the researcher has not ruled out **alternative explanations.**

An alternative explanation is a reasonable explanation of the results that does not depend upon the hypothesis, IV → DV. When we state that a study is internally valid, we have concluded that the research design has allowed us to control for and rule out alternative explanations.

Threats to Internal Validity

There are four broad categories of threat to internal validity. In some cases, we can avoid these threats through good research design and attention to detail while collecting the data.

Any threat to internal validity is a **confounding variable.** As a generality, a confounding variable is any extraneous or uncontrolled condition related to the independent variable. Specifically, any variable correlated with the independent variable, that the researcher cannot control or manipulate, is a confounding variable. Because the researcher cannot control the confounding variable, he or she cannot be sure whether the results reflect the effect of the independent variable or the effect of the confounding variable. The four major categories of confounding variable that we will examine include: (a) unintentional sequence of events, (b) nonequivalent groups, (c) measurement errors, and (d) ambiguity of cause and effect.

Unintended sequence of events

The first threat to internal validity is the **unintended sequence of events.** As the name implies, the data may reflect a sequence of events that the researcher did not or could not control. There are cases when a researcher will want to study how a sequence of events changes behavior. A developmental psychologist, for example, may want to study changes in children's cognitive and intellectual abilities when they enter middle school. There are, however, instances when an unintentional sequence of events is the confounding variable. The following are examples of such unintentional sequences.

Carryover effects. **Carryover effects** refer to the participants' experience in one part of the study that affects their performance in another part of the study. One example is taking the same test twice. Taking the test the first time may influence the participants' scores the next time they take the test. Consequently, if we used this procedure in a research project, we would not know if the changes in test scores reflect the effect of the independent variable or that participants knew the answers to the questions.

Maturation. **Maturation** is another example of unintended sequence of events. If the research project covers a long time, it is possible that the observed changes represent the passage of time or the maturation of the person. For example, some depressed people will gradually improve without treatment. Consequently, the researcher must ensure that the observed improvements are greater than those that are due to the maturation effect.

Intervening events. Another problem related to maturation is the effect of **intervening events.** If the research covers a long time, the participants may experience environmental or outside influences that will affect their behavior regardless of the independent variable. Imagine that you conducted a research project that spanned a month. Participants in the study could talk to each other or other people about the research. Similarly, a host of random events could occur to each participant. These outside factors, over which you have little control, may greatly influence the dependent variable.

Nonequivalent groups

The second threat to internal validity is the problem created by nonequivalent groups. The goal of an experiment is to find differences among groups that reflect the effects of the independent variable. Saying that the independent variable causes the dependent variable implies that two groups will be identical to each other until one group of participants experiences the independent variable. Therefore, a problem arises when the groups are different from each other due to factors besides the independent variable. Two conditions that may cause the groups to be different are mortality and the uncontrolled effects of subject variables.

Mortality. This rather morbid word applies to any loss of participants from the research. People find many reasons to drop out of a study—they may become bored, embarrassed, or move to another city. The consequence of participant **mortality** is that the differences among the groups may represent the effect of the mortality, not the independent variable. A particular problem with subject mortality is that the people who drop out of the study may represent an important subgroup in the population.

Subject variables. For many research projects, the independent variable is a **subject variable.** Because the researcher does not have direct control over this variable, he or she can examine the relation between the independent and dependent variables, but cannot automatically assume cause and effect. Imagine, for example, that we compared two teaching methods, one applied to a psychology course taught at 8:00 AM and the other method to a section taught at 5:00 PM. Time of day is a subject variable in that the students elected to take the early morning or evening section of the course. Consequently, we will have a hard time answering the question, *"Are the differences between the groups due to teaching method or to the type of students enrolled in morning or afternoon courses?"*

Measurement errors

The third threat to internal validity includes problems created by measurement errors. Using a test that is not a valid measure of the independent or dependent variable raises questions about the internal validity of any cause and effect conclusion. Even if the test is valid, other problems may arise.

Ceiling and floor effects. Sometimes a researcher may select a test that is not sensitive to changes in the dependent variable. As an example, imagine that a researcher wants to examine the effectiveness of a new method of teaching mathematics. At some point, the researcher is going to have to measure the participants' mathematics ability. Using too easy a test creates a **ceiling effect** because everyone will do well on the test, and the researcher will not be able to find differences among the participants' scores. By contrast, using too difficult a test creates a **floor effect** because everyone will do poorly.

Reliability. Measurement errors may also influence internal validity to the extent that the test has low reliability. In some cases, the error occurs when the researcher classifies people into different groups.

Regression to the mean. In some circumstances, the change in the scores represents the regression to the mean phenomenon. This effect occurs when people receive exceptionally high or low scores on a test or measure. When tested a second time, the scores will tend to be closer to the average. For example, some people may receive a poor score on a test because they do not feel well or for reasons unrelated to their knowledge of the material. When we test them again a few weeks later, their scores will probably be closer to normal. Consequently, the change in test scores may reflect regression to the mean and not the effects of the independent variable.

Ambiguity of cause and effect

The final threat to internal validity refers to the assumptions of cause and effect. According to British philosopher, John Stuart Mill (1843/1986), before we assume cause and effect we must show that the cause occurs before the effect, find evidence for a correlation between the cause and effect, and rule out other explanations. There are many cases when the method for collecting the data does not allow us to address one or more of these criteria. Two of the major problems we encounter are determining the **temporal order** of the variables and the **third variable problem.** I will review these threats to internal validity later in this chapter. Table 3.1 lists the general threats to internal validity, their characteristics, and an example of each threat.

TABLE 3.1
Threats to internal validity

Specific threat	Description of threat	Examples of threat
Unintended sequence of events: • Carry-over effects • Maturation • Intervening events	Changes in the dependent variable that are the results of experiences with the testing procedure (carry-over effect), changes in the participant (maturation), and intervening events that may occur between phases of the experiment.	• Taking the same or similar tests allows the participant to practice or become more skillful at taking the test. • The participant grows older or changes in some way unrelated to the independent variable. • The participant learns something about the experiment from another participant.
Nonequivalent groups: • Subject variables • Participant mortality	The difference among the groups is due to one or more variables related to characteristics of the participants that are unrelated to the independent variable.	• The researcher assigns the participants to different groups based on a subject variable (e.g., sex) that also influences the dependent variable. • Participants in one group are more likely to withdraw from the study.
Measurement problems: • Ceiling-floor effect • Measurement error • Regression to the mean • Instrumentation	The measurement used to assess the independent or dependent variables does not adequately measure the variable, or it introduces additional variance to the data, thus hiding the effect of the independent variable.	• The test may not be sensitive to differences among the participants. • The test may create error because of low reliability or validity. • Participants who receive exceptionally high or low scores tend to receive scores closer to the mean when tested a second time. • People responsible for collecting the data change the measurement criteria or use different criteria for different groups.
Ambiguity of cause and effect: • Temporal order • Third variable	We cannot determine that the independent variable preceded the dependent variable or we cannot rule out a third variable that causes the dependent variable to change.	• Observing a correlation between television viewing preferences and aggressiveness does not allow us to determine which variable caused the other or whether the variables are due to a third variable.

External Validity

External validity refers to the type of generalizations we can draw from the data, specifically that the results of a study will generalize to the population. In other words, the more confident we are that the sample represents the population, the greater the external validity of our interpretation of the results.

There are two types of external validity, **generality of findings** and **generality of conclusion.** The generality of findings refers to the link between the sample and the target population. If we assume that the sample represents the population, then we can generalize conclusions from the sample data to the population.

The generality of conclusions refers to our ability to generalize the findings from one population to other populations. In many cases, we conduct a study using a specific group of people, but we may want to extend the results to other groups. For example, a researcher may find that a specific type of motivational strategy works well for factory workers. He or she wishes to generalize the results to the staff in managerial positions. In such a situation, we need to question whether the results found for one population will generalize to a second population.

Figure 3.1 illustrates the difference between internal and external validity. Both forms of validity come between the data and the population, indicating that validity is a process that allows us to link the sample data to the population. As you can see, external validity consists of two parts, generality of findings and generality of conclusions.

External Validity and the "Real World"

Some people complain that psychology experiments, conducted in the laboratory, have no bearing in "the real world." The general sentiment is that laboratory studies are contrived, unrealistic, and bogus. Furthermore, the participants in the experiments are mere college students. To make things worse, in the eyes of some, psychologists conduct their experiments in clearly artificial situations, and the students participating in the experiment know

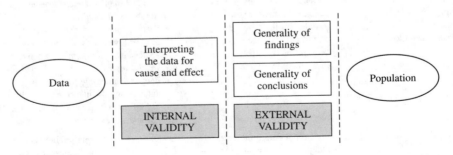

FIGURE 3.1
The difference between internal and external validity. Internal validity refers to the interpretation of the data for a cause-and-effect relation. External validity refers to generalizing the results to the target population.

that they are participating in an experiment! The sentiment expressed in these observations is that the results of research conducted in the laboratory have little or no relevance to the behavior of real people living in the real world. These sentiments are stereotypes that I hope to dispel. As you learn more about psychology, you will discover that much of what we know about behavior comes from sound laboratory research. There is no doubt that laboratory research provides considerable external validity.

Consider the statement that the laboratory is artificial. This is a silly argument because reality does not stop at the door of the laboratory. Students who participate in research projects do not become irrational once they agree to participate in an experiment. Furthermore, the principles that govern their behavior do not cease to exist when a psychology experiment begins. The laws of behavior continue to apply in the laboratory setting as much as they do on the street. Saying that psychological research conducted in the laboratory has little or no external validity is like saying that physics or chemistry experiments conducted in the laboratory are invalid.

The value of the laboratory is that we can control the environment and examine how the independent and dependent variables relate to each other. To illustrate the value of laboratory research, Anderson and Bushman (1997) offered a detailed review of how laboratory research has helped psychologists understand the nature of human aggression. They reviewed the many experiments examining aggression and showed how the results matched the results of research conducted in the real world. The point of their article was to demonstrate that many real world studies of aggression confirmed laboratory research.

There are other examples where laboratory research has led psychologists to discover important phenomena. A classic example comes from research conducted by Martin Seligman and his colleagues (Maier & Seligman, 1976; Overmier & Seligman, 1967; Seligman & Maier, 1967). Seligman had planned a set of experiments to examine an important theory related to classical and operant conditioning. The results of those experiments were startling. To make a long story short, what began as highly controlled laboratory research, using dogs, became the foundation for an extremely influential theory of human depression—learned helplessness theory.

The moral of this brief section is that an experiment is not automatically trivial or invalid because the researchers conducted their work in a laboratory. Much of what we know about human behavior comes from laboratory research. Laboratory research and research conducted in natural settings are valuable and complementary tools for the researcher. As Anderson and Busman (1997) concluded:

> The laboratory is still the best place to test causal hypotheses derived from theories. . . . On the other hand, the real world is often the best place to observe and define new phenomena, and to create new theoretical propositions about human psychology. The real world is still the best place to devise, test, refine, and put into practice specific applications. (p. 37)

Threats to External Validity

What are the factors that limit or reduce the external validity of a research project? Cook and Campbell (1979) identified three broad threats to external validity: a) recruitment of participants, b) effects of situation, and c) effects of history.

TABLE 3.2
Threats to external validity

Specific threat	Description of threat	Examples of threat
Recruitment of participants	Participants in the sample do not represent the population.	• Generalizing results from one age group to another. • People who volunteer in response to a newspaper advertisement may not represent the typical person.
Effects of situation	The environmental context of the research is unique and does not generalize to other settings.	• An experiment conducted in a church may not generalize to phenomena observed in other settings.
Effects of history	Unique events, fixed in time, limit the generality of the data.	• Results conducted many years ago may not generalize to present conditions because of changes in political and social conditions.

Recruitment of participants

How do we get people to participate in our research projects? In most cases, we ask people to volunteer. At many colleges, students in the introductory psychology course receive extra credit for participating in one or more research projects. Most researchers use college students for the sake of convenience.

In some cases, our method of recruiting participants may limit the number and range of target populations to which we can generalize. Consider a few examples. Imagine that a researcher wanted to study the effects of child care on a child's social and cognitive development. Because the researcher works at a large state university that has a child-care center, the researcher decides to track children from the center and a group of children from the community not in child care. The researcher works hard to ensure that both groups of children are similar in all respects except for the experience of day care. Can the researcher generalize the results of his or her study to all children at day-care centers?

You probably see the potential threat to external validity. How well does a college-operated day-care center represent the typical day-care facility? Do children who attend a college-operated day-care center represent the typical child who attends day care? These questions raise a potential threat to the external validity of the results. Day-care centers operated at colleges may represent the best of the best. The staff may be well educated and the facilities of good quality. Consequently, the sample from the college-operated day care may not well represent the population of typical day-care centers.

How do we overcome this threat to external validity? One way is to repeat a study in a different location or with a different sampling population. For example, many researchers have examined the effects of child care using an array of child-care settings. The child-care settings vary regarding their location, quality and training of staff, student-to-staff ratios, and other critical variables. As a whole, the research allows us to understand the effects of child care on developmental processes. Although we may question the external validity of a single study, observing similar results across an array of settings gives us greater confidence in the conclusions.

Effects of situation

Will the results of an experiment conducted at your college generalize to my college? What if we conducted an experiment on the motivation of employees working on an assembly line—will the results generalize to employees at the management level? Is it possible that a treatment will work in one setting because of unique circumstances that do not generalize to other situations?

Assume that a researcher found that workers on an assembly line are less likely to call in sick if they received extra pay for using fewer than average sick days. Can we generalize these results to people who work in management—will extra money increase a manager's productivity? Notice that taking sick days and productivity are not the same. Consequently, it is possible that extra pay will work in some work settings but not others.

Effects of history

Can the results of an experiment conducted 50 years ago generalize to current situations? What about an experiment conducted during a series of unique political and social conditions? Does the time during which we conduct a study affect the results and thereby compromise the external validity of the results? There are cases where the results of a study are relevant to a particular era and do not necessarily generalize to contemporary situations.

Consider the familiar achievement tests that most college-bound students take during their senior year of high school. Many years ago, there were large systematic differences between men and women. Women scored higher on the verbal components of the test, whereas men scored higher on the math section of the test. Some people thought that the differences represented a fundamental difference between men and women's cognitive abilities. Researchers now find that the difference between men and women's scores on these achievement tests has declined (Hyde & Lynn, 1988). Women now score higher on the mathematics portions of the tests. What caused the changes in the test scores? Things have changed during the last 50 years. Women may now receive better math and science education than 50 years ago because teachers are more likely to encourage women to study and excel in these subjects.

ACHIEVEMENT CHECK

(1) Explain why internal and external validity refer to a researcher's interpretation of the data and not the data.

(2) A researcher claims that there is a cause-and-effect relation between two variables. You believe that there is a significant threat to the internal validity. Can the researcher continue to claim that the interpretation has external validity?

(3) A psychology instructor wants to examine the effectiveness of a new teaching method. On the first day of classes, she administers to all the students a 100-item multiple-choice test that reviews the major content areas of psychology. She uses a similar test as the final exam. List the potential threats to internal validity that you believe could apply to this study.

(4) A researcher believes that changes in physiological reaction (e.g., heart rate and amount of sweat on the hands) indicate when someone is lying. To test this hypothesis he conducts a study using college students. He gives students an envelope that contains either a blank piece of paper or a $100 bill. He then tells all the students to say that they found a blank piece of paper in the envelope during a lie-detection test. Assume that the researcher finds evidence supporting the claim that one can detect a lie based on physiological reactions

and that the police can use lie-detector tests in criminal investigations. What issues related to external validity does the researcher need to consider when interpreting the data?

(5) Miranda found an article published in the early 1960s that examined short-term memory, but decided not to read it because it is over 40 years old. She told her friend, "Why read the paper? The results are no longer relevant today." Comment on her conclusion.

SURVEY OF EMPIRICAL METHODS

The following sections review different empirical research methods. In each section, I will give you a brief description of the method, its role in contemporary psychology, and its potential advantages and disadvantages. I will also add a few points about issues related to internal and external validity.

True Experiments

We begin by reviewing the **true experiment** not because the method is popular among psychologists or because it offers the best source of data. We begin with the true experiment because it is the best technique we can use to determine cause and effect. The value of the true experiment is that it allows us to control for and remove potential threats to internal validity. Specifically, the true experiment allows us to ensure that the independent variable comes before the dependent variable, that the independent and dependent variables are related, and that we can account for alternative explanations.

Several critical features set a true experiment apart from other research methods. These features are:

1. The independent variable is a manipulated variable under the researcher's control,
2. the researcher uses random assignment to place individuals into the different research conditions, and
3. the researcher can create one or more control conditions.

Manipulated independent variable

The hallmark of a true experiment is that the researcher directly controls the levels of the independent variable. In the other research designs, the researcher uses subject variables that he or she cannot control. By contrast, in the true experiment, the researcher can select an independent variable and then select different conditions to use in the experiment.

A **qualitative independent variable** represents a variable that uses a nominal scale. For example, a psychologist may use different forms of psychotherapy (e.g., psychoanalytic, behavioral, family systems, and rational-emotive) to determine which is the most effective for the treatment of depression. In this example, psychotherapy is a qualitative independent variable in that the forms of treatment represent mutually exclusive types of therapy.

A **quantitative independent variable** is a variable represented by an ordinal or more sophisticated measurement scale. For instance, the researcher may vary the time that students practice before a test. For such an experiment, time is the independent variable and measured using a ratio scale. Similarly, the researcher may vary the complexity of the task. In this situation, the researcher may have used an ordinal scale to rate the task as easy, moderately challenging, or difficult.

Whether the independent variable is qualitative or quantitative, the researcher has control over the **treatment condition** the participants experience. In the example of psychotherapies, each type of psychotherapy would represent a level of the independent variable.

In an experiment that examines memory, the researcher may vary the time that people study a problem. For this experiment, time is the independent variable, and the treatment conditions might include 0 minutes, 1 minute, 5 minutes, and 10 minutes of study time. In other words, study time represents the independent variable and has four levels.

Random assignment

Random assignment is another critical component of the true experiment. **Random assignment** means that each participant selected for the experiment has an equal chance of experiencing one of the research conditions. The value of random assignment is that it reduces alternative explanations of the results.

Figure 3.2 illustrates the logic and steps of a true experiment. In this example, the researcher begins by selecting 30 participants from the sampling population and then randomly assigns them to one of the three treatment conditions. At this point, the three groups

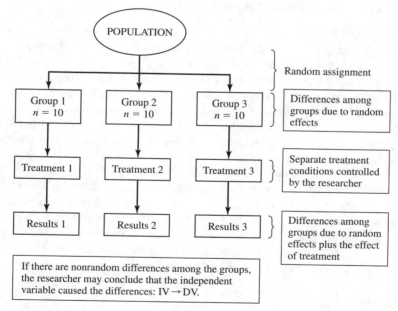

FIGURE 3.2

A true experiment. The researcher selects participants from the sampling population and randomly assigns them to treatment conditions. The researcher then exposes the groups of participants to specific levels of a manipulated independent variable. In the last stage, the researcher examines the differences among the groups.

should be similar to each other. Will they be identical? No, if we were to compare the three groups, we would find minor differences among them. These differences will be trivial, however. Recognize that any difference among the groups reflects chance or random effects. Once we form the three groups, we then expose the participants in each group to a different level of the independent variable.

The final step in the illustration is examining the differences among the groups. These differences will reflect the effects of the independent variable and random factors. In most cases, we use statistical techniques to determine the proportion of the difference due to the independent variable and the proportion of the difference due to random factors.

Using random assignment is an important technique to ensure the internal validity of the experiment. By randomly assigning participants to the treatment conditions, we prevent the confound between their selection and the treatment condition. Consider the following example. A researcher assigns all the women to one treatment condition and all the men to the other condition. If we find a difference between the two groups, what variable caused the difference, the sex of the participants or the level of the independent variable to which they were exposed? We cannot tell because the sex of the people is confounded with the treatment they received. Specifically, the sex of the participants correlates with the treatment they received. Using random assignment, there should be equal proportions of men and women in both groups causing the characteristics' treatment condition to be independent of the participant's characteristics. Therefore, we can conclude that the difference between the groups reflects the levels of the independent variable.

Use of control groups

The final hallmark of a true experiment is the control group. **Control groups** are essential to the true experiment because they help us rule out a host of alternative explanations. In its basic form, a control group is the group of participants who experience the same treatment as the other participants except for exposure to the independent variable. Although this definition sounds simple enough, control groups can become sophisticated. First, there are many types of control groups. In addition, it is possible to use several control groups in a single experiment. Selecting the appropriate control condition or conditions allows the researcher to make a more convincing case that the independent variable, and not some other variable or variables, caused the differences among the groups.

The placebo treatment is one of the more familiar control conditions. Researchers frequently use placebos to determine the effectiveness of a drug. A placebo is a treatment, such as a pill or an injection, which does not include the active ingredient. In a drug study, the researcher will randomly assign some of the participants to the placebo treatment group. If the researcher finds a meaningful difference between the treatment and placebo groups, then he or she can make a convincing argument that the drug caused the difference.

Utility for Psychology

The true experiment is perhaps one of the most important tools that psychologists have to study behavior because it allows us to determine cause and effect. Although other research techniques may indicate the meaningful relation between the independent and dependent variables, only the true experiment offers an unambiguous opportunity to determine cause and effect.

Potential Limitations

The true experiment is without equal for determining cause and effect. The true experiment does, however, have limitations. First, researchers cannot manipulate some independent variables because of ethical or practical concerns. Imagine a developmental psychologist who wants to study the effects of physical abuse on children. No one in their right mind would conduct an experiment that randomly assigns parents to a treatment condition requiring them to beat their children.

Second, it is impossible to manipulate subject variables. For example, personality, intelligence, and sex are unique characteristics of people that may help us understand why they do the things that they do. These characteristics are variables that researchers cannot control. Therefore, we must use other research techniques to collect and examine the data.

INTACT GROUPS DESIGNS AND QUASI-EXPERIMENTAL STUDIES

There are many times when a researcher cannot control the independent variable. As I noted previously, these situations arise when it is impossible to manipulate the independent variable or it would be unethical do so. Although we may not be able to control the independent variable, we can still study its relation with the dependent variable. Two commonly used research methods are the intact groups design and the quasi-experimental designs. For both designs, the researcher treats a subject variable or some other condition as if it was an independent variable.

Intact Groups Designs

Figure 3.3 presents an example of a simple **intact groups design.** There are some important differences between this design and the true experiment. First, the researcher does not select participants from a single population. Instead, there are several populations each representing a different set of subject variables. For example, a clinical psychologist may want to select clients who fit within different diagnostic categories. Thus, one group represents people diagnosed with schizophrenia, another group represents people diagnosed with depression, and the third group represents people diagnosed with obsessive-compulsive disorder.

We cannot use random assignment to create the groups. Because we use a subject variable to define the populations, random assignment to the groups is impossible. Therefore, all we can do is assume that each sample represents its sampling population.

In the last stage we collect data and compare the differences among the groups. As with the true experiment, we assume that the differences among the groups represents random variation as well as factors associated with the subject or grouping variable. Unlike the true experiment, we cannot use these data to assume that the subject variable caused the differences. We can compare, however, the group averages. Therefore, we can test the hypothesis that $\mu_1 = \mu_2 = \mu_3$.

POPULATIONS

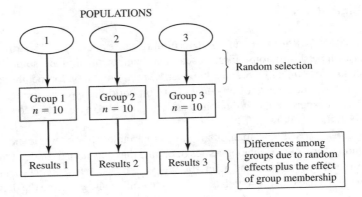

FIGURE 3.3
An intact groups design. In this design, the researcher randomly
selects participants from different sampling populations. The
researcher then compares the differences among the groups.

Quasi-Experimental Designs

A **quasi-experiment** is similar to a true experiment except that we cannot randomly assign
participants to the treatment and control conditions. Figure 3.4 presents an example of a
hypothetical quasi-experiment. As you can see, there are two groups. Because this is a
quasi-experiment, we have not randomly assigned participants to the groups; the grouping
existed before the research began. We measure both groups for the dependent variable and
then expose one group to a treatment condition. After the treatment we measure both
groups again. Therefore, this study consists of a grouping variable as well as a manipulated
variable. In this type of study, we call the independent variable a **quasi-independent variable** to indicate that the researcher can manipulate the variable but cannot randomly assign
participants to the treatment conditions.

Consider the following example of a quasi-experiment in which a researcher wants to
study the effect of a college's alcohol policy on student drinking. The researcher finds two

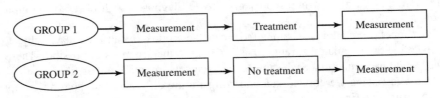

FIGURE 3.4
A quasi-experiment. The researcher uses two preexisting groups of participants and
measures each for one or more relevant dependent variables. The researcher then
exposes one group to a treatment using the other group as a control condition, and
then reevaluates both groups.

equivalent colleges. After assessing the amount of drinking on both campuses, one college establishes a "dry-campus" policy. The introduction of the policy represents the treatment. The researcher can then return to both campuses and measure students' alcohol consumption. For this example, the researcher wants to test the hypothesis that the level of drinking at one campus will be less than the other campus, or $\mu_1 < \mu_2$.

What conclusions could the researcher reach if she found that after adoption of a "dry-campus" policy there was a radical reduction in drinking among the students? Can the researcher conclude that the introduction of the treatment caused the change? The answer to this question leads us to examining the utility and limitations of the intact groups design and quasi-experiments.

Utility to Psychology

There is no doubt that the intact groups design and the quasi-experiments are useful to psychologists. Many of the variables that affect behavior are subject variables. For instance, it is common for psychologists to examine the ways men are different from women. Similarly, we can ask whether children raised by a single parent have different emotional attachments than children raised in two-parent homes. We can address these interesting topics with an intact groups design. Similarly, the quasi-experiment allows us to conduct research when random assignment of participants to treatment conditions is impossible, impractical, or unethical.

Potential Limitations

The most important limitation of the intact groups design and the quasi-experiment is the inability to form definitive conclusions regarding cause and effect. We cannot assume cause and effect because we do not have direct control over the independent variable. In other words, these designs cannot ensure the internal validity of the link between the independent and dependent variables. There are two major threats to internal validity to review: (a) the third variable problem and (b) the temporal order problem.

The third variable problem

The **third variable problem** is that some condition, other than the independent variable, may affect the dependent variable. Figure 3.5 presents an illustration of the problem. Assume that a researcher took a random sample of men and women and compared their verbal and writing skills. If the researcher finds that women are better writers and have better verbal skills, can he or she assume that sex causes the difference? No, other variables may account for the difference. For example, the women in this study could have taken more courses that enhance writing and verbal skills. Therefore, the number of English and other courses that require reading and writing produces the difference, not the sex of the people.

As you can see in Figure 3.5, the third variable links to both the independent and the dependent variable. Because of this relation, we cannot be sure if the independent variable or the third variable causes changes in the dependent variable.

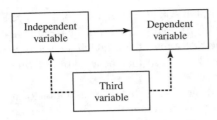

FIGURE 3.5
The third variable problem. In this example, we assume that there is a direct link between the independent and dependent variables. But there may be a third variable correlated with both. The third variable is a confounding condition because it correlates with both the independent and dependent variables. The third variable prohibits us from assuming a cause-and-effect relation between the independent and dependent variables.

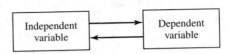

FIGURE 3.6
The temporal order problem. This problem occurs when one uses a subject variable or measures both variables at the same time. We cannot be sure which variable produces or causes the other variable.

Temporal order problem

The **temporal order problem** is a fancy title for the chicken–egg problem: Which came first—the chicken or the egg? Figure 3.6 illustrates this problem. Because we do not control the independent variable, we cannot be sure if the independent variable caused the dependent variable or whether the opposite is true.

Imagine that you compared the self-esteem of depressed and nondepressed people, finding that people with low self-esteem are also depressed. Can you use these data to assume that low self-esteem causes depression? The problem is that in this type of research, the researcher will measure the constructs, self-esteem and depression, at the same time. Therefore, we do not know which came first, the low self-esteem or the depression.

SURVEYS

Researchers use **surveys** to estimate population parameters. As you may recall from chapter 2, we write this hypothesis as $M \approx \mu$. The following is an example of the contemporary use of survey research.

Teen pregnancy is a serious problem in the United States. Each year, thousands of young unmarried women become pregnant. The consequences of these pregnancies are staggering. According to a report by the Anne E. Casey Foundation (1999),

> "The combination of lost tax revenues and increased spending on public assistance, child health care, foster care, and the criminal justice system totals about $7 billion annually for births to teens" (p. 8).

To understand the prevalence of teen pregnancy, we need to collect objective data. The report, *When Teens Have Sex: Issues and Trends* (Anne E. Casey Foundation, 1999), documents the prevalence of pregnancy within each state. This report pulled together the results of health data collected by different surveys conducted by different research teams. These data are of considerable value to researchers and policymakers.

Researchers can use the data to determine the course of future research. For example, some states have exceptionally high rates of teen pregnancy whereas others have much lower rates. What causes this difference? Additional survey research may yield an answer. A researcher may develop a questionnaire that asks teenagers about their attitudes toward premarital sex, the use of birth control, and other factors. The results of the survey may help explain why one group of young women is more likely to become pregnant than another group.

Policymakers may use the data to change a state's policies or funding for various health programs. Finding exceptionally high pregnancy rates in a state may prompt lawmakers into action to find a legislative solution.

There are countless examples of surveys. The general feature of any survey is that it consists of a representative sample of the population. Having a representative sample allows us to generalize from the sample data to the population. Another feature of surveys is the collection of objective information. In most cases, people responding to a questionnaire can answer *Yes* or *No,* rate their response on a 7-point scale, or select from one of several options. Chapter 7 offers a comprehensive review of how to design questionnaires.

Utility to Psychology

Surveys are extremely useful ways of obtaining information and they give us accurate estimates of important population parameters. Surveys also allow us to collect information quickly and with minimal expense.

Potential Limitations

Surveys suffer from several potential limitations. First, people do not always tell the truth. How would you respond if you received a questionnaire in the campus mail asking you to describe your sexual behavior or about cheating on exams? Would you be honest? Researchers who conduct surveys are aware of this problem and attempt to use techniques that produce honest results. These techniques are not always effective, however.

A second problem is that what we say and what we do are often two different things. The answer to a survey question that a person gives may reflect their ideal view of themselves or reflect the socially acceptable thing to say. For example, some people might say that they have no sexist attitudes and that they believe that men and women should receive equal treatment. When confronted with a real life dilemma, we may see less honorable behaviors from the person who claims the moral high ground.

CORRELATIONAL STUDIES

Correlational studies evolve from surveys and allow us to test the hypothesis, $\rho > 0$ or $\rho < 0$. For a survey project, we want to estimate a population parameter. In other words, we want to know how much, how often, or how many. For a correlational study, we want to know the extent of the correlation among two or more variables.

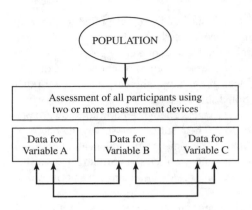

FIGURE 3.7
A correlational design. The researcher selects participants from the sampling population and measures two or more variables. The researcher then examines the correlation among the different variables.

Figure 3.7 presents the steps of a correlational study. In the first step, we create a sample and then administer two or more tests to the participants. The tests could take any form. One test might be a personality inventory and the other test a survey of attitudes. The essential characteristic of a correlational study is that we collect two or more bits of information from each participant.

In Figure 3.7 I used lines with arrows on both ends to connect the variables. I did this to emphasize that when we use a correlation, we cannot assume cause and effect. For example, can you assume that hours studying cause higher grades if you found that there is a correlation between hours spent studying and grades? No, GPA and hours studying are subject variables that the researcher does not directly control. Therefore, we cannot easily resolve the third variable or the temporal order problems.

Utility to Psychology

The correlational design is popular in psychology, especially in the study of social psychology, personality assessment, and industrial/organizational psychology. By examining the correlation among variables we may be better able to understand complex behaviors. For example, industrial/organizational psychologists examine the relation between personality and work behavior. Knowing the relation between these variables allows psychologists to predict how people will perform on the job.

Potential Limitations

Like the intact groups design and the quasi-experimental design, the correlational design cannot support conclusions of cause and effect. Specifically, the correlational design cannot resolve the third variable problem or the sequence of events problem.

SINGLE-PARTICIPANT RESEARCH METHODS

When most people think about research, they have a vision of vast groups of people assigned to different treatment conditions. The researcher then combines and examines the data as a group. Although a popular image of psychological research, it is not completely correct. There are many cases where a researcher will use only one or two participants as the focus of the research. Instead of examining the behavior of many people, the psychologist will examine, in detail, the behavior of one person. Single-participant research methods have a long history in psychology. Fechner and Ebbinghaus, two important figures in the history of psychology, conducted much groundbreaking research using single-participant designs, and their work and methods are still relevant.

Single-participant experiments

A **single-participant experiment** is conducted using one participant. I know that that definition is a bit circular, so let me elaborate. In all true experiments, we have an independent variable and a dependent variable. We then try to determine if the independent variable causes the dependent variable to change. Another feature of an experiment is that we measure the dependent variable in the presence of the independent variable as well as in its absence. We can meet these requirements using a single-participant experiment. We will review the principles of the single-participant experiment in chapter 14.

Case studies

The **case study** may be one of the more familiar forms of single-participant methods. The essential feature of a case study is the intense review of the behavior of one person. Sigmund Freud made extensive use of case studies to develop his theory of personality and abnormal behavior. For example, he used his famous case of Anna O. to develop his theories of hysterical disorder. He also used the case study to show the effectiveness of psychoanalysis as a diagnostic tool and treatment technique (Freud & Breuer, 1895/1976).

In some cases, a person will suffer an unfortunate accident that allows us to gain insight into the workings of the brain. For example, a person known by the initials HM underwent brain surgery in the 1950s as a cure for epilepsy. Although the surgery cured HM's epilepsy, it destroyed HM's ability to create long-term memories. Many psychologists have studied HM's inability to form long-term memories and have made important discoveries about the relation between different parts of the brain and their role in memory formation (Milner, 1966; Milner, Corkin, & Teuber, 1968).

Utility for Psychology

Single-participant experiments serve an important role in psychology. The real advantage of this method is that we can use sound experimental techniques to determine how to influence a person's behavior. For example, behavior modification techniques, derived from laboratory research, help children and adults with behavioral and emotional problems. Using a single-participant research design, the clinical psychologist can tailor the therapy for the particular needs of the client and then collect objective data to determine whether the treatment works. The internal validity of single-participant experiments can be good, depending on how well the researcher controls the independent variable and other situational variables.

Case studies serve as important teaching tools and exemplars of basic principles. There are many times when psychologists will use a case study as a part of their work. When I teach my courses, I often use my children's behavior as examples of a particular psychological principle. Although my children hate that their behavior is on public display, the examples allow me to give my students illustrations that help them learn the material.

In a more serious tone, a researcher may use a case study to demonstrate the utility of a specific principle. David Premack (1959, 1965) used the behavior of several students to demonstrate the value of his theory of positive reinforcement. The single-participant experiments allowed Premack to demonstrate that his theory had practical applications as well as important theoretical applications.

Potential Limitations

The problem with this research method is that we are looking at the behavior of a single person or a small group of people. The case study, for example, does not allow us to make sweeping generalizations about the population. Although we may learn much about the motivations and history of a single person, we cannot conclude that what was true for the person in the case study is true of all people.

Case studies

Although case studies offer interesting information, we must interpret the information with some care. What are some of the potential limitations of case studies? The following is a short list of several of the more severe problems.

Verification of facts. Many times, the person collecting the information for the case study has no way of confirming the facts that are a part of a person's history. Elizabeth Loftus (Loftus & Ketcham, 1994) provided compelling evidence that the questions people ask us can distort our memories. Therefore, a major weakness of any case study occurs when we must rely exclusively upon the individual's memory for critical facts about their lives.

Potential for bias in examples. In many cases, an author will present a case study because the case fits his or her theory. Howard Gardner's book, *Leading Minds* (1995), is an example. In the book, Gardner presented an interesting theory of leadership. He then presented case studies of 10 great leaders from history (e.g., Margaret Mead, George Marshall, and Eleanor Roosevelt). Although the theory and case studies are interesting, we must ask if they are proof of the accuracy of the theory. One problem is that Gardner may have selected people who demonstrate his theory while ignoring great leaders who do not fit his theory of leadership. Similarly, because Gardner is recounting the history of another person, he may have selected only those episodes of the person's life that fit his theory.

META-ANALYSIS

Listening to news reports of research findings can sometimes be frustrating. You may hear that a group of researchers claims that they found the cure for a terrible disease. Later, another team of researchers reports that the treatment is not effective. These experiences cause many people to think that science must be only one step removed from witchcraft. The problem is not with the scientists but with how we look at individual research reports.

No single experiment can offer definitive proof by itself. Each experiment is subject to a host of random factors that affect the results. Specifically, an experiment is a sample, and only a sample, of the population. Hence, there is always a chance that a single experiment or research study, no matter how well conducted, may produce misleading results. This is the reason replication is such an important part of research.

If a researcher reports an interesting finding, the chances are that he or she will conduct more studies to examine the effect in detail. Other researchers will join in and publish their results. How will we evaluate the accumulated collection of research findings?

Many researchers write *literature reviews* that summarize the findings of many research projects. The author reads all the relevant research and then describes what he or she believes to be the general findings. Literature reviews are important because they allow us to take a step back from the individual studies and look for the broader significance of the research. There are some problems, however. Literature reviews tend to be subjective, and they are not quantitative. When the author reads the results of a study, he or she has to judge whether the results are meaningful. There are better ways to examine the outcomes of empirical research.

In 1978, Glass developed a method to objectively analyze the outcomes of many studies. This technique, called meta-analysis, allows the reviewer to quantify the results of the individual studies. In other words, **meta-analysis** allows us to do a statistical analysis of statistical outcomes. The logic of meta-analysis is rather straightforward. The more often one samples from a population, the greater the accuracy of the sample average. The goal of meta-analysis is to offer a quantitatively based and objective review of the research literature.

Utility for Psychology

Since its introduction, meta-analysis has become a popular review method for psychology and other research disciplines. You will find that researchers in psychology, medicine, political science, sociology, education, and other empirical sciences use meta-analysis extensively. It is an almost essential component of any literature review.

Potential Limitations

Although meta-analysis uses objective mathematical techniques to examine the data, there remains a subjective component—selection of the studies for the review. To conduct a meta-analysis, one must first determine whether the researcher used proper research methods to collect the data. The reviewer will examine the method and determine whether the data afford valid interpretations. If the reviewer finds an error in the study, he or she will exclude the results from the meta-analysis. Many people complain that this step biases the results of the meta-analysis.

RESEARCH IN ACTION: EFFECTIVENESS OF PSYCHOTHERAPY

As you learned in this chapter, internal and external validity are central concepts in all research. In this section, we will review a research project that examined the effectiveness of psychotherapy.

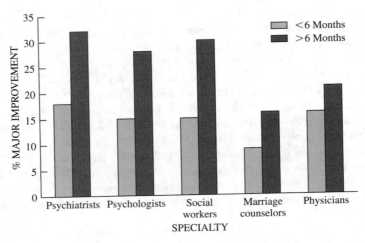

FIGURE 3.8

Percentage of individuals reporting a major improvement in their mental health depending on the type of psychotherapist they saw and the length of treatment. The data are based on a figure presented by Seligman (1995).

Washing machines, tires, compact cars, and psychotherapy: Do they work—are they worth the money? *Consumer Reports* is a magazine devoted to rating the quality, safety, and economic value of different products that consumers buy. The editors take great pride in their well-deserved reputation for scrutiny, objectivity, and fairness.

In 1995, the magazine published an article that examined the effectiveness of mental health treatment. We can use this research to further examine internal and external validity. To do so, we must first examine the methods the researchers used. We can begin our analysis of the study by exploring how the authors collected the data.

Each year, *Consumer Reports* sends questionnaires to its over 4 million subscribers (Kotkin, Daviet, & Gurin, 1996). In 1994, *Consumer Reports* sent 184,000 subscribers a comprehensive survey that examined their experience with different forms of psychotherapy. Of the 184,000 subscribers contacted, 22,000 people completed the questionnaire. Of the returned questionnaires, 6,900 people indicated that they had sought professional help for emotional problems within the past three years.

Figure 3.8 presents a summary of the data. The graph presents several pieces of important information. First, the figure displays the data by the type of professional: psychiatrists, psychologists, social workers, marriage counselors, or physicians. The figure also distinguishes between people who saw the professional for less than 6 months and those who saw the professional for more than 6 months. We can treat these variables (type of provider and time in therapy) as independent variables. The dependent variable was the percentage of people who reported a "major improvement" in their condition.

The results of the survey, based on this sample, led some people to make several conclusions:

1. People benefited from psychotherapy.
2. Long-term treatment was more effective than short-term treatment.

3. Psychotherapy alone was as effective as medication and psychotherapy combined. This conclusion presumes that psychiatrists prescribed medication as a part of their treatment.
4. Mental health professionals were more effective than marriage counselors and physicians (Seligman, 1995).

Now comes the tricky part. What confidence can we have in conclusions drawn from these data? For the sake of argument, we can focus our attention on the first conclusion: *People benefited from psychotherapy*. We can rewrite the statement in several different ways:

1. People responding to the questionnaire reported being satisfied with the psychotherapy they received.
2. People receiving psychotherapy are generally satisfied with the treatment they received.
3. Psychotherapy caused people's mental health to improve.

Can you see the differences among the statements? What are the implications for these differences? Statement 1 is a report of fact. The focus of the statement is the sample of respondents. In addition, there is no particular conclusion other than a summary of the results. Now compare Statement 1 with Statement 2.

Statement 2 takes a step away from the sample and makes an inference about the population. The focus of the generalization is descriptive in that it implies that because the sample of respondents expressed satisfaction we can assume that the population will express the same level of satisfaction.

By contrast, Statement 3 is a dramatic shift from the first two statements. Not only does the conclusion generalize from the sample to the population, it also assumes that there is a cause-and-effect relation between psychotherapy and improved mental health.

Earlier in this chapter, I said that the data are not valid or invalid—only the researcher's interpretations. Can you use what you have learned so far to determine the types of inferences we can make from these data? Specifically, evaluate the internal and external validity of the conclusions.

What type of research design does this research represent? At one level, the research is a survey. The staff of *Consumer Reports* mailed a detailed questionnaire to some of its subscribers and then reported the results of the survey. From a different perspective, you can see that we have an intact groups design because we have different groups of people receiving treatment from different providers. Can we use these data to assume a cause-and-effect relation as implied in Statement 3?

What are the conditions necessary to assume cause and effect? Are these conditions present in the *Consumer Reports* study? The three characteristics of a true experiment are: (a) manipulated independent variable, (b) random assignment of participants to treatment conditions, and (c) control conditions. Are these conditions present in the study?

First, the researchers could not manipulate the independent variables. The people responding to the survey selected the type of therapist they saw. In addition, the researchers could not control how long the people spent in therapy. Therefore, the type of psychotherapist and the time in therapy are subject variables. In addition, the researchers could not randomly assign the people to the different categories of treatment provider or the length of treatment.

Second, are there control conditions? In a true experiment, the most extreme control condition would be a group of people who receive no psychotherapy during the course of the study. We need control groups because some mental health problems improve spontaneously.

Like the old saying, *Time heals all wounds,* some people may feel better as they put some distance between themselves and the situation that caused their distress. They may also find ways of coping with the problem. Thus, the purpose of a control group is to determine if psychotherapy has a greater effect than the passage of time. Clearly, there is no control group in this study.

Because the design of the study does not meet the criteria of a true experiment, we cannot conclude that psychotherapy caused people's mental health to improve. In making this observation we have criticized the conclusion, not the data. The specific objections we raised concern the internal validity of the interpretation. We determined that we cannot assume that the independent variable (psychotherapy) caused the dependent variable (improvement in mental health).

What about the external validity of conclusions drawn from this study? Statement 2 implies that the data are representative of the population of people who seek psychotherapy. The statement also implies that clients are generally satisfied with the treatment they receive. Strupp (1996) argued that evaluating a patient's sense of well-being is an important part of any research on the effectiveness of psychotherapy. He, like many psychotherapists, believes that research of this type should examine the client's adaptive behavior, personality structure, and sense of well-being. Therefore, the information concerning the client's evaluation of the treatment they received is an important part of the research examining psychotherapy. Consequently, the *Consumer Reports* study has the potential of telling us how people reacted to the treatment they received.

Do the data allow us to generalize from the sample to the population? Several researchers criticized the external validity of this conclusion (Brock, Green, & Reich, 1998; Brock, Green, Reich, & Evans, 1996; Jacobson & Christensen, 1996). These researchers raised several questions about who responded to the questionnaire.

In an ideal world, we would prefer a random sample of all people who received psychotherapy. The current data reflect only people who received psychotherapy *and* who subscribe to *Consumer Reports*. Although we may agree that *Consumer Reports* is a good magazine, we must ask whether people who subscribe to the magazine represent the typical person seeking psychotherapy or the typical person who may require psychotherapy.

Another issue to examine is the return rate of the questionnaires. As Brock et al. (1998) noted, only a small proportion of the original sample indicated seeking help from a therapist. There may be some self-selection bias in who returned the surveys. We cannot be sure whether the data represent the population or only those satisfied with their experiences. Brock et al. argued that the sample did not represent the population and therefore do not support inferences about the population of people seeking psychotherapy.

Where does all this criticism lead us? Can we conclude that psychotherapy does not work? No, there is no information that would warrant such a reckless conclusion. Many research reports confirm the effectiveness of psychotherapy. Jacobson and Christensen (1996), for example, offered a readable account of this research. Our review of this case merely illustrates that you must interpret the *Consumer Reports* data with caution.

ACHIEVEMENT CHECK
(6) Describe how one's hypothesis will determine the research design that one will use.
(7) How does the inclusion of one or more control groups help us determine cause and effect in a true experiment?

(8) How does random assignment help ensure the internal validity of our interpretation of the data?

(9) There is a strong correlation between whether a mother smokes and the health of her children. The children of mothers who smoke have more health problems than the children of mothers who do not smoke. Do these data allow us to conclude that smoking causes poor health in children?

(10) The following are short descriptions of research projects. For each scenario, identify the:

    (a) Independent variable(s) and the dependent variable.

    (b) Hypothesis that the researcher appears to be testing (you will have to infer this from your reading of the scenario).

    (c) Empirical method that the researcher used.

    (d) Aspects of the research design influencing our evaluation of internal validity.

    (e) Aspects of the research design influencing our evaluation of external validity.

    (f) Changes you would make to the study to improve the internal and external validity.

       (i) A researcher wants to determine if there is a sex difference in altruism. To study this difference, the researcher has a male friend pose as a motorist who needs help changing a tire. The researcher counts the number of men and women who offer to help. The data suggest that men are 50 times more likely to offer help to the motorist. The researcher concludes that men are more altruistic than women.

       (ii) A psychologist was interested in examining the effects of a freshman seminar course. The researcher assumed that students' appreciation for the course would increase as they progressed through school. The psychologist distributed a survey to the seniors and found that the majority of the students endorsed the statement, "I enjoyed my freshman seminar." The psychologist reported to the dean that the course had succeeded at preparing students for college.

       (iii) A psychologist convinced a large corporation that she had a year-long training program that increases the effectiveness of a salesperson. Impressed by the claim, the personnel director required 15 newly hired salespeople to participate in the training program. All 15 had worked for approximately 18 months as salespeople. During the year, the salespeople continued their sales work as well as spending three hours a week in the sales seminar. At the end of the year, sales for all 15 salespeople had increased a significant amount. The personnel director decided that all new salespersons would take the seminar as a part of their training.

CHAPTER SUMMARY

This chapter provided a broad overview of the research methods that behavioral researchers use to conduct their research. A research design is a plan to collect data. More specifically, the purpose of a research design is to allow the researcher to collect data that answer a research hypothesis.

Whenever we prepare to design a study, we need to consider two important forms of validity, internal validity and external validity. As you learned, internal and external validity refer to the interpretations one can make from the results of the study.

Internal validity refers to the researcher's ability to show a cause-and-effect relation between two variables, the independent and dependent variables. Cause-and-effect relations are difficult to demonstrate because of the number of threats to internal validity. Careful attention to research design can help the researcher avoid the threats to internal validity including (a) unintentional sequence of events, (b) nonequivalent groups, (c) problems with measurement, and (d) ambiguity of cause and effect.

External validity refers to our ability to use the results to make inferences beyond the study. Specifically, we can ask how the findings generalize to the target population. We can also ask whether the results reached with one study will generalize to different populations and different applications of the variables.

There are many threats to external validity including bias in the methods used to recruit the participants for the study, situational factors unique to the study, and historical events that may be unique to a group of participants.

The remainder of the chapter reviewed the major research designs including the true experiment, intact groups design and quasi-experiments, surveys and questionnaires, correlational studies, single-subject methods, and meta-analysis.

The defining characteristic of a true experiment is the ability to manipulate systematically the independent variable and to randomly assign participants to the levels of the independent variable. In addition, true experiments include a control group. Participants in the control group experience the same things as the other subjects except for exposure to the independent variable.

Although true experiments are useful for psychology, they are sometimes impractical or impossible to perform. The intact group design and the quasi-experiment are alternatives to the true experiment. The distinguishing feature of these designs is that the researcher cannot randomly assign the participants to the different levels of the independent variable.

In our review of the quasi-experiments and intact groups design, we examined two important threats to internal validity, the third variable problem and the temporal order problem. The third variable problem is that some condition, other than the independent variable, affects both the independent and dependent variable. The temporal order problem is that the research design does not allow us to determine whether the independent variable preceded the dependent variable.

Surveys and questionnaires are useful to psychology because we can measure an interesting psychological construct by asking participants objective questions.

Correlational studies allow us to examine the relation among two or more variables. These research designs are useful for studies of personality or business administration where we are interested in the relation between one set of behaviors and other behaviors.

As the name implies, single-subject designs allow us to study one or two people. In some single-subject designs we can use experimental techniques to study the behavior of one person. For other situations, we will examine the individual's history to create a case study.

Meta-analysis is the study of research studies. Researchers who use meta-analysis use statistical techniques to combine the results of many studies. The goal of meta-analysis is to come to some uniform conclusion about a phenomenon.

The "Research in Action" section used a report on the effectiveness of psychotherapy to examine how researchers can apply different research techniques to address specific empirical questions. The review of the research illustrated that the research design affects the internal and external validity of the data.

CHAPTER GLOSSARY FOR REVIEW

Alternative Explanation   Another method of explaining the results that does not depend upon the independent variable.

Carryover Effects   A form of unintentional sequence of events threat to internal validity wherein the participants' experiences during one part of the research affects their performance in subsequent parts of the research.

Case Study   An empirical research method for which the researcher examines the history and behavior of a single person. In some situations, the researcher will use case study to describe a patient's reaction to treatment.

Ceiling and Floor Effects   A form of measurement error threat to the internal validity wherein the measurement device cannot adequately measure high-level (ceiling) or low-level (floor) performance.

Confounding Variable   A variable related to the independent variable that the researcher cannot control and that threatens the internal validity of the cause and effect hypothesis, IV → DV.

Control Group   A treatment condition in which the participants experience all aspects of the experiment except for the independent variable.

Correlational Studies   An empirical research method for which the researcher takes two or more measurements of characteristics for each participant and then examines the correlation among the variables.

External Validity   The degree to which we can generalize the results and conclusions reached with a sample to the population.

Generality of Conclusions   The degree to which the conclusion reached in one population will generalize to different populations.

Generality of Findings   The degree to which we can use the sample data to generalize about the population from which the data were drawn.

Intact Group Design   A form of research for which the researcher divides participants into separate groups on the basis of one or more subject variables. The goal of the research is to determine whether there are differences among the populations represented by the groups.

Internal Validity   The degree to which we can assume that changes in the independent variable caused changes in the dependent variable.

Intervening Events   A form of unintentional sequence of events threat to internal validity wherein the participants experience extraneous events, outside the researcher's control, that affects their behavior.

Maturation   A form of unintentional sequence of events threat to internal validity wherein the participants grow older and consequently change their behavior.

Meta-Analysis   A collection of statistical techniques used to combine the results of separate research projects to help one determine the relation between the independent and dependent variables.

Mortality   A form of nonequivalent groups threat to internal validity wherein the participants withdraw from the research.

Qualitative Independent Variable   An independent variable best described by a nominal scale.

Quantitative Independent Variable An independent variable described by an ordinal, interval, or ratio scale.

Quasi-experimental Design A form of research for which the researcher can identify an experimental group that is exposed to the variable of interest and a control that is not exposed to the variable of interest, but cannot randomly assign the participants to the two conditions.

Quasi-independent Variable A variable that the researcher may be able to manipulate but cannot randomly assign participants to different levels of the variable.

Random Assignment Each participant has an equal probability of assignment to one of the treatment conditions.

Research Design A procedure or plan for collecting data that will answer one or more empirical questions.

Regression to the Mean A form of measurement error threat to the internal validity wherein participants who obtain exceptionally high or low scores when first tested will tend to have average scores when tested a second time.

Reliability A form of measurement error threat to the internal validity wherein measurement device produces large inconsistencies of measurement.

Single-participant Experiment A form of a true experiment for which the researcher examines the behavior of a small group of participants. Each participant experiences the control and treatment conditions.

Subject Variables A form of nonequivalent groups threat to internal validity wherein the researcher uses a subject variable to group participants. The researcher will not be able to determine whether differences among groups reflect the independent variable or selection variable.

Survey or Questionnaire An objective method of obtaining information from members of a population. In most cases, the researcher will ask participants to answer a series of questions.

Temporal Order Problem A threat to internal validity. Because the researcher measures two variables at the same time, or is unable to control one of the variables, there is no way to determine which is the cause and which is the effect.

Third Variable Problem A threat to internal validity. The problem arises when a third variable correlates with both the independent and dependent variables.

Treatment Condition A level or setting of the independent variable. The differences among the treatment conditions may represent qualitative or quantitative differences.

True Experiments A form of empirical research in which the researcher randomly assigns participants to different independent groups, uses one or more control conditions, and uses a manipulated independent variable.

Unintended Sequence of Events A category of confounding variables that threaten the internal validity of the research. The threat arises when the researcher cannot control extraneous events that occur during the research.

4 LEARNING ABOUT PSYCHOLOGY AND FORMING HYPOTHESES

CHAPTER OUTLINE

- ✦ Introduction
- ✦ Bibliographic Research
- ✦ The Internet
- ✦ Developing a Search Strategy
- ✦ Searching the Literature: The Library
- ✦ Reading a Research Article

*Libraries are reservoirs of strength, grace and wit, reminders of order,
calm and continuity, lakes of mental energy, neither warm nor cold, light
nor dark. The pleasure they give is steady, unorgastic, reliable, deep and
long-lasting. In any library in the world, I am at home, unselfconscious,
still and absorbed.*

—Germaine Greer

INTRODUCTION

In this chapter we will review how to use the library and other resources to find information. In addition, we will examine how researchers share information with others. Finally,
we will explore how you can find information to help you design your research project.
Learning these skills will help you develop ideas for your research hypotheses.

BIBLIOGRAPHIC RESEARCH

The last step of a successful research project is publication. To paraphrase an age-old riddle:
*If a scientist conducts an experiment, but does not share the results, did the research really
happen?* Progress in the sciences occurs because researchers share their work with others. As
you learned in chapter 1, almost all research evolves from previous research. You also learned
that no research study by itself offers complete and final answers. At best, a good study will
answer one or two questions. A good study will raise as many questions as it solves. Reading
what others have discovered allows us to know how we should proceed with our research.

You can develop a research hypothesis by reading current research papers. As you
learn more about a particular topic, you may find unanswered interesting questions that
require additional research. At the same time, you may find that you have a different way
of looking at a problem. This chapter will help you learn where to get the best and most current information related to contemporary research in the behavioral sciences. In the first
section, we will consider three levels of bibliographic sources called tertiary, secondary,
and primary sources. Each has a different role in your bibliographic research.

Tertiary Bibliographic Sources

Tertiary bibliographic sources (also called third level) provide the most general and
nontechnical review of a topic. Almost all textbooks and articles in popular newspapers or
magazines are examples of tertiary sources. The essential feature of tertiary sources is their
generality and casual review of a topic. Unfortunately, the authors of these sources do not
have the luxury of time and space to review the topic in detail.

For example, many people recognize David Myers's (2001) introductory psychology
textbook as a rigorous and thoughtful survey of psychology. In a book of several hundred
pages, he dedicated only a few to attitudes and behavior, a popular topic in social psychology.

If you take an advanced course in social psychology, you may find that the author of the textbook will devote a whole chapter to attitudes. You may also find whole books that exclusively examine attitudes. Authors of general textbooks must review a nearly inexhaustible amount of information quickly and for readers not particularly familiar with the topic.

Therefore, the advantage of a textbook is that it gives you a quick and easy-to-understand introduction to a topic. This advantage is also its limitation. Textbook authors review the topics already well understood and typically do not discuss current trends in research. Although authors work hard to keep their books current and accurate, several years can pass between a new discovery and its description in a textbook.

You will find that textbooks are a good resource to help you begin to understand an important topic. As you read the book, take note of the boldface text. These are often the technical terms researchers use to describe different phenomena. At the same time, take note of the research articles that the author references. These papers are often good examples of research on the subject; you may want to read these references as you plan your research.

Psychology dictionaries and encyclopedias are also tertiary sources. As with textbooks, these sources have a specific but limited function. These sources are useful to someone who wants a quick answer for a general question and does not have the time and inclination to investigate a topic at length. You should not use textbooks, dictionaries, or encyclopedias as authorities on a topic. Although they may help you understand the meaning of specific terms or psychological phenomena, they are too general to serve as the foundation of your research. When you write your research paper, you will most likely use primary and secondary sources.

Secondary Bibliographic Sources

As you can infer from the name, **secondary bibliographic sources** stand between tertiary and primary sources. Secondary sources are more in-depth than textbooks or other tertiary sources. In general, secondary sources are comprehensive reviews and written by an expert on the topic. There are many outlets for secondary sources. The two categories that I will review are books and literature reviews.

Books

Each year, many researchers publish insightful and useful commentaries on different phenomena in psychology. For instance, all introductory psychology textbooks review Pavlov's classical conditioning experiments. Textbooks dedicated to learning may devote four or five chapters to various topics related to classical conditioning. By contrast, a secondary source may exclusively review a single topic within classical conditioning or review the state of the art regarding current theories and trends in research.

The advantage of secondary sources is that they bring you closer to the heart of the research problem. Unlike textbooks, secondary sources are more likely to examine important issues related to the methods of conducting research on the phenomenon. These sources also give comprehensive summaries of current theories and trends in research. Therefore, you will find secondary sources as useful guides to a topic and often a source of good ideas for additional research.

There are limitations with secondary sources. Although secondary sources offer more focused reviews than textbooks, they are still less focused than primary sources. In addition, there remains the time lag between the publication of primary sources and their discussion in secondary sources. Although secondary sources tend to be more up-to-date than textbooks, nothing is as current as a primary resource.

Literature reviews

A literature review shares some features with secondary sources. There are some important differences, however. First, you will find most literature reviews published in specialized professional journals. Second, literature reviews tend to be more topic-specific than those published in textbooks. Like secondary sources, literature reviews provide a comprehensive summary of the current research. The author or authors summarize the relevant research reports and then describe the important factors or variables that explain the phenomenon.

There are several good sources of literature reviews. For example, the American Psychological Association publishes the journal *Psychological Bulletin,* which includes nothing but literature reviews. Many psychologists consider *Psychology Bulletin* to be a premier journal that has a well-deserved reputation for publishing some of the best and most influential reviews of psychological research. Other journals also publish literature reviews. For example, the American Psychological Society publishes the journal *Current Directions in Psychological Science.* You will also find that other journals will publish a combination of original research articles and literature reviews.

Another valuable resource is the annual book *Annual Review of Psychology.* This resource includes many chapters covering different areas of psychology. Although these reviews tend to be broader than literature reviews published in scientific journals, they are a good resource to help you learn more about a specific topic.

Primary Bibliographic Sources

Primary bibliographic sources are the original research reports that you will find published in research journals. A **research journal** is a special type of magazine that publishes scientific research articles. Many professional societies publish journals. For example, the American Psychological Association, the American Psychological Society, the Psychonomic Society, and the Society for Research on Child Development each publish one or more scholarly journals. In other cases, corporations publish scholarly journals. In all cases, the editorial board of these journals consists of prominent researchers in the field. You will find that these journals list the names and academic affiliation of the editorial board, and that the editors are well-regarded professionals working in academic or other professional institutions.

Research articles represent the greatest level of focus and detail of all the bibliographic sources. The advantage of the primary source is that there is no filtering of information. For other sources, the author must condense and remove much critical information to keep the review short and focused. Consequently, you may not learn everything about a particular experiment even when you read a secondary source. Thus, only the primary source will provide a detailed account of the research methods, the data analysis, and the complete research results.

Although primary sources contain a considerable amount of information, the reading is sometimes difficult. Professional researchers use the primary resource to communicate with other researchers. Therefore, you will find the primary source filled with pages of technical language. Don't despair! Any person who can gain entry into college can read and understand original research articles.

Peer review

Before moving on, I want to comment on an important characteristic of research journals and professional books, peer review. The goal of **peer review** is to filter out bad research and make the good research as clear and compelling as possible. Peer review is a part of the normal editing process during which experts read a manuscript to ensure that the researchers used appropriate methods to collect and analyze the data, and then made reasonable inferences from the data.

When a researcher submits a manuscript to a scientific journal, the editor will ask at least three other researchers, who are experts in the area, to read and comment on the merits of the report. Using the reviewers' comments, the editor can reject the manuscript, require that the author revise it, or accept it for publication. If the editor accepts the manuscript for publication, it means that the reviewers and editor agreed that the study met the basic requirements for sound scientific research and that other researchers will be interested in the paper.

Although the peer review system works well, errors can and do occur. There are cases of poorly designed research or faulty conclusions finding their way into the published literature. Similarly, one editor will sometimes reject important and insightful research that another editor will publish. The peer review process involves a large subjective component that no amount of tinkering can remove. Despite its flaws, the peer review system does have an essential feature; it is self-correcting.

Sometimes, published articles become the center of considerable controversy. As a part of this controversy, many question whether the peer review system works. In 1998, the *Psychological Bulletin* published the article, "A meta-analytic examination of assumed properties of child sexual abuse using college samples" (Rind, Tromovitch, & Bauserman, 1998). Some readers, especially several politically motivated individuals, objected to the article arguing that its authors advocated pedophilia. (The authors made no such claim. Rather, they argued that several commonly held beliefs regarding the effects of pedophilia are not accurate and required clarification.)

In response to intense political pressure, the American Psychological Association (APA) requested that the American Association for the Advancement of Science (AAAS) conduct an independent review of the peer review process that the journal had used in evaluating the original article. The AAAS declined the request. In their letter to the APA, the AAAS noted that,

> We see no reason to second-guess the process of peer review used by the APA journal in its decision to publish the article in question. While not without its imperfections, *peer review is well established as a standard mechanism for maintaining the flow of scientific information that scientists can refer to, critique, or build on* [italics added]. . . . Uncovering [a problem with a manuscript is] the task of those reviewing it prior to publication *[and] to the reader of the published article* [italics added]. . . . (Lerch, 1999)

I believe that the AAAS made the correct decision and offered an important message in their response. Science depends upon an open and free exchange of ideas. The peer review process should be a filter for faulty and flawed work, but should not become a barrier that censors unpopular ideas. Furthermore, the reader has the ultimate responsibility to think critically about the information and conclusions presented in any published article. You, as the reader, must assume the responsibility to analyze and critique the ideas presented in a published article.

Errors in the published literature do not last long. If an author publishes a paper with an error, other researchers will be quick to note the mistake. In most cases, when researchers disagree with the findings printed in an article, they will conduct research to support an alternative perspective or interpretation. The researcher will then put the new results into the publication cycle. Therefore, bad ideas, poor research, and faulty inferences do not last long in the scientific community. Researchers quickly ignore and forget findings and conclusions that cannot withstand the scrutiny of systematic and direct replication. In the same vein, novel and unique results that researchers can replicate receive considerable attention in the research community.

THE INTERNET

Although many people find the Internet a fascinating and interesting resource, it has limitations. First, there is no peer review for the vast majority of Internet web pages. There are currently few, if any, restrictions on what one may post on a web page. In many ways, the Internet is the modern soapbox. Any person can publish his or her ideas on the Internet without fear of censorship, a constitutional right for all Americans.

The second problem with the Internet is that it is an ever-changing medium with no permanent record. Books, journals, and other print media are tangible, permanent products. There is no equivalent for web pages.

Although the Internet is a wonderful resource, you should use it with care and a strong dose of skepticism. You cannot trust everything you read on the Internet. In fact, you should be careful with everything you read, regardless of its source. There are some important differences, however, between what you will find on the Internet and in professional journals. This raises the question, *"How should we use the Internet?"*

Click, Check, and Double Check

If you use the Internet, you should be aware of some things. First, search engines and subject directories are not complete and exhaustive reviews of current web pages (Brandt, 1996, 1997). Therefore, when you are searching the Internet, you should recognize that a search will be incomplete and that different search engines will produce different results.

Second, you should be cautious about the material you find on the web. As with any research project, you should not rely on one source of information. When you read something, from the Internet or some other source, you need to determine whether the information is credible. Here are a few tips you should follow as you examine a web page:

- **Check the credentials of the author.** I tend to be skeptical of web pages that have no clearly identified author or if the author does nothing to indicate his or her credentials or professional affiliation.
- **Check how well the author annotates the web page.** If the web page contains lots of claims and conclusions but no supporting information, be suspicious. Serious authors include a bibliography with their text. The bibliography allows the reader to double check

the original sources to ensure that the author has presented the information accurately. You should use this practice for any information you use, Internet or print.

- **When in doubt, doubt.** There is an old saying about free advice—you get what you pay for. You should not rely on a web page as your primary source of information. Find corroborating evidence from other sources before you make an assertion and run the risk of embarrassing yourself with incorrect information. Also, check with your professor before using references from the web; some professors may not want you to use the Internet for your research.

- **Print a copy of the web page.** If you plan to use information from a web page, it is a good practice to print a copy of the web page. This tactic will allow you to have a permanent record of the information in case the author revises or removes the material from the Internet or if your reader (e.g., your professor) wants to read the reference.

DEVELOPING A SEARCH STRATEGY

A common observation is that there are more scientists living now than in any time in history. This is especially true for psychology. Each year, more than 4,000 people receive their Ph.D. in psychology. Furthermore, there are at least 1,700 journals directly and indirectly related to psychology. If we use a conservative estimate that each journal publishes 500 pages a year, then there are 850,000 psychology journal pages published each year! This means there is an incredible amount of information about psychology, and you will need to develop a strategy for finding articles that interest you.

Find a Topic That Interests You

What are things in psychology that you find fascinating? Can you remember reading about an experiment in one of your psychology courses and thinking that it was interesting? If you are looking for a research topic, it is a good idea to begin with your interests.

Sometimes, students find it useful to sit down as a group and talk about the areas of psychology that they find interesting. As you and your fellow students talk, you may find that you have common questions about why people behave as they do. Another way to find interesting topics is to read psychology textbooks. Perhaps you took a course in the psychology of gender, child development, or social psychology. Dust off and reread those books. Chances are that you will find one or more interesting topics for your research.

Read Tertiary and Secondary Sources

Once you find a topic that you find interesting, keep reading. Begin with tertiary sources; they are the easiest to read and offer the broadest coverage. Assume, for example, that you want to learn more about altruistic behavior. As you read the general sources, you may find that altruism is a broad topic and that it includes many subcomponents. While you are reading, take note of several things. Specifically, look for specialized terms, researcher's names, notable experiments, important independent and dependent variables, and recommendations for new research. This information will help you later when you begin to search the primary literature.

Specialized terms

These words or phrases are important because they often describe special aspects of research. If you read a chapter on altruistic behavior, you are likely to read terms such as *diffusion of responsibility, empathic concern, negative-state relief,* and *norm reciprocity.* Any one of these concepts can serve as a focal point for research on altruism. Consider *empathic concern* as an example. The phrase refers to feelings of pity for another person in distress. We can ask many empirical questions about this concept:

- Are there ways to increase and decrease the level of empathic concern that people experience, and how do these changes affect helping behavior?
- Are people more likely to feel empathic concern for people like themselves?
- Are people more likely to feel empathic concern if they feel good about themselves or are happy?

Researchers' names

When searching for information on a topic, why not look for people who seem to be doing the interesting research. From my reading on altruism, I have learned that Batson is a leading researcher on helping behavior. I also learned that Cialdinei, Dovidio, Schreoder, and Sibicky are other researchers who have conducted innovative studies on helping behavior. Therefore, I will want to see if these people have done additional research on the topic.

Notable experiments

You will often find reference to one or two classic experiments in tertiary reviews. It is a good idea to read these articles as they provide a historical context for the current research. If you wanted to study helping behavior, for example, you may want to read Darley and Latané's (1968) research on the diffusion of responsibility phenomenon. You may also want to find a literature review on the topic. For example, Latané & Nida (1981) reviewed the literature on the diffusion of responsibility research and found that many researchers have verified Darley and Latané's conclusion. This background reading may help you understand the purpose of more recent research.

Talk to Your Instructors

Another good source of information is to talk with your professors about your interests. Faculty enjoy talking about their research. As you talk about your interests, your professor may be able to give you invaluable guidance by recommending additional readings or by helping you refine your research questions.

SEARCHING THE LITERATURE: THE LIBRARY

Many people have the misconception that a library is a place that stores books. Nothing could be farther from the truth. A library is a place to find information. Furthermore, size does not matter; access to information is the essential service of any contemporary library. For example, I did my graduate training at The University of Georgia, which has an exceptionally large library. When I was there, the university maintained two huge library buildings. I then taught at a small college of approximately 1,100 students whose library is tiny by comparison to Georgia's. Although the library was small, I never had a want of information. Through the college's library, I could obtain any piece of information that I desired. You can do the same at your library; all you need to do is learn how to ask the right questions. Thus, the focus of this section will be to examine the resources typically found in a college library.

Library Staff

It has been my experience that students typically overlook one of the greatest resources in the library, the professional staff. All libraries use complex storage and retrieval systems that allow librarians to store and find information efficiently. Librarians have a master's of science degree in library science, which means that they know a lot about how to find information. Many librarians also have an additional master's degree in an academic area such as psychology. At a large university, there may be a reference librarian for each general subject matter. In other words, a person with training in library science and psychology may be the reference librarian for psychology and sociology.

Search Tools

At one time, the only search tools in the library were the card catalog and various readers' guides. The computer has revolutionized and replaced many of these tools. For example, the chances are that your college's library uses an online catalog. In addition, your college probably subscribes to several specialized search tools such as *Proquest* ©, *PsycInfo* ©, *ERIC* ©, and others. These specialized search tools allow you to find specific research articles quickly.

Online catalog

All libraries keep their bibliographic material in a well-organized system that you can use to find information quickly. Specifically, most colleges use the Library of Congress classification scheme that uses a combination of letters and numbers to classify each book, document, and other materials such as films and records. For example, the Library of Congress gives books on psychology the prefix "BF." After the letter heading are numbers that indicate the specialized topic within psychology. Books on general experimental psychology receive a number between 180 and 210. The next set of numbers is the author notation that determines the exact location of the book on the shelf. This complete set of numbers and letters is the **call number.** Each book, journal, recording, and other reference in the library has a unique call number.

Because psychology is such a broad and interdisciplinary subject, you will find psychology-related books throughout the library. For instance, librarians place books on abnormal psychology, or psychopathology, in the internal medicine section (RC) and books on animal behavior in the zoology section (QL). Therefore, you can expect to roam throughout the entire library as you search for bits of information.

Most colleges allow you to search for books using an online catalog. There are many different catalog systems, too many to describe in detail. The common feature of these systems is that you can search by the author's name, the title of the book, the topic, or a keyword. Most students find these systems easy to use and provide much useful information. For example, most systems will indicate whether the book you want is on the shelf or has been checked out. In some cases, you can use the program to browse through the titles on the same shelf. This is a useful feature. Because the librarians store the books in logical categories, you may find surrounding books that may be useful.

PsycInfo

PsycInfo is a comprehensive database that contains references to books and to more than 1,700 journals of interest to psychologists. Therefore, *PsycInfo* is a powerful research tool that gives you access to all the most recent research related to psychology. Using this system, you can find research articles and literature reviews on specific topics.

Each college and university has a slightly different way of gaining access to the *PsycInfo* database. The following information will apply regardless of the system you use. Ask the reference librarian to show you how to use the resource if you have questions.

PsycInfo allows you to search the database using commonly used words or keywords. A **keyword** can be any term or phrase you want to use for the search. It can be a commonly used word or a technical term used by psychologists to describe a specific phenomenon. You can also use **Boolean operators** to condition your search. The two primary Boolean operators that you will use are **AND** and **OR.** For the sake of an example, assume that you are interested in learning more about eating disorders such as anorexia nervosa and bulimia and their treatment. You can use the terms *anorexia nervosa, bulimia,* and *treatment* as keywords.

The AND operator causes the search process to collect references that contain two or more keywords. Figure 4.1 presents an example of the search "anorexia and treatment." The two circles represent the articles containing the separate terms. The shaded area where the two circles overlap represents articles containing both words. Therefore, the AND operator is a fast way to scale down the number of references in a search.

In some cases, it is useful to increase the breadth of the search and examine more rather than fewer topics. Figure 4.2 represents a search using the OR operator. Specifically,

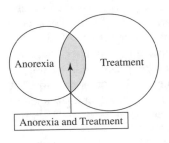

FIGURE 4.1
A search using the AND operator. Each circle represents the articles containing the word "anorexia" or the word "treatment." The shaded area where the two circles overlap represents the articles where both words are in the same reference.

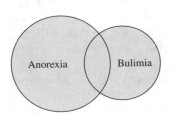

FIGURE 4.2
A search using the OR operator. Each circle represents the articles containing the word "anorexia" or "bulimia." Because the search command used OR, the search retrieves articles containing either word.

the figure represents articles that contain "anorexia or bulimia." The shading in both circles indicates that the search will include articles that contain either keyword. If you had used the command, "*anorexia AND bulimia*," the computer would only produce articles where both words appear. To summarize, AND *decreases* the number of articles included in the search whereas OR *increases* the number of articles.

Thesaurus

You may be wondering what keywords you should use. There are two answers to this question. First, if you followed my previous recommendations, you will read tertiary and secondary texts and note terms that the authors used to describe the phenomenon you want to study. The second answer is to use the *Thesaurus of Psychological Index Terms* (American Psychological Association, 2001), which contains a long list of all the keywords that librarians use to classify psychological articles and will help you select the keyword that will allow you to conduct efficient *PsycInfo* searches. If you are having trouble conducting your search, such as getting too many unrelated references or not enough relevant references, you should use the thesaurus to find and select alternative keywords. Using the thesaurus will help you to select the most representative articles.

Each entry of the thesaurus has a brief definition of the term and a series of related terms. Figure 4.3 presents an example of the entry for anorexia nervosa. As you can see, the APA librarians introduced the term as a keyword in 1973.

The third line begins a brief technical definition of the term that librarians use to classify articles by subject. You should use this definition to ensure that you use the term correctly and that the keyword will identify the articles you want.

Depending on the keyword you use, the thesaurus will provide several additional keywords that may help you in your search. These terms are alternatives that can narrow your search (using the AND command), broaden your search (using the OR command), or make your search more accurate by using the proper keyword.

The keywords following the B are broader terms that encompass the specific keyword. For example, the phrase Eating Disorders is a broader term for anorexia nervosa. Terms listed under the heading R are related terms. Related terms have some logical association with the keyword. In this example, Body Image Disturbance, and Nutritional Deficiencies are psychological disabilities related to anorexia.

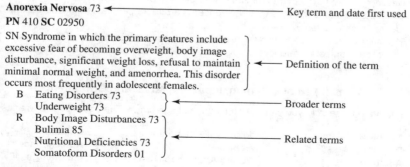

FIGURE 4.3

Entry for anorexia nervosa in the *Thesaurus of Psychological Index Terms* (2001).

Some entries will contain additional categories. One of these categories is UF, which stands for *used for*. The UF line is important to use because it is preferred to other terms that someone might use. As an example, *anoxia* is an absence or reduction of oxygen in body tissue and is the preferred term for words such as *asphyxia* and *hypoxia*.

Another category of terms is N or narrower terms. These keywords are more specific terms than the keyword. For example, if you were to look up the keyword Appetite Disorders, you would find that the thesaurus lists Anorexia Nervosa and Bulimia as narrower terms.

PsycInfo fields

Each entry in the *PsycInfo* database consists of a number of fields. A field represents a specific type of information. Box 4.1 lists these fields and their descriptions. As you can see, there are fields for the title of the article, the author's name, and the journal that published the article. You can use several of these fields to your advantage to help make your search more productive.

Consider the language field, LA. At first glance, this field seems rather trivial until you realize that there are many foreign language journals. When you conduct a search on a

---

BOX 4.1   List of the Search Fields Used in *PsycInfo*

The table lists the abbreviation for the field and its contents.

TI The title of the article.
AU The list of the author(s) name.
JN The name of the journal, the date of the publication, the volume and issue numbers, and the page numbers of the article.
LA The language of the text. Be careful—sometimes the citation will have an English title and abstract, but the text of the paper will be a different language. If you do a search that produces many references, it is a good idea to remove the foreign language articles using the command *English IN LA*.
AB The abstract is a brief discussion of the purpose and main findings of the study. Reading the abstract should tell you whether reading the entire paper would give you the information that you need.
KC Key concepts are general descriptive terms to classify the article. Sometimes these phrases can help you in your search process.
DE Descriptors are terms that librarians use to classify papers. The difference between key concepts and descriptors is that key concepts are more general terms whereas descriptors are technical terms used by the APA librarians.
PO This field stands for the population of subjects. If you wanted to find all the articles using animals as subjects referenced in *PsycInfo,* enter the command *animals IN PO*. The specific populations are:

Animal, Female, Human, Inpatient, Male, and Outpatient

AG For human research, you can search by general age group. The age groups and ages are:

Neonatal (0–1 month)	**Infancy** (2–23 months)	**Childhood** (0–12)
Preschool Age (2–5)	**School Age** (6–12)	**Adolescence** (13–17)
Adulthood (18+)	**Young Adulthood** (18–29)	**Middle Age** (40–59)
Aged (65+)	**Very Old** (85+)	

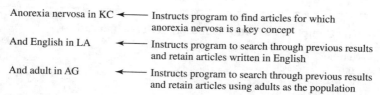

FIGURE 4.4
Commands used to conduct a search using *PsycInfo*.

popular topic, it is common to find articles written in Russian, French, German, or Japanese. Therefore, unless you can read these languages, you should filter them out of your search. The easiest way to do this is use the AND operation. As an example, the command *anorexia nervosa AND English in LA* retrieves only those articles written in English and related to anorexia nervosa. You can use the same logic and other search strategies to prune your search.

Assume that you conducted a search using *anorexia nervosa in KC*. This search would yield all the articles for which anorexia nervosa is an explicit keyword. In other words, you can be sure that the articles discuss self-starvation. Your next command might be *AND English in LA*. This command instructs the computer to search through the previous results and retain only those articles written in English. Even with this filtering, you may still want to reduce the number of articles to a manageable size. One tactic might be to focus on a specific population. For example, the command *AND adults in AG* instructs the computer to retain only those articles examining anorexia in adult-aged populations. Figure 4.4 outlines these steps. By the end of your search you should have a collection of articles examining anorexia nervosa, written in English, and focusing on adults.

Practical matters and *PsycInfo*

There is as much art as there is science to conducting a good search using *PsycInfo*. Much of the success in using this valuable tool comes from planning, practice, and patience. Searching through the *PsycInfo* database is like panning for gold. In some cases you may have to use many filtering techniques to find the right set of articles. You should not expect to find five great articles in five minutes. Rather, plan to spend quality time at the computer searching for the articles you need.

Selecting articles

Once you have a list of potential articles, you need to select the articles that you will want to read in detail. The best way to make this judgment is to read the abstract for the article. All articles published in scholarly journals have an abstract, which *PsycInfo* allows you to read. In most cases the abstract is a short paragraph of 120 words or fewer that describes the purpose or thesis of the article, a brief review of the author's method, and a synopsis of the major findings. Reading the abstract should allow you to determine if you want to invest the time and energy reading the entire article.

Box 4.2 is an example of a record for an article written by Casper and Jabine (1996). As you can see, the program provides a lot of information including the authors' names,

BOX 4.2   The Complete *PsycInfo* Record for a Published Article

Accession Number
1996-06702-007
Author
Casper, Regina C.; Jabine, Leslie N.
Affiliation
Stanford U, School of Medicine, Dept of Psychiatry & Behavioral Sciences, Stanford, CA, USA
Title
An eight-year follow-up: Outcome from adolescent compared to adult onset anorexia nervosa.
Source
Journal of Youth & Adolescence. 1996 Aug Vol 25(4) 499–517
ISSN/ISBN
0047-2891
Language
English
Abstract
(from the journal abstract) 75 women were traced and reassessed on average 8 yrs after the onset of anorexia nervosa. All patients received treatment and 88% were hospitalized at least once. Comparisons between early (11–15 yrs; N = 35), late (16–18 yrs; N = 24) adolescent and adult (19–27 yrs; N = 14) onset revealed no significant differences in outcome for age at onset. For 70% of adolescent and 42% of adult onset patients the outcome was good, meaning that the weight was within ±15% of norm with regular cyclical menstruation, 17% and 21% had an intermediate, and 9% and 21%, respectively, had a poor outcome, 5.3% had died. Taken together, 59% had physically recovered and were free of any eating disorder. Severity of illness reflected in a low body mass index, excessive exercise, and poor psychosocial functioning at intake were poor prognostic indicators; length of illness and food restriction or bulimia as eating patterns were unrelated to outcome. . . . (© 1997 APA/PsycINFO, all rights reserved)
Key Concepts Identifiers
early vs. late adolescent vs. adult onset & illness severity, prediction of clinical outcome, 18–40 yr old females with anorexia nervosa, 8 yr followup
Keywords (Thesaurus Terms)
Age Differences; Anorexia Nervosa; Prognosis; Severity (Disorders); Onset (Disorders); Adulthood; Disease Course; Followup Studies; Treatment Outcomes; Human Females
Classification Codes
3260 Eating Disorders
Population Group
300 Adulthood (18 yrs & older)
Population Location
Form/Content Type
0800 Empirical Study; 0840 Followup Study
Table of Contents (Book Records only)
Publication Year
1996

academic affiliation, and a complete citation to the journal in which the article appeared. The program also lists the ISSN/ISBN number. This is an important piece of information if you must use interlibrary loan to request a copy of the article. The ISSN number helps the librarians locate the journal in other libraries; the ISBN identifies the particulars about books listed in *PsycInfo*.

Reading the abstract provides a fair review of the content of the article. In this case, the authors examined the differences among persons diagnosed with anorexia nervosa eight years after the initial diagnosis. Specifically, the authors compared groups of patients for whom the onset of the disorder occurred during childhood, adolescence, or adulthood. The authors also examined the effectiveness of treatment as it related to the age of onset and the severity of the self-starvation. (By the way, can you recognize the type of research design they used? This appears to be an intact groups design because the researchers created the groups depending upon the age of onset of the disorder.) Depending on your interests, you may be willing to read the entire article or move on to the next abstract.

If you want to find similar articles, you can use several tricks. Look at the Key Concepts and Keywords fields. These contain words and phrases that characterize this article and that may help you search for similar articles. For example, the phrases "prediction of clinical outcome" and "Treatment Outcomes" combined with "Anorexia Nervosa" may focus your search on those articles that examine the effectiveness of psychotherapies for anorexia nervosa.

READING A RESEARCH ARTICLE

Once you have selected several articles, you are ready to begin reading. Don't expect the journal article to be easy reading. Remember, the author is a professional writing a research article for other professionals to read and will assume that you understand basic concepts. In addition, you may find the sentence structure more challenging than the typical textbook. Although the reading may be demanding, a little patience will allow you to learn much. Keep a dictionary by your side to find the meaning of unfamiliar words. Write down questions concerning information you do not understand; your professor will be glad to help you understand the more complex material.

All research articles consist of several primary parts. The following is a brief review of the general purpose and content of each section.

Introduction

The introduction establishes the rationale for the research. In most cases, the researcher will describe the problem and give a short historical account of previous research. Usually, the start of the introduction is general in that the author describes the general problem and the importance of the topic. Next, the author will describe the results and findings of previous research. Toward the end of the introduction, the author will focus on the purpose of the research and then describe the specific purpose of the research project.

Method

The method section describes all the details of how the researcher collected the data for the study and should allow you to learn how to repeat the study. The typical method section includes three subsections called participants, materials, and procedure.

In the participants section the author will tell you how he or she obtained the people for the research. Generally, this section describes the population from which he or she selected the sample. In addition, the author will describe any unique features of the participants.

The materials section describes the equipment used to conduct the study. Again, there should be enough information in this section to allow you to repeat the study. For example, if the researcher used a test to collect the data, he or she will describe the features of the test and its source.

Finally, the procedure section should offer a systematic account of the study. In this section, the researcher will describe the conditions created for each group and the method used to collect the data.

Results

Of all the sections in the journal article, this is the most technical because the author describes the various statistical tests he or she used to analyze the data. A good results section will contain a balanced combination of clear writing, statistical analysis, and graphs and tables.

Later in this book, we will review many of the statistical tests that researchers use to analyze their data. For our purpose, recognize that there are several classes of statistics, including (a) descriptive statistics, (b) correlational statistics, and (c) inferential statistics.

The descriptive statistics are the most basic and describe important features of the data. For example, most researchers use the mean (M) to describe the typical score in the data. In some cases, the researcher will use the median (MDN) to represent the typical score. The standard deviation (SD) indicates the variability of the scores.

Another group of statistics examines the correlation of groups of scores. The correlation coefficient, represented as r, is a statistical test that indicates whether there is a relation between the two variables. For example, a researcher could examine the correlation between a test of body image (whether a person believes he or she is under- or overweight) and self-esteem. A large correlation means that there is a close relation between the two variables. A small correlation means that there is no relation between body image and self-esteem.

A third class of statistics examines the differences among groups. You will probably read about many of these tests including t-ratios, ANOVAs, ANCOVAs, and other tests. The primary purpose of these tests is to determine whether the mean for one group of participants is meaningfully different from the means of other groups. For example, a researcher may compare men's and women's performance on a specific task. Using a statistical test, the researcher will ask the statistical question: *Is there a meaningful difference between men's and women's performance?* If the difference between the two groups is sufficiently large, the researcher may write that the difference is "statistically significant." Statistically significant indicates that the researcher has statistical evidence that led him or her to infer that the difference is not due to chance. You may, for example, read a sentence such as:

The difference among the groups was statistically significant, $F(2, 38) = 9.82, p < .05$, $\omega^2 = .30$.

The numbers represent the type of statistical test the researcher used. In this example, the researcher used an analysis of variance, a statistical tool we will examine in chapter 11. The "$p < .05$" is a probability statement that means that if there were no differences among the population means, the probability of obtaining the difference among the sample means observed in the study is less than 5 times in 100.

A good results section also includes graphs or tables. In many cases, you may find the graphs easier to understand than the statistical test. Take time to look at the graph and see what it tells you about the results. Then read the corresponding results section for additional information.

Discussion section

The discussion section allows the researcher to interpret the data. As they write their discussion section, most authors attempt to answer three questions: *What have I contributed here? How has my study helped to resolve the original problem? What conclusions and theoretical implications can I draw from the research?* The content of the discussion section is different from the analysis used in the results section.

In the results section, the author will describe the statistical procedures used to analyze the data. By contrast, the discussion section allows the researcher to interpret the implications of the results. In many ways, the discussion section is like an editorial. Whereas the results section presents the bare facts of the research, the discussion section offers a commentary of the results and a description of their meaning.

There is no typical discussion section. In some cases, the results of the research verify the researcher's hypotheses. In these cases, the researcher proclaims victory and describes how the results of the study verify an important theory of set of hypotheses that he or she tested. In other cases, the results of the research produce findings that conflict with previous research or with the researcher's expectation. In these cases, the researcher attempts to explain the disparity between the expected and actual results.

RESEARCH IN ACTION: DOES LISTENING TO MOZART MAKE YOU SMARTER?

In this section we will review an experiment conducted by Steele, Ball, and Runk (1997) as an example of how to read a journal article. Steel and his colleagues examined what has now become know as the Mozart effect. In essence, some people believe that listening to Mozart's music can help improve one's IQ. Steele et al. conducted an experiment to determine whether they could replicate the effect. We will begin with the introduction of the article.

Begin by reading the text in Box 4.3. The text is the introduction of the Steele et al. (1997) article.

BOX 4.3   Introduction from Steele, Ball, and Runk (1997) Experiment

Rauscher, Shaw, and Ky (1993) reported that 36 undergraduates increased their mean spatial reasoning scores the equivalent of 8 or 9 IQ points on portions of the Stanford-Binet Intelligence Scale: Fourth Edition (Thorndike, Hagen, & Sattler, 1986) after listening to 10 min. of Mozart's Sonata for Two Pianos in D Major, K448 (hereafter labeled the "Mozart effect"). The Mozart effect was temporary, having disappeared within 10 to 15 minutes. Rauscher, Shaw, Levine, Ky, and Wright (1994) reported further that short periods of music education in school produced both a temporary effect, immediately after music training, and a permanent increase over a school year in performance by preschool children on the Object Assembly portion of the Wechsler Preschool and Primary Scale of Intelligence-Revised (Wechsler, 1989).

BOX 4.3 *Continued*

The hypothesis that musical experiences of short duration can have powerful effects on IQ scores on both a short-term and long-term basis is important for both practical and theoretical reasons. However, attempts to replicate the original report by Rauscher et al. (1993) have been unsuccessful. Kenealy and Monsef (1994) were unable to produce a Mozart effect on performance using portions of the Stanford-Binet test, the Paper Folding and Cutting task and the Matrices task. Studies by Newman, Rosenbach, Burns, Latimer, Matocha, and Vogt (1995) and by Stough, Kerkin, Bates, and Mangan (1994) did not yield a Mozart effect when items from the Raven's Progressive Matrices (Raven, 1986) were the dependent measure. Carstens, Huskins, and Hounshell (1995) reported no Mozart effect when the dependent measure was the Revised Minnesota Paper Form Board Test, Form AA (Likert & Quasha, 1948).

Rauscher, Shaw, and Ky (1995) have reported a replication of the Mozart effect, using elaborations of the Stanford-Binet Paper Folding and Cutting task as the dependent measure. Further they specified that an appropriate task was one that involved not just spatial recognition but that it should incorporate spatial and temporal transformations. This observation was the basis for the dependent measure used here, a backwards digit span task. A backwards digit span task requires that a person listen to a string of digits and then reproduce them in reverse sequence. Theoretically, the backwards digit task is of interest as a spatial reasoning task because it requires rotation or transformation of the sequence (Carroll, 1993; Das, Kirby, & Jarman, 1979). Empirically, performance scores on this task correlate strongly with scores on memory for designs (Schofield & Ashman, 1986), performance with Raven's Progressive Matrices (Banken, 1985), and is a good predictor of performance with the Rod and Frame task (Haller, 1981). Right-hemisphere dysfunction reduces backwards digit span performance while left-hemisphere dysfunction reduces forward digit span performance (Rapport, Webster, & Dutra, 1994; Rudel & Denckla, 1974), although this difference does not occur in all types of disorders (Gupta, Mahto, Tandon, & Singh, 1986).

The purpose of the experiment reported here was to examine whether a Mozart effect would be produced following the procedure of Rauscher et al. (1993), using backwards digit span performance as the dependent measure.

ACHIEVEMENT CHECK

(1) What is the problem being studied?
(2) What is the authors' hypothesis?
(3) How was the hypothesis developed?
(4) How does this study relate to the problem?
(5) What type of research design did Steele et al. use?

Steele et al. (1997) provided a short and clear rationale for their study. They began by reviewing the previous research that has examined the Mozart effect and found that the results are inconsistent. In their review, they noted that several research teams did not replicate the Mozart effect when using different dependent variables. As a part of their review, Steele et al. focused on Rauscher, Shaw, and Ky's (1995) hypothesis that the Mozart effect works when the task incorporates "spatial and temporal transformations" (p. 1180). The focus of this hypothesis provides the foundation for the study. In the last paragraph of the introduction, Steele et al. made clear that they conducted the experiment to determine whether they could replicate the Mozart effect following Rauscher, Shaw, and Ky's (1993) procedures.

The next section is the "Method" section in which the authors described the people who participated in the study, the materials they used, and the systematic procedures they followed (see Box 4.4).

BOX 4.4   Method Section for Steele, Ball, and Runk (1997) Experiment

Method

Participants

Thirty-six Euro-American upper-division university students (28 women and 8 men) from two sections of a psychology course volunteered and received course credit for their participation.

Apparatus

Two stimulus tapes of approximately 10 min. duration were created. One contained the Mozart Sonata for Two Pianos in D Major (K448) and the other contained the sound of a gentle rainstorm ("Spring Showers") from an environmental sounds recording. Sequences of digits were recorded on separate tapes for the digit span task. Tapes were played on a good quality portable system.

Procedure

The experiment took place in a room reserved for that purpose. The participant was told that the experiment concerned the effect of relaxation on recall and was instructed to sit in a large, comfortable, recliner chair. The chair faced away from the experimenter who operated the tape player that had been placed on a table by the left arm of the recliner chair.

Each participant listened in turn to the Mozart tape, the rainstorm tape, or sat quietly following the verbal instruction "to relax." The order of stimulus conditions was counterbalanced across participants using a Latin square design. Following exposure to a stimulus condition, each participant listened to three nine-digit sequences. Digits were presented on the tape at the rate of one every 2 sec. After each nine-digit sequence, the participant attempted to repeat that sequence in reverse order. The score recorded was the sum of number correct across the three sequences, the maximum score being 27. Each participant heard nine sequences of digits across the experimental session, three per stimulus condition. Digit sequences were created by a random-number generator and no sequence was repeated in a session to a participant. Three different units of digit sequences were created and assigned in a balanced fashion across participants.

The number of digits correctly recalled in reverse order was recorded for each subject for each condition. A correct recall was defined as the correct digit in the correct serial location. For example, if the original sequence was 7-5-3-1-9 and the recalled sequence was 9-1-3-4-7 then the score would be 4 correct. The Rauscher et al. prediction is that the number of digits correctly reversed in recall should be enhanced in the Mozart condition relative to both the silence and the rainstorm condition.

ACHIEVEMENT CHECK

(6) What are the independent and dependent variables?

(7) Why do you think that Steele et al. used three conditions?

(8) What controls did Steele et al. use to control for confounding variables?

(9) Why did Steele et al. use the backwards digit span task?

The next section of the paper is the "Results" section wherein Steele et al. (1997) offer a narrative account of their analysis of the data. Note how they combine the use of descriptive text, tables of descriptive statistics, and inferential statistics to describe their data (see Box 4.5).

BOX 4.5   Results Section for Steele, Ball, and Runk (1997) Experiment

Table 1 shows three descriptive measures of mean recall on the backwards digit span task. The headings under "Stimulus Condition" show mean performance as a function of the type of stimulus that immediately preceded the recall task. There was no difference overall in mean recall as a function of the preceding stimulus condition, $F(2, 70) = 0.03$, $p = .97$. The outcomes of specific inferential contrasts were consistent with this observation, Music versus Rain, $t(35) = 0.03$, $p = .98$ and Music versus Silence $t(35) = 0.21$, $p = .83$.

The lack of differences in performance among stimulus conditions was not due to unsystematic variability. For example, a clear practice effect overall was observed $F(2, 70) = 21.92$, $p < .001$. Although serial position was completely counterbalanced in stimulus presentation, we calculated performance as a function of serial position. The headings under "Order of Task" in Table 1 give mean recall as a function of the serial position of the stimulus condition. The data indicate that mean recall was improved by additional experience in the task. This observation is confirmed by inferential tests, First versus Second $t(35) = 4.24$, $p < .001$ and Second versus Third $t(35) = 2.41$, $p = .02$.

All three stimulus conditions were administered in a single session as was done by Rauscher et al. (1993). Although the effect of music is supposed to be short-lived, it is possible that there was some carryover effect of music onto the other stimulus conditions or the reverse. Therefore we compared performances after the first stimulus condition only, when there would be no such effects. The headings under "First Stimulus" in Table 1 indicate recall following a stimulus condition presented first in the session. Overall there was no significant difference among treatments $F(2, 22) = 1.26$, $p = .30$. The mean recall after music is not different from that after silence, $t(11) = 0.38$, $p = .71$. Although mean recall after the rainstorm condition was lower than after music, the difference was not statistically significant, $t(11) = 1.26$, $p = .23$.

TABLE 1
Mean scores on backward digit span

Condition	M	SD	n
Stimulus condition			
Music	18.53	4.14	36
Rain	18.50	6.07	36
Silence	18.72	5.09	36
Order of task			
First	15.64	4.70	36
Second	19.14	4.87	36
Third	20.97	4.29	36
First stimulus			
Music	16.67	2.77	12
Rain	14.17	5.70	12
Silence	16.08	5.13	12

Note. Maximum score = 27. Number of scores in comparison indicated by n.

ACHIEVEMENT CHECK
(10) Did Steele et al. find evidence of the Mozart effect?
(11) Why did Steele et al. also examine the "Order of Task" and "First Stimulus" effect?

The last section of the paper is the "Discussion" section in which the authors review the implication of their research (see Box 4.6).

BOX 4.6   Discussion Section for Steele, Ball, and Runk (1997) Experiment

Exposure for 10 min to a recording of the Mozart Sonata for Two Pianos in D Major (K448) was not followed by an enhancement in performance on a backwards digit span task, a task chosen because it required a temporally extended quasispatial solution as did the paper folding and cutting task. The lack of effect here is inconsistent with the findings of Rauscher et al. (1993, 1994, 1995) but is consistent with reports from other laboratories (Carstens et al., 1995; Kenealy & Monsef, 1994; Newman et al., 1995; Stough et al., 1994). This difference is made more puzzling by the observation that Rauscher et al. have reported large effects in their studies while both Newman et al. (1995) and Stough et al. (1994) conclude confidently that there was no Mozart effect in their experiments. One explanation for the failure of this and other experiments to obtain a Mozart effect could be related to the use of different dependent measures. But different measures cannot be the entire explanation because Kenealy and Monsef (1994) did not obtain a Mozart effect even though they used a paper folding and cutting task as did Rauscher et al. Kenealy and Monsef (1994) used silence as their control condition. Rideout and Laubach (1996) reported recently a positive effect with a paper folding and cutting task but they compared exposure to a Mozart sequence against exposure to a progressive relaxation tape only. The lack of a silence-only control condition means that one cannot state whether listening to Mozart improved performance or listening to the progressive relaxation tape reduced performance. Rauscher et al. (1993) reported a Mozart effect relative to both silence and a relaxation-tape control condition.

There seems to be some important methodological difference between Rauscher et al.'s work and that of other experimenters that has not yet been elucidated. The nature of this difference constitutes a puzzle since the experimental design seems straightforward. Rauscher et al. (1994) emphasized the potential beneficial effects of increases in time and money allocated to music education in the grade-school curriculum. These practical considerations add to the importance of the solution of this scientific puzzle.

ACHIEVEMENT CHECK

(12) How do the results of this experiment relate to previous research?

(13) Steele et al. noted that the Rideout and Laubach (1996) study did not incorporate a silence control group. What is the relevance of that observation?

(14) Have Steele et al. resolved the inconsistencies in the Mozart effect?

(15) Why do you think Steele et al. commented on the requests to allocate more money to grade-school music education?

CHAPTER SUMMARY

The advance of any science depends upon an exchange of information. Psychologists, like other scientists, share the results of their research in professional research journals. Because psychology is a popular and complex topic, there is a monumental amount of information about various behavioral topics. Libraries are, therefore, important resources to help you find what researchers have discovered about psychological phenomena.

There are three classes of bibliographic source: tertiary, secondary, and primary. Tertiary sources are the most general resource, but are a useful introduction to different topics. Secondary resources are more specific and offer a more detailed review of the research that has been conducted on a specific topic. Primary resources are the original articles written by researchers.

An important component of professional research journals is peer review. Peer review means that fellow professionals review a researcher's manuscript to determine whether it is worthy of publication. In other words, peer review is a form of quality control to ensure that a journal publishes only good quality research.

The Internet is a fascinating resource, but is still in its infancy. There are few checks and balances for reviewing information posted on the Internet. Consequently, you must be cautious of information that you gather from the Internet.

We reviewed many ways that you can develop your interest in psychology and develop a research hypothesis. One of the more important resources is reading the research that has already been conducted. This background work will help you understand what psychologists know about a specific topic and what issues remain a mystery.

There are many resources you can use to locate useful information. One of the most useful resources is *PsycInfo,* a comprehensive database of primary and secondary resources. You can search the database using a search engine. These search engines use Boolean operations that allow you to find specific topics. The AND operator causes the search engine to select articles where two or more specific keywords describe the research. The OR operator allows you to conduct a broader search of related topics.

When you find an interesting research article, you will find that it is divided into several sections. The introduction offers a brief history of the research on the topic and a review of the researcher's hypotheses. In the method section, the researcher describes the techniques used to collect the data. The results section provides a detailed account of the results the researcher obtained. Finally, the discussion section includes the researcher's commentary of the meaning of the data with regard to his or her hypotheses.

In the "Research in Action" section, we reviewed a recently published article to illustrate how to read a research article.

CHAPTER GLOSSARY FOR REVIEW

AND   A Boolean operator that requires that two or more keywords be present in the citation.

Boolean Operators   Logical terms that control the search process for keywords.

Call Number   A combination of letters and numbers used in a library classification system to store and locate recorded information.

Keyword   A word or phrase used to search *PsycInfo* or other databases.

OR   A Boolean operator that requires that either keyword be present in the citation.

Peer Review   Part of the editorial process for professional books and journals in which professionals in the area review a manuscript for its scientific merits.

Primary Bibliographic Sources   A class of text resource that includes original research reports.

Research Journal   A periodic publication that contains original research articles, summaries, and commentaries. The editorial board consists of fellow researchers who have expertise on the primary topic of the journal.

Secondary Bibliographic Sources   A class of text resources, which includes specialized books and articles, that offers a comprehensive review of the literature for research on a specific topic.

Tertiary Bibliographic Sources   A class of text resource that includes textbooks and general reviews of a topic.

Thesaurus of Psychological Index Terms   A book that contains the definition and related terms of specific psychological keywords.

5 ETHICS AND BEHAVIORAL RESEARCH

CHAPTER OUTLINE

The essence of morality is a questioning about morality; and the decisive move of human life is to use ceaselessly all light to look for the origin of the opposition between good and evil.

—Georges Bataille

INTRODUCTION

Every day we face choices, decisions, and consequences. From the moment we wake up in the morning until we return to sleep in the evening, we confront situations that require us to act in one way or another. Typically, the choices that we make have little bearing on the lives of others. The decision whether to have a second cup of coffee or trudge off to the library to study may characterize the typical dilemma we face. There are, however, cases where our actions do affect the lives of others. These choices represent a special case of decision making because they involve moral behavior.

Anyone who conducts research must be sensitive to and mindful of moral principles and ethical reasoning. As you will learn in this chapter, psychologists and other behavioral researchers take seriously their responsibility to act morally. All behavioral research affects the lives of the people who and the animals that participate in the research. Therefore, before we begin any research, we must examine with considerable care the justification for and the consequences of our actions.

Professional researchers have a personal stake in examining the moral principles that guide their work. Foremost among these principles is the belief that the researcher should do no harm. Although scientific research is important, the value of the research is not an automatic license to act without regard to the welfare of others.

There are also practical reasons for researchers to examine the morality of their work. Most professional organizations have a set of clearly stated ethical guidelines. The American Psychological Association (APA), which represents well over 140,000 psychologists, has an elaborate ethical code of conduct that establishes the foundation for the moral behavior of all its members (APA, 1992). Other authoritative organizations have similar codes of conduct that require the researcher to justify his or her research.

For example, the federal government requires that all researchers receiving federal grants to conduct research on humans or nonhuman animals must submit a proposal of their research to an **Institutional Review Board (IRB)** for approval. An IRB is a group of people who examine the researcher's proposed methodology to ensure that the researcher will protect the basic rights of the participants in the study. Most large research universities and colleges have an IRB and require all researchers, regardless of the funding source, to obtain IRB approval for any human research. Chances are that you will have to seek approval from your IRB to conduct research.

In this chapter, we will examine the ethical issues that arise when psychologists conduct research. First, we will examine several broad ethical principles and perspectives that are a part of any ethical decision. We will then examine the ethical principles established by the APA as they apply to research with humans and animals. Finally, we will examine an array of case studies that will allow us to examine ethical dilemmas that researchers in the behavioral sciences often face.

WHAT IS ETHICS?

What does it mean to be moral or to act morally? What is ethics? Morality and ethics represent a set of interconnected principles and ways for making choices. As we progress through this chapter, we will use ethics and morality to describe how researchers make decisions about their research design. For example, we will ask, "Is this procedure moral?" or "What is the ethical thing to do in this experiment?"

Although many people use the words morals and ethics interchangeably, there is an important difference between the two. In general, **morals** are the principles or rules that define what is right and wrong. For example, you may have learned that it is wrong to lie to others and that is good to help others. By contrast, **ethics** is the process of studying moral standards and examining how we should interpret and apply them in various situations. An example of ethics is asking whether it is acceptable to lie to another person to spare them the shock and pain created by the truth or if it is acceptable to steal something to save the life of another person.

You should recognize that ethics is more than "doing the right thing." Although it is important that you behave correctly, it is also important that you understand why you make the decisions you do. One might even argue that your behavior is not moral unless you can justify your actions. Consequently, whenever you conduct research, you must ask yourself whether your actions are right or wrong and be able to justify your decision.

Although there are many moral standards or principles, they all share four general characteristics. Understanding these characteristics will help set the stage for our review of specific moral principles and ethical deliberation.

Moral principles address the well-being of others

At the heart of morality is the well-being of people whom our behavior affects. This concern for others is an integral component of our religions, laws, and social codes. Your parents, for example, have taught you to believe that it is bad to hurt others intentionally. Consequently, you probably believe that assault, child abuse, theft, and murder are wrong because they harm others. The well-being of others is the central feature of all codes of conduct. The APA (1992), for example, has developed its code of conduct to protect people and animals from harmful research practices.

Moral principles transcend other standards including self-interest

Moral principles direct us to act without regard to our personal goals and interests. For example, during the 1960s, many people protested the segregation laws practiced in the southern states. These people believed that they had a moral obligation to oppose laws that systematically denied African Americans their civil liberties. By traveling to the southern states, participating in marches, and helping with voter registration programs, these people took considerable personal risk to stand for what they believed was right.

There is nothing wrong with pursuing self-interest; it is a reasonable goal. The question arises, however, when we must choose between a morally correct behavior and personal gratification. Would you cheat on an exam or submit a plagiarized paper to get an "A" in a course? When faced with a conflict between self-interest and moral behavior, morality should lead the way. The application of this principle to research is clear. No matter how valuable the data may be to us, we cannot overlook the rights of the participants in the research.

Moral principles are constants and universals

The laws our governments make are often arbitrary and reflect many compromises among lawmakers. By contrast, moral principles are not arbitrary and do not reflect mere agreement among a few people. For example, there is no moral principle supporting the law that we drive on the right side of the road. That law represents an arbitrary (we could change the law to require that people drive of the left side of the road) and convenient standard for motorists to follow. Another example of the arbitrary nature of laws is that each state has a different set of laws. In many cases, what is legal in one state may be illegal in a neighboring state.

By contrast, we treat moral principles as if they are self-evident facts that apply to all people in all situations. Consequently, we follow moral principles because they reflect a universal virtue, not because some authority directs us to do so.

Moral principles are impartial

When we examine moral problems, we attempt to solve the problem consistently and impartially. For example, some people oppose any research that uses animals because they believe that the research harms the animal's well-being. A person who opposes animal research may begin by endorsing the moral principle that one should act to maximize happiness and minimize suffering. Next, they will argue that animals, like humans, can feel pain and do suffer. These observations lead some people to believe that the dividing line between humans and animals is arbitrary and irrelevant. The conclusion from this line of reasoning is that the moral principle of maximizing happiness and minimizing suffering must be impartially and equally applied to humans and animals.

Ethics and Ethical Codes

Ethics is a process of investigation, criticism, and decision making. When I say that someone studies ethics, I mean that they examine how basic moral standards and the facts of a situation lead to a consistent moral conclusion. An **ethical code,** or **code of conduct,** is a set of rules established by and for a group of people. As I noted previously, the APA has an ethical code that consists of a set of rules that governs its members. Like any set of laws, parts of the ethical code of psychologists consist of regulations agreed upon through a process of compromise and consensus. Therefore, like any collection of laws created by a group of people, the APA's code of conduct is subject to criticism and revision.

Although the APA ethical code (1992) offers a useful guideline for your research, you should not treat it as the final and authoritative word on moral behavior. Remember that ethics is the process of examining moral principles and behavior. Consequently, anyone who conducts research should consider carefully the moral implications of his or her research. There may be situations where you will have to defend the morality of your study. In these situations, saying, "*I was just doing what the APA code allows me to do*" will not be sufficient. Questions about moral behavior require you to recount the ethical deliberations you used to reach your conclusions.

APPROACHES TO ETHICAL ANALYSIS

Throughout history, people have devised different approaches to determine how to behave. I cannot examine all of these in this chapter. Instead, I will examine two of the more influential approaches and encourage you to enroll in a philosophy of ethics course. The two approaches that I will review are the principle of utilitarianism and the principle of rights.

The Principle of Utilitarianism

Jeremy Bentham (1748–1832) and John Stuart Mill (1808–1873) were two philosophers who wrote much about the principles of utilitarianism. The fundamental perspective of **utilitarianism** is that ethical behaviors are those where the total positive outcomes are greater than the total negative outcomes produced by one's actions. For utilitarianism, the primary focus of the ethical analysis is the consequence of our behavior. As Bentham often quipped, "the . . . truth is that it is the greatest happiness of the greatest number that is the measure of right and wrong." Therefore, a behavior is morally correct if the positive consequences outweigh the negative consequences for the greatest number of people.

Mill, like Bentham, agreed that we must consider the consequences of our actions, but was specific about the types of consequences we should examine. According to Mill, we should select behaviors that maximize happiness while minimizing suffering. Therefore, from Mill's perspective of utilitarianism, actions that create the greatest good or happiness for the most people are morally correct behaviors. How would we apply this principle to behavioral research?

The goal of research, according to utilitarianism, should be to maximize happiness. Consequently, psychologists must justify a research project by satisfying two conditions. First, the researcher should be able to show that the results will produce a useful outcome that will benefit others. Therefore, if the research jeopardizes the well-being of the participants, the researcher must demonstrate that the benefits of the study outweigh the discomfort experienced by the participants. Second, the researcher must demonstrate that the specific methods employed are better than all the available options for collecting the data. In other words, the researcher must show that there is no other way to collect the same quality of data. Here is an example of how we might use utilitarian reasoning in an experiment that examines the effectiveness of psychotherapy.

In a true experiment designed to test the effectiveness of a new treatment for depression, we must randomly assign some people to a control condition. By definition, people in this condition will receive nothing that will improve their mood. The other people in the experiment will receive what we believe to be an effective treatment. How can we justify withholding a useful treatment from the people in the control group? We know that these individuals are distressed and we believe that the treatment would make them feel better. Furthermore, our actions prevent these people from feeling better because we purposefully withhold the treatment.

We can justify the experiment by using the utilitarian perspective if we can successfully support two arguments. First, we must show that the results of the experiment have the potential of bringing the greatest happiness to the greatest number of people. If the experiment is successful, we can say with confidence that we have a valid treatment for depression and thereby be able to treat countless people of this distressing condition. Second, we must show that this experiment is the only way to assess the effectiveness of the treatment. We would have to prove that this research design, more than any other research design, will produce the results we need to evaluate the effectiveness of the treatment. If we can make these claims, then we can conclude that the experiment is morally acceptable because we have determined that the potential happiness for many people outweighs the temporary discomfort of a few people in a control group.

In the behavioral sciences, many experiments can cause temporary distress for the participants. For example, to understand the sensation of pain, the researcher has to inflict pain. To understand aggression, many psychologists create situations where one person can express hostility toward another person. Although the people who take part in the research may agree that the conditions are unpleasant, the researcher can justify the research if the results, in the long run, improve the lives of many and if there is no other reasonable way to collect the data.

Disadvantages of utilitarianism

How are we to know the true effect of any experiment? How do we determine the relative cost of a person's discomfort or their happiness? Although we use these terms every day, how do we weigh or measure discomfort and happiness? What accounting system do we use to ensure that our experiments do not go into debt by creating more discomfort than happiness? What counts as a cost? What counts as a benefit? I may think that the results are of considerable theoretical significance and thereby serve science. You, however, may think that the results are trivial and of no known practical value. Therefore, one of the essential problems with utilitarianism is that value, discomfort, and happiness are vague terms that are hard to quantify.

Advantages of utilitarianism

One advantage of utilitarianism is that it offers a clear rationale for conducting research that creates temporary discomfort. The researcher can justify the temporary discomfort of a few people if he or she can show that the results have a recognized value and that there is no other reasonable way to collect the data.

Another advantage of utilitarianism is that it allows us to use common sense when evaluating the morality of any research project. The common sense perspective allows us to recognize that there are exceptions to some moral principles. Consequently, we can use utilitarianism to find a balance between two moral principles that are incompatible with each other. For instance, we may believe that each participant has the right to receive information concerning his or her performance in a research project. Does this mean that the researcher must reveal everything about the participant's performance? What if the participant completed an intelligence test as a part of the study; are we obligated to disclose the results of the test to the person? Using the utilitarianism perspective would allow us to balance the benefits and costs of the disclosure. Therefore, we may withhold information if we believe that sharing the results will do more harm than good. In other situations, however, our analysis of the situation may compel us to share the test results with the participant.

The Principle of Rights

The utilitarian perspective requires that we examine the consequences of our actions to determine if a behavior is morally right or wrong. The perspective of rights is a completely different method of studying ethics because it requires us to recognize that the rights of other people must guide our actions. When we speak of moral rights, we mean that every person is entitled to certain privileges regardless of who they are. That is, moral rights are universal principles applied to every person equally and impartially. The philosopher most often associated with the concept of moral rights is Immanuel Kant (1724–1804).

Kant formulated the principle of the categorical imperative as a means to determine fundamental moral principles. As you will see, the categorical imperative allows us to define moral principles and to identify our duty as moral agents. For Kant, doing the "right" thing was not enough. We often do the right thing because it serves our goals. Some people give money to charity because they can use the donation as a tax deduction, to win the admiration of others, and to express pity for the less fortunate. Although giving money to a charity may be a nice thing to do, it is not automatically the morally right thing to do. According to Kant, the individual's sense of moral duty must drive his or her actions. Consequently, a true charitable act would be to donate the money in such a way that no one knows who gave the money.

Following Kant's categorical imperative, it is not enough to accept blindly the APA's code of conduct as a field guide of the right and wrong things to do in research. Rather, you should examine the moral principles that guide your work as a researcher.

The ethical perspective created by the principle of rights is different from the utilitarian perspective. As I noted previously, the utilitarian perspective considers only the consequences of our behavior. By contrast, the principle of rights requires that we examine the intention of our behavior. In addition, the principle does not focus on the balance of positive and negative outcomes. Rather, the principle of rights examines the universal rights each person has and the duty we have to respect those rights.

An essential formulation of the **categorical imperative** is, "Act in such a way that you always treat humanity, whether in your own person or in the person of any other, never simply as a means, but always at the same time as an end" (Kant, 1750/1964, p. 96). This formulation of the categorical imperative establishes that all people are equal, as are their moral rights. More specifically, this moral code requires that we respect the dignity of other people and refuse to treat them merely as a way to serve our self-interests. We must ensure that our behavior as researchers does not deny others their basic rights. The principle also requires that we avoid actions that diminish the dignity or self-worth of other people.

This formulation of the categorical imperative is a cornerstone of the APA's ethical guidelines (APA, 1992).[1] For example, Principle D of the code requires psychologists to respect the rights and dignity of all people. Specifically, the definition of this principle includes the passage,

> Psychologists accord appropriate respect to the fundamental rights, dignity, and worth of all people. They respect the rights of individuals to privacy, confidentiality, self-determination, and autonomy, mindful that legal and other obligations may lead to inconsistencies and conflict with the exercise of these rights. (p. 1598)

---

[1]The APA is currently revising its code of conduct. You may review the revised code of conduct at http://www.apa.org/ethics/

Disadvantages of principle of rights

There are several criticisms that we can aim at Kant's perspective. The first is that the system has no way to balance the conflicting rights of individuals. I am an experimental psychologist who believes that all people should participate in research when given informed consent and the choice not to participate. To me, helping expand the body of scientific knowledge is a moral duty. By contrast, another person may believe that scientific research is misguided and that no one should act to help researchers. Kant's categorical imperative treats these conflicting rights as equal and gives us no way to decide between them. Because Kant's perspective does not consider the consequences of our behavior, we have no way of resolving the conflict.

A second problem with Kant's perspective is that it can sometimes be too absolute and create conditions that we find intuitively unacceptable. For example, I may believe that confidentiality is a moral right that must be accorded to all research participants. According to Kant's categorical imperative, I must never divulge what someone did or said to me as a part of my research.

Imagine that I am conducting an interview as a part of my research. In response to one of my questions, a participant tells me, "I've been having sexual relations with the little girl who lives next door." According to the categorical imperative, the right to confidentiality is absolute, and I must maintain the confidentiality of the participant's confession. According to Kant's perspective, the consequences of maintaining confidentiality are immaterial. If I believe that confidentiality is a universal rule then I cannot violate the participant's confidentiality. If I call the police or warn the little girl's parents, I will violate my rule and can no longer say that confidentiality is a universal moral right of all people.

Advantages of principle of rights

Kant's philosophical principles make clear that all people are equal and that we cannot treat them as if they were pieces of equipment. This perspective is in keeping with our beliefs about morality and is an integral part of the APA's (1992) code of conduct. Specifically, the code of conduct recognizes that we cannot conduct research merely to serve our self-interests. Our research procedures must respect the dignity of the people who participate in our research and recognize that they have the capacity to act freely. Following this principle saves us from committing dreadful acts in the self-serving name of science.

MAKING ETHICAL DECISIONS

Life is complex and often unpredictable. Consequently, there is no way that we can create a set of rules that prescribes what you should do in every situation that you will encounter. Instead, we try to formulate general standards or principles that guide our decisions. Such is the case for deciding how to behave ethically.

Thus far, you have learned that the perspective of utilitarianism and the perspective of rights have different ways of resolving ethical problems. In addition, each perspective has its relative advantages and disadvantages. These two perspectives can often lead to conflicting conclusions. Because research is a practical enterprise, we need to find some way to make practical decisions.

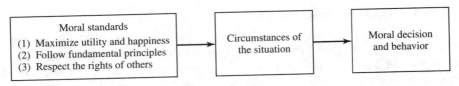

FIGURE 5.1
Ethical decision making. Using fundamental moral principles and the facts of the situation, a person can come to a rational and logical decision.

As I have already noted, ethical reasoning requires careful thought and deliberation. To examine an ethical issue, we must begin by examining the moral principles that we hold to be true. Next, we examine the specific circumstances of the situation. Using consistent and objective reasoning, we can determine how to behave.

Figure 5.1 represents the sequence of events that we use to come to an ethical decision. The moral standards are those principles that we hold to be true. This approach requires that we attempt to balance these moral standards within the circumstances of the research project. The result of this discourse is the moral decision and our course of action. As you will see, the ethical code of the APA follows this pattern to examine ethical principles.

THE ETHICAL CODE OF THE AMERICAN PSYCHOLOGICAL ASSOCIATION

Research on humans is a relatively new phenomenon (Resnik, 1998). Before the 20th century, most scientists conducted research on topics unrelated to human behavior and the body. Toward the end of the 19th century, however, scientists began to study humans in detail. During this time, psychology emerged from philosophy to assert itself as an empirical science. At the same time, physicians began to use the scientific method to study various diseases and their cures. Soon, research using living people became commonplace. Unfortunately, there was no ethical code to guide researchers except their personal beliefs and conscience. The need for an ethical code for researchers studying humans became apparent in the late 1940s.

At the end of World War II, the Allied powers charged Nazi officials with a long list of war crimes. Included in the charges were allegations that Nazi scientists conducted cruel experiments on Jews and other groups of people held in the concentration camps. These experiments were little more than protracted torture. As a response to these atrocities, researchers developed the *Nuremberg Code* (Resnik, 1998). The *Nuremberg Code*, listed in Box 5.1, consists of nine fundamental principles that researchers must use when conducting research with humans.

Unfortunately, horrible and immoral experiments on humans were not the sole providence of Nazi scientists. Recently released documents from the United States Department of Energy reveal that during the 1940s and 1950s, government researchers conducted experiments on unsuspecting American citizens to determine the effects of nuclear radiation

BOX 5.1   The *Nuremberg Code* of Principles Governing Research Using Humans

1. **Informed Consent:** The participant must understand what will happen to him or her in the research and then volunteer to participate.
2. **Social Value:** The results of a study should benefit society.
3. **Scientific Validity:** Only trained scientists who employ careful and well-designed studies should conduct research.
4. **No Malfeasance:** Researchers must conduct studies that are safe and minimize risk of harm to the participants.
5. **Termination:** The participant may withdraw from the study for any reason, and the researcher must stop the study if the participant is at risk of injury or death.
6. **Privacy:** The researcher must preserve the privacy/confidentiality of the participant.
7. **Vulnerable Populations:** Researchers need to use special caution to protect the rights of those who cannot act for themselves, including children, the developmentally delayed, or the mentally disabled.
8. **Fairness:** Selection of the participants for the research and assignment to treatment conditions must be fair, consistent, and equitable.
9. **Monitoring:** The researcher must continually monitor the study to ensure the safety of participants.

Note: The original *Nuremberg Code* included Principles 1–5. Principles 6–9 are more recent additions to the code (Resnik, 1998).

(Welcome, 1999). None of the people knew that they had been exposed to these deadly conditions. In another case, physicians at the Tuskegee Institute purposefully withheld treatment from 399 people who had contracted syphilis, for the sole purpose of studying the long-term effects of this dreadful disease (Jones, 1982). Unfortunately, these examples are not isolated cases. There are other instances of unethical experiments conducted by American scientists (Resnik, 1998).

This bleak history illustrates the need to create and enforce clear ethical guidelines. The *National Research Act,* which became law in 1974 (PL–93–348), established the IRB that I described earlier. The law requires that researchers receiving federal money to conduct research with humans and animals must demonstrate that their research methods meet minimal ethical standards and that the IRB review the research proposal.

In the late 1960s and early 1970s, the American Psychological Association created its first ethical guidelines. Since then, the APA has revised the code, with the current version published in 1992. The *Ethical Principles of Psychologists and Code of Conduct* establishes a set of principles that psychologists must use to make decisions about their professional behavior. Box 5.2 lists the general ethical principles the code identifies for all psychologists.

The complete code is long and covers many professional domains including therapy, psychological testing, psychological research, and other activities such as teaching and supervising employees. In the following sections, we will examine the basic APA ethical principles as they apply to conducting research with humans and animals.

BOX 5.2 The General Ethical Principles for All Members of the American Psychological Association. Based on the APA's *Ethical Principles of Psychologists and Code of Conduct* (1992)

(A) Competence: Psychologists develop and maintain the competence necessary to perform their professional duties.

(B) Integrity: Psychologists are fair and honest in all aspects of their professional duties.

(C) Professional and Scientific Responsibility: Psychologists act in accord with the ethical codes of conduct that govern their professional duties. When necessary, psychologists consult with other psychologists to avoid unethical behavior.

(D) Respect for People's Rights and Dignity: Psychologists "respect the fundamental rights, dignity and worth of all people" (p. 1598).

(E) Concern for Other's Welfare: Psychologists work to preserve the welfare of others (humans and animals) and strive to minimize the harm to others.

(F) Social Responsibility: Psychologists strive to promote human welfare and reduce human suffering. In addition, psychologists work to prevent the misrepresentation of psychological information.

SEEKING APPROVAL FOR RESEARCH: THE INSTITUTIONAL REVIEW BOARD

In this section, we will examine how psychologists seek approval for their research and the interplay between the IRB and the ethical code of the APA. The size and complexity of an IRB will vary depending on the size of the institution and the type of research conducted there. Typically, the board consists of researchers and other professionals who understand the legal and ethical standards that guide research. In some cases, research using specialized procedures or unique populations requires special members of the IRB. For example, the *National Bioethics Advisory Commission* (1998) offered specific recommendations for cases when the proposed research will use people with a mental disability (e.g., schizophrenia or a developmental disability). Specifically, the commission recommended that the IRB include at least two professionals familiar with the disability; a family member of a person with the disability or a representative of an advocacy group; and, when possible, a person with the disability. This recommendation ensures that the members of the IRB understand the nature of the disability and preserve the rights of people with the condition.

Planning research and seeking IRB approval

The first APA ethical principle is relatively straightforward. All research conducted with humans must use valid research methods, follow legal and ethical standards, and be approved by the institution's IRB.

Researchers submit a detailed description of their research by answering a series of questions. The members of the IRB review the material and then inform the researcher whether he or she may proceed with the research. In some cases, the IRB may require minor or substantial modifications to parts of the research to protect the rights of the participants. Box 5.3 presents an example of the IRB form that my college uses. The questions

BOX 5.3   An Example of an Institutional Review Board Application Form for Proposed Research Using Humans

Proposal for Research Involving Humans

1. Title of Project: _____

2. Type of research: Faculty _____   Student Honor's Project _____
                       Student Project _____   Class Project _____

3. Starting date for the investigation: _____

4. Name(s) of investigator(s) and campus phone number(s):

5. Name of supervising faculty member and campus telephone number(s):

6. Has previous research or pilot studies indicated any significant dangers or risks in the proposed procedures?   Yes ____   No ____

7. Does this research involve any active deception of the participants?   Yes ____   No ____

8. Will any information from this investigation be confidential?   Yes ____   No ____
   Signature of investigator(s): _____ date: _____
   Signature of faculty supervisor: _____ date: _____

Respond to each of the following:

9. Describe the general purpose of the research.

10. Describe the procedures and tests used in the investigation.

11. Describe how you will obtain Informed Consent or justify why you will not obtain Informed Consent. Attach a copy of the Informed Consent Contract you plan to use.

12. Describe how you will recruit participants. Describe any special requirements of the population and any criteria for inclusion or exclusion of participants.

13. Identify how you examined potential hazards of this research. Give references when appropriate.

14. Describe and assess the potential hazards (physical, psychological, or legal) and estimate their likelihood and seriousness.

15. Describe any procedures that you will employ for minimizing potential hazards and give an assessment of their potential effectiveness.

16. Indicate how and when you will inform participants of the purpose of the research.

17. Describe what you know about the ethical guidelines for treating humans within your discipline.

If you answered "yes" to Question #7 then provide the following information:

18a. Explain the rationale for the deception. How and when will the participants learn of the deception?

18b. Describe the expected reactions (immediate or long-term) of the participants to the deception, particularly any potential negative reactions.

If you answered "yes" to Question #8 then respond to the following:

19a. What information obtained through this research is confidential?

19b. Who will have access to that information?

19c. How will you protect confidentiality?

19d. What will happen to this information at the end of this investigation?

require the researcher to examine all aspects of his or her research. You should recognize, however, that each IRB creates its own application and review procedures.

Responsibility and qualifications

This requirement ensures that the researcher will protect the dignity and welfare of the participants and has the qualifications to use the procedures involved in the study. Qualification is important, especially when the researcher uses invasive techniques. Consider a few examples. Imagine that I wanted to conduct a study that monitored participants' physiological reactions to different conditions. Measuring physiological reactions requires electronic equipment. Therefore, I must demonstrate to the members of the IRB that my recording equipment is safe and that I know how to operate it safely. In another experiment, I may want to collect blood samples from the participants. Because I am not certified to draw blood, I would have to hire a certified medical technician who can do this procedure safely, or I need to receive the necessary training and certification.

The principle of responsibility and qualifications makes clear that students cannot conduct research without supervision. A faculty member must verify that he or she will supervise the student. This stipulation allows students to learn how to conduct research and protects the participants from potential mistreatment.

Voluntary informed consent

Voluntary **informed consent** is the hallmark of all research involving humans. Researchers cannot coerce or force people to participate in any research. For all human research, the researcher must show that the people who participate in the study did so of their own free will. In addition, the participants must understand that they are free to withdraw from the study at any time and for any reason without penalty.

For informed consent, the researcher must offer an easy to understand, accurate, and complete description of the research. Specifically, the APA (1992) requires that researchers use clear language that the participants can understand and:

(a)   Describes the nature of the research,
(b)   Indicates that participation is voluntary and that the participant may withdraw from the research at any time without penalty,
(c)   Describes any potential risks from participating in the study or withdrawing from the research,
(d)   Describes how the researcher will protect the confidentiality and anonymity of the participant,
(e)   Describes if and how the participant will be compensated for his or her participation in the research,
(f)   Describes what information the researcher will share with the participant, and
(g)   Describes who is responsible for supervising the research process.

Box 5.4 presents a hypothetical informed consent contract that a student might use for his or her research. The format of the document is similar to a contract. The informed consent document is a pledge from the researcher to the participant that stipulates the rights of the participant and the duties of the researcher. The participant and the researcher should each keep a copy of the signed document.

BOX 5.4   An Example of an Informed Consent Contract

Memory for Words

Informed Consent Contract

I, _____, hereby agree to participate voluntarily in an experiment conducted by Jane Mnemonic, "Memory for Words." This research is conducted under the supervision of Dr. David J. Pittenger and has been approved by the Institutional Review Board of the University of Tennessee at Chattanooga. The researcher has explained to my satisfaction the following points:

1. My participation is voluntary. I am under no direct obligation to participate in this research. Furthermore, I understand that I may withdraw from this project at any time without penalty. If I do withdraw, the data I generated, to the extent that they may be attributed to me, will be destroyed.

2. I may receive extra credit for my Psychology 101 course for participation in this experiment. The amount of credit I receive will not reflect my skill, ability, or performance in the study.

3. All records of my behavior will remain confidential. The data for this research will be published as group averages. The researcher will not publish or share with others personally identifiable information about me without my written consent.

4. There are no inherent risks involved in participating in this research.

5. The purpose of this research is to study memory. I will be asked to listen to audiotapes of words and then recall that list.

6. The researcher will provide a complete review of the purpose of this research and expected findings at the end of my participation. In addition, the researcher will attempt to answer all reasonable questions I ask about the research.

7. Dr. Pittenger's campus telephone number is: 5-1234

   Ms. Mnemonic's campus telephone number is: 6-7890

The campus telephone number of the University of Tennessee at Chattanooga IRB is: 5-4321

Participant's Signature

Date

Jane Mnemonic

Date

Dr. David J. Pittenger

Date

An important consideration is how much information to give the participant. You do not need to describe your hypothesis or your research methods. Instead, you should describe the types of things you will ask the person to do and the conditions to which they may be described in enough detail to allow the person to decide whether they wish to participate in the experiment.

Informed consent and minors. Minors (people younger than 18) and people afflicted with a medical, mental, or developmental disability cannot give informed consent. To include people from these populations, you must obtain approval from their parent or legal guardian. For example, if you wanted to conduct a study that examined children's memory, you would first need to obtain the consent of the child's parents to conduct the research. You will then need to ask the child to participate in the study. As with all research, the parents and the child have the right to withdraw from the study at any time.

Filming or recording behavior. If you plan to videotape or photograph the participant's behavior, you must first obtain informed consent from the participant. In addition, you will need to explain how you will use the recording. For example, if you were studying facial expressions you might tell the participants that you will videotape their facial reactions, but never present the tapes outside of the laboratory unless you have the written permission of the participant.

Using college students in research. Many departments of psychology require students in the introductory psychology course to participate in psychological research or offer extra credit for participating in research. The rationale for the requirement is that participation in psychological research is educational. If the researchers take their responsibilities seriously, they will offer each participant a detailed explanation of their research and its importance.

When you use fellow students for your research, you need to ensure several safeguards. Each student must have a legitimate and equivalent alternative to participating in the study. For example, students may want to select between participating in an experiment, attending a guest lecture, or reading a short article related to psychology. Remember that you cannot coerce a person to participate in research. Telling them that they must be in an experiment or fail the course is coercive.

You should also assure your fellow students that their performance has no effect on the credit received for the course. If a student receives extra credit for participating in a study, you cannot offer more or less credit based on their performance in the study. Similarly, you cannot penalize participants if they decide to withdraw from the study.

When no informed consent is needed. There are special conditions when you do not need informed consent. These conditions occur where you will passively and unobtrusively observe people's behavior in natural contexts. For example, you might go to a playground and observe how the children play with each other. If you do not plan to interact with the child or alter the environment, you can collect data without asking the children for their permission to observe their play.

State law may control recording people's actions and conversations. For example, some states make it illegal to record a telephone conversation unless both people understand that the conversation is being recorded. Therefore, you may want to consult a legal authority concerning what you can and cannot record without consent.

In other cases, you might use public domain data. Many agencies collect data open for inspection. For example, you can go to your county's board of elections and obtain the names of registered voters, their political affiliation, and whether they voted in the previous elections. You can also review police records to determine who has been arrested, the charges, and the court's action.

Anonymous questionnaires and surveys are also exempt from the informed consent requirement. Therefore, if you wanted to send a questionnaire through campus mail to all students, you would not have to have the students' informed consent unless the data you collected allowed you to learn who completed the questionnaire.

Although these are examples of cases where you do not need informed consent, you will still need approval from your institution's IRB. According to the APA, the rule is simple: You cannot begin to collect data until the IRB approves your research proposal. Seeking the IRB's approval ensures that your decision not to use informed consent conforms to the board member's interpretation of the ethical principles.

Deception in research

Deception in research means that you lie to the participants about some important part of the research. You may lead a person to believe that the other people sitting at the table are fellow students who volunteered to participate in the study. The truth may be that the other people are part of the experiment and are following a script that you prepared. A placebo is another type of deception because the researcher may tell a participant that the treatment is effective when it is not.

There are two types of deception, **deception by omission** and **deception by commission.** Deception by omission means that you withhold important facts from the participant. Deception by commission means that you purposefully lie to or mislead the participant about an important component of the research. Figure 5.2 is a cartoon that represents deception by commission at its worst.

THE FAR SIDE   By GARY LARSON

FIGURE 5.2
Although deception in psychological research is permissible, there are limits. Participants in psychological research should understand that they are participating in a research project and be allowed to withdraw voluntarily from the experiment at their discretion. (*THE FAR SIDE* © 1993 *FARWORKS, INC. Used by permission. All rights reserved.*)

Deception by omission occurs in all research because it is impossible and impractical to tell the participant everything about the purpose and details of the research. For example, we do not describe the hypothesis we want to test, nor do we describe every aspect of the research design. If we did, the information will bias their behavior. Therefore, we describe the general themes of the research that will allow the potential participants to know what may happen to them during the study. For instance, we would not tell a person whether they are in the placebo treatment condition. Instead, we would tell them that there is a chance that they will receive a placebo.

Deception by commission raises serious ethical concerns because the researcher is lying to the participant. Although deception by commission has many negative consequences, there are times when we must use it as a part of the research. For example, in many social psychology experiments, the researcher will create an elaborate cover story for the experiment. The cover story diverts the participant's attention from the true purpose of the study and may thereby reduce any bias in the participant's behavior.

According to the APA ethical guidelines (1992), we can use deception under special conditions. First, we must demonstrate that the participant will still obtain sufficient information about the research to offer voluntary informed consent. In the case of the placebo treatment condition, the participants should understand that the researcher will randomly assign them to either the placebo or the treatment conditions.

Second, the researcher must demonstrate to the members of the IRB that the deception is essential to collect the data. This is an example where the researcher must examine the utility of the research. In particular, the researcher must show that the deception will cause minor or no negative consequences for the participants and that the data produced by the study have legitimate scientific value.

Finally, the researcher must demonstrate that there is no other way to collect the data other than to use the deception. Your use of deception by commission must be the last resort and the only reasonable way to conduct the study.

Confidentiality

All information that you collect must be confidential. Confidentiality means that the identity of your participants remains a secret. In most cases, confidentiality is easy to preserve. One way to maintain confidentiality is to use a meaningless number to identify the participants. For example, you might use the number "2–3–47" to record the data of a person. The number is meaningless in that it does not identify the person, but does allow you to file the data. In addition, when we publish the results of the research, we present the data as averages across groups rather than the performance of individual people.

Informing participants of the results of the research

You have a duty to explain your research to your participants. Most researchers debrief the participants at the end of the study. **Debriefing** means that you tell the participants the details of your research. If you used deception, you must describe the purpose of the research and why you used the deception. You also use the debriefing to answer the participants' questions and ensure that they understand why you conducted the research.

Debriefing does not mean that you need to tell the participant everything about the research. For example, imagine that you used a personality test as a part of your research.

Can you or should you share the results of the test with the participant? In most cases, the answer is no. Only licensed psychologists are qualified to interpret individual personality test results. I am a psychologist, but not licensed to administer psychological tests for diagnostic purposes. Therefore, I can use a personality test in research, but I should not review the individual results with the participants. Instead, I can offer generalities such as, "Researchers believe that people with this personality dimension are more likely to behave in this manner." By contrast, I could not say, "The results show that you are extroverted, therefore you are likely to . . . ."

In most cases, researchers do not share the individual results with others; the results remain confidential. There are two general exceptions to this rule. First, if you discover that the person committed a crime, you may need to report the facts to the police. For example, if in the course of an interview, a parent indicated that he or she abused a child, you would need to report the incident. The second condition arises when the researcher discovers that the person is likely to do harm to self or others or suffers from a life-threatening illness. Fortunately, these exceptional conditions do not occur in most research projects. You should, however, be aware that there may be cases where you could obtain information that would cause you to break the conditions of confidentiality.

MILGRAM'S EXPERIMENT—COULD IT BE REPEATED TODAY?

Any review of research ethics would be incomplete without a discussion of Milgram's (1963) study of obedience. His experiments attracted much attention and generated considerable debate. In this section, I want to raise the question, "If you were a member of an IRB, would you approve the research?"

Milgram's Obedience Research

Stanley Milgram (1963, 1974) conducted a series of experiments to study the conditions under which one person would obey the order to hurt another person. Milgram placed an advertisement in a local newspaper calling for people to participate in a psychology experiment. When the participants arrived at the laboratory, the researcher told them that they would take part in an experiment on learning, and that one person would be the learner and the other person would be the trainer. In fact, the learner was a member of the research team.

The researcher explained that the purpose of the study was to examine the effects of punishment on learning. The trainer would read a list of word pairs (e.g., blue–box, nice–play, windy–sky, bright–night) and then read the first word of a pair with four alternatives (e.g., blue: sky, paint, box, boy). The other person would then indicate which of the four words went with the first word. For each mistake, the trainer had to press a button that delivered an electrical shock to the learner. As a demonstration, the researcher administered a mild shock to the trainer.

For the first part of the experiment, all went well. The trainer read the words and the learner responded correctly. After a few trials, however, the learner began to make mistakes. With each error, the trainer had to give a progressively stronger shock (15 to 450 volts in 15-volt increments). The learner, who was not really receiving the shocks, responded to the shock with a clear reaction. He began with grunts in response to the 75-volt shock. At higher voltages, he shouted " . . . get me out of here! I won't be in the experiment any more! I refuse to go on!" (Milgram, 1974, p. 23). At 300 volts, the learner shouted that he would no longer respond. At 330 volts, the learner made no more responses.

If the trainer objected and wanted to stop the experiment, the researcher would say, "Please continue" or "The experiment requires that you continue" (Milgram, 1974, p. 21). The experiment continued until the trainer refused to administer another shock or had administered the strongest shock. At the end of the experiment, Milgram debriefed the participants.

In the first experiment, Milgram (1963, 1974) found that 26 of the 40 trainers administered the complete range of shocks. Furthermore, he found that all the trainers administered shocks of 300 volts or greater.

Milgram was the first psychologist to study obedience in the laboratory, thus it was anyone's guess what the participants would do. Before he conducted the experiment, Milgram (1974) had surveyed psychiatrists, college students, and middle-class adults and asked them to predict how far the typical person would go in the experiment. All three groups predicted that the typical person would stop when they began to administer "strong shocks" (around 135 volts).

What would happen if someone wanted to repeat Milgram's experiment? Would the typical IRB approve the research? What would you decide if you were on the IRB? What conclusions would we reach if you followed the ethical perspectives reviewed earlier in the chapter?

The Principle of Utilitarianism

How would we evaluate Milgram's experiment from this perspective? Can we justify the experiment, or should we reject Milgram's proposed experiment? As you recall, the answers to these questions will arise from a cost and benefit analysis of the experiment. What are the costs of the experiment? How would you feel if you thought that you were hurting another person? There is no doubt that the experiment was stressful. It is also possible that the participants would become distressed to learn that they were capable of committing a horrible act.

On the other hand, there are clear benefits to conducting the experiment. Milgram's studies demonstrated that an average person could be induced to do terrible things under certain circumstances. These data are valuable to psychology because they help us understand an important behavior. Consequently, we could justify conducting the experiment given the cost/benefit analysis if we can show that the cost to the people who participate is far less than the value of the data. Furthermore, Milgram used extensive debriefing techniques to ensure that the people who participated in the experiment did not suffer long-term consequences. Hence, we could show that we have minimized the harm to the participants. Finally, we may approve the research if we can be convinced that there is no other way to collect the data. Therefore, we can conclude that as long as the researcher followed the requirements of informed consent and debriefing, we should approve the research.

We can take several tactics to use the principle of utilitarianism to reject Milgram's request. The first objection is that we cannot overlook the cost to the participants. We could argue that the emotional stress created by this experiment is not trivial. In this case, we may argue that the threat to the individual does not justify the data that will come from the experiment. Although we are still using the utility principle, we reached a different decision because we concluded that the participants' discomfort outweighs the value of the data.

Another way we can object to Milgram's experiment is to ask if there are other ways to collect the data. Would it be possible to conduct an experiment on obedience that was not as stressful or did not require deception? If we can find alternative methods to obtain similar data, then we can conclude that parts of the experiment are unacceptable. If we find that we can create the same effect through less stressful means, then we should reject the experiment.

The Principle of Rights

How would you respond to this experiment from the principle of rights? Using this perspective, you would *not* examine the cost/benefit ratio of the research. Instead, you would examine the moral principles that guide our decisions. For our purposes, we can focus on Kant's categorical imperative that requires us to determine whether the researcher respects the inherent dignity of the people who participate in the study. We have to ask if the researcher respects the participants' dignity or treats them merely as a self-serving means of collecting data.

From the perspective of rights, deception in any form treats participants as mere opportunities to collect data and ignores their dignity. For example, someone studying grief could claim he or she needed to deceive participants by telling them that their parents have been murdered. In these situations, it may appear that the researcher has placed his or her interest in collecting data before the dignity of the participant. Thus, manipulating a person's emotions to satisfy one's scientific curiosity is unacceptable. Similarly, we could argue that the participants were not free to choose how to respond. The researcher's request to continue the shocks is a form of coercion. The researcher assumed a role of authority over the participant and consequently caused the participant to do things that they would normally avoid doing. Thus, the perspective of rights is most likely to find Milgram's experiment unacceptable.

What Is the Right Answer?

You may be asking, "What is the right answer? Should I or should I not use deception?" I cannot give you the correct answer. You must come to the answer on your own. Ethics is a process of investigation, and you, as an intelligent and thoughtful person, must resolve the dilemma.

Part of the answer may come from examining the APA's code of conduct. You could, for example, examine the problem and determine whether the proposed research meets certain minimal qualifications. For example, you can ask: "Is there sufficient evidence of informed consent?" "Do the people really have the opportunity to stop the experiment?" "Has the researcher minimized the risks?" The answers to these questions are important for part of your ethical deliberation.

At the same time you should examine the broader moral principles involved in your research. For example, you may find that there are some procedures that the APA ethical code treats as permissible that you find unacceptable. Thus performing the experiment would be morally wrong from your perspective although acceptable within the APA's code of conduct. For instance, although the APA's ethical code permits psychologists to conduct research on animals, many psychologists find the practice morally wrong.

RESEARCH WITH ANIMALS

Although the vast majority of the research conducted by psychologists involves humans, animal research remains an important and vital component of psychology. Psychologists who study physiological processes, such as the working of the brain, use animals for their research. We can conduct experiments on animals that we clearly cannot conduct on humans. Although the reason to use animals is simple, the ethical rationale is not. Many people believe that subjecting animals to research is morally wrong. In this section, I will examine the general principles on both sides of the issue and review the APA's ethical position on animal research.

The Case Against Animal Research

In 1975, Peter Singer, a philosopher, published the first edition of *Animal Liberation* (1990). The book quickly became a bestseller and, for many, the authoritative statement against using animals in research. Singer used the principle of utility to establish the rights of animals as equal to humans. As Singer (1990) noted, "the basic principle of equality does not require equal or identical *treatment;* it requires equal consideration" (p. 2). Singer also argued that we must recognize that animals, like humans, experience pain and suffer in uncomfortable situations. Therefore, the ability to experience pain is an equally important consideration for human and animal research.

Singer coined the term **speciesism** to refer to the attitude many people use to judge the treatment of animals. Speciesism is analogous to racism and sexism. Both racism and sexism refer to differential treatment based on trivial or immaterial attributes. The color of a person's skin or a person's sex is irrelevant when we consider fundamental human rights and privileges. For example, it is racist to prohibit people from seeking an education or obtaining a job based on skin color. Being Asian, African American, Hispanic, or European has no relevance to one's ability. Therefore, denying a person a privilege based on his or her heritage is racist and unethical.

The argument against speciesism is the same as the argument against racism or sexism. Because all animals, human and nonhuman, have a central nervous system and the capacity to experience pain, we cannot give special treatment to one species that we do not extend to another species. Singer (1990) refers directly to Bentham and other utilitarian philosophers to support the notion that "taking into account . . . the interests of the being, whatever those interests might be—must, according to the principle of equality, be extended to all beings, black or white, masculine or feminine, human or nonhuman" (1990, p. 5). In summary, Singer argued that the principle of utility places the well-being of nonhuman animals on the same level as humans.

The Case for Animal Research

Is there any way to justify animal research using the principle of utility? Although there are many arguments in favor of animal research, we will only examine one. Steinbock (1978) used the principles of utilitarianism to show that one could build a logical rationale of animal research given specific conditions.

Steinbock (1978) disagreed with Singer on several points. Although she agreed that animals can experience pain, and that experiencing pain is relevant, she noted that Singer's philosophy leads to unacceptable conclusions. She also argued that recognizing differences among species is important and that we have an obligation to defend and care for our species. Consequently, as humans we have a moral obligation to ensure the welfare of our species. Furthermore, this obligation transcends the welfare of other species.

As an example, Steinbock (1978) noted that if our home were invaded by disease carrying rats that bit the children, we should place the welfare of the family above the rats even if we have to kill the rats. In defense of animal research, she noted that, "if we can free human beings from crippling diseases, pain and death through experimentation which involves making animals suffer, and if this is the only way to achieve such results, then I think that such experimentation is justified" (p. 250).

The argument in favor of animal research is that some information cannot be obtained by other means and that the data have utility for humans. Therefore, we can justify putting animals into painful situations where the results will clearly benefit humans. Indeed, research with animals has generated many insights the led to better understanding of human behavior. Our knowledge of how the brain works comes from, in large part, animal research. In addition, many principles of behavior that we accept with little question come from animal research. As an example, Seligman discovered the learned helplessness phenomenon when studying dogs' reactions to inescapable shock.

The APA Ethical Guidelines: Animal Research

The APA ethical guidelines for animal research follow many of the same principles as the guidelines for human research. Researchers submit their research proposals to a review board that specifically evaluates research with animals. The researcher must demonstrate that the results are useful, that the researcher has no other ethical means of collecting the information, and that the subjects will experience minimal pain and suffering. Box 5.5 lists the general ethical guidelines governing research with animals.

BOX 5.5   Summary of the APA's Ethical Guidelines for the Treatment of Animals. Based on the APA's *Ethical Principles of Psychologists and Code of Conduct* (1992)

1. **Humane Treatment:** Psychologists raise, house, and care for animals in a humane manner.
2. **In Accordance with Relevant Laws:** The researcher's treatment of the animals conforms to all federal, state, and local laws governing the care and treatment of animals.
3. **Competence of Researcher:** The researcher and his or her assistants have the necessary competence to care for the animals and conduct the research.
4. **Appropriate Techniques:** The researcher uses commonly accepted practices for conducting the research with the animals.
5. **Minimal Discomfort:** The researcher ensures that any discomfort is minimized or avoided.
6. **Only Option:** For procedures that cause pain or death, the researcher must verify that there are no other means for gathering the data.
7. **Use of Euthanasia:** The researcher will use fast-acting and humane euthanasia procedures when the animal's life must be terminated.

RESEARCH IN ACTION: ETHICAL DILEMMAS

The following are short scenarios describing various research practices. Read each with care and then examine the ethical issues raised by the scenario. Some of the ethical issues can be answered using the APA's ethical guidelines. Others may require additional ethical analysis.

Another Look at Conformity

Mark wants to study conformity and use deception in his research. When the participant arrives for the study, he or she will meet the researcher and another person who appears to be another participant. In fact, the other person is Mark's associate and is a part of the experiment. The researcher says that the study requires the participants to complete several questionnaires, and then asks the participants to read and sign an informed consent contract. The informed consent says nothing about the deception. Next, Mark distributes the questionnaire and leaves the room. There are three experimental conditions. In the control group, the accomplice does nothing other than fill out the questionnaire. In another situation, the accomplice says, "Let's screw up the results and answer 'Highly Disagree' for each answer," and then laughs as he completes the questionnaire and continues to encourage the real participant to "screw up the results." For the third group, the accomplice says, "Gee, this seems like a really important research project. I'm going to answer as honestly as I can." One of the questionnaires is a legitimate test that measures how honestly a person responds.

ACHIEVEMENT CHECK

(1) Is the deception in this experiment acceptable? What would be the arguments for and against approving the research?

(2) If the research is approved, what should Mark say in his debriefing statement?

Eavesdropping on Conversations

Sid is a psychologist and interested in dating behavior. To test one of his theories, he goes to a local college "pick-up" bar. He discretely stands next to couples engaged in conversation and observes their behavior. Using a small notebook, he records the frequency of different types of comments each person makes. He also notes how often and where the couples touch each other. Finally, he records whether the two people leave the bar with each other. At no time does Sid indicate that he is a researcher listening to the conversations.

ACHIEVEMENT CHECK

(3) Should Sid be allowed to conduct this research?

(4) Should he inform the couple that he has observed them and give them the opportunity to have him destroy the data?

(5) Could Sid use a tape recorder to record the couple's conversation for later analysis?

Requiring Students to Participate in Research

Mythical University is a large state institution. The Department of Psychology requires all the graduate students to do research as a part of their training and dissertation. Most of the graduate students conduct at least one experiment each semester and use students from the campus. In addition, the faculty members conduct research. To ensure that there are sufficient numbers of students to participate in the research, the psychology faculty requires all students enrolled in Psychology 101 to participate in 10 experiments during the semester. If they miss an appointment, the students must do two additional experiments (one to replace the missed appointment and one as a penalty). Students who do more than the 10 experiments can earn extra credit for the course. Students who do not want to do any experiments may write a five-page paper as an alternative to each experiment.

ACHIEVEMENT CHECK

(6) Is the department's policy defensible? Develop arguments in favor of and opposed to the policy.

(7) What potential ethical problems does this practice create?

(8) What modifications, if any, would you propose for this policy?

Questionnaire About Sex

Courtney is interested in college students' attitudes about date rape. She prepares a long questionnaire concerning different aspects of sexual behavior. Some of her questions concern the types of sexual behavior students have performed (e.g., genital-genital sex, oral sex, anal sex) as well as the frequency of each. She also asks students if they have ever been forced/coerced to perform a sexual act they did not wish to perform or if they ever forced/coerced another person to perform a sexual act against his or her will. She plans to ask students to come to a classroom and complete the questionnaire.

ACHIEVEMENT CHECK

(9) Should Courtney obtain informed consent before distributing the questionnaire? Why or why not?

(10) What should Courtney do if a person completing the questionnaire indicated that he raped another student?

(11) Are there any precautions that Courtney needs to take when collecting the data?

Real-World Study of Altruism

Richard studies altruism. For the current project, he wants to know if the color of the person in need of help will influence a person's willingness to help. He hires two students, one white and the other black, to act as an injured person needing help. The test consists of the following situation: The actor stands next to an open car trunk, is neatly dressed, and wearing a plaster cast that covers his entire right arm. In the car trunk is a large and bulky box. The actor stops people walking on the sidewalk and asks if they will help carry the box into a nearby house. The researcher records the proportion of people who help the white and the black actors.

ACHIEVEMENT CHECK

(12) Does Richard need informed consent for this experiment?

(13) Is Richard's use of deception defensible?

(14) Should Richard debrief the people the actor asks for help? What are the consequences of debriefing and failing to debrief the people the actor stops on the street?

Assessing Students' Depression

Rebbecca is an undergraduate student interested in the effects of academic stress on depression. She plans to administer two valid inventories several days after the start of the semester and two days before the final exams. The first test is a survey of academic and personal stress. The second test is one that many clinical psychologists use to assess severity of depression.

ACHIEVEMENT CHECK

(15) Should Rebbecca be allowed to conduct this study?

(16) What should Rebbecca do if she finds that one of the students is severely depressed?

Use of a Control Group

For many years, Drug X has been the treatment of choice for the treatment of depression. Profit Labs has discovered a new medication, Drug Y, that researchers believe is a superior medication. Researchers for the company are in the process of designing the initial research projects to determine whether Drug Y is a superior treatment for depression. People diagnosed as severely depressed will be randomly assigned to one of three treatment conditions: Placebo Treatment, Drug X Treatment, Drug Y Treatment. The treatment phase will last for six months. A licensed clinical psychologist and a psychiatrist will evaluate each participant's condition once every 14 days.

ACHIEVEMENT CHECK

(17) Is it appropriate to use a control group for this experiment?

(18) What should we do if we find that people in the control group begin to become more depressed?

(19) Midway through the experiment, the researchers find that Drug Y is much more effective than Drug X. Should they continue with the experiment for the full six months?

Brain Research on Cats

Chet is a psychologist who studies the visual system using cats because their visual cortex is similar to humans. He plans to conduct a series of experiments that will improve our knowledge of how the visual system works. These experiments require that Chet implant electrodes into the brains of the cats. In addition, the cats must be killed at the end of the experiment so that the brains can be studied in detail.

ACHIEVEMENT CHECK

(20) Should Chet be allowed to do this research?

(21) Would your opinion change if you learned that (a) Chet was doing "basic" research that had no known immediate application or that (b) Chet was finding a way to allow stroke victims to recover their sight?

CHAPTER SUMMARY

All researchers bear a responsibility to act in a moral manner. This responsibility is especially critical for psychologists because their research directly affects the lives of the people and animals that are a part of their research. This chapter reviewed basic moral principles and the process of ethics. Moral principles are the beliefs we have that help us distinguish between right and wrong. Ethics is the process of examining how we react to specific situations and make decisions on how we should act.

The four moral principles at the heart of psychological research are: (a) the concern for the welfare of other beings, (b) the belief that moral principles stand before our interests and secular laws, (c) the belief that moral principles are universal truths that do not change across time or situations, and (d) the belief that moral principles are impartial and treat everyone equally.

Two of the major philosophical systems that guide ethical analysis are the principle of utility and the principle of rights. Utilitarianism directs us to seek ways to maximize happiness and minimize discomfort. Therefore, when a researcher examines a research design, he or she must consider the consequences of conducting the study. Specifically, the researcher must show that the results of the study justify the method by demonstrating that there is no other way to collect the data, and that the importance of the data outweighs any discomfort the people or animals in the study may experience. By contrast, the principle of rights requires that the researcher focus on preserving the dignity and self-worth of the people participating in the research. Research that puts the interest of the researcher above the welfare of the participants is morally wrong.

Each researcher must resolve any moral problems created by the research design by considering basic moral principles and the specific circumstances of the particular research project. The American Psychological Association developed an ethical code of conduct to help all psychologists evaluate their professional behavior.

For any research project using humans or animals, the researcher should first receive approval from the IRB. The IRB is a committee of fellow professionals that examines the research design to ensure that the researcher preserves the participant's rights. When applying for IRB approval, the researcher must demonstrate that (a) he or she is qualified to conduct the research or is being supervised by a responsible person with the necessary qualification, (b) the participants in the study have provided voluntary informed consent to participate in the study, (c) any deception used in the research is justified in that there is no other way to collect the data and that the consequence of the deception has minimal harm to the participant, (d) the data will remain confidential, and (e) at the end of the study the researcher will provide a reasonable account of the purpose of the research to the participant.

To practice an ethical deliberation, we examined Milgram's classic experiments that examined obedience. Specifically, we examined the research from the perspective of utility and the perspective of rights.

We also reviewed our moral obligation to animals used in psychological research. Some people believe that animals should not be used in any psychological research because of the extreme suffering they experience. Others believe that animal research is justified if one can demonstrate that there is no other way to obtain the data and that the benefits of the many outweigh the suffering experienced by the animals in the study.

The "Research in Action" section presented a number of ethical dilemmas that researchers often face.

CHAPTER GLOSSARY FOR REVIEW

Categorical Imperative   An ethical perspective developed by Kant that requires that we always respect the humanity and dignity of other people and never treat others as a means to an end.

Debriefing   Explaining to the participants of a study why you conducted the study and the importance of the study.

Deception by Commission   The intentional act of deceiving the participants by telling them something incorrect about the research.

Deception by Omission   A form of deception where the researcher withholds information about some conditions of the research from the participant.

Ethical Code or **Code of Conduct**   A list of rules and guidelines that direct and guide the behaviors of members of an organization.

Ethics   The process of examining one's moral principles and behavior.

Informed Consent   A requirement for all human research that ensures that the participant understands the purpose of the research, his or her rights as a participant, and the potential hazards of participating in the research.

Institutional Review Board (IRB)   A group of people who examine the researcher's proposed methodology to ensure that the researcher will protect the basic rights of the participants.

Morals   Fundamental principles that distinguish right from wrong.

National Research Act   A federal law (PL–93–348) that established the existence of the Institutional Review Board (IRB). The law requires that any researcher receiving federal funds to conduct research on humans must first receive IRB approval of the research.

Speciesism   The attitude that humans and animals have different moral rights with regard to be free of pain and suffering.

Utilitarianism   A perspective of ethics that requires one to examine the consequences of one's behavior and to ensure that it maximizes happiness and minimizes suffering.

6 SAMPLING, THE FIRST STEPS IN RESEARCH

CHAPTER OUTLINE

◆ Introduction

◆ The Nature of Samples

◆ Probability Sampling

◆ Sampling Methods

◆ Nonprobability Sampling

◆ Central Limit Theorem

◆ Applications of the Central Limit Theorem

◆ Sources of Bias and Error: A Reprise

◆ Statistics Behind the Research: A Supplement

It is a capital mistake to theorize before one has data.

—Sir Arthur Conan Doyle

INTRODUCTION

Much of what we know we learn from samples. Consider some common examples. Your knowledge of the world and the decisions you make come from samples. When someone asks you if the lunches at a restaurant are good, you use your experiences to answer the question. Your meals at the restaurant are samples. The establishment may produce thousands of meals and has served hundreds of customers since its opening. You have no way of being sure that each meal was prepared well and enjoyed. Yet, based on your experience with the restaurant, you make a single and confident conclusion, "The food is good."

The same is true when you meet a person for the first time. Social psychologists tell us that we make long-lasting conclusions based on our first impressions of people. Think for a moment of what happens in such situations. After a mere five minutes, many people are willing to state confidently that they have formed a good impression of another person. That is, an extremely small sample of behavior creates a lasting impression of that person. Given the complexity of human behavior, this is an amazing conclusion based on such a limited sample.

As you will recall from chapter 1, Bacon warned about the Idols of the Cave, relying too much on our personal experience for seeking truth. Objective or scientific sampling is a way of overcoming the Idols of the Cave because it ensures that our experiences are as broad and representative as possible. Moreover, as you learned in chapter 3, having a representative sample of the population ensures the external validity of the conclusions we draw from the data.

What are the common features of samples and sampling? First, we use samples to describe and compare things. Consider as an example, describing someone's personality. Each of us is affected by many things ranging from situational factors, interactions with others, and a host of variables too numerous to list. Even for an individual, it would be impossible to observe all the things he or she would do under different situations. However, based upon a representative sample of that person's behavior, we may be able to predict how he or she will react to specific situations. This observation leads us to the second feature of sampling. We use samples to help us make predictions and conclusions about other things or conditions. As the quotation at the start of this chapter suggests, our theories are the product of the data we collect. Perhaps, by extension, we can also suggest that no theory is any better than the data that inspired its creation.

How can we be sure that what we observe in the sample accurately represents the population? This is a critical question. As you learned in chapter 3, such a question goes to the heart of external validity. If the sample is not representative of the population, then the data will be of little value to us because they do not support inferences about the population.

Therefore, the purpose of this chapter is to examine the foundations of samples and sampling. In the following pages, we will examine the methods researchers use to collect accurate samples of the population. In addition, we will review how statistics, based on sample data, allow us to make inferences about population parameters. Hence, we will begin with a more detailed analysis of the characteristics of samples.

I assume that you have had a course in statistics and understand the foundations of descriptive statistics such as measures of central tendency (e.g., mean and median), measures of dispersion (e.g., variance and standard deviation), and z-scores. If you are not familiar with these statistics, or wish to brush up on your skills, you may want to check the "Statistics Behind the Research" section at the end of this chapter.

THE NATURE OF SAMPLES

There are several ways that we can define samples. The primary emphasis of this definition is to show that the sample is a valid representation of the population. One way to define a sample is to contrast samples with things that are not samples. We can also define samples by the methods used to create them. As you may recall from our previous discussions of validity, we cannot directly assess the external validity or the representativeness of a sample. Rather, we examine the methods used to create the sample to infer its validity. Consequently, researchers work hard to ensure that their sampling techniques produce useful data.

Scientific Samples versus Anecdotal Evidence

What is the difference between a sample and other types of information? We can begin by considering personal experiences and anecdotal evidence and compare them to a scientific sample. Imagine a person who traveled to Paris for a short vacation and then pronounces the French to be rude and inconsiderate people. Such a conclusion is indefensible. A moment's thought will reveal that many factors bias this unflattering conclusion. Specifically, a stranger traveling abroad, spending a short time in a small portion of the country, and interacting with a minuscule proportion of the population, cannot come to a meaningful conclusion about the manners of a nation of people.

Anecdotal evidence and personal experience are not sampling in the technical sense of the word. Our hypothetical traveler probably did meet several rude and inconsiderate people, an experience likely to occur when traveling to any large city. Therefore, we cannot deny the person's experiences. We do deny the conclusion, however, because we do not consider the personal encounters representative of the population.

We can use the criteria of representativeness to distinguish anecdotal evidence and personal experience from scientific samples and empirical conclusions. The goal of scientific research is to create samples that represent the population that we study and support reasonable and valid conclusions. When we collect the data, we use procedures that ensure that the samples will be free of bias and thereby represent the population. By contrast, anecdotal evidence is typically a haphazard collection of personal experiences that may be biased.

Unfortunately, anecdotal evidence too easily sways many people's opinions, an observation that Bacon noted when he described the Idols of the Tribe and Idols of the Cave. Social psychologists have long studied the poor decision-making processes that many people follow (Plous, 1993). A well-known phenomenon is the "person-who" effect that occurs when someone uses anecdotal evidence to discount a statistical generalization. For example, a smoker may dismiss the risk of smoking by noting that his or her father smoked two packs of cigarettes a day and lived to be 75. In this case, the person seems to ignore the larger body of evidence that people who smoke have a shorter life expectancy and an increased risk of health problems.

The problem we all must confront is the pervasive nature of anecdotal evidence and its influence on decision making. As researchers, we must remain vigilant to ensure that our data are representative of the population. Finally, you should recognize that the plural of anecdote is not data. Anecdotes, like rumors, cannot be trusted to be accurate, reliable, or valid no matter how often repeated.

PROBABILITY SAMPLING

Before we do anything else, we must define the meaning of random. **Random** means that each possible outcome has an equal probability of occurring and that the outcome of one event has no influence on the probability of subsequent outcomes. Imagine a balanced six-sided die. Each time you throw the die, the probability of any one side landing face-up is always 1/6. In addition, each time you throw the die, the results of the previous tosses have no effect on the current toss. That one event has no effect on other events is the principle of **independence.** Random sampling is an example of independence because selecting one object from the population will not influence the selection of other objects.

Understanding randomness is important for sampling because it allows us to link individual samples to the population. According to the **law of large numbers,** any large number of items chosen at random from a population will have, on average, the same characteristics as the population. This law is the cornerstone of probability sampling and allows us to infer that what is true of the sample is also true of the population. In this section, we will examine how we can use random events and other procedures to create samples that represent the population.

Populations and Samples

In chapter 2, I introduced you to the concepts of the population, the sampling population, and the sample. As you should recall, the population consists of all the individuals or things that the researcher wants to describe. Researchers define the population by developing the criteria that determines membership in the population. Defining the population is essential as it determines the conclusions that the researcher may draw from the data (Wilkinson, 1999).

When referring to a population, many researchers refer to the **target population** or the **universe.** For example, a researcher may study the self-attributions made by people suffering depression. In this example, the target population is any adult diagnosed with depression as defined by the *Diagnostic and Statistical Manual of Mental Disorders–IV* (American Psychiatric Association, 1994).

In some cases, it is impractical or impossible to draw a representative sample from the target population. Consequently, researchers will use a sampling population. For our purposes, a **sampling population** consists of an accessible group of people who share the same characteristics as the target population. In most behavioral research, the sampling population consists of people who live or work near the researcher. When they report their results, researchers define the characteristics of the sampling population. Doing so allows the reader to determine whether the sampling population is representative of the target population.

Some researchers refer to a **subject pool,** another term related to the sampling population. The subject pool refers to a group of people to whom the researcher has easy access. At many colleges and universities, the department of psychology maintains a subject pool of students enrolled in introductory psychology who may receive extra credit for participating in a study.

A related concept is the **sampling frame.** A sampling frame is a list of names that identifies the members of the population (Babbie, 1998). If you wanted to conduct a survey of voter opinion in your community, you could use the list of registered voters maintained by the local board of elections as the sampling frame. The main difference between the subject pool and the sampling frame is that people in the subject pool are willing to participate in a research project. By contrast, the sampling frame is merely the list of people who belong to a population.

Detailed descriptions of the characteristics of the population, sampling population, and sampling frame help us evaluate the external validity of inferences made from a sample. Consider, as an example, the sampling frame. How accurate and complete is the list? Does the list include all members of the sampling population, or does it systematically exclude important groups of people? What about our subject pool? Is the fact that the participants of an experiment were students enrolled in the Psychology 101, Fall Term, 2003 at Mythical College important to our interpretation of the results? The answer is yes.

The connection between external validity and the sampling population, subject pool, and sampling frame is important. If any of these subgroups is not representative of the population, then it will be impossible to assume a meaningful link between the sample and the population. For these reasons, researchers spend considerable time analyzing and describing the sources of their data. Doing so allows the researcher to establish a connection between the sample statistics and the population parameters. With these concerns in mind, we can turn our attention to the business of creating samples.

Characteristics of Probability Sampling

There are many ways to take a representative sample from a population. We can use techniques known as simple random sampling, stratified sampling, systematic sampling, or cluster sampling, to name just a few. Although there are many types of sampling procedures, they all have one thing in common; they are **probability sampling** techniques.

All probability sampling techniques share common features. First, they treat each member of the population as a potential member of a sample. This is a critical feature as it ensures that the sampling technique does not systematically exclude portions of the population from the sample and thereby bias the results. By implication, the procedures employed in the sampling procedure are objective and systematic. All sampling procedures create a set of rules, known as a protocol, for selecting members of the population. In some

TABLE 6.1
All potential samples of 2 drawn from a population consisting of the values 1 through 6

S_1 (1, 2)	S_2 (1, 3)	S_3 (1, 4)	S_4 (1, 5)	S_5 (1, 6)
S_6 (2, 3)	S_7 (2, 4)	S_8 (2, 5)	S_9 (2, 6)	S_{10} (3, 4)
S_{11} (3, 5)	S_{12} (3, 6)	S_{13} (4, 5)	S_{14} (4, 6)	S_{15} (5, 6)

cases, the protocol for sampling may be minimal, in other cases the sampling protocol may be extremely elaborate. We follow the rules for creating the sample to ensure that the data are not biased.

The second feature of probability sampling is that we can determine the probability of selecting any specific sample (Cochran, 1977). This may sound a bit strange, but it is an important assumption that allows us to connect the results of the sample to the parameters of the population. Consider the following example of probability sampling.

Assume that you have a population containing the whole numbers 1 to 6, inclusive. Using sampling without replacement, and with a sample size of 2, you could create the 15 potential samples listed in Table 6.1. If we use probability sampling, we can determine the probability that we will select any one of these samples. In this example, there is an equal likelihood that we will select any one of the samples. Specifically, for each sample, $p = 1/15$ or $p = .0667$. The probability (p) that we will select any one of these samples is approximately 6.67%.

You may object and say that we rarely know the true nature of the population, and if we did, why would we need sampling? You are correct; we rarely know the parameters of the population. This illustration shows the logic of probability sampling. For any given population, we can draw an infinite number of samples. Using mathematical techniques that we will soon review, we can estimate the probability of selecting any one of those samples. Armed with this knowledge, we can then make several interesting inferences about the population.

SAMPLING METHODS

There are many methods of drawing samples from the population. Each method shares a common goal; ensure that the sample is an unbiased depiction of the population. In this section we will review several of the more frequently used sampling methods including simple random sampling, sequential sampling, stratified sampling, and cluster sampling. This section can provide only a general introduction to sampling methods. Sampling is a science, and there are many sophisticated techniques researchers use for specific purposes (Babbie, 1998; Cochran, 1977; Salant & Dillman, 1994).

Simple Random Sampling

Simple random sampling is the most basic of the sampling procedures. Simple random sampling occurs whenever each member of the population has an equal probability of selection. The steps involved in conducting a simple random sample are clear cut. First,

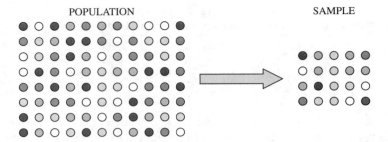

FIGURE 6.1
Random sampling. The block on the left represents the population. Each
circle has an equal chance of selection. The block on the right represents
the sample.

estimate the size of the population. Next, generate random numbers to determine which members of the population to select. In the final stage, collect the data and conduct the study.

Figure 6.1 illustrates random sampling. The block of circles on the left represents members of a population. The block of circles on the right represents a random sample of the population. In this example, there are five types of circle; each represented by a different shade. Because there is no bias in the sampling procedure, the sample should be similar to the population, and any difference between the sample and the population represents chance or random factors.

Imagine that you want to conduct a survey of student opinion at your college. The college's Institutional Review Board approved your research, and you are ready to collect the data. The first step is to determine the size of the population. This should be relatively easy. Go to the college's records office and ask the registrar for the number of students currently enrolled at the college. For the sake of the illustration, assume that there are 7,584 students enrolled at your college and that you have decided that you will create a random sample of 250 students.

For the next step, you will need 250 **random numbers.** Random numbers are a series of numbers with no order or pattern. Technically, random numbers are independent of each other. Independence means that each number has an equal chance of selection and the selection of one number has no effect on the selection of another number. Before the advent of personal computers, many researchers used a random number table created by the Rand Corporation (1955) that contains 1 million random digits. The authors of the book went to great pains to build and test a machine that produced random digits. Table A.2 of Appendix A is an example of a random number table.

Many researchers now use their computer to generate random numbers. Different computer programs can produce a string of random numbers between specific values. In the current example, we need 250 random numbers between 1 and 7,584, inclusive. Table 6.2 presents 20 random numbers between 1 and 7,584 that I created using a spreadsheet program. Once you have the 250 numbers, you could go to an alphabetic list of all students and select the students whose position on the list corresponds to the random numbers. If everyone cooperates with your request to complete the questionnaire, your sample will be an unbiased representation of the population.

TABLE 6.2

Twenty random numbers between 1 and 7,584 generated using a spreadsheet program and rank ordered from lowest to highest

23	147	450	496	871	1529	2629	2660	2898	3311
3775	4020	4035	4484	4852	5565	5790	6438	6699	7558

Many computer programs generate random numbers. Researchers call these numbers pseudorandom numbers because generating truly random numbers is difficult (Pashley, 1993). For most cases, however, these pseudorandom numbers are sufficient for behavioral research.

Sequential Sampling

Although simple random sampling is the gold standard of probability sampling, many researchers find it inefficient and impractical (Babbie, 1998). A suitable alternative is **sequential sampling.** For a sequential sample, we list the members of the sampling population and then select each kth member from the list.

The steps for sequential sampling are straightforward. First, we need to determine the **sampling interval** that identifies which members of the list to select. The sampling interval is merely:

$$\text{Sampling Interval} = \frac{\text{Size of Population}}{\text{Desired Size of Sample}} \tag{6.1}$$

In our previous example, we wanted to create a sample of 250 from a population of 7,584 students. Therefore, the sampling interval is 30 ($30.336 = 7,584/250$). Now all you need to do is obtain a current list of all students and then select every 30th student on the list. This procedure assumes that the list is a complete sampling frame.

Stratified Sampling

Stratified sampling is a refinement of simple random and sequential sampling. This technique is especially useful in situations where the population contains different subgroups that the sample must include. Researchers who conduct public opinion polling, for example, want to ensure that the sample represents the population for gender, age, political affiliation, education, annual income, and a host of other variables that may affect public opinion. Figure 6.2 illustrates how stratified sampling works. In this example, the population contains five distinct subgroups of different sizes. The researcher wants to include a sample of each subgroup in the sample. In order not to bias the sample, the size of the subgroups in the sample should equal the relative size of the subgroups in the population.

Figure 6.2 offers a hint of how a researcher would conduct a stratified random sample. First, the researcher would identify the specific subgroups in the population and attempt to estimate their relative size. Next, the researcher can use simple random or sequential sampling within each subgroup. The result is a representative sample. If all goes well, the size of the subgroups in the sample will be the same relative size as the population.

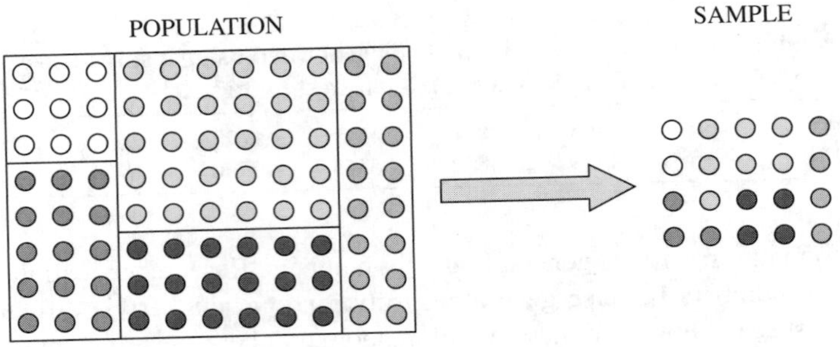

POPULATION   SAMPLE

FIGURE 6.2
Stratified sampling. The box on the left represents a population
consisting of smaller subgroups or strata. The researcher randomly
selects from each stratum to create the sample. The sample will have
approximately the same proportions of the subgroups as the population.

Cluster Sampling

Cluster sampling is a form of sampling that researchers use when it is not convenient to
pull one or two people out of their environment for the research or when other methods of
sampling are impractical. Researchers often use this technique when working with intact
groups. An example would be a research project examining the effectiveness of different
teaching techniques.

Imagine that Figure 6.3 represents students enrolled in 20 different sections of the same
course. The researcher may want to know if differences in teaching method affect students'
performance in the course. It may be impractical to randomly select students and create special sections of the course. As an alternative, the researcher can select different sections at random for the research. In Figure 6.3, the researcher randomly selected five different clusters.

In other cases, the clusters may represent cities, neighborhoods, schools, or other naturally occurring clusters. The researcher can then select clusters randomly or systematically. If the researcher knows that particular clusters contain important portions of the population, he or she may then purposely select those clusters.

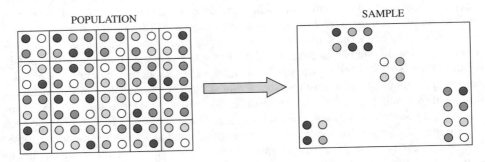

POPULATION   SAMPLE

FIGURE 6.3
Cluster sampling. The small blocks of individuals in the left square identify separate clusters
of individuals. The researcher then randomly selects several clusters for the sample.

NONPROBABILITY SAMPLING

Although probability sampling is the ideal, it is often beyond the budget, time, and personal resources of the researcher. Therefore, in many situations researchers will resort to **nonprobability sampling.** These methods are convenient for the researcher, but the results need to be interpreted with caution. As you should recall from your reading in previous chapters, using a nonprobability sampling method may limit the inferences that you can make from the data. On the other hand, these methods can produce useful data when collected and interpreted under the right conditions (Cochran, 1977).

Convenience Sampling

There is an important difference between probability sampling and **convenience sampling.** Probability sampling means that each member of the sampling population is a potential member of the sample. By contrast, convenience sampling means that the researcher uses members of the population who are easy to find. Interviewing people at a shopping mall or people who walk by a particular street corner are examples of convenience sampling. In these cases, the researcher allows the individual's behavior to determine who will, and more importantly who will not, be a part of the study.

Do you see the difference between probability sampling and convenience sampling? For all forms of probability sampling, the *researcher's method* of sampling determines who will be a potential member of a sample. For convenience sampling, the *individuals' behavior* determines whether they could become part of the sample. Consequently, convenience sampling can bias the results and interpretation of the data. Imagine that you wanted to conduct a survey of students at your college. Do you think you would get different results if you surveyed students lounging around the college's student union versus students studying in the library? In many ways, convenience sampling suffers the same problems as anecdotal evidence because the sample does not represent the population.

There are times, however, when a convenience sample may be the only way to collect the data. For example, a researcher interested in studying homeless people may use people who eat at a cafeteria for the homeless. Although there may be many homeless people who do not eat at the facility, this may be the only way for the researcher to interview these people.

Snowball Sampling

A cohort is a group of people who share a particular feature. Sometimes the members of a cohort are difficult to find and recruit for research. The members of the cohort may wish to remain anonymous, or there is no list identifying the members of the cohort. In such situations, the researcher may wish to use **snowball sampling.** To sample from the cohort, the researcher needs to find a member of the cohort and use him or her to find other members of the cohort.

In the 1940s, homosexual men and women took extraordinary precautions to keep their sexual orientation a secret. Evelyn Hooker was able to gain the trust of several homosexual men. Once they trusted her and the motives of her research, they helped Hooker recruit homosexual friends and associates for her research. Consequently, Hooker was one of the first psychologists to publish empirical research demonstrating that homosexuals and heterosexuals experience the same rates and types of mental health problems (Hooker, 1956, 1957, 1958). Without the snowball sampling technique, Hooker may never have been able to conduct this important and groundbreaking research. Her research did much to help reduce the unfounded stereotypes many people, including clinical psychologists and psychiatrists, held about homosexuality.

ACHIEVEMENT CHECK

(1) What are the differences between anecdotal evidence and scientific sampling?

(2) What are the potential problems with relying on personal experience to make decisions?

(3) Describe the similarities and differences among simple random sampling, sequential sampling, stratified sampling, and cluster sampling.

(4) Anne is selecting courses for next semester and must take an English literature course, but does not know which professor she should select. To solve her dilemma, she decides to ask three of her friends, who are English majors, for their recommendations.
   a. What type of sampling is Anne using?
   b. Describe the factors that may bias the information Anne receives.

(5) The dean of academic affairs at a small college wants to examine the study habits of students attending the college. He randomly selects 50 students from the college and asks them to record the number of hours they work on homework each day for one week (assume that all the students participate and answer honestly). According to the results, the typical student studies an average of 3.2 hours a day.
   a. Can we conclude that the dean has a valid estimate of the students' study habits?
   b. Are there factors that can bias the results of the data?

(6) Professor Smith distributes a survey to 45 students in his English Composition 101 course. Professor Jones distributes the same survey to 45 students in her Organic Chemistry 250 course.
   a. What are the factors that may bias the results of these samples?
   b. Is one sample more likely to be representative of the students at the college?

(7) A national magazine publishes the results of a survey of its readers. The magazine argues that the results are valid because of the large number (e.g., 12,592) of readers who responded to the questionnaire. Do you agree that the results are valid?

(8) A researcher in a large city wishes to conduct a survey and ensure that the sample includes a representative sample of each of the five major ethnic groups that live in the city. Describe how the researcher could use each probability sampling technique to create such a sample.

(9) A researcher wants to examine the opinions of members of different Christian denominations (e.g., Baptist, Catholic, Episcopal, Lutheran, and Presbyterian). What might be the most cost-effective method of generating a representative sample?

(10) Do you agree with the statement, "A sample of convenience is little better than anecdotal evidence"? Defend your answer.

CENTRAL LIMIT THEOREM

You may be wondering how I can continue to assert that a sample statistic is an unbiased estimate of the population parameter. How do we know that the mean or the standard deviation of a sample accurately estimates the mean and the standard deviation of a population (e.g., $M \approx \mu$ and $SD \approx \sigma$)? To answer that question, we need to examine an important principle in statistics known as the central limit theorem. The central limit theorem is important because it allows us to use the sample to describe the population.

The central limit theorem describes the distribution of probability samples. As I noted previously, one of the characteristics of probability sampling is the ability to predict or to estimate the probability of selecting a specific sample. We can use the central limit theorem and a sampling distribution to estimate the probability of obtaining, at chance, any potential sample from the population. Before we proceed, however, we need to define some terms.

A **sampling distribution** represents the result of taking many samples of a specific size from a population and plotting the frequency of a sample statistic such as the mean. A sampling distribution is the theoretical distribution of the potential values of a sample statistic that would occur when drawing an infinite number of equal-sized random samples from the population. We can use a thought experiment as an illustration.

Imagine that you have access to a population of college students you want to survey. You draw a random sample of 25 students, test each person, and then calculate the mean score. You can now repeat these steps to produce the mean for a second sample. Chances are that the two sample means will be different from each other. If you continue to collect samples from the population, you will eventually have a large collection of sample means. When you create a graph of the frequency of the values of the means, you will form the sampling distribution for the means.

Not all the sample means will be equal to each other; there will be variability among the sample means. Specifically, many of the sample means will be slightly greater or less than the population mean, and some will be much different from the sample mean. We use the concept of **standard error (ε)** to describe the difference between the individual sample means and the population mean ($\varepsilon = M - \mu$). Because we used random sampling to create the samples, the difference among the sample means represents random or chance factors. The central limit theorem allows us to describe the shape of the sampling distribution of sample means and the amount of standard error.

The **central limit theorem** makes several specific propositions or statements about the shape of the sampling distribution of the sample mean. The propositions are:

1. As the size of the individual samples increases, the shape of the sampling distribution of sample means will become progressively normal regardless of the shape of the population.
2. The mean of the sampling distribution of sample means (μ_M) will equal the mean of the population (μ), $\mu_M = \mu$.
3. The standard deviation of the sampling distribution of sample means (σ_M) will equal the standard deviation of the population (σ) divided by the square root of the sample size ($\sqrt{n}$), $\sigma_M = \sigma/\sqrt{n}$.

What are the implications of these propositions? Why are they important for statistics? We will consider the answers to these questions in the following sections.

Shape of the Sampling Distribution

One of the most interesting predictions of the central limit theorem is that the shape of the sampling distribution of sample means will be normal especially as the size of each sample increases. Figure 6.4 illustrates this prediction. The top panels of the figure represent the

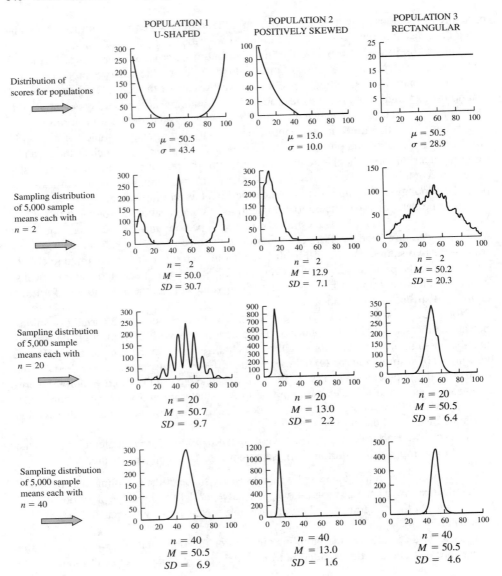

FIGURE 6.4

The central limit theorem. The top panels represent the shape of the populations from which the samples are drawn. The lower three rows of graphs represent the sampling distribution of the mean for sample sizes of 2, 20, and 40. Each sampling distribution represents 5,000 random samples generated by a computer program. According to the central limit theorem, the shape of the sampling distribution will become normal as the sample size increases. In addition, $\mu_M = \mu$ and $\sigma_M = \sigma/\sqrt{n}$. The mean ($M$) of each sampling distribution is close to the mean of the population, and the standard deviation of each distribution (SD) is approximately $\sigma/\sqrt{n}$.

shape of three populations: U-shaped, positively skewed, and rectangular. The lower panels represent the sampling distributions of means for sample sizes of 2, 20, and 40. Each sampling distribution represents 5,000 random samples taken from the population. As you can see, as the size of the sample increases, the distribution of means becomes progressively normal in shape.

Mean of the Sampling Distribution: $\mu_M = \mu$

The symbol μ_M represents the theoretical mean of the sampling distribution of means. In words, the quantity represents the mean of means. As an equation,

$$\mu_M = \frac{\sum M}{N} = \frac{\text{Sum of all sample means}}{\text{Number of samples}} \tag{6.2}$$

This equation indicates that we take the sum of all sample means drawn from the population and divide by the number of samples created. You should be clear about the difference between *sample size* and *number of samples*. Sample size, represented as *n*, refers to the number of observations in each sample. The number of samples, represented as *N*, refers to the number of samples drawn from the population. For Equation 6.2, we assume that the sample size is constant and that *N* is an extremely large number. As an example, look at the bottom row of graphs in Figure 6.4. Each graph represents 5,000 random samples. Therefore, $N = 5,000$. Each of the samples consists of 40 scores. Consequently, $n = 40$.

You should now be able to see that the sample mean is an unbiased estimate of the population mean. Although there is standard error in any sampling distribution, the error is random and nonsystematic. Therefore, any individual sample mean is equally likely to be above or below the population mean. Using these facts allows us to conclude that the sample mean is an unbiased estimate of the population mean, or that $M = \mu$.

Standard Error of the Mean: $\sigma_M = \dfrac{\sigma}{\sqrt{n}}$

The **standard error of the mean (*SEM*)** is the standard deviation of the sampling distribution of sample means. The equation for *SEM* tells us that as sample size increases, the distribution of sample means will cluster closer to the population mean. As sample size increases, the sample mean will be a more accurate estimate of the population mean.

To summarize, the central limit theorem allows us to make several inferences concerning the relation between sample statistics and population parameters. First, the sample mean is an unbiased estimate of the population mean if we use a probability sampling procedure to generate the sample. Furthermore, the sample mean becomes a better estimate of the population mean as the sample size increases. Because of these properties, researchers prefer to use the sample mean as the descriptive statistic to infer the population parameter. Second, the central limit theorem allows us to determine the probability of obtaining various sample means.

APPLICATIONS OF THE CENTRAL LIMIT THEOREM

In this section we will examine how we can use the central limit theorem to our advantage. As you will see, we can use the central limit theorem to answer two important questions, "How reliable is my sample mean?" and "How large should my sample be?" We can answer the first question by calculating the standard error of the mean and the confidence interval. Once we review these basic statistical tools, we can begin to address the second question.

Standard Error of the Mean

We use *SEM* to describe the standard deviation of the sampling distribution of means. This value allows us to estimate the range of potential sample means drawn from a population.

Figure 6.5 represents the hypothetical results of taking 20 samples at random from a population mean. Assume that the mean of the population equals 100 ($\mu = 100$), that the standard deviation of the population equals 30 ($\sigma = 30$), and that we draw 20 random samples of 9 observations each ($n = 9$). We can calculate the standard error of the mean as $\sigma_M = 10.0 = 30/\sqrt{9}$.

The normal distribution in Figure 6.5 represents the hypothetical sampling distribution for sample means where $\mu_M = 100.0$ and $\sigma_M = 10.0$. The box-and-whisker plots below the graph represent the 20 individual samples. As you can see, there is variability among the individual sample means. If you look closely, almost all of the sample means fall between 80 and 120, within two standard deviations of the mean, $\pm 2\sigma$. Most fall between 90 and 110, within one standard deviation of the mean, $\pm 1\sigma$. One sample is greater than 120, but it seems to be the exception rather than the rule. This figure illustrates how we can use the sample statistics and sample size to determine the accuracy of the sample mean as an estimate of the population mean.

Confidence Interval

You are probably familiar with the concept of the confidence interval (CI). Whenever you read or hear about a political poll, you may hear that the results are accurate to ± 5 points or ± 3 points. This statement represents the confidence interval. The confidence interval indicates the potential range of values that would occur if the researchers drew another sample under identical conditions from the population.

For example, if Strickland[1] and Hollister are running for public office and a poll of registered voters shows Strickland with 60% of the popular support ± 5 points, we can conclude that between 55% and 65% of the registered voters favor Strickland. Statisticians call these estimates the **point estimate** and the **interval estimate.** The point estimate refers to the use of a sample statistic to estimate the corresponding population parameter. In this example, we estimated that 60% of the voters would vote for Stickland. The interval estimate allows us to describe the accuracy of the statistic as an estimate of the population parameter.

---

[1]Dr. Ted Strickland was the first psychologist to be elected to the House of Representatives. He represents the voters in southeastern Ohio.

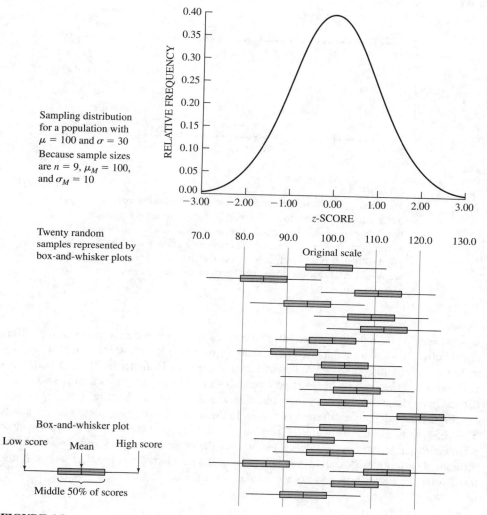

FIGURE 6.5

Illustration of the central limit theorem. The box-and-whisker plots represent 20 random samples drawn from a population where $\mu = 100.0$ and $\sigma = 30.0$. For each box-and-whisker plot, the long horizontal line represents the range between the lowest and highest scores. The rectangle represents the middle 50% of the sample. The vertical line within the box is the sample mean. The sample size of each sample is $n = 9$. The four long vertical lines represent the location of $\pm 1\sigma_M$ and $\pm 2\sigma_M$. For the sampling distribution of means, $\mu_M = 100.0$ and $\sigma_M = 10.0$, $10.0 = 30/\sqrt{9}$.

Because a poll is a sample, subsequent samples may yield different values. The interval estimate allows us to estimate the potential range of sample means we would obtain if we simultaneously collected an infinite number of samples. In this example, we predict that if we were to continue generating samples, the proportion of voters endorsing Strickland would range between 55% and 65%.

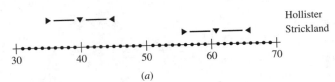

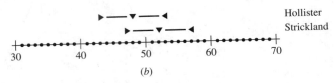

FIGURE 6.6

Two examples of how we can use point and interval estimates to make inferences about the difference between two point estimates. In (a) there is no overlap of the interval estimates, which allows us to infer that Strickland is clearly favored over Hollister. In (b) the point estimates occur within the interval estimates. Consequently, we would infer that the difference between 48 and 52 represents sampling error.

We can also use the point and interval estimates to make inferences about the differences between population parameters. Consider two examples. First, imagine that the estimate for Strickland is 60% ±5 points and the estimate for Hollister is 40% ±5 points. As you can see in Figure 6.6a, there is no overlap of the interval estimates for the two candidates. Given these data, we may infer that Strickland is the clear favorite.

Figure 6.6b depicts a different situation. In this example, the estimate for Strickland is 52% ±5 points and the estimate for Hollister is 48% ±5 points. Because the two sample point estimates are within the interval estimate of the other sample, we would infer that the difference between 52% and 48% may represent the standard error. In other words, registered voters do not clearly favor one candidate over the other.

Calculating the Confidence Interval

There are several ways to calculate the confidence interval depending on the type of data one collects. Specifically, there are confidence intervals for the proportion and for the mean. As you will see, they share common elements.

Confidence interval for proportions

A proportion is a special type of mean. In the political example regarding the Strickland–Hollister race, we might find that for Strickland, $p = .60$. To obtain this number, a pollster may have randomly contacted 400 registered voters who indicated that they are very likely to vote. Of these, 240 indicated that they favor Strickland. Therefore, $p = .60 = 240/400$. What would happen if we conducted another random sample? Assuming that people have not changed their opinion of Strickland, what range of proportions would we expect to find? To answer this question, we first need to calculate the standard error of the proportion using the following equation,

$$SE_p = \frac{\sqrt{p(1 - p)}}{\sqrt{N}} \qquad (6.3)$$

For this equation, p represents the proportion that we want to examine and N represents the total number of people we sampled. Applying the equation to this example, we proceed with the following steps,

$$SE_p = \frac{\sqrt{.60(1 - .60)}}{\sqrt{400}} \qquad SE_p = \frac{\sqrt{.60(.40)}}{20} \qquad SE_p = \frac{\sqrt{.24}}{20}$$

$$SE_p = \frac{.4899}{20} \qquad SE_p = 0.0245$$

Once we have the standard error of the proportion, we can then determine the confidence interval using the equation,

$$CI = p \pm z_{(1-\alpha)/2}(SE_p) \qquad (6.4)$$

For this equation, $z_{(1-\alpha)/2}$ represents the z-score that indicates the lower and upper levels of the confidence interval. To determine the appropriate z-score, you will first need to determine the confidence interval that you want to use. For example, if you set $1 - \alpha = .90$, then you want to have a range that represents 90% of potential means. If you set $1 - \alpha = .95$, then you have established a 95% confidence interval. To determine the corresponding z-score, divide $1 - \alpha$ by 2 [e.g., $(1 - \alpha)/2$], then turn to Table A.1 of Appendix A. Looking down Column B, find the proportion that matches $(1 - \alpha)/2$ and use the corresponding z-score for your calculations. Table 6.3 represents the z-scores that correspond with different confidence intervals and the corresponding z-scores.

As you can see in Table 6.3, if we had selected a 95% confidence interval, the confidence interval is $.60 \pm 0.0480$. By multiplying the values by 100, we can convert the proportions to percentages—$60\% \pm 4.8\%$. Therefore, if we collected additional random samples of 400 registered voters, we would expect the percentage of people supporting Strickland to range between 55.5% and 64.8%.

TABLE 6.3
Calculating the confidence interval for a proportion

Confidence interval			
68%	**90%**	**95%**	**99%**
$(1 - \alpha)/2 = .34$	$(1 - \alpha)/2 = .45$	$(1 - \alpha)/2 = .475$	$(1 - \alpha)/2 = .495$
$z_{(1 - \alpha)/2}$ scores			
$z_{(1 - \alpha)/2} = 1.00$	$z_{(1 - \alpha)/2} = 1.65$	$z_{(1 - \alpha)/2} = 1.96$	$z_{(1 - \alpha)/2} = 2.58$
$CI = .60 \pm 1.0(0.0245)$	$CI = .60 \pm 1.65(0.0245)$	$CI = .60 \pm 1.96(0.0245)$	$CI = .60 \pm 2.58(0.0245)$
$CI = .60 \pm 0.0244$	$CI = .60 \pm 0.0404$	$CI = .60 \pm 0.0480$	$CI = .60 \pm 0.0632$
.5755–.6244	.5595–.6404	.5552–.6480	.5367–.6632

Confidence interval for means

We can apply the same logic used in the previous section to determine the confidence interval for the arithmetic mean. You should recognize some familiar terms in Equation 6.5; M represents the mean of the sample, and $\frac{SD}{\sqrt{n}}$ is the standard error of the mean. In this form of the equation, we use SD to estimate the population standard deviation, σ. The other term in the equation, $t_{(1-\alpha)/2}$, may be new to you. This variable is similar to $z_{(1-\alpha)/2}$ in that it determines the specific values for the upper and lower limits of the confidence interval. The difference between $z_{(1-\alpha)/2}$ and $t_{(1-\alpha)/2}$ is that $z_{(1-\alpha)/2}$ represents the normal distribution whereas $t_{(1-\alpha)/2}$ represents the sampling distribution of the mean for specific sample sizes. We can work through a problem to illustrate how to use Equation 6.5.

$$CI = M \pm t_{(1-\alpha)/2} \left(\frac{SD}{\sqrt{n}} \right) \tag{6.5}$$

Assume that you create a random sample of 16 people and give each person a test. According to your calculations, $M = 75.0$ and $SD = 5.0$. What is the confidence interval for your mean? The first thing you will need to do is determine the appropriate value for $t_{(1-\alpha)/2}$. To obtain this value, turn to Table A.3 of Appendix A. In the instructions, you will see that you need to convert the sample size to the degrees of freedom (df) by calculating $n - 1$. For this example, the $df = 15(df = 16 - 1)$. Using the value of df, select the appropriate value of t for the equation. To find this value, use the column of numbers labeled "Level of Significance of a Two-Tailed or Nondirectional Test" and the appropriate level of $1 - \alpha$. This column of numbers represents that we want to estimate a symmetrical area about the mean of the distribution with α split equally between the two extreme ends of the table. For example, if we set $1 - \alpha = .95$ we find that $t_{(1-\alpha)/2} = 2.131$. Table 6.4 presents an example of these calculations.

If we had set $1 - \alpha = .95$ then the confidence interval is 72.4–77.6. Therefore, if we continue to create random samples of 16 from this population, we can expect that 95% of them will be between 72.4 and 77.6. We can also conclude that the probability of obtaining at random a sample with a mean less than 72.4 or greater than 77.6 is 5%.

TABLE 6.4
Calculating the confidence interval for a sample mean for $df = 15$

Confidence interval		
90%	95%	99%
$1 - \alpha = .90$	$1 - \alpha = .95$	$1 - \alpha = .99$
	$t_{(1 - \alpha)/2}$ **scores**	
$t_{(1 - \alpha)/2} = 1.753$	$t_{(1 - \alpha)/2} = 2.131$	$t_{(1 - \alpha)/2} = 2.947$
$CI = 75 \pm 1.753(1.25)$	$CI = 75 \pm 2.131(1.25)$	$CI = 75 \pm 2.947(1.25)$
$CI = 75 \pm 2.191$	$CI = 75 \pm 2.638$	$CI = 75 \pm 3.684$
72.8–77.2	72.4–77.6	71.3–78.7

Interpreting the Confidence Interval

The confidence interval allows us to estimate the potential range of sample means that would occur if we continued to draw samples from the population under identical circumstances. Consider the 95% confidence interval, one that many researchers use. For the example in Figure 6.5, the 95% confidence interval extends between 80.0 and 120.0, inclusive. The confidence interval indicates that if we were to take an infinite number of samples from the population, each with a sample size of 9, we would expect 95% of the sample means to be between 80.0 and 120.0.

Factors that Affect SEM

What are the factors that influence the size of the standard error? Are there ways that we can reduce the standard error and thereby increase the accuracy of the sample mean as an estimate of the population mean? According to the central limit theorem, two factors influence the standard error of the mean, the standard deviation of the population (σ), and the sample size (n). As the standard deviation of the population decreases, the size of the SEM will also decrease, all else being equal.

How can you change the value of σ if it is a constant value and parameter of the population? Technically, you cannot change σ, but you can change the way you define your population. One way to reduce σ is to refine your definition of the population. Broad and sweeping definitions of the population tend to correspond with large variability in individual scores. As you begin to refine your definition of the population, the members of the population may tend to become more homogeneous (similar) to each other. Having a more specific definition of your population may also help you better understand the phenomenon you are studying.

Adults who suffer from depression, for example, may experience an extremely wide range of symptoms. If you defined your population as anyone who has experienced depression, your population would include about every living person. By contrast, if you defined your population as young adult (18 to 29 years of age) women who had met the criteria for a major depressive episode lasting between one and two years, your population would probably be much more homogeneous; that is, σ will be smaller. You may find that this more narrow definition of the population will allow you to understand depression for this population. In addition, you might be able to make more accurate statements about how depression expresses itself in different populations (e.g., men versus women; older versus younger people; short-term versus long-term depression).

As the researcher, you can directly control the size of your sample. According to the central limit theorem, the sample size affects the SEM by $1/\sqrt{n}$. Specifically, as the sample size increases, the SEM will decrease. Figure 6.7 presents the relation between the SEM and sample size. The message presented in the graph is clear; as the sample size increases, the magnitude of the SEM decreases. Therefore, if you want the sample mean to accurately represent the population mean, you should maximize the sample size.

Another important message in the graph is that increasing sample size has diminishing returns. Specifically, greater increases in sample size produce minor reductions in the SEM.

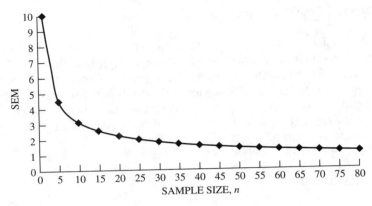

FIGURE 6.7
The size of the standard error of the mean (*SEM*) as the sample size
increases. As sample size increases, the size of the *SEM* decreases by $1/\sqrt{n}$.

As you can see on the left side of the graph, small increases in sample size (e.g., $n = 5$ to
$n = 25$) produce large drops in the *SEM*. As the sample size increases, however, the
changes in *SEM* decrease. Why is this fact important?

Sampling is expensive. Selecting individuals from the population and collecting the
necessary information is time consuming. In addition, recruiting and collecting data from
each participant adds to the cost of the research. Therefore, it is not always practical or fea-
sible to collect exceptionally large samples. Because of the economic impact that sample
size has on the cost of the research, determining the optimal sample size of the research is
an important part of any research plan. We will examine methods to determine the optimal
sample size in subsequent chapters when we review specific research methods. Although
these techniques vary depending on the type of research, they all depend on the propositions contained in the central limit theorem.

SOURCES OF BIAS AND ERROR: A REPRISE

The focus of this chapter has been sampling. We have examined different methods of obtaining samples that we hope are representative of the population. At different points in
the chapter, we have reviewed bias and error. As a generality, *bias* refers to nonrandom
and systematic factors that cause the sample mean to be different from the population
mean. By contrast, *error* refers to random events that we cannot control. The goal of research design is to identify ways that we can eliminate bias and reduce error as much as
possible.

Figure 6.8 presents an outline of the relation between the target population, sampling
population, sampling distribution, and individual sample. Each level in the figure indicates
a potential source of bias or error.

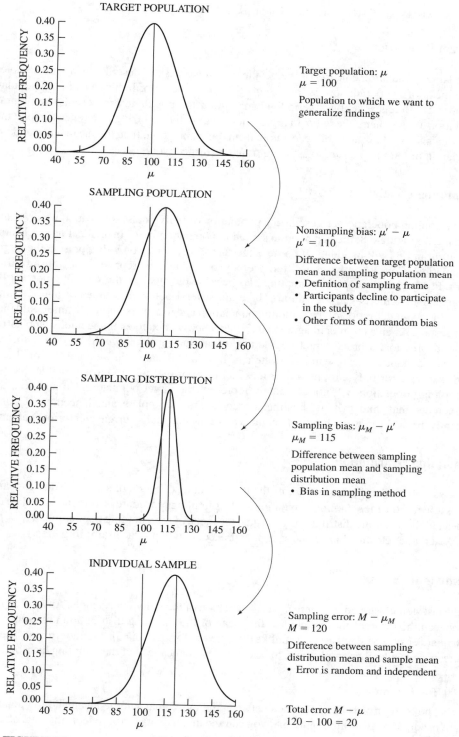

FIGURE 6.8

Potential sources of bias and error when creating samples.

Target Population

The target population consists of the people whom we wish to describe using our sample. The mean of the population, μ, represents the typical score of individuals in the population, and differences among the individuals within the population represents the natural variation among them. We use σ to represent the naturally occurring differences among individuals. If we draw an unbiased sample from this population, then the mean and standard deviation of the sample should estimate μ and σ, respectively.

Sampling Population

The sampling population represents the population of individuals from which we draw the sample. In Figure 6.8, the mean of the sampling population is μ'. In an ideal research situation, μ and μ' will be identical because the sampling population will represent the target population. Consequently, any difference between μ and μ' represents a **nonsampling bias.** Figure 6.8 depicts a nonsampling bias because the mean of the sampling population is greater than the target population. There are several potential sources of nonsampling bias. First, our definition of the sampling population and use of a sampling frame could bias our results. As an example, imagine that a researcher wanted to examine adults who suffer from depression, a broad target population. What do you think would happen if the researcher conducted the research at a veterans' hospital? Because the veterans' hospital provides service for only current and former members of the military, it is possible that the sampling population will not accurately represent the target population. In addition, the researcher may find that the hospital's records are incomplete and inaccurate. Consequently, he or she may not be able to contact all of the hospital's current and former patients.

Sampling Distribution

The sampling distribution represents the theoretical distribution of sample means for samples drawn from the sampling population. If the sampling procedure is truly random, then the mean of the sampling distribution will equal the mean of the sampling population, $\mu_M = \mu'$. A systematic selection bias in the sampling procedure will produce **sampling bias.**

Individual Sample

The last step illustrated in Figure 6.8 is the creation of the individual sample. Any difference between the mean of the sample and the mean of the sampling distribution represents the standard error. The standard error, unlike the different forms of bias, is a random event. Therefore, we consider the sample mean to be equivalent to the mean of the sampling distribution.

Total error

The total error is the difference between the individual sample mean and the population mean, $M - \mu$. From Figure 6.8, you can see that the total error reflects the total effects of nonsampling bias, sampling bias, and the sampling error.

Inferences from the sample to the population

At the start of the chapter, I noted that we cannot directly assess the external validity or the representativeness of a sample merely by inspecting the sample data. Because we never know the true value of μ, we cannot determine what proportion of the total error reflects bias and what proportion reflects the standard error. Therefore, we need to ensure that our sampling and research methods are free of bias.

RESEARCH IN ACTION: TRENDS IN HIV-RELATED RISK BEHAVIORS

Human immunodeficiency virus (HIV) is a serious health risk. During 1997, HIV was the seventh leading cause of death among persons aged 15–24 in the United States (Ventura, Anderson, Martin, & Smith, 1998). The virus is bloodborne and spreads when there is an exchange of blood. Many people contract HIV while engaged in intimate contact, including sexual intercourse. Although there are many treatments for the symptoms of HIV and acquired immunodeficiency syndrome (AIDS), there is no cure for these dreadful conditions. Therefore, health experts and policymakers have worked hard to educate the public about the threat of HIV and AIDS. Part of this education has been to discourage adolescents from engaging in risky sexual behaviors (e.g., sexual relations without a condom and with multiple partners) that increase the risk of contracting HIV.

Since 1991, a division of the Centers for Disease Control (CDC) has gathered extensive data on the prevalence of risky sexual behaviors among high school-aged adolescents. To collect the data, the researchers used a two-stage cluster sampling method. First, they selected seven large-city school districts including Boston, Chicago, Dallas, Fort Lauderdale, Jersey City, Miami, and Philadelphia. The researchers selected these cities because the spread of HIV is greatest in urban areas. In addition, these cities represent the major geographic regions of the nation. Next, the researchers randomly selected schools within these cities to conduct their survey. The survey was anonymous and contained questions about the students' age, ethnic group, and sexual behaviors. The CDC collected data in 1991, 1993, 1995, and 1997. During these years, the return rate for the questionnaires ranged between 60% and 85% (Centers for Disease Control, 1999).

Figures 6.9 and 6.10 represent the changes in adolescent sexual behavior practices between 1991 and 1997. Specifically, Figure 6.9 represents the percentage of adolescents who had had four or more sexual partners during their lifetime. There are differences among the seven major metropolitan areas—students in some cities reported having, on average, more sexual partners than students in other cities. Using the confidence interval, you can see that there is also variability within each metropolitan area. Finally, you should see a general trend between 1991 and 1997, the percentage of adolescents reporting multiple sexual partners decreased. Furthermore, the greatest relative change appears to have occurred in Chicago and Dallas.

Figure 6.10 represents the percentage of adolescents who reported using condoms during their sexual encounters. These data represent a clear trend. With the exception of Boston, each metropolitan area showed a considerable increase in condom use. In some cases, the rate of reported condom use nearly doubled.

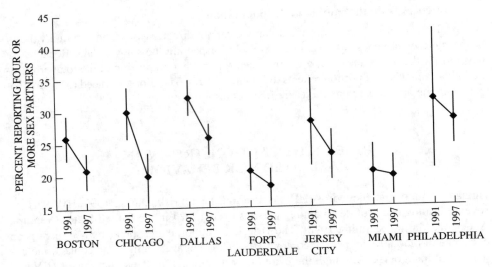

FIGURE 6.9
Percentage of adolescents living in seven metropolitan areas reporting having had four or more sex partners during their lifetime. The diamonds represent the average and the vertical lines represent the 95% confidence interval. Data based on report published by the Centers for Disease Control (1999).

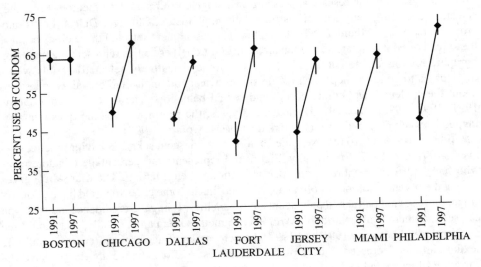

FIGURE 6.10
Percentage of adolescents living in seven metropolitan areas reporting that they used a condom during a sexual encounter. The diamonds represent the average and the vertical lines represent the 95% confidence interval. Data based on report published by the Centers for Disease Control (1999).

There are important components of this example. First, you can see that basic statistical principles and sampling methods allow researchers to address an important issue of great social importance. Second, the example offers a real-life example of the application of sampling techniques. Finally, the data allow us to show how the confidence interval helps us interpret the data. Without the confidence intervals, we would not be able to say whether the differences among the means were relatively trivial or represented a stunning change.

There are some things that the statistics can and cannot tell us. It does appear that students' reported sexual behaviors have changed, and that this change represents less risky sexual behavior. Can we conclude that educational programs and AIDS awareness campaigns helped reduce risky sexual behaviors? Have these programs been a success? Is there anything missing—should the researchers collect additional information? If you had the opportunity to repeat this research, what would you do differently?

Are these data representative of all adolescents? What would happen if we collected similar data for rural areas or smaller cities? Is it possible that students in urban areas receive greater exposure to AIDS awareness campaigns or are more likely to have a friend or family member contract HIV and develop AIDS?

Although there has been an increase in condom use, do we really want to say that the educational programs are a success? From one perspective, condom use among adolescents is much higher at the end of the decade rather than at the start. From another perspective, condom use among adolescents is still low. If 40% of the adolescents are still engaged in unprotected sexual intercourse, there is still an incredible health risk for those individuals. Adolescents who do not use condoms may well contract and spread HIV to others. From this perspective, the data are encouraging, but far from great. Recognize that the same results can afford different interpretations.

We might also question the validity of the data we collected. Were the students being honest when they completed the questionnaire? The truth is, people lie, especially about sex. Is it possible that these students say that they use condoms when they do not? Is it possible that the AIDS awareness program taught students what to say about condom use but had no effect on their behavior?

Finally, we can ask if we have taught adolescents the right thing. Many religious leaders and policymakers believe that adolescents should be encouraged to abstain from sexual intercourse until marriage. Some people may see the data as the results of a failed policy. Some may argue that the AIDS awareness programs continue to encourage immoral behaviors.

Some of the questions I raised are empirical. We can collect more information to understand changes in adolescents' sexual behavior. Researchers can conduct surveys in different parts of the country to determine if there are differences between urban and rural areas. Similarly, researchers can collect data concerning the rates of HIV among age groups. If the students are telling the truth about their sexual behavior, then there should be a decrease in the rate of HIV.

The other questions are equally important but require different intellectual tools. Is 60% condom use high or low? To answer this question, you need to examine your priorities. If you believe that the goal of AIDS awareness is to increase condom use, then 60% is far better than 40%. If you had hoped for perfect results, the 60% rate may be encouraging, but still disappointing.

ACHIEVEMENT CHECK

(11) What is the difference between a sampling distribution and the distribution of sample scores?

(12) Assume that you were to create sampling distributions by creating random samples. Describe the factors that will affect the shape of the distribution.

(13) What is the relation among M, μ, and μ_M?

(14) What is the relation among SD, σ, and σ_M?

(15) For an individual random sample:
   a. What accounts for $X - M$?
   b. What accounts for $M - \mu$?

(16) For the research described in the "Research in Action" section, describe the sampling techniques that the researchers may have used to collect the data.

(17) Some people are surprised to learn that some samples used to represent national trends consist of "only 500" participants. Based on what you know about sampling, why might a sample size of 500 be sufficient?

(18) A researcher wants to conduct a study of people who abuse crack cocaine. Why would probability sampling be difficult to use in this situation? How could the researcher use nonprobability techniques to create a sample of this population?

(19) The president of a prestigious private college reports that the average graduate of the college makes 2.5 times more money that the average graduate of other colleges. When asked about the source of the numbers, the president claims that the staff of the alumni office called a random number of the college's alumni and requested current information, including annual income. The president then says that the average income for other college graduates comes from the most recent census data that indicates the median income of college graduates. Do you accept the president's claim that graduates of the college are more affluent than the typical college graduate?

(20) A researcher believes that his or her sampling procedure may be biased. Will increasing the sample size help the researcher collect data to better represent the population?

CHAPTER SUMMARY

The primary focus of this chapter was how researchers use samples to make inferences about populations. Specifically, we examined the purpose of samples, how researchers construct useful samples, and ways to ensure that the sample represents the population.

Sampling is not a haphazard and casual method of collecting information. We examined how scientific evidence is different from personal experience and anecdotal evidence. When we depend on anecdotal evidence and personal experience, we are likely to come to the wrong conclusion. Bacon recognized this problem when he described the Idols of the Cave. Personal experience is not sufficient for understanding complex behavioral phenomenon. Rather, we need to depend upon objectively constructed samples to represent the population.

Probability sampling ensures that the sample will represent the population. According to the law of large numbers, if we randomly select members of the population, the sample will share the same features as the population. Random selection means that every element of the population has an equal and independent probability of being selected. Using probability sampling, we can predict the probability of selecting different samples from the population.

When we describe sampling procedures, we make distinctions between different types of populations. The target population represents the group that we hope to describe with our research. The sampling population is the group from which we create our sample. If the sampling population is representative of the target population then we can use the sample to make inferences about the target population. The sampling frame represents the list or resource that identifies the members of the sampling population. For all cases, the researcher creates operational definitions of the target and sampling populations.

There are several probability sampling techniques. For random sampling, each member of the population has an equal and independent probability of selection. Sequential sampling allows us to select each kth member from the sampling frame. Another sampling tactic is stratified sampling where we identify important subgroups in the population and then take random or sequential samples from each subgroup. Finally, in cluster sampling, we identify clusters of individuals and then randomly select several clusters for the research.

In some situations, nonprobability sampling procedures are the only ways of creating a sample. For convenience sampling, we allow the participants' behavior to determine whether they are included in the sample. Convenience sampling means that the participants are easy to locate. Another technique is snowball sampling where we ask the participants to help the researcher locate or recruit additional participants for the research.

The central limit theorem is a statement about the shape of a sampling distribution. The central limit theorem states that for any population, the sampling distribution of means will tend to be normally distributed, especially when the sample size is large; that the mean of the sampling distribution will equal the mean of the population; and that the standard deviation of the sampling distribution will equal the standard deviation of the population divided by the square root of the sample size. The central limit theorem, therefore, allows us to predict the probability of various samples.

Given the predictions of the central limit theorem, we examined how the researcher can change the standard error by increasing sample size or changing σ by redefining the population.

Creating a sample is not easy to do because there are several sources of bias and error. We examined how different factors, such as a poor quality sampling frame, can bias our results. Similarly, we distinguished among nonsampling bias, sampling bias, and sampling error. Nonsampling bias occurs when the sampling population differs from the target population. Sampling bias occurs when we use nonprobability sampling procedures. The standard error, by contrast, represents random differences among sample means.

We ended the chapter by reviewing a comprehensive and national research study of risky sexual behavior. The example illustrated the use of various sampling procedures and demonstrated how sample data allows us to make inferences about population parameters.

CHAPTER GLOSSARY FOR REVIEW

Anecdotal Evidence   A brief and typically personal account, which may not represent true events. Anecdotal evidence is often a biased and unrepresentative sample of a population.

Central Limit Theorem   A mathematical postulate that states that the sampling distribution of randomly generated sample means will: (1) tend to be normally distributed especially as sample size increases, (2) have a mean equal to the population mean, and (3) have a standard deviation equal to the standard deviation of the population divided by the square root of the sample size.

Convenience Sampling   Selecting members of the population who are easy to find and study.

Independence   A condition that exists when each event has no effect on subsequent events.

Interval Estimate   An estimate of the accuracy of the sample statistic as an estimate of the population parameter, specifically the potential range of sample statistics that would occur when creating additional samples.

Law of Large Numbers   Prediction that any large number of items chosen at random from the population will, on average, represent the population.

Nonprobability Sampling   Any method of sampling that does not use random events or probability methods to create the sample.

Nonsampling Bias   A nonrandom and systematic set of conditions that causes the mean of the sampling population to be different from the mean of the target population.

Point Estimate   Using a sample statistic to estimate the value of the corresponding population parameter.

Probability Sampling   A method of creating a representative sample that uses random and independent procedures for selecting individuals from the population.

Random   Each potential event has an equal probability of occurring, and the occurrence of one event has no influence on the probability of subsequent events.

Random Numbers   A sequence of numbers having no pattern or sequence because there is an equal probability of selecting each number, and the selection of one number has no effect on selecting another number.

Sampling Bias   A nonrandom and systematic set of conditions that causes the mean of the sampling distribution to be different from the mean of the sampling population.

Sampling Distribution   A theoretical probability distribution of the potential values of a sample statistic that would occur when drawing an infinite number of equal-sized random samples from the population.

Sampling Frame   A list or some other resource that identifies the members of the sampling population.

Sampling Interval   The number used in sequential sampling to select members of the population for the sample. Sampling Interval $= \dfrac{\text{Size of Population}}{\text{Desired Size of Sample}}$

Sampling Population   An accessible population that shares the same characteristics as the target population and from which the researcher draws the sample.

Sequential Sampling   A method of sampling where one selects every k^{th} member from a list.

Simple Random Sampling   A method of creating a representative sample of a population. Each member of the population has an equal probability of selection, and the selection of one member has no effect on the selection of other members of the population.

Snowball Sampling   Asking members of the sample to identify additional members of a population who could participate in the research.

Standard Error, ε   The random difference between a sample statistic and the corresponding population parameter.

Standard Error of the Mean (*SEM*, σ_M)   The standard deviation of the sampling distribution of means. $\sigma_M = \frac{\sigma}{\sqrt{n}}$.

Subject Pool   A group of individuals available and willing to participate in research projects.

Target Population or **Universe**   All members of a group who share one or more common characteristics defined by the researcher.

STATISTICS BEHIND THE RESEARCH: A SUPPLEMENT

I wish to God these calculations had been executed by steam.

—Charles Babbage

INTRODUCTION

I assume that you have already had a course in statistics and have learned the basics of descriptive and inferential statistics. I also assume that you, like many students, appreciate the opportunity to review several of the basic concepts related to statistical procedures. Therefore, this section will provide you with a brief review of commonly used statistics. If you believe that you understand concepts such as measures of central tendency, measures of dispersion, and z-scores then you may skip this section. If, however, you want a quick review of these concepts, this section provides an overview of the critical concepts you need to know.

The quotation at the start of this chapter reflects how many people feel about mathematics and statistics; like Babbage, they dislike doing long and tedious calculations. Fortunately, many computer programs will conduct statistical tests for you quickly and efficiently. Thus while you study statistics, your goal should be to understand why researchers use these statistical tools. I hope that reading this chapter will allow you to understand how to interpret and use basic statistics. This chapter should also help you prepare for the material presented in the subsequent chapters.

VARIABLES *X, Y, N, n*

For all equations in this book, the letters X, Y, N, and n have a consistent meaning. In all cases, X and Y represent the variables. More specifically, X and Y represent sets of data. In correlational research, for example, we might use X and Y to represent the two tests we administer to participants in the study. For example, we might collect data for 10 people using two measures. In this case, we use X to represent the data for the first variable and Y to represent the data for the second variable. Here are two sets of data:

$$X \quad \{18 \quad 10 \quad 11 \quad 13 \quad 8 \quad 11 \quad 6 \quad 10 \quad 3 \quad 10\}$$
$$Y \quad \{18 \quad 17 \quad 13 \quad 6 \quad 6 \quad 7 \quad 4 \quad 9 \quad 3 \quad 10\}$$

We use the letters N and n to indicate the number of observations we have for a study. The distinction between N and n is one of scope—N represents all the observations used in a study whereas n represents the number of observations in a set. For this example, we would write $N = 20$ to indicate that there are 20 individual data points. For each group there are 10 observations. Therefore, we would write $n_X = 10$ and $n_Y = 10$.

SUBSCRIPTS (X_1) AND SUPERSCRIPTS (X^2)

Mathematicians use subscripts and superscripts to indicate types of information and indicate specific mathematical operations, respectively. Whenever you see a subscript, such as X_1 or Y_1, the subscript represents the individual score within a specific group. Using the two data sets we have, we can identify the individual scores as:

$X_1 = 18$	$X_6 = 11$	$Y_1 = 18$	$Y_6 = 7$
$X_2 = 10$	$X_7 = 6$	$Y_2 = 17$	$Y_7 = 4$
$X_3 = 11$	$X_8 = 10$	$Y_3 = 13$	$Y_8 = 9$
$X_4 = 13$	$X_9 = 3$	$Y_4 = 6$	$Y_9 = 3$
$X_5 = 8$	$X_{10} = 10$	$Y_5 = 6$	$Y_{10} = 10$

We can also use letters in the subscripts to help identify the groups. For example, n_X and n_Y represent the samples sizes for the groups X and Y. In a true experiment, we might use X_{a1} and X_{a2} to represent two groups of participants. The symbol X_{a1} represents the first group whereas X_{a2} represents the second group. In several of the later chapters, I will introduce you to subscripts that are more complex. For now, remember that we use subscripts to identify different variables and observations within sets of data.

A superscript, such as X^2 or Y^2, represents a mathematical operation. The most commonly used superscript in statistics is squaring or X^2. Thus if $X_2 = 10$, then $X_2^2 = 100$.

Population Parameters

In statistics, Greek letters (μ, σ, ρ) represent population parameters. A parameter is a statistic that describes a characteristic of a population. We use Roman letters (e.g., M, SD, and r) to represent sample statistics. The more commonly measured population parameters and the equivalent sample statistics are:

Measure	Population parameter	Sample statistic
Mean	μ	M
Variance	σ^2	VAR
Standard deviation	σ	SD
Correlation	ρ	r

Summation $\sum$

Sum of scores $\sum X$

The Greek letter Σ (sigma) is a mathematical symbol that tells us to find the sum of a group of numbers. Specifically, it indicates the sum of all values in a set. For example, $\sum X$

represents the sum of all scores in the set, X; $\sum Y$ represents the sum of all scores in the set, Y. For example, if

$$X \quad \{18 \quad 10 \quad 11 \quad 13 \quad 8 \quad 11 \quad 6 \quad 10 \quad 3 \quad 10\}$$
$$Y \quad \{18 \quad 17 \quad 13 \quad 6 \quad 6 \quad 7 \quad 4 \quad 9 \quad 3 \quad 10\}$$

Then,

$$\sum X$$
$$\sum X = 18 + 10 + 11 + 13 + 8 + 11 + 6 + 10 + 3 + 10 \qquad \sum X = 100$$

$$\sum Y$$
$$\sum Y = 18 + 17 + 13 + 6 + 6 + 7 + 4 + 9 + 3 + 10 \qquad \sum Y = 93$$

Sum of squared scores $\sum X^2$

In many cases you will see a summation sign that looks like $\sum X^2$ or $\sum Y^2$. This symbol means that you first square each score in the set and then add all the squared scores. For example,

$$\sum X^2 = 18^2 + 10^2 + 11^2 + 13^2 + 8^2 + 11^2 + 6^2 + 10^2 + 3^2 + 10^2$$
$$\sum X^2 = 324 + 100 + 121 + 169 + 64 + 121 + 36 + 100 + 9 + 100$$
$$\sum X^2 = 1144$$

$$\sum Y^2 = 18^2 + 17^2 + 13^2 + 6^2 + 6^2 + 7^2 + 4^2 + 9^2 + 3^2 + 10^2$$
$$\sum Y^2 = 324 + 289 + 169 + 36 + 36 + 49 + 16 + 81 + 9 + 100$$
$$\sum Y^2 = 1109$$

Sum of scores squared $\left(\sum X\right)^2$

You will also see a summation sign that looks like $\left(\sum X\right)^2$ or $\left(\sum Y\right)^2$. These symbols call for a different set of steps than $\sum X^2$ and $\sum Y^2$. The expression $\sum X^2$ means that you first square each score in the set and then add all the squared scores. By contrast, the expression $\left(\sum X\right)^2$ means that we first add all the scores in the set and then square the total. For example,

$$\sum X = 100 \qquad\qquad \sum Y = 93$$
$$\left(\sum X\right)^2 = 100^2 \qquad\qquad \left(\sum Y\right)^2 = 93^2$$
$$\left(\sum X\right)^2 = 10,000 \qquad\qquad \left(\sum Y\right)^2 = 8,649$$

Sum of cross products $\sum XY$

Another common summation operation is $\sum XY$, which we call the sum of cross products. $\sum XY$ is not the same thing as $\left(\sum X\right)\left(\sum Y\right)$. To calculate the cross products, we first multiply each number by its pair and then add the individual cross products. For example,

	X		Y		Cross products XY
	18	×	18	=	324
	10	×	17	=	170
	11	×	13	=	143
	13	×	6	=	78
	8	×	6	=	48
	11	×	7	=	77
	6	×	4	=	24
	10	×	9	=	90
	3	×	3	=	9
	10	×	10	=	100
$\sum X = 100$		$\sum Y = 93$		$\sum XY = 9330$	

For these data $(\sum X)(\sum Y) = 100 \times 93 = 9300$ whereas $\sum XY = 9330$. This important difference cannot be overlooked.

MEASURES OF CENTRAL TENDENCY

The measures of central tendency are descriptive statistics that summarize the data with a single number that represents the typical score. We use measures of central tendency because we believe that most scores cluster around the typical or most common score in the data. Consequently, the measure of central tendency is a convenient way to indicate the most typical score in a set of data.

Selecting an appropriate measure of central tendency depends upon the measurement scale used to represent the variable, the symmetry of the data, and the inferences to be made from the measure of central tendency. In the following sections we will review the mode, median, and arithmetic mean.

MODE M_O

Of the many measures of central tendency, the mode is the easiest to calculate. The definition of the mode is:

$$M_O = \text{Most frequently occurring score or scores in the data} \qquad (6.6)$$

Here is an example of how to calculate the mode using the data set X.

$$X \quad \{18 \quad 10 \quad 11 \quad 13 \quad 8 \quad 11 \quad 6 \quad 10 \quad 3 \quad 10\}$$

Step 1: Rank the numbers from lowest to highest.

$$X \quad \{3 \quad 6 \quad 8 \quad 10 \quad 10 \quad 10 \quad 11 \quad 11 \quad 13 \quad 18\}$$

Step 2: Find the most frequently occurring score.

$$M_O = 10$$

The mode is easy to determine and a useful tool to indicate the location of a cluster of high frequency scores. The statistic is also useful when there are several "peaks" in the data. In such cases, we describe the data as bimodal (two modes) or multimodal. The mode is most often used to report data represented by a nominal scale. In addition, the mode can be useful when the data are discrete values that have no intermediate values, such as the number of children in a family.

MEDIAN *Mdn* OR Q_2

The median is another popular measure of central tendency. The definition of the median is:

$$Mdn \text{ or } Q_2 = \text{Score that divides the ranked data in half} \qquad (6.7)$$

Here is an example of how to calculate the median using two data sets X and Y. For this example, $n_X = 10$ and $n_Y = 9$.

$$X \quad \{18 \quad 10 \quad 11 \quad 13 \quad 8 \quad 11 \quad 6 \quad 10 \quad 3 \quad 10\}$$
$$Y \quad \{18 \quad 17 \quad 4 \quad 6 \quad 6 \quad 13 \quad 7 \quad 9 \quad 10\}$$

Step 1: Rank the numbers from lowest to highest.

$$X \quad \{3 \quad 6 \quad 8 \quad 10 \quad 10 \quad 10 \quad 11 \quad 11 \quad 13 \quad 18\}$$
$$Y \quad \{4 \quad 6 \quad 6 \quad 7 \quad 9 \quad 10 \quad 13 \quad 17 \quad 18\}$$

Step 2: Add 1 to n and then divide by 2.

$$X: \quad 5.5 = (10 + 1)/2$$
$$Y: \quad 5.0 = (9 + 1)/2$$

Step 3: Starting with the lowest score, count up to the value from Step 2.

$$X \quad \{3 \quad 6 \quad 8 \quad 10 \quad 10 \quad 10 \quad 11 \quad 11 \quad 13 \quad 18\}$$
$$\uparrow$$

$$Y \quad \{4 \quad 6 \quad 6 \quad 7 \quad 9 \quad 10 \quad 13 \quad 17 \quad 18\}$$
$$\uparrow$$

Step 4: If the midpoint falls between the two numbers, add them and divide by 2.

$$X \quad Mdn = 10.0 = (10 + 10)/2$$
$$Y \quad Mdn = 9.0$$

The median is a useful descriptive statistic especially for skewed (nonsymmetrical) distributions of data. The median, unlike the arithmetic mean, is not affected by the presence of outliers (one or two extremely high or low scores).

ARITHMETIC MEAN M

One of the most common measures of central tendency in the behavioral sciences is the arithmetic mean, M. The mean is the sum of all observed scores divided by the number of observations in the data set. We define the arithmetic mean as:

$$M = \frac{\sum X}{n} \tag{6.8}$$

Here is an example of how to calculate the arithmetic mean using two data sets X and Y.

$$X \quad \{18 \quad 10 \quad 11 \quad 13 \quad 8 \quad 11 \quad 6 \quad 10 \quad 3 \quad 10\}$$
$$Y \quad \{18 \quad 17 \quad 4 \quad 6 \quad 6 \quad 13 \quad 7 \quad 9 \quad 10\}$$

Step 1: Calculate the sum of scores for each set.

$$\sum X = 18 + 10 + 11 + 13 + 8 + 11 + 6 + 10 + 3 + 10 = 100.0$$
$$n_X = 10$$
$$\sum Y = 18 + 17 + 4 + 6 + 6 + 13 + 7 + 9 + 10 = 90.0$$
$$n_Y = 9$$

Step 2: Divide the sum of scores $\left(\sum X\right)$ by the sample size, n_x.

$$M_X = \frac{100.0}{10} = 10.0 \qquad M_Y = \frac{90.0}{9} = 10.0$$

The mean has a number of unique features. By definition, the mean is the point in the distribution that is the smallest total difference between itself and each observation. Therefore, $\sum(X - M) = 0$ and $\sum(X - M)^2 = $ minimal value (the second relation is the least squares criterion). In addition, the arithmetic mean is an unbiased estimate of the population mean, μ. The statistic is, however, sensitive to outliers and to skewed distributions. When the data are positively skewed, the mean will be greater than the median (e.g., $M > Mdn$). When the data are negatively skewed, the mean will be less than the median (e.g., $M < Mdn$). Table 6.5 provides a summary of the main measures of central tendency.

TABLE 6.5
Summary of frequently used measures of central tendency

Statistic	Definition	Scale of measurement	Features/properties
Mode Mo	Most frequent score or scores in sample	Nominal or higher scales	Imprecise and potentially misleading for ordinal or higher scales
Median Mdn	Midpoint of the distribution of ranked scores	Ordinal or higher scales	Good to use when extreme scores skew data
Arithmetic mean M	$M = \frac{\sum X}{n}$	Interval or ratio scales	Commonly used measure of central tendency, $\sum(X - M) = 0$, $\sum(X - M)^2 = $ minimal value, and M is an unbiased estimate of μ

MEASURES OF VARIABILITY

The measure of central tendency indicates only one characteristic of the data, the typical score. Although this is a useful bit of information, we need additional information to describe the data. One of the more important characteristics of the data is the amount of variability. Variability indicates the extent to which the data differ from the measure of central tendency. It is important to know whether the data are clustered close to the measure of central tendency or if the data are spread across a broad range of scores. Much like the measures of central tendency, selecting an appropriate measure of variability depends upon the measurement scale used to represent the variable, the symmetry of the data, and the inferences to be made from the measure of variability.

Simple Range

The range is the easiest measure of dispersion to calculate. The definition of the range is:

$$Range = X_{highest} - X_{lowest} \tag{6.9}$$

Like the mode, the range is easy to calculate, however, it is greatly affected by outliers. Therefore, most researchers use it only as a general descriptive tool. Here is an example of how to calculate the range.

$$X \quad \{18 \quad 10 \quad 11 \quad 13 \quad 8 \quad 11 \quad 6 \quad 10 \quad 3 \quad 10\}$$
$$Y \quad \{18 \quad 17 \quad 4 \quad 6 \quad 6 \quad 13 \quad 7 \quad 9 \quad 10\}$$

Step 1: Rank the scores from lowest to highest.

$$X \quad \{3 \quad 6 \quad 8 \quad 10 \quad 10 \quad 10 \quad 11 \quad 11 \quad 13 \quad 18\}$$
$$Y \quad \{4 \quad 6 \quad 6 \quad 7 \quad 9 \quad 10 \quad 13 \quad 17 \quad 18\}$$

Step 2: Determine the difference between the highest and lowest scores.

$$Range_X = 15.0 = 18 - 3$$
$$Range_Y = 14.0 = 18 - 4$$

Semi-Interquartile Range

Another measure of dispersion is the semi-interquartile range (*SIR*). The semi-interquartile range is the difference between the 75th percentile and the 25th percentile divided by 2. The mathematical definition of the semi-interquartile range is:

$$SIR = \frac{Q_3 - Q_1}{2} \tag{6.10}$$

In this equation, Q_3 represents the 75th percentile and Q_1 represents the 25th percentile. The 75th percentile indicates that 75% of the scores are at or below Q_3—for the 25th percentile, 25% of the scores are at or below Q_1. The following example illustrates how to calculate the *SIR*.

$$X \quad \{18 \quad 10 \quad 11 \quad 13 \quad 8 \quad 11 \quad 6 \quad 10 \quad 3 \quad 10\}$$
$$Y \quad \{18 \quad 17 \quad 4 \quad 6 \quad 6 \quad 13 \quad 7 \quad 9 \quad 10\}$$

Step 1: Rank the scores from lowest to highest.

$$X \quad \{3 \quad 6 \quad 8 \quad 10 \quad 10 \quad 10 \quad 11 \quad 11 \quad 13 \quad 18\}$$
$$Y \quad \{4 \quad 6 \quad 6 \quad 7 \quad 9 \quad 10 \quad 13 \quad 17 \quad 18\}$$

Step 2: Add 1 to the sample size and divide by 2.

$$X \quad 5.5 = (10 + 1)/2$$
$$Y \quad 5.0 = (9 + 1)/2$$

Step 3: Starting with the lowest score, count up to the value from Step 2.

$$X \quad \{3 \quad 6 \quad 8 \quad 10 \quad \underset{\uparrow}{10} \quad 10 \quad 11 \quad 11 \quad 13 \quad 18\}$$

$$Y \quad \{4 \quad 6 \quad 6 \quad 7 \quad \underset{\uparrow}{9} \quad 10 \quad 13 \quad 17 \quad 18\}$$

Step 4: Determine the midpoint of the upper and lower halves using the same procedure described in Step 2. Specifically, add 1 to the number of scores in each half and divide by 2.

$$X \quad 3.0 = (5 + 1)/2$$
$$Y \quad 2.5 = (4 + 1)/2$$

Step 5: Using numbers from the previous step, determine Q_1 and Q_3.
If the location of Q_1 or Q_3 falls between two numbers, take the average of the two.

$$X \quad \{3 \quad 6 \quad \underset{\underset{Q_1}{\uparrow}}{8} \quad 10 \quad \underset{\underset{Q_2}{\uparrow}}{10} \quad 10 \quad \underset{\underset{Q_3}{\uparrow}}{11} \quad 11 \quad 13 \quad 18\}$$

$$X \quad Q_1 = 8.0 \qquad Q_3 = 11.0$$

$$Y \quad \{4 \quad \underset{\underset{Q_1}{\uparrow}}{6} \quad 6 \quad \underset{\underset{Q_2}{\uparrow}}{7} \quad 9 \quad 10 \quad \underset{\underset{Q_3}{\uparrow}}{13} \quad 17 \quad 18\}$$

$$Y \quad Q_1 = 6.0 = (6 + 6)/2 \qquad Q_3 = 15.0 = (13 + 17)/2$$

Step 6: Calculate *SIR*.

$$SIR_X = 1.5 = (11 - 8)/2$$
$$SIR_Y = 4.5 = (15 - 6)/2$$

Like the median, extreme scores do not affect the semi-interquartile range. Therefore, researchers often use the statistic to describe skewed data.

Variance and Standard Deviation

The variance and standard deviation are two of the most commonly used measures of dispersion. In the following table you will see that there are several ways to write the equations for these statistics. There are the definitional and computational equations. Statisticians use the definitional equation to help describe and explain the purpose of the variance and standard deviation. The computational equations, as the name implies, are equations people use when they have to calculate these statistics by hand.

There are two forms of the variance and standard deviation equations. The first form, the sample statistic, determines the variance and standard deviation when the data are the population. The second form, the unbiased estimate of the population, allows us to estimate the population parameter using sample data. In most cases, you will use the unbiased estimate of the population form of the equations.

We can examine the definitional equations for the variance and standard deviations to help understand what these statistics mean. If you look at the numerator of the equations, you will see the expression $\sum(X - M)^2$. The name of this equation is the sum of squares. More specifically, the sum of squares is the sum of the squared deviation scores—the deviation score is $(X - M)$, which indicates the difference between the mean and an observed score. As you can see, the larger the difference between the mean and the observed score, the greater the deviation score. Because $\sum(X - M) = 0$, we square each deviation score. Squaring the deviation scores ensures that there are no negative deviation scores. Therefore, $\sum(X - M)^2$ will always be greater than 0 unless all the scores in the data are the same number.

Once we determine the sum of squares, we divide by the denominator. For the unbiased estimate of the population equation, the denominator is $n - 1$. We call the denominator the degrees of freedom. Thus the variance is an estimate of the typical squared deviation between the scores and the mean. The final step is to calculate the square root of the variance. This step returns the value of the variance to the scale used to measure X. This means that the standard deviation is an index of the typical deviation of scores in the sample.

Sample statistic	Unbiased estimate of population
Variance	
Definitional equations	
$s^2 = \dfrac{\sum(X - M)^2}{N}$	$VAR = \dfrac{\sum(X - M)^2}{n - 1}$ (6.11)
Computational equations	
$s^2 = \dfrac{\sum X^2 - \dfrac{(\sum X)^2}{N}}{N}$	$VAR = \dfrac{\sum X^2 - \dfrac{(\sum X)^2}{n}}{n - 1}$ (6.12)
Standard deviation	
Definitional equations	
$s = \sqrt{\dfrac{\sum(X - M)^2}{N}}$	$SD = \sqrt{\dfrac{\sum(X - M)^2}{n - 1}}$ (6.13)
Computational equations	
$s = \sqrt{\dfrac{\sum X^2 - \dfrac{(\sum X)^2}{N}}{N}}$	$SD = \sqrt{\dfrac{\sum X^2 - \dfrac{(\sum X)^2}{n}}{n - 1}}$ (6.14)

The following is a step-by-step example of how to determine the variance and standard deviation of a set of data. We can begin by using a sample of data.

$$X \quad \{18 \quad 10 \quad 11 \quad 13 \quad 8 \quad 11 \quad 6 \quad 10 \quad 3 \quad 10\}$$

Step 1: Calculate the sum of scores.

$$\sum X = 18 + 10 + 11 + 13 + 8 + 11 + 6 + 10 + 3 + 10$$

$$\sum X = 100$$

Step 2: Calculate the sum of squared scores.

$$\sum X^2 = 18^2 + 10^2 + 11^2 + 13^2 + 8^2 + 11^2 + 6^2 + 10^2 + 3^2 + 10^2$$

$$\sum X^2 = 324 + 1100 + 121 + 169 + 64 + 121 + 36 + 100 + 9 + 100$$

$$\sum X^2 = 1144$$

Step 3: Complete the equations.

	Sample statistic	Unbiased estimate of population
Variance		
	$s^2 = \dfrac{\sum X^2 - \dfrac{(\sum X)^2}{N}}{N}$	$VAR = \dfrac{\sum X^2 - \dfrac{(\sum X)^2}{n}}{n-1}$
	$s^2 = \dfrac{1144 - \dfrac{(100)^2}{10}}{10}$	$VAR = \dfrac{1144 - \dfrac{(100)^2}{10}}{10-1}$
	$s^2 = \dfrac{144}{12}$	$VAR = \dfrac{144}{9}$
	$s^2 = 14.4$	$VAR = 16.0$
Standard deviation		
	$s = \sqrt{14.4}$	$SD = \sqrt{16.0}$
	$s = 3.7947$	$SD = 4.00$

Figure 6.11 presents four distributions with means of 50 and standard deviations of 5, 10, 15, and 20. As the standard deviation increases, the spread of data becomes much wider. For the distribution with a standard deviation of 5, the majority of the scores are close to the mean of 50. Also, the majority of the scores, about 95%, fall between 40 and 60. By contrast, the distribution with the standard deviation of 20 has scores running across the entire scale. For that distribution, the majority of scores fall between 10 and 90.

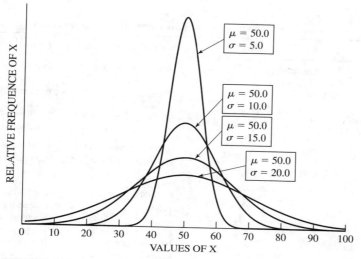

FIGURE 6.11

Four distributions of data, each with a mean of 50 and standard deviations of 5, 10, 15, and 20. As the standard deviation increases, the spread of the scores becomes much wider.

THE STANDARDIZED OR z-SCORE

The z-score allows us to convert observed scores to standardized scores. There are advantages to using the z-score. First, it allows us to convert the data from different groups to a common scale. This transformation is important when the groups have different means and standard deviations as z-score allows us to compare scores from different groups. Later in the book you will see that we use the z-score transformation to calculate the correlation coefficient between two variables. Another advantage of the z-score is that it can help us interpret or make inferences about specific observations. If we assume that the normal distribution represents the data, we can also use the z-score to convert observed scores to percentiles.

There are two ways to calculate the z-score. The first method assumes that the data represent an intact group. Therefore we use s to calculate the standard deviation of the data. The equation for this version of the z-score is:

$$z = \frac{(X - M)}{s} \tag{6.15}$$

In the second method, if the data are a sample that we use to estimate the population parameters, we may use SD to estimate the standard deviation. In this case, we use the following equation to calculate the z-score.

$$z = \frac{(X - M)}{SD} \tag{6.16}$$

Consider the following example. Imagine that you give 10 people two tests, Test A and Test B. We will assume that these data represent an intact group. Therefore we will

TABLE 6.6
Summary of frequently used measures of central tendency

Statistic	Definition	Scale of measurement	Features/properties
Range	$Range = X_{highest} - X_{lowest}$	Ordinal or higher scales	Imprecise and potentially misleading when the data contain outliers
Semi-interquartile range, SIR	$SIR = \dfrac{Q_3 - Q_1}{2}$	Ordinal or higher scales	Good to use when extreme scores skew data
Variance of sample, s^2	$s^2 = \dfrac{\sum X^2 - \dfrac{(\sum X)^2}{N}}{N}$	Interval or ratio scales	Used when the data represent the population of scores
Standard deviation of sample, S	$s = \sqrt{\dfrac{\sum X^2 - \dfrac{(\sum X)^2}{N}}{N}}$	Interval or ratio scales	Used when the data represent the population of scores
Unbiased estimate of standard variance, VAR	$VAR = \dfrac{\sum X^2 - \dfrac{(\sum X)^2}{n}}{n-1}$	Interval or ratio scales	Used when the data represent a sample. This is the more commonly used statistic in behavioral research
Unbiased estimate of standard deviation, SD	$SD = \sqrt{\dfrac{\sum X^2 - \dfrac{(\sum X)^2}{n}}{n-1}}$	Interval or ratio scales	Used when the data represent a sample. This is the more commonly used statistic in behavioral research

calculate s to determine the standard deviation. Looking at Table 6.6 you can see the tests have different means and standard deviations. For Test A, $M_A = 100$ and $s_A = 75$. For Test B, $M_B = 3.0$ and $s_B = 1.0$.

Table 6.7 also presents the z-scores for the tests. The means and standard deviations of the z-scores for Test A and Test B are $M = 0.0$ and $s = 1.0$. This occurs because the z-score always standardizes the scores to a scale whose mean is 0.0 and whose standard deviation is 1.0. This fact is true for both forms of the z-scores. When you calculate z-scores using s for the standard deviation, then

$$\sum z = 0.0 \qquad \sum z^2 = n \qquad M_z = 0.0 \qquad s_z = 1.0$$

When you use SD to calculate z-scores, then

$$\sum z = 0.0 \qquad \sum z^2 = n - 1 \qquad M_z = 0.0 \qquad s_z = 1.0$$

Once we convert the observed scores to z-scores, we can directly compare pairs from different groups. As an example, consider person B's scores on the two tests. Person B earned a score of 560 on the first test and a score of 2.4 on the second test. We can say that B scored better than average on Test A because the z-score is $z = 0.80$. The score is 0.8 standard deviations greater than the mean. However, B did below average on Test B because the z-score is $z = -0.6$. Specifically, B's test score is -0.6 standard deviations below the mean.

TABLE 6.7

Example of z-scores. Each person completed two tests. Next to each test score is the corresponding z-score. The z-score represents the relative difference between the observed score and the group mean.

Person	Test A	Test A z-scores	Test B	Test B z-scores
A	440	$(440 - 500)/75 = -0.8$	3.4	$(3.4 - 3.0)/1.0 = 0.4$
B	560	$(560 - 500)/75 = 0.8$	2.4	$(2.4 - 3.0)/1.0 = -0.6$
C	515	$(515 - 500)/75 = 0.2$	2.8	$(2.8 - 3.0)/1.0 = -0.2$
D	395	$(395 - 500)/75 = -1.4$	4.2	$(4.2 - 3.0)/1.0 = 1.2$
E	500	$(500 - 500)/75 = 0.0$	3.0	$(3.0 - 3.0)/1.0 = 0.0$
F	545	$(545 - 500)/75 = 0.6$	2.6	$(2.6 - 3.0)/1.0 = -0.4$
G	605	$(605 - 500)/75 = 1.4$	1.2	$(1.2 - 3.0)/1.0 = -1.8$
H	425	$(425 - 500)/75 = -1.0$	3.6	$(3.6 - 3.0)/1.0 = 0.6$
I	605	$(605 - 500)/75 = 1.4$	4.8	$(4.8 - 3.0)/1.0 = 1.8$
J	410	$(410 - 500)/75 = -1.2$	2.0	$(2.0 - 3.0)/1.0 = -1.0$

$\sum X_A = 5000$		$\sum Z_A = 0.0$	$\sum X_B = 30.0$	$\sum Z_B = 0.0$
$\sum X_A^2 = 2556250$		$\sum Z_A^2 = 10.0$	$\sum X_B^2 = 100.0$	$\sum Z_B^2 = 10.0$
$M_A = 500$		$M_{Az} = 0.0$	$M_B = 3.0$	$M_{Bz} = 0.0$
$s_A = 75$		$s_{Az} = 1.0$	$s_B = 1.0$	$s_{Bz} = 1.0$

Thus, using the z-score, we can quickly determine whether a person's score is above or below the mean and the relative magnitude of the difference. For example, z-scores of -0.2 and 0.1 indicate that the scores are not too far below or above the mean. By contrast, z-scores of -1.95 or 1.64 indicate scores far below and far above the mean.

Determining the Percentile Using the z-Score

Once we have converted the observed score to a z-score we can then convert the z-score to a percentile. A percentile is a number that represents the percentage of individuals that received the same or a lesser score. For example, if you took a test and learned that you scored at the 90th percentile, then you can conclude that you did as well as or better than 90% of the people who took the test. If, however, your test score was at the 45th percentile, you should conclude that your score was less than average. A score at the 45th percentile means that you did as well as or better than 45% of the people who took the test.

Converting z-scores to percentiles is rather easy especially if we use Table A.1 of Appendix A. If you look at that table, you will see that there are three columns. Column A represents the z-scores. Because the normal distribution is symmetrical, we can use this column to examine positive as well as negative z-scores. Column B of the table represents the area of the normal distribution that exists between the mean and the z-score. Column C represents the area of the curve beyond the z-score. Using this table, we can convert the z-score to a percentile. The following instructions show you how to convert negative and positive z-scores to percentiles.

Negative z-scores

If the z-score is negative or equal to 0 ($z \leq 0$) then use the following procedure.

Step 1: Convert the observed score to a z-score.

$$X = 440 \qquad M = 500 \qquad s = 75$$
$$z = (440 - 500)/75 = -0.8$$

Step 2: Locate the value of the z-score, ignoring the sign, using Column A from Table A.1 of Appendix A, and then note the value listed in Column C. This value represents the proportion of the distribution beyond the z-score.

$$z = 0.80 \qquad \text{Proportion beyond } z\text{-score} = .2119$$

Step 3: Multiply the proportion beyond z-score by 100 and round to the nearest whole number, the product is the percentile.

$$21.19 = .2119 \times 100 \qquad \text{Percentile} = 21$$

In this example, we can conclude that only 21% of people taking the test will earn a score of 440 or less. In other words, if you gave this test to 100 people, you would expect that only 21 of them would have a score of 440 or lower. You could also conclude that 79% (100% − 21%) of the people taking the test would have a score greater than 440.

Positive z-scores

If the z-score is positive ($z > 0$) then use the following procedure.

Step 1: Convert the observed score to a z-score.

$$X = 515 \qquad M = 500 \qquad s = 75$$
$$z = (515 - 500)/75 = .20$$

Step 2: Locate the value of the z-score using Column A from Table A.1 of Appendix A, and then note the value listed in Column B. This value represents the proportion of the distribution between the mean and the z-score.

$$z = 0.20 \qquad \text{Proportion between mean and } z\text{-score} = .0793$$

Step 3: Add the value found in Step 2 and .5000. This step accounts for the half of the normal curve that falls below the mean.

$$.5793 = .5000 + .0793$$

Step 4: Multiply the result of Step 3 by 100 and round to the nearest whole number. The product is the percentile.

$$57.93 = .5793 \times 100 \qquad \text{Percentile} = 58$$

Therefore, a score of 515 represents the 58th percentile, indicating that 58% of the people taking this test would be expected to score at or below 515. What percentage of people taking the test will score greater than 515? Given the mean and standard deviation of the test, we would expect that 42% (100% − 58%) will receive a score of 515 or greater.

Figure 6.12 and Table 6.8 illustrate how to determine the percentile score for each of the 10 scores recorded for Test A. When you convert z-scores to percentiles, it is a good idea to draw a sketch of the normal distribution and label the mean and relative location of the z-score.

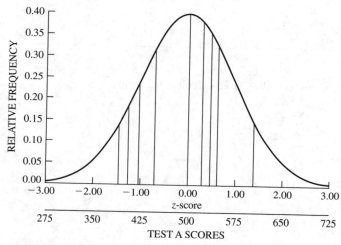

FIGURE 6.12
The normal curve. The vertical lines represent the location of values of X presented in Table 6.8.

TABLE 6.8
A complete illustration of converting observed scores to percentiles

X	z	Area below* z-score	Percentile
395	$-1.40 = (395 - 500)/75$	.0808	$8 = .0808 \times 100$
410	$-1.20 = (410 - 500)/75$	.1151	$12 = .1151 \times 100$
425	$-1.00 = (425 - 500)/75$	.1587	$16 = .1586 \times 100$
440	$-0.80 = (440 - 500)/75$	.2119	$21 = .2119 \times 100$
500	$0.00 = (500 - 500)/75$	.5000	$50 = .5000 \times 100$
515	$0.20 = (515 - 500)/75$	$.5793 = .5000 + .0793$	$58 = .5793 \times 100$
545	$0.60 = (545 - 500)/75$	$.7257 = .5000 + .2257$	$73 = .7257 \times 100$
560	$0.80 = (560 - 500)/75$	$.7881 = .5000 + .2881$	$79 = .7881 \times 100$
605	$1.40 = (605 - 500)/75$	$.9192 = .5000 + .4192$	$92 = .9192 \times 100$
605	$1.40 = (605 - 500)/75$	$.9192 = .5000 + .4192$	$92 = .9192 \times 100$

*From Table A.1 of Appendix A.

ACHIEVEMENT CHECK

Use the data in the following table to complete the questions.

X_{a1}	z_{a1}	Percentile	X_{a2}	z_{b1}	Percentile
26	1.2000	88	11	−1.2000	12
23			29		
17			17		
29			41		
22			27		
19			25		
11			5		
20			23		
18			19		
15			33		

Using the data in the preceding table calculate the following:

(a) $\sum X_{a1}$ $\sum X_{a2}$

(b) $\sum X_{a1}^2$ $\sum X_{a2}^2$

(c) $\left(\sum X_{a1}\right)^2$ $\left(\sum X_{a2}\right)^2$

(d) Mdn_{a1} Mdn_{a2}

(e) M_{a1} M_{a2}

(f) s_{a1}^2 s_{a2}^2

(g) s_{a1} s_{a2}

(h) VAR_{a1} VAR_{a2}

(i) SD_{a1} SD_{a2}

(j) Using the data, and M and s for each group, convert each score to a z-score.

(k) Using the z-scores you just calculated, determine the percentile for each score.

(l) Calculate the standard error of the mean for each sample using a 90% confidence interval.

(m) Calculate the standard error of the mean for each sample using a 95% confidence interval.

7 CREATING AND USING TESTS, SURVEYS, AND OBJECTIVE MEASURES

CHAPTER OUTLINE

- ✦ Introduction
- ✦ Purpose of Measurement
- ✦ Caveat Tester
- ✦ Creating a Measurement Scale
- ✦ Constructing Interviews, Questionnaires, and Attitude Surveys
- ✦ Preparing the Questions
- ✦ Writing Good Questionnaire and Survey Items
- ✦ Naturalistic Observation

Psychology cannot attain the certainties and exactness of the physical sciences, unless it rests upon a foundation of experiment and measurement.

—James McKeen Cattell

INTRODUCTION

Measurement is at the heart of all the empirical sciences. Without objective measurement, there can be no science. This fact did not escape Cattell's (1890) attention or that of the generations of psychologists who followed him. Therefore, the task of this chapter is clear; it will show you how researchers create questionnaires and surveys.

PURPOSE OF MEASUREMENT

There are two goals of measurement. The first goal is to replace the ambiguity of words with operationally defined constructs. In our day-to-day language we say that someone has an "extraverted personality," is a "senior citizen," or is "adept at mathematics." We may also want to know if reinforcement will "reduce a child's intrinsic motivation." Although these phrases share much information, there is ambiguity. What, for example, is a senior citizen, someone over 65, 75, or 85? Picking an age clarifies our meaning of senior by offering an operational definition. As Wilkinson (1999) noted, the value of an operational definition is that it provides a specific method for converting observations to a specified range of potential values. Using operational definitions helps researchers achieve the goal of public verification of observation because other researchers can use and, if necessary, critique and revise the operational definition.

The second goal of measurement is standardization or consistency in measurement. Consistency of measurement allows us to compare people using a common set of procedures and scales. Standardization also implies that the numbers have a constant meaning. For example, a score of 110 on a standardized test, such as intelligence, has a meaning that does not change over time, across situations, or across people.

CAVEAT TESTER

There are two common misperceptions of psychological tests and measurements. It is interesting that these misperceptions oppose each other. The first is too great a mistrust in measurement, and the second is too great a trust in measurement.

How many times have you heard something such as, "There are some things that you cannot measure" or "Some human behaviors are too complex to measure objectively"? This is a common complaint that often arises when people want to discredit a research finding or to argue that psychology cannot be a science. The problem with this belief is that it is inconsistent to say that you cannot objectively measure a construct described by words. That we use words to describe some human characteristic means that we must have the ability to recognize those characteristics. If we can recognize those characteristics using words, then the steps to objective measurement are not far away.

The other error associated with any measurement is the uncritical trust in the numbers. Kaplan (1964) called this problem the **mystique of quantity,** which he defined as "an exaggerated regard for the significance of measurement, just because it is quantitative, without regard to what has been measured . . . [the] number is treated as having intrinsic scientific value" (p. 172).

One consequence of the mystique of quantity is what philosophers of science call **reification.** Reification means that one treats a measurement as if it represents a real thing. As Dewdney (1997) noted, because we have a word for something does not mean that the thing exists independent of the word. The reification problem is an example of Bacon's Idol of the Market-place we reviewed in chapter 1. As you may recall, we examined how psychologists' use of phrases such as "maternal absence" influenced how they conducted and interpreted the results of their research on the effects of child care.

Consider the words beauty, anxiety, and intelligence, words we use routinely. For example, I might say that a painting by Mary Cassett is "beautiful." There is nothing in the painting that is, by itself, beautiful. What does exist is Cassett's pigmented paint and their arrangement, all material things on the canvas. There is nothing in the picture that is beauty; rather beauty describes my perceptions of, and reactions to, the painting.

We invent words or constructs to help us make predictions and offer explanations. In most cases, we can operationally define these words for the purpose of our research. In chapter 2, I used the example of anxiety. Anxiety is an abstract concept that we use to pull together different conditions and to explain various behaviors. If we have a clear operational definition of the construct, we might find that the concept helps us explain the relation among several variables.

There is nothing inherently wrong with using hypothetical terms like intelligence. We use these words to help us describe, predict, and explain the world. The problem arises when we forget that some of our variables are inventions, and we begin to treat them as if they are real things. Gould (1981) complained that the reification of intelligence has caused many biologists, psychologists, and sociologists to search for its genetic component much as one would search for the genetic foundation of eye color, sickle-cell anemia, Hodgkin's disease, or other heritable conditions. Many believe that such a search is a fool's errand because intelligence is not a biologically determined process like eye color.

Another serious problem that arises from the mystique of quantification and reification is that some people forget that the numbers cannot capture or express all the important characteristics associated with a particular phenomenon. No measurement, quantitative or qualitative, can represent all the important components of human behavior. Unfortunately, many people believe that a test measures the "real thing" and forget that the test may ignore critical characteristics of an individual. Miles-Tapping (1996) provided a good example of this problem. While she was examining the quality of life of people who must use wheelchairs, she noted an important difference in how people used the word "independence." Many researchers used independence to mean that a person walks without the assistance of a cane, walker, or wheelchair. Therefore, a person who is wheelchair bound is, by that definition, not independent. By contrast, Miles-Tapping found that persons who must use a wheelchair perceive the chair as a symbol and instrument of their independence.

In summary, we need to view testing and measurement with guarded enthusiasm. With sufficient planning, analysis, and revision we can develop useful measures of the constructs that interest us. In most cases, we will be able to create a measure that suits our needs, to a point. At the same time, we must remember that our measures are tentative, subject to error and bias, and forever in need of refinement.

CREATING A MEASUREMENT SCALE

In the following sections, I will show you how to create measurement procedures for various applications including observational research, interviews, and surveys. Although each study is unique, the process of creating a measurement technique will follow a common set of steps. I will introduce these steps as a series of questions that the researcher must answer.

What Questions Are You Trying to Answer?

The best way to answer this question is to read the hypothesis. If you have a well-crafted hypothesis, you should be able to define your independent and dependent variables. Identifying the variables is half the battle as it helps you identify the types of behaviors you want to assess.

The more specifically you can describe the variables, the better. Consider the hypothesis "Children who participate in cooperative-learning projects will demonstrate fewer racial stereotypes and prejudicial behaviors." This is a good start. From this hypothesis, we know that the dependent variable has something to do with racial stereotypes and prejudicial behaviors. All we need is an operational definition of these terms. How will we measure a stereotype? How will you know if a child is prejudiced?

What Is the Most Convenient Method for Producing the Data?

Identifying observable behaviors related to the dependent variable will help determine how you will collect the data. Using the previous example, the definition of prejudicial behavior may focus on how children play with each other. Specifically, do the children from different ethnic groups play together or do they fight? In this case, you may find that an observational technique will supply the data that you need.

On the other hand, you may want to know how the children perceive members of different ethnic groups. Because you are interested in the child's perceptions, you may want to use a questionnaire or an interview. As you will see in the following sections, each method has its relative advantages and disadvantages. Therefore, you will need to weigh these as you consider your options.

What Is the Most Accurate Measurement Technique?

There is no such thing as a perfect measurement technique. Because all measurements have some form of error, you will need to consider methods that will help reduce bias and random errors. For observational research, we can use several trained observers to help ensure that we capture all the relevant information. For questionnaires, we can focus on the wording and design of the questions to ensure accurate results.

CONSTRUCTING INTERVIEWS, QUESTIONNAIRES, AND ATTITUDE SURVEYS

There are many ways that we can ask people questions ranging from face-to-face interviews to questionnaires sent through the mail. The questions we ask can be open-ended and allow the person to tell us about his or her beliefs, or the question can request a "Yes–No" answer. As with all research, the selection of specific procedures represents a balancing act between the need for information and the feasibility of the procedure.

The following is a review of different data collection techniques and their relative advantages and disadvantages. Consider my comments a general introduction to what can be a fascinating, albeit a complex, form of behavioral research.

Personal Interviews

The personal interview, either face-to-face or through the telephone, is a popular and useful way to understand human attitudes and beliefs (Fontana & Frey, 1994). Personal interviews, especially face-to-face interviews, tend to have a high level of cooperation. In addition, people are likely to answer an interviewer's questions rather than check the "Don't Know" box on a questionnaire. Other advantages are that the interviewer can ensure that the participant understands the questions, and the interviewer can ask follow-up questions. In sum, personal interviews can be a rich source of information.

There is no single format for the personal interview. Interviews can be highly structured or unstructured. Similarly, the interview may be limited to two people or may involve a small group. Fontana and Frey (1994) described many types of interviewing formats, each of which has a specific role for contemporary research. These formats take place in different settings, require different roles of the interviewer, involve different numbers of people in the discussion, and use different formats for the questions. Furthermore, no single interview technique is better than another; each serves its purpose. Table 7.1 presents a review of the different types of interview methods.

Potential limitations of interviews

Although interviews produce good data, the information comes at a price. Interviews are time intensive and expensive to conduct. First, you need a staff to conduct the interviews. Unless you can find a team of volunteers, you will need to pay the staff. Second, conducting a good interview requires much practice, a bit of acting, and the ability to respond to unpredictable situations. The staff need to be trained in how to use the interview

TABLE 7.1
Review of various interview methods and their characteristics

Type	Characteristics	Question format	Use
Brainstorming	Unstructured interaction among members of the group	No format; interviewer asks questions to facilitate discussion	Generate ideas for a project that will be examined in detail later
Case study	Intensive study of one person's history and current situation	Unstructured and guided by interaction between interviewer and participant	Demonstration of a general principle or application of a clinical intervention; often the source of ideas for later research
Focus or Delphi group	Structured interaction between interviewer and a small group of people	Interviewer uses a script of questions, but can ask follow-up questions for additional information	Gather information regarding people's reactions to a specific topic; often used to assess people's opinions
Formal interview	Highly structured interaction between interviewer and participant	Interviewer follows a script with little or no room for deviation	Collection of specific information typically for a larger program of research

technique, how to answer a participant's questions, and how to react to the participant's many comments that may or may not apply to the questions asked.

Conducting interviews is especially difficult when there are significant racial and cultural barriers between the interviewer and the people interviewed. Consider the following example. During the 1930s, the Federal Writers' Project funded in-depth interviews of African Americans living in the southern states (Davidson & Lytle, 1992). In one case, two people independently interviewed Susan Hamlin, a former slave. During part of the first interview she said,

> Mr. Fuller [Susan's owner] was a good man and his wife's people been grand people, all good to their slaves. Seem like Mr. Fuller just git his slaves so he could be good to dem. He made all the little colored chillen love him. (p. 161)

During the second interview she said,

> . . . but our master ain't nebber want to sell his slaves. But dat didn't keep Clory [a mulatto slave owned by Mr. Fuller] frum gittin' a brutal whippin'. Dey whip' 'er untul dere wasn't a white spot on her body. Dat was de worst I ebber se a human bein' got such a beatin'. (p. 165)

Clearly, Susan told different stories about her life as a slave. In the first interview, she described the slave owner as a gentleperson who treated his slaves well. The second interview tells a story about ruthless behavior. Davidson and Lytle (1992) discovered that the first interviewer was white whereas the second interviewer was black. Clearly, Susan was distrustful of white people and unwilling to tell them of her horrible experiences.

The previous example illustrates the need to exercise caution when planning an interview. Good interviewing is not just reading the questions from a script. In many cases, the interview is successful only after the interviewer has gained the participant's trust and willingness to answer honestly. This important skill takes time and practice to cultivate.

Personal interviews are useful sources of information but require considerable financial support, professional staff, and time. Consequently, researchers are most likely to use personal interview techniques only as a part of a well-funded grant.

Self-Administered Surveys

An alternative to the personal interview is the self-administered survey. The survey is the model of simplicity; give many people a few questions and ask them to mark their answers on a sheet of paper. The advantages are obvious. First, the cost of photocopying and distributing a survey is a fraction of the cost of a personal interview. Second, this method does not require staff to conduct interviews. Finally, self-administered surveys are easy to distribute. We can mail the survey along with a stamped return envelope or hand them out to a class of students or some other well-defined group.

Self-administered surveys have their cost, however, in the quality of the data. Many people are likely to throw away surveys they receive in the mail. Therefore, survey data may be biased if the responses are not representative of the population. In addition, the researcher has little control over the questionnaire once it is delivered. There is no way to be sure that the person we wanted to answer the questions completed the questionnaire.

Although there are many potential liabilities with self-administered surveys, they are extremely popular among behavioral researchers. In those situations where many people complete the questionnaire, self-administered surveys are a cost-effective method of obtaining data. There are a few ways one can maximize compliance with a survey. The following sections to review these techniques.

Use a captive audience

When you can, distribute your survey where there is a natural grouping of people. Many researchers ask students to complete a survey that may take 5 or 10 minutes of class time. At some universities, there may be 300 or more students enrolled in an introductory psychology course. These large courses provide an opportunity to gather much data quickly.

Use social psychology to your advantage

According to Salant and Dillman (1994), there are many things that you can do to increase the return rate of surveys sent through the mail. Plan to send several letters to potential participants. The first letter should be an advanced notice telling the individuals that they will receive the questionnaire within several days. This letter should convey the importance of the research and the need for the person's response. The second mailing is the survey along with a cover letter that reiterates the importance of the research. If necessary, you can send a third and fourth letter to remind the participants to return the completed questionnaire.

Salant and Dillman (1994) also recommend using a distinctive envelope, priority mail, or both. Although you do not want your package to look like a sweepstakes mailing, you do want it to create the impression that it contains an important document. Finally, make the cover letter as personal as possible, and convey the impression that you eagerly await the person's comments. Figure 7.1 presents examples of the type of letters a researcher

The University of Tennessee at Chattanooga
Department of Psychology   *Chattanooga, TN*

September 23, 2002

Ms. M. Barnas
1234 Cloverleaf Dr.
Chattanooga, TN 37403

Dear Ms. Barnas:

Good quality health care is important to all people who live in Hamilton County. That is why Chattanooga Community Hospital is looking for ways to improve its services. The staff of the hospital believes that the best way to improve services is to listen to people in the community. Therefore, the hospital is currently conducting extensive research to find ways to improve the care it provides. They have asked me to help with this important research project.

You were selected as one of a small group of people who will soon receive a survey. This survey will ask for your opinion on how well Chattanooga Community Hospital does its job and where it could improve its services. Your answers to this survey will help the staff of the hospital understand the needs of our community.

You should receive the survey within the next 7 to 10 days. The packet will contain the survey, a stamped self-addressed envelope, and a pen. Completing the survey will require about 10 minutes of your time.

Your answers will be completely confidential. No one will ever know how you answered these questions. The information from all the surveys will be combined and reported as a group.

If you have any questions about the survey or the research, please feel free to contact me at (423) 555-1234.

Sincerely,

David J. Pittenger
Professor of Psychology

ee at Chattanooga
Chattanooga, TN

Dear Ms. Barnas:

Please find enclosed the survey that I mentioned in my letter of September 23. You should find enclosed the survey, a self-addressed stamped envelope, and a pen. The survey should take about 10 minutes to complete. I hope that you will be able to complete the survey quickly and return it through the mail.

I can assure you that your answers will be completely confidential. Therefore, I hope that you feel comfortable answering the questions as honestly and completely as possible.

The information from all the surveys will be combined and reported as a group. Chattanooga Community Hospital plans to use the data from this project to find ways that it can improve services to patients living in Hamilton County. Your answers will do much to ensure that our hospital meets the future needs of the community.

If you have any questions about the survey or the research, please feel free to contact me at (423) 555-1234.

Sincerely,

David J. Pittenger
Professor of Psychology

FIGURE 7.1
An example of the letters that one might send to participants in a survey. The letters are simple, to the point, and convey the importance of the project.

might use. The first is a note to introduce the participants to the purpose of the project and tell them of the forthcoming survey. The second is a cover letter for the survey. Both letters emphasize the importance of the research and the need for a timely response from the participant.

Another successful method for increasing return rates is to give the person a gift. Social psychologists call this phenomenon normative reciprocity. If I do something nice for you, you will feel obligated to return the favor. Salant and Dillman (1994) noted that attaching a $1 bill to a questionnaire increases response rates by 5 to 8%. Larger denominations ($5 or $20) increase response rates even higher (probably not a practical option for most student research). Finally, do not give people an excuse for not completing the survey immediately. Include a sharpened pencil or a pen with the questionnaire along with a stamped return envelope.

PREPARING THE QUESTIONS

Once you select a method for obtaining the data, you will need to prepare the questions for the survey. As a generality, you can ask two types of questions. The first is the **open-ended question** that asks the person to give a short answer to the question. The alternative is the **closed-response question** that requires the person to select from a set of options.

Open-Ended Questions

An advantage of the open-ended question is the rich and complex data that you can obtain that is not possible from a closed-response question. Consider the typical course evaluation form that most colleges use. At the end of each semester, my college has students complete a course evaluation for each course. Most of the questions are closed-response, such as,

Overall, I would rate the instructor as:

⑤ Outstanding   ④ Very Good   ③ Average   ② Below Average   ① Poor

In addition, there are also two open-ended questions, "What do you like most about the instructor's teaching?" and "In what ways can the instructor improve as a teacher?" Although the answers to the closed-response questions let me know what students think of my teaching, their written comments can often be extremely informative. Each semester I receive comments that are sometimes flattering, sometimes humbling, but always illuminating.

The written comments provide information difficult to obtain with closed-response questions. This does not mean that open-ended questions are always the preferred format. First, many people provide minimal or vague answers to open-ended questions, especially when they have to write their response. Second, written responses can be difficult to evaluate objectively. For example, how should I respond to the written comment, "This course is difficult and requires a lot of reading"? Is the student stating a fact or complaining about the course? Because of these ambiguities, many researchers prefer to use closed-response questions for surveys. One compromise is to ask closed-response questions and then provide room for written responses.

Closed-Response Questions

The primary feature of the closed-response question is that the researcher supplies the response options for the person. You can use many alternative formats for a closed-response question.

Nominal category response

The answer options for this category represent a nominal scale. In some cases, the question will treat the options as mutually exclusive and force the person to select only one category. In other cases, the question will allow the person to select several separate categories. Table 7.2 is an example of nominal category response items.

Forced Choice Alternatives

For these questions, we ask the participants to select a response that best represents their answer to the question. In this case, we assume that the alternatives represent an underlying scale that ranges between the two extremes. Table 7.3 presents examples of forced choice alternative items.

TABLE 7.2
Example of nominal category response items

Mutually exclusive response options:

Sex: _____ Female   _____ Male

I am: _____ Single   _____ Married   _____ Divorced   _____ Widowed

Multiple nominal responses:

I use the following sources to learn about national news:

Mark all that apply.

_____ Newspapers   _____ News Magazines   _____ Television News

_____ Radio   _____ Internet

TABLE 7.3
Examples of forced choice alternatives

Forced choice alternatives along a scale

For each of the following pairs of words, mark the word that best describes you:

_____ Liberal   vs.   _____ Conservative

_____ Shy   vs.   _____ Outgoing

_____ Leader   vs.   _____ Follower

_____ Assertive   vs.   _____ Passive

_____ Introverted   vs.   _____ Extraverted

Mark the statement that best describes your belief*

(a) _____ In the long run, people get the respect they deserve in this world.

or

(b) _____ Unfortunately, an individual's worth often passes unrecognized no matter how hard he or she tries.

---

*Item from Rotter's (1966) Internal-External locus of control scale.

Likert Format

The Likert format is perhaps one of the most popular options for the closed-response format questionnaire because it has a couple advantages. First, it offers a clear and unambiguous ordinal scale of measurement. Second, you can use the same format for many questions. Therefore, you can combine the answers to produce an average score. Table 7.4 presents several examples of the Likert format.

In its most common form, the Likert format consists of 4 to 10 points that represent potential reactions to the question or statement. The response may reflect the person's appraisal of something or whether they agree or disagree with a statement. Several researchers examining the reliability and validity characteristics of the Likert format recommend that one use between 4 and 10 items (Chang, 1994; Preston & Colman, 2000).

Guttman Format

A Guttman format, like the Likert format, represents a continuum that ranges from one extreme to another. For this format, the researcher arranges the answer options by levels of acceptance. When the person responds, we assume that he or she agrees with the statement and all the preceding statements as well. Consider the examples in Table 7.5. For each question, I have ranked the alternatives such that if you agree with one statement, you are likely to agree with the preceding statements.

TABLE 7.4
Examples of the Likert format

Overall, I believe that Mayor Matthews is doing a good job.

①	②	③	④	⑤
Strongly Agree	Agree	Neutral	Disagree	Strongly Disagree

If the election were held tomorrow, I would

①	②	③	④	⑤	⑥	⑦
Definitely Vote Democrat			Unsure			Definitely Vote Republican

The meals prepared by the food service are

①	②	③	④	⑤	⑥	⑦
Consistently Good						Consistently Poor

TABLE 7.5
Example of a Guttman format response alternative

Which of the following best represents your opinion regarding abortion? Select only one option.

(1) _____ Abortion may be performed when the mother's life is in danger.
(2) _____ Abortion may be performed if the fetus has a severe disability.
(3) _____ Abortion may be performed in cases of rape.
(4) _____ Abortion may be performed as a type of family planning.
(5) _____ Abortion may be performed for any reason.

The Guttman format, although useful, can be difficult to prepare because you cannot rely on your opinion for the best order of the items. To create the scale, you should distribute the individual items to a small and representative sample of the target population, and ask the participants to identify the items with which they agree. The order of the items for the final Guttman format represents the percent agreement for each item—items with high levels of agreement come first followed by items receiving lower percentages of agreement.

ACHIEVEMENT CHECK

(1) Describe the "reification problem" in your words.

(2) What is meant by the phrase "mystique of quantity"?

(3) How are the concepts of "reification" and "mystique of quantity" related?

(4) Consider the terms "intelligence," "personality," and "anxiety." What are the differences between the way a researcher would use these terms and the way another person would use these terms?

(5) Can a science exist without measurement? Justify your opinion.

(6) Describe in your words the goals and characteristics of measurement.

(7) Why are operational definitions essential for creating a measurement instrument?

(8) Assume that you wanted to collect data concerning students' attitudes toward minorities. What would be the relative advantages and disadvantages of using a personal interview or a self-administered questionnaire?

(9) Describe in your words the similarities and differences between the Likert and Guttman formats.

(10) What do you see as the differences between conducting a face-to-face interview versus a telephone interview?

(11) A researcher wants to conduct a survey by posting the question on a web page. What do you see as the advantages and disadvantages of this option?

WRITING GOOD QUESTIONNAIRE AND SURVEY ITEMS

The real work of preparing a good questionnaire is writing questions that sample the opinions, attitudes, or beliefs that you want to measure. The following are some guidelines for preparing survey items.

Ask Single Questions or Make Single Statements

EXAMPLE. Do you agree with the college's plan to build a new student recreation center and increase the student fee to $500 to help pay for the building?

This question has two parts, building the new student recreation center *and* increasing the student fee. Some people may agree with both statements, some may disagree with both, and others will agree with one statement but not the other. Because of the inherent ambiguity created by asking two questions in one, the question should be broken into two parts. The results will provide an unambiguous indication of student sentiment.

Alternatives: (1) Do you agree with the college's plan to build a new student recreation center?

(2) Would you pay $500 in student fees to help pay for a new student recreation center?

Ask Specific Questions and Avoid Vague Terms

EXAMPLE. Do you actively support the college's decision to build a new student recreation center?

What does *actively support* mean? Although people recognize the difference between "support" and "oppose," we have no way of determining the extent of their support. Therefore, we need to find an alternative wording that will indicate the extent to which students support this construction project.

Alternatives: I believe that the college should build a new student recreation center as soon as possible.

①	②	③	④	⑤
Strongly Agree	Agree	Neutral	Disagree	Strongly Disagree

or

Which of the following building projects should be started as soon as possible? Pick one:

_____ An addition to the library.

_____ A new arts and sciences building.

_____ A new student recreation center.

_____ Renovations to the Mary Beach and Russell residence halls.

Write Neutral Statements and Avoid a Biased Tone

EXAMPLES. (1) Many people believe that it is bad to spank children. Do you?

(2) Do you believe that all students must complete two semesters of English composition regardless of their writing skills?

Both questions come to the reader with a chip on their shoulder. The first question makes it clear that you should agree with the majority and condemn spanking children. Similarly, the second question makes it clear that the English composition courses are not necessary. By contrast, notice how the following alternatives merely ask for an opinion.

Alternatives: (1) Do you believe that parents should spank their children?

(2) Do you favor or oppose a new policy requiring all students to complete two semesters of English composition?

Ask Questions That Don't Embarrass or Anger the Participant

EXAMPLES. (1) Are you still a virgin?

(2) How often do you get drunk?

Highly personal questions such as these can offend some people. In addition, these questions seem to imply a moral overtone about one's sexuality and drinking habits. The questions should take a neutral tone, and the answer options should allow the individual to respond in a neutral manner.

Alternatives: (1) With how many people have you had sexual intercourse?

_____ 0   _____ 1   _____ 2   _____ 3   _____ 4 or more

(2) During the typical month, how many times do you drink until you are intoxicated?

_____ 0   _____ 1–2   _____ 3–5   _____ 6–7   _____ 8 or more

Whenever Possible, Use Simple Words and Concepts

EXAMPLE. Do you believe that you received sufficient time to consider your alternatives before you were required to purchase your computer?

This question uses many formal and long words that may be difficult for some readers to understand. Good questions use simple words and sentence structure. Most word processors have a function that examines the readability of a sentence and estimates its reading level. The previous question received a rating at the 12th grade reading level. The following alternatives are easier to understand.

Alternative: (1) Did you feel rushed to buy the computer?
(2) Did you have enough time to think about buying the computer?

Ask Questions That the Person Can Easily Answer

EXAMPLE. What percentage of the typical week do you spend studying?

This question asks the participant to do a lot of guestimating in their heads. In addition, most people do not do a good job of estimating percentages. Consequently, you may not get valid results. As an alternative, ask the participants to estimate the actual amount—you can then determine the percentages.

Alternative: During the typical weekday (Monday–Friday), how many hours do you

_____ Attend classes
_____ Study or work on homework and class assignments
_____ Work at a job
_____ Socialize or party with friends
_____ Sleep
_____ Other activities
_24_ Total hours

Recognize That One Question May Not Be Enough

EXAMPLE. All in all, I am inclined to feel that I am a failure.*

Many psychological constructs, such as opinions, attitudes, and personality, cannot be accurately measured with a single question. In these cases, it is appropriate to ask several highly related questions. The average answer to a group of questions is a more reliable measure of the person's opinion, attitude, personality, or whatever construct that you are measuring. Asking a series of related questions also creates a **priming cue** for the participant. If you ask a series of related questions, the participant will have more time to think about the issue and thereby offer a more thoughtful answer to the questions.

Alternatives: (1) All in all, I am inclined to feel that I am a failure.
(2) I feel that I have a number of good qualities.
(3) I am able to do things as well as most other people.
(4) I feel that I do not have much to be proud of.
(5) On the whole, I am satisfied with myself.
(6) I certainly feel useless at times.

---

*All items are from Rosenberg's (1965) Self-esteem Scale.

You should be cautious of the order of questions because each question sets the stage for how the participant will answer subsequent questions. For example, Dillman (2000) reported that 21% of college students agreed with a policy that a student should be expelled from college for plagiarism. However, 34% of another sample of students endorsed expulsion of the student if the preceding question asked whether a faculty member should be fired for plagiarism. The difference in the response rates raises the question, which data set represents the students' opinion? Results like these represent what researchers call the **order effect,** that the sequence of questions can influence a participant's response to specific questions.

There is no easy solution to the order effect other than to recognize that it exists. Dillman (2000) recommended that if you suspect that the order of the questions will influence the participants' responses to critical questions, you should create several versions of the questionnaire with different sequences of questions. The alternative is to identify the order of questions in the report of the data, thus allowing the reader to understand the context in which the participants answered the questions.

Word Questions That Reduce the Risk of a Response Set

Look at the six alternative statements in the previous section. These questions all assess a person's self-esteem. Although they measure the same thing, look at their wording. If the participant has a high level of self-esteem, then he or she will have to agree with some questions and disagree with others. If all the questions were worded in the same manner, then the person may become lazy and be tempted to give the same answer to each question without really reading the question. Researchers call this habit a **response set** (Cronbach, 1950).

One way to avoid the response set is to reword the questions and statements so that half are stated in the positive (e.g., "I am a good person.") and the remaining stated in the negative (e.g., "There is little to like about me."). Barnette (2000) also recommended that one switch the response scale among the questions. Using this tactic, you would word the questions/statements as you choose. For half the items, you would use one response set such as:

①	②	③	④	⑤
Strongly Agree	Agree	Neutral	Disagree	Strongly Disagree

For the remaining items, you would use the response set:

①	②	③	④	⑤
Strongly Disagree	Disagree	Neutral	Agree	Strongly Agree

Avoid Questions and Statements That Have an Obviously Correct Answer

EXAMPLES. (1) Women are generally not as smart as men.
(2) I would not want a woman as my boss.

In some cases, being straightforward is not the best policy. Most people know that the previous statements about women are not popular. Therefore, respondents may tell you what they think you want to hear, not what they believe. One alternative is to reframe the questions to obscure the intent. For example, Swim, Aiken, Hall, and Hunter (1995) developed a test that measures sexism using subtly worded statements.

Alternatives: (1) Discrimination against women is no longer a problem in the United States.
(2) Women often miss out on good jobs due to sexual discrimination.
(3) On average, people in our society treat husbands and wives equally.

Resources for Tests and Measurements

Why reinvent the wheel when there are many sources for tests and measures that have already been written and evaluated for reliability and validity? You can find many of these tests in published literature. Therefore, before you run out and create a test or survey, see if someone has already done the hard work for you. You can use *PsycInfo* to search for tests that have been published in the psychological literature.

Determining Sample Size for a Survey

In chapter 6, I introduced you to the central limit theorem and the standard error of the mean. As you learned, we use these mathematical concepts to determine the accuracy of the sample mean as an estimate of the population mean. We can also use these concepts to determine the optimal sample size for surveys.

In this section, we will examine how to determine sample size for questionnaires where you require the person to select one response from several options. The common example of this questionnaire is a political poll wherein you ask potential voters whom they favor in an election. We can treat the answer as a **binary response** because we want to know whether voters will vote for a candidate. Specifically, we want to estimate the probability (P) that voters will vote for a particular candidate.

Cochran (1977), in his influential text on sampling, demonstrated that Equation 7.1 allows us to estimate sample size, n', given P and α. We use α to determine the width of the confidence interval of the mean. Also in the equation is $z^2_{(1-\alpha)/2}$, which represents the absolute value that defines the boundaries of α. We reviewed how to find $z_{(1-\alpha)/2}$ in chapter 6. Equation 7.1, therefore, allows us to estimate sample size when given specific conditions.

$$n' = \frac{(z^2_{(1-\alpha)/2})(P)(1-P)}{\alpha^2} \tag{7.1}$$

There are several steps for estimating sample size. First, we need to determine what we would consider an acceptable margin of error for our research. Smaller values of α will give us greater precision in our estimate. For example, if we accept $\alpha = .05$, then we are comfortable with our margin of error being ± 5 percentage points. To increase the accuracy of our estimate, we could use $\alpha = .01$, which would mean that the margin of error becomes ± 1 percentage points.

Next, we need to guesstimate the value of P that we will observe when we collect the data. If you have no way to make this prediction, you can use the conservative option by setting $P = .5$.

TABLE 7.6
The relation between α, P, and estimated sample size

95% confidence interval $\alpha = .05$ $z_{(1-\alpha)/2} = 1.9600$		97.5% confidence interval $\alpha = .025$ $z_{(1-\alpha)/2} = 2.2414$		99% confidence interval $\alpha = .01$ $z_{(1-\alpha)/2} = 2.5785$	
P	n'	P	n'	P	n'
.9	138	.9	723	.9	5,971
.8	245	.8	1,286	.8	10,615
.7	322	.7	1,688	.7	13,933
.6	368	.6	1,929	.6	15,923
.5	384	.5	2,009	.5	16,587
.4	368	.4	1,929	.4	15,923
.3	322	.3	1,688	.3	13,933
.2	245	.2	1,286	.2	10,615
.1	138	.1	723	.1	5,971

Table 7.6 presents the relation among α, P, and estimated sample size. As you can see, when $P = .5$ and $\alpha = .05$ you need 384 participants in your survey to obtain a relatively reliable estimate of the population. As we reviewed in chapters 6, the accuracy of the sample statistic depends upon the method we use to create the sample.

Table 7.6 also illustrates that increasing sample size will greatly increase your precision, but at a cost. For example, doubling the precision of measurement ($\alpha = .05$ to $\alpha = .025$) requires a considerable increase in sample size (384 to 2,009).

Small populations

If you are working with a small population, you can adjust your estimated sample size using Equation 7.2. You can use this equation whenever you know the size of the population. If the population is small, you may find that you need fewer participants to maintain your confidence interval.

$$n'' = \frac{N(n')}{N + n'}$$

(7.2)

For this equation, n' represents the estimated sample size from Equation 7.1 and N represents the size of the population. Here is an example. Assume that you want to conduct a survey of students at your college and ask them if they support the faculty's decision to use a plus/minus grading system. For the sake of the example, assume that you want to be accurate to within ±3 percentage points ($\alpha = .03$), that you set $P = .5$, and that there are 7,500 students at your college. Given these facts, $1 - \alpha = .97$, $(1 - \alpha)/2 = .485$, $z_{(1-\alpha)/2} = 2.17$,

$$n' = \frac{\left(z^2_{(1-\alpha)/2}\right)(P)(1-P)}{\alpha^2} \qquad n' = \frac{(2.17^2)(.5)(1-.5)}{.03^2} \qquad n' = 1{,}308.03 \quad n' = 1{,}308$$

$$n'' = \frac{N(n')}{N+n'} \qquad n'' = \frac{7500(1308)}{7500 + 1308} \qquad n'' = 1{,}113.74 \quad n'' = 1{,}113$$

Therefore, you should survey at least 1,113 students to meet the objectives of your study.

The preceding example illustrates how to determine sample size for binary responses. Determining sample sizes for other response scales, such as the Likert format, that measure quantities using ordinal, interval, or ratio scales require a different set of procedures. We will examine these procedures in a subsequent chapter.

NATURALISTIC OBSERVATION

For many types of research there are no better tools than a pair of eyes, a sharp pencil, and a sheet of paper. Although good observational research is difficult to conduct, it can produce a wealth of useful information. With proper planning and work, one can conduct observational research that includes systematic manipulation of independent variables and the recording of dependent variables all in a natural setting. In other words, one can conduct experiments and produce data that have clear external validity.

Observational techniques go by many names including "Field Studies," "Naturalistic Observation," or "Natural Experiment." The essential feature of this research technique is that we watch and record the individual's ongoing behaviors. Here are three examples of how one might use observational techniques.

An experiment in anxiety

Many developmental psychologists study separation anxiety, the emotional reaction that children have when separated from their parents (e.g., Ainsworth & Bell, 1970; Ainsworth, Blehar, Waters, & Wall, 1978). To study separation anxiety, a researcher may invite parents to bring their toddlers to the department's laboratory. The researcher can then observe the children's reaction to different situations through a two-way mirror or with a hidden video camera. In this type of research, the researcher is able to control many of the different variables such as the child's age and the test situation. One can easily use naturalistic observation in a true experiment.

Watching the bully on the playground

Many psychologists and educators study bullying behavior (e.g., Pepler & Craig, 1995). A popular method of studying bullying is to watch children's play during school recess. As in the previous example, the researcher finds some inconspicuous place where he or she can observe the children's play. As with all observational research, the person collecting the data will watch for and record the duration, frequency, or intensity of specific behaviors.

Who said what to whom?

In some cases, the target behavior will be what people say to each other. For this type of research, we make a record of what people say in a conversation. DePaulo and Kashy (1998) conducted an interesting example of this type of research by asking participants to keep a daily journal of the lies they told their friends, family, and associates. Using an objective scoring procedure, research assistants who did not know the hypotheses being tested read and scored the episodes described in the journals. DePaulo and Kashy found that the participants did not lie often to friends, but occasionally told "white lies" to protect their friends' feelings. By contrast, the participants were more willing to tell self-serving lies to casual acquaintances and strangers.

What to Observe

The steps we take to create a survey are the same steps we can follow to develop a strategy for observing and recording behavior. First, we need to decide what behaviors we want to observe. Unless you are observing the behavior of slugs, most creatures engage in many behaviors, too many to observe in a single study. Therefore, we need to identify a manageable set of behaviors that we can observe and document. As with all research, we select variables that correspond to the hypothesis we want to test.

Once we select the variables we want to measure, we need to ensure that there is a clear operational definition of the behaviors to be monitored. Some variables may be easy to define. We can count the number of cigarettes smoked in an hour, the time spent watching television and the name of the shows selected, or the number of four-letter curses. Other behaviors are not as readily defined. For example, what do we mean by an aggressive act? Is a tackle in a football game an aggressive act or part of playing a game? If one person accidentally hurts another, is the behavior aggressive? What about verbal threats; will you include these in your definition of aggression?

Consider children's social behavior. Assume that a researcher wanted to study how children react when they are the new member of a group. The focus of the study is to determine how a child behaves when he or she is the new member of a group. Will the child immediately join the group, or will he or she be cautious and watch the other children from afar? As a part of the study, the researcher may observe the child's play and use definitions of play like those presented in Table 7.7.

TABLE 7.7
Example of definitions for behaviors that are to be observed

Unoccupied	Child is not engaged in play or other specific activity.
Solitary play	Child is playing alone with toys and is not seeking interaction with others.
Interactive play	Child is playing with one or more children. There is an exchange of toys, play activities, and cooperation among the children.

Strategies for Collecting Observational Data

Once you have defined the behaviors to observe, you will need to select the type of data to collect. As a generality, there are three types of recording techniques: frequency recording, duration recording, and interval recording. As with all aspects of research, selection of the recording technique depends upon the definition of the variable and the research hypothesis.

Frequency recording

As the name implies, for frequency recording we count the number of times that a behavior occurs during a specified interval. Most researchers use frequency recording to count discrete behaviors that generally have a fixed duration. Therefore, we can count the number of times one student interrupts another student, the number of times a child offers to share a toy, or the number of cigarettes a person smokes. Other behaviors, such as studying, reading a book, napping, and watching television are behaviors better measured using other recording techniques because they are ongoing behaviors that may occur infrequently, but last a long time.

Duration recording

Duration recording focuses on the amount of time a person spends engaged in one behavior. This method is useful for measuring ongoing behavior that may last for an unpredictable amount of time. A researcher may use duration recording to monitor a child's behavior during a stranger-situation study. Specifically, the researcher could time how quickly the child stopped playing and returned to the parent when the stranger entered the room, how long the child stayed close to the parent, and the how long it took for the child to return to playing with the toys.

Interval recording

For interval recording, the researcher plans to observe one or more individuals for a fixed time. The researcher then divides the session into intervals of equal lengths. The interval length is short enough that the individual can engage in only one behavior during the interval. During each interval, the researcher indicates the presence or absence of the relevant behavior. In most cases, there may be a pause or delay between intervals.

Although this technique is often recommended to researchers, it has also been the target of criticism (Altmann, 1974; Murphy & Goodall, 1980; Tyler, 1979). Altmann concluded that the method has no general value for behavioral research because it does not accurately measure the frequency or the duration of behavior. She also criticized interval recording because the method cannot adequately indicate the proportion of time the individual engages in a behavior.

Special Considerations for Observational Research

As with all research procedures, there are special controls that you should consider to collect accurate, reliable, and valid data. The essential question to ask is, "Who is collecting the data and do they know what they are doing?" The reliability of the data depends upon the vigilance of the person observing and recording the data. The most common method to ensure that the data are reliable is to have two or more observers record the data and then report the average of the observations.

Before you aggregate the data, however, you need to ensure that the observers agree with each other by determining the **interrater reliability.** The interrater reliability is a statistical index that represents how the observers' records match. If the interrater reliability is high, we can place greater confidence in the data and proceed with their analysis. If the interrater reliability is low, analysis of the data may not be useful because the measurement error is too great. Low interrater reliability can indicate that the observers need to be better trained, that the definitions need to be clarified, that the recording procedure needs to be revised, or some combination of these solutions.

There are many ways to assess interrater reliability. The following sections examine the more popular options.

Coefficient Kappa

One of the more popular methods of determining interrater agreement is Cohen's kappa, κ. Researchers use κ to assess interrater reliability when the data represent a nominal or an ordinal scale. As an example, consider the data presented in Table 7.8. In this example, two raters independently observed the same person and counted the number of times one of three behaviors occurred. The numbers in the table represent their assessments. Look down Column A of the table. The numbers are 15, 2, and 1. These numbers represent agreements and disagreements. Raters 1 and 2 agreed 15 times on the occurrence of Behavior A, but disagreed on the classification of 3 other behaviors. The numbers along the diagonal of the table represent agreements; the numbers in the other cells represent disagreements.

Cohen's κ allows us to determine the level of agreement among the raters. To calculate κ, we use the following equations.

$$\kappa = \frac{P_A - P_C}{1 - P_C}, \quad \text{where } P_A = \frac{\sum O_{ii}}{T} \quad \text{and} \quad P_C = \frac{\sum R_i C_i}{T^2} \tag{7.3}$$

In this equation, P_A represents the proportion of agreement between the raters. To determine P_A, we add the observed agreements, O_{ii}, and divide by the total number of observations, T. The second component of κ is P_C, which estimates the number of agreements that would have happened by chance.

TABLE 7.8

Example of data from two independent raters who classified the same people or behaviors into one of three categories

		Rater 1 Category A	Rater 1 Category B	Rater 1 Category C	Row totals $\sum$
Rater 2 Category	**A**	15	1	1	$R_1 = 17$
	B	2	21	2	$R_2 = 25$
	C	1	1	16	$R_3 = 18$
Column totals $\sum$		$C_1 = 18$	$C_2 = 23$	$C_3 = 19$	$T = 60$

Procedure for calculating coefficient kappa, κ

$$P_A = \frac{\sum O_{ii}}{T} = \frac{15 + 21 + 16}{60} = \frac{52}{60} = .8667$$

$$P_C = \frac{\sum R_i C_i}{T^2} = \frac{(18 \times 17) + (23 \times 25) + (19 \times 18)}{60^2} = \frac{1223}{3600} = .3397$$

$$\kappa = \frac{P_A - P_C}{1 - P_C} = \frac{.8667 - .3397}{1 - .3397} = \frac{.5270}{.6603} = .7981$$

$$\kappa = .80$$

TABLE 7.9

Example of steps to calculate coefficient kappa for more than two observers

Person	Categories of behavior			$n_{ij}(n_{ij}-1)$			$\sum n_{ij}(n_{ij}-1)$	$\dfrac{\sum n_{ij}(n_{ij}-1)}{j(j-1)} = A_j$
	C_1	C_2	C_3	C_1	C_2	C_3		
1	5	0	0	5(4) + 0	+ 0		= 20	20/20 = 1.0
2	0	5	0	0	+ 5(4)	+ 0	= 20	20/20 = 1.0
3	0	1	4	0	+ 1(0)	+ 4(3)	= 12	12/20 = 0.6
4	4	1	0	4(3)	+ 1(0)	+ 0	= 12	12/20 = 0.6
5	0	0	5	0	+ 0	+ 5(4)	= 20	20/20 = 1.0
6	4	1	0	4(3)	+ 1(0)	+ 0	= 12	12/20 = 0.6
7	0	0	5	0	+ 0	+ 5(4)	= 20	20/20 = 1.0
8	0	5	0	0	+ 5(4)	+ 0	= 20	20/20 = 1.0
9	1	4	0	1(0)	+ 4(3)	+ 0	= 12	12/20 = 0.6
10	5	0	0	5(4)	+ 0	+ 0	= 20	20/20 = 1.0

$C_1 = 19 \quad C_2 = 17 \quad C_3 = 14$ $\qquad\qquad\qquad\qquad \sum A_j = 8.4$

$T = \sum C_i = 19 + 17 + 14 = 50$

$\sum (C_i/T)^2 = (19/50)^2 + (17/50)^2 + (14/50)^2$

$\sum (C_i/T)^2 = (0.38)^2 + (0.34)^2 + (0.28)^2 \qquad j = 5$

$\sum (C_i/T)^2 = .1444 + .1156 + .0784 = .3384 \qquad N = 10$

$P_C = \sum (C_i/T)^2 = .3384$

$P_A = \sum A_j/N = 8.4/10 = .84$

$\kappa = \dfrac{P_A - P_C}{1 - P_C} = \dfrac{.84 - .3384}{1 - .3384} = .7582$

$\kappa = .76$

Notes: A_i = proportion of agreement for each person
$\quad\quad C_i$ = total of columns for the categories
$\quad\quad j$ = number of judges
$\quad\quad n_{ij}$ = number of judges who agree within each row for each category
$\quad\quad N$ = total number of people or objects rated
$\quad\quad T$ = total number of observations made by the judges

In some situations, there may be more than two observers. Although the calculations are more cumbersome, we can still calculate κ to determine the interrater agreement among the observers. Table 7.9 presents an example for calculating κ for more than two observers. The example presents hypothetical data for 5 judges evaluating 10 individuals. The column labeled "Person" represents the individuals being evaluated. The next three columns, C_1, C_2, and C_3, represent the behavioral categories the judges use to classify the participant's behavior. The number of categories can be as few as two or as many as the researcher needs for the study. The number within each cell (n_{ij}) indicates the number of judges who agree on a classification for that person. For example, for person 3 the numbers are 0, 1, and 4. These values indicate that none of the judges classified person 3 within C_1, one judge listed person 3 as a case of C_2, and the other four judges rated person 3 within C_3. The rest of the table presents the details of the calculations.

TABLE 7.10
**General guidelines for interpreting
the size of κ***

Value of κ	Level of agreement
<.20	Poor
.21– .40	Fair
.41– .60	Moderate
.61– .80	Good
.81–1.0	Excellent

*Based on Altman (1991).

Interpreting κ is straightforward, the larger the better. Values of κ can range between 0, which represents no interrater reliability, and 1.0, which represents perfect interrater reliability. Most researchers strive to have κ be greater than .75. When $\kappa < .50$ there is too much disagreement among the judges to produce useful information. Table 7.10 lists a general guideline for interpreting the size of κ.

Pearson Correlation Coefficient, *r*

The Pearson correlation coefficient, r, can also describe the interrater reliability. Researchers use this statistic specifically when they use an interval or a ratio scale to measure the variable. Therefore, the statistic might be used for determining the reliability of frequency and duration measures. I devote the next chapter to the review of this important statistic. In brief, we interpret the r as we do κ. As with κ, the absolute values of r can range between 0 and 1, with larger values representing greater levels of interrater agreement.

Improving Interrater Reliability

There are a number of things that you can do to maximize the reliability and validity of observational data. One of the most important is to keep the rater from knowing your hypothesis. If the raters know what you expect to find in the study, they may be tempted to score their observations in favor of your expectations.

Another is to train the observers. Barkhof et al. (1997) provided an example of the need for training to ensure reliable data. The researchers examined the ability of five novice researchers and five expert researchers to read magnetic resonance images (MRIs) and rate the lesions of patients with multiple sclerosis (MS). Lesions are scar tissue in the central nervous system and appear as white spots on the MRI. As you might guess, the interrater agreement for the novice researchers was low compared to the experts (novice $\kappa = .37$ versus expert $\kappa = .65$). After intensive training, the interrater reliability of the novices and experts improved κ (novice $\kappa = .65$ versus expert $\kappa = .74$).

Observing behavior is not easy work. It can be difficult to do well for long uninterrupted periods. Therefore, researchers who do this type of work limit their observation time to short periods or work in shifts with other observers. Altmann (1974) described her experiences observing primate behavior and the difficulty of remaining alert during the observation session. She wrote that, "even with two observers, one 15-minute sample per hour was near the upper limit of our capacity when obtaining an accurate record" (p. 246). The implication of this is that observational sessions should be relatively short (e.g., less than 15 minutes) and punctuated with ample rest.

Fortunately, video cameras make the task of observing behavior easier. Cameras do not get tired or bored, and they record all the behaviors that occur. Furthermore, the researcher has access to a permanent and rich source of information of all behaviors. Therefore, the researcher can review and score the behaviors at his or her convenience and at a pace that is not exhausting.

Another important feature of the video camera is that it is easy to hide. Hiding the video camera helps to ensure that the people being observed act naturally. If you wanted to study bullying behavior among children, using a hidden camera will record the more natural behavior than having an adult researcher obviously watching the children. As you learned in chapter 5, however, there are significant ethical issues that the researcher must confront before conducting this type of research.

Participant Observation Research

A variant of naturalistic observation is participant observer research. There is an important difference between naturalistic observation and participant observation. For the most part, the observer in naturalistic observation is not an immediate part of the ongoing behavior as he or she attempts to record the data unbeknownst to the individuals being observed. By contrast, the participant observer joins the group to study the group's behavior.

Participant observation does allow one to study a group of people, especially if their behavior is covert or underground. This technique is especially popular among anthropologists and sociologists who study small social groups. There are several notable examples of participant observation that psychologists used to their advantage. For example, Robert Cialdini (1984), a social psychologist, wanted to learn more about how salespeople persuade others to buy various products. As Cialdini described it, "when I wanted to learn about the compliance tactics of encyclopedia (or vacuum-cleaner, or portrait-photography, or dance lesson) sales organizations, I would answer a newspaper ad for sales trainees and have them teach me their methods" (p. xiii). Cialdini used what he learned in the field as the basis for his laboratory research on social influence.

The participant observation technique has some serious risks, however. An infamous example is Laud Humphreys's (1970) research for his book *Tearoom Trade*. Humphreys wanted to study the men who engaged in homosexual acts in public places. To study these men, Humphreys began to hang out at public restrooms, known as tearooms among homosexuals, and acted as a lookout while the men had their sexual encounters. He then secretly followed the men to their homes and later interviewed them. Many commentators have criticized Humphreys's tactics because they violated the men's right to privacy. Therefore, conducting participant research cannot be entered into lightly.

Participant research can also be dangerous. The cartoon in Figure 7.2 illustrates the potential risk you run if you attempt to join a group as an imposter. Many groups of people wish to remain closed to outsiders and react poorly to a stranger in their midst. For example, Thompson (1985), studying the Hell's Angels, received a severe beating from the members of the gang he had attempted to join.

"So, you're a *real* gorilla, are you?
Well, guess you wouldn't mind munchin' down
a few beetle grubs, would you? ... In fact,
we wanna see you chug 'em!"

FIGURE 7.2
There is a real risk to conducting participant observer research, especially when members of the group discover that you are not one of them.

RESEARCH IN ACTION: ANALYSIS OF ASSAULTS

Acquaintance rape, or date rape, is an unfortunate experience that too many people encounter. Although this behavior has been examined for many years, Larimer, Lydum, Anderson, and Turner (1999) believed that much of the research was biased against men. Larimer and her colleagues noted that for many of the previous studies, the researchers examined women's experiences exclusively or used sex-biased survey techniques. Therefore, Larimer et al. attempted to document the prevalence of unwanted sexual encounters experienced by men and women and the role that alcohol consumption played in these encounters.

Larimer et al. (1999) asked participants to complete a series of questionnaires that examined the prevalence of unwanted sexual encounters and the use of alcohol. All of the questionnaires were scales developed and published by other researchers. Table 7.11 presents a portion of two of the scales examining unwanted sexual experiences and the relation between alcohol consumption and unwanted sexual encounters. For their first questionnaire, Larimer et al. revised the *Sexual Experiences Survey* (Koss & Oros, 1982) to ensure that questions were not sex-biased.

Larimer et al. (1999) used 296 (165 males, 131 females) students who were new members of fraternities and sororities at a large West Coast public university. The majority of the students were freshmen and sophomores.

Figure 7.3 presents the results for the *Sexual Experiences Survey*. One notable feature of these data is the percentage of men reporting that they had experienced unwanted

TABLE 7.11

Example of questions Larimer et al. (1999) used to examine the prevalence of unwanted sexual encounters and the use of alcohol during unwanted sexual encounters

1. In the past year, have you been in a situation where your partner became so sexually aroused that you felt it was useless to stop them even though you did not want to have sexual intercourse?
2. In the past year, have you had sexual intercourse with someone who didn't really want to because you felt pressured by their continual arguments?
3. In the past year, have you been in a situation where someone used some degree of physical force (twisting your arm, holding you down, etc.) to get you to have sexual intercourse with them when you didn't want to, whether or not intercourse actually occurred?
4. In the past year, have you had someone attempt sexual intercourse with you by giving you alcohol or other drugs, but intercourse did not occur?
5. In the past year, have you had sexual intercourse when you didn't want to because a person gave you alcohol or other drugs?

Items based on the *Sexual Experiences Survey* (Koss & Oros, 1982) as revised by Larimer et al. (1999).

1. Has drinking ever gotten you into sexual situations which you later regretted?
2. Because you had been drinking, have you ever had sex when you really didn't want to?
3. Because you had been drinking, have you ever had sex with someone you wouldn't ordinarily have sex with?
4. Have you ever been pressured or forced to have sex with someone because you were too drunk to prevent it?
5. Have you ever pressured or forced someone to have sex with you after you had been drinking?

Items based on the *Young Adult Alcohol Problem Severity Test* (Wood, Johnson, & Sher, 1992) as presented by Larimer et al. (1999).

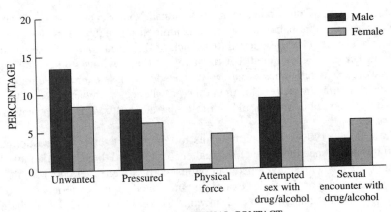

FIGURE 7.3
Percentage of participants reporting various types of unwanted sexual encounters. Graph based on data presented by Larimer et al. (1999).

sexual encounters or had felt pressured into a sexual encounter. Also apparent in the data is that women reported higher percentages of some form of coercion (physical force or alcohol/drug use) to engage in sexual intercourse. These data are important. First, the data support previous research by replicating the finding that women often experience some forms of coercion during an unwanted sexual encounter. Second, the data suggest that men and women experience unwanted sexual encounters. These data are interesting as they conflict with the stereotype that men are perpetrators and women are victims of these situations.

Figure 7.4 presents the percentage of participants who had sexual encounters related to their drinking behavior. The data make clear that nearly half of the men and women in the study later regretted a sexual encounter related to their drinking.

Finally, Figure 7.5 presents the mean number of alcoholic drinks consumed per day during the previous three months. Two interesting trends appear in these data. First, men claim to consume more drinks per day than do women. Second, participants who reported an unwanted sexual encounter appear to drink more than those who had not experienced an unwanted sexual encounter.

The data led Larimer et al. (1999) to conclude that men and women experience unwanted sexual intercourse. Their data also implicate alcohol as a major contributor to sexual victimization of both men and women. Because sexual coercion and unwanted sexual intercourse can have a dramatic impact on one's emotional well-being, it is essential that researchers better understand this phenomenon. As Larimer and her colleagues concluded, "further empirical study of the emotional consequences of these events and the context surrounding them for both genders is warranted" (p. 307).

Before we embrace the data too quickly, we need to examine several features of the study. To their credit, Larimer et al. (1999) recognized and described many of the problems with their research and called for additional and more refined studies. We can begin by examining the population and the sample.

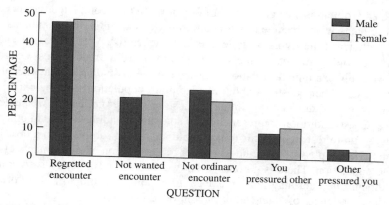

FIGURE 7.4

Percentage of participants reporting various types of unwanted sexual encounters related to drinking. Graph based on data presented by Larimer et al. (1999).

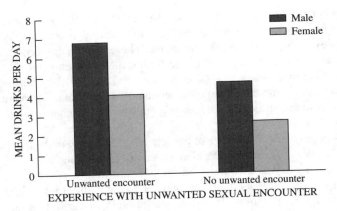

FIGURE 7.5

Mean number of alcoholic drinks consumed per day during last three months for men and women who had or had not experienced an unwanted sexual encounter. Graph based on data presented by Larimer et al. (1999).

The sampling population consisted of students who had joined a Greek-letter society. Although fraternities and sororities are popular on many college campuses, their membership may not be representative of the student population. Greek-letter organizations may be attractive to only a segment of the contemporary college student body. Similarly, the life experiences of students living in a fraternity or sorority may be different than life in a residence hall. For example, most Greek-letter organizations sponsor intensive training programs that sensitize their members to the dangers of alcohol abuse and sexual coercion. Thus, we cannot be sure that life in a fraternity or sorority is representative of the typical college student.

A related problem is the age of the participant when they completed the survey. Most of the participants were freshmen or sophomores. Consequently, these students may not have had sufficient time living at college to experience the types of sexual encounters experienced by older students. If the sample had included a broader cross section of all students, we could examine the relation between the age of student and the risk of assault.

We can raise other questions about the sampling population. Are the experiences of students at large state universities similar to those of smaller colleges? Are students who attend West Coast institutions representative of students attending college in other parts of the country? Future research on this topic should attempt to sample from a broader range of students. The sample would include a greater representation of all segments of the typical college population. There is no reason that we must limit our analysis to college students. Although the data may not be as easy to obtain, it would still be informative to examine the experiences of young adults not enrolled in college.

We can also question whether the sample is sufficiently large. Although 296 participants is a large sample, it may not be sufficiently large to detect small differences between men and women's behavior or events that do not occur frequently. Consequently, those who wish to replicate this study should consider a larger sample size.

Finally, we can ask if the wording of the questions produce the answers we need. For example, do men and women "regret" unwanted sexual relations for the same reasons? Similarly, is the phrase "pressured or forced" as clear as it can be? The phrase seems to require considerable interpretation on the part of the participant.

Larimer et al. (1999) studied an interesting and important topic. Moreover, they reported findings that challenge several preconceived beliefs. Their research also demonstrates that one can examine interesting topics using questionnaire methods. At the same time, this research confirms a theme that recurs throughout this book—no individual study is complete by itself. The Larimer et al. study is one of many studies that examine the relation between date rape and alcohol and will surely not be the last such report.

ACHIEVEMENT CHECK

(12) Why is it necessary to pretest a questionnaire before using it in a research project?

(13) Can a researcher use closed-response questions in a face-to-face interview?

(14) A researcher developed a series of open-ended and closed-response questions. What are three ways the researcher could collect the data? What are the relative advantages and disadvantages of each?

(15) Describe in your words the advantages and disadvantages of open-ended and closed-response questions.

(16) Imagine that you are planning to conduct a survey and need to estimate the number of participants you need to include in your sample. You decide that for most of the questions, $P = .50$ and that $\alpha = .02$. How many participants will you need in the sample if your population consisted of:

    (a) 1,000 people

    (b) 5,000 people

    (c) 25,000 people

    (d) 50,000 people

(17) Dr. Blume has trained observers to use frequency recording to record the behavior of 12 schizophrenic clients. According the analysis of the data $\kappa = .47$, do you think the observers are sufficiently trained to allow Dr. Blume to proceed with the research?

(18) Imagine that you have been hired to assess the content of children's television shows. You are to determine how often the different children's shows depict aggressive acts versus altruistic acts.

    (a) How would go about selecting the children's shows to watch?

    (b) How would you define aggressive acts?

    (c) How would you define altruistic acts?

    (d) Which measurement technique (frequency, duration, or interval recording) would you use and why?

(19) Assume that you used two trained observers to watch the episodes from various children's shows. The observers were to watch a segment, typically 20 to 30 seconds long, and classify the behavior as aggressive, altruistic, or other. The following table presents the data. How well do the raters agree with each other?

	Aggressive	Altruistic	Other
Aggressive	121	13	57
Altruistic	3	67	45
Other	12	10	93

(20) As a researcher, what ethical responsibilities do you have when conducting personal interviews or self-administered questionnaires?

(21) If you were going to use a hidden video camera to record the behavior of a group of people, what ethical issues would you need to resolve?

CHAPTER SUMMARY

All the sciences depend upon objective measurement, and psychology is no exception. Although the primary focus of this chapter was creating and using questionnaires, the concepts reviewed in this chapter apply to any situation wherein the researcher must collect data.

Many people do not understand the uses and limitations of measurement. Two common errors include reification of the measurement and denial of the measurement. Reification is an example of mystique of quantity and occurs when people infer too much meaning from a single measurement. In contrast, some people dismiss many psychological tests believing that the underlying construct cannot be measured. We create psychological tests to help us describe and explain the phenomenon that we are studying.

Creating an appropriate test or measure of the dependent variable depends on the hypothesis we wish to test, the conditions of our research, and the accuracy of various techniques.

Several of the more common ways of collecting information include personal interviews and self-administered surveys. Personal interviews, while time consuming and expensive to conduct, can provide valuable forms of information. By contrast, self-administered surveys are inexpensive and can produce much valuable information.

For much of the chapter, we reviewed techniques to create questions and scales to collect data. The goal of these techniques is to prepare simple and objective questions that the participants will answer honestly.

When we plan any research project, it is important to determine the optimal sample size for the research. Therefore, we reviewed one method for estimating sample size. This technique allows us to predict, and thereby control, the accuracy of the population estimates.

Observational techniques are also common in behavioral research. Two of the more commonly used methods for observational research are frequency recording and duration recording. These research techniques, like the questionnaire, require clear operational definitions of the behavior we wish to observe and attention to the procedures for collecting the data.

Whenever we use a measurement technique, we need to assess its reliability or consistency in measurement. We reviewed how the coefficient kappa, κ, allows us to evaluate the interrater reliability among two or more raters.

In the "Research in Action" section, we examined how researchers used a survey method to evaluate the interrelation between alcohol abuse and date rape. We used this research to illustrate how the researchers selected a series of questionnaires to measure the relevant dependent variables. The example also allowed us to practice a critique of the data.

CHAPTER GLOSSARY FOR REVIEW

Binary Response   A response that has only two answers, such as yes or no.

Closed-Response Question   A question that the participants answer by selecting from among alternative statements provided by the researcher.

Interrater Reliability   A descriptive statistic that indicates the degree to which two or more observers agree on the classification of a behavior or an object.

Mystique of Quantity   An uncritical trust in the meaning and importance of the numbers produced by measurement.

Open-Ended Question   A question that requires the participants to state or write their answer to the question.

Order Effect   The effect of asking a sequence of questions on how the participant answers subsequent questions.

Priming Cue   Questions that cause the participant to think about a topic and to more thoughtfully respond to subsequent questions.

Reification   To treat an abstract construct as if it has material existence independent of the word.

Response Set   Tendency to give the same answer to all questions regardless of the true answer.

8 CORRELATION STATISTICS: THEIR USE AND INTERPRETATION

CHAPTER OUTLINE

*Give a researcher three weapons—correlation, regression, and a pen—
and he or she will use all three.*

—Anonymous

INTRODUCTION

Correlational research allows us to study the relation between two or more variables. Finding a correlation between two variables can help us in many ways. We can use the correlation to make predictions about one variable using another variable. This prediction might help us explain the dependent variable using the independent variable. For instance, a psychologist might use a personality test to predict how someone will respond in specific situations. Similarly, an employer may use an aptitude test to determine whether applicants have the skills necessary to perform a job. As you will learn in this chapter, studying the correlations among variables is a powerful tool for understanding various behavioral phenomena.

In this chapter, we will review several of the more common applications of correlation statistics. We will examine the Pearson product-moment correlation and regression analysis. Although these are not the only statistical tools for analyzing the relation among variables, they are the most frequently used in the behavioral sciences. The primary focus of the chapter will examine how to use and interpret these statistics. The last section of this chapter illustrates how to calculate these statistical tests.

As a brief preview of what you are about to read, you should understand that there is a distinction between correlation research methods and correlational statistics. When we speak of the method, we are describing how we go about gathering the data. The most general account of the correlational method is that the researcher gathers two or more bits of information about participants in the study. In some cases, the researcher may gather the information during one session. For instance, a psychologist may examine the participants' self-esteem and attitudes toward minority groups by asking the participants to complete several questionnaires.

In other situations, the researcher will want to determine if one variable will predict another variable. For this type of study, the researcher will collect data on two or more occasions. As an example, a researcher could administer a math aptitude test to a group of students at the start of the school year. At the end of the school year, the researcher could give the students a math achievement test. The researcher may hope to find that there is a correlation between the aptitude test and the achievement test. Using this information, teachers could use the aptitude test to predict which students may need extra help with math and which students would benefit from a more challenging review of math. In correlation research, the researcher often examines the relation among subject variables and does not necessarily place the participants into different research conditions, as is the case for a true experiment. A researcher uses correlational research to determine whether two or more variables are interrelated.

A researcher can use correlation statistics for any data set regardless of the method of collecting the data. A researcher may conduct a true experiment, a quasi-experiment, or a correlational study and then turn to correlation statistics to examine the relation between the variables. As you will learn throughout this book, there are many ways that the researcher can examine the relation among the many variables examined in a study. In this chapter, we will focus our attention on the **correlation coefficient.**

CONCEPTUAL REVIEW OF CORRELATION

Although there are many ways to determine the correlation between two variables, all correlation coefficients share features. First, the correlation examines two or more sets of measurements taken from the same individual. Second, the correlation coefficient is a descriptive statistic that describes the **linear relation** between two variables. A linear relation refers to a pattern of data best described by a straight line. In addition, correlation coefficients range between −1.0 and +1.0.

Figure 8.1 presents six scatter plots representing correlations that are: $r = +1.0$, $r = .80$, $r = .50$, $r = 0$, $r = -.50$, and $r = -1.0$. As the value of the correlation becomes closer to +1.0 or −1.0, the data are more likely to fall on a straight line. A **positive correlation,** $r > 0$, indicates that *in*creases in one variable correspond to *in*creases in the other variable. A **negative correlation,** $r < 0$, indicates that *in*creases in one variable correspond to *de*creases in the other variable.

Finally, a correlation coefficient, regardless of its size, is not evidence of a cause-and-effect relation. As we reviewed the issue in chapter 3, we cannot infer a causal relation from a correlational research design because we can neither control for the third variable problem nor resolve the temporal order problem (see chapter 3). Thus a correlation between two variables, regardless of the size of the correlation, is not evidence of a cause-and-effect relation.

PEARSON'S r

Carl Pearson created one of the most commonly used correlation coefficients. The full name for the statistic is the Pearson product-moment correlation coefficient, but most researchers refer to it as Pearson's r. We can use the definitional equation, presented in Equation 8.1, to examine how the statistic summarizes the data.

$$r = \frac{\sum z_X z_Y}{N} \tag{8.1}$$

First, we convert each observed score to a z-score and then determine the cross products by multiplying the pairs of z-scores. The sum of the cross products ($\sum z_X z_Y$) divided by the number of pairs (N) is the correlation coefficient. The advantage of using z-scores is that they convert the data to a common scale. The mean and standard deviation of z-scores are always $M = 0$ and $SD = 1.0$ (see the "Statistics Behind the Research" section in chapter 6). Because the z-score converts the data to the same scale, we can examine the correlation between any two variables regardless of their means and standard deviations.

INTERPRETING THE CORRELATION COEFFICIENT

The correlation coefficient is a descriptive statistic that indicates the degree to which changes in one variable correspond with changes in a second variable. As you have already

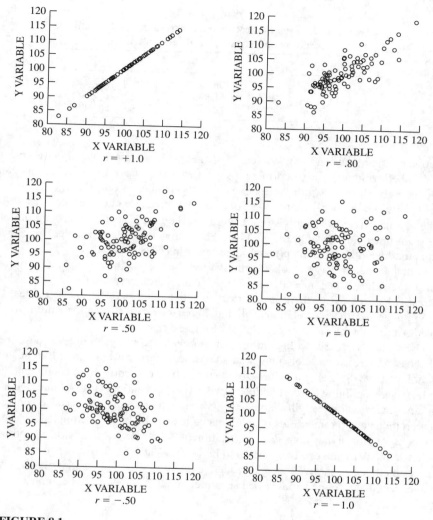

FIGURE 8.1

The scatter plots for six pairs of data where the correlations are: $r = +1.0$, $r = .80$, $r = .50$, $r = 0$, $r = -.50$, and $r = -1.0$.

learned, the correlation coefficient can range between -1.0 and $+1.0$. In this section we will examine how to interpret the size of the correlation coefficient.

Magnitude and Sign of r

There are two important pieces of information contained in the correlation coefficient, its sign and its magnitude. The sign of the coefficient indicates whether there is a positive or a

TABLE 8.1

Ranges of correlation coefficients corresponding to small, medium, and large correlation coefficients

r		r
$-.29 - -.10$	Small	$.10 - .29$
$-.49 - -.30$	Medium	$.30 - .49$
$-1.00 - -.50$	Large	$.50 - 1.00$

negative relation between the variables. Many people misinterpret the sign of the correlation and believe that positive correlations are better than negative correlations. Nothing could be farther from the truth. A negative correlation indicates only that there is an inverse relation between the two variables—as one variable increases the other decreases. An example of a negative correlation is the relation between one's score for a round of golf and time spent practicing. In golf, the goal is to get as low a score as possible. Hence, we can predict that the more a person practices, the lower his or her score.

Perhaps a better way to look at and interpret the correlation coefficient is to examine its absolute value. When $|r| = 0$, there is no linear relation between the two variables.[1] By contrast, when $|r| = 1.0$, there is a perfect linear relation between the variables. Cohen (1988) suggested that correlations fall into three categories, small, medium, or large. Table 8.1 presents the range of correlations for these categories.

Use Cohen's criteria with caution. Cohen developed his guidelines to describe general behavioral research. You may find that researchers working in different areas of psychology have different guidelines for the magnitude of a correlation coefficient. For example, when examining the correlation between two conventional tests of intelligence, you may find that researchers will dismiss any correlation less than .90 because considerable research indicates that measures of intelligence tend to be highly correlated. By contrast, another psychologist may consider a correlation of .40 between a standardized aptitude test and academic performance (e.g., GPA) to be large. Academic performance reflects many factors (intelligence, motivation, and academic major to list a few), and it may be impossible to expect that a single variable will accurately predict something as complex as grades.

Coefficients of Determination and Nondetermination

Another way to examine the correlation coefficient is to square its value. The statistic r^2 is the **coefficient of determination.** The coefficient of determination indicates the proportion of variance shared between the two variables. If, for example, the correlation between two variables is $r = .82$, then $r^2 = .67$, and we can conclude that because of the linear relation between the two variables that 67% of the variability of the Y variable can be predicted or explained by the differences in the X variable.

We can also calculate the **coefficient of nondetermination,** $1 - r^2$. For the current example, $1 - r^2 = .33$. The coefficient of nondetermination is an estimate of the proportion

---

[1]The || symbol converts the value within the lines to a positive number regardless of its original sign. For example, $|-.45| = .45$ and $|.32| = .32$.

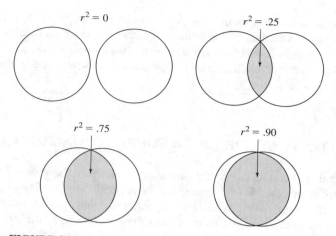

FIGURE 8.2

The coefficient of determination, r^2. Each circle represents a variable, X and Y. The amount of overlap indicates the magnitude of the correlation between the two variables.

of unshared variance between two variables. Thus, when $1 - r^2 = .33$, 33% of the variability of Y cannot be explained by X.

Figure 8.2 presents a conceptual illustration of the meaning of r^2 and $1 - r^2$. Imagine that the circles represent the X and Y variables. When $r = 0$, there is no overlap between the two circles. As the magnitude of the correlation increases, the amount of overlap increases. The overlap of the two circles represents the coefficient of determination between two variables and the unshaded areas represent the coefficient of nondetermination.

Causality

A large correlation coefficient, positive or negative, is not evidence in itself of a cause-and-effect relation. The problem is that when we use the correlation coefficient there is no direct way to resolve the temporal order problem or the third variable problem. Recall from chapter 3 that the temporal order criterion for cause and effect requires the cause to occur before the effect. In much correlational research, we collect the data for the variables at the same time. As an example, a researcher may examine the correlation between levels of anxiety and smoking behavior. To collect the data, the researcher asks the participants to estimate the number of cigarettes they smoke each day and to complete a standard measure of anxiety. Because the researcher collected the data at the same time, we cannot be sure whether the anxiety brings about smoking or if smoking creates anxiety.

The third variable problem refers to a third, and unmeasured variable, that may influence the two measured variables. As an example, a researcher may find that there is a positive correlation between the amount of time a child watches television and his or her aggressiveness with other children. Although we cannot deny the correlation between the two variables, we cannot assume that watching television causes aggressiveness. It is possible that the contributing factor to both variables is the level of parental supervision. Parents who spend little time with their children may allow them to watch more television and may not teach their children to control their aggressive behaviors. By contrast, parents who spend much time with their children may limit television watching and teach their children to cooperate with others.

FACTORS THAT CORRUPT A CORRELATION COEFFICIENT

If you are planning to conduct a correlational study, you need to be aware of several factors that can corrupt the magnitude of r causing it to be artificially high or low. These factors include nonlinearity of the data, truncated range, extreme populations, outliers, and multiple populations. In this section we will examine how these factors affect the size of the correlation coefficient, how to detect their effects in the data, and how to avoid these problems.

Nonlinearity

A primary assumption of the correlation coefficient is that a straight line best represents the relation between the variables. Knowing the correlation coefficient allows us to draw a straight line through the scatter plot that describes the relation between the variables. A **curvilinear relation** means that a curved line best describes the relation between the two variables. Consider Figure 8.3 as an example. Clearly, there is a systematic relation between X and Y, but the relation is far from a straight line. The relation between X and Y in this case is U-shaped. Using Pearson's r, the correlation between the variables is $r = .144$, which suggests a small linear relation between the two variables.

From one perspective, the correlation coefficient is correct; a straight line cannot explain the relation between the variables. However, if we did not draw a scatter plot of the data, we would have assumed that there is a small or trivial relation between the two variables. Looking at Figure 8.3 it appears that there is a strong nonlinear relation between the

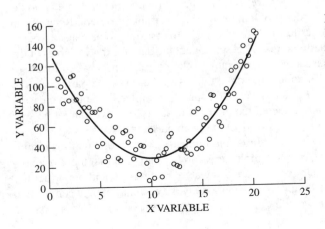

FIGURE 8.3
Data in which a curved line represents the relation between the X and Y variables.

X and *Y* variables. Consequently, we need to use different statistical tools to analyze the data. Fortunately, many computer programs, such as Excel© and SPSS©, can quickly and efficiently perform the mathematics necessary to analyze these data.

Therefore, a nonlinear relation between two variables is not a problem unless you fail to recognize its existence. Finding a curved rather than a linear relation may produce useful insights into the phenomenon that you are studying. That curvilinear relations exist demonstrates that you cannot rush the data through a simple-minded computer analysis. A carefully planned research design implies a careful statistical analysis of the data as well.

Truncated Range

The **truncated range** problem refers to a form of bias created by poor sampling techniques. A representative sample is one where the characteristics of the sample match the parameters of the population. A truncated range occurs when the variance of the sample is much smaller than the variance of the population. Figure 8.4 represents what happens to the correlation coefficient when we have a truncated range.

Assume that the entire scatter plot in Figure 8.4 represents what would happen if you created a true representative sample of the population. For all the data, the correlation is $r = .71$, a strong linear relation. What would happen if your selection procedure created bias and you selected only those people who have scores on the *X* variable of 15 or greater? The smaller x-y axis within the graph represents this biased sample. For those data, the correlation is $r = .10$, a small correlation that does not well represent the true correlation between the variables.

The problem is that the correlation coefficient represents the shared variance of the two variables. If your sampling procedure restricts the variance of the data, then the statistic cannot provide an accurate estimate of the correlation. The solution to this potential problem is to use a good sampling procedure. When you devise your sampling strategy, you will need to ensure that your sample will capture the natural range of potential scores for both variables.

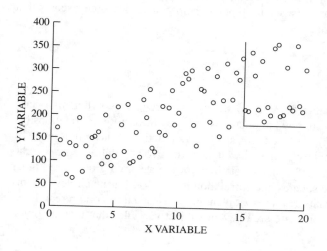

FIGURE 8.4

The effects of truncating the range of scores on the correlation coefficient. The correlation for the entire data set is $r = .71$. However, if the sample included only those scores with values of $X > 15$, as is represented by the smaller graph, the correlation is low, $r = .10$.

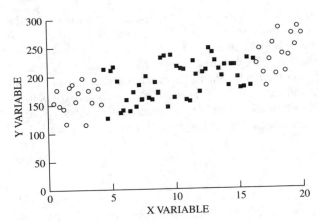

FIGURE 8.5
The consequence of sampling from extreme ends of one variable. The correlation coefficient for the data represented as circles is $r = .83$. However, the correlation for all the data is $r = .69$.

Extreme Populations

Another problem with nonrepresentative sampling is selecting groups that represent extreme ends of the distribution for one variable. Consider Figure 8.5 as an example of this problem. There are two sets of data, one represented by circles and the other by squares. If we examine only the circle data, the correlation is $r = .83$. By contrast, if we examine all the data presented in the scatter plot, the correlation is lower, $r = .69$. As a generality, analyzing data from the extreme ends of the variables tends to inflate the correlation coefficient.

Outliers or Extreme Scores

As with any statistical test, outliers or extreme scores can affect the value of the correlation coefficient. Hence, it is important that you review your data to ensure that you have accurately recorded all the data. Drawing a scatter plot can help you see a score or scores that stand apart from the rest of the data.

Multiple Populations

Another problem that can create artificially high or low correlation coefficients occurs when the sample contains data from two populations that may have different relations between the two variables. In Figure 8.6, there are two populations, one represented by squares and the other represented by circles. If we ignore the two populations, the correlation of the entire data set is $r = .58$. The correlations for the separate groups are higher than the combined data. For the squares, the correlation is $r = .79$; for the circles the correlation is $r = .82$. The important lesson is that planning is essential to good research. As you analyze the data, determine if there are relevant subject variables that may help you better describe the data.

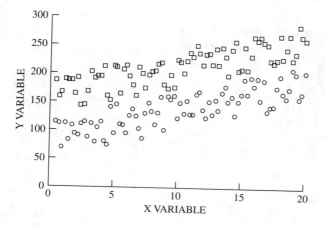

FIGURE 8.6
The effect of having two populations within one data set. The correlation for the entire data is $r = .58$. The correlation for the data represented by circles is $r = .82$. The correlation for the data represented by the squares is $r = .79$.

SAMPLE SIZE AND THE CORRELATION COEFFICIENT

The correlation coefficient is a descriptive statistic. It is also an unbiased estimate of the population parameter, ρ (rho), the correlation between populations. Thus, as we use the sample mean, M, to estimate the population mean, μ, we can use r to estimate ρ. As you learned in chapter 6, the confidence interval about any estimate of a population parameter is a function of the sample size. As sample size increases the confidence interval decreases. Smaller confidence intervals imply that the sample statistic more closely estimates the corresponding population parameter.

Determining the confidence interval for the correlation coefficient is complicated because the sampling distribution for the correlation coefficient is not symmetrical. The skew of the sampling distribution for r increases when it moves toward -1.0 or $+1.0$. A section at the end of this chapter includes the formula for determining the confidence interval for Pearson's r. Although we will not examine those calculations here, we can use them to help guide us in determining the relation between sample size and width of the confidence interval.

Table 8.2 presents the confidence intervals for population correlations ranging between $\rho = .20$ and $\rho = .90$. For each correlation, the table presents the 95% confidence interval for specific sample sizes. We can use an example to illustrate how the table works.

Imagine that you plan to conduct a study to examine the correlation between two variables and believe that the correlation will be moderate, say $\rho = .40$. According to Table 8.2, if you collect data from 50 participants, you would predict that 95% of the sample correlations would range between $r = .14$ and $r = .61$, a wide range of values. What would happen if you increased your sample size? As you would expect, the width of the 95% confidence interval will decrease. Using 450 participants, for example, the 95% confidence interval is $r = .32$ to $r = .47$. Samples larger than 450 produce marginal reductions in the width of the confidence interval. If you could reasonably expect to have a higher population correlation, then you may not require as many participants to estimate accurately the correlation coefficient.

TABLE 8.2
**The estimated 95% confidence interval for correlation coefficients
and sample size of different sizes**

N	$\rho = .2$ $r_{low}-r_{high}$	$\rho = .4$ $r_{low}-r_{high}$	$\rho = .6$ $r_{low}-r_{high}$	$\rho = .8$ $r_{low}-r_{high}$	$\rho = .9$ $r_{low}-r_{high}$
50	−.08–.45	.14–.61	.39–.75	.67–.88	.83–.94
100	.00–.38	.22–.55	.46–.71	.72–.86	.85–.93
150	.04–.35	.26–.53	.49–.69	.73–.85	.86–.93
200	.06–.33	.28–.51	.50–.68	.74–.84	.87–.92
250	.08–.32	.29–.50	.51–.67	.75–.84	.87–.92
300	.09–.31	.30–.49	.52–.67	.76–.84	.88–.92
350	.10–.30	.31–.48	.53–.66	.76–.83	.88–.92
400	.10–.29	.31–.48	.53–.66	.76–.83	.88–.92
450	.11–.29	.32–.47	.54–.66	.76–.83	.88–.92
500	.11–.28	.32–.47	.54–.65	.77–.83	.88–.92
600	.12–.28	.33–.47	.55–.65	.77–.83	.88–.91
700	.13–.27	.34–.46	.55–.65	.77–.83	.88–.91
800	.13–.27	.34–.46	.55–.64	.77–.82	.89–.91
900	.14–.26	.34–.45	.56–.64	.78–.82	.89–.91
1000	.14–.26	.35–.45	.56–.64	.78–.82	.89–.91
2000	.16–.24	.36–.44	.57–.63	.78–.82	.89–.91

Note: The sampling distribution of the correlation coefficient is not symmetrical, especially when the sample size is small. Therefore, the confidence intervals will not be symmetrical around ρ.

ACHIEVEMENT CHECK

(1) Explain in your words how we can examine the correlation between two variables even when the means and standard deviations of the two variables are radically different.

(2) Why does a correlation of −.75 represent a stronger relation between two variables than a correlation of +.60?

(3) An instructor distributes a questionnaire to students asking them to estimate the number of hours they study each week and their current GPA. According to the data, the correlation between the two variables is +.93. Can we use these data to show students that studying causes improved grades?

(4) Paula conducted a correlational study using 100 pairs of scores and found that $r = .10$. This correlation is far less than she expected. Describe in your words what could have caused this small correlation.

(5) Devin is the director of admission of a prestigious liberal arts college. He has learned that there is a new aptitude test designed to predict students' college academic performance. To test the value of the new test, he plans to randomly select 500 students currently enrolled at the college and pay them to take the test. He will then examine the correlation between the students' test scores and their current GPA. Do you believe that Devin has created a research design that will allow him to evaluate the correlation between test scores and academic performance?

APPLICATIONS OF THE CORRELATION COEFFICIENT

Like most statistical tests, the correlation coefficient has many applications. In the following sections, we will see how we can use the correlation coefficient to examine the reliability and validity of tests and other measures that we create.

Using Correlation to Determine Reliability

In the previous chapter, you learned how to use coefficient kappa (κ) to determine the interrater reliability for nominal and ordinal scales. As you might guess, we can use Pearson's r to determine the reliability of a test that uses an interval or ratio scale. The comparison between κ and r is straightforward; the closer the statistic is to 1.0, the greater the reliability of the test or measurement device. In this section we will examine the many ways that we can use the correlation coefficient to examine the reliability of a test.

Test-Retest Reliability

One of the most common measures of reliability is test-retest reliability. To determine test-retest reliability, the researcher will administer the same test, or similar versions of the test, on two occasions. The correlation coefficient between the two scores indicates the stability of the measure over time. We can use the test-retest reliability to determine the degree to which random events that we do not want to measure affect the test scores. If the test-retest reliability is 0, we must conclude that the test scores are not stable over time and are subject to considerable fluctuation. By contrast, if the test-retest reliability is 1.0, we can conclude that the test measures the construct consistently and is unaffected by random events.

Interrater Reliability

In the previous chapter I showed you how to use coefficient κ to determine interrater reliability when there are two or more observers and they are using either a nominal or an ordinal scale. In this section we will see how we can use the correlation coefficient to calculate the interrater reliability among observers if the measurement scale is interval or ratio. For interrater reliability, the pairs of scores represent the scores given by the two observers. Specifically, X_1 would represent the score assigned by the first rater, and X_2 would represent the score assigned by the second rater. As with Cohen's κ, the larger the correlation coefficient the greater the interrater agreement. If the interrater reliability is sufficiently large, then you can average the ratings of the two reviewers as the final observation.

Split-Half Reliability

The split-half reliability of a test is similar to the interrater reliability. The only difference is that we are looking at the correlation among items or measurements within a test rather than the correlation between observers' ratings. The goal of split-half reliability is to assess the test's **internal consistency.** Internal consistency, like interrater reliability, refers to the degree to which items in a test agree with one another. If a test has high internal consistency, then each test item produces the same or similar score for each person taking the test. Remember that internal consistency refers to how items in a test correlate among each other not to the variability among test scores. For our purposes, internal consistency is a way of determining the reliability of a test. If the internal consistency is low, then the test may not be measuring the variable we want to measure. Therefore, researchers strive to ensure high levels of internal consistency.

A common measure of internal consistency is Cronbach's (1951) **coefficient alpha, r_α.** This statistic is a special type of correlation coefficient that represents the correlation among all the items in the test. In other words, r_α is another way to determine interrater agreement, specifically, the level of agreement among questions or items in a test. Coefficient alpha can range from 0, which represents no internal consistency, to 1.00, which represents perfect agreement among all the items in the test. The "Statistics Behind the Research" section at the end of this chapter shows how to calculate this statistic.

For our purposes, the primary concern is how we should interpret coefficient alpha. Unfortunately, many people misinterpret the meaning of r_α (Cortina, 1993; Schmitt, 1996). Some people make the mistake and assume that a large value of r_α means that all the questions measure the same construct. This interpretation is not correct, as Cortina and Schmitt have demonstrated. Thus, you should be careful when you read about or use r_α. Keep your interpretation of r_α straight; it indicates the extent to which items within a test, or a part of a test, correlate with each other—nothing more, nothing less.

Improving Test Reliability

There are several things that you can do to improve the reliability of a test or measurement technique. One of the more simple methods is to increase the number of items or measurements. All other things being equal, the longer the test or the more times you measure something, the more reliable the score. Imagine that a researcher wants to time how long it takes people to solve an anagram. During a preliminary experiment, the researcher asks participants to solve two anagrams (i.e., convert "rdow" and "kcab" to "word" and "back"). The researcher timed how long it took each participant to solve each anagram. Using these data, the researcher then determined the internal consistency of the measure by calculating the correlation coefficient between times required to solve the two anagrams. According to the results, the internal consistency is $r = .5$. The researcher can use the Spearman-Brown formula presented in Equation 8.2 to estimate the increase in reliability that will occur if he or she used more anagrams.

$$r' = \frac{P(r)}{1 + (P - 1)r} \tag{8.2}$$

In this equation, r is the original measure of internal consistency and r' is the estimated internal consistency for a test with more items or measurements. The P in the equation represents the number of times the test is lengthened or shortened. For example, if $P = 2$, then the test will be twice as long. When $P = 0.50$, the test length is cut in half. What would happen if the researcher decided to require the participants to solve 10 rather than 2 anagrams? In this case, $P = 5$ because the new measure will have five times the number of measurements. According to Equation 8.2,

$$r' = \frac{5(.50)}{1 + (5 - 1).50} \qquad r' = \frac{2.5}{1 + (4).50} \qquad r' = \frac{2.5}{3} \qquad r' = .83$$

Collecting more data from each participant will increase the reliability of the measure. The average of 10 measurements will be more reliable than the average of 2 measurements. Therefore, the researcher can use the average time to solve 10 anagrams as the dependent variable for the study.

Collecting more data comes at a cost. In some cases, doubling the length of a test may not be practical. For example, converting a 20-item test to a 40-item test may make the test boring and tedious. Consequently, participants may want to rush through the test, not taking the time to answer each question accurately or honestly. In this case, you will need to consider finding a more reliable test or include more participants in your study.

You can also increase reliability by using more accurate and sensitive measurement techniques. For example, if you are measuring the time it takes participants to complete a task, you will find that using a stopwatch that is accurate to within 1/100 second is more reliable than a watch that is accurate to within one second. Increases in precision correspond to increases in reliability. The invention of the personal computer has also helped researchers increase the accuracy and reliability of their measurement techniques. Researchers can program the computer to control the experiment and collect the data. The speed and consistency of the computer often allows the researcher to improve the reliability of the data collection procedures.

Using the Correlation to Determine Validity

Reliability is a necessary but not sufficient requirement for validity. To determine that a test is valid, we need data that demonstrates that the test measures what we intended it to measure. We can turn to the correlation coefficient as one way to demonstrate the validity of a test. To demonstrate validity, we would want to show that the test scores correlate well with some measures and do not correlate with other measures.

Imagine that a psychologist wants to develop a new test of depression. The advantage of such a test is that it is faster and less expensive than an assessment interview conducted by a psychologist or psychiatrist. To test the validity of the instrument, the researcher could first administer the new test to a large group of people. A clinical psychologist or psychiatrist would then independently evaluate these individuals. If the test is valid, the test scores for depression should correlate with a professional's rating of the person's emotional state. At the same time, we would expect that the depression test scores do not correlate with the presence of other mental health conditions.

Researchers hope to show that their tests show evidence of convergent and discriminant validity (Campbell & Fiske, 1959). A high correlation between two measures of the *same* construct is evidence of **convergent validity.** A low correlation between two measures of *different* constructs is evidence for **discriminant validity.**

Figure 8.7 illustrates an example of convergent validity and discriminant validity. For convergent validity, we would expect large correlations between the new test of depression and other tests of depression. By contrast, the new test of depression should not correlate with schizophrenia or anxiety as these are different psychiatric conditions. Evidence of convergent validity and discriminant validity indicates that the instrument measures what the author of the test intended the test to measure.

Another component of validity assessment is **criterion validity.** For criterion validity, we hope to show that there is a correlation between the test score and some important characteristic of the person. Specifically, researchers use criterion validity to demonstrate that one can use a test to make predictions about a person's behavior. Two forms of criterion validity are **concurrent validity** and **predictive validity.** Concurrent validity means that we

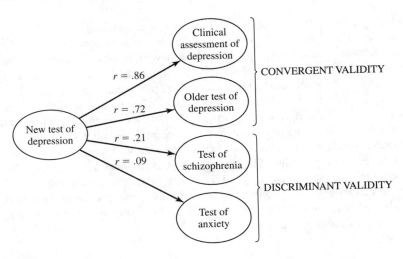

FIGURE 8.7
Convergent validity and discriminant validity. For convergent validity, we
would expect the test to correlate highly with other measures of the same
construct. Discriminant validity indicates that the test does not correlate well
with measures of other constructs. Convergent validity and discriminant
validity is evidence that the test measures the identified construct and not other
constructs.

can use the test to predict some condition within the person that currently exists. Predictive
validity means that we can use the test to predict the person's behavior.

As an example, a math achievement test should be able to measure a student's current
skills at mathematics. Large correlations between the test score and current math grades,
for example, would be evidence of concurrent validity for the math achievement test. By
contrast, an aptitude test attempts to predict whether a person will be successful at a specific task. To determine the predictive validity of an art aptitude test, we may administer the
test to students to determine whether scores on the test predict success in an art class.

The utility of a test determines its validity. Utility refers to the extent to which the
test produces useful information that allows us to understand a specific behavior. The implication of this definition is that the use and interpretation of a test determines its validity.
The interpretation of test results may be valid in one situation and not valid in another.
Therefore, the validity of a test is much like the internal and external validity of a research
project. Validity is not a characteristic inherent in the test scores or the data; validity is a
characteristic of the interpretations we draw from the data. You can find comprehensive reviews of this issue in the work of Cronbach (1988) and Messick (1980, 1988, 1989).

REGRESSION ANALYSIS

The correlation coefficient, whether it is positive or negative, indicates the presence of a
linear relation between the two variables. We can use this relation to make predictions
about one variable using the other. For example, in general, the longer you stay in school,

the higher your annual income. As you will soon see, we can use the correlation coefficient to convert general statements like this into a specific mathematical equation. This equation defines a straight line that best describes the linear relation between the two variables. Using this equation, we can then make specific empirical predictions.

Whenever we have two variables, X and Y, we can use Equation 8.3 to define a straight line.

$$Y' = a + b(X) \qquad (8.3)$$

In this equation, X represents the variable that we want to use to predict levels of Y. In regression analysis, we use Y' (pronounced "Y-prime") or $\hat{Y}$ (pronounced "Y-hat") to represent the predicted scores along the regression line. Do not confuse Y' and Y; Y represents the original scores and Y' represents the scores predicted by the regression equation. In most cases, Y and Y' will not be the same. The other components of the equation, a and b, are constants that define the line. Specifically, a is the **intercept** and b is the **slope** of the line. The intercept (a) represents the value of Y' when $X = 0$. The slope of the line indicates how much Y' changes as X changes. Equation 8.4 represents a conceptual formula for determining the slope in a line. b represents a ratio of the changes in Y that correspond with changes in X.

Figure 8.8 will help you see how we use Equation 8.4 to create a straight line in a simple graph. Figure 8.8 is a graph with four regression lines. For each graph, the intercept is 50, but the slopes are different. We can describe the slope as

$$b = \frac{\text{Change in } Y}{\text{Change in } X} \qquad (8.4)$$

For example, when $b = 5$, for every one-point increase in X there is a five-point increase in Y. By contrast, when the slope is $b = -5$ every increase in X corresponds to a five-point decrease in Y. When the slope is 0, the line is horizontal; there are no changes in Y that correspond with changes in X.

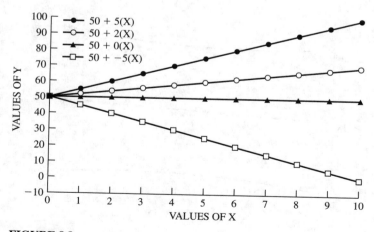

FIGURE 8.8

Four regression lines with the same intercept ($a = 50$) and different slopes: $b = 5$, $b = 2$, $b = 0$, and $b = -5$.

Characteristics of a Regression Line

The regression line has several important features we need to review. First, the regression line shares much in common with the arithmetic mean. One property of the mean is that the sum of the differences between the mean and each score in the sample is always 0. Specifically, $\sum(X - M) = 0$. The mean represents the balance point of the small and large scores in the sample. The regression line does the same thing; it represents the smallest total distance between the regression line and each value of Y. The sum of the differences between each value of Y and its predicted value, Y', is always 0; that is, $\sum(Y - Y') = 0$. The regression line represents a special type of average. Consequently, many people also call the regression line the line of best fit.

Interpreting the Regression Equation

Unless there is a perfect correlation between the two variables, the regression line represents only an estimate of the values of Y. Therefore, we need a statistic that will indicate the accuracy of Y'. As you may recall, the standard deviation is a descriptive statistic that allows us to describe how far scores typically differ from the mean. We can do the same thing for Y' using a statistic called the **standard error of estimate.** The standard error of estimate is the standard deviation of scores around the regression line. Using the standard error of estimate, we can then determine the confidence interval for Y'. This confidence interval is similar to the one reviewed in chapter 6 in that it allows us to estimate the range of potential scores for a specific value of Y'. The section at the end of the chapter shows how to calculate the standard error of estimate for Y'.

Figure 8.9 presents the original scores, the regression line, and the 95% confidence interval about the regression line. The figure makes clear that values of X much less than or much greater than M_X create a broader confidence interval than values of X close to M_X.

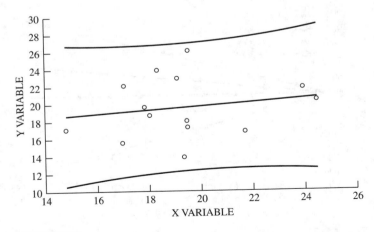

FIGURE 8.9
A scatter plot of the correlation between two variables. The line in the center of the data represents the regression line. The outer curved lines represent the upper and lower limits for the 95% confidence interval.

REGRESSION TO THE MEAN

In chapter 3 I told you that regression to the mean is a potential threat to the internal validity of a study. You may also recall a promise to explain the phenomenon in this chapter. I saved the explanation of the regression toward the mean phenomenon because of its relation to measurement of constructs and the reliability of our measurements.

Sir Francis Galton (1889) first recognized the regression toward the mean phenomenon when he was studying various inherited traits such as height. Galton noted that tall parents tend to have taller than average children, but not as tall as the parents. Similarly, the children of short parents tend to be taller than their parents, but shorter than average.

We can summarize the regression toward the mean phenomenon with a few simple generalizations. When the correlation is less than 1.0, the relative difference between X and its mean [e.g., $(X - M_X)$] will be greater than the difference between the predicted score, Y', and the mean of Y [e.g., $(Y' - M_Y)$]. Consider the example of heights of parents and the heights of their children. The expression $(X - M_X)$ represents the difference between the parents' height and the average heights of parents. The expression $(Y' - M_Y)$ represents the difference between the children's height and the average height of the other children. What Galton observed was that exceptionally tall or short parents tended to have taller or shorter than average children, but that the children tended to be closer to the average height than their parents.

Mathematically, regression toward the mean states that $|(X - M_X)| > |(Y' - M_Y)|$. In addition, the amount of regression toward the mean effect increases as the difference between X and M_X increases. Finally, the regression toward the mean phenomenon is greatest when $r = 0$ and absent when $r = 1.0$. Stated from a different perspective, as the correlation between X and Y moves closer to 0, predicted values of Y' are closer to M_Y. When $r = 0$, all predicted scores equal the mean of the Y variable. Specifically $Y' = M_Y$.

Figure 8.10 presents an illustration of regression toward the mean. The scatter plot represents a correlation of $r = .50$. The regression line for these data is $Y' = 45.0 + .55(X)$. The other line in the graph represents the regression line had the correlation been $r = 1.0$. The shaded area between the two regression lines represents regression

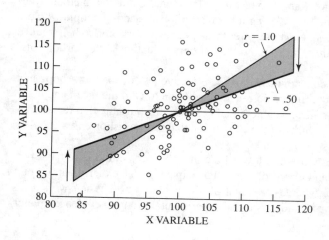

FIGURE 8.10
Regression toward the mean. The scatter plot represents $r = .50$. The bold line represents the regression line for the data. The other line represents the regression line had the correlation been $r = 1.0$. The shaded area represents the regression toward the mean. According to the regression toward the mean phenomenon, $|Y' - Y|$ is less than $|X - M_X|$.

TABLE 8.3
An example of regression to the mean

| High scores for Test 1 | | | Low scores for Test 1 | | |
Test 1	Test 2	$T_2 - T_1$	Test 1	Test 2	$T_2 - T_1$
95	33	−62	21	15	−6
95	92	−3	21	48	27
94	27	−67	21	17	−4
91	42	−49	18	3	−15
89	21	−68	16	23	7
87	81	−6	13	21	8
84	91	7	12	98	86
80	8	−72	10	49	39
79	20	−59	5	81	76
78	26	−52	4	94	90
M 87.2	44.1	−43.1	14.1	44.9	30.8

toward the mean. The arrows at either end of the regression lines indicate the direction of the regression. This graph clearly shows that a value of X above or below M_X predicts scores of Y' relatively closer to M_Y when $r = .50$. When $r = 0$, then all values of Y' equal the mean of Y.

Here is another example of regression toward the mean. I generated two pairs of 50 random numbers ranging between 0 and 100. Think of these pairs of numbers as if they were scores on two psychology exams that I gave, one on Monday and the other on Friday. The first set of numbers represents Test 1; the second set represents scores for Test 2. Table 8.3 presents the highest 10 and the lowest 10 scores for Test 1. Next to each Test 1 score is the score for Test 2. The regression to the mean effect is dramatic. Almost every high score on Test 1 has a lower Test 2 score. Similarly, almost every low Test 1 score has a higher Test 2 score. There is a clear regression to the mean. The amount of regression toward the mean is large in this example because I used random numbers where the correlation between the two variables is $r = 0$.

This example of regression toward the mean has practical applications for designing research projects. Imagine that we wanted to test the effectiveness of a new method to reduce people's fear of public speaking. We begin the research by selecting people who are extremely anxious giving a speech. Next, we offer these people a workshop to help reduce their anxiety. After completing the workshop, we repeat our evaluation of the participants' anxiety while giving a speech.

Is a large drop in anxiety scores evidence of the effectiveness of the workshop? Not necessarily. The drop in anxiety scores could reflect regression toward the mean and nothing more. Regression toward the mean is a potential confounding variable that raises serious questions about the internal validity of the conclusion that the workshop eases people's fear of public speaking.

How would we control for regression toward the mean? One method is to have two groups, an experimental group and a control group. Participants in the experimental group would complete the workshop, whereas the control group would not. When we subsequently evaluate both groups, we would expect the experimental group to evidence greater improvement than the control group. According to the regression toward the mean effect, participants in both groups should show some improvement. If the public speaking workshop is truly effective, then the participants in the experimental group should evidence greater average improvement.

RESEARCH IN ACTION: SEARCHING SHORT-TERM MEMORY

During the mid- to late-1960s, Saul Sternberg (1966) conducted a series of revolutionary experiments that examined how short-term memory works. You probably learned in your introductory psychology course that short-term memory can hold approximately 7 ± 2 chunks of information. Once we have information in short-term memory, how do we use the information? Sternberg wanted to know how we search through information stored in short-term memory. As an example, what are the last two digits of your social security number? How did you come to the answer? Did you automatically recall the last two numbers, or did you have to recite the entire number until you came to the end?

To answer these questions, Sternberg (1966) conducted an experiment. Figure 8.11 presents the sequence of events for the experiment. For each trial, Sternberg presented his participants a set of randomly selected letters to memorize. The number of letters ranged between 1 and 6 and changed on each trial. After the participants had sufficient time to study the letters, Sternberg presented a single letter and asked the participants to indicate whether the probe letter belonged in the just memorized set of letters. For a random half of the trials, the probe letter was a letter contained in the memorized set; for the other trials, the probe letter was not in the set.

Sternberg (1966) timed how long it took participants to determine whether the probe letter belonged in the memorized set. Because these mental processes are fast, Sternberg measured the reaction time in milliseconds (1 millisecond = .001 of a second). This experiment allowed Sternberg to determine whether the size of the memorized set affected the time to answer the question. To ensure high reliability in the data, Sternberg tested each participant many times in each condition and then calculated the average response across all participants.

Before we look at the results that Sternberg obtained, we should review several of the potential outcomes for the experiment. Figure 8.12 presents three potential outcomes, each representing a different type of search strategy for short-term memory.

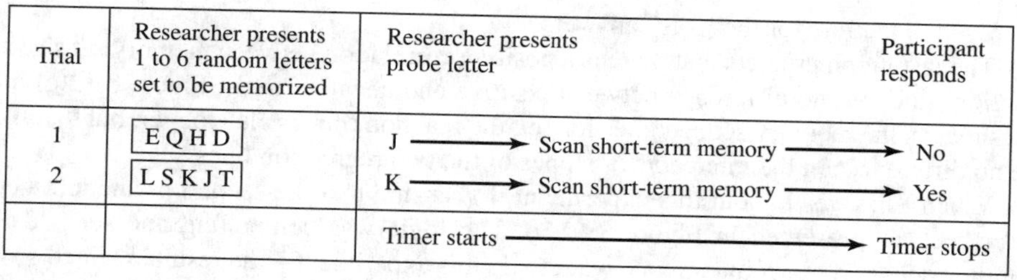

Trial	Researcher presents 1 to 6 random letters set to be memorized	Researcher presents probe letter	Participant responds
1	E Q H D	J ——→ Scan short-term memory ——→ No	
2	L S K J T	K ——→ Scan short-term memory ——→ Yes	
		Timer starts ————————————→ Timer stops	

FIGURE 8.11
Sequence of events Sternberg (1966) used to study short-term memory.

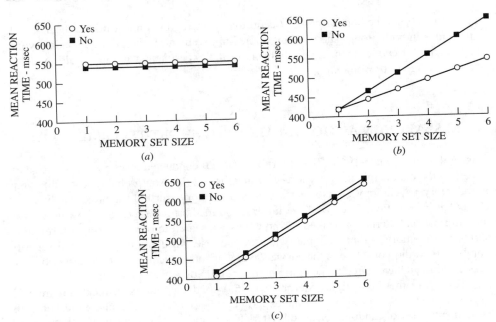

FIGURE 8.12

Potential outcomes for Sternberg's (1966) experiment.

The first potential pattern represents a parallel search, represented by Figure 8.12(a). There is no correlation between the size of the memory set and the reaction time. According to this hypothesis, we search through short-term memory at the same rate regardless of the size of the memory set. Because there is no correlation between the two variables, the regression lines are flat.

The next graph predicts that there is a positive correlation between the size of the memory set and the reaction time. An additional prediction is that the search is longer when the probe letter is not a member of the memory set. The logic of this prediction is that one must compare each letter of the memory set with the probe letter. For the negative trials, the person must search through the entire set before saying "No." By contrast, the person can say "Yes" as soon as the probe letter matches a letter in the memory set and stop the search. As Figure 8.12(b) shows, the slope of the regression line for the "No" answers is steeper than the line for the "Yes" answers.

The last graph predicts that there is a positive correlation between memory set size and reaction time, but no difference between positive and negative trials. Figure 8.12(c) indicates that as the memory set becomes longer, the reaction time is also longer, but that there are no differences in the intercepts or slopes of the two regression lines.

When I first read about this experiment, I was sure that the second prediction would be correct, as presented in Figure 8.12(b). The logic was compelling and seemed like common sense. Why would anyone want to do this experiment—the results seemed so obvious? Fortunately, Sternberg was not lulled into trusting what seemed to be an obvious answer.

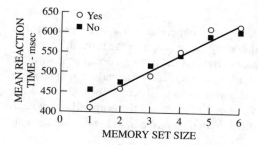

FIGURE 8.13
Results produced by Sternberg's (1966) experiment on the time required to search short-term memory.

Figure 8.13 presents an example of the data that Sternberg's experiment generated. There are two important features of these data. First, as the size of the memory set increases, the reaction time also increases. Second, the pattern for "Yes" trials and "No" trials is the same. Both sets of data appear to follow the same linear trend. The results did not confirm what seemed to be the obvious and common sense outcome. Instead, the data confirmed the exhaustive serial search strategy. Even more impressive is that other researchers replicated the results using different tasks and populations (Searleman & Hermann, 1994).

There are lessons we can take from this example. First, do not trust common sense explanations of the data without empirical verification. The data, not our beliefs, should guide our understanding of psychological processes. Second, we can use the concept of correlation and regression analysis in many different research applications.

STATISTICS BEHIND THE RESEARCH

In this section we will examine the statistical procedures reviewed in this chapter. We will examine Pearson's product-moment correlation coefficient, regression analysis, the standard error of estimate, the confidence interval of r, and coefficient alpha. In addition, I will introduce you to the Spearman rank-order correlation coefficient. Spearman's correlation is a useful alternative to Pearson's coefficient when an interval or ratio scale does not represent the data.

Pearson Product-Moment Correlation Coefficient

This section provides a quick review of the calculation formula for the correlation coefficient. Although Equation 8.1 presented the definitional equation for r, it can be tedious to use. Therefore, if you must calculate the correlation manually, you should use the following equation.

$$r = \frac{\sum XY - \frac{(\sum X)(\sum Y)}{N}}{\sqrt{\left(\sum X^2 - \frac{(\sum X)^2}{N}\right)\left(\sum Y^2 - \frac{(\sum Y)^2}{N}\right)}} \tag{8.5}$$

Worked example

Assume that a student repeated Sternberg's (1966) experiment. Table 8.4 presents the data the student collected. The dependent variable represents the average time, measured to the nearest $1/100^{th}$ of a second, the participants required to make a correct response for each condition. For example, it took participants, on average, 0.41 seconds to indicate that the probe letter was in the set. The student chose to multiply all scores by 100 to remove the decimal points. We will use the data in Table 8.4 to calculate the correlation between memory set and reaction time for both conditions. As you can see in Table 8.5 the correlation between the variables is $r = .97$.

TABLE 8.4
Data replicating Sternberg's (1966) experiment

	Memory set size X	X^2	Reaction time Y	Y^2	XY
Probe letter in set	1	1	41	1681	41
	2	4	45	2025	90
	3	9	49	2401	147
	4	16	56	3136	224
	5	25	62	3844	310
	6	36	62	3844	372
Probe letter not in set	1	1	45	2025	45
	2	4	46	2116	92
	3	9	51	2601	153
	4	16	55	3025	220
	5	25	60	3600	300
	6	36	61	3721	366

$\sum X = 42 \qquad \sum X^2 = 182 \qquad \sum Y = 633 \qquad \sum Y^2 = 34{,}019 \qquad \sum XY = 2{,}360$

$M_X = 3.5 \qquad\qquad\qquad\qquad\qquad M_Y = 52.75$

$s_X = 1.7078 \qquad\qquad\qquad\qquad\quad s_Y = 7.2356$

TABLE 8.5
Worked example of Pearson's correlation coefficient

$$r = \frac{\sum XY - \frac{(\sum X)(\sum Y)}{N}}{\sqrt{\left(\sum X^2 - \frac{(\sum X)^2}{N}\right)\left(\sum Y^2 - \frac{(\sum Y)^2}{N}\right)}}$$

For this equation, XY represents the cross product for each pair of scores—N represents the number of score pairs.

$$r = \frac{2360 - \frac{(42)(633)}{12}}{\sqrt{\left(182 - \frac{(42)^2}{12}\right)\left(34019 - \frac{(633)^2}{12}\right)}}$$

$$r = \frac{2360 - 2215.5}{\sqrt{(182 - 147)(34019 - 33390.75)}}$$

$$r = \frac{144.5}{\sqrt{(35)(628.25)}}$$

$$r = \frac{144.5}{148.2860}$$

$$r = .9745$$

Additional Tests

Once you calculate the correlation coefficient, there are additional tests that you can conduct. For this chapter we will examine the confidence interval of r and regression analysis.

Confidence interval of r

This statistic allows one to determine the confidence interval for the correlation coefficient r. For this example, we will assume that,

$$95\% \text{ confidence interval:} \quad r = .97, \quad N = 12, \quad \alpha = .05$$

Step 1: Convert r to a z-score using Table A.8 of Appendix A. For this example, Table A.8 indicates that when $r = .97$,

$$z_r = 2.092$$

Step 2: Determine the lower and upper bounds of the confidence interval using the equations,

$$z_L = z_r - \frac{z_{(1-\alpha)/2}}{\sqrt{n-3}} \qquad z_U = z_r + \frac{z_{(1-\alpha)/2}}{\sqrt{n-3}}$$

$z_{(1-\alpha)/2}$ represents the z-score associated with the confidence interval you wish to create, and z_L and z_U represent the lower and upper bounds of the confidence interval. For the 95% confidence $\alpha = .05$, therefore, $z_{(1-\alpha)/2} = 1.96$

$$z_L = 2.092 - \frac{1.96}{\sqrt{12-3}} \qquad z_U = 2.092 + \frac{1.96}{\sqrt{12-3}}$$

$$z_L = 1.4387 \qquad\qquad z_U = 2.7453$$

Step 3: Determine the upper and lower bounds of the confidence interval using the equations,

$$r_L = \frac{e^{2 \times z_L} - 1}{e^{2 \times z_L} + 1} \qquad r_U = \frac{e^{2 \times z_U} - 1}{e^{2 \times z_U} + 1}$$

For these equations, e is the constant 2.71828

$$r_L = \frac{2.71828^{2 \times 1.4387} - 1}{2.71828^{2 \times 1.4387} + 1} \qquad r_U = \frac{2.71828^{2 \times 2.7453} - 1}{2.71828^{2 \times 2.7453} + 1}$$

$$r_L = \frac{2.71828^{2.8774} - 1}{2.71828^{2.8774} + 1} \qquad r_U = \frac{2.71828^{5.4906} - 1}{2.71828^{5.4906} + 1}$$

$$r_L = \frac{17.7680 - 1}{17.7680 + 1} \qquad r_U = \frac{242.4017 - 1}{242.4017 + 1}$$

$$r_L = .89 \qquad\qquad r_U = .99$$

Therefore, the student concludes that the 95% confidence interval for the correlation coefficient is .89–.97–.99.

Regression analysis

Upon calculating the correlation coefficient, one can determine the equation that defines the linear relation between X and Y. The linear equation has an intercept (a_Y) and a slope (b_Y).

Slope:

$$b_Y = r \left(\frac{s_Y}{s_X} \right) \tag{8.6}$$

Intercept:

$$a_Y = M_Y - b_Y (M_X) \tag{8.7}$$

Regression equation:

$$Y' = a_Y + b_Y (X) \tag{8.8}$$

EXAMPLE

$$r = .97, \quad M_X = 3.5, \quad M_Y = 52.75, \quad s_X = 1.7078, \quad s_Y = 7.2356$$

Step 1: Calculate the slope.

$$b_Y = r \left(\frac{s_Y}{s_X} \right) \qquad b_Y = .97 \left(\frac{7.2356}{1.7078} \right) \qquad b_Y = .97(4.2368)$$

$$b_Y = 4.1097$$

Step 2: Calculate the intercept.

$$a_Y = M_Y - b_Y (M_X) \qquad a_Y = 52.75 - 4.1097(3.5) \qquad a_Y = 52.75 - 14.3840$$

$$a_Y = 38.366$$

Step 3: Using the results of Steps 1 and 2, create the regression equation.

$$Y' = a_Y + b_Y (X)$$
$$Y' = 38.366 + 4.1097(X)$$

We can use this equation to create a series of predicted scores. Table 8.6 presents the predicted reaction time scores using the regression equation.

TABLE 8.6
Predicted reaction time scores using the data presented in Table 8.4 and the regression equation, $Y' = 38.366 + 4.1097(X)$

X	$Y' = 38.366 + 4.1097(X)$
1	42.4757
2	46.5854
3	50.6951
4	54.8048
5	58.9145
6	63.0242

Standard error of estimate

The regression line is an estimate of probable values of Y given X. The accuracy of the prediction depends upon the value of the correlation between the two variables. In addition, the variances of the two variables affect the range of potential scores for the estimate. The standard error of estimate allows us to predict the range of potential scores given the regression equation.

$$Y_T = Y' \pm s_{estY} \sqrt{1 + \frac{1}{N} + \frac{(X - M_X)^2}{\sum X^2 - \frac{(\sum X)^2}{N}}} \quad \text{where } s_{estY} = s_Y \sqrt{\frac{N(1 - r^2)}{N - 2}} \qquad (8.9)$$

Using the data in Table 8.4,

$$r = .97, \quad M_X = 3.5, \quad M_Y = 52.75, \quad s_X = 1.7078, \quad s_Y = 7.2356, \quad N = 12$$

Step 1: Calculate the standard error of the estimate.

$$s_{estY} = 7.2536 \sqrt{\frac{12(1 - .97^2)}{12 - 2}} \qquad s_{estY} = 7.2536 \sqrt{\frac{12(1 - .9409)}{12}}$$

$$s_{estY} = 7.2536 \sqrt{\frac{12(0.0591)}{12}} \qquad s_{estY} = 1.9317$$

Step 2: Apply the standard estimate to a specific predicted score of Y.

Assume that $X = 4.0$. Using the regression equation, we calculate $Y' = 54.8048$.

Step 3: Complete the calculations.

$$Y_T = Y' \pm s_{estY} \sqrt{1 + \frac{1}{N} + \frac{(X - M_X)^2}{\sum X^2 - \frac{(\sum X)^2}{N}}}$$

$$Y_T = 54.8048 \pm 1.9317 \sqrt{1 + \frac{1}{12} + \frac{(4 - 3.5)^2}{182 - \frac{(42)^2}{12}}}$$

$$Y_T = 54.8048 \pm 1.9317 \sqrt{1.0904}$$

$$Y_T = 54.8048 \pm 2.0171$$

$$Y_T = 52.7877 - 56.8219$$

Spearman Rank-Order Correlation Coefficient

The Spearman rank-order correlation coefficient, or Spearman's r_S, is an alternative to the Pearson product-moment correlation coefficient that researchers use when the data are ranked (e.g., using an ordinal scale) or if the data are skewed. As with the conventional correlation coefficient, the values of r_S can range between -1.00 and $+1.00$. Correlations close to 0 represent no linear relation between the two variables. Correlations close to ± 1.0 represent large linear relations.

$$r_S = 1 - \frac{6 \sum D_i^2}{n(n^2 - 1)} \tag{8.10}$$

Assume that a researcher wanted to examine the correlation between two variables X and Y.

Step 1: Convert the individual scores for X and Y to ranks

Original scores

$$X \quad \{90 \quad 85 \quad 80 \quad 75 \quad 71 \quad 73 \quad 72 \quad 64 \quad 66 \quad 50\}$$
$$Y \quad \{3.1 \quad 3.5 \quad 3.55 \quad 3 \quad 2.5 \quad 2.1 \quad 2.4 \quad 1.9 \quad 1.1 \quad 1.2\}$$

Rank scores and assign rank from lowest to highest

$$X \quad \{50 \quad 64 \quad 66 \quad 71 \quad 72 \quad 73 \quad 75 \quad 80 \quad 85 \quad 90\}$$
$$\text{Rank}_X \quad \{ 1 \quad 2 \quad 3 \quad 4 \quad 5 \quad 6 \quad 7 \quad 8 \quad 9 \quad 10\}$$

$$Y \quad \{1.1 \quad 1.2 \quad 1.9 \quad 2.1 \quad 2.4 \quad 2.5 \quad 3 \quad 3.1 \quad 3.5 \quad 3.55)$$
$$\text{Rank}_Y \quad (1 \quad 2 \quad 3 \quad 4 \quad 5 \quad 6 \quad 7 \quad 8 \quad 9 \quad 10\}$$

Step 2: Determine the difference between ranks for the paired data and then square the differences.

Participant	X	Rank_X	Y	Rank_Y	$D = (\text{RANK}_X - \text{RANK}_Y)$	D^2
A	90	10	3.10	8	2	4
B	85	9	3.50	9	0	0
C	80	8	3.55	10	-2	4
D	75	7	3.00	7	0	0
E	71	4	2.50	6	-2	4
F	73	6	2.10	4	2	2
G	72	5	2.40	5	0	0
H	64	2	1.90	3	-1	1
I	66	3	1.10	1	2	4
J	50	1	1.20	2	-1	1
						$\sum D^2 = 20$

Step 3: Complete the calculations.

$$r_S = 1 - \frac{6(20)}{10(10^2 - 1)} \qquad r_S = 1 - \frac{120}{990} \qquad r_S = 1 - .1212$$

$$r_S = .8788$$

Confidence interval for r_S

The sampling distribution of r_S is similar to the sampling distribution of the Pearson product-moment correlation coefficient, r. Consequently, you can use the same procedures for determining the CI of r_S as you did for r.

Coefficient Alpha

Coefficient alpha is a special form of the correlation coefficient that allows one to determine the internal consistency of items in a test. The value of coefficient alpha ranges between 0 and 1.0. Higher values of coefficient alpha greater levels of agreement among the individual test items. Table 8.7 presents hypothetical data for a 10-item test administered to 8 people. The equation for coefficient alpha is,

$$r_\alpha = \left(\frac{I}{I-1}\right)\left(1 - \frac{\sum s_I^2}{s_T^2}\right) \tag{8.11}$$

Step 1: Determine the variance for each item treating each person's score on the item as an observation. For Item 1,

$$s_i^2 = \frac{\sum I_i^2 - \frac{(\sum I_i)^2}{N}}{N} \qquad 1.8594 = \frac{135 - \frac{(31)^2}{8}}{8}$$

The i in the equation refers to each item in the test; N represents the number of people taking the test and I represents the number of test items.

Step 2: Add the variance for each item.

$$\sum s_I^2 = 1.8594 + 1.1875 + 0.6094 + \cdots 1.7344 = 14.6875$$

TABLE 8.7
Worked example of coefficient alpha, r_α

Test item	Person A	B	C	D	E	F	G	H	Item variance $\sum I$	$\sum I^2$	s_i^2
1	5	2	4	3	4	2	6	5	31	135	1.8594
2	3	3	5	2	5	3	5	4	30	122	1.1875
3	4	4	4	4	4	2	4	5	31	125	0.6094
4	6	2	5	3	6	3	6	5	36	180	2.2500
5	3	4	3	3	4	4	5	6	32	136	1.0000
6	4	3	4	4	3	1	6	5	30	128	1.9375
7	6	5	3	4	5	3	5	4	35	161	0.9844
8	7	3	4	3	4	2	6	5	34	164	2.4375
9	4	4	5	2	6	3	5	6	35	167	1.7344
10	5	5	4	3	5	4	3	5	34	150	0.6875
$\sum X$	47	35	41	31	46	27	51	50		$\sum s_i^2 = 14.6875$	
$(\sum X)^2$	2209	1225	1681	961	2116	729	2601	2500			

Step 3: Determine the variance among test scores for each person taking the test.

$$s_T^2 = \frac{\sum\sum X^2 - \dfrac{\sum(\sum X)^2}{N}}{N}$$

$$\sum\left(\sum X\right) = 328 = 47 + 35 + 41 + \cdots 51 + 50$$

$$\sum\sum X^2 = 14022 = 2209 + 1225 + 1681 + \cdots 2601 + 2500$$

$$s_T^2 = 71.75 = \frac{14022 - \dfrac{(328)^2}{8}}{8}$$

Step 4: Complete the calculations.

$$r_\alpha = \left(\frac{10}{10-1}\right)\left(1 - \frac{14.6875}{71.75}\right) \qquad r_\alpha = (1.1111)(1 - .2047)$$

$$r_\alpha = 0.8837$$

For this example, we can conclude that the internal consistency of the test is high.

ACHIEVEMENT CHECK

(6) Why might the test-retest reliability of peoples' weight be greater than the test-retest reliability of their personality?

(7) In what ways are coefficient κ and r similar to each other?

(8) What does coefficient alpha, r_α, represent?

(9) Imagine that a researcher found that $r_\alpha = .34$. What conclusions could you draw from this statistic?

(10) What are some ways to increase the reliability of a test?

(11) Explain in your words the importance of convergent and discriminant validity for examining the validity of a test.

(12) Imagine that we randomly selected 25 students who scored extremely well on a math achievement test. We then administer a similar math achievement test to these students. What predictions can you make about the second set of scores?

CHAPTER SUMMARY

The correlation coefficient is a descriptive statistic that indicates the degree to which changes in one variable relate to changes in a second variable. Specifically, the correlation describes a linear relation between two variables. The size of the correlation coefficient ranges between -1.0 and $+1.0$. When the correlation coefficient is 0, then there is no meaningful linear relation between the two variables. Correlation coefficients closer to -1.0 or $+1.0$ represent strong linear relations between the two variables.

Pearson's correlation coefficient is the most commonly used statistic to examine the relation between two variables. The statistic works by examining the sum of the standard score cross products ($\sum z_X z_Y$) of the two data sets. Using the standard scores (z-score) allows us to compare two variables even when the means and standard deviations of the two groups are extremely different.

The absolute value of the correlation coefficient indicates the strength of the relation between the two variables. One way to describe the size of the correlation coefficient is to use the coefficient of determination, r^2, that indicates the proportion of variance in one variable that the other variable can predict.

There are several errors that people often make when interpreting the size of the correlation coefficient. One common error is to use the correlation coefficient as evidence of cause and effect. Correlational research designs do not allow the researcher to control the independent variables or randomly assign participants to different levels of the independent variable. Therefore, we cannot resolve the ambiguity of cause and effect created by the third variable problem or the temporal order problem.

It is also possible to have an exceptionally low correlation because of a curvilinear relation between the two variables or because the sampling procedures did not adequately draw a representative sample from the population. These sampling errors can create a truncated range in the variances of the variables, extreme groups or outliers, and multiple unrecognized populations.

As with other descriptive statistics, we can use the concept of the standard error and the confidence interval to estimate sample size. For the correlation coefficient, the sample size needs to be large ($N = 500$) if the researcher believes that the correlation coefficient for the population is small. If the correlation is larger, however, the researcher may be able to use a smaller sample size.

The correlation coefficient has many applications for researchers. We examined how the correlation coefficient can help the researcher determine the test-retest reliability of a test or the internal consistency between two observers.

A special version of the correlation coefficient, known as coefficient alpha r_α, allows researchers to examine the internal consistency of test items. A high coefficient alpha indicates that the questions in the test are highly interrelated.

Knowing the test-retest reliability or the coefficient alpha can allow the researcher to adjust the length of a test to enhance its reliability. For example, making a test longer can improve the reliability of an instrument. This increased reliability will decrease measurement error of the dependent variable.

The correlation coefficient also allows us to examine the validity of a test. By correlating a test with tests that measure the same construct, we can determine the test's convergent validity. Tests that measure the same construct should produce high correlations. By contrast, tests that measure different constructs should not correlate with each other. Researchers call this discriminant validity.

We can use regression analysis to make a formal statement about the relation between the two variables. The regression line allows us to describe the specific linear relation between X and Y. We can also calculate a confidence interval about the regression line.

Knowing the position of the regression line allows us to describe the regression to the mean phenomenon. If an observed value of X is greater than the mean, then the predicted value of Y' will be closer to the mean of Y.

In the "Research in Action" section, we showed how Sternberg's study of short-term memory can be analyzed using regression statistics.

CHAPTER GLOSSARY FOR REVIEW

Coefficient Alpha r_α   A common measure of internal consistency. The magnitude of r_α indicates whether the participants' responses to the individual test items correlate highly with each other thus indicating internal agreement among the questions.

Coefficient of Determination, r^2   A descriptive statistic that indicates the percentage of shared variance between two variables.

Coefficient of Nondetermination, $1 - r^2$ A descriptive statistic that indicates the percentage of unshared variance between two variables.

Concurrent Validity   A form of criterion validity that indicates that the test scores correlate with the current behaviors of the individuals.

Convergent Validity   An index of the validity of a test that requires that different methods of measuring the same construct correlate with each other.

Correlation Coefficient   A descriptive statistic that describes the linear relation between two variables. The statistic can range between $r = -1.0$ and $r = +1.0$ and indicates the degree to which changes in one variable correspond with changes in the other variable.

Criterion Validity   An index of the validity of a test that requires that the test score predict an individual's performance under specific conditions.

Curvilinear Relation   A systematic relation between two variables that is described by a curved rather than a straight line.

Discriminant Validity   An index of the validity of a test that requires that measures of different constructs should not correlate with each other.

Intercept, a   The value of Y' when $X = 0$.

Internal Consistency   A measure of the degree to which questions in a test agree or correlate with each other.

Linear Relation   The correlation between two variables best described as a straight line.

Negative Correlation   When $r < 0$, increases in one variable correspond with decreases in the other variable.

Positive Correlation   When $r > 0$, increases in one variable correspond with increases in the other variable.

Predictive Validity   A form of criterion validity that indicates that the test scores afford accurate predictions concerning future behavior of the individual.

Regression to the Mean   A phenomenon in regression analysis where $|(X - M_X)| > |(Y' - M_Y)|$.

Slope, b   The change in Y' that occurs when X increases by one unit.

Standard Error of Estimate   The standard deviation of predicted scores about Y'.

Truncated Range   A condition that occurs when the range of observed scores for both variables is smaller than the range of potential scores. This condition tends to reduce the size of the correlation coefficient.

9 RESEARCH DESIGN I: BETWEEN-SUBJECTS DESIGNS

CHAPTER OUTLINE

✦ Introduction

✦ A Model for Research Design

✦ What Is the Independent Variable?

✦ What Is the Dependent Variable?

✦ Are There Any Confounding Variables?

✦ What Are the Research Hypotheses?

✦ Mathematical Hypotheses

✦ Evaluating Hypotheses

✦ Evaluating Hypotheses: Practical Matters

To call in the statistician after the experiment is done may be no more than asking him to perform a postmortem examination: He may be able to say what the experiment died of.

—Sir Ronald A. Fisher

INTRODUCTION

The art of good science is turning an interesting question into a productive research design. A research design refers to the methods used to collect data that will decisively answer an empirical question. Consequently, a good research design must do three things. First, it must be efficient. The design should produce the best quality data for the least amount of time, effort, and money. Second, the design must eliminate factors that bias the results. Finally, the research design should produce useful data that clearly addresses the research question and accounts for alternative explanations. In this chapter we will examine the details of good research design for projects that incorporate two levels of the independent variable. Using this format, we can review the principles of design that we can apply to all research.

A MODEL FOR RESEARCH DESIGN

A common myth is that the researcher is an introverted, white lab-coat wearing, dispassionate, and objective umpire of the data who "calls 'em as I sees 'em." Unfortunately, there are too many examples in the history of science to treat this statement as anything but an ideal rarely, if ever, reached. There are many examples of biologists, chemists, physicists, and psychologists who lost their objectivity and allowed their preconceived beliefs to cloud their judgment and interpretation of the data. As you learned in chapter 1, the four idols that Bacon described 400 years ago continue to affect how people make decisions. In many cases these idols or perspectives lead us to the wrong conclusion and prevent us from considering alternative perspectives. Consequently, the purpose of any research design is to protect researchers from lapses in objectivity and the bias inherent in personal judgment.

In psychology, we have an additional source of bias, the people who participate in our research. Participants in our research come to us with their anxieties, biases, and awareness that they are participating in a psychological study. Being a good behavioral researcher requires knowledge of human behavior and research design in order to conduct useful scientific studies.

I could easily fill this book with examples of the factors that can bias the results of a research project. That tactic would not be an efficient use of your patience or my time. An alternative is to use a model that highlights the phases of research that are most sensitive to different forms of bias. Figure 9.1 illustrates the potential sources of bias arising from the

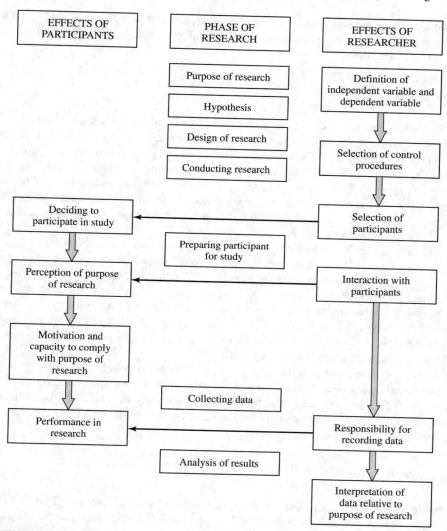

FIGURE 9.1

Potential sources of bias arising from the interaction among the researcher, the design of the study, and the people participating in the research. The column on the left represents the behavior of the participants. The column on the right represents the behavior of the researcher. The central column represents the phases of research. The horizontal lines represent instances where the participants' and researchers' behavior interact. Based in part on Rosnow and Rosenthal (1997) and Hyde (1991).

interaction among the researcher, the design of the study, and the participants. Many of the ideas presented in this illustration come from the work presented by Rosnow and Rosenthal (1997) and Hyde (1991).

Purpose of Research

The first encounter we have with personal bias is with us, the researcher. Most research projects are rarely the product of divine inspiration. Rather, the vast majority of research ideas come from a researcher's theoretical orientation and personal experience.

In chapter 1 we reviewed the reactions that psychologists had when Garcia (1980) attempted to publish his research on taste aversion. Garcia faced much opposition because the results of his research did not fit other psychologists' theories of classical conditioning. The prevailing theories of classical conditioning biased the type of experiments that researchers did and did not conduct.

The influence of a researcher's orientation can have considerable influence on how he or she will view a problem. Consider a group of psychologists who want to study depression. A psychologist with a cognitive perspective will examine the participant's attributions regarding his or her ability to control life's events. A physiological psychologist may focus on the level or imbalance of various neurotransmitters. Finally, a psychologist with a psychodynamic perspective will explore unresolved psychological conflicts. Although each psychologist will say that they are studying the same thing (why a person is depressed), the variables that they examine are radically different.

Perhaps the best way to avoid the bias of preconceived beliefs is to remain open to alternative explanations and ideas. No one has yet cornered the market on good ideas and explanations for the complexity for psychological phenomena. Therefore, be willing to examine alternative explanations until the data clearly indicate that you need to move onto a different perspective.

Design of Research

After identifying the purpose and the hypothesis, the next step presented in Figure 9.1 is the design phase during which the researcher develops controls for potential confounding variables. As we reviewed in chapter 3, confounding variables are conditions that reduce the internal validity of the study. A confounding variable is an uncontrolled condition that creates a plausible alternative hypothesis for the results of the study. As we progress through this book, we will examine different research designs that help reduce or eliminate the effects of well-known confounding effects.

Selection of Participants

When the researcher begins to select participants for the study, the opportunities for bias increase dramatically. In chapter 6, you learned how to develop a representative sample of the population. I am hopeful that you now accept without question the need to ensure that your selection procedure will yield a representative sample of the population.

Critics of psychological research often find fault with the sampling procedures researchers use. Some critics have argued that psychologists too often use college students for behavioral research (e.g., Rosnow & Rosenthal, 1997). Joining this argument are the complaints that much of the classic research in psychology relied on male-dominated (e.g., Hyde, 1991) and Caucasian samples (Samuda, 1975). We cannot brush off these concerns as trivial. Therefore, it is important that you clearly define the target population you wish to study and ensure that your sampling population is a fair representative of that population.

Volunteer participants

Related to our selection of participants is the question of who chooses to participate in our research. Do people who volunteer to participate in our research represent the typical person? The answer is no. Remember the objections raised in chapter 3 about the *Consumer Reports* study of the effectiveness of psychotherapy? The central objection to that report was that people volunteered to return the survey. Because these people decided to participate in the research, we cannot be sure that the results are representative of the population we want to describe.

Preparing the Participant for the Study

Have you ever been driving on the interstate and seen a patrol car enter the flow of traffic? What do you do? The first thing I do is slow down to make sure that I am not speeding. I become self-conscious of my driving while I can see the patrol car. The same type of self-conscious reaction occurs in people who participate in a research project; they know (or perhaps dread) that a psychologist is scrutinizing everything they do.

In Figure 9.1 you can see that there is a link between the researcher's interaction with the participants and the participants' perception of the purpose of the research. This link indicates that the researcher's behavior influences how each participant behaves during the study. Specifically, the participants' ideas about the purpose of the research may cause them to do what they think the researcher wants them to do. We can review this interaction between the researcher's behavior and participants' perceptions using a classic example.

Almost all textbooks on research methods refer to the **Hawthorne effect** as an example of how the researcher's behavior and the participants' perceptions of the research affect the data. The name refers to research conducted at the Hawthorne plant of the Western Electric Company during the late 1920s and early 1930s. The researchers wanted to find ways to improve assembly-line productivity by varying working conditions. Much to their surprise, the researchers found that almost any change, even returning to the original working conditions, improved productivity (Sundstorm, McIntyre, Halfhill, & Richards, 2000). Unfortunately, the available data do not allow us to do much more than speculate why any change in the assembly room increased productivity. Perhaps the workers believed that they would be fired if they did not work hard enough and that the researchers where there to observe who was the most and least productive.

The Hawthorne plant episode is a frequently told story, with different versions that have their own lessons. The history of what happened at the Hawthorne plant is murky at best. Nevertheless, many use the Hawthorne episode to illustrate how a person's behavior changes when he or she knows that someone is watching. The lesson from this version of the story is that we need to ensure that our research design and our behavior as the researcher do not create a **demand characteristic** that contaminates the results of the study. A demand characteristic is any condition created by the design of the study that leads the participants to infer the purpose of the research. The participants' misperception of the purpose of the research may cause them to act differently than they normally would, thereby biasing the results.

Another version of the Hawthorne story is that the researchers inadvertently created a confounding variable in their study. During the study, the workers' pay reflected their productivity; the more components they made, the more money they earned. Therefore, the workers' behavior reflected a well-known behavioral and economic principle, people work harder for more pay (Parsons, 1974). Therefore, we can use the Hawthorne study to emphasize the need to pay attention to the design phase of the study to rule out alternative explanations of the results.

The Hawthorne effect and demand characteristics are more than historical episodes and interesting phenomenon described in textbooks; they are real threats to the internal validity of any research project. If we study history to avoid making the same mistakes, then we should heed the lesson learned from the Hawthorne episode when we design our research projects.

Recording and Analyzing the Results

Hamlet: Do you see yonder cloud that's almost in shape of a camel?
Polonius: By the mass, and 'tis like a camel, indeed.
Hamlet: Methinks it is like a weasel.
Polonius: It is backed like a weasel.
Hamlet: Or like a whale?
Polonius: Very like a whale.

Shakespeare (1604)

Polonius is quick to see what Hamlet claims to see in the random formation of clouds. A single cloud quickly becomes a camel, a weasel, and then a whale all upon Hamlet's suggestion. Clearly, Polonius is a sycophant and agrees with everything Hamlet says. Are researchers like Polonius? Do they allow their research hypothesis to influence their perception?

Do researchers see what they want to see when observing a person's behavior? The answer is yes. If we believe something to be true, we tend to interpret things within that context and act in ways that brings about the expected result. Psychologists call this phenomenon the **self-fulfilling prophecy.**

One of the classic examples of the self-fulfilling prophecy is the Pygmalion in the classroom effect (Rosenthal, 1994; Rosenthal & Jacobson, 1968). To demonstrate the effects of the self-fulfilling prophecy, researchers told grade school teachers that several of the students were "late bloomers" and would soon begin to excel in school. However, the late bloomers were randomly selected students. Nevertheless, many of these students had moderate increases in their IQ scores by the end of the year. This increase in IQ may have been due to the way the teachers interacted with the students. Because they expected the students to blossom academically, the teachers may have given the late bloomers extra attention, support, and encouragement during the year.

As a generality, we refer to the self-fulfilling prophecy in research as **experimenter bias or effect.** Experimenter bias refers to the researcher's treatment of the participant. If the person collecting the data knows the research hypothesis, he or she may treat the participants in the groups differently, thus affecting the participants' behavior and confounding the results.

Finally, once we collect the data, what will convince us that they support or refute our hypothesis? Can we look at the data and shout, "Eureka, I have solved the problem!"? The data do not "speak for themselves." Analyzing the data is an interpretative process and therefore prone to a host of personal and subjective biases. Consequently, we rely upon statistical analysis and objective reasoning to reduce further opportunities for subjective inference and unsubstantiated conclusions.

Some of the answers to the problems raised thus far will come in the following pages and the other chapters of this book. Each research project is unique, however, and no single textbook can offer a fixed set of rules that covers every potential experiment and the design problems that will arise. The preferable alternative is to work through the framework illustrated in Figure 9.1 and use it to consider potential problems and suitable improvements for each research project.

To help me explain and for you to understand these principles, I want to use two research projects as examples. These examples will help me illustrate the many choices and design questions that researchers must resolve. Although the projects come from recently published empirical studies, I have simplified the design of the studies to fit the purpose of our review.

Sex differences and memory for emotional events

Do men and women differ when asked to recall emotionally significant events in their lives? Are men or women more likely to focus on the positive events in their lives? Who is more likely to ignore negative events, men or women? Seidlitz and Diener (1998) addressed these questions in their research.

Changing attitudes by writing essays

Imagine that someone asked you to write an essay that supported a 5% increase in your college's tuition. Would completing this request change your attitude regarding hikes in tuition? Will the task strengthen your beliefs or cause you to switch your opinion? The inspiration for these questions comes from an article by Stalder and Baron (1998).

WHAT IS THE INDEPENDENT VARIABLE?

It is critical to ensure that we define all of our terms as clearly as possible. Consider the research examining sex differences for memory of emotional events. The independent variable is sex[1]—men versus women. (Technically, sex is a quasi-independent variable

---

[1]We use the word "sex" when the biological distinction is the predominant characteristic differentiating groups. We use the word "gender" to refer to men and women as members of social groups or to traits associated with each sex—see the current *Merriam-Webster's Collegiate Dictionary* for details. Seidlitz and Diener (1998) treated their study as one that examined sex differences.

because the researcher cannot randomly assign participants to the different conditions. Nevertheless, the researcher can use the variable to predict the dependent variable.) What could be simpler? The questions do ask about sex differences, but is this the only way we can look at the problem?

Many psychologists study gender role, which refers to one's sexual identity. Some psychologists believe that gender-role identity is a continuous scale with masculinity and femininity on opposite ends of the scale. Although there are only two sexes, there are many levels of gender identity.

Using gender role rather than sex is an interesting alternative for our research question. Bem (1974, 1977) developed a scale that assesses one's gender-role identity. Using this scale, we can identify men and women who have masculine or feminine traits. We could then determine if people with feminine traits have different recall rates for emotional events than people with masculine traits.

The main goal of this example was to illustrate that there may be many ways to define the independent variable. In this example, either definition of the independent variable (sex or gender role) is acceptable, but each represents a different research project. For this study, we will focus on sex differences and compare men and women.

What Type of Independent Variable?

The type of independent variable can have profound effects on the design of the research project as well as the conclusions we can draw from the data. There are several ways we can classify independent variables.

Subject versus manipulated

For the study examining the recall of emotional life events, sex is a *subject* variable because the condition existed before the person's participation in the study. In addition, it is impossible for the researcher to randomly assign people to be men or women. By contrast, the study examining the effects of essay writing on attitude change uses a *manipulated* independent variable because the researcher can decide what type of essay each participant will write.

The difference in the type of independent variable is important because it determines the control we have over alternative explanations. If we use a manipulated variable, we can create one or more control conditions for our experiment. Consider the essay writing project. What control groups could we create, and what function would they serve?

The simplest control would be to have a group of people who do not write an essay; they just tell us what they think about a 5% tuition increase. This control will help us determine whether writing the essay had any effect on the students' attitudes. Will this single control group account for other alternative explanations?

What would happen if we asked students to write an essay on a topic unrelated to tuition? This control has the advantage that it makes the two groups comparable with the exception of the critical component, the topic of the essay. People in both groups will write an essay and experience all the things involved in writing. The only difference is that one group of people will write an essay to support an unpopular idea.

Is it also possible that people will justify the increase in tuition by saying nice things about the college? The change in opinion may reflect positive feelings about the college, not taking a disagreeable stand. If you agree with my argument, you might have a group of people who write an essay describing the good things about their college. The other group of people would write an essay supporting the tuition hike.

Can you think of other control conditions? With some time and thought you might be able to find better examples than mine. The purpose of this discussion was to reiterate the importance of defining the meaning of the independent variable. The exercise will help ensure that you measure the variable correctly and consider alternative definitions of the variable. In addition, the exercise will help you design control conditions that will allow you to account for alternative explanations.

Between-subjects versus within-subjects variables

We can also classify independent variables as being either a between-subjects or a within-subjects variable. Figure 9.2 illustrates the difference between the two types of variable. The distinguishing feature is the number of times we test the individual.

For a **between-subjects variable,** we test the individual under only one treatment or research condition. By contrast, for a **within-subjects variable,** we test the same person under two or more research conditions. Sometimes, researchers will call a within-subjects variable a repeated-measures variable. An example follows.

A person's sex is a between-subjects variable; it does not make sense to test the same person once as a male and then again as a female. An independent variable is also a between-subjects variable if we randomly assign participants to experience only one treatment condition.

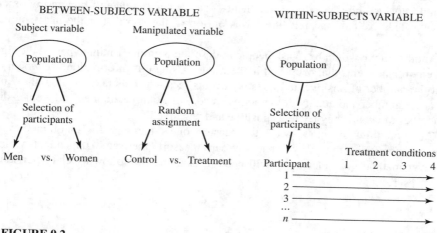

FIGURE 9.2

The difference between a between-subjects variable and a within-subjects variable. For the between-subjects variable, the researcher assesses the participant's behavior under one level of the independent variable. For the within subjects variable, the researcher assesses each participant under multiple treatment conditions.

If we observe the behavior of a participant under different research conditions, that variable is a within-subjects variable. Time can be a within-subjects variable if we test or observe our participants' behavior on different occasions. For example, we may test our participants before and after some important event. Similarly, we may also test the same person under different levels of the independent variable. We call these variables within-subjects variables because we compare the same person's performance under different conditions or at different times.

Recognize the difference between between-subjects and within-subjects variables because they require special considerations for research design as well as statistical analysis. For now, we will focus on between-subjects designs. We will review within-subjects research designs in a subsequent chapter.

WHAT IS THE DEPENDENT VARIABLE?

As with the independent variable, we will need to create an operational definition of the dependent variable. We can use the two studies to examine how we will define the appropriate dependent variable. How will we evaluate the emotional memories of men and women? How will we determine if we have changed people's attitudes toward tuition increases? As you should recall from chapter 2, we are revisiting the concepts of operational definitions, measurement, and validity.

For the study examining sex differences and memory, we could ask people to describe the happiest or saddest moments in their lives. We could then rate the emotional content contained in the statement. For instance, we might give the statement, "I remember when Mom and Dad gave me a puppy for Christmas" a low score. By contrast, we might give a high score to the statement "I can remember when I bought my first car. I was thrilled, excited, and felt like I was on top of the world. For the next couple of days . . . ."

Another tactic would be to ask people to describe within a 3-minute period the significant emotional events that happened in their lives. Using this information, we would then count the number of positive and negative events recalled. This tactic would allow us to look at the number and quality of memories listed. For example, do men and women differ in the types of events they recall as positive and negative?

Can you think of other ways to measure one's memory for emotional events? There are many different ways that we can measure the same dependent variable. Whatever method you select, you will need to examine the following characteristics of your measure.

Reliability and Validity

As you learned in chapter 8, reliability refers to the consistency in a measurement whereas validity refers to the legitimacy of the measure. The downfall of many research projects comes from selecting tests or measurement techniques that were unreliable, invalid, or both.

There are many ways to ensure the reliability and validity of a measure. One is to use techniques that other researchers use. As you read reports on a specific topic, you will begin to find that researchers examining a common topic tend to use similar tests. Although this is not an ideal method of guaranteeing reliability and validity, it is a good start. Psychologists also study the reliability and validity of tests. You can easily find published research that evaluates the efficiency of specific testing procedures.

Objective Recording of the Data

In chapter 7 we reviewed the importance of using consistent and systematic measurement procedures that do not bias the results. Examining the validity of the recording method is one way to remove or reduce potential bias. Other procedural techniques help reduce potential bias in our recording.

One of the most useful methods for reducing experimenter bias is to use what researchers call the single- and double-blind procedures. Blind means that specific people involved in the research do not know the purpose of the study or the relevant independent variables that the participant experienced. Almost all researchers use some form of **single-blind** and many use a double-blind procedure.

The single-blind procedure indicates that the person participating in the research does not know the specifics of the researcher's hypothesis. The goal of the single blind is to reduce any demand characteristics that may result from the participants' knowledge of the researcher's hypothesis. In a true experiment, for example, the participants would not know whether they were in one of the treatment conditions or in a control group. If the single blind is successful, the participants' behavior will reflect natural reactions to the research conditions.

How did the researchers use single-blind techniques in the study of sex differences and the study of attitude change? In the sex-difference study, the participants knew that the researchers were examining memory for emotional events. What the participants did not know was why the researchers were collecting the data or how the data would be analyzed. Similarly, in the attitude change study, the participants did not know the hypothesized effect of essay writing until the researcher debriefed them.

Placebo

A placebo is a common technique used to create a single blind. For example, in most drug studies, some people receive a placebo treatment. The people participating in these studies understand that the researcher is examining the effectiveness of a drug. What they do not know is whether the pill is the real drug or a tablet that does not have the active ingredient being studied. This control procedure ensures that the participants' reactions are not affected by their knowledge of whether they received the drug.

A control group is another form of placebo treatment. Previously, we examined different types of control conditions for the essay writing and attitude change experiment. One recommendation was to ask students to write an essay unrelated to increases in tuition. This control is a type of placebo in that it requires the participants to engage in the same type of behavior, writing an essay. Using this control condition helps us ensure that the topic of the essay, not its production, is the essential factor for attitude change.

Cover story—deception

A cover story is another way to create a single blind. A cover story misleads the participants about the true purpose of the research. Graziano and Bryant (1998) examined how men perceived pictures of women when they received bogus information about changes in their heart rate. The researchers predicted that men would rate women as more attractive if they had been led to believe that their heart rates increased while looking at a picture of the woman.

How did Graziano and Bryant (1998) create this cover story? When each participant arrived for the study the researcher took him to a small room filled with physiological recording devices and attached a sensor to his finger. The researcher then told the participant,

> Most of our research is conducted over at the Medical School Building. We have all sorts of electronic wizardry and soundproof chambers over there. Right now, there are several experiments being conducted and our facilities are overcrowded. Because of this situation, we are doing this experiment here and are forced to use a fairly crude but adequate measure of heart rate and other physiological measures. . . . Here, we are recording the heart rate the way they used to do it 30 years ago. These sensors measure your pulse rate. . . . This machine gives us signals on your pulse and thus your heart rate. . . . Unfortunately, this recording method makes it necessary to have audible sounds. . . . Just try to ignore the heart sounds. I will present 10 slides to you at regular intervals and my assistant will record your heart rate along with other physiological measures. (p. 254)

This cover story offered a plausible account for the conditions surrounding the experiment. To be sure that the cover story worked, Graziano and Bryant (1998) conducted a **manipulation check.** A manipulation check is merely a test to determine whether the cover story or deception worked. In this case, Graziano and Bryant asked the participants at the end of the study if they had any suspicions about the purpose of the research. Only 3 of the 103 volunteers expressed any suspicion that the researchers had faked the heart rate sounds, evidence that the cover story worked.

Cover stories can be extremely effective. Their use raises ethical concerns, however. As you learned in chapter 5, all participants have the right to know the relevant details of a project so that they can make an informed decision on whether they will participate in the research. Therefore, if you plan to use deception or a cover story in your research, you will need to ensure that the deception does not deny a person's ability to know the potential threats of participating in the study. In addition, if you use a cover story, you must fully explain to the participants the deception and its purpose at the end of the research.

Some research projects require additional controls to reduce the risk of experimenter bias. The **double-blind** procedure means that the person participating in the study and the person collecting or scoring the data does not know the researcher's hypothesis and the treatment the participant received. Consider the sex-difference study for recall of emotional events. If we decide to evaluate the content of the individual's memory, then the person scoring the comments must not know the hypothesis and the sex of the participant writing the essay.

ARE THERE ANY CONFOUNDING VARIABLES?

Each research project runs the risk of confounding. What are the potential confounding variables in the studies that we are examining?

The study examining the sex differences for memory of emotional events may create a confound depending on how we collect the data. What would happen if we asked 20 women and 20 men to create a list of their positive memories and then create a second list of their negative memories? Is it possible that the order of the lists will affect the data? Writing about their positive memories first may influence the participants' ability to remember negative events.

Any time we expose a participant to a sequence of events there is a threat of a **carryover effect.** The carryover effect refers to the effect that previous experiences have on subsequent behavior. As an example, if we use the same test on two occasions, the participants may remember the questions and their answers, and this memory may bias the results. Using the same test twice may also give the participants cues about the purpose of the research.

Another potential confound may be that women are more verbal than men and use more words to describe their memories. We could ask that people limit their comments to three to five words, or we could wait until we collect the data to determine whether one group is wordier than the other.

What if the women in our study were happier than the men; will the difference bias our data? Again, the participants' mood during the study could influence how well they recall positive and negative events. To account for this confounding variable, we can use any number of scales that assess a person's mood. The data from the measure of mood will help us determine if there are significant differences between women's and men's mood at the time of the study.

ACHIEVEMENT CHECK

(1) Answer these items after reading each of the short descriptions of research projects that follow.

(a) Identify the independent variable(s) and the dependent variable.

(b) What is the hypothesis that the researcher appears to be testing (you will have to infer this from your reading of the scenario)?

(e) Identify the empirical method that the researcher used.

(f) What aspects of the research design would influence our evaluation of the internal validity of the research?

(g) What aspects of the research design would influence our evaluation of the external validity of the research?

(h) What changes would you make to the study to improve the internal and external validity of the study?

(A) A researcher wants to test the effects of a counseling program on assertiveness behavior. For the first part of the study, students completed a test that measured their assertiveness. Those students who received the lowest scores received the counseling. Two months later the researcher retested the participants. All participants showed a marked improvement in assertiveness. The researcher concludes that the counseling is a success.

(B) An instructor wants to demonstrate to her students the value of elaborated rehearsal. She randomly divides the class into three groups. She tells the students in the first group that they are in the control group and do not need to read the next chapter in the textbook. She tells the students in the second group to read the next chapter in the textbook as if they were preparing for an exam. For the third group, she tells the students to write a letter to their mother explaining the material presented in the chapter. The following week, all students complete a test of the material covered in the assigned chapter. On average, students who wrote the essay score 10% higher than the other groups.

(C) A researcher wanted to evaluate the effectiveness of a lie detector procedure. Fifty students enrolled in an introductory psychology class volunteered to participate for extra credit in the course. The researcher gave each participant an envelope that contained a $100 bill and instructed the participant to lie about the contents of the envelope during a lie detection investigation. The researcher told the participants that they could keep the money if they passed the lie detection test. After evaluating the results of the lie detector test, the researcher claimed that he could detect 80% of the participants as liars. Using these results, the researcher concluded that lie detectors are effective at detecting deception.

(D) A researcher wishes to examine the effect of pornography on aggression. She asks 30 men to watch a 15-minute segment of a sexually explicit videotape. After viewing the film, the researcher leads the men to believe that they will now participate in a second experiment wherein they will deliver electrical shocks to another person. The dependent variable was the length of the shocks that the men delivered. The average length of the shocks was 2.46 seconds. Using these data, the researcher claims that watching pornography increases level of aggression.

WHAT ARE THE RESEARCH HYPOTHESES?

Preparing the research hypothesis is an integral part of preparing a research design. Indeed, the format of the research hypothesis shapes the design of the research and the statistical analysis of the data. When we write a hypothesis, we want to be sure that it clearly states the relation between the independent and dependent variables and the type of results we expect to obtain. For the memory of emotional events and essay writing examples, we are interested in the differences between two groups. Therefore, we will frame each hypothesis as a statement of the relation between the groups.

Directional versus Nondirectional Hypothesis

A research hypothesis describes the relation among population parameters. There are, however, different ways that we can write the hypothesis. The major difference is whether we use a **directional hypothesis** or a **nondirectional hypothesis.**

In a directional hypothesis we predict the specific relation between the two groups using either *greater than* or *less than*. Examples of directional hypotheses include "Women are more likely to remember positive emotional events than men" and "People are more likely to agree with an unpopular opinion after writing an essay supporting that opinion." Both predictions use words to indicate that the behavior of one group would be greater than the behavior of the other group.

By contrast, a nondirectional hypothesis predicts that there will be differences between groups, but does not specify the type of difference that will occur. We can rewrite the previous hypotheses as "Men and women will differ in their recall of positive emotional events," and "Writing an essay supporting an unpopular topic will affect a person's opinion of the topic." We have retained the emphasis on the relation between the groups, but have not indicated which will be greater.

Which type of hypothesis should you use? There is no clear answer to this question, but plenty of opinions. Some researchers believe that if there is a clear prediction about the direction of the results, then one should use a directional hypothesis. The justification for this tactic is that if the researcher is confident in his or her prediction, then he or she should expect only one type of dependent.

By contrast, the justification for the nondirectional hypothesis is that we, as researchers, should examine all results regardless of the direction of the outcome. From this perspective, we would say that any evidence of a statistically significant difference between the groups is important and worthy of our analysis.

Some researchers believe that directional tests are superior to nondirectional tests. Others believe that researchers should use nondirectional hypotheses exclusively. Directional and nondirectional hypotheses have their place in science. In many ways, selecting between directional and nondirectional hypotheses is much like resolving an ethical dilemma. Specifically, the researcher needs to examine his or her philosophical stance on hypothesis testing and then develop a rationale for selecting one type of hypothesis. If you believe that it is imperative to prove that $\mu_1 > \mu_2$, then you should use a directional hypothesis. By contrast, if you believe that it is essential to explore the differences between μ_1 and μ_2, then use a nondirectional hypothesis, $\mu_1 = \mu_2$ (Jones & Tukey, 2000).

MATHEMATICAL HYPOTHESES

In the previous section, we used words to write each hypothesis. In this section, you will learn that it is easy to convert a well-written hypothesis into a series of mathematical or logical statements. These mathematical statements then help us interpret the results of the study.

At one level, the hypothesis refers to the relation between the independent and dependent variables. For example, our hypothesis might imply that one's sex affects the memory of emotional events or that writing essays forms attitudes. The hypothesis also refers to the parameters of the populations. According to what you learned in chapter 6, the sample data should be representative of the target population, and we can use the sample data to generalize about the population. Consequently, the hypothesis describes what we believe to be true of the target populations.

When we prepare the mathematical hypothesis we write two complementary hypotheses, the null hypothesis and the alternative hypothesis. In its basic form, the null hypothesis implies that there is no relation between the independent and dependent variables by indicating that the individual groups are equivalent. The alternative hypothesis, by contrast, implies that there is a relation between the independent and dependent variables, and, by implication, that the groups will be different from each other.

We can use the sex-difference study to illustrate the null and alternative hypotheses. For the null hypothesis, we would say that one's sex is independent of memory for emotional events. As a mathematical statement, we can write the null hypothesis as H_0: $\mu_M = \mu_F$. A translation of the equation is "The population mean of men's recall of positive emotional

TABLE 9.1

Examples of null and alternative hypotheses for directional and nondirectional hypotheses using a two-group design

| Hypothesis | Directional hypothesis | | Nondirectional hypothesis |
	Greater than	Less than	
Research hypothesis	"Men will remember more positive emotional events than women."	"Men will remember fewer positive emotional events than women."	"Men and women will differ in their recall of positive emotional events."
Null hypothesis	$H_0: \mu_M \leq \mu_F$	$H_0: \mu_M \geq \mu_F$	$H_0: \mu_M = \mu_F$
Alternative hypothesis	$H_1: \mu_M > \mu_F$	$H_1: \mu_M < \mu_F$	$H_1: \mu_M \neq \mu_F$

events equals the population mean of women's recall of positive events. The alternative hypothesis is $H_1: \mu_M \neq \mu_F$. In writing the alternative hypothesis, we replace the equals ($=$) with not equals ($\neq$). Table 9.1 presents examples of the null and alternative hypotheses for directional and nondirectional hypotheses.

There are several important points in Table 9.1. First, we use H_0 and H_1 to refer to the null and alternative hypotheses, respectively. This practice is a convention that has evolved among statisticians and researchers. Second, and more importantly, compare the equality sign we use in the null and alternative hypotheses. In the alternative hypothesis, the equality sign ($>$, $<$, or $\neq$) matches the adjective in the research hypothesis (greater than, less than, not equal to). We use the complementary equality sign in the null hypothesis. For example, $=$ and $\neq$ are complementary signs as are the signs $\geq$ and $<$. Finally, the null hypothesis always implies that there is no relation between the independent and dependent variables, whereas the alternative hypothesis implies that there is a meaningful relation between the variables.

EVALUATING HYPOTHESES

You may be wondering why we use the null and alternative hypotheses. It seems rather odd that we would use two hypotheses when one would seem to be enough. The practice of using null and alternative hypotheses has evolved during the past century as a way to make inferences about sample data. We can use the example of the differences between men and women's recall of life events to illustrate the reasoning behind null hypothesis testing.

When conducting empirical research, the researcher's primary responsibility is to provide evidence to support his or her claim about the relation between the variables described in the research hypothesis. The research hypothesis and alternative hypothesis are the same thing, and the researcher must collect data that will convince us of the accuracy of his or her prediction. Therefore, we begin with the null hypothesis as a "true" statement and require that the researcher convince us that the null hypothesis is "false." In the sex-difference study, the null hypothesis states that there is no meaningful difference between men and women. To reject this statement, the researcher must present data to convince us that the alternative hypothesis, not the null hypothesis, is the more accurate description of the relation between sex and the recall of emotional life events. We require the researcher to demonstrate that there is a sizable, or meaningful, difference between men and women's recall of emotional events before we are willing to accept the alternative hypothesis as accurate.

The decision to reject the null hypothesis is an inference; the researcher uses sample data to generalize about the population. There are two important characteristics of an inference. First, whenever we make an inference, we use the experience created by samples to describe the population. Second, whenever we make an inference, we must assume that there is a probability that we are wrong. As you know, the sample mean is an unbiased estimate of the population mean. The important word is estimate. There is always a probability that your inference will be wrong. By implication, then, all hypothesis testing is conditional or based on probabilities.

We use the data to determine whether to reject the null hypothesis. Look at Table 9.1. We use μ to describe the two populations. If we find that the sample means, drawn at random from the populations, are sufficiently different, we will reject the null hypothesis in favor of its alternative. Will we make mistakes when evaluating the null hypothesis? Yes.

There are two mistakes we can make when judging the null hypothesis. In the first case, we can be misled by the data and reject a true null hypothesis. Researchers call this error a **Type I error.** Consider the following example to illustrate a Type I error. Assume that we give two groups of patients suffering from depression a placebo drug treatment. For this experiment we would expect that $\mu_1 = \mu_2$ because both groups experience the same treatment, a placebo. Consequently, a Type I error would occur if we decided that the two groups were not equal to each other.

The decision is a Type I error because both groups of participants received the same treatment; we would expect that their reactions to the treatment should be identical. The Type I error occurred because of random events. It is possible there is a difference between the groups that reflects nothing besides the effects of chance.

Another error is a **Type II error.** A Type II error occurs when a null hypothesis is wrong and we fail to recognize it as false. For example, it is true that the average height of adult men is greater than the average height of adult women. Therefore the statement $\mu_{Men} = \mu_{Women}$ (where μ represents average height) is a false statement. Imagine that you measure the heights of 10 adult women and 10 adult men and find that the average heights are equal. Because the average heights are equal you decide not to reject the statement $\mu_{Men} = \mu_{Women}$. The decision is a Type II error.

This is an example of a Type II error because there is a real difference between the heights of men and women that you could not detect with your data. The Type II error occurred due to random error that you selected men and women whose average heights happened to be equal.

The Type I and Type II errors describe the decisions concerning the null hypothesis, not the decisions regarding the alternative hypothesis—a Type I error means that we rejected a true null hypothesis, a Type II error means that we failed to reject a false null hypothesis. Table 9.2 presents an illustration of Type I and Type II errors.

The Greek letters, α and β, are probability estimates; α represents the probability of committing a Type I error, β represents the probability of committing a Type II error. The

TABLE 9.2
Illustration of Type I and Type II errors

	Population parameters "Reality"	
	$\mu_1 = \mu_2$ H_0 is correct	$\mu_1 \neq \mu_2$ H_0 is false
Reject H_0 and accept H_1	Type I error α	Correct decision $1 - \beta$
Researcher's decision Do not reject H_0	Correct decision $1 - \alpha$	Type II error β

probability of a Type I error is under the direct control of the researcher because he or she can determine the criterion for deciding to reject the null hypothesis. Therefore, if the researcher wants to be conservative and lower the risk of committing a Type I error, he or she can use a small value of α. Many people call α the **significance level** or the **significance criteria,** because α determines the requirement for rejecting the null hypothesis.

The value of β is more difficult to determine. As you will learn in the next chapter, sample size, the difference among the groups, and α each contribute to the size of β. Consequently, researchers can influence the probability of a Type II error by carefully planning their research. When designing their studies, researchers attempt to minimize β to ensure that they will correctly detect and reject false null hypotheses.

Generally, decreasing α will increase β. As you lower the risk of committing a Type I error you increase the risk of committing a Type II error. Consequently, all research designs must attempt to balance the relative risk of these two errors. With careful planning, you can design your research in such a way to reduce the risk of committing a Type I and a Type II error, but you will never be able to eliminate both errors.

In many ways, evaluating the null hypothesis is like the decision a jury must make in a criminal case. According to American legal theory, every person accused of a crime is innocent until proved guilty. The presumption of innocence is the legal equivalent of the null hypothesis. The prosecution must provide ample evidence to persuade the members of the jury to reject this assumption. In criminal cases, the jury must find the defendant guilty *beyond a reasonable doubt*. A guilty verdict means that there is ample and compelling evidence to reject the presumption of innocence. Does a *not guilty* decision prove the defendant's innocence? No, a verdict of not guilty means that there is insufficient evidence to convict the defendant; it does not prove innocence. Similarly, we can never *accept* the null hypothesis. To accept means to prove true. Because we use inferential reasoning in hypothesis testing, we can never prove a hypothesis true. The only decisions we can make regarding the null hypothesis are to reject or not to reject the null hypothesis.

How are Type I and Type II errors related to a jury's verdict? A Type I error is the same as convicting an innocent person. Finding an innocent person guilty is similar to a Type I error because we incorrectly reject a true null hypothesis. Similarly, a Type II error is the same as setting a criminal free. A Type II error occurs because we fail to be sufficiently convinced that the null hypothesis is wrong just as a jury may not be convinced that the defendant is guilty.

EVALUATING HYPOTHESES: PRACTICAL MATTERS

Our decision of whether to reject the null hypothesis depends upon the context in which we interpret the data. When we look at the data, we need to answer one question: *Is there sufficient evidence to reject the null hypothesis as a false statement?* One way to answer this question is to examine the relative difference between the groups. In this section, we will examine the concept of effect size, one of the primary factors in determining whether to reject the null hypothesis.

Effect Size

Imagine that we collect data for two groups. The mean of the first group is $M_1 = 100$; the mean of the second group is $M_2 = 105$. What can we say about the difference between the two means other than they are different from each other? What could cause the difference between the two means? Is the difference trivial or meaningful? One way to answer this important question is to examine the **effect size** of the difference between the groups.

Equation 9.1 presents how to determine the effect size for the difference between two groups. Specifically, the effect size allows us to evaluate the relative difference between two sample means.

$$d_2 = \frac{M_1 - M_2}{\sqrt{\dfrac{VAR_1 + VAR_2}{2}}} \tag{9.1}$$

For the equation, d_2 is the effect size for the difference between two sample means, M_1 and M_2 represent the sample means, and VAR_1 and VAR_2 represent the sample variances. We assume that the two variances are equivalent ($VAR_1 \approx VAR_2$) and that the sample sizes are the same ($n_1 = n_2$).

The effect size is nothing more than a simple ratio. It is the ratio of the differences between the means to the variability within the groups. The larger the absolute value of d_2, the greater the relative difference between the two sample means. Figure 9.3 illustrates three examples of effect size for a two-group comparison. Each curve represents the distribution of scores. For all the data sets, the standard deviation of the samples is 10.0. The pairs of means in each panel are: (a) $M_1 = 100$, $M_2 = 102$; (b) $M_1 = 100$, $M_2 = 105$; and (c) $M_1 = 100$, $M_2 = 108$. With all else being constant, as the difference between the means increases, the effect size increases. In his influential book on statistics, Cohen (1988) described the three effect sizes shown in Figure 9.3 as (a) small, (b) moderate, and (c) large.

As you might guess, the size of d_2 has a lot to do with our interpretation of the null hypothesis. The larger the size of d_2, the stronger the relation between the independent and

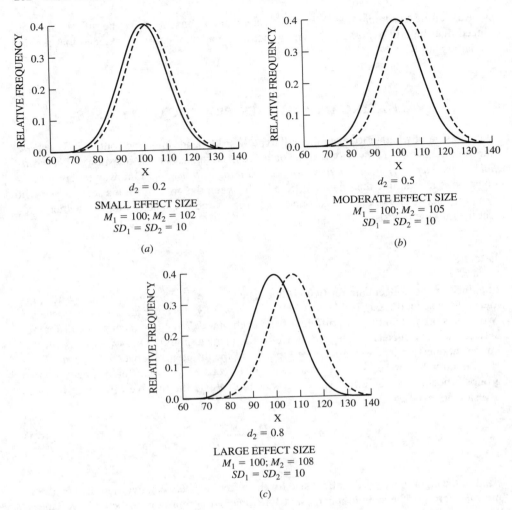

FIGURE 9.3
Effect size with $d_2 = 0.2, 0.5$, and 0.8. Effect size is the ratio of the difference between the two population means to the standard deviation of the groups.

dependent variables. Therefore, when we design any research project, we need to find ways to increase the effect size as much as possible.

Factors That Influence Effect Size

Two factors influence effect size, the between-groups variance and the within-groups variance. There are many things that we can do to control these sources of variance and therefore improve the quality of our results. Figure 9.4 depicts the two types of variance. The

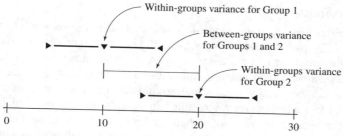

FIGURE 9.4
The between-groups and within-groups variances. The between-groups variance represents the difference between the two group means. The within-groups variance represents the differences between individual observed scores and the group mean.

difference between the two group means represents the between-groups variance. The variability of scores with both groups represents the within-groups variance.

Between-groups variance

The **between-groups variance** represents the difference among the group means. This variance represents the true difference between the population means plus the effect of random sampling or measurement errors.

There are several ways that you can increase the difference between the population means. If you are using a manipulated independent variable, you will want to use levels of the independent variable that you believe create the greatest possible effect.

To increase the effect of the independent variable in the attitude-change study, you could tell the students that they must include five specific arguments in favor of the tuition increase. In addition, you could give the students general facts (e.g., the hard-working faculty receive low salaries, the student union needs a new roof, and the price of library books increased by 18%) to help them write their essays. The goal of these tactics is to increase the effect that writing the essay has on a student's opinion.

For a subject variable, you want to be sure that the two groups are as different as possible. In the sex-difference study, our use of sex as an independent variable does not easily lend itself to further modification because there are only two sexes. There are, however, subject variables that have different levels. In these cases, we would want to define the sampling populations to maximize the differences between the groups. Consider a few examples. Imagine that you are interested in the introversion-extroversion personality dimension and its relation to other variables. When defining the populations, you would want to select participants who are clearly introverted or clearly extroverted. In another study you may want to examine the effects of alcohol consumption on memory. For such a study you might want to select adults who abstain from drinking, those who are moderate social drinkers, and those who have had a long history of alcohol abuse. You should use these tactics with caution, however, as some procedures may produce spurious results. One such tactic to avoid is the median split, discussed next.

Avoid median splits

Some researchers use a technique called a **median split** to create two intact groups. This technique creates two intact groups by using the score of a continuous measure to group people. For example, if you wanted to compare the relation between gender and recall of emotional memories, you could compare the difference between masculine and feminine individuals. Specifically, you would administer the Bem Sex-Role Inventory (Bem, 1974, 1977) to students currently enrolled in the introductory psychology course and determine the median score. You would then label people on one side of the median as masculine and people on the other side of the median as feminine. Although this may sound like a good idea, it is not.

A moment's thought will reveal the problems with the median split procedure. First, the technique looses information. The median split converts scores measured on an interval score to an ordinal scale. This loss of information means that you loose the opportunity to examine an interesting relation between two variables. Second, most measures of subject variables are normally distributed, and the majority of scores are close to the median. Consequently, a small difference between two scores (e.g., 99 and 101) can put people into radically different groups. Finally, median splits can make it difficult to detect differences between groups and thereby lead to bogus conclusions (Bissonnette, Ickes, Bernstein, & Knowles, 1990; Maxwell & Delaney, 1993).

Median splits are not a good idea. If you use a subject variable to classify people, ensure that it naturally places people into discrete groups. A better technique would be to use correlational techniques. You could examine the correlation between gender-role identity and number of positive or negative emotions recalled. Using this tactic would mean that you do not have to exclude people from your study. Rather, you would create a large representative sample and then examine the correlation between the subject variables and the dependent variable.

Within-groups variance

The **within-groups variance** represents the difference among individuals within each condition. As Figure 9.4 illustrates, the variability among scores within a group represents the within-groups variance.

Two factors contribute to the within-groups variance. The first is the natural variation within the population. Look at all the students in your course; their heights and weights are different. These differences represent the natural variation that occurs for these variables. The second factor that affects within-groups variance is measurement error. Because no test is perfectly reliable, each test score includes some amount of error. Highly reliable tests contribute little measurement error, tests with lower reliability contribute more measurement error. These facts allow us to find ways to reduce the within-groups variance.

Homogenous samples

Whenever possible, try to use participants as similar to each other as possible. Researchers prefer to use **homogenous** rather than **heterogeneous samples.** A homogenous sample refers to a condition wherein all the participants are similar to each other. By contrast, a heterogeneous sample refers to a condition wherein there is considerable variability among the members of the sample.

TABLE 9.3
Summary of techniques to increase effect size

Increase between-groups variance	
Independent variable	Select levels of the independent variable maximally different from each other
Decrease within-groups variance	
Homogeneity of variance	Ensure that participants within groups are similar to each other
Reliability of measure	Increase the reliability of the dependent variable measure by selecting good-quality tests or by using multiple measures of the variable

There are several ways to increase the homogeneity of a sample. For example, in animal studies, researchers use animals that come from the same litter or are raised in highly controlled breeding environments. In many cases, researchers are able to use animals that are virtually identical to each other on almost all characteristics.

We can do the same with human research by selecting participants with similar characteristics. The trick is finding the relevant characteristics. In studies of developmental psychology, age is an obvious grouping characteristic. Therefore, rather than lumping children into one large group (e.g., preadolescent) it may be better to create several smaller age groups (e.g., 5–7, 8–10, and 11–13). The goal of the researcher then is to identify the relevant subject variables and use these to create homogeneous groups.

Reliable measures

You can also decrease the within-groups variance by increasing the reliability of the measurement procedures. Measurement error is a random variable that increases some scores and decreases other scores. Therefore, anything you can do to increase the reliability of a test, as we reviewed in chapters 7 and 8, will help you detect any meaningful difference between the groups. Table 9.3 offers a short review of tactics one can use to increase between-groups variance and decrease within-groups variance.

RESEARCH IN ACTION: SEX DIFFERENCES AND MEMORY FOR EMOTIONAL EVENTS

We can begin with the questions regarding sex differences and the recall of emotional events. Seidlitz and Diener (1998) used students enrolled in an introductory psychology course at a large state university. The participants first completed a portion of the Satisfaction with Life Scale (Diener, Emmons, Larsen, & Griffin, 1985). The test consists of a series of 11-point scales that allows one to indicate their general mood. Figure 9.5 presents several items from the inventory.

Once the participants completed the Satisfaction with Life Scale, they listed as many positive or negative life events as they could within 3 minutes. The researcher asked the participants to use a short phrase (three to five words) to describe each event. After completing the first list, participants created a second list of the opposite emotion. The researcher randomly determined the order in which the participants listed the positive and

Mark the number that best describes you.

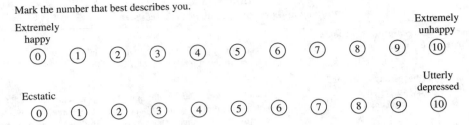

FIGURE 9.5
From the Satisfaction with Life Scale (Diener, Emmons, Larsen, & Griffin, 1985).

TABLE 9.4

Observed scores for number of recalled positive and negative life events and score on the satisfaction with life scale

| | Number of positive and negative life events recalled | | | | Satisfaction with life scale | |
| | Positive events | | Negative events | | | |
	Women	Men	Women	Men	Women	Men
	13 13	12 9	9 11	7 6	4 7	5 7
	8 11	10 10	5 10	6 7	7 3	7 5
	7 11	7 10	4 8	3 4	6 4	5 8
	9 14	9 6	6 8	6 3	9 2	3 4
	10 10	6 7	7 7	8 4	7 6	9 2
	10 12	10 8	7 7	7 8	7 8	2 6
	7 12	8 7	4 9	5 6	9 6	6 6
	10	7	6	3	7	5
n	15	15	15	15	15	15
M	10.47	8.40	7.20	5.53	6.13	5.33
VAR	4.55	3.11	4.17	3.12	4.27	4.10
SD	2.13	1.76	2.04	1.77	2.07	2.02

negative life events. A research assistant, who did not know the purpose of the study, counted the number of responses for each participant and scored the Satisfaction with Life Scale. Table 9.4 presents the hypothetical data for the study.

RESEARCH IN ACTION:
CHANGING ATTITUDES BY WRITING ESSAYS

For this experiment, the researcher randomly assigned 20 participants to one of two groups. The participants in the control group completed an attitude survey that contained a series of questions regarding their attitudes toward tuition increases. Scores for this scale can range from 0 (*complete disagreement*) to 4 (*complete agreement*).

TABLE 9.5
**Total attitude toward tuition increase score
for the control and essay writing groups**

	Control		Essay	
	8	7	13	14
	15	10	8	16
	9	11	11	12
	10	9	12	14
	8	8	17	13
n	10		10	
M	9.50		13.00	
VAR	5.17		6.44	
SD	2.27		2.54	

The participants in the essay group wrote a persuasive essay supporting an increase in the college's tuition. Students writing the essay were free to form their own arguments and had 30 minutes to complete the essay. These participants then completed the same tuition increase attitude scale. Table 9.5 presents the hypothetical data for the two groups.

ACHIEVEMENT CHECK. Use the data for each of the two studies to complete the following tasks.

(2) Select a research hypothesis that best fits the purpose of the research. Describe the hypothesis in words and prepare the corresponding H_0 and H_1.
(3) Calculate the effect size for each set of data. What inferences can you draw about the data given this statistic? For each data set, what factors contribute to the between-groups variance and the within-groups variance?
(4) For each data set, describe the implications of committing a Type I or a Type II error.

CHAPTER SUMMARY

The primary theme of this chapter was designing a research project that reduces the effects of unwanted sources of error and bias. Because research is a uniquely human enterprise, there are many opportunities for the researcher's behavior to bias the participants' behavior as well as the researcher's interpretation of the data. Thus, we examined the sequence of events for the research process from defining the purpose of the study to the final interpretation of the data to examine where and how bias can enter the research process.

The first source of potential bias is the effect that volunteer participants may introduce to the study. People who volunteer for a research project may not represent the typical person we hope to describe in our population.

Once we begin a study, there is a risk of the participants responding to an unintended demand characteristic. Most people know that they are participating in a research project and may want to modify their behavior to match what they believe to be the purpose of the research. A classic example of a demand characteristic is the Hawthorne effect.

A related source of bias is the researcher's expectations. If the persons interacting with the participants or recording the participants' behavior know the hypothesis under study and the treatment that the participants received, their knowledge may create subtle and not-so-subtle forms of bias. The researcher may bias the results by inadvertently treating the participants differently or interpret the behavior of the participant to be in keeping with the research hypothesis.

We then examined how the researcher can define the independent and dependent variables. The independent variable may be either a subject variable or a manipulated variable. The critical difference between the two variables is whether the researcher can randomly assign participants to different levels of the variable. If the researcher can randomly assign participants to different levels of the independent variable, then it is a manipulated variable.

The independent variable may also be characterized as either a between-subjects variable or a within-subjects variable. For a between-subjects variable, we compare and contrast different groups of people against each other. For a within-subjects variable, we observe the same person's behavior under several conditions.

There are several ways that the researcher can reduce the effects of the demand characteristic and experimenter bias. These techniques fall under the general heading of a blind. A single-blind study means that the participant does not know the researcher's hypothesis or the specific treatment condition to which he or she has been assigned. In addition, the researcher may use a placebo or a cover story to control what the participants believe about the purpose of the study and the treatment they receive. In a double-blind study, the participant and the person collecting the data are not aware of the research hypothesis being tested or the participant's treatment condition.

A critical component of any research project is converting the research hypothesis into a mathematical hypothesis. The research hypothesis is a general description or prediction of the relation between the variables in the study. The mathematical hypothesis is a specific statement regarding the pattern of results that the study should produce. A mathematical hypothesis may be either general, as occurs in the nondirectional hypothesis, or specific, as occurs in the directional hypothesis.

Mathematical hypotheses contain two parts, a null hypothesis and an alternative hypothesis. The null hypothesis states that there is no meaningful relation between the variables in the study. The alternative hypothesis is the mathematical equivalent of the research hypothesis. The goal of the researcher is to collect data to allow him or her to reject the null hypothesis and accept the alternative hypothesis.

When evaluating the null and alternative hypotheses, a researcher can make one of two errors. The first error, a Type I error, occurs when the researcher rejects the null hypothesis as false when the null hypothesis is correct. The second error, a Type II error, occurs when the researcher fails to reject a false null hypothesis.

The researcher can directly control the risk of committing a Type I error by establishing a criterion called the significance level, or α. The size of α determines the probability that the researcher will commit a Type I error if the null hypothesis is a correct statement. The researcher can also influence, $1 - \beta$, the probability of correctly rejecting a false null hypothesis.

The effect size is a statistic that reflects the relative difference between two groups and is a statistic that can help us understand how to increase the chances that we will successfully reject a false null hypothesis.

One way to increase the likelihood of rejecting a false null hypothesis is to increase the between-groups variance. The between-groups variance reflects the difference between the group means. If the independent variable does influence the between-groups variance, then selecting levels of the independent variable that create the greatest possible effect can increase the chance for rejecting a false null hypothesis.

The researcher can also attempt to reduce the within-groups variance. The within-groups variance represents the variability among scores within each treatment condition. If there is much heterogeneity of variance, then it will be more difficult to detect a statistically significant difference among the groups. If the researcher can make the data more homogeneous, then the within-groups variance will decrease and the researcher will be better able to detect differences among the groups.

In the final section of the chapter, we reviewed examples of two contemporary research projects. These studies demonstrated the application of good research design and demonstrated how one can collect useful data. The examples will also serve as a foundation for material in the next chapter.

CHAPTER GLOSSARY FOR REVIEW

α (Alpha)   The probability of committing a Type I error. The level of α is under direct control of the researcher.

β (Beta)   The probability of committing a Type II error. The size of β reflects many factors including the design of the research, sample size, and level of α selected.

Between-Groups Variance   The difference or variance among group means. The difference reflects differences among the population means and the effects of sampling error.

Between-Subjects Variable   A form of independent variable for which the researcher tests the participant on one occasion or under one level of the independent variable.

Carryover Effect   A form of bias in which the effect of the participant's previous experiences in a study influences his or her performance.

Demand Characteristic   Any unintended condition created by the design of a study that leads the participants to misinterpret the purpose of the research and respond accordingly.

Directional Hypothesis   A research hypothesis that the researcher uses to predict the relation among groups using either a *greater-than* or a *less-than* prediction.

Double Blind   A control procedure where the person interacting with the participants and recording the data does not know the hypothesis of the research or the relevant details of the independent variable the participant experienced. In addition, the participant does not know the details of the project or the level of independent variable.

Effect Size   A standardized index of the difference between-groups means or the relation between two variables.

Experimenter Bias or Effect   When the experimenter's expectancies and knowledge of the anticipated results alters the way he or she treats the participants in the different research conditions or alters his or her objectivity when recording the data.

Hawthorne Effect   Used to describe any situation wherein the participants' assumptions about the purpose of the research bias their performance.

Heterogeneous Sample   A sample for which the members are dissimilar to each other regarding one or more relevant variables.

Homogenous Sample   A sample for which all the members are similar to one another on one or more relevant variables.

Manipulation Check   Any procedure that a researcher uses to ensure that the participants in the study accepted the cover story as the explanation for the purpose of the research.

Mathematical Hypothesis   A statement that describes the relation between population parameters using relational symbols (e.g., $=$, $\neq$, $<$, $>$, $\leq$, and $\geq$). The null and alternative hypotheses use complementary relations (e.g., $=$ vs. $\neq$, $\geq$ vs. $<$, or $\leq$ vs. $>$).

Median Split   A technique for creating two intact groups by first administering a test of a subject variable and then dividing the participants into two groups based on the median score.

Nondirectional Hypothesis   A research hypothesis that the researcher uses to predict a general difference among groups.

Self-Fulfilling Prophecy   Within the research context, the tendency for a researcher to treat the participants differently based upon preconceived ideas about the participants or the treatment condition that the participants receive.

Significance Level or Criteria   A level of α the researcher selects to determine whether to reject the null hypothesis.

Single Blind   Any procedure used to prevent the participants from knowing the researcher's hypothesis or the treatment condition received.

Type I Error   When the null hypothesis is correct and the researcher treats it as false.

Type II Error   When the null hypothesis is false and the researcher does not reject it.

Within-Groups Variance   The variability among scores within a group. This variability represents the natural variability among the members of the population and measurement error.

Within-Subjects Variable or Repeated Measure Variable   A form of independent variable for which the researcher tests the same participant on more than one occasion or under more than one level of the independent variable.

10 INTRODUCTION TO STATISTICAL INFERENCE

CHAPTER OUTLINE

✦ Introduction

✦ Student's t-Ratio for Independent Groups

✦ Review of Hypothesis Testing

✦ Testing Statistical Hypotheses: Preparation

✦ Common Errors in Interpreting the Meaning of p

✦ The Power of a Test

✦ Estimating Sample Size

✦ Computers and Statistics

✦ Statistics Behind the Research

Statistics is no substitute for judgment.

—Henry Clay

INTRODUCTION

In chapter 9 we reviewed the foundation of the research design for a two-group study. In that chapter, we examined ways to design a research project that allows us to collect data relevant to the research hypothesis. Once we collect the data, we must begin the process of analysis and interpretation. In most cases, we use inferential statistics to help us determine whether to reject the null hypothesis. In the first part of this chapter we will review the logic of inferential statistics and their use. As a part of this review, we will examine the types of inferences these statistics do and do not allow us to make.

Inferential statistics are important to all the behavioral sciences. Unfortunately, some researchers abuse, misapply, and misinterpret these tools. Because statistical analysis forms the basis of decision making, you need to understand what conclusions, or inferences, you can and cannot draw from these statistics tests.

I hope that you will take heed of Clay's comment about statistics and judgments. Statistics are wonderful tools for helping us find patterns and trends in the data. They also help us solve problems and come to decisive conclusions. I hope that you will also learn that statistical inference requires careful consideration. Statistics may help us make judgments, but do not, cannot, and should not replace our ability to make rational decisions.

In another section of this chapter we will review how inferential statistics help us solve other important questions. For example, many researchers ask, "How many participants do I need in my research?" This is an important question because the sample size affects the accuracy of the results and conclusions of our research.

I will continue to use the two-group experiment for my examples not because it is the most popular research tool, but because it is a good way to describe the important topics in this chapter. We will review more complex research designs in subsequent chapters. Fortunately, the principles you mastered in chapter 9, and the ones you will learn in this chapter, apply to all good research designs and inferential statistics.

Finally, I will close the chapter with a few comments about using computers to conduct statistical tests. Computers have done much to revolutionize the use of statistics in contemporary behavioral research. Although computers make statistics easy to perform, you need to be aware of some common pitfalls.

STUDENT'S *t*-RATIO FOR INDEPENDENT GROUPS

One of the most important advances in modern inferential statistics was the development of Student's sampling distributions and the inferential statistics using those distributions. This statistic, known as **Student's *t*-ratio,** is a commonly used statistical procedure in the behavioral sciences and sets the standard for using inferential statistics. Once you master the principles used for this inferential statistic, you will be able to use and understand other inferential statistics. The "Statistics Behind the Research" section at the end of this chapter presents the t-ratio and its alternatives, in detail.

The t-ratio gets its name because it is a ratio of two measures of variability. Specifically, it is the ratio of the difference between two group means relative to the variability within groups. Equation 10.1 presents a conceptual formula for Student's t-ratio.

$$t = \frac{\text{Difference between means}}{\text{Standard error of the difference between means}} \qquad (10.1)$$

The numerator of the equation represents the difference between the two means. As you recall from chapter 9, the difference between the two means reflects the effect of the independent variable and the effects of random error. Because the t-ratio compares the difference between two means, the t-ratio can be a negative value when $M_1 < M_2$, a positive value when $M_1 > M_2$, or 0 when $M_1 = M_2$.

The denominator is the **standard error of the difference between means,** which allows us to estimate the variability within-groups. Recall that the within-groups variability represents normal differences among individuals in the population and sampling error. The standard error of the difference between means is similar to the standard error of the mean. Therefore, we can use what we have learned about the standard error of the mean and apply it to the standard error of the difference between means.

According to the central limit theorem, the distribution of sample means is normally distributed with a standard deviation of $s_M = SD/\sqrt{n}$. The same occurs when we examine the difference between means drawn from separate populations. Imagine that we have two populations where $\mu_1 = 5.0$, $\sigma_1 = 1.0$ and $\mu_2 = 5.0$, $\sigma_2 = 1.0$. We draw a random sample with $n = 2$ from each population. For the first sample, the scores might be 3 and 5. For the second sample, the scores could be 4 and 6. Therefore, $M_1 = 4$ and $M_2 = 5$. The difference between the means is $M_1 - M_2 = -1$. If we continue this sampling procedure infinitely, we can create a sampling distribution of the difference between the means.

What would this sampling distribution look like? Figure 10.1 presents an illustration of what would happen. The sampling distribution at the bottom of the figure represents the distribution of the difference between means, $M_1 - M_2$. Because the null hypothesis states that $\mu_1 = \mu_2$, we predict that the mean of the sampling distribution will be $\mu_{\mu_1-\mu_2} = 0$ and that values above and below 0 represent random sampling error. According to the central limit theorem, we can predict that the distribution of the difference between means will be symmetrical and bell-shaped.

We use the term $\sigma_{\mu_1-\mu_2}$ to represent the standard error of the difference between means. When we calculate the t-ratio, we use the variances of the two samples to estimate $\sigma_{\mu_1-\mu_2}$. Specifically, $SD_{M_1-M_2}$ is an unbiased estimate of $\sigma_{\mu_1-\mu_2}$, just as the SD is an unbiased estimate of the population standard deviation, σ.

Many statisticians refer to $SD_{M_1-M_2}$ as the **error term** because we use it to estimate the random error that occurs when we take random samples from the population. Thus sampling error and random error are synonymous and estimated by $SD_{M_1-M_2}$. Using this information, we can turn our attention to hypothesis testing.

What does the t-ratio tell us? Using Equation 10.1, you can conclude that the larger the absolute value of the t-ratio, the greater the relative difference between the means. The magnitude of the t-ratio, therefore, allows us to determine whether to reject the null hypothesis.

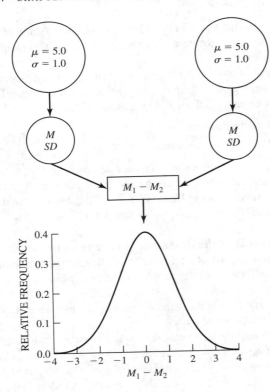

H_0: $\mu_1 = \mu_2$. The two population means are the same. Thus H_0 is a true statement.

Assume that we use random sampling to create the individual samples. Therefore, M is an unbiased estimate of μ and any difference between M and μ is the result of sampling error.

Because the two population means are the same, $\mu_1 = \mu_2$, the typical difference between the sample means will be $M_1 - M_2 = 0$. Differences between the means reflect sampling error.

FIGURE 10.1

The standard error of the difference between means. According to the null hypothesis, $\mu_1 = \mu_2$. Therefore, if we were to create an infinite number of sample pairs, the difference between the pairs would fall into the sampling distribution at the bottom of the figure. The mean of the sampling distribution will be 0 and the standard deviation will equal $\sigma_{\mu_2 - \mu_2} = \sqrt{\sigma_1^2/n_1 + \sigma_2^2/n_2}$.

The typical two-group nondirectional null hypothesis states that H_0: $\mu_1 = \mu_2$. Consequently, we predict that the average difference between the means of samples drawn from the two populations will be 0. Sampling error may cause the difference between some sample means to be greater or less than 0. However, if a t-ratio is sufficiently large, we can use its magnitude to reject the null hypothesis. The question before us is what we mean by sufficiently large.

REVIEW OF HYPOTHESIS TESTING

How do we decide whether to reject the null hypothesis? We use estimates of probability. Imagine that your friend claims to be able to toss a coin and cause it to land heads. To test your friend's skill, you ask that he or she toss a coin 10 times in a row. If your

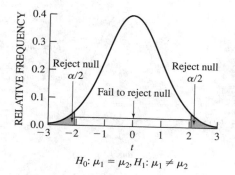

$H_0: \mu_1 = \mu_2, H_1: \mu_1 \neq \mu_2$

FIGURE 10.2

A hypothetical sampling distribution of the t-ratio and testing the nondirectional null hypothesis $H_0: \mu_1 = \mu_2$. The shaded areas represent the criterion for rejecting the null hypothesis. If the t-ratio falls in the shaded area, we reject H_0 in favor of H_1. If the t-ratio falls in the clear area, we fail to reject the null hypothesis.

friend produces only 5 heads out of 10 tosses, you will probably not be impressed because your friend seems to be tossing heads at random. However, if your friend can toss 10 heads in a row, you may be impressed because the probability of a run of 10 heads is less than 1 in 1,000.[1] Could your friend have been lucky and tossed 10 heads by chance? Yes, but the probability is small enough that you decide that the 10 heads must represent a unique skill.

We use the same reasoning when we evaluate the t-ratio. We ask, "If the null hypothesis is a true statement, what is the probability of obtaining a t-ratio at least this large?" If the probability is sufficiently small, we can infer that the null hypothesis is a false statement.

As you learned in chapter 9, we use α to represent the probability of committing a Type I error (rejecting a correct null hypothesis). Most researchers use α to establish the criterion for determining when to reject the null hypothesis and set $\alpha = .05$. The α-level indicates that if the null hypothesis is correct, there is a 5% probability of committing a Type I error (rejecting H_0 when we should not). In some cases, the researcher may want to be more cautious and will set $\alpha = .01$, thus lowering the risk of a Type I error to 1%.

Figure 10.2 represents an example of a sampling distribution for a t-ratio where the nondirectional null hypothesis is $H_0: \mu_1 = \mu_2$. Using this sampling distribution, we can determine the probability of obtaining any specific t-ratio and thereby determine whether to reject the null hypothesis. You should recognize that the null hypothesis in Figure 10.2 is a nondirectional hypothesis and that the alternative hypothesis is $H_1: \mu_1 \neq \mu_2$. In this case, we will reject the null hypothesis if the t-ratio is considerably less than or considerably greater than 0. As you can see, the tail ends of this figure are shaded and marked "Reject null $\alpha/2$." If the null hypothesis is correct, then the probability that the t-ratio will fall within either shaded area is equal to α. Because the null hypothesis is nondirectional, we divide α equally between the two ends of the sampling distribution.

Let's return to the study we discussed in chapter 9 where we wanted to compare men and women's recall of emotional events. In that example, we asked the question "Do men and women differ when asked to recall emotionally significant events in their lives?" This is a nondirectional hypothesis because we want to determine if there is a difference between the two groups. In this example, the null hypothesis is that men and women will recall approximately the same number of positive emotional events. If the null hypothesis is

---

[1]Assume that the probability of heads is .5. Because there are 10 coin tosses, the probability of all heads is $p = .5^{10} = .000977$ or $p = .001$.

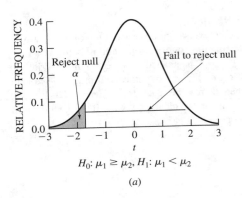
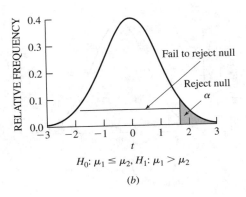

$H_0: \mu_1 \geq \mu_2, H_1: \mu_1 < \mu_2$

(a)

$H_0: \mu_1 \leq \mu_2, H_1: \mu_1 > \mu_2$

(b)

FIGURE 10.3

(a) A hypothetical sampling distribution of a t-ratio and testing the null hypothesis, $H_0: \mu_1 \geq \mu_2$.
(b) A hypothetical sampling distribution of a t-ratio and testing the null hypothesis, $H_0: \mu_1 \leq \mu_2$.
The shaded areas represent the criterion for rejecting the null hypothesis. If the t-ratio falls in the
shaded area, we reject H_0 in favor of H_1. If the t-ratio falls in the clear area, we fail to reject the
null hypothesis.

correct, the t-ratio for the difference between means should be close to 0, and any difference from 0 would represent the effect of random events.

Assume we decide to set $\alpha = .05$. According to Figure 10.2, the probability of obtaining a t-ratio in the upper shaded area is $p = .025$ $(.025 = .05/2)$. Similarly, the probability of obtaining a t-ratio in the lower shaded area is also $p = .025$. Added together the two
shaded areas comprise .05 or 5% of the distribution. If a t-ratio falls within either shaded
area, we reject the null hypothesis because the probability of such a t-ratio is sufficiently
small, so we are willing to infer that null hypothesis is incorrect. By contrast, if the t-ratio
falls between the two shaded areas, we do not reject the null hypothesis.

Figure 10.3 presents how we would proceed if we use a directional hypothesis. Because the directional hypothesis predicts the relation between the means (using < or >) we
place the entire α region on the side of the sampling distribution representing the hypothesized difference between the mean. Specifically, Figure 10.3(a) represents the test we create using the null hypothesis, $H_0: \mu_1 \geq \mu_2$; Figure 10.3(b) represents the test created using
the null hypothesis, $H_0: \mu_1 \leq \mu_2$.

TESTING STATISTICAL HYPOTHESES: PREPARATION

Statisticians and researchers invented inferential statistics during the early part of the 20th
century (Oakes, 1986). Over time, general rules and principles for using inferential statistics became common practice. For example, most researchers now routinely include a null
and alternative hypothesis as a part of their statistical test. In this section we will examine
the specific steps involved in hypothesis testing.

One important feature of all hypothesis testing is that we form the hypothesis *before*
we collect or examine the data. All of us can describe the past with accuracy; predicting the

future, however, is a talent. Thus, we are more impressed by and have much greater confidence in a prediction of the future that comes true. As you will see in the following steps, much of the work associated with hypothesis testing comes before we collect or analyze the data.

Steps for Hypothesis Testing

State the null and alternative hypotheses

As you learned in the previous chapter, the null hypothesis, H_0, is the mathematical statement we want to disprove. More specifically, the typical null hypothesis states that there is no relation between the independent and dependent variables. If we can reject the null hypothesis, then we can accept the alternative hypothesis, the focus of the study. Typically, the alternative hypothesis is the central thesis of the research and states that there is a meaningful difference between the group means.

The null hypothesis can be either nondirectional or directional. The nondirectional hypothesis for a two-group study will be $H_0: \mu_1 = \mu_2$. This version of the hypothesis states that the two population means are identical and that any observed difference between the group means is due to random events unrelated to the independent variable. By contrast, the directional null hypothesis can be either $H_0: \mu_1 \geq \mu_2$ or $H_0: \mu_1 \leq \mu_2$. The directional hypothesis predicts that one population mean is less than the other mean with the exception of the effects of random sampling error.

The alternative hypothesis is always the mathematical complement of the null hypothesis. The complementary relational signs are $=$ and $\neq$, $\geq$ and $<$, and $\leq$ and $>$. As a rule, each null hypothesis has only one alternative hypothesis.

Identify the appropriate statistical test

This step may seem obvious, but is often the downfall of many students and researchers. Part of the problem is that you can apply any statistical test to any set of data. One question you could ask is "Can I use this statistic to analyze these data?" The answer will always be "Yes" because you can use any statistical test to analyze any set of data. A better question is, "Will this statistical test allow me to answer the question I posed in my hypothesis?" Different statistical tests provide different perspectives of the data. Some allow you to compare groups whereas others examine the correlation between groups. Therefore, your null and alternative hypotheses will determine the type of test you use.

Other factors also influence the selection of the appropriate statistical test. Many inferential statistics require that the data meet specific criteria to produce valid results. For example, the t-ratio for independent groups assumes that the observations for the two groups are independent, that the data are normally distributed, and that the variances of the two groups be equivalent. Failure to meet these criteria can produce spurious results.

As you plan your research, you should identify the appropriate statistical tests for analyzing the data and identify the requirements for using that test. In addition, you should identify alternative strategies for analyzing the data in the case that your data do not conform to the requirements of a specific test.

There are many ways to analyze the data from a research project. Consider the study described in chapter 9 where the researchers wanted to compare the number of positive and negative memories that men and women recall. The researchers could use Student's t-ratio for independent groups to analyze the data. If, for some reason, the data do not conform to the requirements of the statistic, there are alternative statistical tests. For example, if the variances of the two groups are not equivalent, the researchers could use a special form of t-ratio that corrects for the inequality of variances. Similarly, the researchers could use the Mann-Whitney U-test, another alternative to the t-ratio. The "Statistics Behind the Research" section at the end of the chapter includes an example of these alternatives.

Determine the significance level

Determining the significance level is another important step. As you learned in the previous chapter, researchers want to avoid making a Type I error. We can control the probability of committing a Type I error by selecting a suitable criterion. Because α represents the probability of committing a Type I error and is determined by the researcher, you have direct control over the probability of committing a Type I error. Recall that the probability of a Type I error and a Type II error are inversely related—as you reduce the risk of a Type I error, you increase the risk of a Type II error. Consequently, you should plan your research with care to ensure that the risk of both errors is at a tolerable level.

Many researchers have gotten into the habit of automatically setting $\alpha = .05$ or $\alpha = .01$ and then continuing with the analysis of the data. There is nothing magical about these criteria but their use is common practice. Selecting an α-level should not be reflexive. Instead, selecting α should be a deliberative process that examines the consequence of committing a Type I or a Type II error.

In many ways, selecting an α-level takes us back to the utilitarian principles of ethics because the process forces us to examine the consequences of our actions. Ask yourself, "What is the cost of committing a Type I versus a Type II error?" For the American legal system, we believe that sending an innocent person to jail (a Type I error) is far worse than letting a guilty person back on the streets (a Type II error). Therefore, the legal criterion for finding guilt—"beyond a reasonable doubt"—is equivalent to setting α to a small value, say $\alpha = .0001$.

Rudner (1953) argued that researchers must make value judgments when deciding whether to reject the null hypothesis. He asserted that,

> [because] no scientific hypothesis is ever completely verified, in accepting a hypothesis the scientist must make the decision that the evidence is *sufficiently* strong or that the probability is *sufficiently* high to warrant the acceptance of the hypothesis. . . . *How sure we need to be before we accept a hypothesis will depend on how serious a mistake would be.* (p. 350)

Rudner recognized two important components of hypothesis tests. First, inferential statistics depend upon samples and probabilities. Consequently, whenever we make a statistical decision, we must recognize the legitimate risk of committing a Type I or Type II error. Second, either error may have grave consequences depending on the purpose of the research. Therefore, as researchers we must examine the utility of our research results and the consequences of our statistical decisions.

For some experiments, committing a Type I error can have serious negative consequences. Will we, for example, use the results to justify an expensive program of research or to alter the treatment that patients currently receive? If the statistical conclusion represents a Type I error, we may end up spending money on a potentially pointless set of experiments or begin to use an ineffective treatment.

In other cases, committing a Type II error is the more serious mistake. A Type II error may cause the researcher to ignore an important relation between two variables or disregard a potentially useful treatment. For many researchers who conduct basic research, a Type II error is the more serious error because it means that they have overlooked a potentially interesting finding.

Because both Type I and Type II errors involve potentially unpleasant consequences, we should design our research to minimize the risk of both errors. Reaching a balance between the two errors is not always easy, but is possible with careful planning. We will return to this important topic later in the chapter.

Once you determine the significance level that you wish to use, you can proceed with the analysis of the data. Using the results of your data analysis, you can then determine whether you have sufficient evidence to support your original research hypothesis.

Determining the significance level for the *t*-ratio

We use Table A.3 of Appendix A to determine the critical value of the *t*-ratio required to reject the null hypothesis. As you learned previously, the table consists of a series of rows and columns. Each column represents the probability level we want to use for our hypothesis. Each row represents the degrees of freedom for the data. For the independent groups *t*-ratio, the degrees of freedom are,

$$df = (n_1 - 1) + (n_2 - 1) \tag{10.2}$$

To determine the critical value of *t*, known as $t_{critical}$, we need to determine the level of α, whether we wish to conduct a directional or a nondirectional test, and the degrees of freedom for the test. As an example, assume that we set $\alpha = .05$ and decide to use a nondirectional test, and that the degrees of freedom are 16. Given these facts, we see that $t_{critical} = 2.120$. What would have happened if we had decided to conduct a directional test? For $df = 16$ and $\alpha = .05$, one-tailed, $t_{critical} = 1.746$.

We can use the data for men and women's recall of positive emotional events as an illustration of the steps for hypothesis testing (see Box 10.1). For the sake of illustration, we will assume that we will use a nondirectional hypothesis.

Because the absolute value of the obtained *t*-ratio exceeds the critical value ($t_{observed} > t_{critical}$; $2.89 > 2.048$), we can reject H_0. If the null hypothesis were true, the probability of selecting at random two samples that differ this much or more is less than 5 times in 100 or $p < .05$.

If you used a computer to calculate the statistic, you may have obtained something like,

$$t(28) = 2.89, \quad p \text{ one-tailed} = .0035, \quad p \text{ two-tailed} = .007$$

Whenever the probability level of the statistic (p) is less than the α-level, you can reject the null hypothesis. In this example, the probability associated with this *t*-ratio is $p = .007$ for the two-tailed or nondirectional test. Because $p < \alpha$, you can reject H_0.

Interpreting the *t*-Ratio

Once we calculate the *t*-ratio and its probability, we can determine whether to reject H_0. Although we have completed one important task, there are still many opportunities to analyze

---

BOX 10.1   Example of Steps Used in Hypothesis Testing

Null Hypothesis:	$H_0: \mu_1 = \mu_2$. The average performance of the participants in the two groups is equivalent.
Alternative Hypothesis:	$H_1: \mu_1 \neq \mu_2$. The average performance of the participants in the two groups is not equivalent.
Statistical Test:	We will use the t-ratio because we wish to compare the difference between two independent groups.
Significance Level:	$\alpha = .05$, two-tailed, $df = 28 = (15 - 1) + (15 - 1)$ $t_{critical}(28) = \pm 2.048$.

Number of positive events recalled

Women	Men
$n_1 = \quad 15$	$n_2 = \quad 15$
$\sum X_1 = \quad 157$	$\sum X_2 = \quad 126$
$\sum X_1^2 = 1707$	$\sum X_2^2 = 1102$
$M_1 = \quad 10.47$	$M_2 = \quad 8.40$

$$t = \frac{M_1 - M_2}{\sqrt{\dfrac{\sum X_1^2 - \dfrac{(\sum X_1)^2}{n_1} + \sum X_2^2 - \dfrac{(\sum X_2)^2}{n_2}}{n_1 + n_2 - 2} \left(\dfrac{1}{n_1} + \dfrac{1}{n_2}\right)}}$$

$$t = \frac{10.47 - 8.40}{\sqrt{\dfrac{1707 - \dfrac{(157)^2}{15} + 1102 - \dfrac{(126)^2}{15}}{15 + 15 - 2} \left(\dfrac{1}{15} + \dfrac{1}{15}\right)}}$$

$$t = 2.89$$

---

the results of our research. In this section we will examine several of the errors that many people make when interpreting the results. We will also examine the conclusions that inferential statistics afford and several statistical procedures that can enhance our interpretation of the data.

Statistically significant

Statistically significant means that we have sufficient statistical evidence to reject the null hypothesis. Unfortunately, many people equate "statistical significance" with "importance." As I hope to show you, this is clearly not the case.

Some researchers like to make the distinction between **statistical significance** and **clinical** or **practical significance.** Statistical significance means that one has reason to reject the null hypothesis. Clinical significance means that the results justify a specific intervention for the target population (Moyé, 2000). In other words, clinical significance means that the results support our conclusion that the size of the effect justifies the cost of the treatment.

Under some circumstances it is possible to obtain statistical significance when $d_2 = .1$ or less (recall that when $d_2 \leq .1$ the effect size is trivial). For example, we can claim that there is a statistically significant difference between men and women's scores on math achievement tests, although d_2 is within the trivial effect size range. The difference between most men and women's math skills is of little practical significance, especially for anything less than the most complex levels of mathematics. Therefore, when you hear that the results are statistically significant, do not automatically assume that the results are of practical or clinical significance unless the researcher has compelling evidence to make such a claim.

Omega squared: $\hat{\omega}^2$

The presence of statistical significance does not automatically confer "importance" on a finding. Given a sufficiently large n, any difference, however trivial, can be statistically significant. One way to clarify the importance of a statistically significant t-ratio is to determine the extent to which variations in the independent variable account for variations in the dependent variable. One of the more popular measures of association is $\hat{\omega}^2$ (**omega squared**). We calculate $\hat{\omega}^2$ by

$$\hat{\omega}^2 = \frac{t^2 - 1}{t^2 + n_1 + n_2 - 1} \tag{10.3}$$

Omega squared is an index of the degree to which the variance in one variable accounts for the variance in another variable. Omega squared can have positive and negative values. Specifically, when the absolute value of $t < 1.00$, $\hat{\omega}^2$ will be negative. For practical purposes, negative values of $\hat{\omega}^2$ have little meaning. Consequently, most researchers calculate $\hat{\omega}^2$ only when the t-ratio is statistically significant.

We can apply the equation for $\hat{\omega}^2$ to the sex difference data. From that example, we know that $t = 2.89$, $n_1 = 15$, and $n_2 = 15$. Therefore,

$$\hat{\omega}^2 = \frac{(2.89)^2 - 1}{(2.89)^2 + 15 + 15 - 1} \qquad \hat{\omega}^s = \frac{8.3521 - 1}{8.3521 + 29} \qquad \hat{\omega}^2 = \frac{7.3521}{37.3521}$$

$$\hat{\omega}^2 = .1968$$

We may interpret $\hat{\omega}^2$ to mean that the independent variable accounts for approximately 20% of the variance in the dependent variable. In some research contexts, accounting for 20% of the variance is a tremendous event and reflects a real advance in the science. In other contexts, 20% is barely worth considering. Consequently, you must use your judgment to evaluate the size of this statistic.

You cannot judge the magnitude of the association by merely looking at the value of the t-ratio or the probability level. For example, imagine that you found a t-ratio of -3.17 with 70 participants in each group. The difference is clearly statistically significant. Under these conditions, the probability for $t = -3.17$ is $p = .00052$. However,

$$\hat{\omega}^2 = \frac{(-3.17)^2 - 1}{(-3.17)^2 + 70 + 70 - 1} \qquad \hat{\omega}^2 = .061$$

Neither the size of the t-ratio nor the size of the p-value can indicate the "importance" of the data. The t-ratio indicates only if there is sufficient evidence to reject the null hypothesis. You must use other statistics such as $\hat{\omega}^2$ or d_2 to further evaluate the results of the study.

Cause and effect

The t-ratio allows us to determine if there is a statistically significant difference between two groups. Before we can use a t-ratio to support conclusions of cause and effect, the research design must meet certain conditions. As you should recall, the experimenter must use a manipulated independent variable and randomly assign the participants to the two groups, one of which must be a control group.

By contrast, intact groups design allow us to infer that the two groups are different from one another. Because we do not control the independent variable, however, we cannot be sure if the difference is due to the independent variable or some other condition beyond our control.

Reporting the *t*-Ratio

Many researchers in the behavioral sciences use the *Publication Manual of the American Psychological Association* (2001) as the editorial guideline when preparing their manuscripts for publication. The recommended format for reporting the results of the *t*-ratio is

$$t(df) = t_{observed}, \quad p = p, \quad \text{or as} \quad t(df) = t_{observed}, \quad p < \alpha$$

As an example, you could write something like,

> Figure 1 presents the average number of positive memories recalled by women and men. An independent groups *t*-ratio confirmed that the women recalled more positive memories than the men, $t(28) = 2.89$, $p < .05$, $\hat{\omega}^2 = .20$.

ACHIEVEMENT CHECK

(1) A researcher conducts a study comparing the behavior of two groups. According to the results, the mean of two groups are $M_1 = 98$ and $M_2 = 107$.
  (a) What are potential explanations for the difference between the means?
  (b) Can the researcher use the difference between the means to conclude that the independent variable has a statistically significant effect on the dependent variable?
  (c) How will changes in the standard error of the difference between means influence our interpretation of the difference between the two means?
(2) Using the previous example, could we potentially reject the null hypothesis if it took the form $H_0: \mu_1 \leq \mu_2$? What if the null hypothesis were $H_0: \mu_1 \geq \mu_2$?
(3) Why should the researcher state the null and alternative hypotheses before collecting and analyzing the data?
(4) What are the factors that will determine your selection of an inferential statistic?
(5) A researcher is determining the significance level of a statistical test. According to Rudner, why is this selection a value judgment? What are the consequences of selecting the significance level?
(6) A researcher finds that the difference between two groups is statistically significant. Under what conditions can the researcher assume that there is a cause and effect relation between the independent and dependent variables?

COMMON ERRORS IN INTERPRETING THE MEANING OF *p*

Many researchers criticize the use of statistical hypothesis testing. Much of the complaint is that some people misuse or misinterpret the results of an inferential statistic. The following is a list of the more common errors. For the most part, the greatest controversy surrounds the interpretation of the probability level associated with inferential statistics.

Change α After Analyzing the Data

Imagine that a researcher set $\alpha = .05$ before collecting the data. After analyzing the data the researcher finds that $p = .003$. Should he or she be able to revise α to $\alpha = .005$ to make the data look "more significant"? What if the researcher had set $\alpha = .01$ but the analysis of the data revealed $p = .03$? Can the researcher revise α to $\alpha = .05$ to say that there are statistically significant results? Shine (1980) argued that the answer to both questions is an emphatic no! The first problem with this type of revision is that it is *unethical*. Researchers should set α before analyzing their data and stick with that decision.

The second reason is that the p-level is not a substitute for α. The mathematical logic is beyond the scope of this text. What you need to understand is that p only estimates the probability of obtaining at least the observed results *if the null hypothesis is true*. Because we estimate p using sample statistics and because the null hypothesis may be false, we cannot work backward and use p to revise α.

Assume That p Indicates That the Results Are Due to Chance

Carver (1978) calls this error the "odds-against-chance" error. Some researchers interpret p to indicate the probability that the difference between the means is due to chance. For instance, a researcher may find that for a specific t-ratio $p = .023$ and conclude that the probability that the results were due to chance is 2.3% or less. This interpretation is incorrect because we begin our statistical test with an H_0 that states that *all differences are due to chance*. H_0 states that the probability of obtaining *any* difference between the means by chance is 1.0. The p-value merely indicates the probability of obtaining a specific or more extreme difference if H_0 is true. Because we do not know the real parameters of the populations, we cannot predict the probability that the results are due to chance.

A related error in the interpretation of the p-value is to assume that p establishes the probability that we will commit a Type I error. If you found that $p = .023$ you could not conclude that the probability committing a Type I error is 2.3%. The value of α determines the probability of a Type I error. As a rule, you should interpret the p-value to mean,

> "If H_0 is a true statement, the probability of obtaining results like these or more extreme is p. If the value of p is small enough, I am willing to reject H_0 in favor of the alternative hypothesis. The probability of committing a Type I error is α."

Assume the Size of p Indicates the Validity of the Results

Some researchers assume that the p-value indicates the probability that the research hypothesis is true. Again, the probability of the statistic does not allow us to determine the accuracy of the alternative hypothesis. The ability to determine the validity of the research hypothesis is an extremely complicated issue. As a generalization, the p-value cannot confirm the validity of the research hypothesis. The only function of the p-value is to determine if there is sufficient evidence to reject H_0.

Some researchers infer that a small value of p indicates the degree to which there is a meaningful relation between the independent and dependent variables. For example, if $p = .001$, the researcher may conclude that the independent variable has a great effect upon the dependent variable or claim that the data are "highly significant." This inference is not true. Only $\hat{\omega}^2$, and related statistics, indicate the relation between the independent and dependent variables.

Assume That p Establishes the Probability That the Results Can Be Replicated

Some people assume that $(1 - p)$ indicates the probability that the experiment will yield the same result if repeated. If, for example, $p = 0.23$, a researcher may assume that the probability of replicating the experiment and rejecting H_0 is $1 - .023 = 0.977$. This is a false statement because the probability of correctly rejecting H_0 is not related to the value of p. The ability to replicate a given finding depends on the difference between the means, the number of participants, the amount of measurement error, and the level of α. It is possible to have a small level of p (i.e., $p = .001$) and a low probability that the results can be directly replicated.

You are probably wondering if you can draw any meaningful conclusion from a statistically significant t-ratio. If you obtain a statistically significant t-ratio at $p \leq \alpha$, you may conclude that there is a statistically significant difference between the two groups. In addition, if your comparison is part of a true experiment, you may conclude that the independent variable affects the dependent variable. You may also conclude the probability of a Type I error is α.

THE POWER OF A TEST

As you may recall from the previous chapter, a Type II error occurs when we fail to reject a false null hypothesis. Researchers want to avoid Type II errors for obvious reasons. We conduct research because we want to discover interesting facts and relations among variables. If our statistical tools overlook these important findings, we will have wasted much time and energy. Therefore, researchers strive to increase the power of their statistical test when they conduct research.

In chapter 9, we also reviewed tactics that we can use to ensure that the data we collect will allow us to correctly reject the null hypothesis in favor of the alternative hypothesis. In this section we will revisit those design tactics and show how they can increase the **power of a statistic.**

For any statistical test, β defines the probability of making a Type II error. The power of a statistic, which we represent as $1 - \beta$, is the probability of correctly rejecting a false null hypothesis. The four factors that influence statistical power are the: (1) difference between the populations, $\mu_1 - \mu_2$; (2) sample size, n; (3) variability in the population, σ^2; and (4) alpha (α) level and directionality (directional versus nondirectional) of the test.

Difference Between Population Means: $\mu_1 - \mu_2$

If the null hypothesis is false, there will be two sampling distributions similar to the ones presented in Figure 10.4(a). Each sampling distribution represents sample means drawn

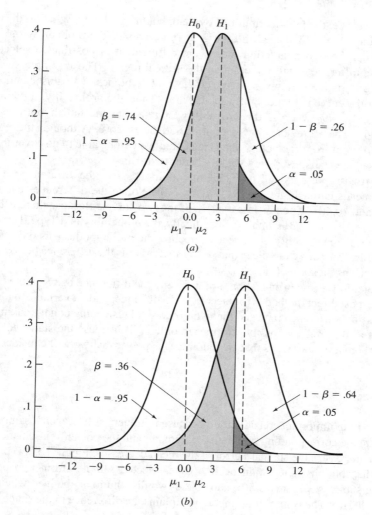

FIGURE 10.4
The effect on power of $\mu_1 - \mu_2$. In (a), the difference is 3.0. The difference in (b) is 6.0. For both pairs of distributions, the shaded areas represent the probabilities of committing a Type I error (α) and a Type II error (β). The power of the statistic is $1 - \beta$. Of the two graphs (b) represents greater power—$1 - \beta = .64$ compared to $1 - \beta = .26$.

from separate populations. The sampling distribution for the null hypothesis is a distribution of sample means for which $\mu_1 - \mu_2 = 0$. The shaded area at the upper end of the scale represents the critical region for $\alpha = .05$ using a directional test. According to the null hypothesis, there is a 5% probability that the difference between any pair of means will be in the critical area. The second distribution is a sampling distribution of means that would occur if we draw samples of a specific size from two populations for which $\mu_1 - \mu_2 = 3$.

As you can see, the two distributions overlap, but not perfectly. What do the different areas represent? The area shaded in light gray represents β, the probability of a Type II error. Although the two population means are different, it is possible to select sample means whose differences will be less than the critical region. Those samples will not be sufficiently different to allow us to reject the null hypothesis. In this example, 74% ($\beta = .74$) of the curve is in the lightly shaded area. Thus, the probability of committing a Type II error is 74% whereas the probability of rejecting the null hypothesis is 26% ($1 - \beta = .26$). Therefore, the power of this statistic is 26%. Although the population means are different from each other, the chance that we will be able to discover this difference using sample statistics is only slightly better than 1 in 4.

Figure 10.4(b) presents a different set of conditions. Now the difference between the population means is much greater ($\mu_1 - \mu_2 = 6.0$). Notice the differences between Figure 10.4(a) and 10.4(b). There is less overlap of the two curves. Because there is less overlap, the area representing β is smaller. Specifically, the probability of a Type II error is now 36%, whereas the probability of correctly rejecting the null hypothesis is 64%. The conclusion to draw from this example is that power increases as the difference between the two population means increases.

In chapter 9, we reviewed tactics for increasing the difference between the two populations. The most direct method is to select levels of the independent variable that create the greatest possible difference between the two groups. All else being equal, making the two populations as different as possible from each other will increase the statistical power of the study. There are other ways that we can increase power that we will consider next.

Sample Size

Sample size is an important consideration because it influences how well a sample statistic will estimate the corresponding population parameter and the power of a statistical test. As sample size increases, the standard error of the mean decreases. Figure 10.5(a) presents the sampling distributions that would occur if one selected samples from two populations using small samples. Figure 10.5(b) shows the two distributions obtained when we use a larger sample size. The central limit theorem explains the difference in the shape of the two sampling distributions.

As a rule, as the sample size increases, the standard error of the mean decreases. Consequently, the degree of overlap of the two sampling distributions decreases and the corresponding power increases.

Although it is true that increasing sample size will increase power, you need to be aware of the cost of this tactic. Increasing sample size sounds easy—you collect more data. The solution can be a problem, however. Collecting data takes time and money. From the cost of purchasing materials to the time you must take out of your schedule, collecting data from each subject adds to the total cost of the research. In some cases, such as administering a set of questionnaires to students in their classes, there will be a minimal cost for collecting more data. In other cases, collecting the data from one subject will be time consuming and expensive. Therefore, you should consider all your options for increasing power before you jump to the conclusion that you need to run more participants through your study.

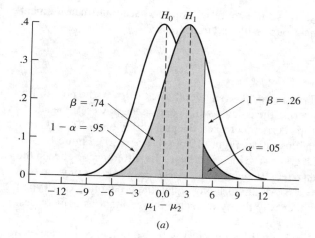

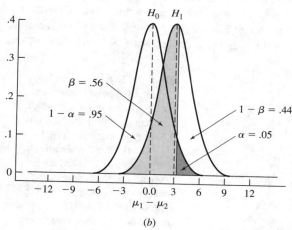

FIGURE 10.5
The effect on power resulting from changes in sample size or changes in population variance. For both distributions, the shaded areas represent the probability of committing a Type I error (α) and a Type II error (β). The power of the statistic is $1 - \beta$, (a) the standard error of the differences between means is larger and power is lower, (b) the standard error of the difference between means is smaller and the power is greater.

Variability

If the population from which you draw the sample has considerable variability, the sampling distribution will also have considerable variance. We can use Figure 10.5 again to represent the effects of population variance on power. The distributions in Figure 10.5(a) represent what would occur when the variance in the population is large. Consequently, there is considerable overlap of the two distributions and the power is small. Reducing the amount of variability in the population will produce a result similar to the one depicted in Figure 10.5(b). Because the magnitude of σ decreased, the overlap depicted in Figure 10.5(b) decreased and the power increased. Therefore, anything you can do to reduce sampling error will improve your ability to detect a statistically significant difference between the means.

As you may recall from chapter 9, there are several ways that we can decrease the within-groups variability. For example, we can use homogenous samples. If the participants in the individual groups are similar to each other, it is easier to detect differences among the group means. Similarly, as we use more reliable and accurate measurement techniques, the variability within the groups will tend to decrease.

Alpha, α

Alpha (α) sets the probability of a Type I error. The smaller the α, the lower the probability of a Type I error. Unfortunately, lowering the α-level will decrease the power of the statistical test. As the probability of the Type I error decreases, the probability of the Type II error increases. Look at Figure 10.6 for an illustration. Figure 10.6(a) has $\alpha = .05$; Figure 10.6(b) has $\alpha = .10$. All other aspects of the graphs are identical. Note the differences between the power for the two conditions. When $\alpha = .10$ the power is $1 - \beta = .39$. Lowering the α to .05 decreases the power to $1 - \beta = .26$. All things being equal, the probability of a Type I error increases as α decreases. Another way to say the same thing is that as α increases, power also increases.

Your selection of a directional and nondirectional test will also influence power. As a generality, a directional test is more powerful than a nondirectional test. The difference is where we place the critical region. Consider a t-ratio with $df = 15$ and $\alpha = .05$. When we use the directional test, we place the critical region at one end of the distribution. In this

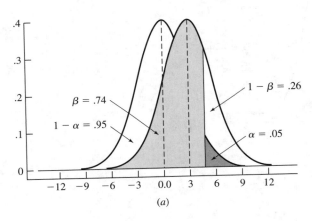

(a)

FIGURE 10.6
The effect of power caused by changes in α. For both graphs, the difference between the means is 3.0. For the distributions in (a), $\alpha = .05$. For the distributions in (b), α is larger ($\alpha = .10$) and the power is greater. For both graphs, the probability of committing a Type I error (α) and a Type II error (β) are represented by shaded areas. The power of the statistic is $1 - \beta$.

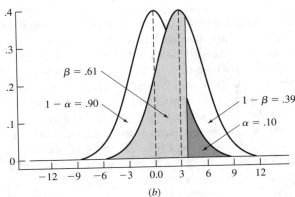

(b)

example, t_{critical} for the directional test is 1.753. When we conduct a nondirectional test, we split the criterion regions between the two extreme ends. Consequently, the t-ratio required to reject the null is larger than the comparable directional test. For the nondirectional test where $df = 15$, $t_{\text{critical}} = 2.131$.

ESTIMATING SAMPLE SIZE

How many participants should you include in your sample? Too few participants will result in small power. Too many participants may make the research too expensive and time consuming to conduct. We can use d_2 to estimate the number of participants we will need for our study.

Look at Tables A.5.1 and A.5.2 of Appendix A, which provide power estimates for two sample t-ratios. Along the left-most column are sample sizes (n), the number of participants in each group. The columns represent values of t_c, the critical t-ratio needed to reject the null hypothesis, and four levels of effect size, d_2. There are two versions of the table, one for directional tests and the other for nondirectional tests. To use the table, select an effect size that you believe represents your research. Then determine the sample size you will need for a specific level of power. Some researchers believe that power of $1 - \beta = .80$ is a good level for power. Others may want their power to be higher or lower.

Here is an example. You want to replicate the sex difference for emotional memories study at your college. How many participants will you need to replicate the effect? What would happen if you used a directional or nondirectional test to compare the differences?

For this example, assume that $\alpha = .05$, two-tailed, and that the effect size for this phenomenon is medium, $d_2 \approx .50$. According to Table A.5.2, you will need approximately 60 participants in each group to have your power set at $1 - \beta = .79$ for a nondirectional test. If you used a directional test, you would require approximately 50 participants in each group to have the power of approximately $1 - \beta = .82$. What would happen if you decided to collect data from 100 students and used a directional test? In that case, $1 - \beta = .98$. The larger sample size means that you will have a 98% chance of rejecting the null hypothesis if the null hypothesis is false.

Caveat Emptor: Sample Size

Increasing sample size should not be the only thing you do to increase the power of a statistical test. The decision to increase sample size should come only after you have examined the design of your research. As you learned in chapter 9, you can increase power by increasing the reliability of the tests you use to measure the dependent variable, ensuring homogeneity of variance among the participants and increasing the difference between the two groups.

ACHIEVEMENT CHECK

(7) Assume that a researcher conducted a two-group study and found that $t(18) = 2.7$, $p < .01$. Determine whether the following statements are correct or incorrect and defend your answer.

(a) The researcher has disproved the null hypothesis, $H_0: \mu_1 = \mu_2$.
(b) The researcher has determined the probability that H_0 is true.
(c) The researcher has proved the research hypothesis is correct.
(d) The researcher can determine the probability that H_1 is correct.
(e) The researcher can be confident that there is an extremely high probability that he or she could replicate the findings by conducting the same experiment.
(f) The probability of the data given the null hypothesis is $p < .01$.

(8) Mark and Mary each conducted an experiment studying the relation between the same independent and dependent variables. Mark used 20 participants in each group and found a statistically significant effect using $p = .045$. Mary used 100 participants in each group and found a statistically significant effect using $p = .045$.
(a) Of the two experiments, which appears to have the greater power?
(b) How would you account for the differences in power between the two experiments?

(9) Khalil wants to conduct an experiment and believes that the effect size for the variables selected is small $d_2 \approx .20$. How many participants should he place into each group to have statistical power of .80 for a two sample t-ratio with $\alpha = .05$—two-tailed? What would be the required sample size if Khalil used $\alpha = .05$—one-tailed?

(10) Khalil wants to find ways to improve the power of his study. What factors, other than increasing the number of participants in each group, should he consider in the design of his experiment that could increase power?

COMPUTERS AND STATISTICS

Charles Babbage (1792–1871), a British mathematician who attempted to invent the first mechanical calculator once exclaimed, "I wish to God these calculations had been [conducted] by steam." Many researchers and students who have calculated statistical tests by hand have often expressed the same sentiment.

Computers have had a profound effect on statistics and research methods by making it easier for researchers to use sophisticated statistical procedures to analyze their data. Before the advent of the computer, most researchers did not use many of the statistical procedures developed by statisticians because these tests required an overwhelming amount of calculation (Pedhazur, 1997). Although most statistical tests require simple arithmetic, the manual calculation of some statistics is impractical because of the computational burden required to complete the work. Even simple descriptive statistics, such as the standard deviation or correlation coefficient, are labor intensive because of the many repetitive calculations required to complete the work. As a generality, the greater the complexity of the statistical procedure, the greater the number of individual operations one must complete. The sample size magnifies the computational burden—the more observations you have, the more individual calculations you must perform.

The first practical computers became available in the late 1950s and early 1960s. Although these machines were huge and expensive, they gave researchers the opportunity to conduct sophisticated statistical tests. Psychologists, along with other scientists, quickly embraced the computer as an essential research tool. Figure 10.7 is an illustration from a statistics textbook published in the 1950s (Dixon & Massey, 1951) that expresses the excitement over the advent of the computer. The image of computer technology is obvious—the computer is a thoughtful and self-reliant machine that cheerfully works through masses of data.

FIGURE 10.7
A cute, although naïve, perspective of computers that was common in the 1950s when they were first available to the researcher. (*Adapted from Dixon, W. J. & Massey, F. J. (1951). Introduction to statistical methods. New York, McGraw-Hill, p. 224.*)

Since the 1950s, computers have grown progressively smaller, become more sophisticated, and much less expensive. The current generation of personal computers is far more sophisticated than many of the multimillion-dollar mainframe computers built 20 years ago. At the same time, statistics software has also evolved. Like the computer, these programs have become easier to use, less expensive, and provide access to many sophisticated statistical tests. The consequence of the computer revolution is that statistical techniques once considered impractical can now be calculated at the click of a mouse button. As useful as computers and computational software are, there are several potential problems that you must consider when using them.

Garbage in–Garbage out

Babbage recognized one of the inherent problems with inventing an automatic calculating machine. He lamented,

> On two occasions I have been asked [by members of Parliament], "Pray, Mr. Babbage, if you put into the machine wrong figures, will the right answers come out?" I [cannot understand] the kind of confusion of ideas that could provoke such a question. (As quoted in Shaw, 2001, p. 14.)

Babbage's quandary is as applicable today as it was then. No computer program or statistical procedure can spin gold from straw; the quality of any statistical analysis depends solely upon the quality of the original data. Unfortunately, many people treat the computer and statistics as magical machines that somehow tell the truth.

Computers do exactly what you tell them to do, even if it is the wrong thing. The phrase "garbage in—garbage out" means that the output of any computer program is no better than the data you ask it to analyze. Statistics packages cannot recognize when you have entered the wrong numbers or request a statistical test that does not address the hypothesis you want to test. These observations mean that we need to proceed with caution when using software packages. Perhaps we should revise the quotation at the start of the chapter to read, "Computers are no substitute for judgment."

Faulty data

The first problem to address is the accuracy of the data to analyze. Software packages treat the numbers .987 and 987 as legitimate values. That there are several orders of magnitude difference between the two numbers is of no concern for the computer. Therefore, you will need to spend a little extra time proofreading the data you have entered in the data file. You can also use several simple statistical tools, called exploratory data analysis, to ensure that you have not entered the wrong data.

Here is an example of how we can use exploratory data analysis to inspect the data for potential errors. I quickly entered 50 numbers that should range between 0 and 20 into a computer program (*SPSS®*) and then had the program create a stem-and-leaf plot and a box-and-whisker plot, which Figure 10.8 presents. Both plots indicate that there is something wrong with the data. The stem-and-leaf plot notes that there are 4 scores greater than 18. The box-and-whisker plot illustrates that I have two scores much greater than the typical range of scores. These outliers (88 and 99) are obvious typographical errors that I need to correct. Fortunately, I could use these graphs to detect obvious errors. Other errors, such as entering 75 rather than 57, require more careful proofreading of the data.

Selecting the right statistical test

The second and far more important problem that we need to address is your knowledge of the statistical tests that the software package allows you to conduct. Most statistical software programs allow you to calculate statistics as simple as the arithmetic mean and as complicated as a multivariate analysis of covariance. Just because the computer will let you use a statistical procedure to analyze the data does not mean that it is the right statistical test to use. Consequently, I cannot emphasize strongly enough the importance

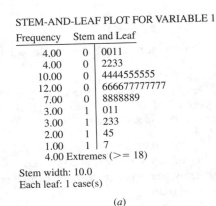

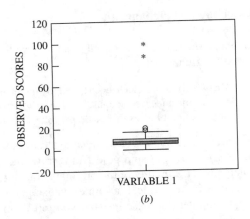

(a)   (b)

FIGURE 10.8

Examples of a (a) stem-and-leaf plot and a (b) box-and-whisker plot used to examine the data entered into a data set. Both plots illustrate that there are several irregular scores in the data set.

that you understand the conceptual foundation of any statistical test that you calculate. Whenever you use a statistic you should be able to justify why you selected it, show how it will help you interpret the data, and know what conclusions you can and cannot draw from the test.

Although many software packages will allow you to conduct similar statistical tests, they may have different ways of printing the final report. Two software packages may produce different reports for the analysis of the same data set and the same statistical analysis. You must practice with the computer program before you use it to analyze the data for your research. Most statistics textbooks give examples of how to calculate various statistical tests. Enter the example data into the computer program and then let the computer program analyze the data. You can then compare the program's output to the textbook example. This exercise should help you understand how the program generates the final report.

Statistical fishing expeditions

Because computer software makes complex statistical tests easy to conduct, many researchers are willing to go on a "fishing expedition" with their data. These researchers conduct statistical test after statistical test in the hope of finding one that will indicate a statistically significant effect. You should select your statistical procedures as a part of your research design, and stick to that plan while analyzing the data. Exploratory analysis, also called data mining, of the data is acceptable as long as it is within the framework of the original research design or if it helps generate new hypotheses for new research projects.

RESEARCH IN ACTION: WORD MEANING AND MEMORY

A psychology major decided to study the effect of word meaning on long-term memory. The student believed that people are more likely to recall related rather than random words. In addition, the student expected participants in the related word condition to recall words that were not in the original list. Finally, the student expected that participants would recite the list of related words faster than the participants who had memorized the unrelated words. The student decided to treat all tests as nondirectional.

To conduct the research, the student created two lists of 20 words each. The related word list consisted of names of common plants (e.g., corn, oak, rose, etc.). The second list consisted of randomly selected words of relatively the same length and familiarity as the words in the related word list (e.g., book, arm, pipe, etc.). The student then randomly assigned 24 participants to either the related word or random word condition. The researcher told all the participants that they were participating in a study of memory, and that they would recite the list 72 hours later. Each participant then had 5 minutes to memorize the words in their list.

When the participants returned for the test, the researcher asked them to speak into a microphone. Later, another student, who did not know the hypotheses, scored the tape recording. The variables measured were (a) the number of words correctly recalled, (b) the number of words recalled that were not in the original list, and (c) the time it took the participant to complete the recitation. Table 10.1 presents the data for the experiment.

TABLE 10.1
Data for free recall of related and random words

	Number of words correctly recalled		Number of new words accidentally recalled		Seconds to complete list	
	Related	**Random**	**Related**	**Random**	**Related**	**Random**
ΣX	185	143	20	9	163.6	199.9
ΣX^2	2963	1787	40	13	2289.6	3519.2
n	12	12	12	12	12	12
M	15.42	11.92	1.67	0.75	13.63	16.66
VAR	10.0833	7.5379	0.6061	0.5682	5.3824	17.1990
SD	3.1754	2.7455	0.7785	0.7538	2.3200	4.1472

BOX 10.2   Statistical Test for Word Meaning and Memory Study

Null Hypothesis:

For each dependent variable:
  $H_0: \mu_1 = \mu_2$

The performance of the related words group (μ_1) will be equal to the performance for the random words list (μ_2).

Alternative Hypothesis:

For each dependent variable:
  $H_0: \mu_1 \neq \mu_2$

The performance of the related words group (μ_1) will not be equal to the performance for the random words list (μ_2).

Statistical Test:

For each dependent variable:

We will use the t-ratio because we estimate $\sigma_{M_1 - M_2}$.

Significance Level:

All tests:
  $\alpha = .05$, two-tailed

Sampling Distribution:

The t-distribution with $df = (12 - 1) + (12 - 1) = 22$. $t_{critical}$ (22) $= 2.179$

Critical Region for Rejecting H_0:

t-tests:

$|t_{observed}| \geq |2.179|$ If $t_{observed}$ is less than -2.179 or greater than 2.179 we can reject H_0.

We can begin by preparing the null and alternative hypotheses for each test, as is presented in box 10.2. The student decided to use a nondirectional hypothesis for each hypothesis and to set $\alpha = .05$. Table 10.2 lists the results of each statistical test.

With the calculations out of the way, the student can now prepare the results section of the manuscript. Figure 10.9 is an example of what the student could write for the results section. For a manuscript, the American Psychological Association (2001) editorial guidelines require that tables be printed at the end of the manuscript. We will review the editorial guidelines in detail in a subsequent chapter.

TABLE 10.2
Statistical analysis for the data presented in Table 10.1

Number of words correctly recalled

$$t = \frac{15.42 - 11.92}{\sqrt{\frac{\left[2963 - \frac{(185)^2}{12}\right] + \left[1787 - \frac{(143)^2}{12}\right]}{12 + 12 - 2}\left(\frac{1}{12} + \frac{1}{12}\right)}} \qquad df = (12 - 1) + (12 - 1)$$

$$|t_{observed}| > |t_{critical}|$$
$$|2.88| > |2.179|$$

$t = 2.88 \qquad df = 22 \qquad$ **Reject** H_0

$$\hat{\omega}^2 = \frac{2.88^2 - 1}{2.88^2 + 12 + 12 - 1} \qquad \hat{\omega}^2 = .24$$

Number of new words accidentally recalled

$$t = \frac{1.67 - 0.75}{\sqrt{\frac{\left[40 - \frac{(20)^2}{12}\right] + \left[13 - \frac{(9)^2}{12}\right]}{12 + 12 - 2}\left(\frac{1}{12} + \frac{1}{12}\right)}} \qquad df = (12 - 1) + (12 - 1)$$

$$|t_{observed}| > |t_{critical}|$$
$$|2.94| > |2.179|$$

$t = 2.94 \qquad df = 22 \qquad$ **Reject** H_0

$$\hat{\omega}^2 = \frac{2.94^2 - 1}{2.94^2 + 12 + 12 - 1} \qquad \hat{\omega}^2 = .24$$

Time to complete list

$$t = \frac{13.63 - 16.66}{\sqrt{\frac{\left[2289.6 - \frac{(163.6)^2}{12}\right] + \left[3519.2 - \frac{(199.9)^2}{12}\right]}{12 + 12 - 2}\left(\frac{1}{12} + \frac{1}{12}\right)}}$$

$$|t_{observed}| > |t_{critical}|$$
$$|-2.21| > |2.179|$$

$t = -2.21 \qquad df = 22 \qquad$ **Reject** H_0

$$\hat{\omega}^2 = \frac{2.21^2 - 1}{2.21^2 + 12 + 12 - 1} \qquad \hat{\omega}^2 = .14$$

Word Meaning   7

Results

Table 1 presents the means and standard deviations for the three dependent measures. Participants in the Related-Words group recalled more words than participants in the Random-Words group, $t(22) = 2.88$, $p < .05$, $\omega^2 = .23$. In addition, participants in the Related-Words group recalled more words that were not part of the original list, $t(22) = 2.94$, $p < .05$, $\omega^2 = .24$. Finally, the difference in the time required to recite the list was also statistically significant, $t(22) = 2.21$, $p < .05$, $\omega^2 = .14$.

Word Meaning   15

Table 1

Means and Standard Deviations for Number of Words Correctly Recalled, Number of New Words Recalled, and Time to Recite List

	Related Word List	Random
Number of Words Correctly Recalled		
M	15.42	11.92
SD	3.18	2.75
Number of New Words Accidentally Recalled		
M	1.67	0.75
SD	0.78	0.75
Time to Complete List, in Seconds		
M	13.63	16.66
SD	2.32	4.15

FIGURE 10.9
Example of the "Results" section and a table of data. In an actual manuscript, all of the text would be double spaced.

STATISTICS BEHIND THE RESEARCH

In this section we will review several statistical tests that allow us to compare the difference between two independent groups. The phrase "independent groups" means that there is no specific correlation between the two groups. One way to ensure the independence of the groups is to randomly assign the participants to the two research conditions, as is done in a true experiment. We can also assume independence of the groups if we use an intact groups design and ensure that our selection of participants for one group has no influence on the selection of participants in the other group.

The three tests that we will examine are Student's t-ratio for independent groups, the Welch t-ratio, and the Mann-Whitney U-test. The Student's t-ratio is an inferential statistic that allows us to determine if the difference between two sample means is statistically significant. Researchers use the test when the dependent variable represents an interval or ratio scale of measurement. The other tests are alternatives that we use when the data do not meet the mathematical assumptions of the statistic.

STUDENT'S t-RATIO FOR INDEPENDENT GROUPS

The complete equation for Student's t-ratio is

$$t = \frac{M_1 - M_2}{\sqrt{\frac{\sum X_1^2 - \frac{(\sum X_1)^2}{n_1} + \sum X_2^2 - \frac{(\sum X_2)^2}{n_2}}{n_1 + n_2 - 2} \left(\frac{1}{n_1} + \frac{1}{n_2} \right)}} \qquad (10.4)$$

The degrees of freedom are calculated as

$$df = (n_1 - 1) + (n_2 - 1) \qquad (10.5)$$

Assumptions of the Test

For the test to work properly, the data must meet several assumptions. The assumptions are independence of groups, normal distribution of the data, and homogeneity of variance.

Independence of groups

The first assumption is that the groups are independent of each other. Chapter 13 reviews procedures for analyzing the data when there is a correlation between the groups.

Normal distribution of the data

A second assumption is that the data are normally distributed. The Mann-Whitney U-test is an alternative to the t-ratio that researchers use when the data are not normally distributed. Related to this assumption is that the data represent interval or ratio data. If the dependent variable represents an ordinal scale, the Mann-Whitney U-test is the preferred alternative test.

Homogeneity of variance

The third assumption refers to homogeneity of variance ($\sigma_1^2 = \sigma_2^2$). As a generality, if the larger variance is 3.0 times greater than the smaller variance, then we should not assume homogeneity of variance, and we should use the Welch t-test or the Mann-Whitney U-test as an alternative.

Forming the Hypothesis

The purpose to the t-ratio is to determine if there is a meaningful difference between the two group means. To conduct the statistical test, you may select either a directional or a nondirectional test.

Nondirectional or two-tailed test	Directional or one-tailed test
H_0: $\mu_1 = \mu_2$ H_1: $\mu_1 \neq \mu_2$	H_0: $\mu_1 \geq \mu_2$ or H_0: $\mu_1 \leq \mu_2$ H_1: $\mu_1 < \mu_2$ or H_1: $\mu_1 > \mu_2$

Sampling Distribution

To determine t_{critical}, establish the level of α and type of hypothesis, and calculate the degrees of freedom. Use Table A.3 in Appendix A to find the degrees of freedom (rows) and appropriate α level (columns). For an example, refer to the following chart.

Nondirectional or two-tailed test	Directional or one-tailed test
$\alpha = .05$, $df = 15$ H_0: $\mu_1 = \mu_2$ $t_{\text{critical}} = 2.131$	$\alpha = .05$, $df = 15$ H_0: $\mu_1 \geq \mu_2$ H_0: $\mu_1 \leq \mu_2$ $t_{\text{critical}} = -1.753$ $t_{\text{critical}} = 1.753$

If you use a directional hypothesis, then you must convert the sign of t_{critical} to conform to the test.

Example

A student decided to repeat the Seidlitz and Diener (1998) study that examined the difference between men and women's recall of emotional events. The student asked randomly selected men and women to describe in two or three words positive or happy events that occurred in their lives. Another student, who did not know whether the author of the comments was male or female, counted the number of episodes recalled. Table 10.3 presents the data.

The student decided to test the hypothesis that women will recall more positive events than men (as Seidlitz and Diener [1998] had found) and decided to set $\alpha = .05$. Accordingly, H_0: $\mu_W \leq \mu_M$ and H_1: $\mu_W > \mu_M$. Using Table A.3 of Appendix A, we find that

TABLE 10.3
Hypothetical data for a replication of the
Seidlitz and Diener (1998) study

1 Males		2 Females		
6	7	8	11	
12	10	10	11	
9	10	12	12	
10	9	9	12	
8	8	10	14	

$n_1 = 10$ $n_2 = 10$ $df = (10-1)+(10-1) = 18$

$\sum X_1 = 89$ $\sum X_2 = 109$ $df = 18$

$\sum X_1^2 = 819$ $\sum X_2^2 = 1215$ $t_{critical} = 1.734$

$M_1 = 8.9$ $M_2 = 10.9$

$SD_1 = 1.7288$ $SD_2 = 1.7288$

$t_{critical} = 1.734$. The value of $t_{critical}$ is positive because the researcher wants to show specifically that $\mu_W > \mu_M$.

$$t = \frac{10.9 - 8.9}{\sqrt{\dfrac{819 - \dfrac{(89)^2}{10} + 1215 - \dfrac{(109)^2}{10}}{10 + 10 - 2}\left(\dfrac{1}{10} + \dfrac{1}{10}\right)}} \qquad t = \frac{2.0}{\sqrt{\dfrac{26.90 + 26.90}{18}}} \text{(.2)}$$

$$t = \frac{2.0}{.7732} \qquad t = 2.5867$$

Because $t_{observed}$ exceeds $t_{critical}$ we can reject the null hypothesis and conclude that there is a statistically significant difference between men and women's recall of positive emotional events and that women recall more such events than do men.

Additional Tests

Confidence interval of the difference between means (*SED*)

This statistic allows you to estimate the confidence interval for potential mean differences given sample statistics.

$$SED = \sqrt{\frac{\sum X_1^2 - \dfrac{\left(\sum X_1\right)^2}{n_1} + \sum X_2^2 - \dfrac{\left(\sum X_2\right)^2}{n_2}}{n_1 + n_2 - 2}\left(\frac{1}{n_1} + \frac{1}{n_2}\right)} \qquad (10.6)$$

$$CI = (M_1 - M_2) \pm t_{critical}(SED) \qquad (10.7)$$

For this equation, $t_{critical}$ represents the value for the two-tailed or nondirectional test using the degrees of freedom, $df = (n_1 - 1) + (n_2 - 1)$. In this example, $df = 18$ and

$t_{critical} = 2.101$. Using the data from the previous example,

$$SED = 0.7732$$

$$CI = 2.0 \pm 2.101(0.7732) \qquad CI = 2.0 \pm 1.6245$$

95% Confidence Interval **0.3765 — 2.0 — 3.6245**

The confidence interval allows us to conclude that if we repeated the study under identical conditions, that there is a 95% probability that the difference between additional sample means will fall between 0.3765 and 3.64. In other words, there is compelling evidence that there is a difference between the two group means.

Omega squared (ω^2)

This statistic is a measure of association that estimates the degree to which the independent variable shares common variance with the dependent variable. The larger the value of $\hat{\omega}^2$, the greater the relation between the variables.

$$\hat{\omega}^2 = \frac{t^2 - 1}{t^2 + n_1 + n_2 - 1} \qquad \hat{\omega}^2 = \frac{-2.5867^2 - 1}{-2.5867^2 + 10 + 10 - 1}$$

$$\hat{\omega}^2 = \frac{5.6910}{25.6910} \qquad \hat{\omega}^2 = 0.2215$$

For this example, we can conclude that the independent variable accounts for approximately 22% of the variance in the dependent variable.

Effect size (d_2)

Effect size is an index of the relative difference between the means. The index is similar to a z-score in that statistics converts the difference between the means into standard deviation units. Box 10.3 presents Cohen's (1988) guide for evaluating effect sizes.

$$d_2 = \frac{|\mu_1 - \mu_2|}{\sigma}, \qquad \sigma = \frac{SD_1 + SD_2}{2} \qquad \text{when } n_1 = n_2. \tag{10.8}$$

Do not use this equation when $n_1 \neq n_2$!

$$d_2 = \frac{|8.9 - 10.9|}{1.7288} \qquad d_2 = \frac{2.0}{1.7288} \qquad d_2 = 1.1218$$

BOX 10.3 Cohen's (1988) Guidelines for Evaluating Effect Sizes

Small effect size	$d_2 = .20$	Generally these differences are small and difficult to detect without large sample sizes. Some researchers believe that when $d_1 \leq 0.10$, the effect is trivial.
Medium effect size	$d_2 = .50$	A medium effect is sufficiently large to be seen by the naked eye when graphed.
Large effect size	$d_2 = .80$	A large effect size is easily seen and requires few subjects to detect the effect.

WELCH *t*-RATIO FOR INDEPENDENT GROUPS—VARIANCES AND SAMPLE SIZES NOT EQUIVALENT

This inferential statistic allows us to determine if the difference between two sample means is statistically significant. Use this test when there are large differences between the variances of two groups. As a generality, when $SD^2_{larger}/SD^2_{smaller} > 3.00$ the Welch *t*-ratio is a more accurate test. Although Student's *t*-ratio is generally robust against violations of the homogeneity of variance requirement, the test will produce spurious results when the difference between the variances is large and when the sample sizes are unequal.

$$\hat{t} = \frac{M_1 - M_2}{\sqrt{\left[\frac{1}{n_1}\left(\frac{\sum X_1^2 - \left[(\sum X_1)^2/n_1\right]}{n_1 - 1}\right)\right] + \left[\frac{1}{n_2}\left(\frac{\sum X_2^2 - \left[(\sum X_2)^2/n_2\right]}{n_2 - 1}\right)\right]}} \tag{10.9}$$

$$df' = \frac{\left[\frac{1}{n_1}\left(\frac{\sum X_1^2 - \left[(\sum X_1)^2/n_1\right]}{n_1 - 1}\right) + \frac{1}{n_2}\left(\frac{\sum X_2^2 - \left[(\sum X_2)^2/n_2\right]}{n_2 - 1}\right)\right]^2}{\dfrac{\dfrac{1}{n_1}\left(\dfrac{\sum X_1^2 - \left[(\sum X_1)^2/n_1\right]}{n_1 - 1}\right)^2}{n_1 - 1} + \dfrac{\dfrac{1}{n_2}\left(\dfrac{\sum X_2^2 - \left[(\sum X_2)^2/n_2\right]}{n_2 - 1}\right)^2}{n_2 - 1}} \tag{10.10}$$

Sampling Distribution

To determine $t_{critical}$, establish the level of α and type of hypothesis, and calculate the degrees of freedom. Use Table A.3 in Appendix A to find the degrees of freedom (rows) and appropriate α level (columns). For example, if $\alpha = .05$ one-tailed and $df = 15$, $t_{critical} = 1.753$. If you use a directional hypothesis, then you must convert the sign of $t_{critical}$ to conform to the test. Table 10.4 presents data for which the sample sizes and the variances of the two groups are not equal.

TABLE 10.4

Hypothetical data representing independent groups with unequal variances and sample sizes

A		B	
3	2	1	6
2	3	3	
2	2	3	
1	1	3	
2	2	3	

A	B
$n_1 = 10$	$n_2 = 6$
$\sum X_1 = 20$	$\sum X_2 = 19$
$\sum X_1^2 = 44$	$\sum X_2^2 = 73$
$M_1 = 2.0$	$M_2 = 3.1667$
$VAR_1 = 0.4445$	$VAR_2 = 2.5667$
$SD_1 = 0.6667$	$SD_2 = 1.6021$

Note lack of homogeneity of variance:
$2.5667/0.4445 = $ **5.77**

Example

$$\hat{t} = \frac{2.00 - 3.167}{\sqrt{\left[\frac{1}{10}\left(\frac{44 - \left[(20)^2/10\right]}{10 - 1}\right)\right] + \left[\frac{1}{6}\left(\frac{73 - \left[(19)^2/6\right]}{6 - 1}\right)\right]}}$$

$$df' = \frac{\left[\frac{1}{10}\left(\frac{44 - \left[(20)^2/10\right]}{10 - 1}\right) + \frac{1}{6}\left(\frac{73 - \left[(19)^2/6\right]}{6 - 1}\right)\right]^2}{\frac{\frac{1}{10}\left(\frac{44 - \left[(20)^2/10\right]}{10 - 1}\right)^2}{10 - 1} + \frac{\frac{1}{6}\left(\frac{\sum X_2^2 - \left[(\sum X_2)^2/n_2\right]}{6 - 1}\right)^2}{6 - 1}}$$

$$\hat{t} = \frac{2.00 - 3.167}{\sqrt{\left[\frac{1}{10}\left(\frac{4.00}{10 - 1}\right)\right] + \left[\frac{1}{6}\left(\frac{12.833}{6 - 1}\right)\right]}}$$

$$df' = \frac{\left[\frac{1}{10}\left(\frac{4.00}{10 - 1}\right) + \frac{1}{6}\left(\frac{12.833}{6 - 1}\right)\right]^2}{\frac{\frac{1}{10}\left(\frac{4.00}{10 - 1}\right)^2}{10 - 1} + \frac{\frac{1}{6}\left(\frac{12.833}{6 - 1}\right)^2}{6 - 1}}$$

$$\hat{t} = \frac{-1.167}{\sqrt{(0.0444) + (0.4278)}}$$

$$df' = \frac{(0.0444 + 0.4278)^2}{\frac{(0.0444)^2}{9} + \frac{(0.4278)^2}{5}}$$

$$\hat{t} = \frac{-1.167}{0.6872}$$

$$df' = \frac{0.22297}{.0368}$$

$$df' = 6.059$$

$$\hat{t} = -1.698 \qquad\qquad df' = 6$$

According to the calculations, the adjusted degrees of freedom = 6. Using $\alpha = .05$ for a two-tailed test $t_{critical} = \pm 2.447$. Because $t_{observed}$ is less than $t_{critical}$, we do not reject H_0.

Additional Tests

Confidence interval of the difference between means (*SED*)

This statistic allows you to estimate the confidence interval for potential mean differences given sample statistics.

$$SED = \sqrt{\left[\frac{1}{n_1}\left(\frac{\sum X_1^2 - \left[(\sum X_2)^2/n_1\right]}{n_1 - 1}\right)\right] + \left[\frac{1}{n_2}\left(\frac{\sum X_2^2 - \left[(\sum X_2)^2/n_2\right]}{n_2 - 1}\right)\right]}$$

$$(10.11)$$

For the previous example,

$$SED = 0.6872$$

$$CI = (M_1 - M_2) \pm t_{\text{critical}} (SED), \quad df = \text{as calculated previously. For this}$$
$$\text{example, } df = 6.$$

$$CI = -1.1667 \pm 2.447(0.6872) \qquad CI = -1.1667 \pm 1.6802$$

95% Confidence Interval $\mathbf{-2.8469 \text{ --- } -1.1667 \text{ --- } 0.5135}$

MANN-WHITNEY U-TEST

The Mann-Whitney U-test is another alternative to the Student's t-ratio for comparing two groups. Many researchers prefer to use the U-test when the data do not fit the assumptions of the t-ratio.

Hypotheses

Null hypothesis
H_0: $U = U'$ The differences between the groups' ranks are due to chance.

Alternative hypothesis
H_1: $U \neq U'$ The differences between the groups' ranks are not random.

Sampling distribution
Table A.15 of Appendix A presents the critical regions for rejecting the null hypothesis. To use the table, find the numbers that correspond to the sample sizes of the two groups. For example, if $N_1 = 10$ and $N_2 = 10$, and $\alpha = .05$ for a nondirectional test, then the critical range is: 23–77. If the values of U and U' are within the critical range, do not reject the null hypotheses. When both values are outside the critical range, reject the null hypothesis.

Equations

$$U = N_1 N_2 + \frac{N_1(N_1 + 1)}{2} - R_1 \quad U' = N_1 N_2 + \frac{N_2(N_2 + 1)}{2} - R_2 \quad (10.12)$$

For these equations, N represents the sample sizes and R represents the sum of ranks for each group. To calculate R for each group, rank all the data from lowest to highest. Assign the ranks and then return the observed scores and their ranks to the original groups.

TABLE 10.5
**Hypothetical example of the use
of the Mann-Whitney U-test**

Experimental		Control	
Rating	Rank	Rating	Rank
66	1	72	5
68	2	80	11
81	12	69	3
70	4	82	13
73	6	83	14
84	15	74	7
76	8	85	16
86	17	77	9
78	10	91	19
89	18	93	20
$R_1 = 93$		$R_2 = 117$	
$N_1 = 10$		$N_2 = 10$	

Example

A student conducted an experiment to examine the effectiveness of listening to classical music on creativity. To conduct the study, the student randomly assigned participants to either an experimental group or a control group. The participants in the experimental listened to 10 minutes of Beethoven's Ninth Symphony; participants in the control group sat in quiet for 10 minutes. After the 10 minutes, all participants wrote a short story describing the first meeting of two people who will later become lovers. Two readers, who did not know the participants' treatment condition, rated the creativity of the story on a 100-point scale. Table 10.5 presents the average of the scores for each participant.

$$U = 10(10) + \frac{10(10 + 1)}{2} - 93 \qquad U = 100 + \frac{110}{2} - 93$$

$$U = 100 + 55 - 93 \qquad U = 62$$

$$U' = 10(10) + \frac{10(10 + 1)}{2} - 117 \qquad U' = 100 + \frac{110}{2} - 117$$

$$U' = 100 + 55 - 117 \qquad U' = 38$$

In this example, the values of U and U' are well within the critical region of 23–77, therefore we fail to reject the null hypothesis.

CHAPTER SUMMARY

In this chapter we examined the foundation of statistical inference using two independent groups and Student's t-ratio. Specifically, we examined how we compare the difference between the means to the standard error of the difference between means. As you learned, the standard error of the difference between means is an estimate of the sampling error present in the data. Therefore, if the relative difference between the sample means is sufficiently large, we can assume that the difference is in excess of sampling error and represents a meaningful difference between the population means.

There are important decisions to make when conducting an inferential statistic. First, we need to determine an acceptable α-level to control for the probability of committing a Type I error. Researchers who find the cost of a Type I error high use a lower α-level. Although lowering the α-level decreases the risk of a Type I error, doing so increases the risk of a Type II error. Consequently, researchers must balance the relative costs of Type I and Type II errors to determine the α-level to select. The researcher must also determine whether to use a directional or a nondirectional test. Another important consideration is the type of test to conduct. Each statistic has a special purpose and role in evaluating hypotheses. Selecting the wrong statistical test will produce misleading information.

Once one finds a statistically significant effect, the results must be interpreted with care. You learned that indices such as omega squared and effect size allow us to describe further the relation between the independent and dependent variables and the relative difference between the sample means. As a review, we can assume cause and effect if the researcher used a true experiment. In other designs, such as an intact groups design, we can use the t-ratio to examine the difference between the groups but cannot assume that the statistically significant results indicate a cause-and-effect relation between the two variables.

We also examined the meaning of the p-value and that many researchers often misinterpret its meaning. The p-value indicates the probability of obtaining the observed t-ratio if the null hypothesis is a correct statement. If the value of p is less than α, then we can reject the null hypothesis in favor of the alternative hypothesis. Other interpretations of p such as (a) indicating that the results are due to chance, (b) indicating the reliability of the results, or (c) indicating the "importance" of the results are incorrect interpretations.

An important component of hypothesis testing is power analysis. The aim of power analysis is decreasing the probability of committing a Type II error. Researchers can increase the power of their research by attempting to increase the difference between the population means, increasing sample size, decreasing sampling and measurement error, and decreasing the α-level.

We concluded by examining the role of computers in statistical analysis. Computers are essential when conducting evenly moderately complex statistical tests. However, computers and statistics software is not foolproof. Misuse of the software and sloppy data entry can lead to meaningless results.

CHAPTER GLOSSARY FOR REVIEW

Clinical or **Practical Significance**   Indicates that the results support rejecting the null hypothesis and that the results represent an effect meaningful in the context of the research.

Error Term $SD_{M_1-M_2}$ estimates the random error that occurs when taking samples from the population, and is an unbiased estimate of $\sigma_{\mu_1-\mu_2}$.

Omega Squared $\hat{\omega}^2$ A statistical index of the degree to which the independent variable accounts for the variance in the dependent variable.

Power of a Statistic, $1 - \beta$ The probability that one will correctly reject H_0.

Standard Error of the Difference Between Means ($\sigma_{\mu_1 - \mu_2}$)   Standard deviation of the sampling distribution of the difference between means.

Statistical Significance   Indicates that the results support rejecting the null hypothesis.

Student's t-Ratio   An inferential statistic that allows us to compare the difference between two means and determine whether there is sufficient evidence to reject the null hypothesis.

11 RESEARCH DESIGN II: SINGLE VARIABLE BETWEEN-SUBJECTS RESEARCH

CHAPTER OUTLINE

- ◆ Introduction
- ◆ Independent Variable
- ◆ Cause and Effect
- ◆ Gaining Control Over the Variables
- ◆ The General Linear Model
- ◆ Components of Variance
- ◆ The F-ratio
- ◆ H_0 and H_1
- ◆ F-ratio Sampling Distribution
- ◆ ANOVA Summary Table
- ◆ Interpreting the F-ratio
- ◆ Effect Size and Power
- ◆ Multiple Comparisons of the Means
- ◆ Statistics Behind the Research

Variance is the spice of life.

—Anonymous

INTRODUCTION

In chapters 9 and 10 you learned about the classic research design that consists of two groups. Although this design is a model of simplicity, it has limitations. Because psychologists study the wondrous complexity of behavior, they often want to compare more than two groups. In addition, events in nature rarely order themselves into two neat categories. Therefore, we need research designs that will help us answer the more complex questions that researchers often ask.

The focus of this chapter will be studies for which there are more than two conditions for a single independent variable. We will also examine an extremely useful statistical technique known as the **analysis of variance (ANOVA).** Since its development by Sir Ronald Fisher in the 1920s, the ANOVA has evolved into an elaborate collection of statistical procedures, perhaps the most commonly used in contemporary behavioral research. Therefore, this statistic, combined with a sound research design, can tell us much about the behavior we want to study. To help me review this research design and the ANOVA, I will again use examples from the contemporary psychological research literature.

Effects of praise on motivation and performance

Most of us like to be praised for our work, and we strive to receive compliments for our best efforts. Although we think of praise as a reward, can some compliments have the opposite effect and decrease one's motivation? Mueller and Dweck (1998) conducted a number of experiments in which they gave school children different types of praise. Do you think that praise for being intelligent would affect children's motivation differently than praise for working hard?

Spotting a liar

Everyone has lied at one time or another. Some people tell the occasional white lie to protect the feelings of others (e.g., "Gee, I REALLY like what you did with your hair!"). Some lies are dishonorable and are intended to hurt others or to protect the guilty. Ekman and O'Sullivan (1991) asked: "How good are we at detecting when someone lies to us?" Specifically, the researchers wanted to know if professionals (e.g., Secret Service agents, judges, and psychiatrists) who routinely work with potential liars could detect lies better than other people could.

INDEPENDENT VARIABLE

In chapter 9 we reviewed the importance of defining the characteristics of the independent variable because its selection influences the type of research we conduct, how we analyze the data, and the conclusions we can draw from the data. In this chapter we will examine the multilevel single variable between-subjects research design. This cumbersome name indicates that the design allows us to examine the relation between the specific levels, or forms, of the independent variable and the dependent variable.

The design of the multilevel study includes more than two **levels** of the independent variable. The term level refers to the form or condition of the independent variable. Consider the experiment conducted by Mueller and Dweck (1998). In that experiment, the independent variable was the type of praise that the children received for completing a project. Specifically, Mueller and Dweck used three levels of the variable: (a) praise for intelligence (e.g., "Very good, you must be smart"), (b) praise for effort (e.g., "Very good, you must have worked hard"), and (c) no praise (this condition was the control condition). In the Ekman and O'Sullivan (1991) study, the independent variable was the person's profession. For the Ekman and O'Sullivan study, there were seven levels of the independent variable: (a) Secret Service agents, (b) judges, (c) psychiatrists, (d) detectives, (e) college students, (f) lawyers, and (g) FBI agents.

This chapter will focus on between-subjects designs. As you will recall, the between-subjects research design is one wherein we compare the behavior of separate or independent groups of people. In the true experiment, such as the Mueller and Dweck (1998) experiment, the researcher randomly assigns the participants to one of the levels of the independent variable. In an intact group design, such as the Ekman and O'Sullivan (1991) study, the researcher uses a subject variable to define the levels of the independent variable.

Advantages of a Multilevel Design

The multilevel design allows a more refined analysis of the relation between the independent and dependent variables. Figure 11.1 presents graphs that represent the results of four hypothetical experiments. Each graph represents a unique and complex relation between the independent and dependent variables that a two-group design would not reveal. For

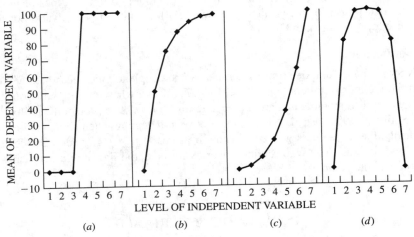

FIGURE 11.1
Hypothetical results of four separate experiments. Each experiment represents a different relation between the independent and dependent variables. A multilevel research design will help find trends like these.

instance, look at Figure 11.1(d), which looks like an inverted "U." Rotton and Cohn (2001) found an inverted U-shaped relation between temperature and the number of aggravated assaults in a large metropolitan city. Specifically, Rotton and Cohn found that the number of assaults increased along with increases in temperature up to a certain point, after which the number of assaults decreased as the temperature continued to increase. What would happen if a researcher conducted an experiment examining the relation between temperature and aggression, but used only two temperature conditions, cold (35°F) and hot (95°F)? According to Rotton and Cohn's data, the researcher would conclude that temperature and aggression are not related.

Another advantage of the multilevel research design is its potential to increase the statistical power of the study. The increase in power occurs if the researcher can identify additional levels of the independent variable that result in less variability among the participants within the groups. Consider the Ekman and O'Sullivan (1991) study. The researchers could have compared three broad categories of professionals including (a) detectives (Secret Service, FBI, and police detectives), (b) lawyers and judges, and (c) mental health personnel. Although this may appear to be a more simple study, it runs the risks of overlooking important differences among groups of professionals. As you will soon see, some groups of professionals are better able to detect liars than others. By grouping people from these professions together, we would overlook these important differences.

A final advantage of this design emerges for a true experiment in which the researcher can incorporate multiple control conditions. By having several control conditions, the researcher can rule out alternative explanations and thereby have greater confidence in describing the effect that the independent variable has on the dependent variable.

CAUSE AND EFFECT

Under certain circumstances, we can use the multilevel between-subjects research design to infer cause and effect between the independent and dependent variables. As a quick review, in a true experiment, the researcher randomly assigns participants to the treatment conditions, uses a manipulated independent variable, and uses control groups and procedures to account for alternative explanations of the data.

Does the fact that a true experiment allows us to infer cause and effect imply that other research designs are not valuable? Absolutely not! The only difference between a true experiment and alternative designs is the ability to infer cause and effect. Finding meaningful differences among intact groups can be helpful. Consider the research examining the ability to detect liars. What would happen if we found that one or two groups of professionals are able to detect lies? Although we could not conclude that being in a specific profession "causes" one to be a good lie detector, the results indicate that we need to discover how and why these groups of people are good at detecting other's lies.

GAINING CONTROL OVER THE VARIABLES

One of the essential factors in determining cause and effect in any research is gaining control of the relevant variables in the study. As a generality, the greater the control that the researcher has over the independent variable and extraneous variables, the better he or she is prepared to argue that there is a cause-and-effect relation between the independent and dependent variables. In this section, I will examine different ways a researcher can exercise control over the variables in the research. For the purpose of discussion, I will divide the methods of control into three broad categories, (a) control through research design, (b) control through research procedure, and (c) control through statistical analysis.

Control through *research design* refers to the tactics we use in designing the research. We randomly assign participants to the treatment conditions, use a manipulated independent variables, and include control groups to demonstrate the relation between the independent and dependent variables. We can also identify additional independent variables that we want to incorporate into the research design. In this chapter and the next two chapters, we will examine research designs that allow the researcher to exercise control over the variables by including additional relevant independent variables in the study.

Control through *research procedure* refers to the methods we use in collecting the data that help eliminate or at least reduce the influence of extraneous variables and thereby increase our ability to examine the relation between the independent and dependent variables. Remember that using a true experiment is not an automatic guarantee that one can show a cause-and-effect relation between two variables. No research design can overcome the effects of sloppy research procedure. Good research procedure reduces alternative explanations.

Control through *statistical analysis* refers to mathematical techniques we can use to remove or account for extraneous variables that we believe affects the dependent variable. Statistical procedures such as the analysis of covariance, multivariate analysis of variance, and multiple regression are techniques that give researchers greater control over different sources of variance. These techniques, while useful, are complex and require familiarity with statistical principles beyond the scope of this book. In addition, statistics cannot overcome a poorly designed research project. Therefore, I will limit my comments to the first two methods.

Control Through Research Design

Our selection of research design greatly influences the control we have over the variables in a study. The common feature of all research designs is that we attempt to determine the extent of the relation between the independent and dependent variables. The difference among these designs is the amount of control we can exert over the variables in the study.

The true experiment provides the greatest level of control for two reasons. First, the researcher can select the levels of the independent variable. By determining the levels of the independent variable, the researcher can also identify the appropriate control group conditions. The second source of control comes from the researcher's ability to randomly assign participants to the different treatment conditions.

Manipulated independent variable as a control

By using a manipulated independent variable, we can vary the experiences of the groups. We can ensure that some groups of participants experience the independent variable whereas others will not. Most importantly, we can create one or more control groups for which we purposefully withhold the independent variable. As you already know, having a control group allows us to determine whether the independent variable is the necessary condition for changing the dependent variable. In the Mueller and Dweck (1998) experiment, the researchers used three levels of the independent variable (praise for intelligence, praise for effort, or no praise) to determine if the type of praise affects the child's motivation.

Random assignment as a control

We treat random assignment as a control procedure because it helps us reduce or eliminate the effect of confounding variables that may influence the dependent variable that we do not want to examine in the study. We can again use the Mueller and Dweck (1998) experiment to illustrate the value of random assignment. The children may differ in their general interest in the task. Some children may enjoy working on the project whereas other children may find the task boring. Consequently, the child's general interest in the task as well as the type of praise will influence the child's motivation. By randomly assigning the children to the three research conditions, we assume that each group contains approximately equal proportions of children who like, dislike, or are neutral in their liking of the task. Therefore, using random assignment, we ensure that the groups are equivalent regarding the subject variables, such as interest in the task, which can influence the dependent variable.

In a quasi-experiment, we cannot randomly assign participants to the treatment conditions, but we can expose different groups of participants to different levels of the quasi-independent variable. Although we cannot randomly assign the participants to the different treatment conditions, we can attempt to design the quasi-experiment to account for alternative explanations. We will consider the design of quasi-experiments in detail in chapter 14.

The intact groups design affords the least amount of control over the independent variable. In the lie-detection study, we use preexisting groups of individuals and then attempt to determine if there are systematic differences among the groups. Although this research design does not allow us to infer cause and effect, it can indicate whether there are important variables related to the dependent variable.

Control Through Research Procedure

Once we select the design for the research, we need to examine ways to control for extraneous variables. In chapter 9 we examined the need for control procedures such as the single- and double-blind techniques. We can continue our study of good laboratory technique to illustrate the need to plan a research project with care.

The primary goal of good research procedure is to ensure that each participant experiences the same common events in the study except for the level of the independent variable. Consider some procedural issues important for the lie-detection study and the praise and motivation experiment.

How can we ensure that each participant in the lie detection study sees and hears the same thing? The answer is to find a way to present the liars and truth tellers consistently. One solution is to videotape people telling a lie or the truth. For their research, Ekman and O'Sullivan (1991) videotaped college students answering questions about a film they were watching. In all cases, the models described positive feelings about a nature film they were supposedly watching. Half the models were watching a nature film and were telling the truth. The other models watched a "gruesome" and emotionally traumatic film. Thus, these models were lying when saying that they felt good watching the film. Ekman and O'Sullivan made the videos of the models as consistent as possible. Each film segment was approximately 60 seconds long and consisted of a head-on view of the full face and body of the model.

How did Mueller and Dweck (1998) ensure that each child experienced the same research conditions save for the type of praise? Reading the method section of their study, you will find that the researchers employed several controls to ensure that the research conditions were nearly identical for all the children. For example, Mueller and Dweck used four female research assistants to test the children. In addition, each assistant followed the same script when explaining the task to the children. The only difference in the script was the presence and type of praise the assistant gave the children. Finally, the researchers conducted the study in an empty classroom free of external distractions that may have affected the child's performance or attention to the task.

There is a fine line between concern for good research design and becoming obsessive-compulsive. All research projects include a near infinite number of factors that the researcher can control. Because we can exert control over a variable does not mean that we need to design an elaborate control technique. The goal of the researcher is to identify the extraneous variables that can influence the dependent variable and then establish the necessary controls. Identifying these variables requires a combination of common sense and learning how to study the dependent variable.

There are several ways you can determine the extraneous variables that you need to control. The first is to carefully read the method section of similar research articles. You will be able to benefit from the collective wisdom of a long tradition of research in a particular field. Another tactic is to talk with people who have conducted similar research. There is often a considerable amount of laboratory lore involved in different types of research. For example, developmental psychologists have found ways to interact with children to ensure the child's cooperation. Many researchers consider these "tricks of the trade" common knowledge to those working in the field and do not describe them in the method section. Finally, you may want to consider conducting a pilot study.

A **pilot study** is a dress rehearsal for the final research project. By conducting the study with a small group of participants, you can determine whether they understand your instructions, that you have reduced the risk of demand characteristics and experimenter effects, and that your method of recording the data works.

THE GENERAL LINEAR MODEL

Now that we have examined the issues surrounding the design of a multilevel single variable between-subjects design, we can turn our attention to the logic we use to analyze the data. In this section we will examine the logic of the multilevel single variable between-subjects research design and the statistical technique used to analyze the data. To help you understand these principles, we can use data for the praise and motivation study.

For this experiment, the researchers randomly assigned 42 fifth-grade students to one of three experimental groups. The researcher asked all students to complete three

TABLE 11.1
Results for the effects of praise on willingness
to continue on task, 0 = low willingness,
10 = high willingness

Praise for intelligence	Praise for effort	Control group
$n_1 = 14$	$n_2 = 14$	$n_3 = 14$
$M_1 = 4.0$	$M_2 = 6.0$	$M_3 = 5.0$
$SD_1 = 1.0$	$SD_2 = 1.0$	$SD_3 = 1.0$
$VAR_1 = 1.0$	$VAR_2 = 1.0$	$VAR_3 = 1.0$

problem-solving tasks. After the child solved the first set of problems, the researcher told him or her, "Wow, you did very well on these problems. You got ___ right. That's a really high score; you did better than 80% of the other children who try to solve these problems." For the children assigned to the Praise for Intelligence Group, the researcher then added, "You must be smart at these problems." By contrast, the researcher told the children in the Praise for Effort Group, "You must have worked hard at these problems." The children in the Control Group received no additional feedback. Notice that each child received the same comments except for the attribution about their good score.

During the next phase of the experiment, the researcher had the children work on a set of difficult problems and then told all of them that they had done poorly. The researcher then asked each child to rate on a 10-point scale their desire to work on the third set of problems (0 = low willingness, 10 = high willingness). Table 11.1 presents the results for the experiments.

Before reviewing the results, I want to draw your attention to an important ethical issue involved in this research; the researchers deceived the children. They misled the children about their performance on the first part of the study and then rigged the second portion of the study to ensure that the children would do poorly. Mueller and Dweck (1998) recognized the ethical responsibility they had to preserve the well-being of the children. Consequently, they ensured that they received informed consent for each child participating in the study. In addition, they developed extensive debriefing procedures that ensured that the children went away from the experiment feeling proud of their efforts and participation in the study.

According to the sample means, children praised for intelligence expressed the least desire to continue with the task ($M = 4.0$), whereas the children praised for effort expressed the greatest desire to continue ($M = 6.0$). The mean for the children in the control condition was intermediate between the two treatment groups ($M = 5.0$). Although we know that there are real differences among the group means, is this difference meaningful? How much of the difference reflects the effects of the praise and how much reflects the effects of random events?

We can use Equation 11.1 to help us understand the variation among the observed scores. The equation will also allow us to return to our discussion of between-groups and within-groups variance. Equation 11.1 is the **general linear model** for the data collected in a single variable study.

$$X_{ij} = \mu + \alpha_j + \varepsilon_{ij} \tag{11.1}$$

In this equation, X_{ij} represents an observation within a specific treatment condition. The i in the subscript represents the individual participant whereas the j represents the group. For example, $X_{2\,3}$ represents the second subject in the third group. The next term, μ, represents the mean for the base population. The α_j represents the effects for each condition on the dependent variable. For the general linear model, the value of each α_j may be 0, positive or negative depending upon the effect of the level of the independent variable. Finally, ε_{ij} represents random error. We assume that the error is a random variable with a mean effect of 0 and a standard deviation equal to σ, the population standard deviation. Figure 11.2 presents an illustration of how the general linear model applies to this experiment.

We begin with the sampling population. In this case, the sampling population consisted of children in the fifth grade (10- to 12-year-olds) in a public elementary school located near the researchers. From this population, we draw a sample of participants. As you learned in chapter 6, the researchers believe that the sample is representative of the sampling population and that the sampling population is representative of the target population.

The next step in the study is the random assignment of the participants to one of the three treatment conditions. As I noted previously, the random assignment causes the three

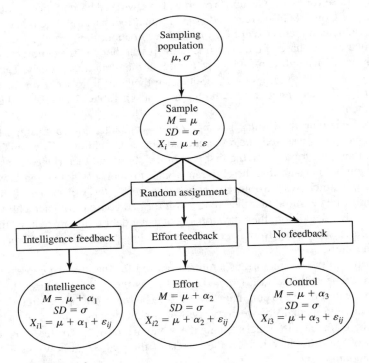

FIGURE 11.2
A single variable study and the general linear model. After creating a random sample from the population, the mean and standard deviation of the sample should be equivalent to the corresponding population parameter. The researcher then randomly assigns the participants into one of three groups. The participants' responses (X_{ij}) represent the combined effects of the treatment condition (α_j) and random events (ε_{ij}).

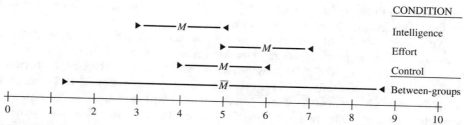

FIGURE 11.3

A graphical depiction of the data presented in Table 11.1. The top three lines represent the praise for intelligence, praise for effort, and the control conditions, respectively. The M represents the mean of each group. The lower line represents the data for all 42 students. The $\overline{M}$ indicates the mean of all 42 children. For each mean, the ▶——◀ represents the limits of one standard deviation above and below the mean. The standard deviation for each group is $SD = 1.0$. The standard deviation for the three group means is $SD = 3.74$.

groups to be equivalent regarding all subject variables. Consequently, the only thing that should differentiate the three groups is the type of feedback the children receive after completing the first task.

The final stage shown in Figure 11.2 represents the data that we collect. According to the logic of the experiment, we believe that each child's performance will reflect three things. First, μ represents the typical interest that fifth-grade students have in the problem-solving task. The second influence on the dependent variable is the effect of the treatment condition, α_j. For the control group, α_3 should equal 0 because the children in this group did not receive any praise. The researchers believe that the type of feedback will influence the participants' interest in the task. Therefore, they will predict that the values of α_j for the intelligence and effort groups will not equal 0. They believe that the effect of the praise will affect each child in the group. The goal of the research is to determine how the type of praise affects the children's interest in the task. The third influence is ε_{ij}, the random error in the equation. ε represents all the random events that can influence the child's interest in the task.

Whenever we conduct a study, we want to determine the proportion of the total variance due to the treatment variable and the proportion due to random error. Figure 11.3 may help you better understand how we will analyze the data and the comparisons that we can make.

The top three lines represent the data for each of the three groups from the Muller and Dweck (1998) study. The Ms represent the three group means, 4.0, 6.0, and 5.0, respectively. The lines surrounding the Ms represent one standard deviation above and below the group mean. For these data, the standard deviation of each group is $SD = 1.0$. Because VAR (recall that $VAR = SD^2$) is an unbiased estimate of the population variance, σ^2, we can conclude that the average within-groups variance is 1.00.

The bottom line represents the variance between[1] the three group means. Specifically, $\overline{M} = 5.0$ represents the mean of all the data. The lines surrounding $\overline{M}$ represent the

---

[1]My apologies to those sensitive to English grammar and diction. The correct preposition is "among," as we are talking about the contrast of more than two things. Researchers and statisticians are in the habit of using "between" regardless of the number of groups being compared.

variance for the three group means, M_1, M_2, and M_3. As you can see, the between-groups variance is greater than the within-groups variance.

What affects the size of the between-groups variance? According to the general linear model, the between-groups variance represents the effect of random error, ε_{ij}, and the effect of the independent variable, α_j. The question that we need to answer is whether the between-groups variance is substantively larger than the within-groups variance. If the between-groups variance is larger than the within-groups variance, we can assume that the difference reflects the effect of the independent variable. The analysis of variance, as the name suggests, is a statistical test that allows us to compare different types of variance. For the single independent variable study, the ANOVA computes three types of variance. The first form of variance is the **total variance,** which represents the variability among all the participants' scores regardless of the treatment condition they experienced.

The second form of variance is the **within-groups variance,** which indicates the average amount of variability among scores that occurs within each treatment condition. We use this measure of variability to estimate the magnitude of ε_{ij}.

The third estimate of variance is the **between-groups variance.** Specifically, we examine the variance among the specific group means. The between-groups variance allows us to determine the joint effects of α_j and ε_{ij}.

The primary statistic for the ANOVA is the F-ratio, the ratio of the between-groups variance to the within-groups variance. We use the size of the F-ratio to determine whether there is sufficient evidence to infer that the differences among the group means is greater than what would be due to random effects.

COMPONENTS OF VARIANCE

In this section we will examine the components of the ANOVA. I assume that you will use a computer to calculate the ANOVA. The section at the end of this chapter provides a step-by-step illustration of how to calculate the ANOVA using conventional computational equations.

A convention among those who use the ANOVA is to call estimates of variance the **mean square,** or **MS.** The term reflects that the variance of any set of numbers is the sum of squares divided by the degrees of freedom. Therefore, whenever you read about a mean square or an **MS,** the author is describing an estimate of variance.

Total Variance

We can begin with the most familiar form of variance, the total variance. The total variance is nothing more than the variance of all participants in the study. As the general linear model suggests, the total variance is the sum of the effects of variance due to the independent variable, represented as α_i, and the effects of random variation among the participants, represented as ε_{ij}. When we conduct an ANOVA, we **partition,** or divide, the total variance into its smaller components—the variance within-groups and the variance between-groups.

Within-Groups Variance

The within-groups variance represents the differences among the observations caused by random error and factors not controlled by the researcher. The mean of random error is 0 and in the long run adds to or takes away nothing from the population mean. Random error is a variable and thus creates variance among the scores. Therefore, it causes individual scores to be greater than or less than the population mean. You can think of the within-groups variance as the average of the variance in each group. For example, examine Table 11.1. As you can see, the variance for each group is 1.0. Therefore, we can conclude that the within-groups variance is 1.0.

When we use the ANOVA we assume that the variances of each group are equal or homogeneous. Homogeneity of variance means that $\sigma_1 = \sigma_2 = \sigma_3 \cdots = \sigma_k$. This is an important assumption because we treat the within-groups variance as an unbiased estimate of the population variance, σ^2. Therefore, if the variance of one group is much larger or smaller than the other group variances, our estimate of the population variance will be inaccurate. Most computer programs automatically test the homogeneity of variance assumption.

Between-Groups Variance

The between-groups variance is a special form of variance that determines the variance among the individual means. Specifically, the ANOVA determines the variance between each sample mean and the mean of the entire data. When we examine the differences among the sample means we assume that some of the difference reflects random variation and that some of the variation reflects the independent variable.

When we conduct this type of ANOVA we assume that the groups are **independent.** The phrase independent groups indicates that the data observed in one group has no influence or relation to the data observed in any of the other groups. There are ways that we can ensure that the groups are independent for the single variable between-subjects research. First, in a true experiment we use random assignment to send the participants to different groups. Because the assignment of participants to research conditions is random we can conclude that the observations are independent of one another. We can also conclude that the data are independent if the researcher tests each participant within only one level of the independent variable. Because the data for each group come from different people, we can assume that there is no correlation among the data from the groups.

THE *F*-RATIO

Once we calculate the three variance estimates, we can then calculate an inferential statistic that helps determine whether the between-groups variance is statistically greater than the within-groups variance. We call this statistic the *F*-ratio in honor of Sir Ronald Fisher, the scholar who invented the ANOVA. This statistic is nothing more than the between-groups variance divided by the within-groups variance. We can write the equation for the F-ratio in one of several ways.

$$F = \frac{\text{Treatment Variance} + \text{Error Variance}}{\text{Error Variance}} \qquad (11.2.a)$$

or as

$$F = \frac{\text{Between-Groups Variance}}{\text{Within-Groups Variance}} \qquad (11.2.b)$$

or as

$$F = \frac{MS_{\text{between}}}{MS_{\text{within}}} \qquad (11.2.c)$$

The F-ratio uses the same logic as the t-ratio because it creates a standardized score or ratio. The F-ratio compares the size of the between-groups variance relative to the within-groups variance. We can use the Mueller and Dweck (1998) experiment to examine how the relation between the independent and dependent variables affects the size of the F-ratio.

No Treatment Effect

Assuming that the independent variable has no influence on the dependent variable, would all the means be equal to one another? If you said no, you are correct. The means would probably not be equal to one another because sampling error, or random error, causes each sample mean to be slightly different from the population mean. We would expect, however, that the means would be relatively close to one another. More to the point, the variance between the means would equal the variance within the groups. Figure 11.4 presents an example of such a situation. For the sake of the example, we will assume that the variance within-groups is 1.0 and that the variance due to the independent variable is 0.0. Therefore,

$$F = \frac{\text{Treatment Variance} + \text{Error Variance}}{\text{Error Variance}}, \quad F = \frac{0.0 + 1.0}{1.0}, \quad F = 1.00$$

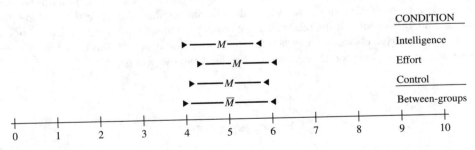

FIGURE 11.4
The within-groups variance is 1.0 and the between-groups variance is 1.0. Therefore, the ratio of the between-groups variance to the within-groups variance is $F = 1.00$. We could interpret these data to indicate that the difference among the three group means is random and that there is no systematic relation between the independent and dependent variables.

The variance between-groups is the same relative size as the variance within-groups. Therefore, whenever the F-ratio is close to 1.0, we can assume that the variance between-groups is due to random factors. As you can see in Figure 11.4, there is variance between the group means. However, because of the considerable overlap among the distributions, we assume that the difference among the means represents chance, the effect of random error. Notice too that the between-groups variance is the same as the within-groups variance.

Treatment Effect Present

What happens to the F-ratio when the levels of the independent variable correspond with changes in the dependent variable? In an experiment, the independent variable may cause the mean of each sample to be greater or less than the population mean. Hence, the between-groups variance will be larger than the within-groups variance. The between-groups variance increases because the treatment variance is greater than 0.0. Figure 11.5 represents what would occur if there were a statistically significant treatment effect. As you can see, the between-groups variance is now extremely large. You can also see that the variability among the three means has increased whereas the variance within each group remains the same as it was for the example in Figure 11.4.

We can represent the variance in Figure 11.5 using the following equation

$$F = \frac{\text{Treatment Variance} + \text{Error Variance}}{\text{Error Variance}}, \quad F = \frac{13.0 + 1.0}{1.0} = 14.00$$

The increase in the treatment variance caused the F-ratio to be greater than 1.00. If the effect of the treatment variance is sufficiently large, we will conclude that the F-ratio is statistically significant and that there is an important relation between the independent and dependent variable. Looking to the example in Figure 11.5, we can interpret the F-ratio to indicate that the variance between the groups is 14 times larger than the variance within-groups. Going a step farther, we may have statistical evidence that changes in the independent variable correspond with changes in the dependent variable.

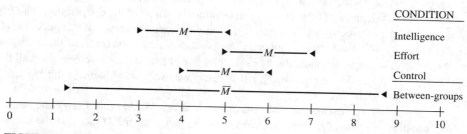

FIGURE 11.5
The within-groups variance is 1.0 and the between-groups variance is 14.0. For this example, $F = 14.00$ and we can infer that the difference among the group means is greater than would be expected by random error alone. We may infer that there is a systematic relation between the independent and dependent variables.

H_0 AND H_1

The null and alternative hypotheses for the ANOVA are similar in form and logic to the null and alternative hypotheses used to test the t-ratio. Specifically, the null hypothesis specifies that the differences in levels of the independent variable are not related to differences in the dependent variable. We write the null hypothesis as

$$H_0: \mu_1 = \mu_2 = \mu_3 \cdots = \mu_j \qquad (11.3)$$

We used a similar null hypothesis for the t-ratio. The only difference is that with the ANOVA we compare simultaneously more than two means. The interpretation of the null hypothesis is that all groups represent the same population and that any observed differences between the means is due to random factors or sampling error.

Because the ANOVA is a general test of variances, we do not make specific statements about how the means will be different from one another in the alternative hypothesis. Remember that the primary purpose of the ANOVA is to determine whether there are any systematic differences among the means. Because we do not specify the relation between the means in the ANOVA, we write the alternative hypothesis as

$$H_1: \text{Not } H_0 \qquad (11.4)$$

The alternative hypothesis for the F-ratio is a nondirectional hypothesis because we do not specify how the means will be different from one another, only that the between-groups variance is greater than the within-groups variance. If we can reject the null hypothesis, we must then use a special form of t-ratio to make specific comparisons among the means.

F-RATIO SAMPLING DISTRIBUTION

Just as Student developed a family of sampling distributions for the t-ratio, Fisher developed a family of sampling distributions for the F-ratio. The concept of the sampling distribution for the F-ratio is the same as that for other sampling distributions. Specifically, the sampling distribution represents the probability of various F-ratios when the null hypothesis is true.

Two types of degrees of freedom (df) determine the shape of the distribution. The first df represents the between-groups variance. For any unbiased estimate of variance, the df always equal one less than the number of observations that contribute to the variance. For the between-groups variance, the df is the number of groups less one. We also call this df the degrees of freedom numerator (df_N) because we use this to calculate the $MS_{between}$, in the numerator of the F-ratio.

The second df represents the within-groups variance. We also call this df the degrees of freedom denominator (df_D) because we use this to calculate the MS_{within}, in the denominator of the F-ratio.

Table A.9 of Appendix A presents the critical values of the F-ratio for various combinations of df_N and df_D. As you will see, the columns represent "Degrees of Freedom for Numerator" and the rows represent the Degrees of Freedom for Denominator. For the single variable ANOVA, the degrees of freedom for the numerator are the $df_{between}$ and the

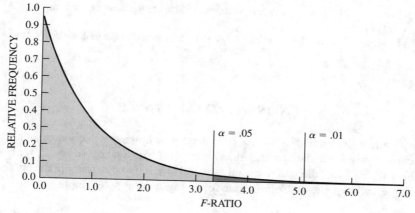

FIGURE 11.6
Sampling distribution for F with $df_N = 2$, $df_D = 39$.

degrees of freedom for the denominator are the df_{within}. For degrees of freedom of $df_N = 2$ and $df_D = 39$, $F_{critical} = 3.235$.

Figure 11.6 represents the sampling distribution for the F-ratio when the degrees of freedom are 2 and 39. The distribution is positively skewed. Because we want to determine if F is greater than 1.00, we place α on the right extreme of the distribution. When the F-ratio is 3.235, 5% of the sampling distribution is to the right of the F-ratio. Therefore, any observed F-ratio that falls in this region will allow us to reject the null hypothesis if $\alpha = .05$.

ACHIEVEMENT CHECK

(1) Describe in your words the advantages of using a multilevel single variable between-subjects research design.

(2) Under what conditions can the researcher use the multilevel single variable between-subjects research design to infer cause and effect?

(3) What is the difference between the between-groups variance and a variance due to the independent variable?

(4) Why is the mean of $\varepsilon = 0$ for all participants in a specific treatment condition?

(5) For a control group used in a true experiment, why would we state that $\alpha_j = 0$?

Comment on the accuracy of the following statements; explain why each statement is correct or incorrect.

(6) When the F-ratio is statistically significant, we can infer that the size of ε_{ij} is small and close to 0.

(7) All else being equal, as the size of ε_{ij} increases, the probability of rejecting the null hypothesis decreases.

(8) If the F-ratio is less than 1.00, the variance between-groups, due to the independent variable, is less than 0.0.

(9) If the F-ratio is not statistically significant, we can assume that the independent variable had no effect on the dependent variable.

(10) Even in a true experiment, the researcher cannot influence the size of α_j.

(11) For a control group in an experiment, we could write the general linear model,
$X_{ij} = \mu + 0 + \varepsilon_{ij}$.

(12) It is impossible for the value of all α_j's to be less than 0 in the general linear model.

ANOVA SUMMARY TABLE

We can use the skills learned in chapter 10 to determine how we will conduct an inferential statistical analysis of the data presented in Figure 11.7. As you should recall, we begin by identifying the null and alternative hypotheses and proceed to determining the criterion for rejecting the null hypothesis. Consider the following steps as an example.

Null Hypothesis

H_0: $\mu_1 = \mu_2 = \mu_3$. The average performance of the children in the three groups is equivalent. The type of praise has no influence on the child's interest in the task. Any observed difference among the three sample means represents chance events.

Alternative Hypothesis

H_1: Not H_0. The average performance of the children in the three groups is not equivalent. The variance among the three groups is greater than what we would expect from the within-groups variance. Therefore, we conclude that the type of praise does influence the children's interest in the task. The test does not indicate, however, which pairs of means are different from each other.

Statistical Test

We will use the single factor independent groups ANOVA because we wish to compare the difference between three independent groups.

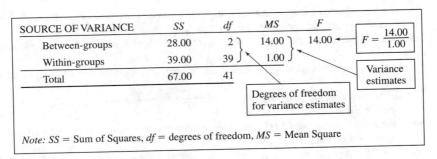

FIGURE 11.7
Example of an ANOVA summary table.

Significance Level

Using $\alpha = .05$ and the degrees of freedom we can determine the significance level as:

$$\alpha = .05, \quad df_N = 2, \quad df_D = 39$$
$$F_{critical}(2, 39) = 3.235$$

Summary Table

Most statisticians report the sum of squares, degrees of freedom, mean squares, and the F-ratio in an ANOVA summary table. The summary table represents the common practice of several generations of statisticians and is now common in the printout of computer programs that perform statistical analyses. The section at the end of the chapter offers a step-by-step analysis of how to calculate the ANOVA summary table by hand. The basic format of the summary table is shown in Figure 11.7.

Because $F_{observed}$ is greater than the $F_{critical}$ $(14.00 > 3.235)$ we can reject the null hypothesis and conclude that the type of praise did influence the children's motivation to continue the task.

According to the *Publication Manual of the American Psychological Association* (2001), the recommended format for reporting the results of an F-test is:

$$F(df_N, df_D) = F_o, \quad p = p \quad \text{or} \quad F(df_N, df_D) = F_o, \quad p < \alpha$$

For this example, we would report the F-ratio as

$$F(2, 39) = 14.00, \quad p = 0.0000261 \quad \text{or} \quad F(2, 39) = 14.00, \quad p < .05$$

The df_N refers to the numerator degrees of freedom, the degrees of freedom for the between-groups effect. The df_D refers to the denominator degrees of freedom, the degrees of freedom for within-groups effect.

When we reject the null hypothesis, we conclude that the difference among the group means is large enough to infer that H_0 is false. We accept the alternative hypothesis, H_1: Not H_0. Although the F-ratio allowed us to take a significant step forward, we need to continue the analysis of our data to learn more about the relation between the treatment and the results.

INTERPRETING THE F-RATIO

All the rules you learned about interpreting the t-ratio apply to the interpretation of the F-ratio. The size of the F-ratio and p value indicates only whether we can reject the null hypothesis given the value selected for H_0. To evaluate the degree to which the independent variable correlates with the dependent variable, we need to convert the F-ratio to omega squared, $\hat{\omega}^2$. The size of $\hat{\omega}^2$ indicates the degree of association between the independent and dependent variables. When I introduced you to $\hat{\omega}^2$ in chapter 10, I told you to calculate $\hat{\omega}^2$ only if the statistic is statistically significant. The same is true for the F-ratio; it is good practice to calculate $\hat{\omega}^2$ only after you have established that the F-ratio is statistically significant. For the current experiment,

$$\hat{\omega}^2 = .382$$

Therefore, we can estimate that approximately 38% of the differences among the three group means reflect the effect of the independent variable, the type of praise the children received.

EFFECT SIZE AND POWER

Cohen (1988) developed a measure of effect size for the F-ratio. The effect size for the F-ratio, represented as f, provides the same type of information as d for the t-ratio. For the current example, $f = .42$ (the equations for $\hat{\omega}^2$, and f are presented in the last section of the chapter). According to Cohen, effect sizes for the ANOVA fall into one of three categories, as presented in Table 11.2. The effect size for this experiment is what Cohen calls a large effect.

You should interpret effect sizes with caution, especially if the effect size is in the small to medium effect size range. Under some circumstances, a small effect size is an extremely important finding. For example, when studying a complex social behavior in a natural environment, one has little direct control over the environment and the treatment of the participants. Furthermore, in this situation, and many others, the measurement procedures may be prone to much error. Therefore, we need always to remember to interpret effect size within a broader context. Sometimes a "small" effect size can represent a major breakthrough in a program of research (Abelson, 1985). In other cases, a "small" effect size is small and the data are soon forgotten.

According to Cohen (1988), effect sizes for most research in the behavioral sciences are in the small to moderate range (e.g., $.10 \le f \le .40$). Why is f small for the behavioral sciences? The problem may arise from factors related to random error. First, most of the phenomena studied by behavioral scientists have many causes, and no single study can account of all these causes.

Another problem related to effect size is the inherent difference among humans. Even in a highly controlled laboratory experiment, each participant walks into the experiment with his or her life's experiences. These experiences create differences among participants that the experimenter cannot control. Finally, measurement in the behavioral sciences contains much error. No questionnaire, attitude survey, or observation technique is free of measurement error. These uncontrolled sources of error combine to reduce the overall effect size of an experiment. The successful researcher recognizes the presence of these inherent sources

TABLE 11.2
Table of Cohen's recommended categories for small, medium, and large effect sizes

Small effect size $f = .10$	Medium effect size $f = .25$	Large effect size $f = .40$

of error and attempts to improve the quality of the research procedure. In time, small effect sizes become progressively larger as the discipline matures.

MULTIPLE COMPARISONS OF THE MEANS

When we reject the null hypothesis tested by the ANOVA, we can only conclude that the variance between the means is greater than sampling error. The F-ratio does not specify where the statistically significant differences among the groups may occur. To determine which means are statistically different from one another we must return to the logic of the t-ratio to compare individual means.

You may be wondering why we would return to the t-ratio after conducting an ANOVA; why not conduct the t-ratios to begin with? The answer comes from an interesting fact related to hypothesis testing: the probability of a Type I error increases depending upon the number of comparisons you make using the same data set.

When we conduct a t-ratio, we assume that the groups are independent of one another. When the groups are independent, the probability of committing a Type I error is α. The problem of inflated Type I error arises when we make many comparisons based on a single experiment with many groups. Consequently, if we were to compare three or more means from the sample experiment, the probability of committing a Type I error is greater than α. Statisticians use Equation 11.5 to determine the probability of committing a Type I error under these conditions.

$$\alpha_e = 1 - (1 - \alpha)^c \qquad (11.5)$$

In this equation, α_e represents the **experimentwise error,** the probability of making a Type I error in any one of the potential comparisons. The other α term represents the **pairwise error.** The pairwise error represents the probability of a Type I error for an individual test. Finally, superscript c represents the number of potential comparisons.

The size of the experimentwise error increases quickly as the number of comparisons increases. For instance, if a researcher were to conduct three t-ratios, the α_e is approximately $\alpha_e = .1426$. Consequently, there is a 14.3% chance that one or more of the statistically significant t-ratios will represent a Type I error. Figure 11.8 will help illustrate this problem. Assume that a researcher conducts a study with three independent groups and proceeds to compare each possible combination of mean pairs. We can also assume that the researcher set $\alpha = .05$ for each comparison. In Figure 11.8, the ☑ represents rejection of the null hypothesis and ⊘ represents failure to reject the null hypothesis. Because $\alpha = .05$, we assume that the probability of a Type I error (represented as ☑) for each comparison is 5%. There are eight potential outcomes ranging from all the comparisons being statistically significant to none to the comparisons being statistically significant.

The column labeled "Probability of Outcome" represents the probability of results if the null hypothesis is a true statement for each of the comparisons. For instance, if H_0: $\mu = \mu$ for each of the three comparisons, then the probability that all three would be statistically significant is $p = .000125$ ($.000125 = .05 \times .05 \times .05$). In other words, the probability that we make a Type I error for each comparison is .0125%. The "Cumulative Probability" column represents probability of obtaining one of the potential outcomes. We will focus our

A vs. B	A vs. C	B vs. C	PROBABILITY OF OUTCOME	CUMULATIVE PROBABILITY	
All three comparisons statistically significant					
☑	☑	☑	$p = .000125 = \alpha^3$	.000125	
At least two comparisons statistically significant					
☑	☑	⊘	$p = .002375 = \alpha^2(1 - \alpha)$		
☑	⊘	☑	$p = .002375 = \alpha^2(1 - \alpha)$		
⊘	☑	☑	$p = .002375 = \alpha^2(1 - \alpha)$	.007250	
At least one comparison statistically significant					
☑	⊘	⊘	$p = .045125 = \alpha(1 - \alpha)^2$		
⊘	☑	⊘	$p = .045125 = \alpha(1 - \alpha)^2$		
⊘	⊘	☑	$p = .045125 = \alpha(1 - \alpha)^2$	.142625	$\alpha_e = 1 - (1 - \alpha)^c$
No comparisons statistically significant					
⊘	⊘	⊘	$p = .857375 = (1 - \alpha)^3$	1.000000	
Note: ☑ Statistically significant			$p = \alpha$	$p = .05$	
⊘ Not statistically significant			$p = (1 - \alpha)$	$p = .95$	

FIGURE 11.8

The experimentwise error rate for multiple comparisons. For this example, we assume that $H_0: \mu_A = \mu_B, \mu_A = \mu_C: \mu_B = \mu_C$ are true statements.

attention on the next to last line. The cumulative probability indicates the probability of obtaining one of the seven outcomes by chance if $H_0: \mu = \mu$ is true for each comparison. For this example, the cumulative probability is $p = .142625$, as predicted by Equation 11.5.

You could lower α (e.g., from .05 to .01) to keep α_e to an acceptable level. The problem with this tactic is that the power for the individual comparisons will be so small that few if any of the t-ratios will reveal statistically significant results. For example, with three potential comparisons we would have to reduce the pairwise α to approximately[2] $\alpha = .01695$ to maintain α_e at .05. Reducing α may reduce the risk of a Type I error, but it will increase the risk of a Type II error. Therefore, we need to find an alternative strategy.

An alternative strategy is to use a post hoc (meaning after the fact) test. Post hoc tests are methods for comparing many sample means while controlling for inflated experimentwise comparison rates. These specialized t-ratios allow you to compare sample means after you conduct the ANOVA and determine which pairs of means are different from one another at a statistically significant level. You will also find that most statistical packages offer a broad menu of post hoc statistical tests. In the following section, we will examine one of the more popular post hoc tests, Tukey's HSD.

---

[2]Use the equation $\alpha = 1 - \sqrt[c]{1 - \alpha_e}$ to estimate the pairwise α required to control the Type I error. To maintain the probability of a Type I error at .05 for three comparisons, the solution is $.01695 = 1 - \sqrt[3]{1 - .05}$.

Post hoc Comparisons: Tukey's HSD

Tukey (1953) developed the Honestly Significant Differences (HSD) procedure to compare all possible pairs of means after one has rejected the null hypothesis using the ANOVA. This procedure strikes a reasonable balance between protecting against inflated Type I errors and preserving statistical power (Jaccard, Becker, & Wood, 1984).

We can use the data from the Mueller and Dweck (1998) experiment to examine the use of Tukey's HSD. Table 11.3 presents a matrix of the differences between the three means from the Mueller and Dweck experiment. The asterisk (*) indicates the statistically significant difference between means. If you are using a computer program to analyze the data, the program will automatically perform the necessary calculations. According to the results, all the group means are different from one another. From the perspective of the purpose of the research, the HSD test confirms that children who received praise for intelligence rated the task lower than did the children in the control condition. Children in the praise for effort condition rated the task higher than did the children in the control condition. Therefore, it appears that the type of praise affects the children's interest in the task.

Estimating sample size

An important, if not essential, step in any research project is determining the number of participants required to reject the null hypothesis. This is not a trivial step; we do not want to spend our time conducting a study only to find that we cannot reject the null hypothesis. Instead, as we design the research project we want to ensure that we do everything possible to increase the probability that we will reject a false null hypothesis. In the language of statistics, we want to increase the statistical power $(1 - \beta)$ of the study. As you should recall, one way to increase power is to increase the sample size for the research. In the following section, we will examine how to estimate the number of participants to include in a single-factor study.

Table A.1 of Appendix A presents a power estimate table that you can use to estimate the number of participants you will need for your research. Figure 11.9 presents a portion of Table A.1. The table includes the two conventional alpha levels (.05, and .01). The column labeled n represents the number of participants in each treatment condition, and the column marked F_c represents the critical F-ratio required to reject H_0. The four other columns represent the small $(f = .10)$, medium $(f = .25)$, large $(f = .40)$, and very large $(f = .55)$ effect sizes. We can use this table to estimate the power of an experiment and to plan our future research projects.

TABLE 11.3
Comparison of all the differences between all pairs of means using the Tukey HSD test

Praise groups	M	Intelligence 4.0	Control 5.0	Effort 6.0
Intelligence	4.0	—	1.0*	2.0*
Control	5.0		—	1.0*
Effort	6.0			—

*The difference is statistically significant at the $\alpha = .05$ level.

TABLE A.13: POWER OF ANOVA

	$\alpha = .05 \quad df_N = 4$					$\alpha = .05 \quad df_N = 5$					$\alpha = .05 \quad df_N = 6$			
		Effect Size, f					Effect Size, f					Effect Size, f		
n	F_c	.10	.25	.40	.55	F_c	.10	.25	.40	.55	F_c	.10	.25	.40	.55
37	2.422	.17	.77	.99	.99	2.256	.19	.82	.99	.99	2.135	.20	.85	.99	.99
38	2.420	.18	.78	.99	.99	2.255	.19	.83	.99	.99	2.134	.21	.87	.99	.99
39	2.419	.18	.80	.99	.99	2.254	.20	.84	.99	.99	2.133	.21	.88	.99	.99
40	2.418	.18	.81	.99	.99	2.253	.20	.85	.99	.99	2.132	.21	.89	.99	.99
45	2.413	.20	.86	.99	.99	2.248	.22	.90	.99	.99	2.128	.23	.93	.99	.99

FIGURE 11.9

A power table for the ANOVA. The n column represents the number of observations in each treatment group. The F_C column represents the critical value of F for the degrees of freedom. The f columns represent the four levels of effect size.

Assume that you want to conduct an experiment with five levels of the independent variable ($df_N = 4$) and set $\alpha = .05$. How many participants do you need to have an 80% chance of rejecting the null hypothesis? According to Cohen (1988), you should assume that your effect size is moderate, $f = .25$ as it reflects the power of most behavioral research. If you wish to be more conservative in your estimate, you can use a smaller effect size estimate (e.g., $f = .10$). Similarly, if you believe that your experiment will produce a large effect size, you can increase your estimate (e.g., $f = .40$).

We can use Figure 11.9 to illustrate how to use Table A.13 for the single-factor study. For this example, there are five groups, therefore, $df_N = 4 = 5 - 1$, and we plan to use $\alpha = .05$. How many participants will this experiment require if we assume that $f = .25$ and we want to set our power to $1 - \beta = .80$? As shown in Figure 11.9, we will need at least 39 participants in each group ($39 * 5 = 195$ participants) to have sufficient statistical power to reject the null hypothesis.

RESEARCH IN ACTION: DETECTING LIES

How good are members of law enforcement at detecting when someone is lying? Ekman and O'Sullivan (1991) asked that question by examining the ability of Secret Service agents, FBI polygraphers, police robbery detectives, judges, psychiatrists, lawyers, and college students to watch a series of videotapes and identify the liars. To conduct the study, the researchers developed 10 videotape presentations. Each tape consisted of a different college-aged woman in an interview. Half of the tapes presented different women lying; the other tapes were of different women telling the truth. The researchers explained to the participants that they would see 10 different women, half of whom were lying, and were to determine who was lying. Table 11.4 presents the hypothetical results for this study. The data represent the number of correct identifications each person made. Ekman and O'Sullivan wanted to know whether members of some professions are better able to detect liars.

TABLE 11.4

Summary statistics and ANOVA summary table for the Ekman and O'Sullivan (1991) study

SS	FBI	D	J	P	L	CS	Total
$n_{a1} = 10$	$n_{a2} = 9$	$n_{a3} = 10$	$n_{a4} = 9$	$n_{a5} = 10$	$n_{a6} = 10$	$n_{a7} = 10$	$N = 68$
$M_{a1} = 6.8$	$M_{a2} = 5.3$	$M_{a3} = 5.2$	$M_{a4} = 5.1$	$M_{a5} = 5.4$	$M_{a6} = 5.3$	$M_{a7} = 5.2$	$\bar{M} = 5.5$

Source	SS	df	MS	F
Between	20.796	6	3.466	4.388
Within	48.189	61	0.790	
Total	68.985	67		

$\hat{\omega}^2 = 0.230$ $\eta^2 = 0.301$

Note: SS = Secret Service agents, FBI = FBI agents, D = detectives, J = judges, P = psychiatrists, L = lawyers, CS = college students.

TABLE 11.5

A matrix of mean differences for the seven groups using the HSD to determine the statistical significance of the differences between pairs of means

Profession	M	J 5.11	D 5.20	CS 5.20	L 5.30	FBI 5.33	P 5.40	SS 6.80
J	5.11	0.00	0.09	0.09	0.19	0.22	0.29	1.69*
D	5.20		0.00	0.00	0.10	0.13	0.20	1.60*
CS	5.20			0.00	0.10	0.13	0.20	1.60*
L	5.30				0.00	0.03	0.10	1.50*
FBI	5.33					0.00	0.07	1.47*
P	5.40						0.00	1.40*
SS	6.80							0.00

Note: * = $p < .05$; J = judges, D = detectives, CS = college students, L = lawyers, FBI = FBI agents, P = psychiatrists, SS = Secret Service agents

The first step is to prepare for the analysis of the data. There are differences between this data set and the one examining the relation between praise and performance. First, the independent variable is a subject variable. This has no real bearing on our analysis of the data; we can continue to use the ANOVA. Second, the nature of the independent variable will influence our interpretation of the data. Third, because we did not use random assignment of participants to the groups, we will not be able to determine that the independent variable causes the dependent variable.

Table 11.4 presents the summary statistics and an ANOVA summary table for the data. Because the F-ratio is greater than the critical F-ratio, we can reject the null hypothesis. Doing so allows us to assume that members of some professions are better able to detect liars than others. We will need to use Tukey's HSD to determine where the difference lies.

Table 11.5 presents the matrix of mean differences and the results of Tukey's HSD test. From these data we can conclude that the Secret Service agents were better able to detect liars than members of other groups.

Figure 11.10 presents the results section that one might prepare for these data. In this example, I included a graph of the data that presents the mean and the standard error of the

Detecting Liars   5

Results

Figure 1 illustrates the differences in the ability of members of different professions to detect when the models were or were not lying. The average accuracy of the Secret Service is greater than the accuracy of the other groups, and there appears to be little difference in accuracy among the other groups. A single factor ANOVA supports this observation, $F(6, 61) = 4.388$, $p < .05$, $\omega^2 = .23$. A Tukey HSD test indicated that the performance of the Secret Service was greater than members in all the other conditions, $p < .05$. There were no other statistically significant differences.

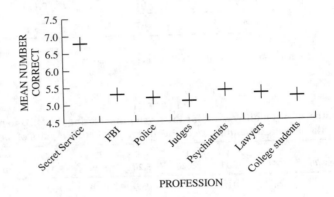

FIGURE 11.10
Results section describing the single-factor between-groups study presented in Table 11.4.

mean. This technique helps to illustrate that the Secret Service agents performed better than the other groups of participants at detecting liars.

STATISTICS BEHIND THE RESEARCH

In this section we will examine the procedures for manually calculating the summary table for the single-factor independent groups ANOVA and the associated statistical tests. For this example, we will use data presented in Table 11.6, which represents the results of the Ekman and O'Sullivan (1991) study.

Assumptions of the Test

The single variable between-groups ANOVA requires that the data meet three specific mathematical requirements. Meeting these assumptions ensures that the ANOVA will produce valid statistical interpretations of the data.

Normal distribution of data

The first assumption is that the data are normally distributed. Extreme skew in one or more of the groups may cause the ANOVA to produce spurious results. A quick review of the data in Table 11.6 indicates no outliers or other conditions that skew the data.

TABLE 11.6
Hypothetical data for the Ekman and O'Sullivan (1991) study

SS	FBI	D	J	P	L	CS
7	6	4	5	5	4	5
7	5	6	6	5	6	4
6	6	5	6	6	6	5
7	4	4	7	5	4	6
6	5	5	4	6	6	4
7	5	6	5	4	5	6
8	7	5	4	5	7	6
7	4	6	4	5	6	5
7	6	5	5	7	5	6
6		6		6	4	5

Totals

$\Sigma X_{a1} = 68$ $\Sigma X_{a2} = 48$ $\Sigma X_{a3} = 52$ $\Sigma X_{a4} = 46$ $\Sigma X_{a5} = 54$ $\Sigma X_{a6} = 53$ $\Sigma X_{a7} = 52$ $\Sigma X_{ij} = 373$

$\Sigma X_{a1}^2 = 466$ $\Sigma X_{a2}^2 = 264$ $\Sigma X_{a3}^2 = 276$ $\Sigma X_{a4}^2 = 244$ $\Sigma X_{a5}^2 = 298$ $\Sigma X_{a6}^2 = 291$ $\Sigma X_{a7}^2 = 276$ $\Sigma X_{ij}^2 = 2115$

$n_{a1} = 10$ $n_{a2} = 9$ $n_{a3} = 10$ $n_{a4} = 9$ $n_{a5} = 10$ $n_{a6} = 10$ $n_{a7} = 10$ $N = 68$

$M_{a1} = 6.8$ $M_{a2} = 5.3$ $M_{a3} = 5.2$ $M_{a4} = 5.1$ $M_{a5} = 5.4$ $M_{a6} = 5.3$ $M_{a7} = 5.2$ $\overline{M} = 5.49$

Note: SS = Secret Service agents, FBI = FBI agents, D = detectives, J = judges, P = psychiatrists, L = lawyers, CS = college students.

Homogeneity of variance

The second assumption is that the variances of the individual treatment conditions be relatively equal. This assumption is critical in that extremely deviant variances in one or more of the groups can produce spurious results. Coupled with this assumption is the general requirement that the sample sizes are the same. Another quick review of the data suggests that the variances of the six groups are equivalent. As an aside, many computer programs, such as *SPSS*©, will conduct a test of homogeneity of variance.

Independence of groups

The final assumption is that the groups are independent. This assumption requires that there be no explicit correlation among the groups. That the researchers use a subject variable that created separate groups means that the groups are independent of each other. Another way to ensure independence is to use a random assignment to place participants into the different treatment groups. There are conditions when there is an explicit correlation between the groups. We will consider this research design in the chapter 13.

Forming the Hypotheses

For the null hypothesis we assume that the independent variable and dependent variable are not related. Therefore, the differences between the group means are the product of chance or random factors. We can write the null hypothesis for this study as:

$H_0: \mu_1 = \mu_2 = \mu_3 = \mu_4 = \mu_5 = \mu_6 = \mu_7$ The type of profession is unrelated to the ability to detect lies.

The alternative hypothesis for the F-ratio is that there is a relation between the independent and dependent variables. Because the ANOVA compares the variance between-groups to the variance within-groups, we cannot specify which group means will be different from one another. Therefore, we write the alternative hypothesis to indicate the null hypothesis is false. Specifically, we write:

H_1: Not H_0 The ability to detect lies corresponds with the type of profession.

Sampling Distribution

To determine whether to reject the null hypothesis we will need to determine $F_{critical}$, after we establish the level of α and calculate the degrees of freedom. As you learned in this chapter, the F-distribution has two degrees of freedom. The numerator degrees of freedom (df_N) is the degrees of freedom associated with the between-groups variance. The denominator degrees of freedom (df_D) is the degrees of freedom associated with the within-groups variance. Table 11.7 presents the $F_{critical}$ for the current example. The value of F-critical allows us to determine whether to reject the null hypothesis for each observed F-ratio. When $F_{observed} \geq F_{critical}$, you can reject the null hypothesis.

We can set $\alpha = .05$, a conventional criterion of basic research that sets the probability of a Type I error to 5%. To determine $F_{critical}$, we first need to calculate the degrees of freedom for the F-distribution. Using Table A.10 of Appendix A, we can find the critical value of F-ratio needed to reject the null hypothesis. Because there is not a listing for $df_D = 61$, we can round the degrees of freedom to 60. Therefore, $F_{critical}(6, 60) = 2.25$, $\alpha = .05$.

Completing the Calculations

We can now proceed with the calculation of the single variable between-groups ANOVA. Table 11.8 presents the computational equations and a worked example for the data presented in Table 11.6. As you proceed with your calculations, ensure that you make clear notes of your calculations. This practice will help you ensure that there are no computational errors. As a double check for your work, you should find that $df_{total} = df_{between} + df_{within}$ and that $SS_{total} = SS_{between} + SS_{within}$. Table 11.9 presents the ANOVA summary table.

TABLE 11.7

Example of determining the degrees of freedom and $F_{critical}$ for each test in the two-variable independent groups ANOVA

Between-groups
$$df_{between} = j - 1 \qquad df_{between} = 7 - 1 \qquad df_{between} = 6$$

Within-groups
$$df_{within} = \Sigma(n_j - 1)$$
$$df_{within} = (10 - 1) + (9 - 1) + (10 - 1) + (9 - 1) + (10 - 1) + (10 - 1) + (10 - 1)$$
$$df_{within} = 61$$
$$F_{critical}(6, 60) = 2.25$$

TABLE 11.8
Worked example for a single-variable independent groups ANOVA

$$SS_{between} = \sum \frac{\left(\sum X_{aj}\right)^2}{n_{aj}} - \frac{\left(\sum X_{ij}\right)^2}{N}$$

$$SS_{between} = \frac{(68)^2}{10} + \frac{(48)^2}{9} + \frac{(52)^2}{10} + \frac{(46)^2}{9} + \frac{(54)^2}{10} + \frac{(53)^2}{10} + \frac{(52)^2}{10} - \frac{(373)^2}{68}$$

$$SS_{between} = 2066.8111 - 2046.7964 \qquad SS_{between} = 20.7956$$

$$df_{between} = j - 1 \qquad df_{between} = 7 - 1 \qquad df_{between} = 6$$

$$MS_{between} = \frac{SS_{between}}{df_{between}} \qquad MS_{between} = \frac{20.796}{6} \qquad MS_{between} = 3.466$$

$$SS_{within} = \sum X_{ij}^2 - \sum \frac{\left(\sum X_{aj}\right)^2}{n_{aj}} \qquad SS_{within} = 2115 - 2066.8111 \qquad SS_{within} = 48.189$$

$$df_{within} = \Sigma(n_j - 1)$$

$$df_{within} = (10 - 1) + (9 - 1) + (10 - 1) + (9 - 1) + (10 - 1) + (10 - 1) + (10 - 1)$$

$$df_{within} = 61$$

$$MS_{within} = \frac{SS_{within}}{df_{within}} \qquad MS_{within} = \frac{48.189}{61} \qquad MS_{within} = 0.790$$

$$SS_{total} = \sum X_{ij}^2 - \frac{\left(\sum X_{ij}\right)^2}{N} \qquad SS_{total} = 2115 - \frac{373^2}{68} \qquad SS_{total} = 68.985$$

$$df_{total} = N - 1 \qquad df_{total} = 68 - 1 \qquad df_{total} = 67$$

$$F = \frac{MS_{between}}{MS_{within}} \qquad F = \frac{3.466}{0.790} \qquad F = 4.388$$

Note: $df_{total} = df_{between} + df_{within}$ $67 = 6 + 61$
$SS_{total} = SS_{between} + SS_{within}$ $68.985 = 20.796 + 48.189$

TABLE 11.9
ANOVA summary table for data present in Table 11.6

Source	SS	df	MS	F
Between-groups	20.796	6	3.466	4.388
Within-groups	48.189	61	0.790	
Total	68.985	67		

$F_{critical}(6, 61) = 2.25$, $\alpha = .05$; reject H_0 because $F_{observed} \geq F_{critical}$

ADDITIONAL TESTS

Omega squared ($\hat{\omega}^2$) is a measure of the degree of association between the independent and dependent variables.

$$\hat{\omega}^2 = \frac{df_{between}(F - 1)}{df_{between}(F - 1) + N} \tag{11.6}$$

$$\hat{\omega}^2 = \frac{6(4.388 - 1)}{6(4.388 - 1) + 68} \qquad \hat{\omega}^2 = \frac{6(3.388)}{6(3.388) + 68} \qquad \hat{\omega}^2 = \frac{20.328}{88.328}$$

$$\hat{\omega}^2 = .2301$$

Effect size (f) is a standardized measure of the relative difference among the groups.

$$f = \sqrt{\frac{\eta^2}{1 - \eta^2}} \quad \text{where } \eta^2 = \frac{df_{\text{between}}(F)}{df_{\text{between}}(F) + df_{\text{within}}} \quad \text{or} \quad \eta^2 = \frac{SS_{\text{between}}}{SS_{\text{total}}} \tag{11.7}$$

For the current example,

$$\eta^2 = \frac{20.796}{68.985} = 0.301 \qquad f = \sqrt{\frac{0.301}{1 - 0.301}} = .656$$

Thus, we can conclude that the effect size is very large.

TUKEY'S HONESTLY SIGNIFICANT DIFFERENCES

Tukey's HSD is a test used in conjunction with the ANOVA to examine the differences between means. The test protects against inflated experimentwise errors. One uses the test to compare means only if there is a significant F-ratio.

EQUATIONS

$$HSD = q_{\text{critical}} \sqrt{\frac{MS_{\text{within}}}{n}} \tag{11.8}$$

For this equation, HSD is the critical difference required to consider the means statistically different, MS_{within} is the mean square within-groups, n is the average sample size, and q_{critical} is the critical value for a given α level for number of means and df_{within}. Use Table A.12 of Appendix A to find q_{critical}. To use Table A.12, you will need to know the number of groups in the analysis and the df_{within}. For this study, $j = 7, df_{\text{within}} = 61, MS_{\text{within}} = 0.790$, and $\alpha = .05$. Therefore, $q_{\text{critical}} = 4.31$.

If the number of subjects in each group is not equal, n' is defined as

$$n' = \frac{j}{\sum \left(\frac{1}{n_j} \right)} \tag{11.9}$$

For the current example, the number of participants in each group is not the same. Therefore,

$$n' = \frac{7}{\dfrac{1}{10} + \dfrac{1}{9} + \dfrac{1}{10} + \dfrac{1}{9} + \dfrac{1}{10} + \dfrac{1}{10} + \dfrac{1}{10}} = \frac{7}{.10 + .11 + .10 + .11 + .10 + .10 + .10}$$

$$= \frac{7}{.72} = 9.72$$

$$HSD = 4.31\sqrt{\frac{0.790}{9.72}} \qquad HSD = 4.31(0.2851) \qquad HSD = 1.23$$

For this study, any difference between a pair of means 1.23 or greater is statistically significant. To create the table of comparisons, order the means from lowest to highest. Then create a table of the difference between the pairs of means as was done for Table 11.5.

ACHIEVEMENT CHECK

(13) A researcher plans to conduct a single-factor ANOVA with four independent groups. If the effect size is moderate, how many participants will the researcher require in each group to ensure an 80% chance of rejecting the null hypothesis when $\alpha = .05$?

(14) Why will decreasing the within-groups variance increase the power of an ANOVA?

(15) Why is the ANOVA considered an omnibus test?

(16) In what ways are the t-ratio and F-ratio similar to and different from each other?

CHAPTER SUMMARY

This chapter is an extension of our previous review of single variable between-subjects research designs. The important difference is that the design we examined in this chapter allows us to simultaneously examine many levels of the independent variable. The statistical test most often used to study the results of this research design is the analysis of variance or ANOVA.

The ANOVA is an omnibus test because it allows us to examine the effect of many different levels of the same independent variable on the dependent variable. As you learned in this chapter, the ANOVA is an extremely flexible design because we can use either quantitative or qualitative levels of the independent variable in our research. We can also use the ANOVA to analyze the data from a true experiment (for which the participants are randomly assigned to the treatment conditions) or an intact groups design (the independent variable is a subject variable).

In this chapter I revisited the themes surrounding cause and effect. Specifically, the researcher must be able to control the independent variable and account for alternative explanations to infer cause and effect. I then examined several ways that the researchers can gain control over the variables in a research project. The two that we examined are control through research design and control through research procedure.

In a true experiment, the researcher can exercise direct control over the independent variable by including control conditions and by randomly assigning the participants to the treatment conditions. Researchers exercise this type of control through the design of their study. A researcher can also exercise control over the research through good procedure. Control through procedure refers to ensuring that the experience of the participants in the different treatment conditions is identical save for the level of the independent variable.

Researchers use the general linear model to describe how the ANOVA analyzes the data. In a true experiment, for example, the participant's observed score is the total of the population mean plus the effect of the level of the independent variable plus the effects of random error. The ANOVA analyzes the variance among the scores in the study. Specifically, the ANOVA allows us to examine the within-groups and between-groups variance. The within-groups variance represents the effects of random events that influence the difference among the scores in the individual groups. The between-groups variance represents the differences among the group means. We use these variance estimates to determine the F-ratio.

The F-ratio is the between-groups variance divided by the within-groups variance. If the F-ratio is equal to 1.00 we must assume that the differences among the group means are due to random error. By contrast, if the F-ratio is "statistically significant" we can assume that the differences among the means are greater than would be expected by chance if the null hypothesis were a true statement. Once we find that there is a statistically significant F-ratio, we can then calculate $\hat{\omega}^2$ or η^2; both indicate the proportion of the differences among the groups related to differences among the levels of the independent variable. Similarly, we can use the post hoc tests, such as Tukey's HSD, to determine which pairs of means are different from each other.

As with any research design, we can determine the power of the study. We can estimate the number of participants required in each treatment condition to ensure that we will have sufficient statistical power to reject the null hypothesis.

CHAPTER GLOSSARY FOR REVIEW

Analysis of Variance   An inferential statistical technique used to examine the difference among group means. The statistics divides the total variance among the participants into variance related to the independent variable and variance related to random error. If the ratio of the between-group variance to the within-groups variance is sufficiently large, one may reject the null hypothesis that all group means are equal.

ANOVA Summary Table   A table that presents the sum of squares, degrees of freedom, mean square, and F-ratio for an analysis of variance.

Between-Groups Variance   An estimate of the variance among the individual group means.

$df_{between}$ Degrees of freedom between-groups, also presented as df_N.

df_{within}   Degrees of freedom within-groups, also presented as df_D.

Effect Size   A descriptive statistic that provides a standardized measure of the relative difference among the group means. Effect sizes greater than 0 indicate a relation between the independent and dependent variables.

Error Variance   Variance among scores within a group and estimated by the within-group variance. The error variance is a random variable with a mean of 0.

Eta Squared η^2   A descriptive statistic that indicates the proportion of the variance between groups that is related to the independent variable.

Experimentwise Error, α_e   The probability of committing one or more Type I errors when conducting multiple t-ratios from a single experiment.

f   A measure of effect size for the analysis of variance.

F-Ratio   The inferential statistic for the analysis of variance. The statistic is the between-groups variance divided by the within-groups variance. If the F-ratio is sufficiently large, one may reject the null hypothesis that all group means are equal.

General Linear Model   A conceptual mathematical model that describes an observed score as the sum of the population mean (μ), the treatment effect for a specific level of a factor (α_j), and random error (ε_{ij}). For the one-variable ANOVA, the general linear model is $X_{ij} = \mu + \alpha_j + \varepsilon_{ij}$.

Independent   For a multilevel between-groups research design, independence indicates that the data collected for one group have no effect or relation to date collected in the other groups.

Level   The magnitude of or a condition within the independent variable. For qualitative variables, such as sex, level refers to the category for the variable (e.g., male versus female). For quantitative variables, level refers to the amount or magnitude of the independent variable.

Mean Square, *MS*   Another term used for an estimate of variance especially within the context of the ANOVA.

Multiple Comparisons   A procedure for examining pairs of means from a multilevel between-groups research design.

Omega Squared, $\hat{\omega}^2$ A descriptive statistic that indicates the proportion of the variance between groups that is related to the independent variable.

Pairwise Error, α   The probability of committing a Type I error for a single *t*-ratio.

Partition   In statistics refers to separating the total variance into its smaller components, the within-groups variance and the variance due to specific variables or combinations of variables.

Pilot Study   A rehearsal of the final research project that allows the researcher to ensure that the procedures will allow him or her to collect the data needed for the study.

Total Variance   An estimate of the variance among all the observations collected in the study.

Within-Groups Variance   An estimate of the average variance among scores within each group of the research.

12 RESEARCH DESIGN III: BETWEEN-SUBJECTS FACTORIAL DESIGNS

Except for the point masses of freshman physics—or the hard round spheres of the earliest models for gas molecules—few phenomena involve only a few variables.

—Tukey, Mosteller, and Hoaglin (1991)

INTRODUCTION

How many times have you heard someone say something like "Television violence causes violence" and thought to yourself, "It's not that simple; there are other factors involved"? As you learn more about psychology, you will discover that most explanations of behavior include several variables. For instance, what causes a person to help others? Researchers who study altruism suggest that many variables influence helping behavior including the number of people in the situation, the cost of helping, and the similarity between the person needing help and the helper. There are few instances where we can use a single variable to explain human behavior. The implication of this is that our research needs to incorporate more than one variable to understand the phenomenon that we are studying.

In this chapter you will learn how to use the two-variable design and the two-factor ANOVA. This research design has many advantages including the ability to: (1) examine the effects of more than one independent variable at a time; (2) examine the interaction between the independent variables; and (3) conduct research that is an efficient use of time and effort.

THE LOGIC OF THE TWO-VARIABLE DESIGN

The logic of the two-variable design is similar to the single-variable design. The primary difference is that the two-variable design allows us to examine the relation between two independent variables and the dependent variable. Specifically, the two-variable design examines how much each independent variable, by itself, influences the dependent variable. In addition, the test determines how much the combination of the independent variables affects the dependent variable.

Figure 12.1 illustrates the logic of the one- and two-variable analysis of variance. As you can see, the single variable ANOVA partitions the total variation among scores into two general components, the between-groups variation and the within-groups variation. The between-groups variation represents, in part, the variance caused by systematic differences among the groups. By contrast, the two-variable design further divides the between-groups variance. Specifically, the two-factor ANOVA divides the between-groups variation into the effects due to each of the independent variables and the interaction of these variables.

We can use the general linear model to examine the logic of the between-subjects two-variable ANOVA. Specifically,

$$X_{ijk} = \mu + \alpha_j + \beta_k + \alpha\beta_{jk} + \varepsilon_{ijk}$$

(12.1)

SINGLE-VARIABLE DESIGN AND ANOVA

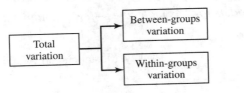

TWO-VARIABLE DESIGN AND ANOVA

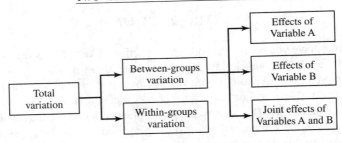

FIGURE 12.1
The difference between a single-variable and two-variable design.
The two-variable design partitions the between-group variation into
three components—effects due to Variable A, Variable B, and the
joint effects of the two independent variables.

In this equation, X_{ijk} represents an observation within a specific treatment condition. The i in the subscript represents the participant in the group, the j represents the level of the first independent variable, and the k represents the level of the second independent variable. As in the single-variable model, μ represents the mean for the base population, and ε_{ijk} represents the sampling error for each observation. The other three terms represent the effects of each independent variable and their interaction. Specifically, α_j represents the effects of the first independent variable, β_k represents the effects of the second independent variable, and $\alpha\beta_{jk}$ represents the unique variation due to the interaction of the two variables.

ADVANTAGES OF THE TWO-VARIABLE DESIGN

There are several advantages of the two-variable design over the one-variable design. The two-variable design allows us to use research resources efficiently, analyze the interaction among variables, and increase statistical power.

Increased Efficiency

What would happen if we conducted two one-variable studies rather than one two-variable study? The first study could examine the effects of three levels of the first independent

TABLE 12.1

The difference between two single-variable studies and one two-variable study

Two single-variable studies

Each study uses 30 participants in each treatment condition for 90 participants total.
Conducting both studies requires 180 participants.

Study 1

	a_1	a_2	a_3	Total
	$n_1 = 30$	$n_2 = 30$	$n_3 = 30$	$N = 90$

Study 2

	b_1	b_2	b_3	Total
	$n_1 = 30$	$n_2 = 30$	$n_3 = 30$	$N = 90$

One two-variable study

This design combines the two studies and requires only 90 participants.

		a_1	a_2	a_3	Total	
	b_1	$n_{11} = 10$	$n_{21} = 10$	$n_{31} = 10$	$n_{b1} = 30$	For each level
B	b_2	$n_{12} = 10$	$n_{22} = 10$	$n_{32} = 10$	$n_{b2} = 30$	of Variable B
	b_3	$n_{13} = 10$	$n_{23} = 10$	$n_{33} = 10$	$n_{b3} = 30$	there are
Total		$n_{a1} = 30$	$n_{a2} = 30$	$n_{a3} = 30$	$N = 90$	30 participants.

For each level of Variable A there are 30 participants.

variable. The second study could then examine the effect of three levels of the second independent variable. Assume for a moment that a power analysis for these experiments indicated that we need 30 participants in each treatment condition to have sufficient statistical power (e.g., $1 - \beta = .80$). Therefore, we will need 90 participants for each study, or 180 participants for both studies. By comparison, the two-variable design requires only 90 participants.

As you can see in Table 12.1, the two-variable design contains the elements of the two one-variable designs and uses fewer participants. The design retains 30 participants for each level of each treatment condition. By combining the two studies, we require half as many participants than if we attempted to conduct two separate studies. Therefore, one two-variable study is more cost effective than two one-variable studies. In addition, the two-variable design provides more information concerning the combined effects of the two independent variables.

Analysis of the Interaction of Variables

Another advantage of the two-variable design is that it helps us understand how combinations of variables influence behavior. Because we can combine different levels of the two variables, we can observe the combined effect of the variables, which we would not be able to see in a single-variable study. These unique results represent the interaction of the two variables. As you will learn, an interaction represents a pattern of results that the independent variables by themselves cannot explain.

Here is an example of how studying two variables can allow us to examine an interaction. Cohen, Nisbett, Bowdle, and Schwarz (1996) conducted an experiment in which they examined the reaction of white male participants who had just been insulted. When the participants arrived for the experiment, a researcher collected a sample of the participants' saliva. Next, the participants walked through a long, narrow hall. For a random half of the men, a research associate, walking in the other direction, bumped into the participant and called him an insulting name. When the participants reached the end of the hall, another researcher greeted the participant, had him complete a short task, and then collected another sample of saliva. Cohen et al. examined the change in testosterone levels for the two saliva samples. Testosterone is a hormone easily measured in saliva and correlates with levels of arousal, especially aggression.

Figure 12.2 represents the results for the study, specifically the average percent increase in testosterone for participants in the control and insult groups. The results seem straightforward. Insulted men produced more testosterone after the insult than men not insulted. Do these data tell the entire story?

Compare Figure 12.2 with Figure 12.3. The results presented in Figure 12.3 represent the relation between changes in testosterone and two independent variables. The first independent variable is whether the participant received an insult. The second independent variable is the regional background of the participants. Cohen et al. (1996) selected the participants for the study such that half of the men had lived most of their lives in the North. The other participants were men who had lived in the South. The insult condition represents a manipulated independent variable because the researcher randomly assigned half the participants to the insult condition and the others to the control condition. The background of the participant is a subject variable as it reflects a characteristic of the participant.

Do you notice a difference between the two graphs? Did men from the North respond to the insult in the same way as men from the South? Clearly, the two groups of men reacted differently to the insult condition. Specifically, in the control condition, there is no distinguishable difference between the two groups of men. The interesting difference occurs in the insult condition. As you can see, men from the North showed little reaction to the insult as indicated by the percent change in testosterone is little different from the mean

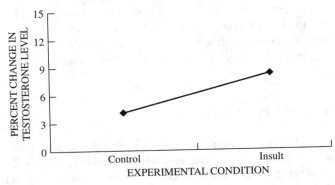

FIGURE 12.2
Relation between changes in testosterone levels and the control and insult conditions.

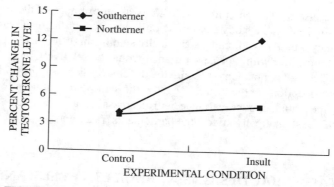

FIGURE 12.3

Relation between changes in testosterone levels and insult
condition for men raised either in southern or in northern states
(based on Cohen et al. 1996).

of the control condition. By contrast, the change in testosterone level for the men from the
South shows a clear reaction. These men produced considerably more testosterone after the
insult than any of the men in the other conditions. The data in Figure 12.3 represent an interaction because the men from the North and the South reacted differently to the same insult condition but showed no difference for the control condition.

Cohen et al. (1996) predicted that men who grew up in the South experience a "culture
of honor" that requires them to protect their character when attacked, whereas men raised
in the North experience a different cultural norm. Because of these cultural differences,
Cohen et al. predicted that men raised in the South would produce greater levels of testosterone indicating greater levels of aggression and offense to the insult.

Look again at Figure 12.2. Is it accurate to say that being insulted increases testosterone levels? Although the statement is accurate, it is incomplete because it does not take
into account the background of the participants. As you can see in Figure 12.3, men raised
in the North did not react to the insult whereas men raised in the South evidence considerable reaction. Therefore, to offer a more complete account of the data, we need to describe
how the combination of insult and regional background affects testosterone levels.

Increased Statistical Power

A third advantage of the two-variable ANOVA is an increase in power. As a generality, the
two-variable design is more powerful than the one-variable design because the within-
groups variance of the two-variable design tends to be smaller than the within-groups variance of a comparable one-variable study. Why is this true?

In the one-variable design, the within-groups variance reflects the effects of sampling
error and the effects of variables that the researcher has not measured. In some research situations, this unmeasured variable may be highly related to the dependent variable. Consequently, measuring an additional variable in a factorial design often allows the researcher
to describe the data more precisely. The benefit of this tactic is that the researcher can reduce the within-groups variance and thereby increase the statistical power of the research.

We can use the Cohen et al. (1996) study as an example. If the researchers had performed a single-variable study examining only the effect of the insult, as presented in Figure 12.2, they would have found a statistically significant difference between the means of the two groups. The within-groups variance would be relatively large, however, because the researchers did not take into account the differences between the northern and southern participants' reactions to the insult. If we use the same data, but now conduct a two-factor ANOVA, the within-groups variance will decrease because we have identified another variable that systematically affects the participants' reactions.

FACTORIAL DESIGNS: VARIABLES, LEVELS, AND CELLS

When researchers talk about the two-variable design, they often refer to concepts such as factorial designs, main effects, and the interaction. These terms refer to the design of the experiment and to the specific components of the general linear model of the two-variable ANOVA. Before we continue, you need to understand the meaning of these terms.

The Concept of a Treatment Combination

One of the advantages of the two-variable ANOVA is that it allows us to examine the effects of two independent variables and their combined effects. When we design a two-variable study, we select the number of levels that we want to use for each variable. Because we combine the two variables into one study, we create a **factorial design.** A factorial design represents a study that includes an independent group for each possible combination of levels for the independent variables. In the Cohen et al. (1996) experiment, for instance, there were two levels of the insult condition (Factor A: control versus insult) and two levels of participant background (Factor B: northerner versus southerner). Consequently, we can say that Cohen et al. used a 2 × 2 factorial design. This design created four independent groups as presented in Table 12.2.

For a 3 × 4 factorial design, there are 12 independent treatment conditions or **cells.** For example, the cell a_1b_2 represents the first level of the first independent variable

TABLE 12.2
**Matrix for a 2 × 2 factorial research design using the
Cohen et al. (1996) study as an example**

Factor B Background of participant		Factor A Insult condition	
		Control a_1	Insult a_2
Northern	b_1	a_1b_1 Control + Northerners	a_2b_1 Insult + Northerners
Southern	b_2	a_1b_2 Control + Southerners	a_2b_2 Insult + Southerners

(Factor A: control condition) and the second level of the second independent variable (Factor B: southerner). Hence, all the participants in a_1b_2 are men from the South assigned to the control condition.

Factorial designs can vary in complexity from the simple 2×2 design to more complex designs such as a 3×5 or a 4×6 factorial. The ANOVA allows us to use any number of independent variables in a study. Some researchers may use three or four independent variables in one experiment. You may, for example, read in a research report that the researcher conducted a $2 \times 3 \times 4$ ANOVA. This information should lead you to conclude that the researcher examined the effects of three independent variables and the interactions among the variables. There were 2 levels for the first variable, 3 levels of the second variable, and 4 levels of the third variable. You should also conclude that there were 24 ($2 \times 3 \times 4 = 24$) independent treatment cells, each representing a unique combination of the three variables. Thus, a distinguishing feature of all factorial designs is that they contain all possible combinations of the treatment conditions the researcher decided to use.

We will focus our attention on the two-variable model. If you need to use a more complex form of the ANOVA you may want to review Hayes (1981); Kirk (1982); or Winer, Brown, and Michels (1991) to learn how to analyze the results from more complex research designs.

EXAMPLES OF FACTORIAL DESIGNS

In this section we will examine how we can use the factorial design to conduct various research projects. The studies differ in the type of independent variables used and the number of levels for each variable.

Reaction to Product Endorsements

How seriously do people take product reviews? Are readers mindful of the credibility of the reviewer? What about the evaluation of the product; do strong endorsements always lead to willingness to buy a product? Chaiken and Maheswaran (1992) conducted an interesting experiment in which they varied the credibility of the review source and the general message of the review. They asked college students to read a review of a new telephone answering machine. The researchers told half the participants that the review came from a flyer printed by the discount store Kmart (low credibility) or from the magazine *Consumer Reports* (high credibility). Each participant then read one of three types of review, an unambiguous strong review, an ambiguous review (the answering machine was better than some machines but not as good as others), or an unambiguous weak review. The researchers then asked the participants to rate on a 10-point scale their willingness to buy the answering machine for $50 (10 = very willing to buy).

What type of research design did Chaiken and Maheswaran (1992) use? Figure 12.4 illustrates the design of the experiment. Clearly, there are two independent variables. The first variable (Factor A) is the credibility of the source, which has two levels, high and low.

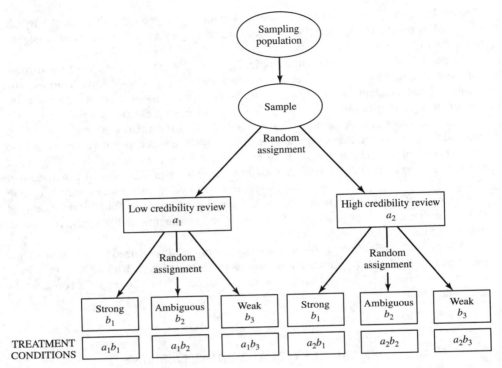

FIGURE 12.4

The research design used by Chaiken and Maheswaran (1992). There are two independent variables, credibility of the review (low versus high) and conclusion of the review (strong, ambiguous, and weak). Because both variables are manipulated variables, the researcher can randomly assign participants to one of the six possible treatment combinations.

The researchers randomly assigned half the participants to the low-credibility condition and the other half to the high-credibility condition. The second variable (Factor B) is the type of review the participants read. There were three levels of this variable: (1) strong review, (2) ambiguous review, and (3) weak review. The researchers randomly assigned the participants to one of the three levels of Factor B. Both factors are manipulated variables because the researchers could randomly determine the type of review the participants read. Therefore the researchers used a 2 × 3 factorial design. As you can see in Figure 12.4, there are six separate treatment conditions representing each possible combination of the two factors.

Table 12.3 and Figure 12.5 present the results of the Chaiken and Maheswaran (1992) experiment. The data in Table 12.3 present the means for each of the six treatment conditions as well as the marginal means. The marginal means represent the average performance for each level of the variable across all levels of the other variable. For example, the average score for all participants who read the low credibility review is 5.70, whereas the average scores for all participants who read the high credibility review is 5.63. By themselves, the means lead us to conclude that the credibility of the review had little effect upon the participants' evaluation of the answering machine.

TABLE 12.3

Mean willingness to buy the answering machine for the six treatment conditions in the Chaiken and Maheswaran (1992) experiment (10 = extremely willing to buy)

Factor B Level of endorsement		Factor A Credibility of source		Row means
		Low a_1	High a_2	
Strong	b_1	$M_{11} = 6.6$	$M_{21} = 5.9$	$M_{b1} = 6.25$
Ambiguous	b_2	$M_{12} = 5.4$	$M_{22} = 8.0$	$M_{b2} = 6.70$
Weak	b_3	$M_{13} = 5.1$	$M_{23} = 3.0$	$M_{b3} = 4.05$
Column means		$M_{a1} = 5.70$	$M_{a2} = 5.63$	$\overline{M} = 5.667$

Note: $\overline{M}$ represents the mean of all the observations across all treatment conditions.

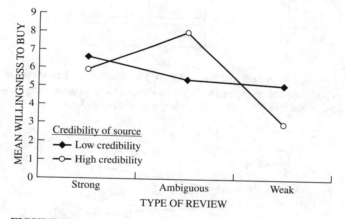

FIGURE 12.5

Results of the Chaiken and Maheswaran (1992) experiment. The interesting finding is the participants' willingness to buy a product that received an ambiguous rating from a highly credible source.

The graph presented in Figure 12.5 reveals an interaction. The lines are not parallel; they cross. The ambiguous review condition creates an interesting pattern of results. The participants who read the ambiguous review from the credible source were the most willing to buy the answering machine. These results clearly illustrate an interaction because the effects of the type of review were not consistent for the source of the review.

Effects of Noise on Children Diagnosed as Hyperactive

Zentall and Shaw (1980) conducted a study to determine the effects of noise on children's ability to complete an academic task. Figure 12.6 presents the design of this study. Specifically, the researchers selected a group of second-grade children diagnosed as hyperactive.

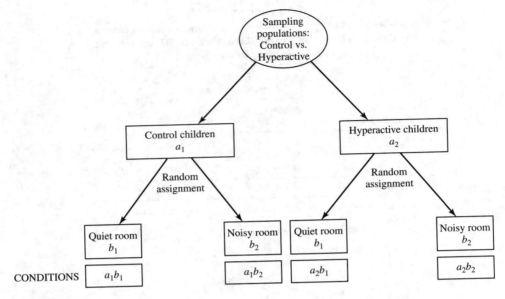

FIGURE 12.6
The research design used by Zentall and Shaw (1980). There are two independent variables, diagnosis of the child (control versus hyperactive) and test conditions (quiet versus noisy). The diagnosis is a subject variable. The testing condition is a manipulated variable.

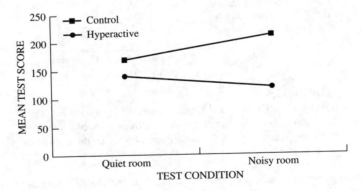

FIGURE 12.7
Results of the Zentall and Shaw (1980) study. The interesting finding in this research is that the children not diagnosed as hyperactive did better in the noisy room rather than the quiet room condition. By contrast, the children diagnosed as hyperactive did better in the quiet room than the noisy room.

The researchers then selected another group of children with no diagnosed learning disability. Next, the researchers had all the children complete a grade-appropriate math test. Half the children completed the task in a quiet room, whereas the other children completed the test in a noisy room. This study is also a factorial study because the design includes each combination of the two variables. This research design is a 2×2 design.

The first variable is a subject variable because the variable (presence of learning disability) is not something the researcher can control. By contrast, the second variable is a manipulated variable because the researcher could randomly assign the students to one of the two conditions.

Figure 12.7 presents the results of the Zentall and Shaw (1980) study. The interesting feature of these results is the different effect that noise had on the children's performance. The children diagnosed as hyperactive did worse in the noisy room than did the hyperactive children in the quiet room. By contrast, the control group performed better in the noisy room than did the control group tested in the quiet room. Again, the different pattern of results suggests an interaction of the two variables.

MAIN EFFECTS AND INTERACTION

The purpose of the factorial design is to examine how the two variables in the research combine and possibly interact with one another. In this section we will examine the potential outcomes for a factorial design and describe how to interpret the results. Specifically, we will examine main effects and interactions. As a brief preview, a main effect represents results wherein one or both factors have a statistically significant effect on the dependent variable. An interaction represents a condition where both variables have an effect on the dependent variable, but the effect differs across the treatment combinations. For the sake of illustration, we can use the study conducted by Cohen et al. (1996) to examine the meaning of main effects and interactions. As a quick reminder, Factor A is the insult condition (control versus insult) and Factor B is the participant's background (southerner versus northerner).

Main Effects

A **main effect** refers to the effect that one independent variable has on the dependent variable holding the effects of the other variables constant. Specifically, a main effect represents a special form of the between-groups variance of a single-independent variable. In a two-variable ANOVA, there are two main effects, one for each factor. When we examine the data using an ANOVA, each main effect can be either statistically significant or not statistically significant. Consequently, there are four potential patterns of results: (1) a statistically significant main effect for Factor A, (2) a statistically significant main effect for Factor B, (3) statistically significant main effects for Factors A and B, or (4) no statistically significant main effect for Factors A and B.

Figure 12.8 represents two types of main effect. In Figure 12.8(a) there is a main effect for Factor A but not Factor B. More specifically, Figure 12.8(a) indicates that the insult condition increased the testosterone of all the participants and that there were no differences between northerners and southerners. By contrast, Figure 12.8(b) indicates that the southerners had a greater change in testosterone than the northerners, but the insult condition had no effect on the results. For both graphs in Figure 12.8, there is no evidence of an interaction. Because the lines are parallel, you can assume that the results are consistent across the treatment conditions.

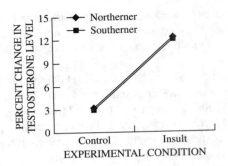

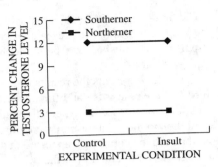

FACTOR A
INSULT CONDITION

Factor B background	Control a_1	Insult a_2	Row means
Northerner b_1	3.25	12.25	7.75
Southerner b_2	3.00	12.00	7.50
Column means	3.13	12.13	7.63

Main effect for Factor A
No main effect for Factor B
No interaction

(a)

FACTOR A
INSULT CONDITION

Factor B background	Control a_1	Insult a_2	Row means
Northerner b_1	3.0	3.0	3.0
Southerner b_2	12.0	12.0	12.0
Column means	7.5	7.5	7.5

No main effect for Factor A
Main effect for Factor B
No interaction

(b)

FIGURE 12.8
Two types of main effect for a 2×2 design. In (a) there is a statistically significant main effect for Factor A, insult condition; men who were insulted had larger changes in testosterone than men who were not insulted. In (b) there is a statistically significant main effect of Factor B, background; southerners had a greater increase in testosterone.

It is also possible to have results where there are statistically significant main effects for the two factors, but no statistically significant interaction. Look at Figure 12.9(a). There is a statistically significant main effect for the insult condition—all the participants in the insult condition had greater increases in testosterone than all the participants in the control condition. The graph also depicts a statistically significant main effect for the participant's background—southerners had greater increases in testosterone than northerners in the control and insult conditions. The lines are parallel, which indicates that the effects of the two factors are consistent across the treatment conditions.

There are times when our research produces no statistically significant findings. Figure 12.9(b) represents results where there are no statistically significant effects. The participant's testosterone showed a slight increase for the control and insult conditions, but there are no systematic differences among the four group means.

The statistically significant main effect represents the **additive effect** of the independent variable. An additive effect means that when we combine two variables, the effect of each variable adds a consistent effect across all treatment conditions. By contrast, the interaction indicates that there is interplay between the two variables that is more than can be explained by either variable alone. An interaction indicates a unique treatment effect that neither independent variable can explain by itself.

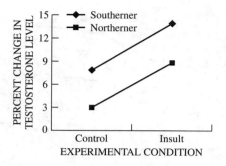
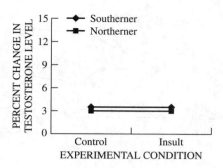

| Factor B background | FACTOR A INSULT CONDITION | | |
	Control a₁	Insult a₂	Row means
Northerner b₁	3.0	9.0	6.0
Southerner b₂	8.0	14.0	11.0
Column means	5.5	11.5	6.5

Main effect for Factor A
Main effect for Factor B
No interaction

(a)

| Factor B background | FACTOR A INSULT CONDITION | | |
	Control a₁	Insult a₂	Row means
Northerner b₁	3.5	3.5	3.5
Southerner b₂	3.0	3.0	3.0
Column means	3.25	3.25	3.25

No main effect for Factor A
No main effect for Factor B
No interaction

(b)

FIGURE 12.9

Two types of main effect for a 2×2 design. In (a) there are statistically significant main effects for the insult condition and the men's backgrounds. The results show that southerners had higher overall increases in testosterone and that the insult condition created greater increases in testosterone. In (b) there are no statistically significant effects.

Figure 12.10 illustrates the additive effect for a 3×2 design with main effects for Variables A and B, but no interaction. For Variable A, each increase in level (e.g., a_1 to a_2 and a_2 to a_3) represents an equal change in the means. The difference between a_1 and a_2 is 20 points for both the b_1 and b_2 conditions. Similarly, the change between a_2 and a_3 is 5 points for both the b_1 and b_2 conditions. Changes in the dependent variable for all two levels of Variable B are consistent across all levels of Variable A. We see this same consistency in the differences for Variable B. The average of the b_2 treatment condition is always 30 points greater than the b_1 treatment condition.

The Interaction

An **interaction** indicates that the effect of one variable is not consistent across all levels of the other variable. As you will see, there are four potential patterns of interaction for the two-variable design. We will begin by examining the situation that arises when there is a statistically significant interaction and one statistically significant main effect.

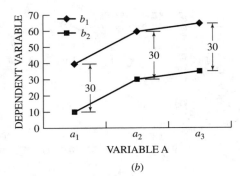

FIGURE 12.10

The additive effect for a 3×2 ANOVA. For this example, there are significant main effects for Variables A and B, but no interaction. For each factor, the differences among the means remain constant.

Figure 12.11 presents two examples of statistically significant interactions. In Figure 12.11(a) there is a statistically significant main effect for Factor A, the insult condition. This main effect indicates that, all else being equal, participants in the insult condition had greater testosterone increases than participants in the control condition. As you can see in the graph, this statement does not take into account the effect of the interaction between the insult condition and the participant's background. Looking at Figure 12.11(a) it is clear that the northern participants' testosterone did not change across the two insult conditions. By contrast, the southern participants had greatly elevated testosterone levels after they had been insulted.

The notable characteristic of the two graphs in Figure 12.11 is that the lines are not parallel. This is a hallmark of the interaction. The interaction represents variation among the treatment conditions that the independent variables alone cannot explain. When there is an interaction, one must examine how the two variables combine to produce unique results. In Figure 12.11, the insult condition, by itself, cannot account for all the differences among the four group means. The effect of the insult condition interacted with the participant's background. In this example, northern men showed little reaction to the insult, as measured by the level of testosterone. By contrast, southern participants showed a considerable reaction to the insult.

Figure 12.11(b) also indicates a statistically significant main effect and interaction. In this example the insult had opposite effects on the southern and northern participants. The insult caused the southern participant's testosterone to increase whereas the testosterone for the northern participants decreased.

Figure 12.12 presents the last set of potential patterns for interactions and main effects. Figure 12.12(a) represents the condition where both main effects and the interaction are statistically significant. As you can see in the means, the insult condition raised the testosterone levels more than the control condition. In addition, southern men had, overall, greater increases in testosterone levels. Although both of these statements are correct, they do not describe all the components of the results. Southern men reacted more, as measured by the change in testosterone, than did northern men.

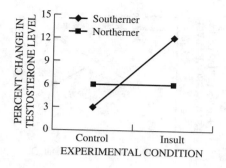

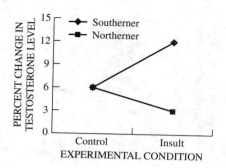

FACTOR A
INSULT CONDITION

| Factor B | Control | Insult | |
background	a₁	a₂	Row means
Northerner b_1	6.0	6.0	6.0
Southerner b_2	3.0	12.0	7.5
Column means	4.5	9.0	6.75

Main effect for Factor A
No main effect for Factor B
Interaction

(a)

FACTOR A
INSULT CONDITION

| Factor B | Control | Insult | |
background	a₁	a₂	Row means
Northerner b_1	6.0	3.0	4.5
Southerner b_2	6.0	12.0	9.0
Column means	6.0	7.5	6.75

No main effect for Factor A
Main effect for Factor B
Interaction

(b)

FIGURE 12.11

Two types of interaction for a 2×2 design. In (a) there is a statistically significant main effect for Factor A and a statistically significant interaction. In (b) there is a statistically significant main effect for Factor B and a statistically significant interaction.

The data presented in Figure 12.12(b) represent a condition when neither main effect is statistically significant, but the interaction is. Do these results mean that the independent variable had no effect on the results? No! Both independent variables influence the dependent variable, but their effects can only be understood within the context of the interaction. In this example, the main effects cancel each other because of the pattern of means.

Figure 12.13 presents another look at a significant interaction. Looking closely at the data, you can see that the changes in the dependent variable are not consistent for the different combinations of the variables. For example, the difference between a_1b_1 and a_2b_1 is 35 points whereas the difference between a_1b_2 and a_2b_2 is 5 points. In addition, the difference between a_1b_1 and a_1b_2 is 0 whereas the difference between a_2b_1 and a_2b_2 is 30 points. This inconsistency across treatment conditions is evidence of an interaction.

You should interpret the differences among the means with care when there is a statistically significant interaction. According to the general linear model, each cell mean reflects the effects of each independent variable and their interaction. Therefore, when you see that the mean of $a_2, b_1 = 45$, you must recognize that its value represents the effect of Variable A, Variable B, and the interaction. We will explore how to examine the contribution of the interaction in a subsequent section.

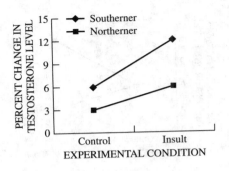

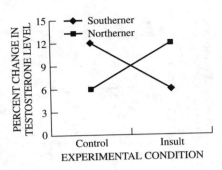

Factor B background	Control a₁	Insult a₂	Row means
FACTOR A			
INSULT CONDITION			
Northerner b_1	3.0	6.0	4.5
Southerner b_2	6.0	12.0	9.0
Column means	4.5	9.0	6.75

Main effect for Factor A
Main effect for Factor B
Interaction

(a)

Factor B background	Control a₁	Insult a₂	Row means
FACTOR A			
INSULT CONDITION			
Northerner b_1	6.0	12.0	9.0
Southerner b_2	12.0	6.0	9.0
Column means	9.0	9.0	9.0

No main effect for Factor A
No main effect for Factor B
Interaction

(b)

FIGURE 12.12
Two types of interaction for a 2×2 design. In (a) there is a statistically significant main effect for the Factor A and Factor B and a statistically significant interaction. In (b) there is a statistically significant interaction, but neither main effect is statistically significant.

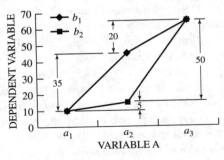

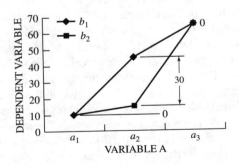

FIGURE 12.13
An interaction along with significant main effects for Variables A and B.

ACHIEVEMENT CHECK. Each of the following represent the cell totals and sample sizes for 2×2 factorial studies. For each study, determine means for the individual treatment conditions as well as the row and column means. Then prepare a graph of the means and determine if there is evidence of main effects for Variables A and B and an interaction.

(1)

	a_1	a_2			a_1	a_2	
b_1	$\Sigma X_{11} = 30.0$ $n_{11} = 15$	$\Sigma X_{21} = 45.0$ $n_{21} = 15$	$\Sigma X_{b1} = 75.0$ $n_{b1} = 30$	b_1	$M_{11} =$	$M_{21} =$	$M_{b1} =$
b_2	$\Sigma X_{12} = 45.0$ $n_{12} = 15$	$\Sigma X_{22} = 60.0$ $n_{22} = 15$	$\Sigma X_{b2} = 105.0$ $n_{b2} = 30$	b_2	$M_{12} =$	$M_{22} =$	$M_{b2} =$
	$\Sigma X_{a1} = 75.0$ $n_{a1} = 30$	$\Sigma X_{a2} = 105.0$ $n_{a2} = 30$	$\Sigma X_{ijk} = 180.0$ $N = 60.0$		$M_{a1} =$	$M_{a2} =$	$\overline{M} =$

(2)

	a_1	a_2			a_1	a_2	
b_1	$\Sigma X_{11} = 100.0$ $n_{11} = 25$	$\Sigma X_{21} = 150.0$ $n_{21} = 25$	$\Sigma X_{b1} =$ $n_{b1} =$	b_1	$M_{11} =$	$M_{21} =$	$M_{b1} =$
b_2	$\Sigma X_{12} = 125.0$ $n_{12} = 25$	$\Sigma X_{22} = 75.0$ $n_{22} = 25$	$\Sigma X_{b2} =$ $n_{b2} =$	b_2	$M_{12} =$	$M_{22} =$	$M_{b2} =$
	$\Sigma X_{a1} =$ $n_{a1} =$	$\Sigma X_{a2} =$ $n_{a2} =$	$\Sigma X_{ijk} =$ $N =$		$M_{a1} =$	$M_{a2} =$	$\overline{M} =$

(3)

	a_1	a_2			a_1	a_2	
b_1	$\Sigma X_{11} = 100.0$ $n_{11} = 25$	$\Sigma X_{21} = 50.0$ $n_{21} = 25$	$\Sigma X_{b1} =$ $n_{b1} =$	b_1	$M_{11} =$	$M_{21} =$	$M_{b1} =$
b_2	$\Sigma X_{12} = 50.0$ $n_{12} = 25$	$\Sigma X_{22} = 100.0$ $n_{22} = 25$	$\Sigma X_{b2} =$ $n_{b2} =$	b_2	$M_{12} =$	$M_{22} =$	$M_{b2} =$
	$\Sigma X_{a1} =$ $n_{a1} =$	$\Sigma X_{a2} =$ $n_{a2} =$	$\Sigma X_{ijk} =$ $N =$		$M_{a1} =$	$M_{a2} =$	$\overline{M} =$

(4)

	a_1	a_2			a_1	a_2	
b_1	$\Sigma X_{11} = 125.0$ $n_{11} = 25$	$\Sigma X_{21} = 225.0$ $n_{21} = 25$	$\Sigma X_{b1} =$ $n_{b1} =$	b_1	$M_{11} =$	$M_{21} =$	$M_{b1} =$
b_2	$\Sigma X_{12} = 75.0$ $n_{12} = 25$	$\Sigma X_{22} = 125.0$ $n_{22} = 25$	$\Sigma X_{b2} =$ $n_{b2} =$	b_2	$M_{12} =$	$M_{22} =$	$M_{b2} =$
	$\Sigma X_{a1} =$ $n_{a1} =$	$\Sigma X_{a2} =$ $n_{a2} =$	$\Sigma X_{ijk} =$ $N =$		$M_{a1} =$	$M_{a2} =$	$\overline{M} =$

(5) Nisbett (1968) conducted a study to examine the relation between food taste and food consumption for obese and underweight people. Nisbett classified participants as obese or underweight by comparing their actual weight to their ideal weights. He then asked people to eat vanilla ice cream. Half the participants ate good tasting ice cream; the others ate bitter tasting ice cream. The dependent variable was the number of grams of ice cream consumed. The following chart presents the average amount of ice cream consumed (assume equal sample sizes).

(a) Draw a graph of the data and write a short essay describing the results.

(b) Given these results, why was it important for Nisbett to include the weight of the person as a variable in the study?

| Factor B | Factor A
Weight of participant | | |
Taste of food	Obese a_1	Underweight a_2	Row means
Good b_1	200	120	
Bitter b_2	45	95	
Column means			

(6) A researcher wanted to study state-dependent learning. To examine the phenomenon, she had half the participants learn a list of 30 unrelated words while listening to a tape of Grateful Dead songs. The other participants learned the list in a quiet room. Two days later, all participants returned to the laboratory to recite the list of words. Half the participants in the music group and half the participants in the quiet group recited the list while listening to the Grateful Dead tape. The other participants recited the list in a quiet room.

(a) Draw a graph of the data and write a short essay describing the results.

(b) Could the researcher have studied the state-dependent learning phenomenon using two single-variable studies? Describe the specific advantages to using the factorial design for this research project.

| Factor B | Factor A
Learned list condition | | |
Recite list	Music a_1	Quiet a_2	Row means
Music b_1	18	9	
Quiet b_2	11	15	
Column means			

DESIGNING A FACTORIAL STUDY

Designing a factorial study is relatively straightforward in that all the principles you have already learned about good research design apply to the two-factor study. In the following section, we will briefly review issues related to the independent and dependent variables and sample size.

Independent Variables

We have already discussed several of the distinguishing features of the factorial design. The factorial design allows us to simultaneously examine the relation between two or more independent variables and the dependent variable. Using two or more independent variables allows us to examine how combinations of treatment conditions relate to different outcomes in the study. Of particular interest, the factorial design allows us to examine the presence of an interaction, something that we could not observe in a single-variable study. Also, we can use manipulated as well as subject variables in the study. This feature allows us to examine the relation among a number of predictor variables and the dependent variable.

Between-subjects variables

The specific research design we examine in this chapter requires that all the variables be between-subjects variables. This requirement means that we test each participant in only one combination of treatment conditions. Consider some of the studies we have examined so far.

In the Cohen et al. (1996) study, both the insult condition and the participant background are between-subjects variables. For the insult condition, Cohen randomly assigned the participants to either the control or the insult treatment condition. Participant background is also a between-subjects variable in that the participants grew up either in the South or the North. The dependent variable, percent change in testosterone level, represents the participants' reaction within one of the four treatment conditions.

The experiment conducted by Chaiken and Maheswaran (1992) also used between-subject variables in that the researchers randomly assigned the participants to one of the six treatment combinations. For that experiment, both independent variables were manipulated variables so that the researcher could select the levels and then randomly assign participants to one of the conditions.

When both variables are between-subjects variables, we can conclude that the individual cells are **independent groups.** In this case, independence means that the data collected for one cell do not correlate with the other cells. The independence of the treatment conditions is an important consideration in that it determines the type of statistical analysis we will use to examine the data. In a following section, we will review how to analyze the data for the two-variable between-subjects design. In the next two chapters we will examine how to analyze the data when one of the variables is a within-subjects variable.

Levels of the variables

An important design consideration is the number of levels to use for each factor. At a minimum, you must have at least two levels of each factor. You can use as many levels for both factors as you need. Consider the Chaiken and Maheswaran (1992) experiment; for their research, it made sense to have two levels of credibility of source and three levels of review endorsement. Similarly, Cohen et al. (1996) chose two levels of each variable for their study. In both cases, the questions that the researchers wished to address determined the number of levels for each independent variable. Can you think of modifications to these studies that might require more levels?

Chaiken and Maheswaran (1992) could have included a third condition for the source of the product review by including an unidentified review. The three levels of review source would then be low-credibility, high-credibility, and unidentified source. The new condition would be a type of control condition because the researcher does not identify the source of the review. Could Cohen et al. (1996) add more levels to their study? For the participant background condition, they could have identified other regions of the country (e.g., West Coast or Rocky Mountain states) or other countries (e.g., men from Asian countries). In addition, Cohen et al. could have used three treatment conditions by adding a condition where the men received a complement rather than an insult.

Adding more treatment conditions may produce results that further enhance our understanding of the phenomenon we are studying. For example, if Cohen et al. (1996) had included men from the West Coast states, they could have determined whether the southerners' reaction to the insult is unique to men raised in the South. Similarly, the addition of a complement condition would help determine if the increase in the testosterone occurs only in the insult condition. Such a study would be an interesting follow-up project.

In the previous chapter, you learned that adding more levels of the independent variable has the advantage of improving our understanding of the relation between the independent and dependent variables. Adding more levels of the variable can also improve the power of a study if adding treatment conditions increases homogeneity of the participants with each condition and increases the range of effect for the independent variable. These same advantages occur in the factorial design.

There is a cost, however, to adding more levels of a variable; you will need to use more participants. Imagine that a researcher begins by planning for a 2 × 2 factorial design and determines that there must be at least 10 participants in each research condition. For this design, the researcher will require 40 participants to conduct the study. After thinking about the purpose of the study, the researcher decides to switch to a 3 × 3 factorial design. This design will require 90 participants, more than twice as many as the 2 × 2 design requires. Even switching to a 2 × 3 factorial design will require 60 participants. This exercise illustrates that selecting the number of levels for each variable requires a balance between the intent of the research and the cost of conducting the study.

Dependent Variables

Several characteristics of the dependent variable require attention when conducting a factorial design. The first characteristic refers to the scale of measurement used for the dependent variable. As a generality, the ANOVA works best when the data are measured using an interval or ratio scale. It is possible to conduct a factorial design for which the data represent a nominal ordinal scale. Data such as these require a different statistical test. Chapter 15 reviews these options.

There are additional considerations to make before we use an ANOVA to examine the results of a factorial design. One is sample size. As a generality, the number of observations in each cell should be the same. Although minor differences in sample sizes have little effect on the validity of the ANOVA, large differences in sample sizes among the cells can cause the ANOVA to produce spurious results. Plan your study with sufficient care to ensure equal sample sizes across all treatment conditions. If circumstances beyond your control cause unequal sample sizes, you should refer to an advanced statistics textbook for recommendations for analyzing the data.

ESTIMATING SAMPLE SIZE

Another critical component of designing the factorial design is determining the number of participants required for each treatment condition. Researchers perform a power analysis of their research to ensure that they have a sufficient number of participants to be able to detect statistically significant main effects and interaction. The steps that we follow for estimating the sample size are essentially the same that we used for the single-factor experiment.

To determine power for the two-factor ANOVA we again turn to Table A.13 in Appendix A. For this example, assume that you want to conduct a 3 × 4 factorial design. Following Cohen's (1988) recommendation, we will assume that and also that the effect size for the main effects and interaction is moderate, $f = .25$ and that we want the power of our statistic to be $1 - \beta = .80$.

The first step is to recognize that the two-variable between-subjects ANOVA will generate three F-ratios: (1) for the main effect of Factor A, (2) for the main effect of Factor B, and (3) for the interaction of Factors A and B.

The next step will be to calculate an adjusted sample size. To complete this step, you will need the degrees of freedom for the ANOVA. Table 12.4 presents the method for determining the numerator degrees of freedom for each F-ratio.

Using these degrees of freedom, we can use the following equation to estimate power using specific sample sizes. We will begin by examining the power of the two-factor ANOVA with 10 participants in each cell. Table 12.5 presents the application of Equation 12.2 assuming $n_{ij} = 10$, $\alpha = .05$ and $f = .25$ for each F-ratio.

$$n'_{\text{effect}} = \frac{jk(n_{ij} - 1)}{df_{\text{effect}} + 1} + 1 \tag{12.2}$$

TABLE 12.4
Equations for determining the numerator degrees of freedom for a factorial design

Equations	Example for 3 × 4 factorial design
Main effect for Factor A	
$df_A = (j - 1)$ j = number of levels of Factor A	$df_A = 2 = (3 - 1)$
Main effect for Factor B	
$df_B = (k - 1)$ k = number of levels of Factor B	$df_B = 3 = (4 - 1)$
Interaction for Factors A and B	
$df_{AB} = (j - 1)(k - 1)$	$df_{AB} = 6 = (3 - 1)(4 - 1)$

TABLE 12.5
Estimated power for a 3 × 4 factorial ANOVA with $n_{ij} = 10$, $\alpha = .05$, and $f = .25$

	df_{effect}		Adjusted sample size	Rounded sample size*	Estimated power
Factor A	2	$n' = \dfrac{12(10 - 1)}{2 + 1} + 1$	$n' = 37$	$n' = 40$	$1 - \beta \approx .68$
Factor B	3	$n' = \dfrac{12(10 - 1)}{3 + 1} + 1$	$n' = 28$	$n' = 30$	$1 - \beta \approx .61$
Factor AB	6	$n' = \dfrac{12(10 - 1)}{6 + 1} + 1$	$n' = 16.429$	$n' = 16$	$1 - \beta \approx .45$

*I rounded the adjusted sample size to conform to the values in the power tables. These power estimates are sufficient for general estimates of the power of the design. If you need exact power estimates, refer to Cohen (1988) or software that performs such calculations.

TABLE 12.6
Estimated power for an interaction in a 3 × 4 factorial ANOVA
with $n_{ij} = 20$, $\alpha = .05$, and $f = .25$

	df_N		Adjusted sample size	Rounded sample size	Estimated power
Factor AB	6	$n' = \dfrac{12(20-1)}{6+1} + 1$	$n' = 33.57$	$n' = 30$	$1 - \beta \approx .76$

According to Table 12.5, the probability of obtaining a statistically significant interaction is less than 50% ($1 - \beta \approx .45$). The probability of obtaining statistically significant main effects is also on the slim side; $1 - \beta \approx .68$ for Factor A and $1 - \beta \approx .61$ for Factor B. One way to increase power is to increase sample size. Table 12.6 presents the predicted power if we increase the sample size to 20. Doubling the sample size does increase the power of the interaction, but at a cost. You will need 240 ($3 \times 4 \times 20 = 240$) participants to conduct the study. Do you have the time and energy to collect this much data?

Are there other things that you can do to increase the effect size of the study? Have you used the best possible measure of the dependent variable? Consider the independent variables. Do you need that many treatment levels? Can you create greater differences among the levels of the variables? Attending to these considerations may help you increase the power without having to use this many research participants.

INTERPRETING THE INTERACTION: ADVANCED CONSIDERATIONS

The interaction represents differences among the group means that cannot be accounted for by the main effects. Consequently, comparing the means for the interaction requires caution. We can use the Chaiken and Maheswaran (1992) experiment to exam how to describe the effects of the interaction.

As you will recall, the interesting finding of the Chaiken and Maheswaran (1992) experiment was that the participants indicated that they were very willing to buy the answering machine if it received an ambiguous review from a highly credible source. If you review Table 12.3, you will see that the mean of this condition is $M_{21} = 8.0$, which is greater than the grand mean, $\overline{M} = 5.667$, a difference of 2.333. How much of the difference reflects the unique combination of credibility and review endorsement? We must subtract the effects of the two main effects using Equation 12.3.

$$\Delta_{ij} = M_{ij} - M_{ai} - M_{bj} + \overline{M} \tag{12.3}$$

In this equation, Δ_{ij} is a **residual.** For this equation, a residual reflects the effect of the interaction after removing the influence of the main effects. Remember that an interaction reflects differences among the group means that neither main effect can explain by itself.

Therefore, the residual reflects the effect of the interaction independent of the main effects. If the interaction is not statistically significant, then the residuals for all group means will be close to or equal to 0.

For this example, the residual is $1.34 = 8.0 - 5.63 - 6.70 + 5.67$. The residual indicates that the mean of treatment condition a_2b_2 is $\Delta_{22} = 1.34$ points higher than we would expect from examining the effects of the main effects alone. Many statisticians and researchers (e.g., Hoaglin, Mosteller, & Tukey, 1991; Rosenthal & Rosnow, 1985) recommend computing the residuals for the factorial design and corresponding ANOVA as a way of interpreting the meaning of the interaction.

If there is no interaction between the two independent variables, then the residuals for each of the treatment combinations will be close to or equal to 0. As the interaction becomes more prominent, the residuals of several or all the treatment cells will become larger. Looking at the ambiguous review condition, the residuals indicate that people were more likely to buy the answering machine if the review came from a high-credibility source, but less likely to buy the device if the review came from the low-credibility source. Remember that the residuals for the means represent the changes that cannot be explained by either main effect alone. Therefore, when you compare the individual cell means, you must remember that the difference will represent the interaction as well as the main effects. Table 12.7 presents the residuals for each of the individual cells; Figure 12.14 presents a graph of the residuals.

Looking at Figure 12.14 indicates that the greatest effect occurred in the ambiguous endorsement condition. In the high-credibility condition, the participants were more likely

TABLE 12.7
Residuals for means presented in Table 12.3

Variable B Review type	Variable A Credibility of source a_1 Low credibility	a_2 High credibility	Row means
b_1 Strong	a_1b_1 $M_{11} = 6.6$ $\Delta_{11} = M_{11} - M_{a1} - M_{b1} + \overline{M}$ $\Delta_{11} = 6.6 - 5.7 - 6.25 + 5.667$ $\Delta_{11} = 0.32$	a_2b_1 $M_{21} = 5.9$ $\Delta_{21} = M_{21} - M_{a2} - M_{b1} + \overline{M}$ $\Delta_{21} = 5.9 - 5.63 - 6.25 + 5.667$ $\Delta_{21} = -0.32$	$M_{b1} = 6.25$
b_2 Ambiguous	a_1b_2 $M_{12} = 5.4$ $\Delta_{12} = M_{12} - M_{a1} - M_{b2} + \overline{M}$ $\Delta_{12} = 5.4 - 5.7 - 6.70 + 5.667$ $\Delta_{12} = -1.33$	a_2b_2 $M_{22} = 8.0$ $\Delta_{22} = M_{22} - M_{a2} - M_{b2} + \overline{M}$ $\Delta_{22} = 8.0 - 5.63 - 6.70 + 5.667$ $\Delta_{22} = 1.33$	$M_{b2} = 6.70$
b_3 Weak	a_1b_3 $M_{13} = 5.1$ $\Delta_{13} = M_{13} - M_{a1} - M_{b3} + \overline{M}$ $\Delta_{13} = 5.1 - 5.7 - 4.05 + 5.667$ $\Delta_{13} = 1.02$	a_2b_3 $M_{23} = 3.0$ $\Delta_{23} = M_{23} - M_{a2} - M_{b3} + \overline{M}$ $\Delta_{23} = 3.0 - 5.63 - 4.05 + 5.667$ $\Delta_{23} = -1.02$	$M_{b3} = 4.05$
Column means	$M_{a1} = 5.70$	$M_{a2} = 5.63$	$\overline{M} = 5.667$

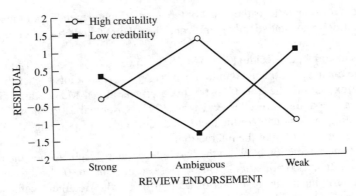

FIGURE 12.14
A graph representing the residuals of the interaction of the Chaiken and Maheswaran (1992) experiment.

to buy the product than would have been expected from the level of credibility or the strength of the endorsement. By contrast, in the low-credibility condition, the participants were less likely to buy the answering machine given the source and type of review. There is also an interesting pattern in the weak endorsement condition where people were less likely to buy the answering machine after reading the high-credibility review but more willing to buy the answering machine after reading the low-credibility review. It is as if the combination of a poor review combined with a credible source makes the answering machine unappealing.

RESEARCH IN ACTION: REINFORCING CREATIVITY

Eisenberger and Armeli (1997) conducted an experiment to answer the question: Does positive reinforcement influence creativity? The researchers predicted that two variables, instruction set and magnitude of reinforcement, would influence creativity. Specifically, they predicted that instructing people to be creative increases creativity. In addition, Eisenberger and Armeli predicted that positive reinforcement for creativity further enhances one's creativity.

The Eisenberger and Armeli (1997) experiment consisted of two phases. During the first phase, the researchers gave fifth- and sixth-grade students common objects and asked them to describe how they might use the object. The researchers told half the students to think of common uses of the objects and told the other students to think of unusual uses for the object. Thus, the first independent variable was instruction (common uses versus novel uses). All the children then received no reward, a small reward (18 cents), or a large reward (90 cents) for their ideas. Therefore, the second variable was the magnitude or reward (0, 18, or 90 cents).

During the second phase of the experiment, the researcher gave students a creativity test. The test consisted of a page with rows of unfilled circles. The researchers asked the

TABLE 12.8

Hypothetical results for Eisenberger and Armeli (1997) experiment

| Factor B Magnitude of reinforcement | | Factor A Instruction for use | | Row means |
		Common a_1	Novel a_2	
0¢	b_1	$M_{11} = 3.9$	$M_{12} = 4.5$	$M_{b1} = 4.2$
18¢	b_2	$M_{12} = 6.5$	$M_{22} = 5.9$	$M_{b2} = 6.2$
90¢	b_3	$M_{13} = 5.4$	$M_{23} = 10.4$	$M_{b3} = 7.9$
Column means		$M_{a1} = 5.27$	$M_{a2} = 6.93$	$\overline{M} = 6.1$

children to use each circle to create a picture. Eisenberger and Armeli (1997) predicted that the creativity of the students' pictures would reflect the effect of the two variables experienced during the first phase of the experiment.

The researchers used a 2 × 3 factorial design. The first variable was the initial training, instruction for use, and consisted of two levels, common versus novel. The second variable was the magnitude of reinforcement the student received for identifying the use of objects and consisted of three levels (0, 18, or 90 cents). Table 12.8 presents the summary statistics for the experiment.

Table 12.9 presents the ANOVA summary table for the 2 × 3 analysis. As you can see, there is a statistically significant main effect for Factor A, instructions for use; a statistically significant main effect for Factor B, magnitude of reinforcement; and a statistically significant interaction of the two variables. Looking at the means in Table 12.8, it is apparent that children in the novel instruction conditions earned higher creativity scores than children in the common instruction conditions. Similarly, it appears that the magnitude of reinforcement affects creativity; children who earned more money earned higher creativity scores. Finally, the interaction appears to reflect high creativity scores for the children in the novel instruction and 90 cent reinforcement condition. The children in this treatment condition earned substantially higher creativity scores than would have been expected by examining the trends seen for the main effects. Box 12.1 presents an example of a results section that one might prepare for this experiment.

TABLE 12.9

Summary table for data presented in Table 12.8

Source	SS	df	MS	F	$\hat{\omega}^2$
A	41.667	1	41.667	8.105*	.106
B	137.200	2	68.600	13.344*	.292
AB	86.933	2	43.567	8.455*	.199
Within	277.600	54	5.141		
Total	543.400	59			

*Reject the null hypothesis, $p < .05$.

The results confirmed our prediction that rewarding unusual responses would increase creative behavior. Figure 1 presents the data for the experiment. Clearly, those children receiving large rewards for novel uses of common objects scored higher on the creativity test than children in the other conditions. This conclusion is supported with a 2 (instructions) × 3 (reward size) ANOVA of the data. There was a statistically significant main effect of instruction type, $F(1, 54) = 8.11$, $\omega^2 = .11$. The main effect for reward size was also statistically significant, $F(2, 54) = 13.34$, $\omega^2 = .29$. The interaction of the two variables was also statistically significant, $F(2, 54) = 8.45$, $\omega^2 = .20$. A Tukey HSD post hoc test indicated that the novel-use and high reward size group produced the highest creativity scores (all $ps < .05$). None of the other differences between groups were statistically significant (all $ps > .05$).

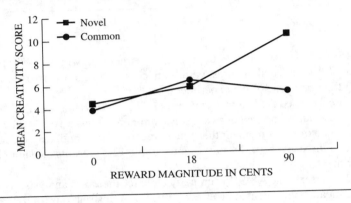

BOX 12.1
Example of results section for data presented in Table 12.9.

STATISTICS BEHIND THE RESEARCH

In this section we will examine the methods used to calculate the ANOVA summary table for the two-variable between-groups ANOVA. Table 12.10 presents the hypothetical data for the Eisenberger and Armeli (1997) experiment presented in the previous section. The table includes the data and the summary information for each treatment condition, as well as the row and column totals.

ASSUMPTIONS OF THE TEST

The two-variable between-groups ANOVA requires that the data meet three specific mathematical requirements known as assumptions. Meeting these ensures that the ANOVA will produce valid statistical interpretations of the data.

Normal distribution of data

The first assumption is that the data are normally distributed. Extreme skew in one or more of the groups may cause the ANOVA to produce spurious results. A quick review of

TABLE 12.10
Hypothetical data for the Eisenberger and Armeli (1997) experiment

	a_1					a_2					
	a_1b_1					a_2b_1					
b_1	1	5	3	5	3	5	5	9	7	4	
	3	6	4	7	2	4	6	3	0	2	
	$\Sigma X_{11} = 39$					$\Sigma X_{21} = 45$					$\Sigma X_{b1} = 84$
	$n_{11} = 10$					$n_{21} = 10$					$n_{b1} = 20$
	$M_{11} = 3.9$					$M_{21} = 4.5$					$M_{b1} = 4.2$
	a_1b_2					a_2b_2					
b_2	5	6	6	5	8	6	7	2	5	5	
	8	10	6	5	6	12	6	8	3	5	
	$\Sigma X_{12} = 65$					$\Sigma X_{22} = 59$					$\Sigma X_{b2} = 124$
	$n_{12} = 10$					$n_{22} = 10$					$n_{b2} = 20$
	$M_{12} = 6.5$					$M_{22} = 5.9$					$M_{b2} = 6.2$
	a_1b_3					a_2b_3					
b_3	4	6	7	5	4	9	10	6	12	11	
	9	7	6	4	2	14	9	8	14	11	
	$\Sigma X_{13} = 54$					$\Sigma X_{23} = 104$					$\Sigma X_{b3} = 158$
	$n_{13} = 10$					$n_{23} = 10$					$n_{b3} = 20$
	$M_{13} = 5.4$					$M_{23} = 10.4$					$M_{b3} = 7.9$
	$\Sigma X_{a1} = 158$					$\Sigma X_{a2} = 208$					$\Sigma X_{ijk} = 366$
	$n_{a1} = 30$					$n_{a2} = 30$					$N = 60$
	$M_{a1} = 5.27$					$M_{a2} = 6.93$					$\overline{M} = 6.10$
											$\Sigma X_{ijk}^2 = 2776$

the data in Table 12.10 indicates that there are no outliers or other conditions that might skew the data.

Homogeneity of variance

The second assumption is that the variances of the individual treatment conditions be relatively equal. This is critical in that extremely deviant variances in one or more of the groups can produce spurious results. Coupled with this is the general requirement that the sample sizes are the same. Another quick review of the data suggests that the variances of the six groups are equivalent. As an aside, many computer programs, such as $SPSS_©$, will conduct a test of homogeneity of variance.

Independence of groups

The final assumption is that the groups are independent. This requires that there be no explicit correlation among the groups. That the researchers randomly assigned the participants to the treatment conditions ensures independence of the groups. There are conditions when there is an explicit correlation between the groups. We will consider this research design in the next chapter.

Forming the Hypotheses

If the data meet the requirements of the ANOVA, we can proceed with creating the null and alternative hypotheses. Because there are three tests in the two-variable between-subjects ANOVA, we will create a null and alternative hypothesis for each test.

Null hypotheses

H_0: $F_A = 1.0$ There is no main effect for Factor A.
H_0: $F_B = 1.0$ There is no main effect for Factor B.
H_0: $F_{AB} = 1.0$ There is no interaction between Factors A and B.

Alternative hypotheses

H_1: Not H_0 There is a main effect for Factor A.
H_1: Not H_0 There is a main effect for Factor B.
H_1: Not H_0 There is an interaction between Factors A and B.

Sampling Distribution

For each F-ratio, we will need to determine $F_{critical}$, after we establish the level of α and calculate the degrees of freedom. As you learned in chapter 11, the F-distribution has two degrees of freedom. The numerator degrees of freedom (df_N) is the degrees of freedom associated with the variance estimate for each F-ratio. The denominator degrees of freedom (df_D) is the degrees of freedom associated with the within-groups variance. Table 12.11 presents the $F_{critical}$ for each test in the current example. The value of $F_{critical}$ allows us to determine whether to reject the null hypothesis for each observed F-ratio. When $F_{observed} \geq F_{critical}$, you can reject the null hypothesis.

Completing the Calculations

We can now proceed with the calculation of the two-variable independent groups ANOVA. Table 12.12 presents the computational equations and a worked example for the data presented in Table 12.10. As you proceed with your calculations, ensure that you make clear notes of your calculations. This practice will help you ensure that there are no computational

TABLE 12.11

Example of determining the degrees of freedom and $F_{critical}$ for each test in the two-variable independent groups ANOVA

Factor A
$df_A = j - 1$ $df_A = 2 - 1$ $df_A = 1$ $F_{critical}(1, 54) = 4.02$

Factor B
$df_B = k - 1$ $df_B = 3 - 1$ $df_B = 2$ $F_{critical}(2, 54) = 3.16$

Factor AB
$df_{AB} = (j - 1)(k - 1)$ $df_{AB} = (2 - 1)(3 - 1)$ $df_{AB} = 2$ $F_{critical}(2, 54) = 3.16$

Within
$df_{within} = \Sigma(n_{jk} - 1)$ $df_{within} = (10 - 1) + \cdots (10 - 1) + (10 - 1)$ $df_{within} = 54$

TABLE 12.12
Worked example for a two-variable independent groups ANOVA

$$SS_A = \sum \frac{(\sum X_{aj})^2}{n_{aj}} - \frac{(\sum X_{ijk})^2}{N} \qquad SS_A = \frac{(158)^2}{30} + \frac{(208)^2}{30} - \frac{(366)^2}{60} \qquad SS_A = 41.667$$

$$df_A = j - 1 \qquad df_A = 2 - 1 \qquad df_A = 1$$

$$MS_A = \frac{SS_A}{df_A} \qquad MS_A = \frac{41.667}{1} \qquad MS_A = 41.667$$

$$SS_B = \sum \frac{(\sum X_{bk})^2}{n_{bk}} - \frac{(\sum X_{ijk})^2}{N} \qquad SS_B = \frac{(84)^2}{20} + \frac{(124)^2}{20} + \frac{(158)^2}{20} - \frac{(366)^2}{60} \qquad SS_B = 137.200$$

$$df_B = k - 1 \qquad df_B = 3 - 1 \qquad df_B = 2$$

$$MS_B = \frac{SS_B}{df_B} \qquad MS_B = \frac{137.2}{2} \qquad MS_B = 68.60$$

$$SS_{AB} = \sum \frac{(\sum X_{jk})^2}{n_{jk}} - \frac{(\sum X_{ijk})^2}{N} - (SS_A + SS_B)$$

$$SS_{AB} = \frac{(39)^2}{10} + \frac{(45)^2}{10} + \frac{(65)^2}{10} + \frac{(59)^2}{10} + \frac{(54)^2}{10} + \frac{(104)^2}{10} - \frac{(366)^2}{60} - (41.667 + 137.20)$$
$$SS_{AB} = 86.933$$

$$df_{AB} = (j - 1)(k - 1) \qquad df_{AB} = (2 - 1)(3 - 1) \qquad df_{AB} = 2$$
$$MS_{AB} = \frac{SS_{AB}}{df_{AB}} \qquad MS_{AB} = \frac{86.933}{2} \qquad MS_{AB} = 43.467$$

$$SS_{within} = \sum X_{ijk}^2 - \sum \frac{(\sum X_{jk})^2}{n_{jk}}$$

$$SS_{within} = 2776 - \left(\frac{(39)^2}{10} + \frac{(45)^2}{10} + \frac{(65)^2}{10} + \frac{(59)^2}{10} + \frac{(54)^2}{10} + \frac{(104)^2}{10} \right)$$
$$SS_{within} = 277.60$$

$$df_{within} = \Sigma(n_{ij} - 1) \qquad df_{within} = (10 - 1) + (10 - 1) + (10 - 1) + (10 - 1) + (10 - 1) + (10 - 1)$$
$$df_{within} = 54$$

$$MS_{within} = \frac{SS_{within}}{df_{within}} \qquad MS_{within} = \frac{277.60}{54} \qquad MS_{within} = 5.141$$

$$SS_{total} = \sum X_{ijk}^2 - \frac{(\sum X_{ijk})^2}{N} \qquad SS_{total} = 2776 - \frac{(366)^2}{60} \qquad SS_{total} = 543.400$$

$$df_{total} = N - 1 \qquad df_{total} = 60 - 1 \qquad df_{total} = 59$$

Note: $df_{total} = df_A + df_B + df_{AB} + df_{within}$ $\qquad 59 = 1 + 2 + 2 + 54$
$SS_{total} = SS_A + SS_B + SS_{AB} + SS_{within}$ $\qquad 543.400 = 41.667 + 137.200 + 86.933 + 277.600$

errors. As a double check for your work, you should find that $df_{total} = df_A + df_B + df_{AB} + df_{within}$ and that $SS_{total} = SS_A + SS_B + SS_{AB} + SS_{within}$. The computations presented in Table 12.12 are the foundation for the ANOVA summary table presented in Table 12.9. To calculate the F-ratios, divide the mean square for the effect by the mean square for the within-groups variance. For example, $F_A = 41.667/277.600 = 8.105$.

Additional Tests

We can determine the residuals for the interaction. In Table 12.9 we see that interaction reflects the unique combination of the two variables. Of particular interest are the data for the children assigned to the largest reward condition. Those children instructed to think of novel uses earned higher creativity scores than their counterparts instructed to think of common applications. Table 12.13 presents the residuals for the cell means.

Omega squared, $\hat{\omega}^2$

Once we find that an F-ratio is statistically significant, we can then calculate $\hat{\omega}^2$ for the effect. As in the single-variable ANOVA, $\hat{\omega}^2$ for the two-variable ANOVA allows us to determine the proportion of the dependent variable accounted for by the particular source of variance. For the two-variable ANOVA, we can calculate $\hat{\omega}^2$ for each main effect and for the interaction. Table 12.14 presents the $\hat{\omega}^2$ for this experiment.

Effect size, f

We can also calculate the effect size for each mean effect and the interaction. Calculating the effect size allows us to estimate the power. As you can see in Table 12.15, the

TABLE 12.13
Residuals for means presented in Table 12.8

Variable B Reward	Variable A Instructions for use a_1 Common	a_2 Novel	Row means
b_1 0¢	a_1b_1 $M_{11} = 3.9$ $\Delta_{11} = 3.9 - 5.27 - 4.2 + 6.1$ $\Delta_{11} = 0.53$	a_2b_1 $M_{21} = 4.5$ $\Delta_{21} = 4.5 - 6.93 - 4.2 + 6.1$ $\Delta_{21} = -0.53$	$M_{b1} = 4.2$
b_2 18¢	a_1b_2 $M_{12} = 6.5$ $\Delta_{12} = 6.5 - 5.27 - 6.2 + 6.1$ $\Delta_{12} = 1.13$	a_2b_2 $M_{22} = 5.9$ $\Delta_{22} = 5.9 - 6.93 - 6.2 + 6.1$ $\Delta_{22} = -1.13$	$M_{b2} = 6.2$
b_3 90¢	a_1b_3 $M_{13} = 5.4$ $\Delta_{13} = 5.4 - 5.27 - 7.9 + 6.1$ $\Delta_{13} = -1.67$	a_2b_3 $M_{23} = 10.4$ $\Delta_{23} = 10.4 - 6.93 - 7.9 + 6.1$ $\Delta_{23} = 1.67$	$M_{b3} = 7.9$
Column means	$M_{a1} = 5.27$	$M_{a2} = 6.93$	$\bar{M} = 6.1$

TABLE 12.14
Example of calculating omega squared for each main effect and the interaction

Equation: $\hat{\omega}^2 = \dfrac{df_{\text{effect}}(F_{\text{effect}} - 1)}{df_{\text{effect}}(F_{\text{effect}} - 1) + N}$

Factor A	Factor B	Factor AB
$\hat{\omega}^2 = \dfrac{1(8.105 - 1)}{1(8.105 - 1) + 60} = .106$	$\hat{\omega}^2 = \dfrac{2(13.344 - 1)}{2(13.344 - 1) + 60} = .292$	$\hat{\omega}^2 = \dfrac{2(8.455 - 1)}{2(8.455 - 1) + 60} = .199$

TABLE 12.15
Example of calculating effect size for the main effects and interaction

Equations: $f = \sqrt{\dfrac{\eta^2_{\text{effect}}}{1.0 - \eta^2_{\text{effect}}}}$ where $\eta^2 = \dfrac{df_{\text{effect}} F_{\text{effect}}}{df_{\text{effect}} F_{\text{effect}} + df_{\text{within}}}$ or $\eta^2 = \dfrac{SS_{\text{effect}}}{SS_{\text{total}}}$

Factor A	Factor B	Factor AB
$\eta^2 = \dfrac{41.667}{543.600} = .077$	$\eta^2 = \dfrac{137.200}{543.600} = .252$	$\eta^2 = \dfrac{86.933}{543.600} = .160$
$f = \sqrt{\dfrac{.077}{1.0 - .077}} = .288$	$f = \sqrt{\dfrac{.252}{1.0 - .252}} = .580$	$f = \sqrt{\dfrac{.160}{1.0 - .160}} = .436$

effects sizes are quite large. The effect sizes are particularly large for the main effect of Factor B, the effects of reinforcement, and the interaction of factors A and B.

ACHIEVEMENT CHECK

(7) Imagine that a researcher conducted a single-factor ANOVA on a set of data and then reanalyzed the same data using a two-factor ANOVA. Explain how the sum of squares total and the sum of squares within would differ between the two statistical tests.

(8) Is it correct to assume that when the F-ratio for a main effect is not statistically significant, one can assume that the factor had no influence on the dependent variable?

(9) Is it correct to conclude that the mean of a treatment combination represents the effect of the interaction alone?

(10) Why will a two-variable ANOVA be more powerful than a single-variable ANOVA?

CHAPTER SUMMARY

This chapter is a further extension of the between-subjects research design as we examined how we can conduct a study that includes more than one independent variable. The two-variable design allows us to simultaneously examine the effect of two variables and their interaction on the dependent variable.

The two-variable design is extremely useful to researchers because it makes better use of research resources, has greater statistical power, and allows us to examine the complex interplay between variables. This interplay between the independent variables is the interaction.

The interaction is an extremely important finding in any research project because it represents an outcome that cannot be explained by either of the independent variables. The interaction indicates results beyond the simple addition of two variables with each other.

In this chapter we reviewed the many possible outcomes for a two-factor research design. As a generality, the results can indicate that one or more main effects is statistically significant, and that the interaction is statistically significant. We also reviewed how to examine a graph and interpret the effects of the independent variables and the interaction.

A large portion of the chapter reviewed the ANOVA for the two-variable design. As with the single-variable ANOVA, the two-variable ANOVA uses the F-ratio to determine whether there is evidence for a statistically significant effect of the independent variables and their interaction.

An important lesson to learn is that a statistically significant interaction means that the data cannot be explained simply by describing the simple effects of the independent variables. Although many researchers examine the pattern of means created by the interaction, several researchers recommend examining the residual, which indicates the effect of the interaction once the effects of the independent variables have been removed.

As with other inferential statistics, we can use power tables to estimate the number of participants that we require to obtain statistically significant effects.

CHAPTER GLOSSARY FOR REVIEW

Additive Effect   In a factorial design, the effect of one variable has a consistent effect upon the other variables.

Cell   Within a factorial design, the cell represents a unique combination of the levels of the independent variables.

Factorial Design   A research design that uses two or more independent variables and all possible combinations of treatment levels the researcher selects.

Independent Groups   A characteristic of the treatment conditions when both variables are between-subjects variables. If the groups are independent, we assume that there is no correlation.

Interaction   In a factorial design, an interaction indicates that the effects of the independent variables are not consistent across all treatment combinations. The interaction represents the differences among the sample means that neither main effect can explain.

Level   A unique condition or magnitude of the independent variable.

Main Effect   Within a factorial design, refers to the primary effect that an independent variable has on the dependent variable, holding the other effects constant.

Residual   For a factorial experiment, the difference between the grand mean and the individual mean less the effects of the independent variables. The residual reflects the effect of the interaction.

13 RESEARCH DESIGN IV: CORRELATED-GROUPS DESIGNS

CHAPTER OUTLINE

- ◆ Introduction
- ◆ Logic of the Correlated-Groups Research Design
- ◆ Repeated-Measures Design
- ◆ Matched-Groups Design
- ◆ Mixed-Model Design
- ◆ Statistics Behind the Research

> *Why speculate when you can calculate?*
>
> —Joan Baez

INTRODUCTION

As you have learned in the previous chapters, we can be creative with our use of the between-subjects design. The primary feature of the independent-groups design is its ability to examine the differences among different groups of people. Using the ANOVA, we can determine whether the between-groups variance is larger than the within-groups variance and thereby infer the relation between the independent and dependent variables. We can also easily modify the ANOVA to fit a wide range of research designs. As you learned in chapter 12, a factorial design allows us to examine the interaction between two variables. We can extend this creative streak by studying the correlated-groups design.

You will learn in this chapter that research designs such as the repeated-measures design and the matched-participants design offer you the opportunity to conduct experiments that have considerable statistical power. These designs allow the researcher to exercise greater control over the variables that influence the dependent variable.

The distinguishing characteristic of the research designs that we will examine in this chapter is that there is a known or intentional correlation among the groups. In the last four research designs we examined, the treatment groups are independent. We achieve this independence by randomly assigning participants to the levels of the treatment groups. Therefore, there should be no correlation between pairs of participants from different groups. In this chapter, we will examine research designs where we intentionally create groups in such a way that there is a correlation among pairs of scores across the groups. The two primary design techniques that we will use are the **repeated-measures design** and the **matched-groups design.** Although the repeated-measures and matched-groups designs are different procedures, we are able to use the same statistical techniques to analyze the data generated by these research designs.

LOGIC OF THE CORRELATED-GROUPS RESEARCH DESIGN

Many factors contribute to the random variation among participants' behavior in a research project. One of the more influential is the individual differences among the participants. The individual differences among the participants contribute to the within-group variance. If the within-group variance is too large, it will be difficult to detect differences among the groups related to the levels of the independent variable. If the variance between-groups is small relative to the size of the variance within-groups then the corresponding F-ratio will be too small to allow us to reject the null hypothesis.

There are several ways we can reduce the within-groups variance. For example, we can try to select participants similar to each other because the more homogeneous the sample, the lower the within-group variance. Another tactic is to treat significant-subject variables, such as sex, as one of the independent variables in a factorial design. If the subject variable systematically contributes to the total variance, identifying it as a variable will reduce the within-groups variance. This tactic works well if the subject variable is a categorical variable (e.g., sex or marital status) or if you can cluster the participants into logical categories (e.g., age groups).

Another way to reduce the within-groups variance is to use a correlated-groups design. This procedure is an exceptionally cost-effective method for increasing statistical power. Like the factorial design, the correlated-groups design allows the researcher to reduce the within-groups variance.

Figure 13.1 presents the difference between the independent groups ANOVA and the correlated-groups research design. For the between-subjects design, the variance among the participants is part of the within-groups variation. The within-groups variation represents variance due to random error and individual differences among participants. Using a correlated-groups design and corresponding ANOVA, we can partition out the variance due to individual differences and treat it as a separate source of variance. Doing so tends to reduce the size of MS_{within} and thereby increases the size of the F-ratio. Consequently, a correlated-samples design usually has greater statistical power than the equivalent between-subjects design.

There are two ways to use the correlated-groups design to our advantage. Specifically, we can use a repeated-measures design or a matched-participants design. Although these are different research procedures, both allow the researcher to exercise greater control over the variables that influence the independent variable. This increased control typically results in greater power.

INDEPENDENT-GROUPS DESIGN AND ANOVA

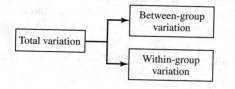

CORRELATED-GROUPS DESIGN AND ANOVA

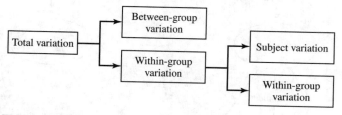

FIGURE 13.1

The difference between a independent-groups and a correlated-groups research design. For the between-subjects design, there is no way of identifying the variation among the participants. Therefore, the within-group variation reflects the random differences among participants and other random factors. The correlated-groups design identifies the variation among participants and separates it from the within-group variation thereby reducing the size of the within-group variance.

REPEATED-MEASURES DESIGN

In the repeated-measures design, we collect the data from the same participants on a series of occasions or under different levels of the independent variable to determine if there are systematic changes in the participants' behavior. There are two types of repeated-measures designs.

The first type of repeated-measures design allows us to test the same participant using several levels of the same independent variable. For example, a researcher might be interested in the effectiveness of different medications for the treatment of schizophrenia. To conduct the study, the researcher uses a placebo, Drug A, and Drug B. Each participant in the study will receive each treatment to determine its effects on the symptoms associated with schizophrenia. The advantage to this procedure is that it requires fewer participants because we test each participant using each treatment rather than assigning separate groups of participants to the three treatment conditions. Another advantage to this design is that we can use each participant as his or her own control condition and thereby reduce the size of the within-groups variance in the ANOVA.

The second type of repeated-measures design allows us to use time as an independent variable. For this type of research, we arrange to test or sample the participants' behavior at specific intervals. Using this procedure we can then determine how the participants' behavior changes as a function of time. This technique is useful when time is a critical predictor variable. Thus we can use this technique when we want to observe a behavior before and after a critical event or when we want to observe changes in the behavior that occur over time.

Figure 13.2 presents an illustration of the difference between an independent-groups design and a correlated-groups design. Both designs begin with a sampling population from which we draw our sample. The difference is the number of samples we draw. For the independent-groups design, we create a separate sample for each treatment condition using

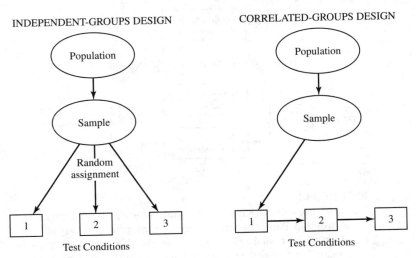

FIGURE 13.2
The difference between an independent-groups and a correlated-groups design.

random assignment. For the correlated-groups design, we create a single sample and then test each participant under each treatment condition.

Example

As an example, imagine that we want to replicate the famous serial position effect. To conduct our study we ask four participants to listen to seven lists of seven abstract, three-syllable words. Immediately after hearing the last word of each list, the participants must repeat the list. If our results replicate the serial position effect, words at the start and end of a list have the greatest probability of recall whereas words toward the middle of a list have a lower probability of recall. The data in Table 13.1 and Figure 13.3 represent hypothetical data for such a study (this example comes from research conducted by Walker & Hulme, 1999).

There is considerable variability among the four participants; some were good at recalling the words, whereas others did not do as well. If you look carefully at each

TABLE 13.1

Hypothetical data for a study of the serial-position effect using four participants

Participant	Position of word							Participant means
	1	2	3	4	5	6	7	
1	4	4	3	2	2	2	3	2.86
2	5	3	2	3	2	2	5	3.14
3	6	4	5	5	3	3	4	4.29
4	7	6	6	5	5	3	5	5.29
Average number of words recalled	5.50	4.25	4.00	3.75	3.00	2.50	4.25	

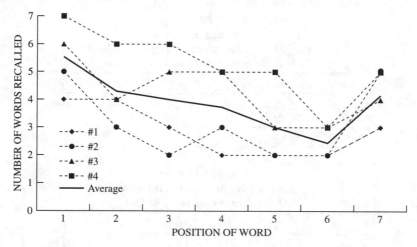

FIGURE 13.3

The number of words each participant recalled. The solid black line represents the average performance of the four participants.

participant's performance, you can see the serial-position effect. Participants recalled the most words that came at the start or the end of the lists. The solid black line in Figure 13.3 represents the average performance of the four participants for each serial position. This line clearly illustrates the serial-position effect. As the position of the word increases, the probability that a participant will remember the word deceases up to the sixth position. Participants recall the word in the seventh position more than the word in the sixth position, as the serial-position effect predicts. What would happen if we analyze the data using a conventional independent-groups ANOVA?

Table 13.2 presents the ANOVA summary table for a conventional independent-groups ANOVA. For this analysis, we treated the seven word positions as if they were independent conditions each consisting of four different people. In other words, we treated the data as if 28 people participated in the study and the researcher randomly assigned each person to one of the seven conditions. The conclusion to draw from this table is that we cannot reject the null hypothesis if $\alpha = .05$.

There is a major problem with analyzing these data using an independent-groups ANOVA; the groups are not independent of each other. If you reread the previous paragraph, you can see that the description of the "assumptions" had no bearing on how the researcher conducted the study. The data for all seven word positions represents the same four participants. Thus, we should assume that a participant's recall of a word in one position will influence the scores in the other positions. Participant 1 does not seem to have done well on the memory test as the scores for this person are generally low. By contrast, Participant 4 generally recalled the most words. If you look closely at the data, although there is much difference between participants 1 and 4, both show evidence of the serial-position effect. Therefore, we should reanalyze the data using another form of the ANOVA that allows us to examine the differences among correlated groups.

Table 13.3 presents a summary table for a correlated-groups ANOVA. There are some differences in the summary table for an independent-groups and a correlated-groups ANOVA. You can see that with the correlated-groups ANOVA we can reject the null

TABLE 13.2
Summary table for an independent-groups ANOVA using data in Table 13.1

	SS	df	MS	F	p
Between	22.4286	6	3.7381	2.166	0.088
Within	36.2500	21	1.7262		
Total	58.6786	27			

TABLE 13.3
Summary table for a correlated-groups ANOVA using data in Table 13.1

	SS	df	MS	F	p
Between	22.4286	6	3.7381	6.634	0.0005
Participants	26.1071	3	8.7024		
Within	10.1429	18	0.5635		
Total	58.6786	27			

hypothesis and conclude that there are statistically significant differences among the seven word positions. According to Table 13.3 the F-ratio increased from $F(6, 21) = 2.166$ to $F(6, 18) = 6.634$. How did this change occur?

For both ANOVA summary tables the $MS_{between} = 3.7381$. This number remains a constant for both forms of the ANOVA because we used $MS_{between}$ as an estimate of the variance among the seven serial position means. Because each ANOVA determines the between-group variance using the same procedures, this value will not change for the two tests. What does change for the two forms of the ANOVA is the value of MS_{within}. Earlier I noted that the importance of the correlated-groups ANOVA is that it divides the variance within-groups into two components, variance due to consistent differences among the participants and variance due to random error. In Table 13.3 you can see that there is a sums of squares (SS) for participants and a SS for within-group variance. Adding $SS_{subjects}$ and SS_{within} in Table 13.3 equals the SS_{within} of the independent-groups ANOVA reported in Table 13.2 ($36.2500 = 26.1071 + 10.1429$). In other words, a sizable proportion of variance within each group reflects the systematic differences among the participants, namely some people are better at recalling the list of words than others. When we divide the $MS_{between}$ by the revised MS_{within} we obtain a much larger F-ratio ($6.634 = 3.7381/0.5635$).

Therefore, the correlated-groups ANOVA allows us to detect the systematic differences among the serial position of the words that the independent-groups ANOVA did not detect. This success occurred because the correlated-groups ANOVA removes from the within-groups variance the variance related to consistent differences among the participants. Hence, we can conclude that the correlated-groups ANOVA is more powerful than the independent-groups design when there are consistent differences among the participants.

We do not need to calculate an F-ratio for the variance due to participants because our primary interest is the differences in the mean number of words recalled across the serial positions, not in the differences among the participants. You could, if you wanted, calculate the F-ratio by dividing the $MS_{subjects}$ by the MS_{within}. The result would tell you what you had anticipated, that there are statistically significant differences among the participants. Because we want to treat the variance among participants as a nuisance variable that we control for, such findings are inconsequential.

Advantages and Disadvantages of the Correlated-Groups Design

The primary advantage of the correlated-groups design is the increase in statistical power we receive from identifying the systematic variance caused by consistent differences among the participants. The increase in power comes from allowing each participant to serve as his or her own control condition, and that the participant's behavior is consistent across treatment conditions. Therefore, we test the same participant under several treatment conditions or across time.

Another advantage of the correlated-groups design is that it requires fewer participants because we test the same participants under more than one treatment condition. This advantage, combined with the increased statistical power, makes the correlated-groups design an extremely attractive procedure.

Repeated measurement of the same participant can introduce unwanted effects in some cases, however. Can you think of some confounding variables that might arise from

TABLE 13.4

Common carryover effects that can confound a repeated measures design

Contrast	In some cases, the change in level of the independent variable creates a contrast effect. For example, a participant switched from 50 to 25 reward points will respond differently than a participant switched from 25 to 50 points or a participant maintained at 25 points.
Fatigue	The participants become tired from or bored by repeating the same task on multiple trials. The effects of fatigue and boredom occur when the individual has little opportunity to rest between trials.
Habituation/ Adaptation	Habituation and adaptation refer to participants becoming used to the effects of the independent variable. In some cases, the participants may develop a tolerance for the independent variable. For example, a stimulus that produces fear the first time will loose its effectiveness if presented repeatedly.
Learning	The participants learn how to perform the task during the first test. Consequently, their performance on subsequent tests reflects the effect of the independent variable and the effect of learning. This form of carryover effect is prevalent whenever one uses the same test or skill-based task.
Pretest sensitization	A pretest, given before the treatment, may alter the participant's reaction to the eventual treatment. For example, asking participants questions about racism or sexism may change how they respond to a treatment condition that causes them to confront these issues.

repeatedly testing the same participants? Consider a study for which we require the participants to complete the same test for each treatment condition. Over time, the participants' performance will change, not because of the effects of the independent variable, but because participants have more experience with the test. We use the phrase **carryover effect** to describe situations where experience in one testing condition affects the participants' performance in the following conditions. Because carryover effects are not part of the purpose of the experiment, they confound the interpretation of the results. Table 13.4 lists several of the more common carryover effects that can confound the interpretation of the results.

Research Designs That Reduce Carryover Effects

There are several research designs that address the threat of a carryover effect. The first is to revert to the between-subjects design. This option may be your only solution, especially when you have irreversible changes in the participants that occur from exposure to the independent variable. Irreversible changes occur whenever you cannot undo the effect of the independent variable. For example, if you were comparing methods of teaching students to multiply, you could not use a repeated-measures design. Once you expose the students to the first teaching method, they have learned something about multiplication, and there is no way of returning the student to the original state of ignorance. Because you cannot undo the effects of the teaching, you cannot directly examine the merits and effect of the second teaching method.

A second option is to use the Solomon four-group design. This procedure is a creative use of control groups that allows you to judge the extent to which there is a carryover effect. This procedure is effective for accounting for the effects described in Table 13.4.

When the changes in the individual are reversible, we can shuffle the order of events for each participant. This shuffling of events will distribute the effects due to the sequence of events across all the participants. The goal of shuffling is to make the sequence effect a random variable that has no consistent effect on the participants' behavior. The two tactics we can use for this strategy are **counterbalancing designs** and **Latin square designs.**

The third option is to recognize that changes in the participant are an important independent variable to examine. The carryover effect is not a confounding variable, but a central focus of the research question we are asking.

In the following sections we will examine the three options for using a correlated-groups design. Specifically, we will examine the Solomon four-group design, counterbalancing designs, and Latin square designs and study the effects of the sequence of events.

Solomon four-group design

Richard Solomon (1949) developed an extremely creative research design, presented in Table 13.5, that makes use of three control groups to account for sequence events. As Campbell and Stanley (1963) noted, the procedure is a superior research design for accounting for carryover effects.

For the Solomon design, only Group 1 and Group 3 experience the treatment condition. The difference between these groups is that Group 1 receives a pretest and a posttest; Group 3 receives only the posttest. Groups 2 and 4 represent special control conditions that do not experience the treatment condition. Group 2 acts as a control condition for Group 1; the participants in both groups complete both the pretest and posttest, but only participants in Group 1 experience the treatment. Similarly, Group 4 acts as a control group for Group 3; the participants in both groups complete the posttest, but only participants in Group 3 receive the treatment.

Figure 13.4 presents an idealized graph of the results of a Solomon four-group design. As the graph illustrates, the participants who experienced the treatment (Groups 1 and 3) show much higher average scores than the participants in the control groups (Groups 2 and 4) for the pretest and posttest measures. There is also evidence of a carryover effect. That the posttest scores for Groups 1 and 2 are higher than the posttest scores of Groups 3 and 4 illustrates that the experience with the pretest has influenced the participants' behavior in some manner. We do, though, need a more objective mechanism for analyzing the data.

Solomon (1949) recommended that researchers use a simple 2×2 ANOVA factorial design to analyze the data. Table 13.6 presents the layout of the design. Braver and Braver (1988) noted that the Solomon four-group design is often underused and frequently misinterpreted. Contrary to popular opinion, the Bravers demonstrated that the Solomon design does not require twice the number of participants even though it has more control groups. They demonstrated that the Solomon design can be a cost-effective research technique if

TABLE 13.5
The Solomon four-group design

	Pretest	Treatment	Posttest
Group 1	O_1	⟶ Treatment ⟶	O_2
Group 2	O_3	⟶	O_4
Group 3		Treatment ⟶	O_5
Group 4			O_6

Note: O_X represents an observation or test score.

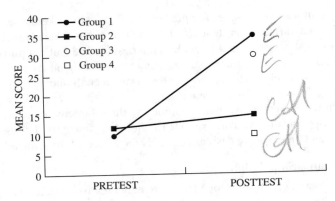

FIGURE 13.4
Idealized results of a Solomon four-group design.

TABLE 13.6
The 2 × 2 factorial analysis of the Solomon four-group design

	Factor A	
	Treatment	
	a_1 Treatment	a_2 No treatment
b_1 Pretest	O_2	O_4
Factor B: Pretesting		
b_2 no Pretest	O_5	O_6

used with the proper statistical analyses. In summary, the Solomon four-group design is a sophisticated research tool that offers considerable methodological and statistical control over carryover effects. It is a research tool often overlooked for little good reason.

Counterbalancing

We can reduce the amount of the carryover effect by randomly changing the sequence of testing for each participant. Researchers call this shuffling procedure counterbalancing. For example, if you wanted to test the effects of three dosages of a drug on the same participants, you would shuffle the order in which each participant receives the different dosages. One participant would receive the pattern 1, 2, 3 whereas another participant may receive the pattern 3, 1, 2.

The number of potential patterns for complete counterbalancing is $k!$, where k represents the levels of the independent variable to be tested (! represents the factorial of a number, and $1! = 1$). For three levels of the independent variable, there are $3!$ or $3 \times 2 \times 1 = 6$ patterns. Because there are six patterns, you will need enough participants for the study to ensure that you use each pattern the same number of times. In other words, if there are three treatment conditions, the number of participants in the experiment must be a multiple of six to ensure equal representation of each counterbalance sequence.

Latin Square Design

Complete counterbalancing can be expensive to conduct because of the number of participants required. Imagine conducting an experiment that used 5 levels of the independent variable. One would require at least $5! = 120$ participants to fill out all the sequence conditions. An alternative is to use a Latin square design.

A Latin square is a collection of counterbalanced sequences that ensures that each treatment occurs once within each position of the sequence. The Latin square also ensures that the sequence of treatments are random, thus controlling for unwanted sequence events. Perhaps seeing how one constructs a Latin square will illustrate the value of the procedure.

Table 13.7 presents the method for generating a Latin square of any size. To use the Latin square in an experiment, randomly assign equal numbers of participants to each treatment order condition specified by the rows of the square. The Latin square is a useful design tool to overcome most carryover effects. The analysis of the data is complex, however. The analysis

TABLE 13.7
Steps to create a Latin square for any number of levels
of the independent variable

	1	2	3	4	5	
1						Step 1: Create a square of k rows and k columns,
2						where k represents the number of levels of the
3						independent variable. For this example, there are
4						five levels of the independent variable.
5						

	1	2	3	4	5	
1	1	2	3	4	5	Step 2: Starting with Row 1, write the numbers 1
2	2	3	4	5	1	through 5. For each subsequent row, start the line
3	3	4	5	1	2	with the number of the line and then continue the
4	4	5	1	2	3	sequence of numbers until you reach k, and then
5	5	1	2	3	4	restart the numbering at 1.

	4	1	5	3	2	
1	4	1	5	3	2	Step 3: Using a random number table, randomly
2	5	2	1	4	3	shuffle the order of the columns.
3	1	3	2	5	4	
4	2	4	3	1	5	
5	3	5	4	2	1	

	4	1	5	3	2	
3	1	3	2	5	4	Step 4: Using a random number table, randomly
1	4	1	5	3	2	shuffle the order of the rows. The numbers within
4	2	4	3	1	5	the grid represent the Latin square. Randomly
5	3	5	4	2	1	assign equal numbers of participants to each of
2	5	2	1	4	3	the five sequences you generated.

of variance for this research design is beyond the scope of this textbook. Fortunately, advanced textbooks on statistics, such as those by Hayes (1981); Kirk (1982); and Winer, Brown, and Michels (1991), review the statistical procedures for the Latin square design.

Examine the Effects of a Sequence

For most repeated-measures research, the carryover effect is not a confounding variable. Rather, the researcher wishes to treat the sequence of events as the independent variable. For many experiments, the researcher intentionally examines the effects of shifting from one condition to another. A classic example of this type of analysis comes from the history of psychology. Crespi (1942) examined the effects of changing the amount of reinforcement that rats received for running through a maze. During the first part of the experiment, rats received 64, 16, or 4 pellets of food for running through the maze. After 20 trials, Crespi changed the amount of food the rats received. The rats that had been receiving 64 pellets began to receive 16 pellets. Similarly, the rats that had received 4 pellet also began to receive 16 pellets.

The results of this experiment demonstrate a clear contrast effect. As you can see in Figure 13.5, rats switched from 64 to 16 pellets began to run slower than the rats maintained at 16 pellets. By contrast, the rats switched from 4 to 16 pellets began to run much faster than rats maintained at 16 pellets.

For this experiment, the carryover effect is the central feature of the experiment because Crespi (1942) wanted to examine how the change in reinforcement would influence the rats' behavior. Many researchers use the repeated-measures design for the same reason.

ACHIEVEMENT CHECK

(1) Describe in your words the meaning and purpose of the matched-groups and repeated-measures designs.

(2) What are the similarities and differences between a matched-participants design and a repeated-measures design?

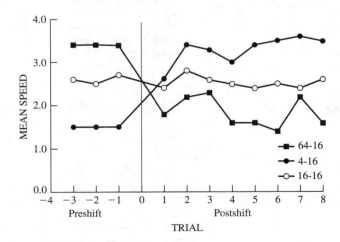

FIGURE 13.5

Results based on Crespi's (1942) research on the effect of changing the magnitude of reinforcement.

(3) What are common carryover effects?

(4) Describe in your words how the Solomon four-group design helps us contend with carryover effects.

(5) In a repeated-measures research design, how does each participant act as his or her own control group?

(6) Why does a correlated-groups design increase the power of the ANOVA?

(7) When is the use of counterbalancing and the Latin square design necessary?

MATCHED-GROUPS DESIGN

The repeated-measures design allows us to examine or test each participant's behavior under more than one condition. Although this procedure has its advantages, there are some shortcomings related to the carryover effect. The largest problem arises when the treatment creates an irreversible change in the participants' behavior. In this section, we will examine another research design that retains the statistical power of the correlated-groups design and allows us to test each participant under only one treatment condition. Specifically, we will examine the matched-groups design.

Researchers use the matched-groups design when they believe that an important subject variable correlates with the dependent variable. The goal of the matched-groups design is to ensure that the groups are equivalent regarding this variable. Therefore, each group in the study contains a separate group of participants; we do not use a repeated-measures procedure. Nevertheless, the matched-groups design allows us to assume that there is a meaningful correlation among pairs of participants across the treatment conditions. This tactic allows us to identify and remove variance due to a subject variable that influences the participant's behavior.

Table 13.8 presents the steps for creating a matched-groups design. First, we test each participant using a measure that correlates with the dependent variable. Second, using the test scores, rank the participants from the highest to the lowest. For the third step, cluster the

TABLE 13.8
Steps used to create a matched-groups design study

Step 1		Step 2		Step 3				Step 4		
Pretest all participants using a measure correlated with the dependent variable.		Rank order participants from highest to lowest based on test score.		Group participants in clusters equal to the number of treatment groups.				Randomly assign participants, by cluster, to treatment groups.		
Participant	**Score**	**Participant**	**Score**							
A	114	A	114						**Group**	
B	101	G	111							
C	104	F	109					**1**	**2**	**3**
D	105	I	106	**1**	A	G	F	A	F	G
E	92	D	105	**2**	I	D	C	C	I	D
F	109	C	104	**3**	H	B	E	E	H	B
G	111	H	103							
H	103	B	101							
I	106	E	92							

participants into groups based on their rank on the test. The size of the cluster must equal the number of treatment conditions used in the study. Finally, randomly assign the participants within each cluster to one of the treatment conditions. What is the result of all this effort?

In the example presented in Table 13.8, the first participant in each group earned one of the highest three scores on the test. Similarly, the second participant in each group earned the next highest level of test scores. This pattern continues for all the participants within each group. Therefore, we can assume that ordered pairs of participants (e.g., the fifth participant in each group) are similar to each other inasmuch as they each received similar scores on the original test.

Some researchers call the matched-groups design a randomized block design. The term block refers to agricultural experiments conducted during the early 1900s. A block was a specific plot of land that the researcher randomly selected to receive a specific treatment. Although behavioral researchers often use the phrases "matched-groups design" and "randomized-block design," I prefer matched-groups design as it emphasizes that the researcher intentionally attempts to equate the groups by measuring a specific subject variable.

We can use a hypothetical example of an experiment examining the effectiveness of several drugs on the treatment of schizophrenia. For this example, assume that the researcher will examine the effects of a placebo, Drug A, and Drug B. Because the researcher believes that the initial severity of the person's schizophrenia will influence results, the researcher first assesses the severity of symptoms for each participant. The researcher would then take the three participants with the highest scores and randomly assign them to one of the three treatment groups. Repeating this procedure for all participants ensures the equivalence among the groups with respect to initial levels of schizophrenia.

There is no reason to limit yourself to one subject variable. In some research projects, researchers find it necessary to match participants across a number of subject variables including age, sex, level of education, income, and other quantitative and qualitative variables that differentiate individuals and correlate with the dependent variable. A caveat is in order, however. Using more than one matching variable can greatly increase the difficulty of achieving a true balance among the participants.

The matched-groups design means that the groups are not independent. As you know, independent means that the behavior of one group of participants has no influence on the behavior of another group of participants. An independent-groups design creates independent groups because we randomly assign participants to the different treatment groups or randomly select participants from different populations. Consequently, the behavior of one group of participants has no influence on the behavior of other groups of participants. In the matched-groups design, we intentionally try to create a correlation among the groups. Therefore, we say that matched-groups design creates correlated groups.

Advantages and Disadvantages of the Matched-Groups Design

There is an advantage to the matched-groups design, the statistical power of the design. As you have already learned, the correlated groups ANOVA reduces MS_{within}. Therefore, any difference among the groups is easier to detect. There is, however, a potential disadvantage to using the matched-groups design. It is lower statistical power. The correlated samples ANOVA treats the scores across the treatment conditions as if they came from the same participants. The result is that the ANOVA acts as if there are fewer participants in the study. In other words, the degrees of freedom for a correlated-groups design are smaller than for the comparable independent-groups design. Review Tables 13.2 and 13.3. The degrees of freedom are (6, 21) for the independent-groups design and (6, 18) for the correlated-groups design. As a generality, small degrees of freedom require larger F-ratios to reject the null hypothesis. Consequently, if the matching technique does not effectively identify a significant subject variable, the statistical power of the test can be lower than a comparable between-groups design. Therefore, the advantage of a matched-groups design occurs only when your matching technique identifies a subject variable with a substantial correlation to the dependent variable.

Yoked-Control Group

Another popular version of the matched-subjects design is the yoked-control group design. In a **yoked-control** study, the researcher randomly pairs a control participant with a participant in the experimental group, and each experience the exact sequence of events or consequences except for the exposure of the independent variable. Researchers use the yoked-control design when the behavior of the participant affects the sequence of events in the study. Perhaps several examples of the use of a yoked-control design would be helpful.

Figure 13.6 presents an illustration of a yoked-control design. In this figure, the participants experience some sequence of events during the course of the experiment. As you

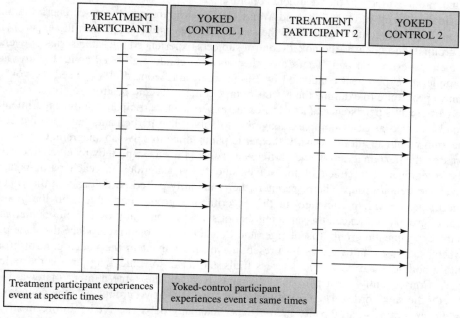

FIGURE 13.6

A yoked-control design.

can see, the order and pattern of events is different for the two participants in the treatment condition. The participants in the yoked-control condition experience the same events in the same sequence and interval as their partner.

Classic examples of the yoked-control group are experiments conducted by Brady (1958) and Brady, Porter, Conrad, and Mason (1958). Brady and his associates exposed monkeys to a series of escapable shocks. Brady selected half of the monkeys to be the "executive" subject in the experimental group. These monkeys could avoid or escape an unsignaled shock by pressing a button. Paired with each executive monkey was a yoked-control monkey. The yoked-control monkey received a shock each time its executive monkey did, but the yoked-control monkey had no way to avoid or escape the shock. Brady reported that the monkeys assigned to the executive condition developed stomach ulcers whereas the yoked-control subjects did not. From these data, Brady concluded that the responsibility of avoiding/escaping the shocks was stressful and created the ulcers.

The Brady et al. (1958) study is an important example, because it contains a serious methodological error—Brady et al. did not randomly assign the participants to the experimental and yoked-control groups. It turns out that Brady et al. pretested the monkeys on a shock-avoidance task and selected the faster learners for the experimental condition and the slower learners for the yoked-control condition. Weiss (1971) recognized the problem with the procedure and repeated the experiment. For his experiment, Weiss randomly assigned rats to either the experimental group or the yoked-control condition. The results of that study were the opposite of the Brady et al. results. The rats in the yoked-control condition developed the stomach ulcers, not the rats in the executive-treatment condition. Therefore, it appears that the Brady et al. findings are the results of a methodological confound, not the effects of the treatment conditions.

In the Brady et al. (1958) and Weiss (1971) experiments, the researchers literally wired the yoked-control subjects to the same apparatus as the subjects in the experimental group. Consequently, the yoked-control subjects experienced the same series of events as their experimental pair. There are other ways to conduct a yoked-control study. For example, an experiment conducted by Eisenberger and Leonard (1980) used the yoked-control procedure to examine the effects of task complexity and positive reinforcement on the participant's persistence at a task. For the experiment, participants in the experimental group received a list of complex anagrams to solve. The participants had to solve each anagram within an allotted time. If the participants failed to solve an anagram, they began work on the next anagram. If the participants solved the anagram, they received a reward. The researchers kept track of the solved and failed anagrams for each participant in the experimental group. The researchers then randomly paired participants in the yoked-control group with participants in the experimental group. Participants in the yoked-control group experienced the same number of successes and failures as their counterparts in the experimental group. Eisenberger and Leonard were able to reproduce the same pattern of successes and failures by presenting the participant in the yoked-control group with a simple anagram for the success trials and an unsolvable anagram for the failure trials. Consequently, each pair of participants received the same number of rewards in exactly the same order. The only difference between the two groups was the complexity of the anagrams—participants in the experimental groups received reinforcement for solving complex anagrams whereas the participants in the control group received reinforcement for solving simple anagrams.

(8) How will using a matched-groups design increase the power of the ANOVA?
(9) In what ways are the matched-groups design and the yoked-control design similar and different from each other?
(10) Describe how a yoked-control design works and how it ensures that participants in the experimental and control groups receive the same treatment except for the independent variable.
(11) How can you distinguish between an independent-groups and a correlated-groups design?

MIXED-MODEL DESIGN

As you might have guessed, we can continue to apply the logic of the ANOVA to various research applications. In this section, you will learn how to conduct a **mixed-model design.** The mixed-model design gets its name because there are two types of variables, a between-subjects variable and a within-subjects variable.

A between-subjects variable is an independent variable to which the researcher randomly assigns the participants. For each level of a between-participants variable there is a different and independent group of participants. The essential characteristic of a between-subjects variable is that participants experience only one level of the variable. Consequently, if participants are exposed to only one level of the variable, it is a between-subjects variable. If the researcher uses a subject variable (e.g., men versus women, depressed versus not depressed) then the variable is also a between-subjects variable. The term between-subjects refers to the fact that the ANOVA compares the differences between independent groups of different participants.

By contrast, a within-subjects variable is a correlated-samples variable. Therefore, if a factor represents a repeated-measures variable or matched-groups variable, we call it a within-subjects variable. The essential characteristic of a within-subjects variable is that we collect data from the same participant on different occasions or under different treatment conditions. We also use within-subjects to describe the matched-groups research design. We will examine the mixed-model design in the "Research in Action" section.

RESEARCH IN ACTION: MEMORY FOR RELATED WORDS

Let's look at a simple experiment to demonstrate how to use a mixed-model ANOVA. A student wants to replicate a classic experiment conducted by Wickens, Born, & Allen (1963) that examined the effects of proactive interference. Proactive interference occurs when you attempt to learn new information and previously learned information interferes with the new material.

For the experiment, the researcher has the participant complete a series of trials. On each trial, the researcher presents the participant with a short list of words whose meanings are highly related (e.g., names of flowers). After seeing the words, the participant must then recall the words in the list. For the experimental and control groups, to which participants are randomly assigned, the first three trials use the same category of words. On the fourth trial, the researchers change the meaning of the words for the experimental group (e.g., names of professions), but leave the meaning of the words for the control group unchanged. Table 13.9 presents the percentage correct for the two groups across the four trials, and Figure 13.7 presents a graph of the group means.

As a quick review, we can examine the components of this experiment. First, the research does incorporate the mixed-model design. The researcher randomly assigned participants to either the experimental or the control groups. Hence the first variable is a between-subjects variable as the researcher tested the participants under one of the conditions. The second variable is the sequence of trials. Because the researcher tested each participant on each trial, we can conclude that trials is a within-subjects design. Specifically, the researcher assumes that there will be a correlation among the groups because each participant completes the entire sequence of trials.

TABLE 13.9

Hypothetical data for an experiment examining release from proactive interference effect

	Participant	Trial 1	Trial 2	Trial 3	Trial 4	
Experimental	1	82	53	48	63	
	2	92	51	39	60	
	3	63	41	10	52	
	4	75	57	51	72	
	5	78	49	43	77	
		$M_{11} = 78.0$	$M_{12} = 50.2$	$M_{13} = 38.2$	$M_{14} = 64.8$	$M_{a1} = 57.80$
Control	6	84	60	47	33	
	7	85	44	42	46	
	8	78	71	34	45	
	9	76	49	38	25	
	10	63	69	55	30	
		$M_{21} = 77.2$	$M_{22} = 58.6$	$M_{23} = 43.2$	$M_{24} = 35.8$	$M_{a2} = 53.60$
		$M_{b1} = 77.6$	$M_{b2} = 54.4$	$M_{b3} = 40.7$	$M_{b4} = 50.3$	$\overline{M} = 55.75$

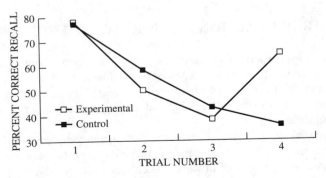

FIGURE 13.7
Graph of the data presented in Table 13.9.

TABLE 13.10
The ANOVA summary table for a mixed-model ANOVA

Source	SS	df	MS	F
A	168.10	1	168.100	0.842
Subjects	1597.40	8	199.675	
B	7354.50	3	2451.500	30.132*
AB	2174.90	3	724.967	8.911*
B × subjects	1952.60	24	81.358	
Total	13247.50	39		

*$p < .05$, Reject H_0.

During the first three trials, the participants' performance in both groups decreased, as is predicted by the proactive interference phenomenon. The data for the fourth trial is interesting. The performance of the participants in the control group continued to decline. By contrast, the performance of the participants in the experimental group improved. We can use these data to demonstrate how to use a mixed-model design.

Table 13.10 presents the ANOVA summary table for the data presented in Table 13.8. There is a statistically significant main effect for the trials and a statistically significant interaction. The results of the interaction between trials and the experimental group indicates that the participants in the experimental group performed just like the participants in the control group until Trial 4. Switching the meaning of the words in the fourth trial undid the effects of the proactive interference.

As with the other forms of the ANOVA we can follow the statistically significant F-ratio with additional tests including post hoc tests of the main effects and interaction and measure of effect size.

STATISTICS BEHIND THE RESEARCH

In this section we will examine two versions of the correlated-groups ANOVA. The first test will examine the computational procedures for the simple one-factor correlated-groups ANOVA. The second test will examine the mixed-model design.

Single-Factor Correlated-Groups ANOVA

To illustrate this version of the ANOVA we will return to the serial-position effect study described at the start of the chapter. Table 13.11 presents an enhanced representation of the data. We need to know the totals for each trial (ΣX_{aj}) and for each participant (ΣX_{si}).

Assumptions

The three primary assumptions for this test are similar to the standard assumptions of the ANOVA. We expect that the group variances are consistent, that the distribution of errors is independent, and that the data are normally distributed. An additional assumption is that there be homogeneity of the correlations among the groups.

TABLE 13.11
Data to be analyzed using a single-factor correlated-groups ANOVA

Participant	|		Position of word						Totals
	1	**2**	**3**	**4**	**5**	**6**	**7**		**Totals**
1	4	4	3	2	2	2	3	$\Sigma X_{s1} = 20$
2	5	3	2	3	2	2	5	$\Sigma X_{s2} = 22$
3	6	4	5	5	3	3	4	$\Sigma X_{s3} = 30$
4	7	6	6	5	5	3	5	$\Sigma X_{s4} = 37$

$\Sigma X_{a1} = 22$ $\Sigma X_{a2} = 17$ $\Sigma X_{a3} = 16$ $\Sigma X_{a4} = 15$ $\Sigma X_{a5} = 12$ $\Sigma X_{a6} = 10$ $\Sigma X_{a7} = 17$ $\Sigma X_{ij} = 109$
$M_{a1} = 5.50$ $M_{a2} = 4.25$ $M_{a3} = 4.00$ $M_{a4} = 3.75$ $M_{a5} = 3.00$ $M_{a6} = 2.50$ $M_{a7} = 4.25$ $\Sigma X_{ij}^2 = 483$

Forming the hypotheses

As with all ANOVAs, we begin with the null hypothesis that states that the differences among the group means represent random variation. The alternative hypothesis states that the variance among the group means is greater than would be expected by chance. For this study,

Null hypothesis

H_0: $\mu_1 = \mu_2 = \mu_3 \cdots = \mu_7$ The differences among the group means represent random variation.

Alternative hypothesis

H_1: Not H_0 The variation among the group means is greater than expected by chance.

Sampling distribution

The sampling distribution of the single-factor correlated-groups ANOVA is the conventional F-distribution. We use the $df_{between}$ and df_{within} to determine $F_{critical}$ for the hypothesis testing.

Completing the calculations

Table 13.12 presents the steps for completing the calculations for the ANOVA summary table. For this analysis, the F-ratio is the variance between-groups divided by the variance within-groups. Using the following calculations, we find that $6.6338 = 3.7381/0.5635$. The degrees of freedom for the F-ratio are 6 and 18. Therefore, $F_{critical}$ (2, 18) $= 2.66$ for $\alpha = .05$. Because $F_{observed} > F_{critical}$ we can reject the null hypothesis.

Mixed-Model ANOVA

To illustrate this version of the ANOVA we will use the data presented in Table 13.9.

Assumptions

This test requires the same assumptions used for the single-factor correlated groups ANOVA.

TABLE 13.12

Steps for creating the ANOVA summary table for a single-factor correlated-groups ANOVA

$$SS_{between} = \frac{\sum \left(\sum X_{aj} \right)^2}{n} - \frac{\left(\sum X_{ij} \right)^2}{nj}$$

$$SS_{between} = \frac{22^2 + 17^2 + 16^2 \cdots + 17^2}{4} - \frac{(109)^2}{4(7)} \qquad SS_{between} = 22.4286$$

$$df_{between} = j - 1 \qquad df_{between} = 7 - 1 \qquad df_{between} = 6$$

$$MS_{between} = \frac{SS_{between}}{df_{between}} \qquad MS_{between} = \frac{22.4286}{6} \qquad MS_{between} = 3.7381$$

$$SS_{subjects} = \frac{\sum \left(\sum X_{si} \right)^2}{j} - \frac{\left(\sum X_{ij} \right)^2}{nj} \qquad SS_{subjects} = \frac{20^2 + 22^2 + 30^2 + 37^3}{7} - \frac{(109)^2}{4(7)}$$

$$SS_{subjects} = 26.1071$$

$$df_{subjects} = n - 1 \qquad df_{subjects} = 4 - 1 \qquad df_{subjects} = 3$$

$$SS_{within} = \sum X_{ij}^2 - \frac{\sum \left(\sum X_{si} \right)^2}{j} - \frac{\sum \left(\sum X_{aj} \right)^2}{n} + \frac{\left(\sum X_{ij} \right)^2}{nj}$$

$$SS_{within} = 483 - \frac{3153}{7} - \frac{1787}{4} + \frac{11881}{28} \qquad SS_{within} = 10.1429$$

$$df_{within} = (n - 1)(j - 1) \qquad df_{within} = (4 - 1)(7 - 1) \qquad df_{within} = 18$$

$$MS_{within} = \frac{SS_{within}}{df_{within}} \qquad MS_{within} = \frac{10.1429}{18} \qquad MS_{within} = 0.5635$$

$$SS_{total} = \sum X_{ij}^2 - \frac{\left(\sum X_{ij} \right)^2}{nj} \qquad SS_{total} = 483 - \frac{(109)^2}{4(7)} \qquad SS_{total} = 58.6786$$

$$df_{total} = nj - 1 \qquad df_{total} = 4(7) - 1 \qquad df_{total} = 27$$

Note: $df_{total} = df_{between} + df_{subjects} + df_{within}$ $27 = 6 + 3 + 18$
 $SS_{total} = SS_{between} + SS_{subjects} + SS_{within}$ $58.6786 = 22.4286 + 26.1071 + 10.1429$

Forming the hypotheses

As with all ANOVAs, we begin with the null hypothesis that states that the differences among the group means represent random variation. The primary factors of interest represent (a) the difference among the between-subjects variable, (b) the difference among the within-subjects variable, and (c) the interaction of the two variables. For this example,

Null hypotheses:

H_0: $F_A = 1.0$ There is no main effect for Factor A, the between-subjects factor.
H_0: $F_B = 1.0$ There is no main effect for Factor B, the within-subjects factor.
H_0: $F_{AB} = 1.0$ There is no interaction between Factors A and B.

Alternative hypotheses:

H_1: Not H_0 There is a main effect for Factor A.
H_1: Not H_0 There is a main effect for Factor B.
H_1: Not H_0 There is an interaction for Factors A and B.

Sampling distribution

The sampling distribution of the single-factor correlated-groups ANOVA is the conventional F-distribution. We use the df_{effect} and df_{within} to determine $F_{critical}$ for the hypothesis testing.

Completing the calculations

Table 13.13 presents the steps for completing the calculations for the ANOVA summary table.

TABLE 13.13

Steps for creating the ANOVA summary table for a single-factor correlated-groups ANOVA

	Participant	Trial 1	Trial 2	Trial 3	Trial 4	Participant totals
Experimental	1	82	53	48	63	$\Sigma X_{s1} = 246$
	2	92	51	39	60	$\Sigma X_{s2} = 242$
	3	63	41	10	52	$\Sigma X_{s3} = 166$
	4	75	57	51	72	$\Sigma X_{s4} = 255$
	5	78	49	43	77	$\Sigma X_{s5} = 247$
		$\Sigma X_{11} = 390$	$\Sigma X_{12} = 251$	$\Sigma X_{13} = 191$	$\Sigma X_{14} = 324$	$\Sigma X_{a1} = 1156$
		$M_{11} = 78.0$	$M_{12} = 50.2$	$M_{13} = 38.2$	$M_{14} = 64.8$	$M_{a1} = 57.8$
Control	6	84	60	47	33	$\Sigma X_{s6} = 224$
	7	85	44	42	46	$\Sigma X_{s7} = 217$
	8	78	71	34	45	$\Sigma X_{s8} = 228$
	9	76	49	38	25	$\Sigma X_{s9} = 188$
	10	63	69	55	30	$\Sigma X_{s10} = 217$
		$\Sigma X_{21} = 386$	$\Sigma X_{22} = 293$	$\Sigma X_{23} = 216$	$\Sigma X_{24} = 179$	$\Sigma X_{a2} = 1074$
		$M_{21} = 77.2$	$M_{22} = 58.6$	$M_{23} = 43.2$	$M_{24} = 35.8$	$M_{a2} = 53.6$
		$\Sigma X_{b1} = 776$	$\Sigma X_{b2} = 544$	$\Sigma X_{b3} = 407$	$\Sigma X_{b4} = 503$	$\Sigma X_{ijk} = 2230$
		$M_{b1} = 77.6$	$M_{b2} = 54.4$	$M_{b3} = 40.7$	$M_{b4} = 50.3$	$\overline{M} = 55.75$
						$\Sigma X_{ijk}^2 = 137570$

$n = 5$: Number of participants in each level of Factor A, the between-subjects variable
$j = 2$: Number of levels for Factor A
$k = 4$: Number of levels for Factor B

$$SS_A = \frac{\sum\left(\sum X_{aj}\right)^2}{nk} - \frac{\left(\sum X_{ijk}\right)^2}{njk} \qquad SS_A = \frac{1156^2 + 1074^2}{5(4)} - \frac{(2230)^2}{(5)(2)(4)} \qquad SS_A = 168.10$$

$$df_A = j - 1 \qquad df_A = 2 - 1 \qquad df_A = 1$$

$$MS_A = \frac{SS_A}{df_A} \qquad MS_A = \frac{168.10}{1} \qquad MS_A = 168.10$$

$$SS_{subjects} = \frac{\sum\left(\sum X_{si}\right)^2}{k} - \frac{\sum\left(\sum X_{aj}\right)^2}{nk}$$

$$SS_{subjects} = \frac{246^2 + 242^2 + 166^2 \cdots 188^2 + 217^2}{4} - \frac{1156^2 + 1074^2}{5(4)} \qquad SS_{subjects} = 1597.40$$

$$df_{\text{subjects}} = (j-1)(n-1) \qquad df_{\text{subjects}} = (2-1)(5-1) \qquad df_{\text{subjects}} = 8$$

$$MS_{\text{subjects}} = \frac{SS_{\text{subjects}}}{df_{\text{subjects}}} \qquad MS_{\text{subjects}} = \frac{1597.40}{8} \qquad MS_{\text{subjects}} = 199.675$$

$$F_A = \frac{MS_A}{MS_{\text{subjects}}} \qquad F_A = \frac{168.100}{199.675} \qquad F_A = 0.842$$

$$SS_B = \frac{\sum\left(\sum X_{bk}\right)^2}{nj} - \frac{\left(\sum X_{ijk}\right)^2}{njk} \qquad SS_B = \frac{776^2 + 544^2 + 407^2 + 503^2}{5(2)} - \frac{(2230)^2}{(5)(2)(4)} \qquad SS_B = 7354.50$$

$$df_B = k-1 \qquad df_B = 4-1 \qquad df_B = 3$$

$$MS_B = \frac{SS_B}{df_B} \qquad MS_B = \frac{7354.50}{3} \qquad MS_B = 2451.50$$

$$SS_{AB} = \frac{\sum\left(\sum X_{jk}\right)^2}{n} - \frac{\left(\sum X_{ijk}\right)^2}{njk} - SS_A - SS_B$$

$$SS_{AB} = \frac{390^2 + 251^2 + 191^2 \cdots 216^2 + 179^2}{5} - 124332.50 - 168.10 - 7354.50 \qquad SS_{AB} = 2174.90$$

$$df_{AB} = (j-1)(k-1) \qquad df_{AB} = (2-1)(4-1) \qquad df_{AB} = 3$$

$$MS_{AB} = \frac{SS_{AB}}{df_{AB}} \qquad MS_{AB} = \frac{2174.90}{3} \qquad MS_{AB} = 724.967$$

$$SS_{B\times\text{subjects}} = \sum X_{ijk}^2 - \frac{\sum\left(\sum X_{jk}\right)^2}{n} - \frac{\sum\left(\sum X_{si}\right)^2}{k} + \frac{\sum\left(\sum X_{aj}\right)^2}{nk}$$

$$SS_{B\times\text{subjects}} = 137570 - \frac{390^2 + 251^2 + 191^2 \cdots 216^2 + 179^2}{5} - \frac{246^2 + 242^2 + 166^2 \cdots 188^2 + 217^2}{4}$$
$$+ \frac{1156^2 + 1074^2}{5(4)}$$

$$SS_{B\times\text{subjects}} = 1952.60$$

$$df_{B\times\text{subjects}} = j(n-1)(k-1) \qquad df_{B\times\text{subjects}} = 2(5-1)(4-1) \qquad df_{B\times\text{subjects}} = 24$$

$$MS_{B\times\text{subjects}} = \frac{SS_{B\times\text{subjects}}}{df_{B\times\text{subjects}}} \qquad MS_{B\times\text{subjects}} = \frac{1952.60}{24} \qquad MS_{B\times\text{subjects}} = 81.358$$

$$SS_{\text{total}} = \sum X_{ijk}^2 - \frac{\left(\sum X_{ijk}\right)^2}{N} \qquad SS_{\text{total}} = 137570 - \frac{(2230)^2}{40} \qquad SS_{\text{total}} = 13247.50$$

$$df_{\text{total}} = njk - 1 \qquad df_{\text{total}} = (5)(2)(4) - 1 \qquad df_{\text{total}} = 39$$

$$F_B = \frac{MS_B}{MS_{B\times\text{subjects}}} \qquad F_B = \frac{2451.50}{81.358} \qquad F_B = 30.132$$

$$F_{AB} = \frac{MS_{AB}}{MS_{B\times\text{subjects}}} \qquad F_{AB} = \frac{724.967}{81.358} \qquad F_{AB} = 8.911$$

Note: $df_{\text{total}} = df_A + df_{\text{subjects}} + df_B + df_{AB} + df_{B\times\text{subjects}}$ $39 = 1 + 8 + 3 + 3 + 24$

$SS_{\text{total}} = SS_A + SS_{\text{subjects}} + SS_B + SS_{AB} + SS_{B\times\text{subjects}}$ $13247.50 = 168.10 + 1597.40 + 7354.50$
$$+ 2174.90 + 1952.60$$

CHAPTER SUMMARY

In this chapter we examined another research design that allows us to increase the power of our research by identifying and removing variance due to differences among the participants. Specifically, we examined the matched-groups design and the repeated-measures design.

For the matched-groups design, the researcher identifies a subject variable that he or she believes influences the dependent variable of interest and then assigns the participants to the treatment conditions in such a way that each group has the same proportion of people who are high and low on the subject variable.

For the repeated-measures design, the researcher tests the same participants under a series of different treatment conditions.

As a generality, the matched-groups and repeated-measures designs can increase the power of the statistical test because the corresponding ANOVA identifies systematic variance among the subjects and removes this variance from the common error term. Therefore, the designs make it easier to detect the differences among the various groups.

The repeated-measures design does have a potential disadvantage, however. In some cases there may be a significant carryover effect that will bias or confound our interpretation of the data. In some cases, the carryover effect can be overcome using a Latin square design. In other cases, the carryover effect may be the focus of the study.

The ANOVA for the correlated-groups design is similar to the ANOVA for between-groups designs. The notable difference is that the ANOVA estimates the variance due to the differences among the participants. This strategy can reduce the common error term and then increase the probability that the differences among the groups will be detected.

Another version of the within-subjects design allows us to mix between-groups and within-groups variables.

A between-subjects variable is one where the participants in one treatment condition are different from the participants in the other treatment conditions. A within-subjects variable is one where there is an intended correlation among the groups. This correlation occurs when we use either a matched-groups or a repeated-measures design.

CHAPTER GLOSSARY FOR REVIEW

Between-Subjects Variable An independent variable that represents different groups of participants. Each level of the variable consists of a different group of participants.

Carryover Effect A form of confounding variable that can occur when using a repeated-measures design. Exposing the participant to one level of the independent can affect the participant's performance when tested under other conditions.

Counterbalancing A technique to reduce the carryover or sequencing effects in a repeated-measures design. The researcher tests the participants under the identified treatment conditions; however, the order of the exposure is different. Specialized tactics for counterbalancing include Latin square designs.

Latin Square Design   A special form of counterbalancing. The procedure balances the sequence of treatment conditions such that order of treatments is balanced across all participants.

Matched-Groups Design   A form of correlated-groups research design in which the researcher matches participants for common characteristics and then assigns them to one of the treatment conditions. The procedure assures that the groups will be similar regarding the relevant subject variables.

Mixed-Model Design   A research design that contains both a between-subjects variable and a within-subjects variable.

Repeated-Measures Design   A form of correlated-groups research design that allows the researcher to test the same participants under different treatment conditions or on different occasions.

Within-Subjects Variable   An independent variable that represents either a repeated-measures condition or a matched-groups design.

Yoked-Control Design   A form of control procedure for which the researcher randomly pairs participants, one member of the pair is assigned to the experimental group and the other to the control condition. The participant in the condition experiences the exact sequence of events as the experimental partner but does not experience the critical feature of the experiment.

14 SINGLE-PARTICIPANT EXPERIMENTS, LONGITUDINAL STUDIES, AND QUASI-EXPERIMENTAL DESIGNS

CHAPTER OUTLINE

- ✦ Introduction
- ✦ Single-Participant Experiments
- ✦ Longitudinal Designs
- ✦ Quasi-Experiments

If we knew what we were doing, it wouldn't be called research.

—Albert Einstein

INTRODUCTION

Many people have the mistaken belief that the results of a research project can be valid only if the researcher used legions of participants randomly selected from the target population and randomly assigned to treatment conditions in a highly controlled experiment. Although it is true that much research in the behavioral sciences uses many participants whom the researcher randomly assigns to various treatment groups, it is also true that behavioral scientists conduct many fine and valid experiments that use only a few participants. Similarly, many researchers conduct revealing studies for which random assignment is impossible or unethical. These alternatives to the typical true experiment offer the researchers valuable tools that allow them to address interesting, albeit complex, questions about human behavior. In this chapter we will review three important research paradigms: (1) single-participant experiments, (2) longitudinal designs, and (3) quasi-experiments.

These methods for conducting research are extremely useful tools that all behavioral researchers can use. Used correctly, these research techniques allow one to examine the relation among variables. Furthermore, these techniques adhere to the same rigorous standards of objectivity and validity as the other research designs we have reviewed in this book. Thus, each of these paradigms offers researchers analytic tools to help them understand various behavioral phenomena.

Single-participant experiments

The features that set these methods apart from other research designs are the methods used to collect and analyze the data. For instance, the single-participant experimental paradigm, as the name implies, is a collection of research techniques used to conduct controlled experiments that focus on the behavior of individuals. Whereas much behavioral research examines the average behavior of groups of participants, the single-participant research examines how the individual responds to the experimental conditions.

Longitudinal designs

The longitudinal design also allows us to examine from a different perspective because it allows us to track the behavior of a group of individuals across time. Longitudinal designs are a special case of the repeated-measures procedure as the researcher tracks changes in the participants' behavior. There is an important difference between longitudinal designs and repeated-measures research. In most cases, longitudinal designs use a time frame that covers months and even years. By contrast, most repeated-measures research examines behavior over a much shorter period. So, the difference between the repeated-measures and longitudinal design is the emphasis and time frame of the research.

In the repeated-measures design, we typically want to know how individuals perform under a series of experimental conditions that we control. We may test the same participants using dosages of a drug to determine its effect on a behavior. In another experiment, we may expose one group of participants to different sequences of events to find how the pattern of events affects behavior.

For a longitudinal study, the researcher is more interested in the development or emergence of behavior that occurs over time. Consider language development as an example. Developmental psychologists who study language examine the profound changes in children's use of language that emerges during early childhood. This research has allowed psychologists to chronicle how language emerges and becomes more complex as the child matures. Clinical psychologists also conduct longitudinal research to examine the long-term effects of various treatments. As an example, clinical psychologists studying alcohol and drug abuse therapies may want to follow the health of the patients over several years to understand the risk of relapses.

Quasi-experiments

The quasi-experiment paradigm is unique because it does not use random assignment in the same way that it is used in true experiments. Quasi-experimental methods have evolved as a way to examine behavior under conditions where meeting the requirements of a true experiment are impossible or impractical. The name quasi-experiment represents that the researcher may have partial control over the independent variable. For most quasi-experimental research, the researcher cannot randomly assign participants to the research conditions. Quasi-experimental designs can yield interesting insights into human behavior.

There is no such thing as the best method for studying any behavioral phenomenon. As you learn more about psychology, you will discover that researchers use many research techniques to study the same behavioral phenomenon. Their selection of technique represents their training and perspective within psychology as well as their belief concerning the best way to conduct a specific research project. With this brief introduction, we can turn our attention to these paradigms.

SINGLE-PARTICIPANT EXPERIMENTS

As the name implies, single-participant experiments examine how individuals respond to changes in the independent variable. There are many examples of famous psychologists who used single-participant experiments. Some psychologists consider Gustav T. Fechner, whom we met in chapter 1, to be the first experimental psychologist. Fechner discovered that he could study the workings of the mind by examining changes in behavior. As an important part of his work, Fechner developed a host of research methods that he described in his book *Elements of Psychophysics* (1966/1860). The research that Fechner conducted typically examined how an individual's perception of specific stimuli (lights, sounds, weights) changed in conjunction with changes in the stimulus. Not only did his work help to establish the science of psychology, psychologists continue to use his techniques when studying topics related to sensation and perception.

Sometime between 1875 and 1878, Hermann Ebbinghaus read Fechner's book and recognized that he could adapt Fechner's research techniques to study memory (Boring, 1957). Ebbinghaus's seminal book, *On Memory* (1913/1885), included many experiments for which he was the sole participant. The results of these studies remain the standard introduction to the analysis of memory and forgetting phenomenon. Similarly, Ivan Pavlov conducted many insightful experiments in classical conditioning using single-participant experiments. Those who read his original research will find that he used two or three dogs for experiments to examine specific conditioning phenomenon. Edward Thorndike and B. F. Skinner adopted the single-participant experimental procedure for their own work on operant conditioning. Indeed, Skinner, and the many behaviorists who followed his lead, developed a comprehensive collection of research techniques that they called the **experimental analysis of behavior.** The experimental analysis of behavior is a perspective of research that focuses on the pattern of behavior produced in individuals by systematic changes in the independent variable. As Skinner (1953) described it, the goal of experimental analysis of behavior is to "predict and control the behavior of an individual organism" (p. 35).

Although researchers originally used the single-participant experiment to examine basic research topics in psychology such as perception, memory, and classical and operant conditioning, researchers now use these techniques for a host of applied and basic research projects. Specifically, researchers use the single-participant experiments when they want to determine how systematic changes in the environment influence an individual's behavior. As Dermer and Hoch (1999) observed, the single-participant experiment is an invaluable tool for research in such diverse areas as audiological rehabilitation, clinical and counseling psychology, and education. A trip to the library will reveal that there are many journals dedicated to single-participant research. The journals, *Behavioral Assessment, Journal of Applied Behavior Analysis, Journal of the Experimental Analysis of Behavior,* and *The Behavior Analyst,* are only a few of the scholarly outlets for single-participant experiments.

Unfortunately, many researchers appear to ignore these important research techniques. Ellis (1999) speculated that single-participant designs are unfairly characterized as "too behavioral, overly simplistic or circumscribed, . . . and too difficult to do" (p. 566). Koehler and Levin (1998) echoed this sentiment in an article wherein they examined the utility of single-participant research designs.

Reprise of Internal and External Validity

You may be suspicious of single-participant designs because of concerns for the internal and external validity of a study based on one, two, or four participants. This is a legitimate concern and one that requires our analysis. We can have confidence, however, in the internal and external validity of single-participant experiments as long as we remember that validity represents how we collect and interpret the data, not the number of participants in the study. The sample size does not determine the internal or external validity of the experiment or the data. Perhaps an example will illustrate my point.

Look at Figure 14.1. The picture contains a series of black squares neatly arranged in rows and columns set on a white background, nothing more. Although the picture is a black and white image, you will perceive faint gray images at the intersection of the white rows and columns. Furthermore, if you stare at the intersection of two white lines, the gray images disappear, but you will see the gray images at the intersections in the periphery of your vision. The gray dots are an illusion in that you perceive something that does not exist.

FIGURE 14.1
The Hermann Grid. As you look at the illustration, you will see faint gray squares at the intersection of the white lines. The gray images are illusions that people with normal vision see.

Psychologists call this figure the Hermann Grid in honor of Ludimar Hermann, the German physiologist who wrote extensively about the fascinating illusion it creates.

What does this illusion have to do with single-participant experiments? The answer is simple—everything. Reread the previous paragraph. I used unambiguous language to describe what you would experience. I did not use qualified statements like "you are likely to see" or "chances are that you will see." Instead, my language was simple and declarative. The fact is that people with normal vision see this illusion. Experiment by showing the picture to the next 10 people you meet. Everyone will have the same experience—they will see the phantom gray dots. How many people do you have to test to conclude that the Hermann Grid produces the illusion of the phantom spots? You could expand your sample to 100 people, but the results will be consistent. Everyone will experience the illusion.

You do not need to show the grid to many people to be convinced that the effect is strong. From a statistical perspective, the Hermann Grid produces a powerful effect. Researchers who study the Hermann Grid and similar sensation-perception phenomenon typically use only two or three participants to conduct their research.

When we speak of external validity, we are concerned about two types of generalization. First, we want to ensure that the participants used in the research represent the broader population we wish to describe. Second, we want to ensure that the phenomenon we observe will occur with samples drawn from different populations. Sample size is not the critical factor in determining external validity. Rather, the critical factor is the types of generalizations we make of the data.

When there is little variability among people, as is the case for the perception of the Hermann Grid illusion, we do not require many participants to represent the population. By contrast, when the differences among individuals in the population are large, then the sample must also be large to represent the population. Remember too that the value of any research finding is the ability to replicate the finding with additional research. Our confidence in a finding increases with the ability of other researchers to replicate a particular finding, not the number of participants used in the research.

What is the status of internal validity for the single-participant experiment? Again, the issue of internal validity does not concern itself with the number of participants. Instead, when we speak of internal validity we mean to show that one has convincing evidence that changes in the independent variable caused changes in the dependent variable. In this regard, the single-participant experiment can support conclusions of cause and effect as well as any true experiment that we have studied in this book. We can use the Hermann Grid as an example.

What are the variables that influence the illusion? You can reproduce the grid using different brightness (shades of gray) for the squares and lines. Similarly, you can use different hues (colors) for the squares and lines. You can also vary the size of the squares and the width and height of the lines separating the squares. You can even change the shape of the squares by using different geometrical shapes (e.g., triangles, squares, pentagons, circles). If you were to vary these conditions systematically, you could determine how changes in these variables influence the strength of the illusion. Specifically, you can ask the same person to look at many different versions of the Hermann Grid to examine how the distance between the squares influences the perception of the illusory gray images.

When to Use Single-Participant Procedures

Those who routinely use single-participant procedures believe that single-participant designs are most useful when the researcher wishes to understand the changes in behavior of the individual that correspond to changes in the individual's environment (Morgan & Morgan, 2001). This definition surely covers many research situations. Some might argue that almost all psychological research should use single-participant research designs because the primary focus of psychology is the study of the behavior of the individual. Such a sweeping perspective ignores many important questions related to human behavior that may not reveal their answer using single-participant designs. Thus it might be helpful to examine some of the general circumstances for which a single-participant design is well suited and circumstances for which a single-participant design might not be appropriate.

The primary goal of the single-participant design is to determine how specific changes in the environment of the individual affect his or her behavior. Consequently, single-participant designs are most frequently used when a researcher wants to examine how the introduction and removal of a specific condition affects the behavior of an individual. For example, a clinical psychologist might want to determine if exposing a person to a therapy will reduce undesirable behaviors and increase desirable behaviors. In such an example, the researcher wants to show that the therapy causes the person's behavior to change, he or she hopes for the better. In one of the following examples, we will review how a team of researchers used a single-participant research design to study the effectiveness of a method of treating panic attacks.

The primary characteristic of the successful application of the single-participant design includes the following characteristics. First, the researcher has direct control over the independent variable. Thus the single-participant design is like a true experiment in that the researcher can control significant elements of the participant's environment and determine when to add and remove the independent variable. Second, the researcher can regularly measure or observe the participant's behavior. Monitoring the participant's behavior allows the researcher to determine how changes in the independent variable correspond to changes in the dependent behavior. A third characteristic is that the researcher will be able to observe the participant across a significant span of time. For many single-participant studies, the research will examine the participant's behavior across many days, even weeks and months.

There are, however, conditions where the single-subject design is not appropriate. In many cases, researchers are interested in defining a population or examining the differences among populations. For example, a researcher may be interested in the emotional development of children who attended preschool and children who did not. For this type of research, we want to know if there are systematic differences among the populations representing the two groups of children. In addition, the predictor variable (preschool versus no preschool) is a variable that the researcher does not control.

Types of Single-Participant Experiments

There are two broad categories of single-participant experiments: **baseline studies** and **discrete trial studies.** As a generality, researchers use baseline studies to examine changes in an ongoing or continuous behavior. For example, a researcher may want to examine how a specific treatment technique changes the social skills of an autistic child. The researcher would use the baseline method to track changes in the child's behavior before, during, and after the treatment. This research will allow the researcher to determine whether the treatment influences the child's social skills.

By contrast, a discrete trial study allows us to examine how a participant reacts to specific test conditions. Consider an experiment studying the Hermann Grid. We could construct many versions of the Hermann Grid by varying the distance between the squares. On each trial, we present one of the grids and determine whether the participant perceives the illusory gray squares. This research will allow us to determine the conditions that produce the illusion.

Baseline studies

Baseline studies examine changes in the frequency of the ongoing behaviors of an individual. Consequently, all baseline studies begin by developing operational definitions of the behaviors to be measured. We reviewed much of this step in chapter 7. We want to develop a reliable method for observing the behavior or behaviors that we want to modify. Once we decide upon the appropriate behavior to observe and the data recording strategy, we can begin by establishing a baseline.

The general format of a baseline design is first to establish a baseline of the individual's behavior and then introduce the change or intervention into the individual's environment. If the intervention is effective, there should be a commensurate and consistent change in the individual's behavior. You may recognize that the single-participant design has much in common with the repeated-measures design discussed in chapter 13. Specifically, we expose the same participant to different treatment conditions to examine how the independent variable influences the dependent variable. The baseline is, therefore, the control condition for the experiment as it represents the participant's behavior in the absence of the treatment condition.

Establishing Cause and Effect

The rules for determining cause and effect are straightforward—use a control condition, demonstrate that there is a relation between the independent and dependent variables, and rule out alternative explanations. There are a number of specific techniques that we can use to achieve these goals for the single-participant experiment.

Establish a baseline

The first step is to establish a baseline that we can use for a frame of reference. The goal of this step is to determine the typical pattern of the behavior that we want to modify. The baseline should be a representative sample of the individual's normal behavior. For example, if we wanted to examine the effectiveness of a social skills training technique for children diagnosed with autism, we would want to examine how often the child engages in specific types of social interactions with other children. Similarly, if we wanted to examine how a tutoring program helps students master math skills, we would need to determine the child's ability to solve specific classes of math problems.

In some cases, the baseline represents a small sample of the individual's behavior. A child with autism may spend little time playing with other children. Alternatively, a child having trouble with math may be able to solve only the most simple of math problems. Because the behavior is extremely consistent, the baseline may be short. For the autistic child, we may observe his or her behavior for three or four sessions to establish the baseline. Similarly, for the student having problems with math, the baseline may consist of the scores on several short math quizzes.

If the target behavior is variable, then the baseline will need to be longer to establish a suitable pattern of the behavior. Sometimes behaviors are cyclical; the behavior increases and decreases. For such cases, the baseline will need to be longer to establish the normal pattern for the behavior. Having the longer baseline will help the researcher determine the extent to which changes in the behavior reflect the independent variable or the cyclical nature of the behavior.

The baseline should contain at least three observations (Barlow and Hersen, 1984). If there is considerable variability of behavior, then the baseline phase needs to be longer to obtain sufficient information to determine the average frequency of the behavior. There is no hard and fast rule to establish the length of the baseline. Sidman (1960) advised his readers that, "there is . . . no rule to follow for the criterion will depend upon the phenomenon being investigated and upon the level of experimental control that can be maintained" (p. 258). Therefore, the researcher needs to exercise common sense to determine whether the baseline is a fair and stable representation of the individual's behavior.

Examine the effects of the intervention

There are a number of general techniques used in the baseline experiment to study the effects of the intervention. The prototypes for these techniques are the **ABA** and the **ABAB designs.** Researchers call the ABA and ABAB designs **reversal designs** because the researcher uses several phases in the research during which they add and remove a treatment condition. As a generality, the "A" phase represents the baseline condition and the "B"

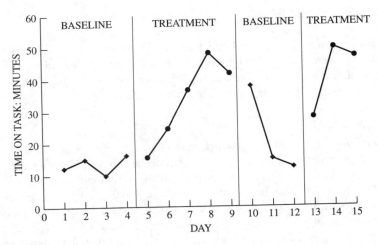

FIGURE 14.2
Hypothetical example of data produced by an ABAB research design.

represents the intervention condition. The goal of the reversal design is to demonstrate that as the research conditions change (A to B and B to A), there is a corresponding shift in the individual's behavior.

Figure 14.2 illustrates the results of a hypothetical ABAB design. The behavior being monitored is the amount of time a second-grade student is "on task" during a classroom assignment. During the baseline condition, the child spends relatively little time on task. At the start of the treatment condition, there is a marked increase in the on-task behavior. When the researcher removes the intervention, the on-task behavior also decreases. Finally, when the researcher reestablishes the treatment condition, the on-task behavior increases. Data such as these would lead the researcher to conclude that the treatment effectively modifies the student's behavior.

Direct replication

A single-participant experiment does not mean that there is only one participant in the study, merely that the researcher does not aggregate the behavior of many participants into a single index such as the arithmetic mean. Instead, the hallmark of the single-participant research design is that the researcher reports the behavior of each individual in the study. **Direct replication** means the researcher will use the same treatment procedures to examine the pattern of behavior for each participant. If the treatment is effective, then there should be similar patterns of behavior change for each participant. Therefore, the single-participant experiment is like other true experiments in that the researcher examines the data of several individuals under highly controlled conditions. The difference, however, is that in most experiments, the researcher examines and reports the average performance of the participants. By contrast, the researcher using a single-participant design will report the individual behavior of each participant.

One of the benefits of the single-participant design is that it uses both inter- and intraparticipant replication to demonstrate the relation between the independent and dependent variables. The intraparticipant replication occurs when one uses ABAB or other reversal designs. By adding and removing the independent variable, we can establish the link between changes in the independent variable and changes in the dependent variable. As you saw in Figure 14.2, changes in the treatment condition corresponded with changes in the behavior of the student, thus replicating the effect intraparticipant. If we use the same procedure on several participants, we will generate interparticipant replication. The inter-participant replication is, therefore, another way of describing direct replication.

Potential problems with reversal designs

In chapter 13 you learned about the threats to internal validity created when using a repeated-measures design. Specifically, we must be concerned with the threats created by a carryover effect. For example, it is possible to remove the intervention and not observe a corresponding change in the underlying behavior. For example, once a child learns to solve math problems, removal of the intervention does not cause the child to forget all that he or she learned. The child will probably continue to do well because of the good grades and other forms of positive reinforcement received for doing well on math tests. In these cases, we can use a reversal design, but the carryover effect will produce an unavoidable confounding variable.

We must also consider the ethics of removing an intervention once we show that it is effective. Why would we want to remove something that we now believe improves the individual's quality of life? In most clinical research, once the researcher finds that the treatment is effective, the researcher will begin to administer the treatment to all the participants receiving the placebo or in the baseline phase of the study. The following is a brief review of several research techniques that overcome the problems created in a reversal design.

Multiple Baseline Design

A suitable alternative to the reversal design is the multiple baseline design. The advantage of this procedure is that it allows us to demonstrate the effectiveness of an intervention when the reversal design is not appropriate. In addition, the procedure allows us to examine the effectiveness of an intervention across behaviors, individuals, or settings.

The primary characteristic of the multiple baseline design is that we monitor the ongoing behavior of the participants and then systematically introduce the independent variable at different times. One of the more popular of these procedures is the **multiple baseline across participants.** To use this procedure, we begin by monitoring the behavior of all the individuals in the study. Once we establish the baseline, we introduce the treatment for one of the participants while the others remain in the baseline condition. After some time has elapsed, we introduce the treatment to the second participant while keeping the remaining participants in the baseline condition. The goal of this procedure is to introduce the independent variable to each participant on a staggered basis to demonstrate that the participant's behavior changes only after the researcher introduces the independent variable.

Figure 14.3 illustrates the application of the multiple baseline across participants procedure. There are three participants. For each participant, we begin to track the behavior

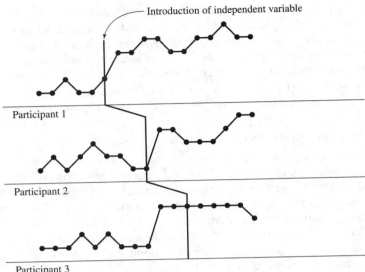

FIGURE 14.3
A multiple baseline across participants procedure.

that we want to modify. Participant 1 is the first to experience the independent variable while the other participants remain in the baseline condition. Later, we introduce the independent variable into the environment of Participant 2. Finally, we add the independent variable to the environment of Participant 3. Using this procedure, we can be sure that the introduction of the independent variable, and not some confounding variable, caused the change in the participant's behavior.

We can also apply the multiple baseline procedure across situations and across behaviors. For the **multiple baseline across behaviors** procedure, the researcher may identify several behaviors that he or she wants to modify with the same intervention. To use this technique, the researcher needs to ensure that the behaviors are independent of each other. As an example, a researcher examining the effectiveness of an intervention with children diagnosed with autism may examine how the intervention works with three behaviors: (1) talking to other children, (2) participating in group activities, and (3) following instructions of the teacher. As with the multiple baseline across individuals procedure, the researcher would collect baseline information for all three behaviors and then stagger the start of the intervention for each behavior. In theory, the intervention should influence the target behavior, but not the other behaviors. The specific behavior will not change until the intervention begins.

The **multiple baseline across situations** works in the same manner except that we identify different situations where the intervention can be applied. Assume that a teacher wants to study the effectiveness of a tutoring technique for a child's academic performance. The teacher can treat the academic subjects (e.g., math, social studies, English, and science) as separate situations. By staggering the start of the tutoring intervention for each subject, the teacher can demonstrate that the tutoring improves the child's academic work when the tutoring begins for the topic.

RESEARCH IN ACTION: TREATMENT FOR PANIC DISORDER

Because we will review three research paradigms, I thought it better to have three "Research in Action" sections, one to illustrate the application of each paradigm. In this section, we will examine a recent application of the single-participant design.

Figure 14.4 presents an example of single-participant experiment conducted by Laberge, Gauthier, Côté, Plamondon, and Cormier (1993). The researchers wanted to demonstrate the

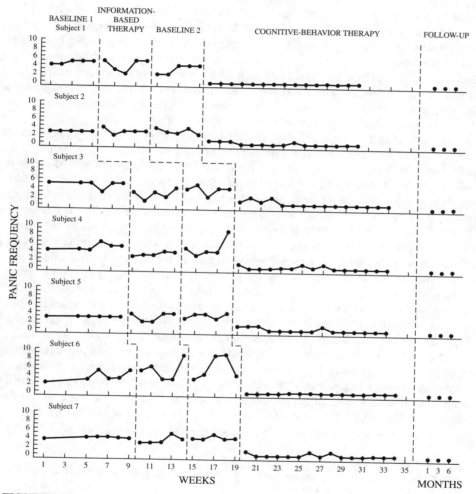

FIGURE 14.4

A multiple baseline across participants design. The dependent variable is the frequency of panic attacks experienced by seven participants over a 35-week period. The vertical dashed lines represent the start of each phase of the experiment for the individual participants. During the first three phases of the experiment, the participants' panic attacks were assessed during three baseline phases. The fourth phase of the experiment included the cognitive-behavior modification treatment. The last three points represent a long-term follow up of the patients. Data from Laberge, Gauthier, Côté, Palmondon, and Cormier (1993).

effectiveness of cognitive-behavioral therapy for the treatment of panic disorder. The researchers examined the frequency of panic attacks of seven individuals using a multiple baseline procedure.

This experiment also contained a slight methodological twist that helps demonstrate the effectiveness of cognitive-behavior therapy. During the first phase, the researchers monitored the frequency of panic attacks to establish a baseline. Then the researchers started a session called "information-based therapy." During this intervention the participants received detailed information about panic attacks and learned how their thinking leads to panic attacks. Laberge et al. (1993) treated this phase of the experiment as a placebo treatment as they believed that it did not include the critical components of a legitimate treatment. Following the information-based therapy phase was another baseline period during which the researchers continued to monitor the frequency of the panic attacks. The first and second baseline conditions allowed the researchers to estimate the frequency of panic attacks while the person was under observation. The second control condition was the information-based therapy session. This condition allowed the researchers to determine if the placebo treatment had any effect on the frequency of panic attacks.

The critical part of the experiment began when Laberge et al. (1993) began to use the cognitive-behavior therapy to treat the participants for the panic attacks. The researchers staggered the start of each phase of the experiment after the initial baseline period across the individuals. By staggering the onset of the different intervention periods, the researchers demonstrated that the change in the panic attack coincided with the start of the legitimate treatment intervention, not other conditions that could have changed in the environments of the individuals. In this example, the researchers used direct replication within the multiple baseline across participants procedure to demonstrate that the intervention brings about a change in the individual's behavior. The researchers also demonstrated the effectiveness of the cognitive-behavior by including the placebo treatment. There were no discernable changes in the frequency of the panic attacks during the first three phases (Baseline 1, information-based therapy, and Baseline 2) of the experiment. The panic attacks stopped, however, when the participants received the cognitive-behavior therapy. Looking at the graph it appears that the effectiveness of the intervention lasted well into the follow-up period.

One thing you may note about single-participant designs is the lack of formal statistical analysis. Many of the early pioneers of single-participant research designs believed that inferential statistical analysis was not appropriate for the analysis of individual participants and believed that the effect of the independent should be clear and unambiguous to visual inspection of the data (Morgan & Morgan, 2001). Therefore, most single-participant designs use simple graphs and basic descriptive statistics to present the data.

ACHIEVEMENT CHECK

(1) Explain why a reversal design, such as the ABAB design, produces results that support conclusions regarding cause and effect.

(2) Imagine that two researchers examined the effectiveness of a new treatment intervention for depression. One researcher used a multiple baseline across participants research design to examine the effect of the treatment on 12 participants. The other researcher randomly assigned 25 participants to a placebo treatment group and another 25 participants to the treatment condition, and then compared the average level of depression between the two groups. Assume that the researchers work at the same institution and sampled from the same subject pool.

(a) Explain why the two studies are comparable with regard to internal validity.

(b) Explain why the two studies are comparable with regard to external validity.

(3) Using the previous example, what are the ethical considerations that would make one research design preferable to the other research design?

(4) Imagine that your professor wants to demonstrate the effectiveness of homework for helping students learn research methods. How could he or she use the multiple baseline across participants or across situations to conduct the research?

LONGITUDINAL DESIGNS

The primary goal of **longitudinal designs** is to examine how behavior changes over time. Developmental psychologists have long used these techniques to examine the systematic changes in children's behavior. Longitudinal designs are also popular in other branches of psychology such as clinical psychology where the researchers wish to study the development of different behavioral and emotional disorders or the risk of relapse after treatment.

The fundamental feature of a longitudinal design is relatively straightforward. The researcher creates a sample of participants and then arranges to monitor their behavior over a predetermined period. For example, a developmental psychologist may be interested in the emotional development of children whose parents use day care or preschool programs and children who spend most of their preschool years at home with an adult. As another example, a clinical psychologist may study the long-term effectiveness of substance abuse treatment programs. In each case, the researcher would identify the appropriate sample of participants to study and then measure the appropriate dependent variables several times afterward. The developmental psychologist would examine the children's emotional development as they begin and progress through kindergarten and the first elementary grades. The clinical psychologist would routinely evaluate the clients for evidence of a relapse or other problems.

During the past two decades, psychologists have become extremely interested in longitudinal research methods due to the development and application of new statistical methods to analyze the data. As you will soon learn, these new statistical tests make the longitudinal research design an extremely useful research tool. Before I describe these new statistics, we should first examine the foundations of the longitudinal design.

The conventional longitudinal design requires that the researcher track one or more groups of individuals over a specified time. The groups can represent an important subject variable (e.g., sex, intelligence, parent's marital status, or other categorical condition) or a treatment condition randomly assigned by the researcher. The researcher then arranges to periodically evaluate the members of the sample.

Although the conventional longitudinal design is popular and produces useful information, it does suffer from some shortcomings. First, the data may take a long time to obtain. Often this is an unavoidable problem. Tracking the progress of a group of patients who have just completed a program of treatment may require a significant follow-up period to evaluate the long-term effectiveness of the treatment.

Another problem related to the length of the study is the problem of participant dropout. With time, members of the sample leave the sample. These people may become bored with the study, move to another city or state, or otherwise become incapable of participating in the study. This problem of attrition (another term for participant dropout) can play havoc with many statistical tests such as the ANOVA. Fortunately, alternative statistical tools can overcome the problems created by participant dropout.

There are other problems related to the longitudinal research that are more difficult to resolve. One of these problems is the cohort effect. The **cohort effect** refers to differences among groups of people born in different eras. A **cohort** is a group of people born at the same time and who had a common experience. A cohort effect occurs when members of one group are consistently different from people born at a different time and who had different experiences. Some cohort effects are the source of the so-called generation gap. For example, my parents, who grew up during the big band era, despise the rock-and-roll music that I listened to as an adolescent. Similarly, I find the music my children listen to intolerable.

There are more serious examples of a cohort effect. For example, some evidence, dubbed the "Flynn effect," indicates considerable increases in intelligence scores during the last century. According to Flynn (1998), intelligence test scores have increased 3 points, on average, each decade over the past 70 years. Children born after 2000 will have an average IQ 21 points greater than great-great grandparents born in the 1930s. As another example, Lewinshon, Rohde, Seeley, and Fischer (1993) reported a large cohort effect for the prevalence of depression and other psychological disorders. Lewinshon et al. found higher rates of depression among people born in more recent decades than in the past.

The presence of a cohort effect forces us to examine the external validity of conclusions based on one cohort and generalized to others. For example, would conclusions about racial stereotypes based on research conducted during the 1920s generalize to contemporary populations?

Cross-Sectional Sequential Designs

Many developmental psychologists study the transitions that children make as they pass through various critical phases of their lives. As an example, a psychologist may want to examine changes in the personality of children as they pass through adolescence (e.g., 8 through 15). Using a conventional longitudinal design would require eight years to collect the data for the study, a considerable test of one's patience and persistence. The **cross-sectional sequential design** is an alternative method that allows the researcher to examine developmental transitions, but in less time.

Figure 14.5 presents the logic of the cross-sectional sequential design. The researcher can select cross sections of the age span that he or she wants to study. Starting in Year 1, for example, the researcher could select participants age 8 through 15. Over the course of the next three years, the researcher can continue to monitor the changes in the participants. By the end of the third year, the researcher will have data that indicate the differences in a wide range of ages and how those changes relate to the passage of time.

The cross-sectional sequential design provides the researcher with much information. First, the researcher can use the data to compare the differences among blocks of ages. For example, the researcher who uses the design illustrated in Figure 14.5 will have three blocks of children aged 10 through 12 and three blocks of children aged 13 through 15. Analyzing these data will indicate if there are systematic differences between these age

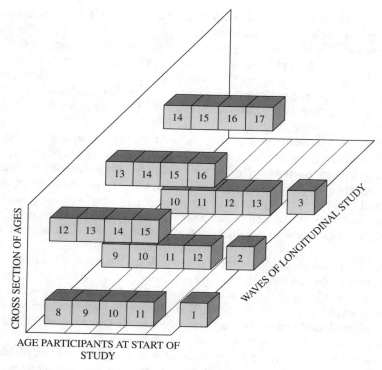

FIGURE 14.5
A cross-sectional sequential design.

groups. Second, the cross-sectional sequential design allows the researcher to examine the changes observed in the children as they grow older.

Survival Analysis

For many years, researchers used the repeated measures ANOVA to analyze the data of longitudinal data. Although this tactic yields useful information, it does have its limitations. First, the correlated groups ANOVA has specific mathematical requirements, or assumptions, of the data that are often difficult to achieve. Failure to meet these requirements can produce invalid F-ratios. Second, the longitudinal design is subject to high levels of participant attrition. Losing large numbers of participants from a longitudinal research project can wreak havoc on the data analysis. Fortunately, statisticians have developed a class of statistical tests that provide researchers an alternative method for analyzing the data generated by longitudinal designs (Greenhouse, Stangl, & Bromberg, 1989; Gruber, 1999; Lewinsohn et al., 1993; Luke & Homan, 1998; Singer & Willett, 1991; Willett & Singer, 1993). These statistical tests overcome the problems created by participants dropping out of the research and the failure of the data to meet the mathematical requirements of the ANOVA.

Survival analysis is a common and popular statistical tool in medical research where the goal is to determine the amount of time it takes for an event to occur. For example, a physician may want to know which of two surgical procedures is the best for the long-term health of patients, such as preventing a second heart attack. To collect the data, the researcher will track the patients after the surgery to determine which surgical technique is more effective at preventing a second heart attack or other significant problems. One characteristic that makes survival analysis unique is that it treats time as a dependent variable rather than an independent variable.

In the conventional longitudinal analysis, we treat time as an independent variable. We then determine whether we can use the passage of time to explain or predict some outcome. A developmental psychologist studying language development might use a child's age to predict when the child will begin to use two words to form simple sentences or when the child will begin to correctly use irregular verbs (e.g., "went" versus "goed"). By contrast, in survival analysis, we treat the time between several events as the dependent variable. Perhaps an example will help illustrate how we can use survival analysis and the longitudinal design.

Stice, Killen, Hayward, and Taylor (1998) examined the onset of the binge-and-purge eating disorder in adolescent girls. The researchers began by creating a sample of 543 young women aged 13 to 17 and then used a comprehensive set of surveys and structured interviews to assess the participants' health and whether they engaged in binge eating and purging. Stice et al. then reassessed the young women each year for the next four years. As the researchers noted, the average annual attrition rate was 15%.

Using the survival analysis procedures, Stice et al. found that the risk of the onset for an eating disorder begins after 14, peaks at approximately 16, and then decreases. Other researchers have used the same techniques to examine the difference between men and women for onset of depressive disorders and also for the risk of relapse among cocaine abusers following treatment (Willett & Singer, 1993). In all these examples, the critical questions are: "How much time typically elapses between two critical events (e.g., treatment and relapse)?" and "If an event has not occurred after a specific interval, what is the probability that it will occur?"

The mathematics that support these statistical tests is beyond the scope of an introductory textbook and requires intensive computational procedures best done by a computer. Fortunately, most professional statistical packages used by psychologists (e.g., *BMDP®*, *SAS®*, *SPSS®*, etc.) include survival analysis routines. The primary message that I want you to appreciate is that these statistical tests are well suited for the types of data collected by psychologists. They correct for dwindling sample size without compromising the validity of the interpretations of the results.

RESEARCH IN ACTION: ONSET OF BULIMIA

For this example of research in action, we can return to the study of the risk of bulimia among young women conducted by Stice et al. (1998). The researchers began with a sample of 543 students from three high schools in California. The average age of the women was 14.9 years and ranged from 13 to 17. At the start of the study, none of the participants showed signs of bulimia.

The researchers then reassessed the participants once a year for the subsequent three years. The assessments consisted of a structured interview conducted by trained researchers who looked for symptoms of eating disorders, especially bulimia. As with most research of this type, some of the participants did not complete the study. Approximately 10% of the original sample moved to another school, the others were absent during the assessment period or chose not to complete the remaining interviews.

Stice et al. (1998) then examined the risk of the women developing bulimia between the ages of 13 (the youngest age of the participants) through 19 (the oldest age by the end of the three years of the study). For most statistical tests, the researchers would have to throw out all the data of the participants who did not complete the study because many statistical tests such as the correlation coefficient, regression analysis, and the ANOVA require a complete record of observations for each participant. Survival analysis does not make this requirement, however, as the statistic uses the available data for each wave of measurement to determine the proportion of participants who show evidence of the syndrome. Even though some women dropped out of the study, we can use their data to make inferences about the presence of bulimia.

Consider, for example, a participant who is 16 at the start of the study and who is available for the first and second measurement sessions, but drops out before the third session. Although she dropped out of the study, she still provided the researchers with five years of data. Recall that at the start of the study, none of the participants showed evidence of bulimia. Therefore, we can assume that the young woman was symptom free when she was 13, 14, 15, and 16.

Using this information, Stice et al. (1998) were able to determine the age when the greatest proportion of women began the binge-and-purge eating pattern associated with bulimia. Because the survival analysis uses proportions (proportion = number of people with condition/total in current sample), the statistic is not affected by loss of participants from the sample. Figure 14.6 presents an example of the data reported by Stice et al.

As Stice et al. (1998) noted, their project was the first to examine the onset of bulimia in a population of young women. Having these data allow researchers to understand the forces associated with the onset of bulimia. Perhaps more importantly, the data can help counselors

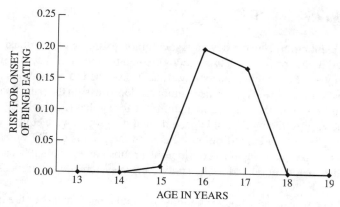

FIGURE 14.6
The risk of onset of binge eating.

and others working with adolescents to find the optimal time to introduce prevention programs and look for risk factors that predict the onset of bulimia and other eating disorders.

QUASI-EXPERIMENTS

In some circumstances, a true experiment is either impractical or unethical. We may not be able to randomly assign participants to different treatment conditions although we can randomly select one group of participants to receive a treatment while the other group acts as a control group. For example, a teacher may not be able to randomly assign students to different classes. However, he or she can randomly select one group to experience a new teaching method while the other class experiences a conventional course. In other cases, it is unethical to subject people to some treatment condition. But fateful events occur naturally that allow us to determine how people react to specific conditions. In this section of the chapter, I will introduce you to two of the more common quasi-experimental techniques, the nonequivalent control-group design and the interrupted time series.

The term quasi-experiment literally means that the research resembles an experiment. In a quasi-experiment there is an independent variable and a dependent variable, and the researcher wants to determine whether introduction of the independent variable produces a change in the dependent variable. In addition, there is a control group of individuals who do not experience the independent variable. Consequently, the researcher can compare the differences in outcome between the treatment and control groups. The missing component from this research is the random assignment of participants to the treatment conditions.

The primary disadvantage of the quasi-experiment is that the lack of random assignment means that we can never rule out alternative explanations to the effect we observe. The primary advantage of the quasi-experiment is that we can collect useful information that will allow us to examine the effects of the independent variable on the dependent variable. The quasi-experiment is another useful tool that the researcher can select when the circumstances of the research prohibit the conventional true experiment.

Nonequivalent Control-Group Design

The nonequivalent control-group design is a common example of the quasi-experimental design. The researcher begins with two groups created by situations beyond his or her control. For example, the researcher may study students assigned to classrooms or who attend different schools. Because the researcher cannot randomly assign the participants to the two groups, we must consider them nonequivalent. If the researcher randomly assigned the participants to the groups, then we would conclude that the groups were equivalent before the start of the experiment, and any difference between the groups would represent sampling error. In a quasi-experiment we must consider the groups nonequivalent because we cannot be sure whether factors unrelated to the study creates systematic differences between the participants.

Although the researcher cannot randomly assign the participants to the treatment conditions, he or she can randomly determine which group will receive the treatment. The main feature of the design includes two observations for both groups. The researcher will assess both groups at the same time, introduce the intervention for the experimental group, and then observe the relevant dependent variable a second time.

Although the nonequivalent control-group design is a popular design that controls for some threats to internal validity (Campbell & Stanley, 1966), there are other threats to internal validity that it cannot directly withstand (West, Biesanz, & Pitts, 2000). The design is subject to threats due to history, regression to the mean, and instrumentation. We will review these threats in the following paragraphs.

History

It is possible that one of the groups will experience an event or change in the environment, unrelated to the purpose of the study, that confounds the analysis of the data. A researcher may wish to study the effects of a binge drinking campaign for college students. After finding two colleges equivalent in size and student body, the researcher randomly selects one of the colleges as the experimental group and the other as a control group. During the course of the study, the researcher cannot control for outside factors that may change one of the campuses. A student at one of the colleges may die due to binge drinking. This tragic and uncontrolled event may affect the students' attitudes toward binge drinking. The event also confounds the results as we do not know whether changes in student attitude represent the treatment program or the student's death.

Regression to the mean

Regression to the mean may be a confounding variable if the researcher selected the experimental and control groups using a test or measure of low reliability. Consider a researcher studying drinking behavior at colleges. It is possible that the time during the semester the researcher collects the data will confound the results. For example, collecting the data just before or just after midterms may cause the researcher to underestimate or overestimate the amount of drinking at the college. Any changes observed may merely reflect regression to the mean.

Instrumentation

Another threat to the internal validity of a nonequivalent control-group design is instrumentation. During the course of the study it is possible that there will be a change in the record keeping of one group but not the other. Consider the binge drinking study. The researcher may require that the student life staff keep track of the number of episodes related to problems related to drinking. It is possible that the staff of the colleges become more selective in what they are willing to ignore and what they document. Thus, the changes in drinking patterns may reflect changes in the way the staff at one of the schools collects and reports the data.

Interrupted Time Series

The interrupted time series is much like an AB design used in single-participant research. The researcher makes repeated measures of the frequency or rate of behavior in a sample of participants before and after a critical event. These data can come from many sources. As with most quasi-experiments, the researcher may not be able to control when the critical event occurs, but can use its presence to examine interesting aspects of human behavior.

Hawton et al. (1999) reported the results of an interrupted time series that examined the effects of a television program on suicide attempts. The researchers learned that the medical television drama, *Casualty* (a popular television show in England), would include an episode in which one of the characters dies of an overdose of the drug paracetamol. Hawton and his associates contacted the emergency rooms of 49 hospitals in England and asked them to monitor the number of cases of self-administered overdoses of paracetamol and other substances. The hospitals tracked the frequency of drug overdoses for three weeks before the episode aired and for three weeks after the broadcast.

Figure 14.7 presents the percent change in the number of reported overdoses for paracetamol after the broadcast of the episode of *Casualty*. Hawton et al. (1999) found that there was a statistically significant increase in all forms of self-administered overdoses. The cases of paracetamol overdoses were greatly elevated and continued at higher rates for two weeks. Data such as these might lead one to conclude that the television show led some of the viewers to mimic the characters in the drama.

The simple time series study suffers from the same problems of internal validity we faced with the simple AB research design. In the current example, we cannot be sure if the television show produced the changes in drug overdoses or if other events, unrelated to the show, contributed to the effect. Therefore, researchers hope to find instances where nature provides the equivalent to the controlled experiment. Can you think of some alternative design options?

One option would be to find two groups for which only one experiences the critical event. Hawton et al. (1999) were able to include this control in their research. They designed their questionnaire to include questions asking patients whether they had seen the particular episode of *Casualty*. Using this information, the researchers were able to compare the rates of self-poisonings for nonviewers and viewers of *Casualty*. The results of this analysis help

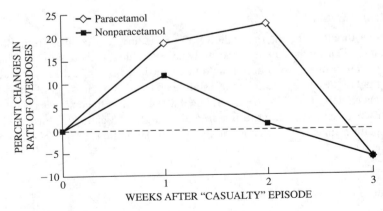

FIGURE 14.7

Percent changes in the rate of overdoses presented in hospitals after an episode of the British television show, *Casualty*. Figure based on data presented by Hawton et al. (1999).

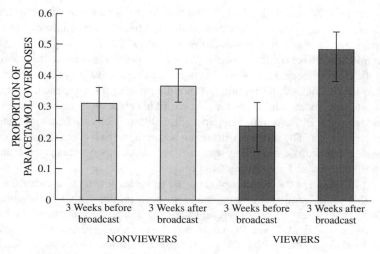

FIGURE 14.8

The proportion of self-administered overdoses of paracetamol that occurred three weeks before and three weeks after the broadcast of an episode of the television drama, *Casualty*. For each bar in the graph, the vertical lines represent the 95% confidence interval of the proportion. The nonviewer and viewer categories represent whether the patients watch *Casualty,* specifically the episode including the paracetamol overdose.

to reinforce the hypothesis that the television episode contributed to the increase in drug overdoses. Figure 14.8 presents the results of this analysis. Among nonviewers of the program, there was no statistically significant difference in the proportion of paracetamol overdoses. By contrast, for the viewers of the program, there was a marked increase in paracetamol overdoses after the *Casualty* episode. Evidence such as this reinforces the conclusion that a television show may influence rates of drug overdoses.

As with the single-participant design, the creative researcher can use many variants of the interrupted time series to examine the relation between two variables. Cook and Campbell (1979) provide a comprehensive review of the more subtle and specialized methods along with a review of the statistical procedures used to study interrupted time-series data.

RESEARCH IN ACTION: TRAFFIC LAWS AND SAFETY

For this example of applied research, we will examine a study conducted by West, Hepworth, McCally, and Reich (1989). The researchers wanted to study the effects of a drunk-driving law that Arizona had adopted during the 1980s.

In 1982, Arizona instituted a drunk-driving law that required those convicted of driving while intoxicated to receive jail sentences. The law required the first-time offenders to be jailed for at least 24 hours, fined $250, and have a temporary suspension of the driver's license. Those who supported the law argued that the benefit of the law would be, among other things, a decrease in traffic fatalities (West et al., 1989).

To examine the effects of the new law, West et al. (1989) reviewed the monthly police reports for the city of Phoenix, Arizona. Recognizing that there are cyclical patterns to traffic fatalities, they reviewed the records 30 months prior to the enactment of the law and 30 months after the enactment of the law. West and his colleagues also collected the same information from the El Paso police department. El Paso is city in Texas that has much in common with Phoenix. The primary difference between the two cities is that Texas had not recently passed any drunk-driving legislation. Thus, this study combines the features of an interrupted time series and a quasi-control group.

Figure 14.9 presents the number of reported fatalities for the two cities. Two characteristics of this graph require explanation. First, both graphs contain a segment labeled "Media Coverage." These months represent the time before the enactment of the law that the Phoenix newspaper, *Arizona Republic,* reported extensively about the pending law. Second, the horizontal lines within the graph represent the average reported fatalities during the period.

Looking at the graphs, it is apparent that the new law did affect Arizona drivers. Prior to enforcement of the law, there were, on average, 14 traffic fatalities each month. During the months prior to the enforcement of the new law, when the media coverage was at its

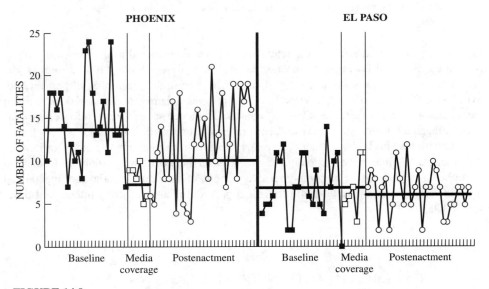

FIGURE 14.9
Number of traffic fatalities reported in Phoenix, Arizona, and El Paso, Texas. The baseline and media coverage phases represent the time before the enactment of the new and stricter drunk-driving law in Arizona. The media coverage phase represents the time during which there was intense media coverage in a Phoenix newspaper. The horizontal lines represent the average monthly fatalities for the specific period.

highest, the fatality rate decreased to 7 deaths per month. Over time, the rate of fatalities did increase to 10. By contrast, the number of traffic fatalities for El Paso remained relatively constant during the changes in Phoenix.

ACHIEVEMENT CHECK

(5) In what ways are repeated-measures designs and longitudinal designs similar to and different from each other?

(6) Explain how time can be a dependent variable.

(7) Describe the similarities between an interrupted time series study and a multiple baseline study.

CHAPTER SUMMARY

The research designs considered in this chapter are alternatives to the conventional experiment. Although single-participant, longitudinal, and quasi-experiments are empirical forms of analysis, they differ from the research designs considered in the earlier chapters.

The distinguishing feature of the single-participant experiment is the attention paid to the individual participant. Rather than average the responses of all the participants for subsequent statistical analysis, researchers who use single-participant research designs focus their analysis on the consistency of behavior observed across individuals.

We revisited the issue of internal and external validity for the single-participant research design. Single-participant research designs can afford substantial internal validity and external validity that compares favorably to other research projects.

The typical research designs for the single-participant baseline experiment are the ABA and ABAB reversal designs and the multiple baseline experiment. In the reversal design, the researcher observes the participant's behavior during a baseline period and then examines how additions to and removal of the intervention influence behavior. The multiple baseline experiment allows the researcher to stagger the onset of the intervention across participants, behaviors, or situations.

Longitudinal research designs allow researchers to track changes in behavior over a long period. An alternative to the longitudinal design that avoids the cohort effect is the cross-sectional sequence procedure. This design allows the researcher to examine the differences among participants of different ages, potential cohort effects, and the effects of growing older.

One of the more recent developments in the analysis of longitudinal research is survival analysis. Survival analysis is a collection of statistical techniques that allows the researcher to examine changes in the participant's behavior over time. The statistical techniques allow researchers to overcome problems with participant dropout and other events that may make statistical tests such as the ANOVA inappropriate.

The quasi-experiment represents a method of conducting research used when the researcher cannot randomly assign participants to the treatment conditions. Two of the more popular quasi-experiments are the nonequivalent control group and the interrupted time series analysis.

CHAPTER GLOSSARY FOR REVIEW

Baseline Study   A form of single-participant research design in which the researcher monitors the changes in an ongoing behavior of the participant during changes in the participant's environment.

Cohort   A group of people born during the same period who experience events different than people born during different periods.

Cohort Effect   A systematic difference between different cohorts due to unique experiences of the cohorts.

Cross-Sectional Sequential Design   A type of longitudinal design for which the researcher selects participants that represent a cross section of ages. The researcher then monitors the relevant variables across a number of subsequent times.

Direct Replication   A tactic used in single-participant experiments to demonstrate that the intervention brought about changes in the behavior. Specifically, the researcher exposes several individuals to the same treatment conditions to determine whether the intervention has the same general effect on all the participants.

Discrete Trial Study   A form of single-participant research design in which the researcher assesses the participant's reaction to a specific event or stimulus.

Experimental Analysis of Behavior   A specific form of single-participant research that emphasizes the analysis of changes in an individual's behavior that result from controlled changes in the environment.

Longitudinal Design   A procedure that allows the researcher to monitor the behavior of participants across a long period.

Multiple Baseline Procedure   A research tactic used in single-participant baseline studies wherein reversal procedures (e.g., the ABAB) design is not appropriate. The researcher staggers the start of the intervention across participants, behaviors, or situations to determine whether the change in behavior occurs with the change in the environment.

Reversal Design: ABA and ABAB Designs   A form of baseline study for which the researcher examines the participant's behavior during which the intervention is added to and removed from the environment.

15 RESEARCH WITH CATEGORICAL DATA

CHAPTER OUTLINE

- ✦ Introduction
- ✦ Goodness-of-Fit Test
- ✦ χ^2 Test of Independence
- ✦ χ^2 Test of Homogeneity
- ✦ Further Analysis of the χ^2
- ✦ McNemar Test

The only relevant test of the validity of a hypothesis is comparison of prediction with experience.

—Milton Friedman

INTRODUCTION

Throughout this book we have examined research projects that used interval or ratio scales to measure the dependent variable. Although much behavioral research relies upon interval and ratio scales, there are many applications of the nominal scale in contemporary research. As you will see, there are many times when we want to know how many people fit into specific categories. Because these research projects examine the frequency of different events, we will need a different set of tools to examine the data. Therefore, the focus of this chapter will be collecting and using categorical data. Before we jump too far ahead, though, we should review some background information.

Nominal and ordinal scales consist of a set of **mutually exclusive** classes. Mutually exclusive means that a person or a measurement fits only one classification. Sex is a mutually exclusive classification system because you are either a male or a female. Political party is also mutually exclusive system—most states require you to register as a Democrat, Republican, or some other political party. By contrast, diagnosis for a psychological disorder may not be mutually exclusive to the extent that a person may have several diagnosed conditions. Because a person can receive a diagnosis of "depression" and "substance dependent," we cannot treat the diagnoses as mutually exclusive.

The independent variable for categorical data research can represent either a nominal scale or an ordinal scale. One's sex and political party are examples of nominal scales in that there is no implied order in the scale. A nominal scale represents any construct that consists of readily identified groups. An ordinal scale suggests that there is a continuum underlying the scale. Most colleges use the terms freshman, sophomore, junior, and senior to identify the students' seniority. These groups are mutually exclusive in that a student can be in only one level. The groups also represent an ordinal scale in that we presume that the classification scheme represents the number of courses or credit hours the student completed.

The dependent variable for categorical research is the number of people who or observations that fit within a category. We count the number of persons and things that occur in specific conditions. For some research projects, we may use a single variable with many classification levels. As an example, a researcher may want to count the number of reported marriages that occur each month to determine if there is a relation between time of year and weddings. The independent variable, month, is clearly a mutually exclusive class as a couple's wedding can occur in only 1 of the 12 months. The dependent variable is the number of weddings reported within each month.

In other research projects, the researcher may want to examine the relation among several variables. An example of a two-variable study would be examining the relation between one's political party (Democrat versus Republican) and support for welfare reform

TABLE 15.1
Example of categorical research examining two variables

		Party affiliation	
		Democrat	Republican
Attitude toward legislation	Favor	103	98
	Oppose	97	102

legislation (favor legislation versus oppose legislation), as presented in Table 15.1. Both variables, political party and attitude toward the legislation, are mutually exclusive categories. The dependent variable is the number of people within each of the four categories.

As with all research, the reliability and validity of the measurement tools are essential to the quality of the research project. The same rule applies to categorical data. Researchers who use categorical data place considerable emphasis on creating clear and useful definitions of the categories used in the research. As you recall from chapter 7, there are many ways to prepare clear definitions of our terms and verify the reliability of those terms.

Research with categorical data has two distinguishing features, the data we collect and the statistical tests we use to analyze the data. In the previous chapters, we studied research projects that examine the average performance of people within specific treatment conditions. For categorical research the data are the frequencies, or number of people, within each condition. Because of this difference, we need to use different statistical procedures to analyze the data. Therefore, this chapter will review several common research procedures for conducting categorical research and the statistics used to analyze the data. Specifically, we will examine the χ^2 statistic.

Karl Pearson, the statistician who invented the correlation coefficient (r), also invented the **chi-square** (χ^2) statistic. The χ^2 is an inferential statistic that allows us to determine whether the number of observations within mutually exclusive classes differs significantly from hypothetical conditions.

GOODNESS-OF-FIT TEST

The purpose of the **goodness-of-fit test** is to determine whether the frequencies of different mutually exclusive categories match or fit a hypothesized population. For an example of how this statistic works, we can examine the relation between month and rate of marriages.

Imagine that a student went to the county courthouse, drew a random sample of 600 marriage licenses issued during the past year, and recorded the month of the marriage. Figure 15.1 presents the data.

For the χ^2 statistic we use O_i to indicate the observed frequency within each class. The symbol T represents the total of all observations. Looking at the data it is clear that June stands out as a popular month for weddings whereas January is not a popular month for exchanging vows. We can now raise the question, "Is the distribution of frequencies different from a known population?"

MONTH	OBSERVED FREQUENCY
January	$O_1 = 26$
February	$O_2 = 41$
March	$O_3 = 36$
April	$O_4 = 41$
May	$O_5 = 62$
June	$O_6 = 75$
July	$O_7 = 60$
August	$O_8 = 67$
September	$O_9 = 58$
October	$O_{10} = 52$
November	$O_{11} = 41$
December	$O_{12} = 41$
TOTAL	$T = 600$

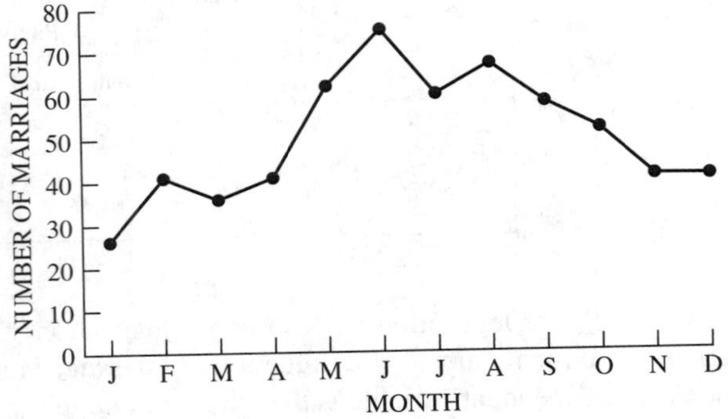

FIGURE 15.1
Hypothetical data of the number of marriages for each month.

TABLE 15.2
An extension of the data presented in Figure 15.1

Month	Observed frequency	Expected proportions	Expected frequency = $p \times T$
January	$O_1 = 26$	0.04	$E_1 = 24 = .04 \times 600$
February	$O_2 = 41$	0.07	$E_2 = 42 = .07 \times 600$
March	$O_3 = 36$	0.06	$E_3 = 36 = .06 \times 600$
April	$O_4 = 41$	0.07	$E_4 = 42 = .07 \times 600$
May	$O_5 = 62$	0.10	$E_5 = 60 = .10 \times 600$
June	$O_6 = 75$	0.12	$E_6 = 72 = .12 \times 600$
July	$O_7 = 60$	0.10	$E_7 = 60 = .10 \times 600$
August	$O_8 = 67$	0.11	$E_8 = 66 = .11 \times 600$
September	$O_9 = 58$	0.10	$E_9 = 60 = .10 \times 600$
October	$O_{10} = 52$	0.09	$E_{10} = 54 = .09 \times 600$
November	$O_{11} = 41$	0.08	$E_{11} = 48 = .08 \times 600$
December	$O_{12} = 41$	0.06	$E_{12} = 36 = .07 \times 600$
Totals	600	1.00	600

Note: The proportions represent data based on national data. The expected values (E_i) equal the hypothetical proportion (p) multiplied by the total number of observations, T.

Table 15.2 presents the observed frequencies along with the expected frequencies. The column listed "Expected Proportions" represents data provided by the Department of Health and Human Services (1995). According to this information, approximately 4% of marriages occur in January whereas 12% of marriages occur in June. Using the proportions from the national sample, we can estimate how many weddings should occur within each month for our sample of 600 couples. According to the results, we would expect 24 marriages in January and 72 marriages in June for any random sample of 600 marriages.

Looking at Table 15.2, you can see that there are slight differences between the observed frequencies and the expected frequencies. For example, the student's sample had more than expected marriages in June and July and fewer than expected marriages in November. Do these differences represent random variation or are the differences statistically significant? To answer that question, we will turn to the χ^2 test of goodness-of-fit.

$$\chi^2 = \sum \frac{(O_i - E_i)^2}{E_i} \tag{15.1}$$

Equation 15.1 defines the χ^2 statistic. The numerator is the squared difference between the observed (O_i) and expected (E_i) scores for each category. The denominator is the expected value for the same class. If the random or chance factors created the difference between the observed and expected scores, then the χ^2 will be relatively small. By contrast, χ^2 will be large if there is a nonrandom difference between the observed and expected scores.

As with the other inferential statistics you have learned to use, the χ^2 statistic has its own family of sampling distributions. The degrees of freedom for the χ^2 statistic is one less the number of classes. Stated mathematically, the degrees of freedom for the Goodness-of-Fit Test is

$$df = k - 1 \tag{15.2}$$

In our example, there are 12 months, therefore the degrees of freedom are $df = 11$ ($df = 12 - 1$). Table A.14 of Appendix A lists the critical values for the χ^2 statistic. As you can see, the critical value to reject the null hypothesis is 19.675.

Like the ANOVA, the χ^2 is a nondirectional statistic. This means that the χ^2 will indicate whether the pattern of observed frequencies deviates from the expected frequencies. It does not indicate whether one particular difference is significantly greater or less than the expected value.

Assumptions of the Goodness-of-Fit Test

The goodness-of-fit χ^2 test requires the data to meet several assumptions. These assumptions include: (a) mutually exclusive categories, (b) exhaustive conditions, (c) independence of observations, and (d) sufficient sample size.

We have already examined the requirement of mutually exclusive categories. In summary, each subject fits into only one category. Examples of mutually exclusive events include one's sex, political party, and marital status. It is critical to ensure that we use procedures that prohibit double counting the individuals. If we allow some people or observations to count in several categories, the results test will produce biased results. Because the couples could list only one wedding date, we can be confident there will be only one reported wedding for each couple.

The issue of an inflated T is a serious problem for the accuracy of the χ^2 test. Counting the same participant several times biases the data. Therefore, researchers who conduct categorical data research spend much time ensuring that their definitions of the categories and the procedures they use to collect the data ensure that the data conform to the mutually exclusive requirement.

The exhaustive conditions assumption indicates that there is a category available for each person in the sample. In the example illustrating the relation between marriages and months, we can consider the conditions exhaustive because the researcher included a category for each month. What if a researcher wanted to examine the relation between political party and attitude toward a new law? To meet the exhaustive conditions requirement, the researcher would need to include a category for each political party (Communist, Democrat, Green, Libertarian, Republican, etc.) or a category for each of the major parties and a category of "Other" party affiliation. The purpose of the exhaustive conditions requirement is to ensure that the researcher classifies each person in the sample. Dropping people from the sample because they do not meet the classification scheme will bias the results.

The independence of observations means that the classification of subjects into one category has no effect on the other categories. To meet the independence requirement, there must be equivalent criteria for entry into each category. For this example, we can assume that the decision of one couple to wed in February had no effect on the plans of the other couples.

The final requirement is that sample size be sufficiently large. The general rule is that none of the expected frequencies be less than 5. If the expected frequencies are too small, the χ^2 will be more likely to produce erroneous results.

In the current example, we can see that we have met all the requirements of the χ^2 test. The groups are mutually exclusive, the conditions are exhaustive, the classification of the people is independent, and the sample size appears to be sufficiently large. Therefore, we can proceed with the test. Table 15.3 presents the χ^2 test for the number of marriages by month. For these data, the null hypothesis is that the observed frequencies will equal the expected frequencies.

The value of $\chi^2_{observed}$ is less than $\chi^2_{critical}$ (2.28 < 19.68). Therefore, we cannot reject the null hypothesis. This result suggests that the distribution of marriages matches the national trends. We must conclude that we have no reason to assume that the difference between the observed and expected frequencies is anything other than chance.

In this example, we used empirical data to determine the values of the expected frequencies. This tactic allowed us to determine if the selection of wedding dates differs from

TABLE 15.3

An extension of the data presented in Tables 15.2 and 15.3. This table shows how one calculates the goodness-of-fit χ^2

Month	O	E	$O_i - E_i$	$(O_i - E_i)^2$	$\dfrac{(O_i - E_i)^2}{E_i}$
January	$O_1 = 26$	$E_1 = 24$	2	4	0.1667
February	$O_2 = 41$	$E_2 = 42$	−1	1	0.0238
March	$O_3 = 36$	$E_3 = 36$	0	0	0.0000
April	$O_4 = 41$	$E_4 = 42$	−1	1	0.0238
May	$O_5 = 62$	$E_5 = 60$	2	4	0.0667
June	$O_6 = 75$	$E_6 = 72$	3	9	0.1250
July	$O_7 = 60$	$E_7 = 60$	0	0	0.0000
August	$O_8 = 67$	$E_8 = 66$	1	1	0.0152
September	$O_9 = 58$	$E_9 = 60$	−2	4	0.0667
October	$O_{10} = 52$	$E_{10} = 54$	−2	4	0.0741
November	$O_{11} = 41$	$E_{11} = 48$	−7	49	1.0208
December	$O_{12} = 41$	$E_{12} = 36$	5	25	0.6944
Totals	600	600			$\chi^2 = 2.2771$

TABLE 15.4
**Hypothetical data representing the number of people admitted to a hospital
for depression during different seasons over a five-year interval**

Season	O	E	$O_i - E_i$	$(O_i - E_i)^2$	$\dfrac{(O_i - E_i)^2}{E_i}$
Spring	495	517.5	−22.5	506.25	0.9783
Summer	503	517.5	−14.5	210.25	0.4063
Autumn	491	517.5	−26.5	702.25	1.3570
Winter	581	517.5	63.5	4032.25	7.7918
Total	2070	2070	0.0		$\chi^2 = 10.5334$

national trends. There are cases where we want to determine if the data are evenly distributed across a set of categories. Consider the following example.

A social worker wants to know if there is a relation between the time of year and the occurrence of depression. Using the data collected by a large metropolitan area hospital, the social worker records the number of admissions for depression that occurred during the past five years. The researcher divides the year into the four seasons (e.g., winter = November, December, January, and February). The data are presented in Table 15.4.

The researcher may want to know whether the frequency of severe depression varies with the time of year. The simplest null hypothesis to propose is that the rate of admission for depression is equal throughout the year. Therefore, the researcher determined that the expected number of admissions in each season should be equal. In other words, the expected frequency for each season is $517.5 = 2070/4$. The remainder of the test follows the same procedures listed previously.

With $df = 3$ and $\alpha = .05$, $\chi^2_{\text{critical}} = 7.815$. Because the observed value of χ^2 is greater than the critical value ($10.5334 > 7.815$), we may assume that the distribution of admissions for depression does deviate from the expected hypothesized values. By casual inspection of the data, it appears that there is an increase of admissions during winter.

χ^2 TEST OF INDEPENDENCE

We can extend the logic of χ^2 to cases where we have two categorical variables. The question that we want to address is whether these variables are independent of each other. The following is an example to help illustrate how to use the χ^2 **test of independence**.

What are the long-term effects of childhood sexual abuse? Are people who experience this type of abuse more likely to suffer severe emotional disorders later in their life? Gladstone, Parker, Wilhelm, Mitchell, and Austin (1999) addressed that question by conducting an extensive review of 171 women receiving treatment for a major depressive episode. Of these women, 40 reported experiencing sexual abuse as children. The researchers then examined the case history of all the women and looked for evidence of self-injurious behavior. The data in Table 15.5 represent the number of patients who attempted to commit suicide.

TABLE 15.5

Contingency table representing the number of women reporting childhood sexual abuse and one or more suicide attempts

| | Childhood sexual abuse | | |
	Abused	Not abused	Row total
Attempted suicide	16	23	39
No suicide attempts	24	108	132
Column total	40	131	171

The χ^2 test of independence allows us to examine the relation between history of childhood sexual abuse and rates of attempted suicide. If the two variables are independent of each other, then the rate of suicide attempts will have nothing to do with the abuse experience. By contrast, if a history of sexual abuse does affect risk of suicide, then we should observe a nonrandom pattern in the data.

As with the goodness-of-fit test, we need to determine the expected value for each cell in the table. The expected value represents the frequency within a cell that we would expect to occur given the independence of the two variables. Perhaps an example would help.

According to the data presented in Table 15.5, we know that 40 women experienced childhood sexual abuse. Converting this number to a percentage, we can say that 23.39% $(23.39 = (40/171) \times 100)$ of the women experienced the abuse. We also know that 39 women attempted to commit suicide. If the rate of suicide attempts and history of abuse are independent of each other, then we can conclude that 23.39% of the women who attempted suicide also have a history of abuse. We would expect that 9.12 ($9.12 = 39 \times$ .2339) women would be in the cell, "Attempted Suicide"/"Abused." We can use the following equation for determining the expected frequencies for each cell.

$$E_{ij} = \frac{R_i C_j}{T} \tag{15.3}$$

In this equation, R_i and C_j represent the row and column totals for each category, and T represents the total number of observations. Therefore, E_{ij} represents the expected frequency for each cell if there is no correspondence between the two variables. Table 15.6 presents the expected values for the data.

If there is no relation between the two variables, then the overall difference between the observed and expected scores should be minimal. Each expected score (E_{ij}) should equal the corresponding observed score (O_{ij}) and χ^2 will equal 0. If the differences between the observed and expected frequencies are sufficiently large, we can infer that there is a relation between the two variables. For this example, a statistically significant χ^2 would allow us to assume a correspondence between a history of childhood sexual abuse and suicide attempts.

The formal mathematical statement for the χ^2 test is:

$$\chi^2 = \sum_{i=1}^{r} \sum_{j=1}^{c} \frac{(O_{ij} - E_{ij})^2}{E_{ij}} \tag{15.4}$$

TABLE 15.6
An extension of the data presented in Table 15.5. This table illustrates how
one calculates the expected values for each cell

| | Childhood sexual abuse | | |
	Abused	Not abused	Row total
Attempted suicide	$O_{11} = 16$	$O_{12} = 23$	$R_1 = 39$
	$E_{11} = \dfrac{40 \times 39}{171}$	$E_{12} = \dfrac{131 \times 39}{171}$	
	$E_{11} = 9.12$	$E_{12} = 29.88$	
No suicide attempts	$O_{21} = 24$	$O_{22} = 108$	$R_2 = 132$
	$E_{21} = \dfrac{40 \times 132}{171}$	$E_{22} = \dfrac{131 \times 132}{171}$	
	$E_{21} = 30.88$	$E_{22} = 101.12$	
Column total	$C_1 = 40$	$C_2 = 131$	$T = 171$

The equation is much like the goodness-of-fit test. The difference is that we need to calculate a ratio for each cell in the matrix. The number of rows, r, and the number of columns, c, determine the degrees of freedom. Specifically,

$$df = (r - 1)(c - 1) \tag{15.5}$$

For Equation 15.5, r represents the number of rows, and c represents the number of columns in the matrix of data. With this information, we can now proceed to our calculations. Carrying out the steps in Equation 15.4 we find,

$$\chi^2 = \frac{(16 - 9.12)^2}{9.12} + \frac{(23 - 29.88)^2}{29.88} + \frac{(24 - 30.88)^2}{30.88} + \frac{(108 - 101.12)^2}{101.12}$$

$$\chi^2 = 8.77$$

Because χ^2_{observed} is much greater than χ^2_{critical} ($8.77 > 3.841$), we can reject the null hypothesis. These data allow the researcher to infer that the risk of suicide attempt corresponds with experiencing sexual abuse as a child. Looking at the differences between the observed and expected values, you can see what should be an obvious effect: Women who experienced sexual abuse as children are more likely to attempt suicide than women who did not experience the abuse.

Interpreting χ^2

We need to interpret a statistically significant χ^2 with caution. Specifically, we need to be mindful of whether a statistically significant χ^2 allows us to infer cause and effect. The primary purpose of the χ^2 test is to determine whether the variables are independent of each other. If we fail to reject the null hypothesis for the χ^2, we must conclude that we do not have evidence for the interdependent between the variables. We must assume that the data represent the random distribution of observed scores. If we do reject the null hypothesis, we can conclude that there is a correspondence between the variables. A correlation between variables is not, by itself, evidence of a cause-and-effect relation between the independent and dependent variables. We can use the current example to illustrate this important consideration.

What were the researcher's independent variables? Both variables are subject variables as they represent conditions of the participants beyond the control of the researcher. The researchers could not randomly assign the participants to the different categories. These observations mean that we cannot rule out alternative explanations of the data.

We also need to examine how the researchers created the sample. Is the sample representative of the general population? The participants in this research were women in therapy for depression. Consequently, this sample may not represent all the women who suffered childhood abuse; some may not have sought treatment from a psychologist. Thus, we cannot automatically assume that all people who experience sexual abuse are at risk for suicide. In determining the long-term effects of childhood sexual abuse, we would need to sample from the general population and find those with a history of childhood sexual abuse, independent of their current treatment for a psychological disorder.

χ^2 TEST OF HOMOGENEITY

Are there conditions when we can assume a cause-and-effect relation for the χ^2 test? Yes, if we conduct the study using a different set of procedures. Imagine that a researcher randomly assigns equal numbers of participants to one of four psychotherapy conditions and then evaluates the clients' conditions after the treatment using three classifications: (a) no change, (b) moderate improvement, and (c) good improvement. The χ^2 test of homogeneity allows us to determine if the pattern of observed frequencies deviate from chance levels. If we find a statistically significant χ^2, we can then assume a cause and effect relation. The data in Table 15.7 represent hypothetical results for such a study.

TABLE 15.7
Hypothetical data for an example of a χ^2 test of homogeneity

| | Psychotherapy condition | | | | |
	Control	Informative	Individual: Type A	Individual: Type B	Total
No change	$O_{11} = 19$ $E_{11} = 14$	$O_{12} = 15$ $E_{12} = 14$	$O_{13} = 7$ $E_{13} = 14$	$O_{14} = 15$ $E_{14} = 14$	56
Moderate	$O_{21} = 21$ $E_{21} = 17$	$O_{22} = 22$ $E_{22} = 17$	$O_{23} = 9$ $E_{23} = 17$	$O_{24} = 16$ $E_{24} = 17$	68
Good	$O_{31} = 20$ $E_{31} = 29$	$O_{32} = 23$ $E_{32} = 29$	$O_{33} = 44$ $E_{33} = 29$	$O_{34} = 29$ $E_{34} = 29$	116
Total	60	60	60	60	240

$\chi^2 = 23.46$ $df = (3 - 1)(4 - 1) df = 6$ $\chi^2_{critical} = 12.592, \alpha = .05$ Reject H_0 because $\chi^2 > \chi^2_{critical}$

In this example, we can treat the type of psychotherapy as a manipulated independent variable because the researcher randomly assigned the participants to one of the conditions. The second variable, the outcome measure, is the condition of the participants at the end of the study. Therefore, this study has all the hallmarks of a true experiment: (a) manipulated independent variable, (b) a control group, and (c) random assignment of participants to the treatment conditions. Data such as these could lead the researcher to conclude that the type of therapy influences the rate at which the clients' condition improves.

The procedures for calculating the χ^2 are identical to those presented for the test of independence. Therefore, the only differences between the χ^2 test of independence and the χ^2 test of homogeneity are the methods used to create the sample and the interpretations we can draw from the test.

To review, for the test of independence, we create a sample and then assess the participants for the variables in the study. In the Gladstone et al. (1999) study, the researchers created a sample of women seeking treatment and then determined the number of individuals who had attempted suicide and the number who had been sexually abused as children. By contrast, for the test for homogeneity, we create as a sample of equal numbers of participants within the different levels of one variable and then assess the dependent variable using an outcome measure.

Reporting χ^2

The style guide published by the American Psychological Association (2001) recommends that we report χ^2 as

$$\chi^2 (df, N = n) = \chi^2, \quad p < \alpha$$
$$\chi^2 (6, N = 240) = 23.46, \quad p < .05$$

The recommended format has us report the degrees of freedom and the number of subjects used in the study. We also indicate whether the probability level associated with the statistic is greater than or less than the α-level selected for the study.

Assumptions of the χ^2 Test

To make a valid interpretation of the χ^2 test, you must ensure that the data meet several specific assumptions of the χ^2 test. These assumptions are similar to the ones we reviewed for the goodness-of-fit test. Specifically, the categories must be mutually exclusive, exhaustive, and independent; the data must represent frequencies; and the sample size must be sufficiently large.

Regarding sample size, many authors offer general guidelines for the χ^2 test of independence. For example, Siegel and Castellan (1988) noted that when either the number of rows or the number of columns is greater than 2, "no more than 20% of the cells should have an expected frequency of less than 5, and no cell should have an expected frequency less than 1" (p. 199). Some researchers have found that the χ^2 test maintains the same rate of Type I errors even with severe violations of this assumption. For example, Good,

Grover, and Mitchell (1970) suggested that expected values could be as low as 0.33 with no change in the probability of committing a Type I error.

Although the χ^2 test appears to be able to withstand the effect of small frequencies, we should not forget the issue of power. As with all inferential statistics, the probability of correctly rejecting the null hypothesis increases as the sample size increases. Therefore, although χ^2 may be valid when the sample size is small, the power may be insufficient to detect an effect.

FURTHER ANALYSIS OF THE χ^2

The χ^2 test allows us to determine whether to reject the null hypothesis, however, the result provides no information for determining the strength of the relation between the variables. In the next two sections, you will learn how to determine the degree of correspondence between the variables and how to examine the differences observed within each cell.

Cramér's Coefficient ϕ

In chapter 8 you learned that Pearson's product-moment correlation coefficient is a statistic used to indicate the degree of association between two variables. The larger the absolute value of r, the greater the association between the two variables. **Cramér's coefficient ϕ** (phi) serves the same purpose as r; it indicates the degree of association between two variables analyzed using the χ^2 statistic.

$$\phi = \sqrt{\frac{\chi^2}{T(S-1)}} \tag{15.6}$$

Equation 15.6 presents Cramér's ϕ. In the equation, T represents the total number of observations and S represents the smaller value of number of rows or number of columns. Because the size of ϕ depends upon the value of χ^2, we can infer that if χ^2 is statistically significant, the same is true of ϕ.

There are important differences between r and ϕ, however. Whereas r can range between -1 and 1, ϕ can only have values between 0 and 1. Nevertheless, we can use the magnitude of ϕ as an index of the relation between the two variables. Another important difference between r and ϕ is that r is a measure of the linear relation between two variables. In chapter 8 you learned that we use r when we assume that a straight line describes the relation between two variables. There are, however, instances when there are systematic relations between two variables best described by curved lines. The ϕ does not assume a linear relation between the two variables. The ϕ is a general test that allows us to estimate how one variable predicts the other variable.

We can use the data from Table 15.6 to illustrate how to calculate Cramér's ϕ.

$$\phi = \sqrt{\frac{8.77}{171(2-1)}} \qquad \phi = \sqrt{\frac{8.77}{171}} \qquad \phi = \sqrt{0.05129}$$

$$\phi = .226$$

Therefore, we can conclude that there is a moderate relation between experiences of childhood sexual abuse and attempted suicides.

Post Hoc Analysis of χ^2

You may recall from our discussion of the analysis of variance that the ANOVA is a general test because it allows us to conclude that there is a relation between several variables, but it does not tell us which specific conditions are significantly different from the others. For the ANOVA, the Tukey's HSD is a commonly used test to compare the differences among specific means.

A similar situation arises for the χ^2 test. We can use the χ^2 test to reject the hypothesis that the two conditions are independent of one another, but we cannot determine from the test which condition or conditions contributed to the statistically significant result. One technique that many researchers use is to convert the differences between the observed and expected values to a statistic called the **standardized residual, e.** The standardized residual allows us to determine the relative difference between the observed and expected frequencies. Using the standardized residual, we can then determine which cells in the data table represent statistically significant differences and which represent chance findings.

Equation 15.7 presents the method of calculating e.

$$e_{ij} = \frac{O_{ij} - E_{ij}}{\sqrt{E_{ij}}} \tag{15.7}$$

Although Equation 15.7 provides an estimate of the standardized residual, many researchers prefer to use a more refined estimate of the residual. Equation 15.8 (Haberman, 1973; Delucchi, 1993) presents the method of calculating the variance for each cell.

$$v_{ij} = \left(1 - \frac{C_i}{T}\right)\left(1 - \frac{R_j}{T}\right) \tag{15.8}$$

Using Equations 15.7 and 15.8 we can now calculate what statisticians call the **adjusted residual, $\hat{e}$.**

$$\hat{e}_{ij} = \frac{e_{ij}}{\sqrt{v_{ij}}} \tag{15.9}$$

The advantage of calculating $\hat{e}$ is that it is normally distributed with a mean of 0 and a standard deviation of 1. Therefore, we can treat $\hat{e}$ as if it were a z-score. If the absolute value of $\hat{e}$ is sufficiently large, we can assume that the difference between the observed and expected values are statistically significant. For example, $z = \pm 1.96$ represents the critical value for $\alpha = .05$, two-tailed. In other words, if $\hat{e} \leq -1.96$ or $\hat{e} \geq 1.96$, we can assume that the difference between O and E is statistically significant at $\alpha = .05$.

Table 15.8 presents the calculations for e, v, and $\hat{e}$. From this work, we can conclude that the difference between the observed and expected frequencies for each cell is statistically significant.

TABLE 15.8
An extension of the data presented in Table 15.6

| | Childhood sexual abuse | | |
	Abused	Not abused	Row total
Attempted suicide	$O_{11} = 16$	$O_{12} = 23$	$R_1 = 39$
	$E_{11} = 9.12$	$E_{12} = 29.88$	
	$e_{11} = \dfrac{16 - 9.12}{\sqrt{9.12}}$	$e_{12} = \dfrac{23 - 29.88}{\sqrt{29.88}}$	
	$e_{11} = 2.278$	$e_{12} = -1.258$	
	$v_{11} = .766 \times .772$	$v_{12} = .234 \times .772$	$.772 = 1 - \dfrac{39}{171}$
	$v_{11} = .591$	$v_{12} = .181$	
	$\hat{e}_{11} = \dfrac{2.278}{\sqrt{.591}}$	$\hat{e}_{12} = \dfrac{-1.258}{\sqrt{.181}}$	
	$\hat{e}_{11} = \mathbf{2.96}$	$\hat{e}_{12} = \mathbf{-2.96}$	
No suicide attempts	$O_{21} = 24$	$O_{22} = 108$	$R_2 = 132$
	$E_{21} = 30.88$	$E_{22} = 101.12$	
	$e_{21} = \dfrac{24 - 30.88}{\sqrt{30.88}}$	$e_{22} = \dfrac{108 - 101.12}{\sqrt{101.12}}$	
	$e_{21} = -1.238$	$e_{22} = 0.684$	
	$v_{21} = .766 \times .228$	$v_{22} = .234 \times .228$	$.228 = 1 - \dfrac{132}{171}$
	$v_{21} = .175$	$v_{22} = .053$	
	$\hat{e}_{21} = \dfrac{-1.238}{\sqrt{.175}}$	$\hat{e}_{22} = \dfrac{0.684}{\sqrt{.053}}$	
	$\hat{e}_{21} = \mathbf{-2.96}$	$\hat{e}_{22} = \mathbf{2.96}$	
Column total	$C_1 = 40$	$C_2 = 131$	$T = 171$
	$.766 = 1 - \dfrac{40}{171}$	$.234 = 1 - \dfrac{131}{171}$	

McNEMAR TEST

The McNemar test is a special form of the χ^2 test that we can use to compare correlated samples. We can use the McNemar test to compare the proportion of participants who fit within a specific category before and after some event or under different conditions. The McNemar test works specifically with a 2×2 table, as presented in Table 15.9.

TABLE 15.9
The layout for a McNemar test

		Condition II	
		1	2
Condition I	1	A	B
	2	C	D

Equation 15.10 presents the basic form of the McNemar test.

$$\chi^2 = \frac{(|B - C| - 1)^2}{B + C}, \quad df = 1 \tag{15.10}$$

Once you calculate the χ^2 test, you can use Table A.14 of Appendix A to determine whether to reject the null hypothesis. An alternative method is to take the square root of the χ^2, which produces a z-score. This transformation works only when the degrees of freedom of the χ^2 tests are $df = 1$.

$$z = \sqrt{\chi^2} \tag{15.11}$$

The null hypothesis of this test is that the difference between the B and C cells is due to chance. A significantly large value of χ^2 indicates that the observed frequencies in the B and C cells do not represent chance factors.

We can use an example from research conducted by Cairns et al. (1989) to illustrate the utility of the McNemar test. Cairns et al. were interested in the developmental changes in aggressive tendencies of children. More specifically, they examined the number of times boys and girls described aggressive tendencies toward other boys and girls. To collect the data, research associates interviewed the children, first in the fourth grade and then again in the seventh grade. During the interviews, the researcher asked the children to describe two recent conflicts with other children. Another research associate, blind to the research questions and nature of the children responding, read and scored verbatim transcripts of the interviews. Part of the coding indicated whether the child described physical aggression toward another child. The data in Table 15.10 present an example of the results for boys that Cairns et al. found.

In this table, the numbers represent frequency of events for two conditions. Look at the data for Grade 4. These data represent the results for the 104 boys interviewed. The question that the researchers wanted to address is the number of times the boys described physical conflicts with other boys and the number of physical conflicts with girls. According to the results, 48 of the boys reported a physical conflict with another boy. These same 104 boys reported 26 physically aggressive conflicts with girls. The research question is if boys are more likely to be physically aggressive with boys than with girls.

According to Table A.14 of Appendix A, the critical value of χ^2 for $df = 1$ and $\alpha = .05$ is $\chi^2 = 3.841$, therefore we can reject the null hypothesis for both the fourth-grade data and the seventh-grade data. We can conclude that the pattern of reported physical conflicts is not random. Specifically, these data suggest that boys are more likely to report themes of physical aggression toward other boys than toward girls and that this pattern appears to become stronger as boys grow older.

TABLE 15.10
The procedure for calculating the McNemar test

Boys' Reports of conflicts: Grade 4

Conflict with:	Physical aggression	No physical aggression	Total
Males	48	56	104
Females	26	78	104

$$\chi^2 = \frac{(|56 - 26| - 1)^2}{56 + 26} \qquad \chi^2 = \frac{(|30| - 1)^2}{82} \qquad \chi^2 = \frac{841}{82} \qquad \chi^2 = 10.2561$$

$$z = \sqrt{10.2561} \qquad z = 3.20$$

$$\phi = \sqrt{\frac{10.2561}{104(2 - 1)}} = 0.314$$

Boys' reports of conflicts: Grade 7

Conflict with:	Physical aggression	No physical aggression	Total
Males	49	55	104
Females	12	92	104

$$\chi^2 = \frac{(|55 - 12| - 1)^2}{55 + 12} \qquad \chi^2 = \frac{(|43| - 1)^2}{67} \qquad \chi^2 = \frac{1764}{67} \qquad \chi^2 = 26.3284$$

$$z = \sqrt{26.3284} \qquad z = 5.13$$

$$\phi = \sqrt{\frac{26.3284}{104(2 - 1)}} = 0.50341$$

ACHIEVEMENT CHECK

(1) Describe in your words the uses of the χ^2 statistic. How are these uses of the χ^2 test similar to and different from each other?

(2) A student conducted a study in which three groups of rats (5 per group) were reinforced under three different schedules of reinforcement (100%, 50%, and 25%). The number of barpressing responses obtained during extinction is as follows: 100%, 615; 50%, 843; 25%, 545. Criticize the use of the chi-square as the appropriate statistical technique.

(3) Neil asked 50 participants to think about their earliest memory of their father and their earliest one of their mother. Then he asked them to evaluate each memory as to whether it is positive or negative. He obtained the results listed in the accompanying table.

	Memory of mother	Memory of father
Positive	35	31
Negative	15	19

Neil plans to analyze his data using χ^2. Do you think such an analysis is appropriate? Explain.

(4) Bill believes that the current generation of students is much different from students in the 1960s. He asks a sample of students at his college the following question:

Which of the following best describes your reason for attending college (pick only one alternative)?

a. Develop a philosophy of life.
b. Learn more about the world around me.
c. Obtain a good paying job.
d. Unsure of reason.

Researchers asked the same question of students at the college in 1965. Here are the results of the two surveys.

	1965	2001
Develop a philosophy of life.	15	8
Learn more about the world around me.	53	48
Obtain a good paying job.	25	57
Unsure of reason.	27	47

Is Bill justified in concluding that there is a difference between the current class of students and students in 1965?

(5) Erin is the chair of a department of psychology. She sent a questionnaire to all students who graduated from the program during the past 10 years. One question asked whether the student attended a graduate program and the type of program attended. Of the students returning questionnaires, 88 indicated that they were in or had completed a Ph.D. program.

Program	Number of students
Clinical	12
Counseling	23
Developmental	8
Experimental	7
Industrial/Organizational	15
Physiological	5
Social	18

Can Erin assume that graduates of the department equally attend each of the seven programs?

(6) Jackie conducted a study in which she compared the helping behavior of passersby under two conditions. What can you conclude from the results shown in the accompanying table?

	Condition A	Condition B
Helped	75	45
Did not help	40	80

Set up this study in formal statistical terms and draw appropriate conclusions.

(7) Robert wanted to determine the effects of a televised debate on voters' preferences. The day before a televised debate, Robert asked 100 randomly selected people their current preference. After the debate, Robert asked the same people to identify their candidate of

choice. Use the following data to describe how voters' preference changed after watching the debate.

	After debate	
	Candidate A	Candidate B
Candidate A	20	25
Before Debate		
Candidate B	30	25

RESEARCH IN ACTION: LONG TERM EFFECTS OF CHILDHOOD ABUSE

In a previous example, we saw that people sexually abused as children are more likely to attempt suicide than people not sexually abused. Mulder, Beautrais, Joyce, and Fergusson (1998) examined the effects of abuse on other emotional and behavioral problems. The researchers were concerned that most of the research that examines the effects of domestic violence used current patients for the sample. Mulder et al. believed that using a random sample of the general population would improve the external validity of the conclusions.

To conduct their research, Mulder et al. (1998) contacted a stratified (for age and sex) random sample of 1,200 registered voters from the Canterbury region of New Zealand. Of the individuals, 1,028 agreed to participate in an in-depth interview that included a review of their history and a structured interview conducted by trained clinical psychologists. One of the characteristics that they examined was dissociative symptoms, which include a disruption of normal functions including "consciousness, memory, identity, or perception" (American Psychiatric Association, p. 477). They decided to measure dissociative symptoms because these symptoms are highly related to other psychiatric illnesses.

Of the people interviewed, 28 reported having been physically, but not sexually, abused as a child. An additional 43 people reported that they experienced sexual abuse as a child. Table 15.11 presents the analysis of the data. The three columns represent three classes of childhood experience, "No Abuse," "Abused," and "Abused and Sexually Assaulted." The rows represent whether the patients evidenced a high level of dissociation disorders. Using these data, we can determine whether there is a relation between the presence of dissociation disorders and childhood abuse.

For these data, $\chi^2_{observed} = 17.97$ is greater than $\chi^2_{critical}$. Therefore, we can conclude that there is a relation between the high levels of dissociation and childhood experiences. Careful inspection of the data reveals an interesting pattern. Higher levels of dissociation occur with reports of physical abuse, not sexual abuse. Mulder et al. (1998) recognized immediately that their findings conflict with popular opinion among clinicians and with previous research. As they noted, however, "our study is one of few, to our knowledge, that have examined this relationship in randomly selected general population samples" (p. 810). They go on to note that using a clinical population for a sampling population introduces substantial bias that may confound the relation among the variables.

These data are interesting and should cause researchers to reconsider with care the relation between sexual abuse and subsequent psychological disorders. The data also beg for

TABLE 15.11
Hypothetical data representing the frequency of various psychological disorders and the presence or absence of physical abuse

	History			
	No abuse	Abused	Abused and sexually assaulted	Total
High dissociation	$O_{11} = 56$ $E_{11} = 60.5107$ $\hat{e}_{11} = -2.28*$	$O_{12} = 7$ $E_{12} = 1.7704$ $\hat{e}_{12} = 4.12*$	$O_{13} = 2$ $E_{13} = 2.719$ $\hat{e}_{13} = -.046$	$R_1 = 65$
Low dissociation	$O_{21} = 901$ $E_{21} = 896.4893$ $\hat{e}_{21} = 2.27*$	$O_{22} = 21$ $E_{22} = 26.2296$ $\hat{e}_{22} = -4.12*$	$O_{23} = 41$ $E_{23} = 40.2811$ $\hat{e}_{23} = 0.46$	$R_2 = 963$
	$C_1 = 957$	$C_2 = 28$	$C_3 = 43$	$T = 1028$

Notes:
*$p < .05$

$\chi^2 = 0.3362 + 15.4478 + 0.7190 + 0.2270 + 1.2255 + 0.0128$

$\chi^2 = 17.97, p < .05; df = 2 = (2 - 1)(3 - 1)$

$$\phi = \sqrt{\frac{17.97}{1028(2 - 1)}}$$

$\phi = .13$

more research. For example, Mulder et al. made a significant contribution by attempting to use a random sample of the general population. This tactic was definitely a step in the right direction, although we should ask whether sampling from a list of registered voters is representative of the general population. We may also want to raise questions concerning the measurement and classification of the various forms of abuse. It is possible that there are other variables lurking in the background. We do not know, for example, how often people experienced episodes of sexual or physical abuse. Perhaps it is not the type of abuse but the frequency of abuse that influences the risk of dissociative symptomology. Similarly, the age when one experienced the abuse affects the risk of dissociative behaviors. Fortunately, one can answer these empirical questions with additional research.

ACHIEVEMENT CHECK

(8) A student conducts a study of binge drinking at her college. She randomly selects 300 students who attend a small liberal arts college and asks them to complete a questionnaire that examines their drinking behavior. The results of the questionnaire allow the researcher to identify students who engage in binge drinking. One question that she wants to address is whether there is a relation between sex and binge drinking. Here are the data from the study.

		Sex	
		Male	Female
Binge drinker	+	28	30
	−	98	144

a. Use these data to determine whether there is a relation between sex and binge drinking.

(9) A social scientist wanted to find if there are ways to increase the return rate of questionnaires sent in the mail. She randomly selected 300 people listed as registered voters and prepared to mail them a short questionnaire with a stamped return envelope. For a random 100 people, the researcher first sent a separate letter explaining that the recipient would receive a survey and that it was essential to return the questionnaire. Another randomly selected 100 people received a telephone call explaining the importance of compliance. The other 100 people received no presurvey contact. The following data indicate the number who returned the survey (compliance) or did not return the survey.

	Presurvey contact		
	Letter	Phone call	Nothing
Compliance	44	68	21
No compliance	56	32	79

a. Is there evidence that there is a relation between the type of contact and the rate of compliance?
b. Which techniques appear to be the most successful in creating compliance?

CHAPTER SUMMARY

Many research projects use a nominal scale to assess the dependent variable. These data require a different statistical method for analysis. Therefore, the purpose of this chapter was to examine the analysis of categorical data using the χ^2 and the binomial tests.

The goodness-of-fit test is a special version of the χ^2 test that allows us to determine whether the observed frequencies differ from the expected values. As with most statistical tests, the χ^2 makes specific requirements of the data for the results to be valid. Specifically, the χ^2 requires that the data the categories represent be mutually exclusive categories, that the observations be independent, and that the sample size be greater than five per category.

The χ^2 test of independence allows us to determine whether two groups are independent. As with the χ^2 goodness-of-fit test, the test of independence compares the difference between the observed and expected frequencies. As with other statistical tests, the χ^2 has a number of post hoc tests that allow us to analyze the data further. For example, Cramér's coefficient ϕ allows us to determine the extent to which one variable predicts the other variable. The adjusted standardized residual allows us to convert the difference between the observed and expected frequencies to a z-score.

The McNemar test is another version of the χ^2 test. It allows us to observe the change in frequencies that occur when monitoring participants on two occasions or when the participants are matched.

CHAPTER GLOSSARY FOR REVIEW

Adjusted Residual, $\hat{e}$ An enhancement of e that fits the normal distribution.

Chi-Square χ^2   A form of inferential statistic used to examine the frequencies of categorical, mutually exclusive classes. The statistic determines whether the observed frequencies equal hypothesized frequencies.

Cramér's Coefficient ϕ   A descriptive statistic used with the χ^2 test of independence to quantify the degree of association between the two categorical variables.

Goodness-of-Fit Test   A version of the χ^2 test that determines whether a statistically significant difference exists between observed frequencies and expected frequencies within mutually exclusive classes.

Mutually Exclusive   A classification scheme for which a person or observation may be placed into only one of the available categories (e.g., sex, political party, and religion).

χ^2 Test of Homogeneity   A version of the χ^2 test that determines whether the distribution of frequencies for independent populations is independent.

χ^2 Test of Independence   A version of the χ^2 test that determines whether the distribution of frequencies for two categorical variables is independent.

Standardized Residual, e   A descriptive statistic that indicates the relative difference between the observed and expected scores for a single condition in the χ^2 test of independence.

16 WRITING THE RESEARCH REPORT

CHAPTER OUTLINE

Writing is not like painting where you add. It is not what you put on the canvas that the reader sees. Writing is more like a sculpture where you remove, you eliminate in order to make the work visible. Even those pages you remove somehow remain.

—Elie Wiesel

INTRODUCTION

The last step in any research project is writing the report wherein you tell the reader why you conducted the research and the importance of the results. In many ways, you are telling a story that has a clear beginning, middle, and end. At the start of the paper, you describe an important and unresolved question. You then describe how you uncovered the clues related to your hypothesis and came to a set of logical deductions. At the end of the paper, you pull the information together and explain how your research has answered the original question. In this chapter we will review the essential characteristics of writing a good research report.

Writing is a unique, intellectual challenge. Your goal is to influence the behavior or thinking of the reader. In most cases, you write to share information and persuade the reader that your interpretation of the facts is correct. The same is true of a research report. At the start of your paper, you introduce the readers to the purpose of your research, and then convince them that you are asking an important and interesting question. By the end of the paper, you will have convinced the reader that your analysis and interpretation of the data were the correct ones and have answered the questions.

Like all skills, learning to write well requires practice. Good writers write well because they write often. Good writers also write well because they have learned from experience and have received useful critiques of their work. I have also observed that good writers are also people who read much. Reading exposes you to many styles of writing and can help you pick up good writing habits. You can learn much about writing by examining how other authors present their ideas.

Finally, good writers never work in isolation; they have others read drafts of their work, and they seek constructive comments. Many students seem to believe that no one should read their paper until they submit it to the instructor. Nothing could be farther from the truth. Asking someone to read a draft of your paper will help you become a better writer.

Having someone else read your paper with a critical eye can help ensure that your work is as clear and concise as possible. As I wrote this book, other psychologists read drafts of the chapters and offered their critical comments. Although there were times when I was frustrated with their critiques, the reviewers' comments allowed me to revise sections that were not as clear and accurate as I thought they were.

There is no mystery to becoming a good writer. Similarly, there are no excuses for why any intelligent person cannot write well. Writing is a craft learned and refined through practice. Thus, a modicum of self-discipline, attention to detail, and willingness to seek help will make you a better writer.

This textbook cannot teach you how to be a good writer anymore than a textbook can teach an artist how to paint masterworks. What I can do is highlight several of the features that are the elements of good writing. Studying these characteristics will help you evaluate your writing.

This chapter will do two things. First, it will review the general stylistic conventions that are the hallmark of good writing. Second, it will introduce you to the editorial guidelines created by the American Psychological Association (APA). What began as a seven-page style handbook has mushroomed into a large reference book: The fifth edition of the *Publication Manual of the American Psychological Association* (APA, 2001) is a hefty 339 pages. This chapter is only 39 pages long and will highlight the basic information that you need to prepare a paper.

WHAT DO READERS APPRECIATE IN GOOD WRITING?

There are many attributes of a good research report. But before we review those qualities, we should examine the elements that are the hallmark of good writing—focus, organization, and integration.

Unfortunately, too many people believe that scientific papers must be dull and boring. There is no reason, however, why writing or reading a scientific report must be an exercise in tedium. True, writing a research report requires that you discuss technical details and complicated issues. It does not follow, however, that your discussion of these details has to be boring. With practice and attention to style, you can prepare a text that captivates the interest and attention of a serious reader.

Focus means that there is a clear purpose for the paper and definite boundaries established for what you will and will not discuss. Some writers fall into the trap of covering too many topics. Consequently, their papers are rambling expositions of many unrelated topics. For a research report, you should focus on your research questions.

The second attribute of good writing is organization, the sequence of arguments that you present. In a well-written paper, each paragraph sets the stage for the next paragraph. As the reader works through the paper, he or she will experience a logical presentation of your ideas that leads to a series of reasonable conclusions.

Finally, good writing integrates information into a coherent message. All writing, even of research reports, is storytelling. Your job as a writer is to bring together a series of facts and observations and show the reader how these relate to each other. Listing all the means, standard deviations, and results of the inferential statistics is not integration. Far more interesting is learning how the results of your research relate to your hypothesis.

ELEMENTS OF APA STYLE

The APA developed its editorial style to promote good writing and to establish a consistent format for presenting the results of research for the behavioral sciences. The editorial style and format are extremely popular. Most professional journals in education, psychology, and sociology require that authors use these guidelines. In this section, we will review several of the fundamental features of APA style.

Issues of Style

Writing a research report requires that you strive for accuracy, brevity, and clarity. You will find that writing and reading a research report is much different from doing so with other forms of writing. I do not wish to imply that one form of writing is better than another, only that different styles serve different purposes. Consider an example from the opening pages of Mark Twain's (1876) *The Adventures of Tom Sawyer,* wherein Twain describes Aunt Polly.

> The old lady pulled her spectacles down and looked over them about the room; then she put them up and looked under them. She seldom or never looked through them for so small a thing as a boy; they were her state pair, the pride of her heart, and were built for "style" not service— she could have seen through a pair of stove-lids just as well. (p. 9)

In this vivid passage, Twain used metaphor and other literary devices to introduce the reader to Aunt Polly. Twain used the glasses to describe Aunt Polly's personality and her relation to Tom. Although these and many other techniques make for good literature, they are not appropriate for technical writing. In research reports, literary techniques such as metaphor, ironic use of words, and intentional ambiguity are distractions. These literary devices require too much inference and subjective interpretation on the part of the reader. Therefore, you should avoid using metaphor (e.g., "Currently, Freud's theories of personality *fly as well as a lead balloon*"), colloquial expressions (e.g., "After *quite a long time,* the effects of the independent variable *kicked in*"), and opaque jargon and euphemistic phrases (e.g., "The individual's behavior created much *collateral disruption* among *interrelated members of the domestic unit*").

Compare the passage from *Tom Sawyer,* with the opening paragraph of an article by Allumbaugh and Hoyt (1999),

> Over 2 million people die in the United States every year (U. S. Bureau of the Census, 1995). For each person who dies, there are numerous people left behind to grieve, many of whom seek help from a therapist. Loss and grief are universal human experiences. The recently bereaved represent a large at-risk population, with higher overall death and suicide rates than age-matched control participants and with an increased incidence of depression, substance abuse, and certain medical disorders. (p. 307)

This paragraph is clear and direct. The authors presented a series of facts that make clear that they have selected an important topic. Furthermore, it does not take a vivid imagination to interpret the meaning of this paragraph. The authors made clear that the death of a person creates grief that can have severe psychological and medical consequences.

Writing for an Audience

You may have learned in a composition course that you should always consider your audience when writing. This advice applies to writing a research report as well. Thus, who is your audience?

The simple answer is your instructor. A better answer, however, is that your audience is a behavioral scientist who understands general principles in the discipline, but who may not be an expert on the topic you chose to study. Knowing your audience should help you determine what you do and do not have to explain to the reader. Because the audience consists of fellow researchers, you can assume that they understand general issues in the discipline, basic research design, and statistical tests. For example, if you use a factorial ANOVA to analyze the data, you will not have to explain the difference between a main effect and an interaction. You can also assume that the reader understands the logic of conventional statistical tests.

Although the reader may understand basic principles, you cannot assume that the reader knows the history and the important questions that are a part of your research. Look again at the Allumbaugh and Hoyt (1999) paragraph. They have few preconceived notions concerning what the reader knows about grief or grief therapy. Although some readers may find the authors' comments obvious, I appreciated that they made clear that grieving can have serious mental and physical health consequences. As I read the rest of the introduction, I learned many things about the history of grief therapy and how different therapies help people overcome the emotional trauma wrought by a loved one's death.

Value-Free Descriptions of Others

The APA has long discouraged biased descriptions of people or groups of people. Biased writing is any description of an irrelevant characteristic of a group of people or of a person. Sexist language, for example, implies that there is a meaningful difference between men and women when one does not exist or draws attention to one's sex when the attention is not necessary. Consider the word "mothering." One connotation of the word refers to caring for others; another connotation is being overly protective. Mothering is a sexist term because both men and women have the capacity to care for others and to be overly protective. Therefore, "parenting," "nurturing," and "protectiveness" are words that avoid linking the underlying behavior to one sex and are thereby value free.

There is no need to refer to a characteristic of a person or group of people unless that trait is the focus of the research. In these instances, the descriptive term should be objective. Select words and phrases that describe the relevant characteristic of the individual's behavior, not the person. Therefore, we replace the terms "fireman," "mailman," and "waitress" with "firefighter," "mail carrier," and "server." The new words and phrases describe the work of the individual without implying their sex.

There are traps you should avoid when writing gender-neutral sentences. Some people use "s/he," or "he/she," or "him/her" to avoid sexist language. Most readers find these alternatives to be well meaning but ungraceful. Fortunately, there are two ways you can avoid this lexical faux pas. First, you can convert the single noun to a plural noun (e.g., change "Each *participant* received *his* . . ." to "The *participants* received *their* . . ."). This option has the advantage of being simple to implement and does not change the meaning of the sentence. The second option is to use the singular noun and use "his or her," "he or she," or an equivalent. The only time you can use a gender specific noun, pronoun, or adjective is when the behavior is clearly sex specific (e.g., "Each woman completed the survey soon after learning that she was pregnant.").

We also extend the editorial policy regarding sexist language to the people who participate in our research or who are afflicted with a psychological or medical condition. Therefore, the APA editorial guideline recommends that we use descriptive nouns to describe the people in our research. All the people in our research are "participants." You can also use nouns such as "children," "college students," "parents," "clients," "individuals," and "respondents" to refer to the participants in the study. Similarly, a diagnosis of a psychological or medical disorder describes the condition of a person, not the person. For example, people are not "schizophrenic," "autistic," or "depressive." Rather, people receive a diagnosis of schizophrenia, autism, or depression based on their cognition and behavior. Just as we avoid sexist language by describing the behavior, we avoid biased language by describing the disability. Consequently, researchers refer to "people diagnosed with schizophrenia," "individuals with low self-esteem," or "individuals who are developmentally delayed." People are not "senior citizens" or "elderly," they are people "over the age of 65" or "over the age of 85."

Integrating Numbers and Text

Table 16.1 presents the general rules governing the use of numbers. Most of the rules are straightforward. A few, however, require special comment. For example, APA style

TABLE 16.1

General rules for reporting numbers in an APA-style paper

- Use numbers to express values equal to or greater than 10.
  Of the people responding, five were engaged to be married.
  Each questionnaire contained 15 questions.

- Use numbers when the value precedes a unit of measurement.
  The dimensions of the floor were 4.5 m × 5.2 m.

- Use numbers when the value is a part of a noun.
  The extinction session began on Trial 5.
  Table 1 and Figure 1 present the results of Experiment 1.

- Use words when the value begins the sentence.
  Fourteen people refused to complete the task.

- Use numbers when the sentence contains several related numbers and at least one is equal to or greater than 10.
  Participants received reinforcement on the first and fifth trials.
  We used the 5th, 8th, and 15th sessions as probe trials.
  All 15 participants completed the 4 questionnaires.

- To make a number plural, add *s* or *es* as necessary. Do not use an apostrophe.
  Skinner's perspectives became popular in the late 1960s and early 1970s.
  Many people believe that tragedies come in threes.

- Use numbers to represent statistical results, fractions, mathematical functions, or the results of mathematical equations.
  Of the participants returning the questionnaire, 63% indicated favoring Option 1.
  We multiplied each score by 4 to equate the groups.

- If a number cannot exceed 1.0, do not use a leading 0 before the decimal point.
  The average reaction time was 0.851 s for the control group and 1.032 s for the experimental group.
  There was a statistically significant correlation between the variables, $r(57) = -.76$, $p < .05$.

TABLE 16.2

Common measurement scale and conversion from tradition to metric units

Scale	Traditional unit	Metric equivalent	Abbreviation	Conversion
Area				
	square foot	square meter	m^2	$m^2 = .09290304 \times foot^2$
	square inch	square millimeter	mm^2	$cm^2 = 645.16 \times inch^2$
Length				
	foot	meter	m	$m = 0.3048 \times foot$
	inch	centimeter	cm	$cm = 2.54 \times inch$
	fraction of inch	millimeter	mm	$mm = .254 \times inch$
	yard	meter	m	$m = 0.9144 \times yard$
Mass				
	ounce	gram	g	$g = 28.34952 \times ounce$
	fraction of ounce	milligram	mg	$mg = 2.834952 \times ounce$
	pound	kilogram	kg	$kg = .45359237 \times pound$
Temperature				
	Fahrenheit	Celsius	°C	$°C = (°F - 32) \times 5/9$
Volume				
	cubic foot	cubic meter	m^3	$m^3 = .02831685 \times foot^3$
	cubic inch	cubic centimeter	cm^3	$cm^3 = 16.38706 \times inch^3$
	fluid ounce	milliliter	ml	$ml = 29.57353 \times f. ounce$
	quart	liter	L	$L = .9463529 \times quart$
Time				
	hours		h	
	minutes		m	
	seconds		s	
	milliseconds		ms	$ms = 1/1000 s$

recommends using the metric system and the International System of Units for reporting specific quantities. Table 16.2 includes a short list of common measures and the method of converting from traditional to metric units.

SPECIAL GRAMMATICAL ISSUES

For the most part, the APA editorial guidelines follow conventional rules of grammar. Thus, what you learned in English composition courses concerning subject-verb agreement, dangling modifiers, and other elements of grammar apply to writing a research report. The APA editorial guidelines also emphasize several grammatical conventions that require extra attention.

Active versus Passive Voice

Active and passive voice refers to the order of the subject, verb, and object of the sentence. Active voice sentences place greater emphasis on the subject, or the actor, of the sentence than the object of the sentence. In an active voice sentence the subject precedes the verb. Consequently, active voice sentences make clear who or what is responsible for the outcome. By contrast, in a passive voice sentence, the object comes before the verb. Passive voice sentences are, therefore, more difficult to interpret. Examples of active voice sentences are:

Mary$_{(subject)}$ caught$_{(verb)}$ the football$_{(object)}$.

The participants completed the questionnaire during the first phase of the study.

Examples of passive voice sentences are:

The football$_{(object)}$ was caught$_{(verb)}$ by Mary$_{(subject)}$.

The questionnaires were completed by the participants during the first phase of the study.

The APA editorial style manual recommends using the active voice sentence. There are two advantages to this convention. First, active voice sentences clearly identify who or what is responsible for the outcome. In passive voice sentences, the cause is either hidden at the end of the sentence or missing. Second, active voice sentences tend to use fewer words and are thereby easier to read and understand.

As another component of active voice, you may identify yourself using personal pronouns (e.g., I or we). The goal of active voice is to make clear who did what to whom. For example, we can revise the passive voice sentence from:

The experiment was designed using the Solomon four-group control procedure.

to

We used the Solomon four-group control procedure for the experiment.

Past and Present Tense

The APA editorial style manual requires the past tense when referring to the work of another author and the data presented in the current report. As an example, you might write, "Freud (1917/1957) believed . . ." or "Freud (1917/1957) argued . . ." because Freud expressed his beliefs long before you began to write your paper. Similarly, you would use the past tense to describe the data you collected. Accordingly, you might write:

The current results confirmed the hypothesis.

or

As expected, there was a significant interaction among the treatment conditions.

When you describe an event or action that did not occur at a specific time, or if the condition remains, you may use the present perfect tense. Examples of the present perfect tense are:

Since the late 1940s, psychologists have used the ANOVA and other inferential statistical techniques for their research.

and

Psychologists have long had an interest in the biological foundations of behavior.

Proper Use of Pronouns

The APA editorial style manual emphasizes specific rules concerning the use of pronouns. Other editorial guidelines (e.g., of the Modern Language Association) do not emphasize these conventions. Therefore, you should pay special attention to this section.

Who versus that

When speaking of humans, and especially individual people, use pronouns such as *who, him,* or *her*. When speaking of nonhumans, use the neuter pronoun *that*. To illustrate the difference, you would write, "The children *who* participated in the study . . ." or "The dogs *that* Pavlov studied . . . ." Similarly, you should write, "The psychologist *who* administered the test . . ." because a psychologist is a person.

That versus which

That and which are relative pronouns that have specific uses. Use *that* in clauses essential to the meaning of a sentence. In the sentence, "Much of the research that psychologists conducted in the past 30 years emphasized the social-cognitive perspective of personality," the reference to the past 30 years is essential to the meaning of the sentence and is, therefore, a restrictive clause.

Use the relative pronoun *which* when the clause is not essential to the meaning of the sentence. For instance, "Gestalt therapy, which focuses on the client's emotions, became popular in the 1970s." The nonrestrictive clause adds information to the sentence, but does not change its meaning. If you can remove the clause without changing the meaning of the sentence, the clause is nonrestrictive (cf., "Gestalt therapy became popular in the 1970s"). Many people tend to use "which" and "that" indiscriminately. Consequently, Strunk and White (1979) recommended that authors go on a "which hunt" when proofreading their work.

Vague pronouns

All style guides warn against the use of vague pronouns. Unfortunately, many people continue to use the pronouns "this," "that," "these," and "those" without an obvious referent. Consider the following passage:

> Many surveys have consistently demonstrated that most people endorse the stereotype that men make better leaders than women. This may prevent women from being promoted to positions of authority. That is an example of the "glass-ceiling" phenomenon.

What do "This" and "That" refer to in the second and third sentences? Does the second sentence mean that the results of the survey prevent women's promotions, or is it the stereotype that creates the barrier? For both sentences, the pronoun has no clear referent. Consequently, the object, or referent, in the sentences is vague. A few simple modifications can clarify these sentences.

> Several surveys of people's attitudes have consistently demonstrated that most people endorse the stereotype that men make better leaders than women. Belief in these stereotypes may cause employers to promote men, but not women, to positions of authority. This discrimination is an example of the "glass-ceiling" phenomenon.

Commonly misused words

Some authors use specific words indiscriminately and incorrectly. Box 16.1 lists many of these commonly misused words and indicates their correct use. As you proofread your manuscript, look out for these problem terms; many spelling and grammar checkers built into word processors overlook these words.

BOX 16.1   Commonly Misused Words

Affect
vs.
Effect

Affect means to influence or to cause a change.
- The independent variable affected the subjects' behavior.

Effect represents the result or the consequence of something.
- There were large treatment effects in the experimental groups.

Among
vs.
Between

Use *among* when discussing more than two people or objects.
- There were minor differences among the 30 participants.

Use *between* when discussing only two people or objects.
- There are minor differences between Hull's and Spence's theories.

Amount

vs.

Number

Use *amount* to refer to a general quantity.
- The amount of reinforcement each participant received depended on the schedule of reinforcement.

Number refers to countable items.
- The number of clients seeking treatment decreased after six months.

Data

Data is the plural form of datum. As a rule, nouns ending with 'a' are plural (i.e., phenomenon vs. phenomena or criterion vs. criteria).
- The data are consistent with the theory.

Ensure

vs.

Insure

vs.

Assure

Ensure refers to procedures that minimize the occurrence of some event.
- We called all participants to ensure that they would return for the second part of the experiment.

Insure refers specifically to the protection against financial loss.
- We instructed the clients to save 10% of their weekly income to insure against possible layoffs from the factory.

Assure means to convince, persuade, or to affirm a pledge.
- The researcher assured the participants that the results of the study would be confidential.

Few
vs.
Little

Few refers to a countable quantity of objects.
- Few people continue to question the importance of this theory.

Little refers to a general quantity.
- The research attracted little attention when first published.

Its
vs.
It's

Its is a possessive pronoun.
- The value of this theory is its ability to make novel predictions.

It's is a contraction of "it is." Never use contractions in technical writing.

That

vs.

Which

That is a relative pronoun used in clauses essential to the meaning of the sentence.
- The author reviewed the evidence that supports Miller's theory.

Use *which* in clauses that are not essential to the meaning of the sentence, but provide additional information.
- The real purpose of the experiment, which the researcher did not tell the participants, was to determine the degree to which people will conform to behavior of a role model.

Utilize
vs.
Use

Utilize is a transitive verb that adds little to a sentence; *use* is sufficient in most cases.

BOX 16.1   *Continued*

While vs.	*While* refers to the simultaneous passage of time for two or more linked events. • While the subjects were involved in filling out the questionnaire, the confederate began to perform various distracting behaviors.
Since vs.	*Since* refers to the passage of time between the past and present. • Since Snyder published his paper in 1974, many researchers have become interested in the self-monitoring construct.
Although vs.	*Although* refers to a contradiction with a statement or fact. • Many people believe in extrasensory perception although psychologists have long questioned the existence of the phenomenon.
Because	Use *because* to indicate the reason for some condition or event. • The external validity of the experiment is questionable because the researcher did not use a random selection procedure.

ACADEMIC INTEGRITY

Academic integrity means that you give complete and fair credit to the sources of the ideas you incorporate in your paper. As a rule, if you state a fact, share an observation, or report the conclusion of another writer you need to acknowledge the origin of that idea. Following this rule allows you to avoid accusations of plagiarism.

Plagiarism comes from a Latin word meaning to kidnap. Thus, someone who plagiarizes steals ideas from others. Most colleges have strict rules against and penalties for plagiarism. Depending on your college's academic policies, you may receive a failing grade for the assignment or the course if the instructor discovers that you have plagiarized.

There are many forms of plagiarism. The most obvious is copying another author's words and presenting them as yours. Other forms of plagiarism may not be as obvious, but are just as wrong. For example, presenting another person's ideas as yours without citing the source is plagiarism. We can use the following passage to look at different forms of plagiarism. Allumbaugh and Hoyt (1999) wrote:

> It is commonly assumed in the psychotherapeutic community that for at least some bereaved individuals, some form of psychotherapy is useful or even necessary to assist in recovering from loss, and numerous theoretical frameworks have been proposed for psychotherapists working with bereaved clients. (p. 370)

What if a student wrote the following sentence?

> Many psychologists believe that some form of psychotherapy is useful and necessary to assist bereaved clients to recover from the loss. Consequently, there are many psychotherapies designed to help bereaved clients.

This passage is an example of plagiarism for several reasons. Although the writer changed a few words and phrases, many of Allumbaugh and Hoyt's (1999) original words remain in the sentence. All the writer has done is a form of editorial recycling. Furthermore, the writer has not credited Allumbaugh and Hoyt's work. To avoid the accusation of plagiarism, the writer should write something like the following sentence:

> According to Allumbaugh and Hoyt (1999), many psychologists believe that psychotherapy can help some people overcome bereavement grief and have created special therapies for this condition.

This sentence gives clear credit to the origin of the idea and is a major revision of the original text.

Citations of Sources in the Text

From the preceding examples, you can see that the APA editorial guidelines require that you credit other's work directly in the body of the text by listing the authors of the source and the date of publication. There are two general methods for citing a source. The first is to include the author's name in the sentence. For this procedure, list the name or names of the authors; include the date of the citation within parentheses.

> Braver and Braver (1988) recommended a meta-analytic procedure for examining the data of a Solomon four-group research design.

The alternative is to treat the citation as a parenthetical statement.

> Some authors (e.g., Braver & Braver, 1988) have argued that psychologists too often overlook the Solomon four-group design.

The ampersand (&) replaces the "and" when placing the references in the parentheses. Box 16.2 presents examples of how to incorporate citations in the text.

Use of et al.

When the reference includes between three and five names, list all the names the first time you refer to the source. For subsequent references to the same source, list the name of the first author followed by the phrase "et al." (which means "and others"). If there are six or more authors in the source, list the first name followed with et al. for all references to the citation.

Listing dates of citations

When you refer to a citation, you must include the date of publication. This practice helps the reader keep track of the different sources you use. The exception is if you refer to the same citation more than once within a paragraph. If you refer to the same citation more than once in a paragraph, include the date with the first citation only. For example,

> Kohn (2000) is a critic of standardized testing commonly used in primary and secondary education. Kohn's primary concern is the emphasis on test scores rather than . . .
>   Much of the research that Kohn (2000) cites reflects . . .

The first paragraph begins with a citation of the date of Kohn's book. The next sentence refers to the same book, but does not include the date. In the second paragraph, however, we include the date of Kohn's book in keeping with the editorial rule.

BOX 16.2 Examples of Citations Within the Text of a Manuscript

Single author/single citation

List the author's last name followed by the date of publication.

- Smith (1998) examined the effects of delayed reinforcement.
- A recent study of delayed reinforcement (Smith, 1998) demonstrated . . .

Single author/multiple citations

List the author's last name followed by the dates of the individual publications

- Smith's research (1996, 1998, 1999) demonstrates that . . .
- Recent research on this topic (Smith, 1996, 1998, 1999) . . .

Two or more authors/single citation

If there are two authors, list both names followed by the date of publication. Use an ampersand when the citation is within the parentheses.

- Allumbaugh and Hoyt (1999) examined the effectiveness of . . .
- In a recent review of grief therapies (Allumbaugh & Hoyt, 1999) . . .

If there are three to five names, list all the names in the first citation. On subsequent citations, list the name of the first author followed with "et al." and the date.

First citation:

- Gutek, Bhappu, Liao-Trouth, and Cherry (1999) examined . . .
- Recent research examining service relationships (Gutek, Bhappu, Liao-Trouth, & Cherry, 1999) . . .

Subsequent citations:

- The Gutek et al. (1999) study indicated . . .
- Several tests of this construct exist (Gutek et al., 1999).

If there are six or more names, list only the first name followed by "et al." and the date.

Multiple citations

If you include several citations from different authors in the same parentheses, list the citations alphabetically by the authors' names. Separate the citations with a semicolon.

- Several studies (Allen, 1980, 1981, 1985; Babcock & Wilcox, 1993; Collins & Zager, 1972) . . .

Translated work

If the original work was translated into English, list the author's name, the date of the original publication, and the date of the translated publication

- Freud (1913/1952) developed the theory of screen memory . . .

Corporate author

List the name of the organization followed by the date of publication.

- Sleep disorders are a common symptom of depression (American Psychiatric Association, 1994).

Newspaper or magazine article with no author

List a short version of the title followed by the date of publication.

- The popular press often sensationalizes psychological research (IQ tests measure nothing, 1999).

Additional Comments on Quotations

Ralph Waldo Emerson quipped, "I hate quotations. Tell me what you know." You should adopt the same attitude when you write a research report. Researchers rarely use quotations because the focus of the research paper is an analysis of ideas, not how the original author expressed them. Your responsibility, as the author of the paper, is to read the work of others and then synthesize that work into a concise statement that supports your argument.

There are at least two instances when you can and should use quotations. First, use a quotation when it is impossible to paraphrase a passage without losing its meaning. For example, you may find that you cannot paraphrase another author's definition of a particular term or concept without altering its meaning. These instances are rare, and you should avoid the temptation of assuming that you cannot put complex ideas into your words.

The more appropriate occasion for using a quotation occurs when the author's ideas and expression of those ideas is the focus of your argument. Imagine that you are writing a paper wherein you examined the effects of positive reinforcement on intrinsic motivation. As a part of your paper, you want to illustrate how another author expressed his or her opinion. You could write something like the following:

> By contrast, some authors believe that positive reinforcement reduces intrinsic motivation. These authors typically make the unqualified claim that reinforcement has detrimental rather than beneficial effects. For example, Kohn (1993) asserted, "But the use of rewards for reading, writing, drawing, acting responsibly and generously, and so on is cause for concern. *Extrinsic motivators are most dangerous when offered for something we want children to want to do"* (p. 87). This sentiment is common . . .

In this case, the quotation is evidence that supports your argument. Using the quote allows you to share with the reader Kohn's tone and sentiment regarding the effects of reinforcement.

If you must use a quotation, try to keep it short. I selected only a few sentences from Kohn's book to illustrate the point I wanted to make. In addition, you should reproduce the quotation exactly as it appeared in its original form. In this example, several words are italicized because they were italicized in the original text. If I had added the italics, I would have included the following note after the italics: "[italics added]". If you drop words or sentences from the original text, replace the missing words with ellipsis points (. . .).

If the length of the quotation is fewer than 40 words, include the quotation as a part of the sentence. For longer quotations, set the material off as a separate indented paragraph. As an example:

> By contrast, some authors believe that positive reinforcement reduces intrinsic motivation. These authors typically make the unqualified claim that reinforcement has detrimental rather than beneficial effects. For example, Kohn (1990) asserted,
>
> > But not only are rewards less effective than intrinsic motivation—they actually undermine it. You started out doing something just because you found it fun. But once you were rewarded for doing it, you came to see yourself as working mostly to get the reward. Your fascination with the task *mysteriously vanished* [italics added] along the way and now you can't be bothered to do it unless there's some reward at stake. (p. 32)
>
> This sentiment is common . . .

I indented the longer quote and separated it from the rest of the paragraph. The example also shows how you can add emphasis to the quotation to draw the reader's attention to a specific phrase in the passage. Whenever you add one of these editorial notes, place them within brackets. For example, to indicate a misspelling in the original text, use "[sic]".

Keep your use of quotations to a minimum. Most professors do not like to read papers that are nothing more than a long collection of quotations embroidered together with a few transitional sentences from the student. Tell the reader what you know. Your work is far more interesting to read than a string of quotations.

PARTS OF THE RESEARCH REPORT

Each research report contains the same elements including the title page, abstract, introduction, method section, results section, discussion section, and references section. In the following pages, we will review the material that goes into each of these sections, along with several additional issues related to APA editorial style.

There are several conventions for formatting a research report in APA style. Box 16.3 lists the general rules for formatting your paper. Most people now use word processors to prepare their papers and find it easy to use the program's setup and formatting options to prepare an APA-style paper. An example of an APA-style research report can be found at the end of this chapter.

Title Page

The title page includes four elements—the running head, the title of the paper, the names of the researchers, and their professional affiliations. The running head, or header, is a short version of the title of the paper and appears at the upper right corner of each page along with the page number. Most word processors allow you to include a running head or header. In addition, the program will allow you to insert the page number as a part of the header.

BOX 16.3   Checklist for Formatting and General Construction

- Set all margins to 1 inch.
- Left justify all text except the title of the paper and the words identifying the start of the major sections.
- Double-space everything. All the text, regardless of section, is double-spaced.
- Running head and page numbers begin on title page and run throughout the entire text. The only pages that do not have the running head and page numbers are the figures.
- Print all text in the same font and size (10 pt. or 12 pt.). Use an easy to read font (e.g., Courier or Times New Roman).
- Insert a single space after each word and punctuation mark including commas, semicolons, and periods.

The first line on the title page consists of the phrase "Running head:" and a short version of the title printed in capital letters. Typically, the running head is an abbreviated version of the title. According to APA style guidelines, the running head cannot be more than 50 characters counting letters, spaces, and punctuation.

Most titles are between 10 and 12 words. Writing a good title requires careful planning. You can get a good impression of how to write your title by looking at the titles or the articles you use in your reference section. Your title should be a short and self-explanatory description of the research. For example, the title "A Study of Human Memory" tells the reader nothing about the purpose of the research as it describes almost any research project on memory. By contrast, the title "A Study Showing That Writing Essays About Traumatic Events in One's Life Helps Reduce Feelings of Anxiety and Guilt Among College Students Who Were Abused As Children" is too long. Examples of better titles are "Proactive Interference in the Memory of Pictures" and "Writing as a Means for Reducing Anxiety and Guilt."

Center the title horizontally on the page. Capitalize the first letter of each major word in the title (you do not need to capitalize smaller words and articles such as *the, and, is, in, of,* and similar words). Do not use abbreviations in the title.

On the line immediately following the title and centered horizontally on the page is your name. Use your full given name rather than nicknames. The following line, also centered, contains the name of your college.

Abstract

The abstract is a short (no more than 120 words) description of the research. Readers use the abstract of a research article to determine whether the article interests them and deserves their attention. Therefore, useful abstracts briefly describe the purpose of the research, the population under study, the method used to collect the data, the primary findings, and the researcher's primary conclusions. Study the abstracts of the research articles you used for the literature review; they will serve as good models to follow.

Introduction

The objectives for writing the introduction are to capture the reader's interest and offer a compelling overview and a rationale for the research. As I noted previously, you should consider the reader to be a well-informed behavioral scientist who may or may not know much about the phenomenon that you chose to study. Consequently, your introduction must help the reader understand the phenomenon and why there is a need for more research.

Although there is no set formula for writing an introduction, you can follow some useful guidelines. Figure 16.1 presents such a guide. Think of your introduction as an inverted triangle. The paper begins with a broad statement of the general problem. As you progress through the introduction, you should focus the text on issues directly related to your research project. In the literature review section, you can describe the findings and conclusions drawn from previous research. This portion of the introduction allows you to help the reader learn about the focus of your study and the necessity for the research. Finally, you

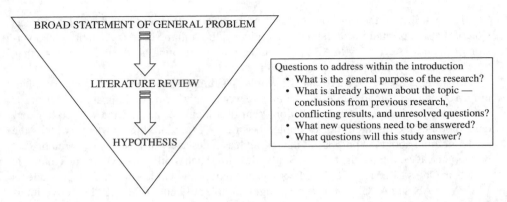

FIGURE 16.1
Inverted triangle model of the introduction.

should end the introduction with a review of the hypothesis or hypotheses that you will examine.

We can use a published article to illustrate the application of this inverted triangle. Eisenberger and Armeli (1997) conducted a set of experiments that examined the effects of positive reinforcement on intrinsic motivation. The opening sentence of their introduction was:

> Over the past quarter century, the view that reward reduces task interest and creativity (Eisenberger & Cameron, 1996) has become widely accepted. (p. 652)

This sentence is a broad introduction to a familiar topic in psychology. In the paragraphs that followed, Eisenberger and Armeli showed the reader that many psychologists and educators believe that positive reinforcement has many negative effects on intrinsic motivation and creativity. After establishing this fact, Eisenberger and Armeli narrowed the focus of their paper with the following sentence:

> Despite these limitations of the behavioral studies, the generally accepted conclusion that reward has inherent detrimental effects on creativity may be premature. (p. 653)

This sentence makes clear that Eisenberger and Armeli do not accept the negative effects of reinforcement as a foregone conclusion. With this transition, the authors began a review of research that suggests that reinforcement does increase creativity and does not harm intrinsic motivation.

Another transitional sentence that narrowed the focus of the introduction was:

> Learned industriousness theory holds that if an individual is rewarded for putting a large amount of cognitive or physical effort into an activity, the sensation of high effort acquires secondary reward properties that lessen, to some degree, effort's innate aversiveness. (p. 654)

With this sentence, Eisenberger and Armeli introduced the theory of learned industriousness and summarized that the theory predicts that reinforcement will increase rather than decrease creativity. The authors then devoted several paragraphs to describing the theory and the supporting research. In these paragraphs, the authors narrowed the scope of the paper to where they could state the purpose of the research. The concluding paragraph of the introduction was:

> In sum, the present research tested two implications of learned industriousness theory: (a) that making explicit the requirement of novel performance for obtaining a large monetary reward in one task should increase the subsequent creativity of performance in an entirely different task and (b) that a decremental effect of reward on intrinsic creative interest should occur with reward for uncreative performance, but not with reward for creative performance. (p. 655)

In 26 paragraphs, Eisenberger and Armeli led the reader through a broad introduction of the problem and a review of previous research and current theory and delivered the reader a concise statement of the purpose of the research and their predictions.

Method Section

The method section provides the reader with a detailed description of how you collected the data for your research. The goal of writing the method section is to allow the reader to evaluate the appropriateness of your data collection techniques. This information will help the reader understand how the data relate to the research hypothesis and evaluate the internal and external validity of your conclusions. Most method sections have three subsections in which you describe how you created the sample you studied, the materials and equipment used to collect the data, and the specific procedures for the study.

Participants/Subjects

The first subsection is the participants or subjects section. If your population is humans, then the title of the subsection is participants. By contrast, if you use nonhuman animals, then the title of the section is subjects. Whatever its name, you will use this subsection to tell the reader the relevant details of your sample and how it was created.

As you learned in chapter 8, sampling is a critical component of any research project. Consequently, you need to define the sampling population and the procedures for creating the sample. Similarly, you need to define the relevant characteristics of the sample. The purpose of your research usually dictates the characteristics of the sample that you should describe. At the very least, you need to indicate the number of men and women in the study as well as the average age of the participants. If your research depends upon specific subject variables, then you should summarize those characteristics as well.

In addition to indicating how you recruited and selected the participants, you should describe whether and how you compensated the individuals. Similarly, you should indicate whether and why you lost the data for any member of the original sample. Mistakes happen. Sometimes the equipment does not work, the researcher makes a mistake, or the participant does not understand the instructions or refuses to complete the study. Report errors like these if they occur. For example, you may have to write, "Of the 120 surveys distributed, 5 could not be scored due to incomplete responses" or "The data for three participants could not be used because of a malfunctioning computer."

If you used nonhuman subjects, report the relevant subject variables including the genus and species name, strain number (if appropriate), supplier or breeder of the animals, and a detailed description of the housing and handling procedures. As with human research, you should then describe additional subject variables that related to the purpose of your research.

Materials/Apparatus

The materials or apparatus subsection includes the description of the devices you used to collect the data. As with all parts of the method section, your description of the materials must be sufficient for another researcher to repeat the research. Because the research report is a short document, you cannot describe every nuance of the materials. Rather, this section should offer the reader a short account of the materials and where you acquired them.

Specialized apparatus. There is no need to describe standard laboratory equipment (e.g., videotape recorders, stopwatches, or projectors) readily available to any researcher. By contrast, if the equipment is highly specialized, then you should indicate the name of the manufacturer and model number of the device. Similarly, if you built a special apparatus for the research, you should offer a brief description of the equipment. Depending on the sophistication of the device, you may want to include a scale drawing of the apparatus.

Tests and questionnaires. You can treat tests and questionnaires the same way you treat a piece of equipment. If you used a published test, then you should include a brief overview of the test (e.g., number of questions and measurement scale used) as well as a reference to the original source of the test. Most researchers also include a reference to research that has evaluated the reliability and validity of the test. If you created your test or questionnaire, you should describe the general nature of the questions included in the survey.

Procedure

The last part of the method section describes the sequence of significant events the participants experienced in the research. Consequently, you should describe how you assigned participants to various conditions of the research as well as your control procedures. You should also describe the instructions you gave the participants.

In some cases, the procedure section may indicate that you distributed a questionnaire to randomly selected classes of students after you had described the purpose of the research. In other cases, the procedure section will be long as there were a series of important stages in the research that require description. Remember, the goal of the method section is to allow your readers to evaluate the quality of your data collection procedure and repeat the study if they so choose.

Results Section

The results section presents your summary of the data and a description of the statistical tests you used to examine the data. This section, like the method section, tends to be expository, or fact oriented. Specifically, you will use this section to lay before the reader the major findings of the research. By contrast, the discussion section allows you to evaluate the broader implications of your data.

The outline of the results section should follow the outline you used to describe the research questions in the introduction. Begin your results section with the general predictions you made for your study. For each hypothesis, you can begin with a general description of the results followed by the specific statistical tests used to confirm your hypothesis.

There is no reason that you must stick to the path implied by your introduction. If you have carefully examined the data, you may find interesting patterns in the data that you did not expect to observe. These serendipitous results can often reveal interesting insights into the phenomenon that you are studying and raise important questions for additional research.

As you prepare your results section, there are a number of editorial questions that you must confront including, "What is the best way to summarize the data?," "How much detail do I need to include?," and "How do I present the results of specific statistical tests?"

There are many ways to summarize the data. Most researchers use a combination of narrative, simple and descriptive statistics, and graphs and tables. Combining these techniques will help the reader quickly understand your primary findings and how the data relate to your research questions. The narrative is relatively straightforward. You describe in words the primary findings of the study with respect to each hypothesis. In many cases, you will find that a table or a graph will do much to augment your description of the data and help the reader visualize the results.

Graphs

Most statistics textbooks (e.g., Runyon, Coleman, & Pittenger, 2000) have extensive reviews of how to prepare good-quality scientific graphs. Therefore, I will only highlight the essentials of a good graph. Figure 16.2 presents a prototype of a good graph.

Graphs for research reports have several distinguishing features. The first significant feature is simplicity. Good graphs contain only essential visual information and are free of distracting and unessential information. For example, many popular computer programs allow you to use 3-D effects, fancy shading, and other features that add little information to the graph and can make the graph difficult to interpret.

Consider Figure 16.3, which contains many unnecessary and distracting elements. Tufte (1983) called much of the unnecessary graphic elements in this graph "chartjunk." Chartjunk refers to anything in the graph that adds nothing to the interpretation of the data.

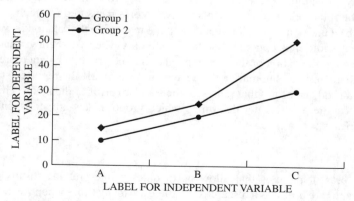

FIGURE 16.2
A line graph and the essential elements contained in any scientific graph.

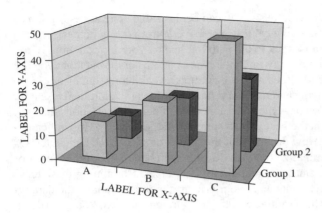

FIGURE 16.3
A graph with much chartjunk. The 3-D effect, shading, and background grid are unnecessary elements of the graph that are distracting and should not be used.

For example, the 3-D effect adds nothing to the display of the information. I find Figure 16.2 far easier to interpret than Figure 16.3.

As a generality, APA-style graphs should be drawn in 2-D and be as simple as possible. Other conventions include that the vertical or y-axis presents the dependent variable whereas the horizontal or x-axis presents the independent variable. The lines or bars in the graph should clearly represent the pattern of the data and not be confused with distracting information.

There is considerable art and science in constructing good graphs, far more than I can describe here. If you want to learn more about preparing good scientific graphs, I strongly recommend the works of Kosslyn (1994), Tufte (1983, 1990), and Wainer (1997). These authors make clear that graphs have a grammar, syntax, and style of their own.

The most commonly used graphs are bar graphs, scatter plots, and line graphs. Figure 16.4 presents an illustration of each. Use bar graphs when the independent variable represents a nominal or categorical scale. Scatter plots present the correlation between two variables. Finally, line graphs present the relation among two or more quantitative variables.

For scatter plots, each dot represents the two scores measured for each participant. In Figure 16.4(b), I added a regression line to help the reader see the relation between the two variables. This addition is optional. Use the option only when you believe that it helps the reader understand the data. For the bar graph and the line graph, the data represent the descriptive statistic used to summarize the dependent variable. If the reported statistic is the mean, you can add error lines that represent the standard error of the mean. This additional information can help the reader determine which group means are statistically different from other means.

Tables

Graphs present pictures that allow us to quickly interpret the results of the data. Although graphs are useful as a research tool, there are many times when we need to present numbers. Constructing useful and easy to read tables is like constructing good graphs. There are some simple rules to follow that will help you present your data well. Ehrenberg (1977) identified six basic features for constructing good tables.

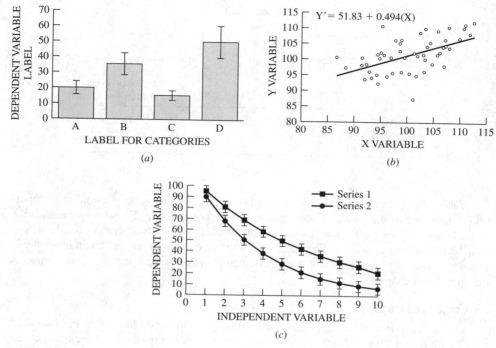

FIGURE 16.4
(a) Bar graph, (b) scatter plot, and (c) line graph. For the bar graph, the heights of the bars represent the statistic used to describe the dependent variable. The lines extending from the bars are optional and represent the standard error of the mean or some other measure of variability that help the reader interpret the difference among the means. For the scatter plot, each dot represents the two observations recorded for each participant. The regression line drawn through the data is optional. If you include the regression line, you should also include the equation that defines its intercept and slope. For the line graph, each point on each line represents the statistic used to describe the dependent variable. The lines extending from each point are optional and represent the standard error of the mean or some other measure of variability that will help the reader interpret the difference among the groups.

First, round the numbers to a meaningful value. As a generality, you can round to whole numbers unless the precision of measurement of your scale requires reporting decimal values. Second, if possible, include row and column averages or totals. These summary statistics help the reader discern general trends in the data and differences among groups. A third consideration is to orient the most important data within the columns. Readers find it easier to scan a column of numbers than to scan a row of numbers. Another helpful tip is to rank the data from largest to smallest or smallest to largest. Ranking the data helps the reader find the extremes in the data. The fifth recommendation is to keep row and column spacing relatively constant. Remember that all the text in your manuscript must be double-spaced. This rule applies to tables as well. Finally, use tables only when it is essential to present the quantitative data or when there is no alternative for presenting the data.

TABLE 16.3
An APA-style table

Table 1.
Proportions of different forms of cheating reported by men and women

Form of cheating	Men[a]	Women[b]	Difference between proportions
Cheat on a test	.277	.161	$z = 1.75, p < .05$
Plagiarize in a paper	.213	.236	$z = -0.32, p > .05$
Copy homework	.375	.328	$z = 0.58, p > .05$

Note: [a]$n = 48$, [b]$n = 124$.

Table 16.3 presents an example of an APA-style table. The table presents the proportion of men and women who reported different forms of cheating. Each row represents the target behavior. The table includes the proportions and the result of the test for the difference between the proportions. This table allows the researcher to present much information in a concise format. You will find more examples of tables in the sample research report at the end of this chapter.

Reporting statistics

Once you have described the general results, you then need to present the statistical tests that justify your observations. Because your audience consists of fellow researchers, you only need to indicate which statistical tests you conducted and the results of the analysis. As with all other parts of the paper, you will present the statistical results in narrative form. The general format is to indicate the statistic that you used and then describe the outcome. Consider the following example from an experiment conducted by Eisenberger and Armeli (1997):

> The average originality of each group's drawings is shown in Figure 1. . . . Planned comparisons revealed the large monetary reward for high divergent thought produce more creative drawings than either no reward or a small reward for high divergent thought, $t(281) = 2.57$, $p < .005$, and $t(281) = 2.25$, $p < .025$, respectively. Further, the large reward for high divergent thought produced subsequent drawings of greater originality than did the same reward for low divergent thought, $t(281) = 3.32$, $p < .001$. (p. 657)

Notice how the authors stated their conclusion and then indicated the statistical test that supported their claim. Eisenberger and Armeli used a student's t-ratio for the inferential statistic. The report of the statistic included the degrees of freedom, 281 in this example; the observed t-ratio; and the probability of the t-ratio. They did not explain the meaning of the t-ratio as they assumed that the reader understands how to interpret this statistical test.

Another important characteristic of the Eisenberger and Armeli (1997) passage is that they chose to report the exact probability of the statistic (e.g., $p < .025$). This is a common practice among many researchers. The alternative is to establish a universal criterion for defining statistical significance and report this if the statistical test meets the criterion. For example, an author may include a sentence similar to the following early in their results section:

> I used the criterion $\alpha = .05$ to establish statistical significance for all inferential statistics.

TABLE 16.4
Commonly used statistics and the format for presenting them in the text of the results section

Descriptive statistics	Presentation in text
Mean	$M^* = 25.67$
Median	$Mdn = 34.56$
Mode	mode $= 45.00$
Standard Deviation	$SD = 1.23$
Standard Error	$SE = 12.01$
Standard Error of Measurement	$SEM = 0.98$
Inferential statistics	**Presentation in text**
ANOVA	$F(2, 25) = 9.32, p < .05$
Chi-Square	$\chi^2(4, N = 55) = 34.10, p < .05$
Mann-Whitney U	$U(12, 15) = 5.67, p < .05$
Pearson's r	$r(98) = .872, p < .05$
Spearman's r	$r_s(74) = -.948, p < .05$
Student's t-ratio	$t(123) = 2.31, p < .05$

*Use italics to present the abbreviation for the statistic.

Later, in the results section, the writer will use $p < .05$ if the test is statistically significant. Specifically, the author would write "$t(281) = 2.25, p < .05$" rather than "$t(281) = 2.25, p < .025$."

The APA editorial guidelines encourage authors to include measures of effect size, such as ω^2 or η^2, along with the results of the inferential statistic. Reporting the effect size helps the reader interpret the relation between the independent and dependent variables.

Table 16.4 presents a list of commonly used descriptive and inferential statistics and the format for reporting them in the text of the results section. For the inferential statistics, the general format is to use a letter associated with the statistic (e.g., t for student's t-ratio and F for the ANOVA), the degrees of freedom, the observed statistic, and the probability of the result. Note that you should italicize the letter representing the statistic.

Discussion Section

During the introduction of the paper, you explain why your research questions were important. In the discussion section, you tell the reader whether your research answers the research questions, and you discuss the implications of your research for future researchers.

The following passages come from the discussion section of an article written by Eisenberger and Armeli (1997). The authors began the discussion section with:

> The present findings indicate that the explicit reinforcement of novel performance for salient rewards enhances generalized creative performance without any loss of intrinsic creative interest. . . . [T]he specific requirement of novel performance in one task (generating uses for physical objects) produced greater subsequent creative performance in an entirely different task (drawing a picture) when a large reward, rather than either no reward or a small reward, was used. (p. 659)

This passage complements the closing sentence of their introduction wherein Eisenberger and Armeli (1997) described the purpose of their research. Moving on, the scope of the discussion broadens to review the implications of the research. Midway through the discussion section, the authors wrote:

> The results contradict the view that any increase in performance that is due to salient reward produces a countervailing decease in intrinsic creative interest (e.g., Condry, 1977; Hennessey & Amabil, 1988). According to the overjustification hypothesis (Lepper et al., 1973), expecting reward for creative thinking would change the perceived cause of one's own performance from an interest in creativity to an interest in the reward. (p. 659)

As you can see, the authors revisited the issues they raised in the introduction. This passage makes clear that the data do not support the consensus view regarding the deleterious effects of reinforcement. By the end of the discussion, Eisenberger and Armeli (1997) concluded:

> Texts in education and business often express the view that creative performance can be increased if course work and jobs are made more intrinsically interesting. This is a laudable goal; however, even the most interesting creative activities require long periods of difficult and unpleasant effort that is necessary for meaningful achievement. The use of periodic salient reward may provide an effective way to help individuals sustain their creative efforts when success comes slowly and with great difficulty. (p. 661)

I have presented only a glimpse of a longer and tightly reasoned set of arguments. Nevertheless, these passages illustrate the editorial triangle illustrated in Figure 16.5. The first portion of the discussion provides a narrative review of the results as they related to the original research question. Specifically, Eisenberger and Armeli (1997) concluded that their research supported the hypothesis that positive reinforcement will enhance, not reduce, intrinsic interest and performance.

Midway through the discussion section, Eisenberger and Armeli (1997) showed how their research contradicts the work of other researchers and theories concerning reinforcement. During this portion of the discussion, the authors presented arguments to convince

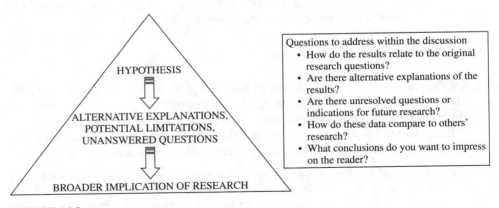

FIGURE 16.5
The triangle model of the discussion. The discussion begins by focusing on how the analysis of the data relates to the original research questions. Depending on the outcome of the study, the scope of the discussion broadens to consider alternative explanations of the data, potential limitations of the current results, and lingering questions. The discussion ends by considering the reasonable conclusions that one may draw from the research.

the reader that their research and conclusions are superior to those of other studies and to show why their results do not agree with other studies.

The closing paragraph makes clear that the results of the research extend well beyond the laboratory. Eisenberger and Armeli (1997) believed that positive reinforcement has many useful applications in many settings.

As I noted at the start of the chapter, reading many research articles will help you see how other authors construct their discussion sections as well as other parts of the research reports. When you read research reports, pay attention to the information the authors present in the paper. At the same time, examine how the authors present their ideas. You can learn a lot by studying the writing style of others.

References Section

The reference section identifies the source of each citation you presented in the paper. Box 16.4 presents the reference style used in APA-style papers. The order of references is alphabetical using the last names of the authors. For each citation, use a hanging indentation that causes the first line to jut out to the left of the other lines in the citation. The reference section, as all other parts of the text, is double-spaced, and there are no extra lines between the citations.

Appendix

The appendix is an optional portion of the paper and used to present detailed information that is not appropriate for the rest of the text. For example, if you created a specialized survey or questionnaire for your research, you may want to include a copy of the instrument in the appendix.

Author Note

The author note serves several functions. It includes your mailing address and other information indicating how the readers can correspond with you. You can also use the author note to acknowledge grants that funded your work and the help you received from colleagues who helped you with portions of the research. In addition, if the manuscript includes material that you have presented in other venues, you should acknowledge that presentation. For example, many authors present portions of their research at professional conferences before they attempt to publish the results in a journal.

Tables

We do not include tables in the body of the text. Instead, we print each table on a separate page after the author note section. Be sure that you double-space the entire text of the table.

BOX 16.4   Formatting the Reference Section of an APA-style Research Report

Journal Articles

Single author:

Flora, S. R. (1990). Undermining intrinsic interest from the standpoint of a behaviorist. *Psychological Record, 40,* 323–346.

Zimmerman, B. J. (1985). The development of "intrinsic" motivation: A social learning analysis. *Annals of Child Development, 2,* 117–160.

Multiple authors:

Balsam, D. P., & Bondy, A. S. (1983). The negative side effects of reward. *Journal of Applied Behavior Analysis, 16,* 283–296.

Hatano, G., Sigler, R. S., Richards, D. D., Inagaki, K., Stavy, R., & Wax, N. (1993). The development of biological knowledge: A multi-national study. *Cognitive Development, 8,* 47–62.

Notes:

- Capitalize the first letter of the first word in the title of the article and of the first word following a colon.
- Capitalize the first letter of each word in the name of the journal.
- Italicize the title of the journal, the volume number, and commas.
- Do not include the issue number unless the journal starts each issue with page 1.
- If there are six or more authors, use the first author's name and "et al." in the text (e.g. "Hatano et al. (1993) examined . . .").

Books

Single author:

Amabile, T. M. (1983). *The social psychology of creativity.* New York: Springer-Verlag.

Toothaker, L. E. (1993). *Multiple comparison procedures.* Newbury Park, CA: Sage.

Multiple authors:

Tegano, D. W., Moran, J. D., & Sawyers, J. K. (1991). *Creativity in early childhood classrooms.* Washington, DC: National Educational Association.

Notes:

- Capitalize the first letter of the first word in the title of the article and of the first word following a colon.
- Italicize the title of the book.
- If the location of the publisher is not well known (e.g., Newbury Park), list the state.

Reprint of a classic text:

Locke, J. (1964). *An essay concerning human understanding.* Edited by A. D. Woozley. Cleveland: Meridian Books. (Original work published 1690)

Translation of a book:

Freud, S. (1961). *Civilization and its discontents.* (J. Strachy, Trans.). New York: Norton. (Original work published 1930)

Notes:

- For the text citation, indicate the original and new publication dates. For example, use Locke (1690/1964) or Freud (1930/1961).

BOX 16.4 *Continued*

Book chapter:

Asher, S. R., & Hymel, S. (1981). Children's social competence in peer relations: Sociometric and behavioral assessment. In J. K. Wine & M. D. Smye (Eds.), *Social competence* (pp. 125–157). New York: Guilford Press.

Corporate author:

American Psychological Association (2001). *Publication manual of the American Psychological Association* (5th ed.). Washington, DC: Author.

Magazines and Newspapers

Magazine:

Lemonick, M. D. (1999, October 4). Smart genes? *Time,154,* (11), 54–58.

Newspaper article

Ray, B. (1999, November 5). Domestic violence growing concern in mid-Ohio valley. *The Marietta Times,* p. A1.

Newspaper article, no author:

Seniors unimpressed with GOP Congress. (1999, November 4). *The Marietta Times,* p. A3.

Other Sources

Computer program:

Allen, J. D., & Pittenger, D. J. (2000). Statistics Tutor (2nd ed.) [Computer software]. New York: Wiley.

Internet website:

National Alliance for the Mentally Ill (November, 1999). Schizophrenia. Retrieved 11/17/1999 from National Alliance for the Mentally Ill: (http://www.nami.org/disorder/990305b.html).

CD recording:

Stray Cats (1990). Rock this town. On *Best of the Stray Cats* [CD]. Hollywood, CA: EMI-USA.

Figures

The figure section contains two parts. The first part contains the figure captions. This page contains the text for the figure caption of each figure. Print the individual figures on separate pages. The pages containing the figures are the only pages that do not include the running head and page number. To identify the figure, print on the reverse side of the figure a short version of the title, the figure number, and the word TOP at the top of the page.

PROOFREADING

Few of us can sit down and write a perfect article. Most authors write and revise their papers several times before they are satisfied with the work. Therefore, proofreading is an essential component of good writing. Now for the bad news and the good news. The bad news is that proofreading is difficult. It is easy to overlook mistakes in your own writing. The good news is that there are many resources you can use to proofread and correct your work.

Computer programs

Most word processors have built in spelling and grammar checkers. These are useful features, but have many limitations. For example, spell checking programs will identify words that are not in its dictionary. Thus, this feature will help ensure that all the words in your paper are correctly spelled. Unfortunately, the spell checker cannot determine whether you used the correct word. For example, you could correctly spell *chose* when you should have written *choose*. The same advantages and disadvantages apply to grammar checkers.

Grammar checkers catch obvious errors and often skip others. For example, my word processor's grammar checker quickly catches passive voice, subject-verb agreement problems, and other common errors. The program also ignores some real whoppers. Consider the following sentences:

> The green bachelor's wife snored furiously against the winter of our discontent.
> May grammars checker does no catch errors a frequently an I wants it too.

My grammar checker found no problem with either sentence, and it indicated that they were easy to read. You, by contrast, should see immediately that both sentences are gibberish. The implications of this example are clear. Spelling and grammar checkers can help you as long as you recognize the limits of these tools and that there are superior methods for proofreading your work.

One tactic is to read the paper aloud. Print your paper and then read it as if it were a speech. In most cases, you will quickly hear the faults. Missing words will become apparent, awkward phrases will stand out, and vague language will sound obscure. As you read your paper, keep a pen at hand, and mark and revise the offensive phrases.

Another tactic is to ask someone else to read your paper. Most colleges and universities have a writing resource center. Typically, the staff will gladly proofread your paper for clarity and style. Although they may know nothing about your topic, they can adopt the role of your intended audience. Therefore, they will point out parts of your paper that are not clear and that require refinement.

A SAMPLE APA-STYLE RESEARCH REPORT

The following paper is an example of an APA-style manuscript for a research report. The research comes from the honors thesis of one of my students, Maleah Thorpe. The manuscript is an edited version of a longer paper published in *College Student Journal.** You can use this manuscript as a checklist and model for your paper.

---

*I wish to thank the editors of *College Student Journal* for the permission to reproduce the manuscript of the article.

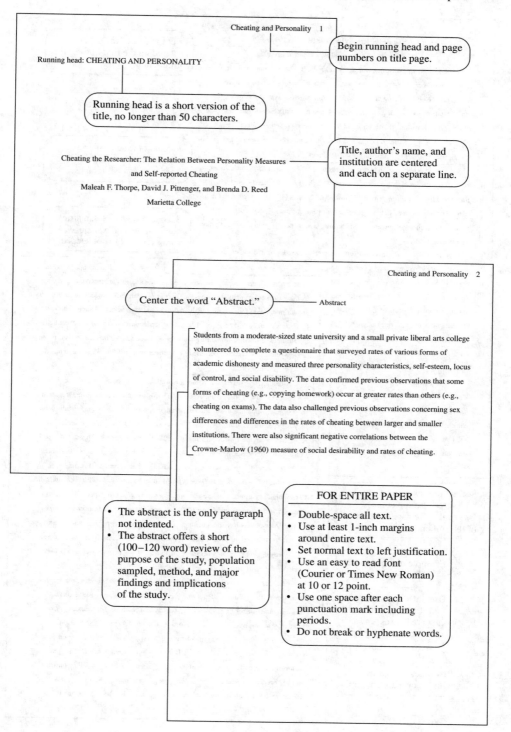

Cheating and Personality   1

Begin running head and page numbers on title page.

Running head: CHEATING AND PERSONALITY

Running head is a short version of the title, no longer than 50 characters.

Cheating the Researcher: The Relation Between Personality Measures
and Self-reported Cheating

Maleah F. Thorpe, David J. Pittenger, and Brenda D. Reed

Marietta College

Title, author's name, and institution are centered and each on a separate line.

Cheating and Personality   2

Center the word "Abstract."

Abstract

Students from a moderate-sized state university and a small private liberal arts college volunteered to complete a questionnaire that surveyed rates of various forms of academic dishonesty and measured three personality characteristics, self-esteem, locus of control, and social disability. The data confirmed previous observations that some forms of cheating (e.g., copying homework) occur at greater rates than others (e.g., cheating on exams). The data also challenged previous observations concerning sex differences and differences in the rates of cheating between larger and smaller institutions. There were also significant negative correlations between the Crowne-Marlow (1960) measure of social desirability and rates of cheating.

- The abstract is the only paragraph not indented.
- The abstract offers a short (100–120 word) review of the purpose of the study, population sampled, method, and major findings and implications of the study.

FOR ENTIRE PAPER

- Double-space all text.
- Use at least 1-inch margins around entire text.
- Set normal text to left justification.
- Use an easy to read font (Courier or Times New Roman) at 10 or 12 point.
- Use one space after each punctuation mark including periods.
- Do not break or hyphenate words.

Cheating and Personality　3

Cheating the Researcher: The Relation Between

Personality Measures and Self-reported Cheating

　　Academic dishonesty, or cheating, is a ubiquitous phenomenon in higher education. Bowers (1964) conducted one of the first and most comprehensive studies of cheating behavior among college students. Although his work defies quick summarization, one can draw several generalizations. First, academic dishonesty of all kinds occurs within all institutions of higher education. Some students copy each other's homework, plagiarize, sneak crib notes into exams or copy from others, and lie to their faculty about the cause of missed deadlines.

　　A second generalization is that students with lower overall academic standing are more likely to cheat. Furthermore, students who cheat are motivated more by high grades and less by the acquisition of knowledge. Bowers (1964) also reported the relation between several demographic variables and cheating. Specifically, men are more likely to cheat than women, and cheating is more pervasive in larger institutions than smaller institutions.

　　During the past 30 years numerous researchers have replicated and expanded upon Bowers's findings (Davis, Grover, Be[...] Franklyn-Stokes, & Armstead, 1996). For [...] Spiller and Crown (1995) reported that con[...] to rates reported 30 years earlier. Similarly,[...] Obenshain, 1994; Baldwin, Daugherty, Rov[...] reported evidence of academic dishonesty i[...] for undergraduate institutions, namely, men[...] students with a history of cheating are likel[...]

　　Other researchers have examined rates[...] Newstead et al. (1996) examined cheating [...] colleges and universities. Their results dem[...] cheating behavior replicate those found am[...] and Dreyer (1994) compared the levels of c[...] students, finding that American students rep[...]

> Print the title of the paper centered on the first lines of the introduction.

> Indent at the start of each paragraph. There are no extra lines between paragraphs.

> Second reference to an article cited earlier in the same paragraph—date not needed.

> Second reference to an article with three or more authors. Use et al. to replace the names of the authors.

> Example of a quotation.

> Use the ampersand (&) for references within the parentheses.

> Reference to an article with six or more authors.

Cheating and Personality　4

counterparts. Davis et al. also found that Australian students are motivated more by learning than by obtaining high grades. By contrast, American students indicated a greater motivation for obtaining high grades. In similar research, Waugh, Godfrey, Evans, and Craig (1995) compared Australian student's attitudes toward cheating to the attitudes of students from other countries. They concluded that Australian students are less tolerant of cheating because of a "cultural emphasis on fair play combined with personal achievement" (p. 73).

　　Although the existence of cheating is well documented, its specific causes have not been extensively studied until recently. During the past decade, several researchers have begun to examine the relation between personality and attritional variables that may help predict cheating behavior. For example, several researchers examined the relation between the Type A personality profile and cheating (e.g., Huss, et al., 1993; Perry, Kane, Bernesser, & Spicker, 1990). One of the defining characteristics of the Type A personality profile is competitive striving for achievement (Friedmand & Rosenman, 1977). As such, the Type A profile may be associated with high motivation to earn high grades and possible cheating. Consistent with this expectation, Davis, Pierce, Yandell, Arnow, and Loree (1995) demonstrated that students characterized by a Type A personality have a higher motivation to learn and earn high grades than Type B students. In addition, Type A students are more likely to cheat on a task designed in which they did not have direct control. There was, however, no correlation between Type A personality and reported levels of cheating.

　　The lack of a correlation between Type A personality and cheating may represent several conditions. First, students who cheat may deny their transgressions thus obscuring the true relation between personality and behavior. Second, this personality scale may not measure aspects of personality that predict cheating. Academic dishonesty is, most likely, a multidetermined behavior that includes environmental conditions, such as opportunity, as well as a host of personality and motivational factors. Finally, current measures of the Type A personality may lack the construct validity needed to detect the covariance among variables (e.g., Matthews, 1982). Therefore, greater attention should be given to examining a broader range of personality factors that will help explain this complex phenomenon.

The purpose of the present study was to achieve several goals. First, we were interested in the degree to which self-reports of cheating are affected by response bias. To date, the majority of researchers studying cheating have depended on students completing anonymous surveys of cheating behaviors. Although this technique has been useful, few researchers have examined personality factors that may affect the veracity of these reports. Given the general negative connotation of cheating, many students may be motivated to deny cheating even in an anonymous form. If true, cheating surveys may actually under represent the rate of academic dishonesty among university students.

A second goal of our research was to examine the relation between two common personality characteristics, locus of control and self-esteem, and cheating. We hoped to determine the degree to which cheating behaviors can be understood by examining the student's perception of self. Locus of control is the attribution concerning whether individuals believe they control their destiny or are controlled by external forces (Leftcourt, 1991; Rotter, 1966). We anticipated that students who believe they have little control over their lives would be more
of control. Self-esteem is a general measure
him or herself as a good person (Blascovicl
relation between self-esteem and cheating t
lower self-esteem are more likely to cheat.

Previously, Antion and Michael (1983
control and self-reports of cheating. The la
First, their sample size was small (e.g., $n =$
present, low rates of the behavior require la
statistical power to detect a relation betwee
Michael also used a non-standard locus of
recent theoretical development in locus of

> For multiple citations, order them alphabetically.

> Begin method section immediately after introduction. Center the word "Method."

> Start the participants section on the next line. Italicize the word "Participants." Start the materials section in the same way.

> When reporting a statistic, use italics for the letter or letters indicating the statistic. For most statistics, one or two significant digits are sufficient.

> Use a comma before the "and" when presenting a list.

Finally, we compared the rates of various cheating behaviors among men and women at both a small private liberal arts college and a moderate-sized state school with an open enrollment policy. We also compared the rates of different forms of cheating (e.g., plagiarism vs. cheating on an exam). Although cheating is a pervasive phenomenon, some forms of cheating are more prevalent than others. For example, Newstead et al. (1996) demonstrated that plagiarism occurs at a much greater frequency than cheating during exams. Previous research has also demonstrated that men are more likely to cheat than women, and that the rate of cheating is greater at larger institutions.

Method

Participants

A total of 310 students completed a questionnaire surveying rates of academic dishonesty and a series of questions measuring various personality dimensions. Of the whole sample, 138 (57 men, 81 women) were enrolled in one of five sections of an introductory psychology course taught at a small (enrollment of 1,000) private liberal arts college located in the eastern Midwest. Some, but not all students, received extra credit for participation in the study. The average age of these students was $M = 20.4$ ($SD = 4.14$). The other 172 participants (48 men, 124 women) were enrolled in introductory psychology courses taught at a moderate sized (enrollment of 5,000) regional state college in the Midwest. All students at the larger institution received extra course credit for their participation in the study. Their average age was $M = 22.6$ ($SD = 5.39$). The difference in mean age between the two institutions was statistically significant, $t(308) = 4.04$, $p < .05$; $\omega^2 = 0.047$, but the effect size was small.

Materials

All participants completed a survey consisting of two parts. The first part contained a questionnaire that recorded demographic information about the student (e.g., age, sex, class standing, work history, and participation in varsity sports) and his or her history of cheating behavior. Specifically, we asked whether or not students had (a) cheated on tests, (b) plagiarized material, (c) submitted another student's paper as their own, and (d) copied another student's homework. If students indicated that they

Cheating and Personality   7

had performed a type of cheating, they were then asked to indicate on a 7-point scale

the relative frequency of the cheating (1 = once or twice, 7 = 13 or more times).

The second part of the questionnaire consisted of 67 questions derived from the

Crowne-Marlowe Social Desirability Scale (Crowne & Marlowe, 1960), Levensen's

Locus of Control Scale, (1973, 1981) and Rosenberg's Self-Esteem Scale (1965). To

ensure consistency in response style, the response scale for all questions was a 6-point

scale ranging from −3 (strongly disagree) to 3 (strongly agree). We randomly

arranged the order of the questions.

Crowne-Marlowe. The Crowne-Marlowe Social Desirability Scale (CM: Crowne

& Marlowe, 1960) consists of 18 the statements that describe desirable but rare

behaviors (e.g., consistently good table manners) and 15 statements describing

undesirable but common behaviors (e.g., seeking revenge). As a generality, the

Crowne-Marlowe scale is an index of impression management and can be used to

determine the degree to which test results are contaminated by the individual's desire

to present a favorable impression of his or her character. Paulus (1991) offered an

alternative interpretation of the test, noting that current research indicates that the

instrument measures an individual's need f[...]

avoid disapproval. Higher scores represent [...]

Locus of Control. Levensen's (1973, [...]

consists of three subscales of eight items [...]

Control-Internal (LOC:I), Powerful Other[...]

internal scale assesses the degree to which [...]

control of his or her life. The other scales [...]

concept of external locus of control. The [...]

degree to which individuals see their lives [...]

authority (e.g., teachers and administrators[...]

reflects the belief that the events in one's [...]

controlled. For each scale, higher scores r[...]

underlying construct. Leftcourt (1991) pr[...]

psychometric properties of the instrument[...]

> This is a level 4 heading used as a subsection for the materials section.

> Use abbreviations to stand for long text used repeatedly in the text.

> Capitalize the name of the test.

Cheating and Personality   8

Self-Esteem. The Rosenberg (1965) Self-Esteem Scale (SE) consists of 10

statements describing positive (e.g., I have good qualities) or negative (e.g., I am a

failure) attributions of self. Higher scores indicate greater levels of self-esteem.

Blascovich and Tomaka (1991) reported the scale has good reliability and validity

indices and is recognized as a unidimensional measure of self-esteem.

Procedure

The first author or the instructor distributed the questionnaire during a class

along with an informed consent form. Instructions accompanying the questionnaire

guaranteed anonymity and confidentiality. All students had the opportunity not to

participate, but none declined.

Results

Figure 1 presents the percentage of students reporting different forms of

cheating while in college. These data are in keeping with previous reports (e.g.,

Bower, 1964; Newstead et al., 1996). Namely, men tend to report higher levels of

cheating than do women for most forms of cheating. Similarly, students at larger

institutions tend to report higher levels of cheating than students at smaller

institutions. Finally, some forms of cheating are more prevalent than others.

Specifically, plagiarism and copying homework are more common than cheating on

tests or submitting another student's paper.

We used the binomial test for the difference between proportions test to examine

levels of reported cheating the occurred during college. Regarding sex differences, the

only statistically significant difference between men and women existed for

submitting a paper written by another author, $z = 2.18$, $p < .05$.

Regarding school size, there were statistically significant differences for

cheating on test, $z = 2.60$, $p < .05$, and for submitting a paper written be another

author, $z = 3.01$, $p < .05$. The differences in the rates for cheating on homework,

tests, and plagiarizing were not statistically significant, $p > .05$.

Table 1 presents the correlations among the five personality dimensions. For

the locus of control dimension, the correlation among the three subscales matches

previously published convergent validity data (Leftcourt, 1991). However, the

> Begin the results section immediately after the method section. Center the word "Results."

correlations between the locus of control scales and the Crowne-Marlowe scales are much higher than previous reports. There is also a moderate correlation between the SE and CM scales. Therefore, it appears that the bias for social desirability contaminated the other scales, and any interpretation of the correlation between these personality measures and cheating should be made with caution.

Table 2 lists the correlations between the reported frequency of admitted cheating and the personality profiles. Specifically, students with a higher need for approval report fewer episodes of cheating. Contrary to our original prediction, the locus of control does not appear to be a reliable correlate with cheating behavior.

Capitalize the words "Figure" and "Table" when referring to a specific figure or table, regardless of position in sentence.

Begin the discussion section immediately after the results section. Center the word "Discussion."

Discussion

The present results confirmed previous findings regarding cheating behavior, challenged several generalizations, and created a vexing paradox. To begin, the data of the present study confirmed previous results. Specifically, cheating of various forms is a prevalent behavior among college students. The differences between the rates of cheating reported by men and women, and for students at larger and smaller institutions appear to replicate previous reports. Our research also demonstrated that the reported rates of cheating are related to

Our findings confirmed the data of Ne showed that different forms of cheating are Specifically, Newstead et al. and Nuss dem during an exam to be a more egregious infr homework assignments. Consequently, as v higher rates of plagiarizing and copying ho the distinction among the types of cheating interprets the rate of cheating among stude cannot be viewed as a highly congruent set treating all cheating behaviors as a whole r variables. Therefore, future research on che distinction among the types of cheating beh motivation and causes of academic dishone

A related question arises from the differences between the two schools. We found that more students from the larger school reported cheating on exams than at the smaller institution. How much of the difference between the two institutions is due to student variables versus numbers and types of opportunities to cheat? Smaller colleges may have less cheating because of the types of tests given. Specifically, faculty at smaller institutions may be more likely to use essay exams, which do not afford the same opportunities for cheating, than multiple choice exams. Similarly, larger class sizes, as typically found at larger institutions, may also afford more opportunities to cheat (Bowers, 1964).

The correlation between the CM scale and the rates of cheating creates an interesting paradox. One interpretation of the data follows from the assumption that the CM scale is an explicit measure of response bias. Therefore, one may conclude that the data concerning rates of cheating are contaminated by the bias to present one's self as a virtuous person. An alternative interpretation presumes that the CM scale is a measure of personality. If the CM is a measure of the degree to which a person wishes to avoid disapproval, then one may interpret the current results to indicate that students who do not cheat do so to avoid the stigma of cheating. Unfortunately, the data from the present study do not afford a rational solution to this conundrum.

These data do reveal the need to consider the dimension measured by the CM scale for future research. For example, we had hoped to demonstrate a clear relation between cheating, self-esteem, and locus of control. However, the dominant nature of the CM dimension appeared to eclipse these relations. Therefore, future research examining the motivations and personalities of students who are prone to cheat need to examine the systematic variance attributed to the CM construct.

Cheating and Personality   11

In summary, academic dishonesty is a complex behavior that defies simplistic
explanation. Studying this behavior is complicated by the fact that the behavior is, by
its nature, covert. Cheating too, like most behavior, is determined by a host of
interrelated variables.

> Begin the reference section on a new page. Center the word "References."

Cheating and Personality   12

References

Anderson, R. W., & Obenshain, S. S. (1994). Cheating by students: Findings,
reflections, and remedies. *Academic Medicine, 69,* 323-332.

Antion, D. L., & Michael, W. B. (1983). Short-term predictive validity of
demographic affective, personal, and cognitive variables in relation to two
criterion measures of cheating behaviors. *Educational and Psychological
Measurement, 43,* 467-482.

> References include the name of the journal and volume number, both italicized.

Baldwin, D. C., Daugherty, S. R., Rowley, B. D., & Schwarz, M. R. (1996). Cheating
in medical school: A survey of second-year students at 31 schools. *Academic
Medicine, 71,* 267-273.

Blascovich, J., & Tomaka, J. (1991) Measures of self-esteem. In J. P. Robinson,
P. R. Shaver, & L. S. Wrightsman (Eds.), *Measures of personality and social
psychological attitudes.* (pp. 115-160). San Diego: Academic Press.

Bowers, W. J. (1964). Student dishonesty and its control in college. (Cooperative
research project No. OE 1672). New York: Columbia Bureau of Applied
Research.

> Alphabetize the references using the authors' last name. For each reference, do not indent the first line but do indent subsequent lines.

Crowne, D. P., & Marlowe, D. (1960). A new scale of social desirability
independent of psychopathology. *Journal of Consulting Psychology, 24,*
349-354.

Dans, P. E. (1996). Self-reported cheating by students at one medical school.
Academic Medicine, 71, 870-872.

Davis, S. F., Grover, C. A., Becker, A. H., & McGregor, L. N. (1992). Academic
dishonesty: Prevalence, determinants, techniques, and punishments. *Teaching
of Psychology, 19,* 16-20.

Davis, S. F., Noble, L. M., Zak, E. N., & Dreyer, K. K. (1994). A comparison of
cheating and learning/grade orientation in American and Australian college
students. *College Student Journal, 28,* 353-356.

Davis, S. F., Pierce, M. C., Yandell, L. R., Arnow, P. S., & Loree, A. (1995).
Cheating in college and Type A personality: A reevaluation. *College Student
Journal, 29,* 439-497.

> Use an ampersand (&) in the references instead of "and."

Friedman, M., & Rosenman. R. H. (1977). The key cause: Type A behavior pattern. In
A. Monat & R. H. Lazrus (Eds.), *Stress and coping* (pp. 203-212). New York:
Columbia University Press.

Huss. M. T., Curnyn. J. P., Roberts. S. L., Davis, S. F., Yandell, L., & Giordano, P.
(1993). Hard driven but not dishonest: Cheating and Type A personality. *Bulletin
of Psychonomic Society, 31,* 429-430.

Leftcourt, H. M. (1991). Locus of control In J. P. Robinson. P. R. Shaver. & L. S.
Wrightsman (Eds.). *Measures of personality and social psychological attitudes.*
(pp. 413-500). San Diego: Academic Press.

Levensen. H. (1973). Perceived parental antecedent of internal, powerful others, and
chance locus of control orientations. *Developmental Psychology, 9,* 268-274.

Levensen, H. (1981). Differentiating among internal, powerful others, and chance. In
H. M. Leftcourt (Ed.). *Research with the locus of control construct.* (Vol. 1, pp.
15-36). New York: Academic Press:

McCabe, D. L., & Bowers, W. J. (1994). Academic dishonesty among males in
college: A thirty-year perspective. *Journal of College Student Development, 35,*
5-10.

Matthews, K. A. (1982). Psychological per[...]
Psychological Bulletin, 91, 293-323.

Newstead, S. E., Franklyn-Stokes, A., & A[...]
student cheating. *Journal of Educatio[...]*

Nuss, E. M. (1988). Academic integrity: C[...]
Improving College and University Te[...]

Paulus, D. L. (1991). Measurement and co[...]
P. R. Shaver, & L. S. Wrightsman (Ed[...]
psychological attitudes. (pp. 17-60). S[...]

Perry, A. R., Kane, K. M., Bernesser, K. J.,[...]
competitive achievement-striving, and[...]
Psychological Reports, 66, 459-465.

Rotter, J. B. (1966). Generalized expectancies for internal versus external control of
reinforcement. *Psychological Monographs, 80(Whole No. 609).*

Rosenberg, M. (1965). *Society and the adolescent self-image.* Princeton; Princeton
University Press.

Spiller, S., & Crown, D. F. (1995). Changes over time in academic dishonesty at the
collegiate level. *Psychological Reports, 76,* 763-768.

Waugh, R. F., Godfrey, J. R., Evans, E. D., & Craig, D. (1995). Measuring students'
perceptions about cheating in six countries. *Australian Journal of Psychology,
47,* 73-80.

Cheating and Personality   15

Author Note

A copy of our survey is available upon request.

We thank Martha Bleeker and Shelby Evans for distributing our survey at Emporia State University.

Portions of this research were conducted as a part of the first author's honors thesis project at Marietta College, and were presented at the annual meeting of the National Undergraduate Research Convention, Austin, TX.

This version of the manuscript is a much edited version of the paper, Thorpe, M., F., Pittenger, D. J., & Reed, B. D. (1999). Cheating the researcher: A study of the relation between personality and measures and self-reported cheating. *College Student Journal, 33,* 49–59, and reproduced with the permission of the editor.

> The author note section is optional and starts on a separate page after the references.

Cheating and Personality   16

Table 1

Correlations Among the Five Personality Measures

	SE	LOC:I	LOC:P	LOC:C	CM
SE	1.000	.410*	−.348*	−.301*	.397*
LOC:I		1.000	−.051	−.112	.174*
LOC:P			1.000	.491*	−.292*
LOC:C				1.000	−.394*
CM					1.000

Note. *$p < .05$, $df = 308$, SE = Self-Esteem, LOC:I = Locus of Control: Internal, LOC:P = Locus of Control: Powerful Others, LOC:C = Locus of Control: Chance, CM = Crowne-Marlow.

> Start each table on a separate page. Number the tables sequentially as they are introduced in the text. Capitalize the first letter of each word in the title. Double-space the text of the table.

> The table note contains text that defines the meaning of symbols and abbreviations.

Table 2

Correlations Between Personality Measures and Reported Frequency of Cheating.

Behavior	SE	LOC:I	LOC:P	LOC:C	CM
Test	−.094	.116	.027	.154	−.268*
Plagiarize	−.216	.031	.131	.064	−.450*
Paper	−.121	.086	−.018	.208	−.156
Home Work	.014	.049	.044	.090	−.311*

Note. *p* < .05, *df* = 308, SE = Self-Esteem, LOC:I = Locus of Control: Internal, LOC:P = Locus of Control: Powerful Others, LOC:C = Locus of Control: Chance, CM = Crowne-Marlow, Test = Cheating on a test, Plagiarize = Plagiarizing in a paper, Paper = Submitting the paper of another person, Home Work = copying the home work of another student.

> Use the note section for each table to include relevant general information as well as the meaning of the acronyms and phrases used in the table.

Figure Caption

Figure 1. Proportion of students at small (men = 57, women = 81) and large (men = 48, women = 124) college. Test = Cheating on a test, Plagiarize = Plagiarizing in a paper, Paper = Submitting the paper of another person. Home Work = copying the home work of another student.

> The figure caption section starts on a separate page. List each figure caption in a separate paragraph starting with the word "Figure" and the number of the figure. Print each figure on a separate page. Do not include the running head with the figures. Write the figure number on the back of the figure.

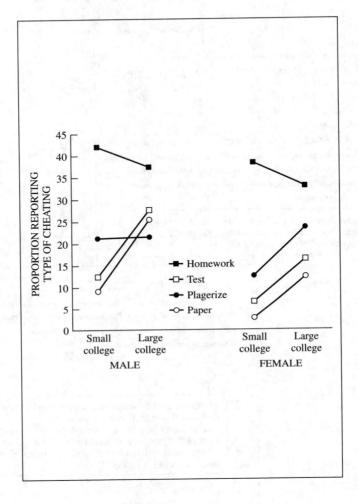

Appendix A
STATISTICAL TABLES

APPENDIX OUTLINE

TABLE A.1: PROPORTIONS OF THE AREA UNDER
THE NORMAL CURVE

Using Table A.1

To use Table A.1, convert the raw score to a z-score using the following equation; X is the observed score, M is the mean of the data, and SD is the standard deviation of the data.

$$z = \frac{(X - M)}{SD}$$

The z-score is a standard deviate that allows you to use the standard normal distribution. The normal distribution has a mean of 0.0 and a standard deviation of 1.0. The normal distribution is symmetrical.

The values in Table A.1 represent the proportion of area in the standard normal curve that occurs between specific points. The table contains z-scores between 0.0 and 3.98. Because the normal distribution is symmetrical, the table represents z-scores ranging between –3.98 and 3.98.

Column A of the table represents the z-score. Column B represents the proportion of the curve between the mean and the z-score. Column C represents the proportion of the curve that extends from to z-score to ∞.

Example

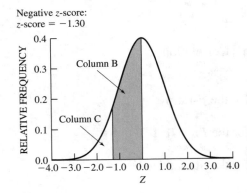

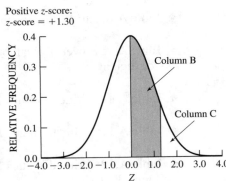

	Column B	Column C	
Negative z-scores z = −1.30			
Area between mean and −z	.4032		40.32% of curve
Area less than −z		.0968	9.68% of curve
Positive z-scores z = 1.30			
Area between mean and +z	.4032		40.32% of curve
Area greater than +z		.0968	9.68% of curve
Area **between** −z and +z	.4032 + .4032 = .8064 or 80.64% of curve		
Area **below** −z and **above** +z	.0968 + .0968 = .1936 or 19.36% of curve		

In the following examples, we add .5000 to the area between the mean and z-score. The .5000 represents the proportion of the curve on the complementary half of the normal curve.

Area at and **below** +z = +1.30   .5000 + .4032 = .9032 or 90.32% of curve
Area at and **above** −z = −1.30   .4032 + .5000 = .9032 or 90.32% of curve

TABLE A.1

A	B	C	A	B	C	A	B	C
	Area between mean and z	Area beyond		Area between mean and z	Area beyond		Area between mean and z	Area beyond
z		z	z		z	z		z
.00	.0000	.5000	.27	.1064	.3936	.54	.2054	.2946
.01	.0040	.4960	.28	.1103	.3897	.55	.2088	.2912
.02	.0080	.4920	.29	.1141	.3859	.56	.2123	.2877
.03	.0120	.4880	.30	.1179	.3821	.57	.2157	.2843
.04	.0160	.4840	.31	.1217	.3783	.58	.2190	.2810
.05	.0199	.4801	.32	.1255	.3745	.59	.2224	.2776
.06	.0239	.4761	.33	.1293	.3707	.60	.2257	.2743
.07	.0279	.4721	.34	.1331	.3669	.61	.2291	.2709
.08	.0319	.4681	.35	.1368	.3632	.62	.2324	.2676
.09	.0359	.4641	.36	.1406	.3594	.63	.2357	.2643
.10	.0398	.4602	.37	.1443	.3557	.64	.2389	.2611
.11	.0438	.4562	.38	.1480	.3520	.65	.2422	.2578
.12	.0478	.4522	.39	.1517	.3483	.66	.2454	.2546
.13	.0517	.4483	.40	.1554	.3446	.67	.2486	.2514
.14	.0557	.4443	.41	.1591	.3409	.68	.2517	.2483
.15	.0596	.4404	.42	.1628	.3372	.69	.2549	.2451
.16	.0636	.4364	.43	.1664	.3336	.70	.2580	.2420
.17	.0675	.4325	.44	.1700	.3300	.71	.2611	.2389
.18	.0714	.4286	.45	.1736	.3264	.72	.2642	.2358
.19	.0753	.4247	.46	.1772	.3228	.73	.2673	.2327
.20	.0793	.4207	.47	.1808	.3192	.74	.2704	.2296
.21	.0832	.4168	.48	.1844	.3156	.75	.2734	.2266
.22	.0871	.4129	.49	.1879	.3121	.76	.2764	.2236
.23	.0910	.4090	.50	.1915	.3085	.77	.2794	.2206
.24	.0948	.4052	.51	.1950	.3050	.78	.2823	.2177
.25	.0987	.4013	.52	.1985	.3015	.79	.2852	.2148
.26	.1026	.3974	.53	.2019	.2981	.80	.2881	.2119

(*continued*)

TABLE A.1 (*Cont'd.*)

A	B	C	A	B	C	A	B	C
z	Area between mean and z	Area beyond z	z	Area between mean and z	Area beyond z	z	Area between mean and z	Area beyond z
.81	.2910	.2090	1.28	.3997	.1003	1.75	.4599	.0401
.82	.2939	.2061	1.29	.4015	.0985	1.76	.4608	.0392
.83	.2967	.2033	1.30	.4032	.0968	1.77	.4616	.0384
.84	.2995	.2005	1.31	.4049	.0951	1.78	.4625	.0375
.85	.3023	.1977	1.32	.4066	.0934	1.79	.4633	.0367
.86	.3051	.1949	1.33	.4082	.0918	1.80	.4641	.0359
.87	.3078	.1922	1.34	.4099	.0901	1.81	.4649	.0351
.88	.3106	.1894	1.35	.4115	.0885	1.82	.4656	.0344
.89	.3133	.1867	1.36	.4131	.0869	1.83	.4664	.0336
.90	.3159	.1841	1.37	.4147	.0853	1.84	.4671	.0329
.91	.3186	.1814	1.38	.4162	.0838	1.85	.4678	.0322
.92	.3212	.1788	1.39	.4177	.0823	1.86	.4686	.0314
.93	.3238	.1762	1.40	.4192	.0808	1.87	.4693	.0307
.94	.3264	.1736	1.41	.4207	.0793	1.88	.4699	.0301
.95	.3289	.1711	1.42	.4222	.0778	1.89	.4706	.0294
.96	.3315	.1685	1.43	.4236	.0764	1.90	.4713	.0287
.97	.3340	.1660	1.44	.4251	.0749	1.91	.4719	.0281
.98	.3365	.1635	1.45	.4265	.0735	1.92	.4726	.0274
.99	.3389	.1611	1.46	.4279	.0721	1.93	.4732	.0268
1.00	.3413	.1587	1.47	.4292	.0708	1.94	.4738	.0262
1.01	.3438	.1562	1.48	.4306	.0694	1.95	.4744	.0256
1.02	.3461	.1539	1.49	.4319	.0681	1.96	.4750	.0250
1.03	.3485	.1515	1.50	.4332	.0668	1.97	.4756	.0244
1.04	.3508	.1492	1.51	.4345	.0655	1.98	.4761	.0239
1.05	.3531	.1469	1.52	.4357	.0643	1.99	.4767	.0233
1.06	.3554	.1446	1.53	.4370	.0630	2.00	.4772	.0228
1.07	.3577	.1423	1.54	.4382	.0618	2.01	.4778	.0222
1.08	.3599	.1401	1.55	.4394	.0606	2.02	.4783	.0217
1.09	.3621	.1379	1.56	.4406	.0594	2.03	.4788	.0212
1.10	.3643	.1357	1.57	.4418	.0582	2.04	.4793	.0207
1.11	.3665	.1335	1.58	.4429	.0571	2.05	.4798	.0202
1.12	.3686	.1314	1.59	.4441	.0559	2.06	.4803	.0197
1.13	.3708	.1292	1.60	.4452	.0548	2.07	.4808	.0192
1.14	.3729	.1271	1.61	.4463	.0537	2.08	.4812	.0188
1.15	.3749	.1251	1.62	.4474	.0526	2.09	.4817	.0183
1.16	.3770	.1230	1.63	.4484	.0516	2.10	.4821	.0179
1.17	.3790	.1210	1.64	.4495	.0505	2.11	.4826	.0174
1.18	.3810	.1190	1.65	.4505	.0495	2.12	.4830	.0170
1.19	.3830	.1170	1.66	.4515	.0485	2.13	.4834	.0166
1.20	.3849	.1151	1.67	.4525	.0475	2.14	.4838	.0162
1.21	.3869	.1131	1.68	.4535	.0465	2.15	.4842	.0158
1.22	.3888	.1112	1.69	.4545	.0455	2.16	.4846	.0154
1.23	.3907	.1093	1.70	.4554	.0446	2.17	.4850	.0150
1.24	.3925	.1075	1.71	.4564	.0436	2.18	.4854	.0146
1.25	.3944	.1056	1.72	.4573	.0427	2.19	.4857	.0143
1.26	.3962	.1038	1.73	.4582	.0418	2.20	.4861	.0139
1.27	.3980	.1020	1.74	.4591	.0409	2.21	.4864	.0136

TABLE A.1 *(Cont'd.)*

z	Area between mean and z	Area beyond z	z	Area between mean and z	Area beyond z	z	Area between mean and z	Area beyond z
2.22	.4868	.0132	2.68	.4963	.0037	3.14	.4992	.0008
2.23	.4871	.0129	2.69	.4964	.0036	3.15	.4992	.0008
2.24	.4875	.0125	2.70	.4965	.0035	3.16	.4992	.0008
2.25	.4878	.0122	2.71	.4966	.0034	3.17	.4992	.0008
2.26	.4881	.0119	2.72	.4967	.0033	3.18	.4993	.0007
2.27	.4884	.0116	2.73	.4968	.0032	3.19	.4993	.0007
2.28	.4887	.0113	2.74	.4969	.0031	3.20	.4993	.0007
2.29	.4890	.0110	2.75	.4970	.0030	3.22	.4994	.0006
2.30	.4893	.0107	2.76	.4971	.0029	3.24	.4994	.0006
2.31	.4896	.0104	2.77	.4972	.0028	3.26	.4994	.0006
2.32	.4898	.0102	2.78	.4973	.0027	3.28	.4995	.0005
2.33	.4901	.0099	2.79	.4974	.0026	3.30	.4995	.0005
2.34	.4904	.0096	2.80	.4974	.0026	3.32	.4995	.0005
2.35	.4906	.0094	2.81	.4975	.0025	3.34	.4996	.0004
2.36	.4909	.0091	2.82	.4976	.0024	3.36	.4996	.0004
2.37	.4911	.0089	2.83	.4977	.0023	3.38	.4996	.0004
2.38	.4913	.0087	2.84	.4977	.0023	3.40	.4997	.0003
2.39	.4916	.0084	2.85	.4978	.0022	3.42	.4997	.0003
2.40	.4918	.0082	2.86	.4979	.0021	3.44	.4997	.0003
2.41	.4920	.0080	2.87	.4979	.0021	3.46	.4997	.0003
2.42	.4922	.0078	2.88	.4980	.0020	3.48	.4997	.0003
2.43	.4925	.0075	2.89	.4981	.0019	3.50	.4998	.0002
2.44	.4927	.0073	2.90	.4981	.0019	3.52	.4998	.0002
2.45	.4929	.0071	2.91	.4982	.0018	3.54	.4998	.0002
2.46	.4931	.0069	2.92	.4982	.0018	3.56	.4998	.0002
2.47	.4932	.0068	2.93	.4983	.0017	3.58	.4998	.0002
2.48	.4934	.0066	2.94	.4984	.0016	3.60	.4998	.0002
2.49	.4936	.0064	2.95	.4984	.0016	3.62	.4999	.0001
2.50	.4938	.0062	2.96	.4985	.0015	3.64	.4999	.0001
2.51	.4940	.0060	2.97	.4985	.0015	3.66	.4999	.0001
2.52	.4941	.0059	2.98	.4986	.0014	3.68	.4999	.0001
2.53	.4943	.0057	2.99	.4986	.0014	3.70	.4999	.0001
2.54	.4945	.0055	3.00	.4987	.0013	3.72	.4999	.0001
2.55	.4946	.0054	3.01	.4987	.0013	3.74	.4999	.0001
2.56	.4948	.0052	3.02	.4987	.0013	3.76	.4999	.0001
2.57	.4949	.0051	3.03	.4988	.0012	3.78	.4999	.0001
2.58	.4951	.0049	3.04	.4988	.0012	3.80	.4999	.0001
2.59	.4952	.0048	3.05	.4989	.0011	3.82	.4999	.0001
2.60	.4953	.0047	3.06	.4989	.0011	3.84	.4999	.0001
2.61	.4955	.0045	3.07	.4989	.0011	3.86	.4999	.0001
2.62	.4956	.0044	3.08	.4990	.0010	3.88	.4999	.0001
2.63	.4957	.0043	3.09	.4990	.0010	3.90	.5000	.0000
2.64	.4959	.0041	3.10	.4990	.0010	3.92	.5000	.0000
2.65	.4960	.0040	3.11	.4991	.0009	3.94	.5000	.0000
2.66	.4961	.0039	3.12	.4991	.0009	3.96	.5000	.0000
2.67	.4962	.0038	3.13	.4991	.0009	3.98	.5000	.0000

TABLE A.2: 1200 TWO-DIGIT RANDOM NUMBERS

Using Table A.2

This table consists of two-digit random numbers that can range between 00 and 99 inclusive. To select a series of random numbers, select a column and row at random, and then record the numbers. You may move in any direction to generate the sequence of numbers.

Example

A researcher wished to randomly assign participants to one of five treatment conditions. Recognizing that the numbers in Table A.2 range between 00 and 99, the researcher decided to use the following table to convert the random numbers to the five treatment conditions:

Range of random numbers	Treatment condition
00–20	1
21–40	2
41–60	3
61–80	4
81–99	5

TABLE A.2

	1	2	3	4	5	6	7	8	9	10	11	12	13	14	15	16	17	18	19	20	21	22	23	24
1	43	41	16	31	22	44	10	41	45	00	47	19	43	67	83	02	79	05	98	92	64	82	06	89
2	26	44	01	04	28	85	11	91	23	02	39	79	44	45	93	20	17	91	35	15	25	82	18	41
3	83	39	26	84	04	16	89	79	68	85	61	63	03	20	17	76	95	80	27	39	35	82	10	86
4	65	94	48	27	77	65	34	95	04	51	78	90	14	76	90	83	17	76	69	50	34	01	25	08
5	89	38	32	05	09	49	87	93	21	24	88	74	30	94	26	19	23	72	94	80	90	24	55	44
6	77	80	30	43	26	01	43	46	66	40	52	00	44	69	84	10	48	96	49	85	49	84	97	41
7	43	42	26	74	51	05	56	43	06	80	58	22	57	02	11	95	00	91	88	17	71	98	32	56
8	76	76	61	17	69	06	73	37	77	06	36	28	05	73	31	04	44	33	40	74	46	26	02	99
9	42	05	88	83	15	05	28	52	88	78	88	66	50	80	24	38	31	20	48	73	18	85	18	90
10	46	74	76	34	97	40	59	34	86	11	50	98	69	59	46	74	59	60	98	76	96	42	34	83
11	67	15	82	94	59	55	27	99	02	34	47	34	88	98	72	15	38	73	57	42	56	09	85	83
12	03	58	51	69	14	89	24	06	35	31	16	65	71	76	04	80	01	36	00	67	78	73	07	37
13	79	98	19	32	25	95	89	54	20	78	29	81	96	34	62	53	26	09	02	04	63	95	03	53
14	56	12	61	36	21	69	96	06	22	06	01	80	57	72	23	55	05	74	42	55	91	45	60	91
15	58	80	33	35	75	33	35	42	06	79	73	29	89	73	99	07	05	54	42	77	78	99	33	92
16	31	51	77	53	92	51	35	71	34	46	79	43	76	15	76	46	40	04	36	84	83	64	56	73
17	25	77	95	61	71	10	82	51	57	88	29	59	55	84	71	89	64	34	38	33	11	45	47	19
18	02	12	81	84	23	80	58	65	74	13	46	09	33	66	86	74	94	96	07	22	52	39	31	36
19	18	38	40	30	34	27	70	62	35	71	48	96	73	74	28	61	15	37	23	16	91	29	03	06
20	31	76	47	77	59	14	66	85	27	10	63	58	48	66	66	17	91	16	55	70	30	53	05	94
21	50	93	33	61	20	55	10	61	08	76	62	14	22	65	44	95	75	68	94	76	51	21	22	12
22	45	75	89	11	64	06	22	39	20	04	91	47	16	48	19	93	12	02	17	15	94	74	77	37
23	17	97	59	42	77	26	29	88	66	62	53	28	95	01	10	85	31	10	25	75	10	35	99	60
24	23	25	86	94	12	75	66	93	87	95	09	48	85	43	20	94	00	38	53	45	11	77	01	66
25	63	17	05	28	67	39	72	85	02	34	69	56	53	66	09	38	72	31	85	29	62	18	29	37
26	99	81	28	63	05	26	66	16	66	69	18	56	26	53	29	38	08	04	27	93	54	83	53	15
27	86	72	54	89	57	45	05	82	32	64	93	24	83	44	56	65	29	68	69	14	70	79	92	39

TABLE A.2 (*Cont'd.*)

	1	2	3	4	5	6	7	8	9	10	11	12	13	14	15	16	17	18	19	20	21	22	23	24
28	42	50	86	19	08	81	57	09	69	35	29	06	52	43	53	99	57	55	30	63	63	67	94	94
29	42	80	75	06	05	62	69	04	90	49	10	48	34	21	63	94	19	99	96	79	83	41	86	38
30	82	48	69	65	59	74	64	25	66	93	32	56	14	57	80	10	36	17	39	48	46	94	88	43
31	24	81	98	33	40	89	60	97	28	64	78	93	07	84	07	02	63	35	64	30	29	49	37	00
32	15	84	59	73	01	21	67	43	43	74	00	28	64	66	03	80	60	08	51	67	51	89	00	46
33	92	31	60	34	23	72	00	19	78	73	80	36	51	54	45	76	17	34	35	74	78	20	49	95
34	05	80	10	40	30	63	25	78	91	13	77	39	90	78	89	17	45	76	28	64	12	37	60	34
35	67	51	92	66	84	33	15	34	42	73	54	93	02	01	19	87	36	58	08	11	58	38	88	98
36	71	44	83	33	92	84	96	76	87	24	59	41	71	36	86	14	54	31	41	25	15	59	74	52
37	43	13	62	58	75	90	94	10	65	16	51	90	01	40	18	21	51	82	69	91	65	91	22	32
38	97	55	94	52	18	65	73	90	55	80	51	05	60	53	01	52	46	57	21	05	76	61	05	23
39	32	75	70	24	04	98	03	79	84	34	50	06	25	00	05	00	04	25	68	58	99	48	06	80
40	23	87	76	65	51	19	93	54	81	09	71	83	97	24	90	01	81	14	70	16	07	16	05	93
41	21	77	33	17	02	64	55	23	21	84	80	02	79	30	61	46	33	94	28	92	44	27	76	20
42	90	11	17	05	24	52	08	39	94	07	43	58	33	72	04	51	81	79	63	70	94	71	71	68
43	89	00	39	09	55	13	96	24	47	81	18	37	82	37	37	01	95	82	38	57	20	20	35	83
44	58	65	18	34	73	85	20	47	04	68	77	28	80	14	37	24	97	62	87	38	09	09	08	50
45	80	35	64	10	03	18	24	41	54	12	99	97	50	14	15	80	71	87	47	79	50	62	87	42
46	87	26	52	18	56	47	76	29	40	08	12	07	40	49	29	70	60	74	20	50	51	00	17	42
47	54	23	81	36	70	93	10	05	39	54	20	49	10	70	49	13	37	59	44	52	98	13	64	48
48	72	08	17	30	70	44	08	10	25	81	53	39	81	67	13	80	74	09	71	06	95	05	17	00
49	34	59	02	12	20	31	15	96	18	12	37	32	25	96	71	52	78	01	77	18	63	66	96	09
50	97	89	00	94	82	17	49	92	29	73	30	17	78	53	45	29	39	24	95	61	63	76	90	86

TABLE A.3: CRITICAL VALUES FOR STUDENT'S *t*-TEST

Using Table A.3

For any given df, the table shows the values of $t_{critical}$ corresponding to various levels of probability. The $t_{observed}$ is statistically significant at a given α-level when it is equal to or greater than the value shown in the table.

For the single sample t-ratio, $df = N - 1$.

For the two sample t-ratio, $df = (n_1 - 1) + (n_2 - 1)$.

Examples

Nondirectional Hypothesis:

$H_0: \mu - \mu = 0$	$H_1: \mu - \mu \neq 0$	$\alpha = .05$	$df = 30$
$t_{critical} = \pm 2.042$	If $|t_{observed}| \geq |t_{critical}|$ then Reject H_0		

Directional Hypothesis:

$H_0: \mu - \mu \leq 0$	$H_1: \mu - \mu > 0$	$\alpha = .05$	$df = 30$
$t_{critical} = +1.697$	If $t_{observed} \geq t_{critical}$ then Reject H_0		
$H_0: \mu - \mu \geq 0$	$H_1: \mu - \mu < 0$	$\alpha = .05$	$df = 30$
$t_{critical} = -1.697$	If $t_{observed} \leq t_{critical}$ then Reject H_0		

TABLE A.3

	Level of significance of a one-tailed or directional test $H_0: \mu - \mu \geq 0$ or $H_0: \mu - \mu \leq 0$					
	$\alpha = .10$ $1 - \alpha = .90$	$\alpha = .05$ $1 - \alpha = .95$	$\alpha = .025$ $1 - \alpha = .975$	$\alpha = .01$ $1 - \alpha = .99$	$\alpha = .005$ $1 - \alpha = .995$	$\alpha = .0005$ $1 - \alpha = .9995$
	Level of significance of a two-tailed or nondirectional test $H_0: \mu - \mu = 0$					
df	$\alpha = .20$ $1 - \alpha = .80$	$\alpha = .10$ $1 - \alpha = .90$	$\alpha = .05$ $1 - \alpha = .95$	$\alpha = .02$ $1 - \alpha = .98$	$\alpha = .01$ $1 - \alpha = .99$	$\alpha = .001$ $1 - \alpha = .999$
1	3.078	6.314	12.706	31.821	63.656	636.578
2	1.886	2.920	4.303	6.965	9.925	31.600
3	1.638	2.353	3.182	4.541	5.841	12.924
4	1.533	2.132	2.776	3.747	4.604	8.610
5	1.476	2.015	2.571	3.365	4.032	6.869
6	1.440	1.943	2.447	3.143	3.707	5.959
7	1.415	1.895	2.365	2.998	3.499	5.408
8	1.397	1.860	2.306	2.896	3.355	5.041
9	1.383	1.833	2.262	2.821	3.250	4.781
10	1.372	1.812	2.228	2.764	3.169	4.587
11	1.363	1.796	2.201	2.718	3.106	4.437
12	1.356	1.782	2.179	2.681	3.055	4.318
13	1.350	1.771	2.160	2.650	3.012	4.221
14	1.345	1.761	2.145	2.624	2.977	4.140
15	1.341	1.753	2.131	2.602	2.947	4.073
16	1.337	1.746	2.120	2.583	2.921	4.015
17	1.333	1.740	2.110	2.567	2.898	3.965
18	1.330	1.734	2.101	2.552	2.878	3.922
19	1.328	1.729	2.093	2.539	2.861	3.883
20	1.325	1.725	2.086	2.528	2.845	3.850
21	1.323	1.721	2.080	2.518	2.831	3.819
22	1.321	1.717	2.074	2.508	2.819	3.792
23	1.319	1.714	2.069	2.500	2.807	3.768
24	1.318	1.711	2.064	2.492	2.797	3.745
25	1.316	1.708	2.060	2.485	2.787	3.725
26	1.315	1.706	2.056	2.479	2.779	3.707
27	1.314	1.703	2.052	2.473	2.771	3.689
28	1.313	1.701	2.048	2.467	2.763	3.674
29	1.311	1.699	2.045	2.462	2.756	3.660
30	1.310	1.697	2.042	2.457	2.750	3.646
40	1.303	1.684	2.021	2.423	2.704	3.551
50	1.299	1.676	2.009	2.403	2.678	3.496
60	1.296	1.671	2.000	2.390	2.660	3.460
70	1.294	1.667	1.994	2.381	2.648	3.435
80	1.292	1.664	1.990	2.374	2.639	3.416
90	1.291	1.662	1.987	2.368	2.632	3.402
100	1.290	1.660	1.984	2.364	2.626	3.390
150	1.287	1.655	1.976	2.351	2.609	3.357
200	1.286	1.653	1.972	2.345	2.601	3.340
500	1.283	1.648	1.965	2.334	2.586	3.310
1000	1.282	1.646	1.962	2.330	2.581	3.300
∞	1.282	1.645	1.960	2.326	2.576	3.290

TABLE A.4: POWER OF STUDENT'S SINGLE SAMPLE *t*-RATIO

Using Table A.4

This table provides the power $(1 - \beta)$ of the single sample *t*-ratio given effect size, sample size (n), α, and directionality of the test.

Example

A researcher plans to conduct a study for which H_0: $\mu = 12.0$ using a single sample *t*-test. The researcher will use $\alpha = .05$ two-tailed and believes that the effect size is .20. Approximately how many participants should be in the sample of power to be approximately .80? According to Table A.4, if the researcher uses 200 participants, the power will be $1 - \beta = .82$.

Note

Effect size

Small $d = .20$ Medium $d = .50$ Large $d = .80$

TABLE A.4

Power table: Single sample *t*-ratio

	$\alpha = .05$ two-tailed				$\alpha = .01$ two-tailed				
n	t_c	.10	.20	.50	.80	t_c	.10	.20	.50	.80
5	2.306	.07	.09	.19	.37	3.355	.02	.03	.07	.16
6	2.228	.07	.09	.22	.44	3.169	.02	.03	.08	.21
7	2.179	.07	.09	.24	.50	3.055	.02	.03	.10	.25
8	2.145	.07	.10	.27	.57	2.977	.02	.03	.11	.30
9	2.120	.07	.10	.30	.62	2.921	.02	.03	.13	.35
10	2.101	.07	.10	.33	.67	2.878	.02	.03	.14	.40
11	2.086	.07	.11	.35	.72	2.845	.02	.03	.16	.45
12	2.074	.07	.11	.38	.76	2.819	.02	.03	.18	.50
13	2.064	.07	.11	.41	.80	2.797	.02	.04	.19	.54
14	2.056	.07	.12	.44	.83	2.779	.02	.04	.21	.59
15	2.048	.07	.12	.46	.86	2.763	.02	.04	.23	.63
16	2.042	.07	.12	.49	.88	2.750	.02	.04	.25	.67
17	2.037	.07	.13	.51	.90	2.738	.02	.04	.27	.71
18	2.032	.07	.13	.54	.92	2.728	.02	.04	.29	.74
19	2.028	.07	.14	.56	.94	2.719	.02	.05	.31	.78
20	2.024	.08	.14	.59	.95	2.712	.02	.05	.33	.80
21	2.021	.08	.14	.61	.96	2.704	.02	.05	.35	.83
22	2.018	.08	.15	.63	.97	2.698	.02	.05	.37	.85
23	2.015	.08	.15	.65	.97	2.692	.02	.05	.39	.87
24	2.013	.08	.16	.67	.98	2.687	.02	.05	.41	.89
25	2.011	.08	.16	.69	.98	2.682	.02	.06	.43	.91
30	2.002	.08	.18	.78	.99	2.663	.02	.07	.53	.96
40	1.991	.09	.23	.89	.99	2.640	.03	.09	.70	.99
50	1.984	.10	.28	.95	.99	2.627	.03	.11	.82	.99

(*continued*)

TABLE A.4 (*Cont'd.*)

Power table: Single sample *t*-ratio

		$\alpha = .05$ two-tailed					$\alpha = .01$ two-tailed			
n	t_c	.10	.20	.50	.80	t_c	.10	.20	.50	.80
60	1.980	.11	.32	.98	.99	2.618	.04	.14	.90	.99
70	1.977	.13	.37	.99	.99	2.612	.04	.17	.95	.99
80	1.975	.14	.42	.99	.99	2.607	.04	.20	.98	.99
90	1.973	.15	.46	.99	.99	2.604	.05	.23	.99	.99
100	1.972	.16	.50	.99	.99	2.601	.05	.26	.99	.99
150	1.968	.22	.69	.99	.99	2.592	.08	.43	.99	.99
200	1.966	.28	.82	.99	.99	2.588	.11	.59	.99	.99
250	1.965	.34	.90	.99	.99	2.586	.15	.72	.99	.99
300	1.964	.39	.95	.99	.99	2.584	.18	.82	.99	.99
350	1.963	.45	.98	.99	.99	2.583	.22	.89	.99	.99
400	1.963	.51	.99	.99	.99	2.582	.26	.94	.99	.99
500	1.962	.61	.99	.99	.99	2.581	.35	.98	.99	.99
600	1.962	.69	.99	.99	.99	2.580	.43	.99	.99	.99
700	1.962	.76	.99	.99	.99	2.579	.51	.99	.99	.99
800	1.961	.82	.99	.99	.99	2.579	.59	.99	.99	.99
900	1.961	.87	.99	.99	.99	2.579	.66	.99	.99	.99
1000	1.961	.90	.99	.99	.99	2.578	.72	.99	.99	.99

TABLE A.5.1: POWER OF STUDENT'S TWO SAMPLE *t*-RATIO, ONE-TAILED TESTS

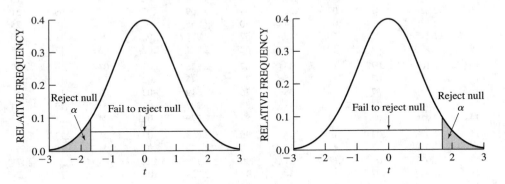

Using Table A.5.1

This table provides the power $(1 - \beta)$ of the two sample *t*-ratio given effect size, sample size (*n*), and α when the researcher uses a directional test.

Example

A researcher plans to conduct a study for which H_0: $\mu_1 \leq \mu_2$ using a two sample *t*-ratio. The researcher will use $\alpha = .05$ one-tailed and believes that the effect size is .20. Approximately how many participants should be in the sample of power to be approximately .80? According to Table A.4, if the researcher uses 300 participants in each sample, the power will be $1 - \beta = .81$.

Note

Effect size

Small $d = .20$ Medium $d = .50$ Large $d = .80$

TABLE A.5.1

Power table: Two sample t-ratio, one-tailed tests

		$\alpha = .05$ one-tailed				$\alpha = .01$ one-tailed			
n	t_c	.10	.20	.50	.80	t_c	.10	.20	.50	.80
5	1.860	.12	.13	.21	.33	2.896	.04	.04	.07	.13
6	1.812	.12	.14	.22	.38	2.764	.03	.04	.08	.15
7	1.782	.12	.14	.24	.42	2.681	.03	.04	.08	.18
8	1.761	.12	.14	.26	.46	2.624	.03	.04	.09	.21
9	1.746	.12	.14	.28	.50	2.583	.03	.04	.10	.23
10	1.734	.12	.14	.29	.54	2.552	.03	.04	.11	.26
11	1.725	.12	.14	.31	.57	2.528	.03	.04	.12	.29
12	1.717	.12	.15	.33	.61	2.508	.03	.04	.13	.32
13	1.711	.12	.15	.35	.64	2.492	.03	.04	.14	.35
14	1.706	.12	.15	.36	.67	2.479	.03	.04	.15	.37
15	1.701	.12	.15	.38	.70	2.467	.03	.04	.16	.40
16	1.697	.12	.16	.40	.73	2.457	.03	.04	.17	.43
17	1.694	.12	.16	.41	.75	2.449	.03	.05	.18	.46
18	1.691	.12	.16	.43	.78	2.441	.03	.05	.19	.49
19	1.688	.12	.16	.45	.80	2.434	.03	.05	.20	.52
20	1.686	.12	.17	.46	.82	2.429	.03	.05	.21	.54
21	1.684	.12	.17	.48	.84	2.423	.03	.05	.22	.57
22	1.682	.12	.17	.50	.85	2.418	.03	.05	.23	.59
23	1.680	.12	.17	.51	.87	2.414	.03	.05	.24	.62
24	1.679	.12	.18	.53	.88	2.410	.03	.05	.25	.64
25	1.677	.12	.18	.54	.89	2.407	.03	.05	.26	.66
30	1.672	.13	.19	.61	.94	2.392	.03	.06	.32	.76
40	1.665	.13	.22	.73	.98	2.375	.03	.07	.44	.89
50	1.661	.14	.25	.82	.99	2.365	.04	.09	.55	.96
60	1.658	.15	.28	.88	.99	2.358	.04	.10	.65	.99
70	1.656	.15	.31	.92	.99	2.354	.04	.12	.73	.99
80	1.655	.16	.34	.95	.99	2.350	.04	.13	.80	.99
90	1.653	.17	.37	.97	.99	2.347	.05	.15	.85	.99
100	1.653	.18	.40	.98	.99	2.345	.05	.17	.90	.99
150	1.650	.21	.53	.99	.99	2.339	.07	.26	.99	.99
200	1.649	.25	.64	.99	.99	2.336	.09	.35	.99	.99
250	1.648	.29	.74	.99	.99	2.334	.10	.45	.99	.99
300	1.647	.33	.81	.99	.99	2.333	.12	.54	.99	.99
350	1.647	.36	.86	.99	.99	2.332	.14	.62	.99	.99
400	1.647	.40	.90	.99	.99	2.331	.17	.69	.99	.99
500	1.646	.47	.96	.99	.99	2.330	.21	.81	.99	.99
600	1.646	.53	.98	.99	.99	2.329	.26	.89	.99	.99
700	1.646	.59	.99	.99	.99	2.329	.30	.94	.99	.99
800	1.646	.64	.99	.99	.99	2.329	.35	.97	.99	.99
900	1.646	.69	.99	.99	.99	2.328	.40	.98	.99	.99
1000	1.646	.74	.99	.99	.99	2.328	.45	.99	.99	.99

TABLE A.5.2: POWER OF STUDENT'S TWO SAMPLE *t*-RATIO, TWO-TAILED TESTS

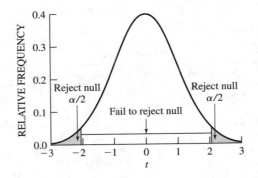

Using Table A.5.2

This table provides the power $(1 - \beta)$ of the two sample *t*-ratio given effect size, sample size (*n*), and α when the researcher uses a nondirectional test.

Example

A researcher plans to conduct a study for which $H_0: \mu_1 = \mu_2$ using a two sample *t*-ratio. The researcher will use $\alpha = .05$ two-tailed and believes that the effect size is .20. Approximately how many participants should be in the sample of power to be approximately .80? According to Table A.4, if the researcher uses 400 participants in each group, the power will be $1 - \beta = .82$.

Note

Effect size

Small $d = .20$ Medium $d = .50$ Large $d = .80$

TABLE A.5.2

		$\alpha = .05$ two-tailed					$\alpha = .01$ two-tailed			
n	t_c	.10	.20	.50	.80	t_c	.10	.20	.50	.80
5	2.306	.07	.08	.13	.22	3.355	.02	.02	.04	.08
6	2.228	.07	.08	.14	.26	3.169	.02	.02	.05	.10
7	2.179	.07	.08	.15	.29	3.055	.02	.02	.05	.12
8	2.145	.07	.08	.17	.33	2.977	.02	.02	.06	.14
9	2.120	.07	.08	.18	.36	2.921	.02	.02	.07	.16
10	2.101	.07	.08	.19	.40	2.878	.02	.02	.07	.19
11	2.086	.06	.08	.21	.43	2.845	.02	.02	.08	.21
12	2.074	.06	.08	.22	.47	2.819	.02	.02	.09	.23

Power table: Two sample *t*-ratio, two-tailed tests

TABLE A.5.2 (*Cont'd.*)

Power table: Two sample *t*-ratio, two-tailed tests

		$\alpha = .05$ two-tailed					$\alpha = .01$ two-tailed			
n	t_c	.10	.20	.50	.80	t_c	.10	.20	.50	.80
13	2.064	.06	.08	.23	.50	2.797	.02	.03	.09	.26
14	2.056	.06	.09	.25	.53	2.779	.02	.03	.10	.28
15	2.048	.06	.09	.26	.56	2.763	.02	.03	.11	.31
16	2.042	.06	.09	.28	.59	2.750	.02	.03	.11	.33
17	2.037	.06	.09	.29	.62	2.738	.02	.03	.12	.36
18	2.032	.06	.09	.30	.65	2.728	.02	.03	.13	.38
19	2.028	.06	.10	.32	.68	2.719	.02	.03	.14	.41
20	2.024	.06	.10	.33	.70	2.712	.02	.03	.15	.43
21	2.021	.07	.10	.35	.72	2.704	.02	.03	.15	.46
22	2.018	.07	.10	.36	.75	2.698	.02	.03	.16	.48
23	2.015	.07	.10	.37	.77	2.692	.02	.03	.17	.51
24	2.013	.07	.10	.39	.79	2.687	.02	.03	.18	.53
25	2.011	.07	.11	.40	.80	2.682	.02	.03	.19	.56
30	2.002	.07	.12	.47	.88	2.663	.02	.04	.24	.67
40	1.991	.07	.14	.60	.96	2.640	.02	.05	.34	.83
50	1.984	.08	.16	.70	.99	2.627	.02	.06	.44	.92
60	1.980	.08	.18	.79	.99	2.618	.02	.07	.54	.97
70	1.977	.09	.21	.85	.99	2.612	.02	.08	.63	.99
80	1.975	.09	.23	.90	.99	2.607	.03	.09	.71	.99
90	1.973	.10	.25	.93	.99	2.604	.03	.10	.78	.99
100	1.972	.10	.28	.96	.99	2.601	.03	.11	.83	.99
150	1.968	.13	.39	.99	.99	2.592	.04	.18	.97	.99
200	1.966	.16	.50	.99	.99	2.588	.05	.26	.99	.99
250	1.965	.19	.60	.99	.99	2.586	.07	.35	.99	.99
300	1.964	.22	.69	.99	.99	2.584	.08	.43	.99	.99
350	1.963	.25	.76	.99	.99	2.583	.10	.51	.99	.99
400	1.963	.28	.82	.99	.99	2.582	.11	.59	.99	.99
500	1.962	.34	.90	.99	.99	2.581	.15	.72	.99	.99
600	1.962	.39	.95	.99	.99	2.580	.18	.82	.99	.99
700	1.962	.45	.98	.99	.99	2.579	.22	.89	.99	.99
800	1.961	.51	.99	.99	.99	2.579	.26	.94	.99	.99
900	1.961	.56	.99	.99	.99	2.579	.31	.96	.99	.99
1000	1.961	.61	.99	.99	.99	2.578	.35	.98	.99	.99

TABLE A.6: CRITICAL VALUES FOR PEARSON'S CORRELATION COEFFICIENT

Using Table A.6

For any given df, the table shows the values of r corresponding to various levels of probability. The $r_{observed}$ is statistically significant at a given level when it is equal to or greater than the value shown in the table.

Examples

Nondirectional Hypothesis:

H_0: $\rho = 0$ H_1: $\rho \neq 0$ $\alpha = .05$ $df = 30$
$r_{\text{critical}} = \pm.3494$ If $|r_{\text{observed}}| \geq |r_{\text{critical}}|$ then Reject H_0

Directional Hypothesis:

H_0: $\rho \leq 0$ H_1: $\rho > 0$ $\alpha = .05$ $df = 30$
$r_{\text{critical}} = +.2960$ If $r_{\text{observed}} \geq r_{\text{critical}}$ then Reject H_0
H_0: $\rho \geq 0$ H_1: $\rho < 0$ $\alpha = .05$ $df = 30$
$r_{\text{critical}} = -.2960$ If $r_{\text{observed}} \leq r_{\text{critical}}$ then Reject H_0

The relation between the correlation coefficient and the t-ratio is:

$$r_c = \frac{t_c}{\sqrt{(n-2) + t_c^2}}$$

TABLE A.6

	Level of significance of a one-tailed or directional test H_0: $\rho \leq 0$ or H_0: $\rho \geq 0$					
	$\alpha = .10$	$\alpha = .05$	$\alpha = .025$	$\alpha = .01$	$\alpha = .005$	$\alpha = .0005$
	Level of significance of a two-tailed or nondirectional test H_0: $\rho = 0$					
df	$\alpha = .20$	$\alpha = .10$	$\alpha = .05$	$\alpha = .02$	$\alpha = .01$	$\alpha = .001$
1	.9511	.9877	.9969	.9995	.9999	.9999
2	.8000	.9000	.9500	.9800	.9900	.9990
3	.6870	.8054	.8783	.9343	.9587	.9911
4	.6084	.7293	.8114	.8822	.9172	.9741
5	.5509	.6694	.7545	.8329	.8745	.9509
6	.5067	.6215	.7067	.7887	.8343	.9249
7	.4716	.5822	.6664	.7498	.7977	.8983
8	.4428	.5494	.6319	.7155	.7646	.8721
9	.4187	.5214	.6021	.6851	.7348	.8470
10	.3981	.4973	.5760	.6581	.7079	.8233
11	.3802	.4762	.5529	.6339	.6835	.8010
12	.3646	.4575	.5324	.6120	.6614	.7800
13	.3507	.4409	.5140	.5923	.6411	.7604
14	.3383	.4259	.4973	.5742	.6226	.7419
15	.3271	.4124	.4821	.5577	.6055	.7247
16	.3170	.4000	.4683	.5425	.5897	.7084
17	.3077	.3887	.4555	.5285	.5751	.6932
18	.2992	.3783	.4438	.5155	.5614	.6788
19	.2914	.3687	.4329	.5034	.5487	.6652
20	.2841	.3598	.4227	.4921	.5368	.6524
21	.2774	.3515	.4132	.4815	.5256	.6402
22	.2711	.3438	.4044	.4716	.5151	.6287
23	.2653	.3365	.3961	.4622	.5052	.6178
24	.2598	.3297	.3882	.4534	.4958	.6074

TABLE A.6 (Cont'd.)

	Level of significance of a one-tailed or directional test $H_0: \rho \le 0$ or $H_0: \rho \ge 0$					
	$\alpha = .10$	$\alpha = .05$	$\alpha = .025$	$\alpha = .01$	$\alpha = .005$	$\alpha = .0005$
	Level of significance of a two-tailed or nondirectional test $H_0: \rho = 0$					
df	$\alpha = .2$	$\alpha = .1$	$\alpha = .05$	$\alpha = .02$	$\alpha = .01$	$\alpha = .001$
25	.2546	.3233	.3809	.4451	.4869	.5974
30	.2327	.2960	.3494	.4093	.4487	.5541
35	.2156	.2746	.3246	.3810	.4182	.5189
40	.2018	.2573	.3044	.3578	.3932	.4896
50	.1806	.2306	.2732	.3218	.3542	.4432
60	.1650	.2108	.2500	.2948	.3248	.4079
70	.1528	.1954	.2319	.2737	.3017	.3798
80	.1430	.1829	.2172	.2565	.2830	.3568
90	.1348	.1726	.2050	.2422	.2673	.3375
100	.1279	.1638	.1946	.2301	.2540	.3211
150	.1045	.1339	.1593	.1886	.2084	.2643
300	.0740	.0948	.1129	.1338	.1480	.1884
500	.0573	.0735	.0875	.1038	.1149	.1464
1000	.0405	.0520	.0619	.0735	.0813	.1038

TABLE A.7: CRITICAL VALUES FOR SPEARMAN'S RANK ORDER CORRELATION COEFFICIENT

Using Table A.7

For any given df, the table shows the values of r_S corresponding to various levels of probability. The $r_{S\text{-observed}}$ is statistically significant at a given level when it is equal to or greater than the value shown in the table.

Examples

Nondirectional Hypothesis:

$H_0: \rho_S = 0$ $\qquad$ $H_1: \rho_S \ne 0$ $\qquad$ $\alpha = .05$ $\quad df = 30$
$r_{\text{critical}} = \pm.350$ $\qquad$ If $|r_{\text{observed}}| \ge |r_{\text{critical}}|$ then Reject H_0

Directional Hypothesis:

$H_0: \rho_S \le 0$ $\qquad$ $H_1: \rho_S > 0$ $\qquad$ $\alpha = .05$ $\quad df = 30$
$r_{\text{critical}} = +.296$ $\qquad$ If $r_{\text{observed}} \ge r_{\text{critical}}$ then Reject H_0
$H_0: \rho_S \ge 0$ $\qquad$ $H_1: \rho_S < 0$ $\qquad$ $\alpha = .05$ $\quad df = 30$
$r_{\text{critical}} = -.296$ $\qquad$ If $r_{\text{observed}} \le r_{\text{critical}}$ then Reject H_0

When $df > 28$ we can convert the r_S to a t-ratio and then use Table A.3 for hypothesis testing.

$$t = r_S \sqrt{\frac{N-2}{1 - r_S^2}}, \quad df = N - 2$$

For example, $r_S = .60$, $N = 42$

$$t = .60\sqrt{\frac{42-2}{1-.60^2}} \qquad t = .60\sqrt{\frac{40}{.64}} \qquad t = .60\sqrt{62.5}$$

$$df = 42 - 2$$

$$t = 4.74, \quad df = 40$$

If $\alpha = .05$, two-tailed

$$t_{\text{critical}} = 1.684 \qquad \text{Reject } H_0: \rho_S = 0$$

TABLE A.7

	Level of significance of a one-tailed or directional test H_0: $\rho_S \le 0$ or H_0: $\rho_S \ge 0$					
	$\alpha = .1$	$\alpha = .05$	$\alpha = .025$	$\alpha = .01$	$\alpha = .005$	$\alpha = .0005$
	Level of significance of a two-tailed or nondirectional test H_0: $\rho_S = 0$					
df	$\alpha = .2$	$\alpha = .1$	$\alpha = .05$	$\alpha = .02$	$\alpha = .01$	$\alpha = .001$
2	1.000	1.000				
3	.800	.900	1.000	1.000		
4	.657	.829	.886	.943	1.000	
5	.571	.714	.786	.893	.929	1.000
6	.524	.643	.738	.833	.881	.976
7	.483	.600	.700	.783	.833	.933
8	.455	.564	.648	.745	.794	.903
9	.427	.536	.618	.709	.755	.873
10	.406	.503	.587	.678	.727	.846
11	.385	.484	.560	.648	.703	.824
12	.367	.464	.538	.626	.679	.802
13	.354	.446	.521	.604	.654	.779
14	.341	.429	.503	.582	.635	.762
15	.328	.414	.485	.566	.615	.748
16	.317	.401	.472	.550	.600	.728
17	.309	.391	.460	.535	.584	.712
18	.299	.380	.447	.520	.570	.696
19	.292	.370	.435	.508	.556	.681
20	.284	.361	.425	.496	.544	.667
21	.278	.353	.415	.486	.532	.654
22	.271	.344	.406	.476	.521	.642
23	.265	.337	.398	.466	.511	.630
24	.259	.331	.390	.457	.501	.619
25	.255	.324	.382	.448	.491	.608
26	.250	.317	.375	.440	.483	.598
27	.245	.312	.368	.433	.475	.589
28	.240	.306	.362	.425	.467	.580
29	.236	.301	.356	.418	.459	.571
30	.232	.296	.350	.412	.452	.563

TABLE A.8: r TO z TRANSFORMATION

Using Table A.8

This table provides the Fisher r to z transformation. Both positive and negative values of r may be used. For specific transformations, use the following equation:

$$z_r = \frac{1}{2} \log_e \left(\frac{1 + r}{1 - r} \right)$$

Example

$$r = .25 \quad z_r = .255$$

TABLE A.8

r	z_r	r	z_r	r	z_r	r	z_r
.00	0.000	.25	0.255	.50	0.549	.75	0.973
.01	0.010	.26	0.266	.51	0.563	.76	0.996
.02	0.020	.27	0.277	.52	0.576	.77	1.020
.03	0.030	.28	0.288	.53	0.590	.78	1.045
.04	0.040	.29	0.299	.54	0.604	.79	1.071
.05	0.050	.30	0.310	.55	0.618	.80	1.099
.06	0.060	.31	0.321	.56	0.633	.81	1.127
.07	0.070	.32	0.332	.57	0.648	.82	1.157
.08	0.080	.33	0.343	.58	0.662	.83	1.188
.09	0.090	.34	0.354	.59	0.678	.84	1.221
.10	0.100	.35	0.365	.60	0.693	.85	1.256
.11	0.110	.36	0.377	.61	0.709	.86	1.293
.12	0.121	.37	0.388	.62	0.725	.87	1.333
.13	0.131	.38	0.400	.63	0.741	.88	1.376
.14	0.141	.39	0.412	.64	0.758	.89	1.422
.15	0.151	.40	0.424	.65	0.775	.90	1.472
.16	0.161	.41	0.436	.66	0.793	.91	1.528
.17	0.172	.42	0.448	.67	0.811	.92	1.589
.18	0.182	.43	0.460	.68	0.829	.93	1.658
.19	0.192	.44	0.472	.69	0.848	.94	1.738
.20	0.203	.45	0.485	.70	0.867	.95	1.832
.21	0.213	.46	0.497	.71	0.887	.96	1.946
.22	0.224	.47	0.510	.72	0.908	.97	2.092
.23	0.234	.48	0.523	.73	0.929	.98	2.298
.24	0.245	.49	0.536	.74	0.950	.99	2.647

TABLE A.9: POWER OF PEARSON'S CORRELATION COEFFICIENT

Using Table A.9

This table provides estimates of the power $(1 - \beta)$ of the Pearson Correlation Coefficient (r) given effect size, sample size (n), α, and directionality of the test.

Example

A researcher plans to conduct a study for which H_0: $\rho = 0$ using a two-tailed test. The researcher will use $\alpha = .05$ two-tailed and believes that the effect size is .30. Approximately how many participants should be in the sample of power to be approximately .80? According to Table A.4, if the researcher uses 90 participants, the power will be $1 - \beta = .82$.

Note

Effect size

Small $r = .10$ Medium $r = .30$ Large $r = .50$

TABLE A.9

	$\alpha = .05$ one-tailed Effect size: r						$\alpha = .05$ two-tailed Effect size: r				
n	.10	.30	.50	.70	.95	n	.10	.30	.50	.70	.95
10	.07	.19	.42	.75	.98	10	.03	.11	.29	.63	.99
11	.07	.21	.46	.80	.99	11	.03	.12	.33	.69	.99
12	.08	.23	.50	.83	.99	12	.04	.14	.37	.74	.99
13	.08	.24	.54	.87	.99	13	.04	.15	.40	.78	.99
14	.08	.26	.57	.89	.99	14	.04	.16	.44	.82	.99
15	.09	.27	.60	.91	.99	15	.04	.17	.47	.85	.99
16	.09	.29	.63	.93	.99	16	.04	.19	.50	.88	.99
17	.09	.31	.66	.94	.99	17	.05	.20	.53	.90	.99
18	.09	.32	.69	.96	.99	18	.05	.21	.56	.92	.99
19	.10	.33	.71	.96	.99	19	.05	.22	.59	.93	.99
20	.10	.35	.73	.97	.99	20	.05	.24	.61	.94	.99
21	.10	.36	.75	.98	.99	21	.05	.25	.64	.95	.99
22	.10	.38	.77	.98	.99	22	.05	.26	.66	.96	.99
23	.11	.39	.79	.98	.99	23	.06	.27	.69	.97	.99
24	.11	.40	.81	.99	.99	24	.06	.28	.71	.97	.99
25	.11	.42	.82	.99	.99	25	.06	.30	.73	.98	.99
26	.11	.43	.84	.99	.99	26	.06	.31	.75	.98	.99
27	.12	.44	.85	.99	.99	27	.06	.32	.76	.98	.99
28	.12	.46	.86	.99	.99	28	.06	.33	.78	.99	.99
29	.12	.47	.88	.99	.99	29	.06	.34	.80	.99	.99
30	.12	.48	.89	.99	.99	30	.07	.35	.81	.99	.99
31	.12	.49	.89	.99	.99	31	.07	.37	.83	.99	.99
32	.13	.50	.90	.99	.99	32	.07	.38	.84	.99	.99
33	.13	.52	.91	.99	.99	33	.07	.39	.85	.99	.99
34	.13	.53	.92	.99	.99	34	.07	.40	.86	.99	.99
35	.13	.54	.93	.99	.99	35	.07	.41	.87	.99	.99
36	.13	.55	.93	.99	.99	36	.07	.42	.88	.99	.99
37	.14	.56	.94	.99	.99	37	.08	.43	.89	.99	.99
38	.14	.57	.94	.99	.99	38	.08	.44	.90	.99	.99
39	.14	.58	.95	.99	.99	39	.08	.45	.91	.99	.99
40	.14	.59	.95	.99	.99	40	.08	.46	.91	.99	.99
50	.17	.69	.98	.99	.99	50	.09	.56	.96	.99	.99
60	.18	.75	.99	.99	.99	60	.11	.64	.98	.99	.99
70	.20	.81	.99	.99	.99	70	.12	.71	.99	.99	.99
80	.22	.85	.99	.99	.99	80	.13	.77	.99	.99	.99

TABLE A.9 (*Cont'd.*)

	α = .05 one-tailed Effect size: r						α = .05 two-tailed Effect size: r				
n	.10	.30	.50	.70	.95	*n*	.10	.30	.50	.70	.95
90	.23	.89	.99	.99	.99	90	.15	.82	.99	.99	.99
100	.25	.92	.99	.99	.99	100	.16	.86	.99	.99	.99
200	.40	.99	.99	.99	.99	200	.28	.99	.99	.99	.99
300	.53	.99	.99	.99	.99	300	.40	.99	.99	.99	.99
400	.63	.99	.99	.99	.99	400	.51	.99	.99	.99	.99
500	.72	.99	.99	.99	.99	500	.60	.99	.99	.99	.99

TABLE A.10: CRITICAL VALUES FOR THE *F*-RATIO

Using Table A.10

This table provides the critical values required to reject the null hypothesis for the analysis of variance. The bold text represents $\alpha = .01$ whereas the regular text represents $\alpha = .05$.

To use the table, you will need to identify the degrees of freedom for the numerator and denominator. The numerator degrees of freedom are those used to determine the mean square for the treatment effect or interaction. The denominator degrees of freedom are those used to determine the mean square for the within-groups or error variance.

Example: One-factor ANOVA

A researcher conducts a study that produces the following ANOVA summary table:

Source	SS	df	MS	F
Between-Groups	28.00	2	14.00	3.50
Within-Groups	156.00	39	4.00	
Total	184.00	41		

From the summary table,

Degrees of Freedom, Numeration: $df_N = 2$
Degrees of Freedom, Denominator: $df_D = 39$
$F_{observed} = 3.50$

From Table A.10:
Because the exact values of the degrees of freedom for the denominator are not listed, you must use the average of the two adjacent numbers:

$F_{critical}(2, 38) = 3.24, \alpha = .05$ $F_{critical}(2, 38) = 5.21, \alpha = .01$
$F_{critical}(2, 40) = 3.23, \alpha = .05$ $F_{critical}(2, 40) = 5.15, \alpha = .01$

Therefore,

$F_{critical}(2, 39) = 3.235, \alpha = .05$ $F_{critical}(2, 39) = 5.18, \alpha = .01$
$F_{observed} = 3.50 > F_{critical} = 3.235$, Reject H_0 $F_{observed} = 3.50 < F_{critical} = 5.18$, Do Not Reject H_0

TABLE A.10
Critical values for the F-ratio

Degrees of freedom for denominator (left) / Degrees of freedom for numerator (columns)

df	α	1	2	3	4	5	6	7	8	9	10	11	12	13	14	15	30	50	100	1000
1	.05	161	199	216	225	230	234	237	239	241	242	243	244	245	245	246	250	252	253	254
	.01	4052	4999	5404	5624	5764	5859	5928	5981	6022	6056	6083	6107	6126	6143	6157	6260	6302	6334	6363
2	.05	18.51	19.00	19.16	19.25	19.30	19.33	19.35	19.37	19.38	19.40	19.40	19.41	19.42	19.42	19.43	19.46	19.48	19.49	19.49
	.01	98.50	99.00	99.16	99.25	99.30	99.33	99.36	99.38	99.39	99.40	99.41	99.42	99.42	99.43	99.43	99.47	99.48	99.49	99.50
3	.05	10.13	9.55	9.28	9.12	9.01	8.94	8.89	8.85	8.81	8.79	8.76	8.74	8.73	8.71	8.70	8.62	8.58	8.55	8.53
	.01	34.12	30.82	29.46	28.71	28.24	27.91	27.67	27.49	27.34	27.23	27.13	27.05	26.98	26.92	26.87	26.50	26.35	26.24	26.14
4	.05	7.71	6.94	6.59	6.39	6.26	6.16	6.09	6.04	6.00	5.96	5.94	5.91	5.89	5.87	5.86	5.75	5.70	5.66	5.63
	.01	21.20	18.00	16.69	15.98	15.52	15.21	14.98	14.80	14.66	14.55	14.45	14.37	14.31	14.25	14.20	13.84	13.69	13.58	13.47
5	.05	6.61	5.79	5.41	5.19	5.05	4.95	4.88	4.82	4.77	4.74	4.70	4.68	4.66	4.64	4.62	4.50	4.44	4.41	4.37
	.01	16.26	13.27	12.06	11.39	10.97	10.67	10.46	10.29	10.16	10.05	9.96	9.89	9.82	9.77	9.72	9.38	9.24	9.13	9.03
6	.05	5.99	5.14	4.76	4.53	4.39	4.28	4.21	4.15	4.10	4.06	4.03	4.00	3.98	3.96	3.94	3.81	3.75	3.71	3.67
	.01	13.75	10.92	9.78	9.15	8.75	8.47	8.26	8.10	7.98	7.87	7.79	7.72	7.66	7.60	7.56	7.23	7.09	6.99	6.89
7	.05	5.59	4.74	4.35	4.12	3.97	3.87	3.79	3.73	3.68	3.64	3.60	3.57	3.55	3.53	3.51	3.38	3.32	3.27	3.23
	.01	12.25	9.55	8.45	7.85	7.46	7.19	6.99	6.84	6.72	6.62	6.54	6.47	6.41	6.36	6.31	5.99	5.86	5.75	5.66
8	.05	5.32	4.46	4.07	3.84	3.69	3.58	3.50	3.44	3.39	3.35	3.31	3.28	3.26	3.24	3.22	3.08	3.02	2.97	2.93
	.01	11.26	8.65	7.59	7.01	6.63	6.37	6.18	6.03	5.91	5.81	5.73	5.67	5.61	5.56	5.52	5.20	5.07	4.96	4.87
9	.05	5.12	4.26	3.86	3.63	3.48	3.37	3.29	3.23	3.18	3.14	3.10	3.07	3.05	3.03	3.01	2.86	2.80	2.76	2.71
	.01	10.56	8.02	6.99	6.42	6.06	5.80	5.61	5.47	5.35	5.26	5.18	5.11	5.05	5.01	4.96	4.65	4.52	4.41	4.32
10	.05	4.96	4.10	3.71	3.48	3.33	3.22	3.14	3.07	3.02	2.98	2.94	2.91	2.89	2.86	2.85	2.70	2.64	2.59	2.54
	.01	10.04	7.56	6.55	5.99	5.64	5.39	5.20	5.06	4.94	4.85	4.77	4.71	4.65	4.60	4.56	4.25	4.12	4.01	3.92
11	.05	4.84	3.98	3.59	3.36	3.20	3.09	3.01	2.95	2.90	2.85	2.82	2.79	2.76	2.74	2.72	2.57	2.51	2.46	2.41
	.01	9.65	7.21	6.22	5.67	5.32	5.07	4.89	4.74	4.63	4.54	4.46	4.40	4.34	4.29	4.25	3.94	3.81	3.71	3.61
12	.05	4.75	3.89	3.49	3.26	3.11	3.00	2.91	2.85	2.80	2.75	2.72	2.69	2.66	2.64	2.62	2.47	2.40	2.35	2.30
	.01	9.33	6.93	5.95	5.41	5.06	4.82	4.64	4.50	4.39	4.30	4.22	4.16	4.10	4.05	4.01	3.70	3.57	3.47	3.37
13	.05	4.67	3.81	3.41	3.18	3.03	2.92	2.83	2.77	2.71	2.67	2.63	2.60	2.58	2.55	2.53	2.38	2.31	2.26	2.21
	.01	9.07	6.70	5.74	5.21	4.86	4.62	4.44	4.30	4.19	4.10	4.02	3.96	3.91	3.86	3.82	3.51	3.38	3.27	3.18

Degrees of freedom for denominator

df	α																		
14	.05	4.60	3.74	3.34	3.11	2.96	2.85	2.76	2.70	2.65	2.60	2.57	2.53	2.51	2.48	2.46	2.31	2.24	2.19	2.14
	.01	8.86	6.51	5.56	5.04	4.69	4.46	4.28	4.14	4.03	3.94	3.86	3.80	3.75	3.70	3.66	3.35	3.22	3.11	3.02
15	.05	4.54	3.68	3.29	3.06	2.90	2.79	2.71	2.64	2.59	2.54	2.51	2.48	2.45	2.42	2.40	2.25	2.18	2.12	2.07
	.01	8.68	6.36	5.42	4.89	4.56	4.32	4.14	4.00	3.89	3.80	3.73	3.67	3.61	3.56	3.52	3.21	3.08	2.98	2.88
16	.05	4.49	3.63	3.24	3.01	2.85	2.74	2.66	2.59	2.54	2.49	2.46	2.42	2.40	2.37	2.35	2.19	2.12	2.07	2.02
	.01	8.53	6.23	5.29	4.77	4.44	4.20	4.03	3.89	3.78	3.69	3.62	3.55	3.50	3.45	3.41	3.10	2.97	2.86	2.76
17	.05	4.45	3.59	3.20	2.96	2.81	2.70	2.61	2.55	2.49	2.45	2.41	2.38	2.35	2.33	2.31	2.15	2.08	2.02	1.97
	.01	8.40	6.11	5.19	4.67	4.34	4.10	3.93	3.79	3.68	3.59	3.52	3.46	3.40	3.35	3.31	3.00	2.87	2.76	2.66
18	.05	4.41	3.55	3.16	2.93	2.77	2.66	2.58	2.51	2.46	2.41	2.37	2.34	2.31	2.29	2.27	2.11	2.04	1.98	1.92
	.01	8.29	6.01	5.09	4.58	4.25	4.01	3.84	3.71	3.60	3.51	3.43	3.37	3.32	3.27	3.23	2.92	2.78	2.68	2.58
19	.05	4.38	3.52	3.13	2.90	2.74	2.63	2.54	2.48	2.42	2.38	2.34	2.31	2.28	2.26	2.23	2.07	2.00	1.94	1.88
	.01	8.18	5.93	5.01	4.50	4.17	3.94	3.77	3.63	3.52	3.43	3.36	3.30	3.24	3.19	3.15	2.84	2.71	2.60	2.50
20	.05	4.35	3.49	3.10	2.87	2.71	2.60	2.51	2.45	2.39	2.35	2.31	2.28	2.25	2.22	2.20	2.04	1.97	1.91	1.85
	.01	8.10	5.85	4.94	4.43	4.10	3.87	3.70	3.56	3.46	3.37	3.29	3.23	3.18	3.13	3.09	2.78	2.64	2.54	2.43
21	.05	4.32	3.47	3.07	2.84	2.68	2.57	2.49	2.42	2.37	2.32	2.28	2.25	2.22	2.20	2.18	2.01	1.94	1.88	1.82
	.01	8.02	5.78	4.87	4.37	4.04	3.81	3.64	3.51	3.40	3.31	3.24	3.17	3.12	3.07	3.03	2.72	2.58	2.48	2.37
22	.05	4.30	3.44	3.05	2.82	2.66	2.55	2.46	2.40	2.34	2.30	2.26	2.23	2.20	2.17	2.15	1.98	1.91	1.85	1.79
	.01	7.95	5.72	4.82	4.31	3.99	3.76	3.59	3.45	3.35	3.26	3.18	3.12	3.07	3.02	2.98	2.67	2.53	2.42	2.32
23	.05	4.28	3.42	3.03	2.80	2.64	2.53	2.44	2.37	2.32	2.27	2.24	2.20	2.18	2.15	2.13	1.96	1.88	1.82	1.76
	.01	7.88	5.66	4.76	4.26	3.94	3.71	3.54	3.41	3.30	3.21	3.14	3.07	3.02	2.97	2.93	2.62	2.48	2.37	2.27
24	.05	4.26	3.40	3.01	2.78	2.62	2.51	2.42	2.36	2.30	2.25	2.22	2.18	2.15	2.13	2.11	1.94	1.86	1.80	1.74
	.01	7.82	5.61	4.72	4.22	3.90	3.67	3.50	3.36	3.26	3.17	3.09	3.03	2.98	2.93	2.89	2.58	2.44	2.33	2.22
25	.05	4.24	3.39	2.99	2.76	2.60	2.49	2.40	2.34	2.28	2.24	2.20	2.16	2.14	2.11	2.09	1.92	1.84	1.78	1.72
	.01	7.77	5.57	4.68	4.18	3.85	3.63	3.46	3.32	3.22	3.13	3.06	2.99	2.94	2.89	2.85	2.54	2.40	2.29	2.18
26	.05	4.23	3.37	2.98	2.74	2.59	2.47	2.39	2.32	2.27	2.22	2.18	2.15	2.12	2.09	2.07	1.90	1.82	1.76	1.70
	.01	7.72	5.53	4.64	4.14	3.82	3.59	3.42	3.29	3.18	3.09	3.02	2.96	2.90	2.86	2.81	2.50	2.36	2.25	2.14
27	.05	4.21	3.35	2.96	2.73	2.57	2.46	2.37	2.31	2.25	2.20	2.17	2.13	2.10	2.08	2.06	1.88	1.81	1.74	1.68
	.01	7.68	5.49	4.60	4.11	3.78	3.56	3.39	3.26	3.15	3.06	2.99	2.93	2.87	2.82	2.78	2.47	2.33	2.22	2.11
28	.05	4.20	3.34	2.95	2.71	2.56	2.45	2.36	2.29	2.24	2.19	2.15	2.12	2.09	2.06	2.04	1.87	1.79	1.73	1.66
	.01	7.64	5.45	4.57	4.07	3.75	3.53	3.36	3.23	3.12	3.03	2.96	2.90	2.84	2.79	2.75	2.44	2.30	2.19	2.08

Degrees of freedom for denominator

(continued)

TABLE A.10 (Cont'd.)

Degrees of freedom for numerator

	α	1	2	3	4	5	6	7	8	9	10	11	12	13	14	15	30	50	100	1000
29	.05	4.18	3.33	2.93	2.70	2.55	2.43	2.35	2.28	2.22	2.18	2.14	2.10	2.08	2.05	2.03	1.85	1.77	1.71	1.65
	.01	7.60	5.42	4.54	4.04	3.73	3.50	3.33	3.20	3.09	3.00	2.93	2.87	2.81	2.77	2.73	2.41	2.27	2.16	2.05
30	.05	4.17	3.32	2.92	2.69	2.53	2.42	2.33	2.27	2.21	2.16	2.13	2.09	2.06	2.04	2.01	1.84	1.76	1.70	1.63
	.01	7.56	5.39	4.51	4.02	3.70	3.47	3.30	3.17	3.07	2.98	2.91	2.84	2.79	2.74	2.70	2.39	2.25	2.13	2.02
31	.05	4.16	3.30	2.91	2.68	2.52	2.41	2.32	2.25	2.20	2.15	2.11	2.08	2.05	2.03	2.00	1.83	1.75	1.68	1.62
	.01	7.53	5.36	4.48	3.99	3.67	3.45	3.28	3.15	3.04	2.96	2.88	2.82	2.77	2.72	2.68	2.36	2.22	2.11	1.99
32	.05	4.15	3.29	2.90	2.67	2.51	2.40	2.31	2.24	2.19	2.14	2.10	2.07	2.04	2.01	1.99	1.82	1.74	1.67	1.60
	.01	7.50	5.34	4.46	3.97	3.65	3.43	3.26	3.13	3.02	2.93	2.86	2.80	2.74	2.70	2.65	2.34	2.20	2.08	1.97
33	.05	4.14	3.28	2.89	2.66	2.50	2.39	2.30	2.23	2.18	2.13	2.09	2.06	2.03	2.00	1.98	1.81	1.72	1.66	1.59
	.01	7.47	5.31	4.44	3.95	3.63	3.41	3.24	3.11	3.00	2.91	2.84	2.78	2.72	2.68	2.63	2.32	2.18	2.06	1.95
34	.05	4.13	3.28	2.88	2.65	2.49	2.38	2.29	2.23	2.17	2.12	2.08	2.05	2.02	1.99	1.97	1.80	1.71	1.65	1.58
	.01	7.44	5.29	4.42	3.93	3.61	3.39	3.22	3.09	2.98	2.89	2.82	2.76	2.70	2.66	2.61	2.30	2.16	2.04	1.92
35	.05	4.12	3.27	2.87	2.64	2.49	2.37	2.29	2.22	2.16	2.11	2.07	2.04	2.01	1.99	1.96	1.79	1.70	1.63	1.57
	.01	7.42	5.27	4.40	3.91	3.59	3.37	3.20	3.07	2.96	2.88	2.80	2.74	2.69	2.64	2.60	2.28	2.14	2.02	1.90
36	.05	4.11	3.26	2.87	2.63	2.48	2.36	2.28	2.21	2.15	2.11	2.07	2.03	2.00	1.98	1.95	1.78	1.69	1.62	1.56
	.01	7.40	5.25	4.38	3.89	3.57	3.35	3.18	3.05	2.95	2.86	2.79	2.72	2.67	2.62	2.58	2.26	2.12	2.00	1.89
38	.05	4.10	3.24	2.85	2.62	2.46	2.35	2.26	2.19	2.14	2.09	2.05	2.02	1.99	1.96	1.94	1.76	1.68	1.61	1.54
	.01	7.35	5.21	4.34	3.86	3.54	3.32	3.15	3.02	2.92	2.83	2.75	2.69	2.64	2.59	2.55	2.23	2.09	1.97	1.85
40	.05	4.08	3.23	2.84	2.61	2.45	2.34	2.25	2.18	2.12	2.08	2.04	2.00	1.97	1.95	1.92	1.74	1.66	1.59	1.52
	.01	7.31	5.18	4.31	3.83	3.51	3.29	3.12	2.99	2.89	2.80	2.73	2.66	2.61	2.56	2.52	2.20	2.06	1.94	1.82
42	.05	4.07	3.22	2.83	2.59	2.44	2.32	2.24	2.17	2.11	2.06	2.03	1.99	1.96	1.94	1.91	1.73	1.65	1.57	1.50
	.01	7.28	5.15	4.29	3.80	3.49	3.27	3.10	2.97	2.86	2.78	2.70	2.64	2.59	2.54	2.50	2.18	2.03	1.91	1.79
44	.05	4.06	3.21	2.82	2.58	2.43	2.31	2.23	2.16	2.10	2.05	2.01	1.98	1.95	1.92	1.90	1.72	1.63	1.56	1.49
	.01	7.25	5.12	4.26	3.78	3.47	3.24	3.08	2.95	2.84	2.75	2.68	2.62	2.56	2.52	2.47	2.15	2.01	1.89	1.76
46	.05	4.05	3.20	2.81	2.57	2.42	2.30	2.22	2.15	2.09	2.04	2.00	1.97	1.94	1.91	1.89	1.71	1.62	1.55	1.47
	.01	7.22	5.10	4.24	3.76	3.44	3.22	3.06	2.93	2.82	2.73	2.66	2.60	2.54	2.50	2.45	2.13	1.99	1.86	1.74

Degrees of freedom for denominator

df (denom.)	α																			
48	.05	4.04	3.19	2.80	2.57	2.41	2.29	2.21	2.14	2.08	2.03	1.99	1.96	1.93	1.90	1.88	1.70	1.61	1.54	1.46
	.01	7.19	5.08	4.22	3.74	3.43	3.20	3.04	2.91	2.80	2.71	2.64	2.58	2.53	2.48	2.44	2.12	1.97	1.84	1.72
50	.05	4.03	3.18	2.79	2.56	2.40	2.29	2.20	2.13	2.07	2.03	1.99	1.95	1.92	1.89	1.87	1.69	1.60	1.52	1.45
	.01	7.17	5.06	4.20	3.72	3.41	3.19	3.02	2.89	2.78	2.70	2.63	2.56	2.51	2.46	2.42	2.10	1.95	1.82	1.70
55	.05	4.02	3.16	2.77	2.54	2.38	2.27	2.18	2.11	2.06	2.01	1.97	1.93	1.90	1.88	1.85	1.67	1.58	1.50	1.42
	.01	7.12	5.01	4.16	3.68	3.37	3.15	2.98	2.85	2.75	2.66	2.59	2.53	2.47	2.42	2.38	2.06	1.91	1.78	1.65
60	.05	4.00	3.15	2.76	2.53	2.37	2.25	2.17	2.10	2.04	1.99	1.95	1.92	1.89	1.86	1.84	1.65	1.56	1.48	1.40
	.01	7.08	4.98	4.13	3.65	3.34	3.12	2.95	2.82	2.72	2.63	2.56	2.50	2.44	2.39	2.35	2.03	1.88	1.75	1.62
65	.05	3.99	3.14	2.75	2.51	2.36	2.24	2.15	2.08	2.03	1.98	1.94	1.90	1.87	1.85	1.82	1.63	1.54	1.46	1.38
	.01	7.04	4.95	4.10	3.62	3.31	3.09	2.93	2.80	2.69	2.61	2.53	2.47	2.42	2.37	2.33	2.00	1.85	1.72	1.59
70	.05	3.98	3.13	2.74	2.50	2.35	2.23	2.14	2.07	2.02	1.97	1.93	1.89	1.86	1.84	1.81	1.62	1.53	1.45	1.36
	.01	7.01	4.92	4.07	3.60	3.29	3.07	2.91	2.78	2.67	2.59	2.51	2.45	2.40	2.35	2.31	1.98	1.83	1.70	1.56
80	.05	3.96	3.11	2.72	2.49	2.33	2.21	2.13	2.06	2.00	1.95	1.91	1.88	1.84	1.82	1.79	1.60	1.51	1.43	1.34
	.01	6.96	4.88	4.04	3.56	3.26	3.04	2.87	2.74	2.64	2.55	2.48	2.42	2.36	2.31	2.27	1.94	1.79	1.65	1.51
100	.05	3.94	3.09	2.70	2.46	2.31	2.19	2.10	2.03	1.97	1.93	1.89	1.85	1.82	1.79	1.77	1.57	1.48	1.39	1.30
	.01	6.90	4.82	3.98	3.51	3.21	2.99	2.82	2.69	2.59	2.50	2.43	2.37	2.31	2.27	2.22	1.89	1.74	1.60	1.45
125	.05	3.92	3.07	2.68	2.44	2.29	2.17	2.08	2.01	1.96	1.91	1.87	1.83	1.80	1.77	1.75	1.55	1.45	1.36	1.26
	.01	6.84	4.78	3.94	3.47	3.17	2.95	2.79	2.66	2.55	2.47	2.39	2.33	2.28	2.23	2.19	1.85	1.69	1.55	1.39
150	.05	3.90	3.06	2.66	2.43	2.27	2.16	2.07	2.00	1.94	1.89	1.85	1.82	1.79	1.76	1.73	1.54	1.44	1.34	1.24
	.01	6.81	4.75	3.91	3.45	3.14	2.92	2.76	2.63	2.53	2.44	2.37	2.31	2.25	2.20	2.16	1.83	1.66	1.52	1.35
200	.05	3.89	3.04	2.65	2.42	2.26	2.14	2.06	1.98	1.93	1.88	1.84	1.80	1.77	1.74	1.72	1.52	1.41	1.32	1.21
	.01	6.76	4.71	3.88	3.41	3.11	2.89	2.73	2.60	2.50	2.41	2.34	2.27	2.22	2.17	2.13	1.79	1.63	1.48	1.30
400	.05	3.86	3.02	2.63	2.39	2.24	2.12	2.03	1.96	1.90	1.85	1.81	1.78	1.74	1.72	1.69	1.49	1.38	1.28	1.15
	.01	6.70	4.66	3.83	3.37	3.06	2.85	2.68	2.56	2.45	2.37	2.29	2.23	2.17	2.13	2.08	1.75	1.58	1.42	1.22
1000	.05	3.85	3.00	2.61	2.38	2.22	2.11	2.02	1.95	1.89	1.84	1.80	1.76	1.73	1.70	1.68	1.47	1.36	1.26	1.11
	.01	6.66	4.63	3.80	3.34	3.04	2.82	2.66	2.53	2.43	2.34	2.27	2.20	2.15	2.10	2.06	1.72	1.54	1.38	1.16

Degrees of freedom for denominator

Example: Two-factor ANOVA

Source	SS	df	MS	F
Variable A	0.067	1	0.067	0.01
Variable B	80.433	2	40.217	6.859
AB	58.233	2	29.117	4.966
Within-groups	316.600	54	5.863	
Total	455.333	59		

From the summary table:

	$\alpha = .05$			Statistical Decision
Variable A:	$df_N = 1$ $df_D = 54$		$F_{observed} = 0.01$	$F_{critical}$ (1, 54) = 4.02, $\alpha = .05$, Do Not Reject H_0
Variable B:	$df_N = 2$ $df_D = 54$		$F_{observed} = 6.859$	$F_{critical}$ (2, 54) = 3.16, $\alpha = .05$, Reject H_0
Variable AB:	$df_N = 2$ $df_D = 54$		$F_{observed} = 4.966$	$F_{critical}$ (2, 54) = 3.16, $\alpha = .05$, Reject H_0

	$\alpha = .01$			Statistical Decision
Variable A:	$df_N = 1$ $df_D = 54$		$F_{observed} = 0.01$	$F_{critical}$ (1, 54) = 7.12, $\alpha = .01$, Do Not Reject H_0
Variable B:	$df_N = 2$ $df_D = 54$		$F_{observed} = 6.859$	$F_{critical}$ (2, 54) = 5.01, $\alpha = .01$, Reject H_0
Variable AB:	$df_N = 2$ $df_D = 54$		$F_{observed} = 4.966$	$F_{critical}$ (2, 54) = 5.01, $\alpha = .01$, Do Not Reject H_0

TABLE A.11: CRITICAL VALUES FOR THE F_{max} TEST

Using Table A.11

To use this table, divide the largest variance by the smallest variance to create F_{max}. The column labeled n represents the number of subjects in each group. If the sample sizes for the two groups are not equal, determine the average n and round up. The other columns of numbers represent the number of treatment conditions in the study. If the observed value of F_{max} is less than the tabled value, then you may assume that the variances are homogeneous, $\sigma_{smallest} = \sigma_{largest}$.

Example

A researcher conducted a study with 6 groups. The largest variance was 20 and the smallest variance was 10, with 15 participants in each group. $F_{max} = 2.00$. The critical value of $F_{max} = 4.70$, $\alpha = .05$. Therefore, we do NOT reject the hypothesis that the variances are equivalent. The data do not appear to violate the requirement that there be homogeneity of variance for the ANOVA.

TABLE A.11

| n | α | \multicolumn{9}{c}{Number of variances in study} |
		2	3	4	5	6	7	8	9	10
4	.05	9.60	15.5	20.6	25.2	29.5	33.6	37.5	41.4	44.6
	.01	23.2	37.0	49.0	59.0	69.0	79.0	89.0	97.0	106.0
5	.05	7.2	10.8	13.7	16.3	18.7	20.8	22.9	24.7	26.5
	.01	14.9	22.0	28.0	33.0	38.0	42.0	46.0	50.0	54.0
6	.05	5.8	8.4	10.4	12.1	13.7	15.0	16.3	17.5	18.6
	.01	11.1	15.5	19.1	22.0	25.0	27.0	30.0	32.0	34.0
7	.05	5.0	6.9	8.4	9.7	10.8	11.8	12.7	13.5	14.3
	.01	8.9	12.1	14.5	16.5	18.4	20.0	22.0	23.0	24.0
8	.05	4.4	6.0	7.2	8.1	9.0	9.8	10.5	11.1	11.7
	.01	7.5	9.9	11.7	13.2	14.5	15.8	16.9	17.9	18.9
9	.05	4.0	5.3	6.3	7.1	7.8	8.4	8.9	9.5	9.9
	.01	6.5	8.5	9.9	11.1	12.1	13.1	13.9	14.7	15.3
10	.05	3.7	4.9	5.7	6.3	6.9	7.4	7.9	8.3	8.7
	.01	5.9	7.4	8.6	9.6	10.4	11.1	11.8	12.4	12.9
12	.05	3.3	4.2	4.8	5.3	5.7	6.1	6.4	6.7	7.0
	.01	4.9	6.1	6.9	7.6	8.2	8.7	9.1	9.5	9.9
15	.05	2.7	3.5	4.0	4.4	4.7	4.9	5.2	5.4	5.6
	.01	4.1	4.9	5.5	6.0	6.4	6.7	7.1	7.3	7.5
20	.05	2.5	2.9	3.3	3.5	3.7	3.9	4.1	4.2	4.4
	.01	3.3	3.8	4.3	4.6	4.9	5.1	5.3	5.5	5.6
30	.05	2.1	2.4	2.6	2.8	2.9	3.0	3.1	3.2	3.3
	.01	2.6	3.0	3.3	3.4	3.6	3.7	3.8	3.9	4.0
60	.05	1.7	1.9	1.9	2.0	2.1	2.2	2.2	2.3	2.3
	.01	2.0	2.2	2.3	2.4	2.4	2.5	2.5	2.6	2.6
∞	.05	1.0	1.0	1.0	1.0	1.0	1.0	1.0	1.0	1.0
	.01	1.0	1.0	1.0	1.0	1.0	1.0	1.0	1.0	1.0

TABLE A.12: CRITICAL VALUES FOR THE STUDENTIZED RANGE TEST

Using Table A.12

This table contains the critical values developed by Tukey for his HSD test. To use the table, you will need the degrees of freedom for the within-groups term in the ANOVA summary table and the number of means to be compared by the HSD test.

Example

A researcher conducted a study with 4 groups. The degrees of freedom denominator (df for the within-groups factor) are 12. Using Table A.12,

$q_{critical} = 3.62, \alpha = .10$

$q_{critical} = 4.20, \alpha = .05$

$q_{critical} = 5.50, \alpha = .01$

TABLE A.12

		2	3	4	5	6	7	8	9	10	11	12	13	14	15	16	17	18
	α							Number of means in set										
1	.10	8.93	13.40	16.40	18.50	20.20	21.50	22.60	23.60	24.50	25.20	25.90	26.50	27.10	27.60	28.10	28.50	29.00
	.05	18.00	27.00	32.80	37.10	40.40	43.10	45.40	47.40	49.10	50.60	52.00	53.20	54.30	55.40	56.30	57.20	58.00
	.01	90.00	135.0	164.00	186.00	202.00	216.00	227.00	237.00	246.00	253.00	260.00	266.00	272.00	277.00	282.00	286.00	290.00
2	.10	4.13	5.73	6.78	7.54	8.14	8.63	9.05	9.41	9.73	10.00	10.30	10.50	10.70	10.90	11.10	11.20	11.40
	.05	6.09	8.30	9.80	10.90	11.70	12.40	13.00	13.50	14.00	14.40	14.70	15.10	15.40	15.70	15.90	16.10	16.40
	.01	14.00	19.00	22.30	24.70	26.60	28.20	29.50	30.70	31.70	32.60	33.40	34.10	34.80	35.40	36.00	36.50	37.00
3	.10	3.33	4.47	5.20	5.74	6.16	6.51	6.81	7.06	7.29	7.49	7.67	7.83	7.98	8.12	8.25	8.37	8.78
	.05	4.50	5.91	6.82	7.50	8.04	8.48	8.85	9.18	9.46	9.72	9.95	10.20	10.40	10.50	10.70	10.80	11.00
	.01	8.26	10.60	12.20	13.30	14.20	15.00	15.60	16.20	16.70	17.10	17.50	17.90	18.20	18.50	18.80	19.10	19.30
4	.10	3.01	3.98	4.59	5.04	5.39	5.69	5.93	6.14	6.33	6.50	6.65	6.78	6.91	7.03	7.13	7.23	7.33
	.05	3.93	5.04	5.76	6.29	6.71	7.05	7.35	7.60	7.83	8.03	8.21	8.37	8.52	8.66	8.79	8.91	9.03
	.01	6.51	8.12	9.17	9.96	10.60	11.10	11.50	11.90	12.30	12.60	12.80	13.10	13.30	13.50	13.70	13.90	14.10
5	.10	2.85	3.72	4.26	4.66	4.98	5.24	5.44	5.65	5.82	5.97	6.10	6.22	6.34	6.44	6.54	6.63	6.71
	.05	3.64	4.60	5.22	5.67	6.03	6.33	6.58	6.80	6.99	7.17	7.32	7.47	7.60	7.72	7.83	7.93	8.03
	.01	5.70	6.97	7.80	8.42	8.91	9.32	9.67	9.97	10.20	10.50	10.70	10.90	11.10	11.20	11.40	11.60	11.70
6	.10	2.75	3.56	4.07	4.44	4.73	4.97	5.17	5.34	5.50	5.64	5.76	5.88	5.98	6.08	6.16	6.25	6.33
	.05	3.46	4.34	4.90	5.31	5.63	5.89	6.12	6.32	6.49	6.65	6.79	6.92	7.03	7.14	7.24	7.34	7.43
	.01	5.24	6.33	7.03	7.56	7.97	8.32	8.61	8.87	9.10	9.30	9.49	9.65	9.81	9.95	10.10	10.20	10.30
7	.10	2.68	3.45	3.93	4.28	4.56	4.78	4.97	5.14	5.28	5.41	5.53	5.64	5.74	5.83	5.91	5.99	6.06
	.05	3.34	4.16	4.69	5.06	5.36	5.61	5.82	6.00	6.16	6.30	6.43	6.55	6.66	6.76	6.85	6.94	7.02
	.01	4.95	5.92	6.54	7.01	7.37	7.68	7.94	8.17	8.37	8.55	8.71	8.86	9.00	9.12	9.24	9.35	9.46
8	.10	2.63	3.37	3.83	4.17	4.43	4.65	4.83	4.99	5.13	5.25	5.36	5.46	5.56	5.64	5.74	5.83	5.87
	.05	3.26	4.04	4.53	4.89	5.17	5.40	5.60	5.77	5.92	6.05	6.18	6.29	6.39	6.48	6.57	6.65	6.73
	.01	4.74	5.63	6.20	6.63	6.96	7.24	7.47	7.68	7.78	8.03	8.18	8.31	8.44	8.55	8.66	8.76	8.85
9	.10	2.59	3.32	3.76	4.08	4.34	4.55	4.72	4.87	5.01	5.13	5.23	5.33	5.42	5.51	5.58	5.66	5.72
	.05	3.20	3.95	4.42	4.76	5.02	5.24	5.43	5.60	5.74	5.87	5.98	6.09	6.19	6.28	6.36	6.44	6.51
	.01	4.60	5.43	5.96	6.35	6.66	6.91	7.13	7.32	7.49	7.65	7.78	7.91	8.03	8.13	8.23	8.33	8.41
10	.10	2.56	3.28	3.70	4.02	4.26	4.47	4.64	4.78	4.91	5.03	5.13	5.23	5.32	5.40	5.47	5.54	5.61
	.05	3.15	3.88	4.33	4.65	4.91	5.12	5.30	5.46	5.60	5.72	5.83	5.93	6.03	6.11	6.19	6.27	6.34
	.01	4.48	5.27	5.77	6.14	6.43	6.67	6.87	7.05	7.21	7.36	7.48	7.60	7.71	7.81	7.91	8.00	8.08

Degrees of freedom for denominator

df	α																	
11	.10	5.51	5.45	5.38	5.31	5.23	5.15	5.05	4.95	4.84	4.71	4.57	4.40	4.21	3.97	3.66	3.23	2.54
	.05	6.20	6.18	6.06	5.99	5.90	5.81	5.71	5.61	5.49	5.35	5.20	5.03	4.82	4.57	4.26	3.82	3.11
	.01	7.81	7.73	7.65	7.56	7.46	7.36	7.26	7.13	6.99	6.84	6.67	6.48	6.25	5.97	5.62	5.14	4.39
12	.10	5.44	5.37	5.31	5.24	5.16	5.08	4.99	4.89	4.78	4.65	4.51	4.35	4.16	3.92	3.62	3.20	2.52
	.05	6.09	6.02	5.95	5.88	5.80	5.71	5.62	5.51	5.40	5.27	5.12	4.95	4.75	4.51	4.20	3.77	3.08
	.01	7.50	7.52	7.44	7.36	7.26	7.17	7.06	6.94	6.81	6.67	6.51	6.32	6.10	5.84	5.50	5.04	4.32
13	.10	5.37	5.31	5.25	5.18	5.10	5.02	4.93	4.83	4.72	4.60	4.46	4.31	4.12	3.89	3.59	3.18	2.51
	.05	6.00	5.93	5.86	5.79	5.71	5.63	5.53	5.43	5.32	5.19	5.05	4.88	4.69	4.45	4.15	3.73	3.06
	.01	7.42	7.37	7.27	7.19	7.10	7.01	6.90	6.79	6.67	6.53	6.37	6.19	5.98	5.73	5.40	4.96	4.26
14	.10	5.32	5.26	5.19	5.12	5.05	4.97	4.88	4.79	4.68	4.56	4.42	4.27	4.08	3.83	3.56	3.16	2.99
	.05	5.92	5.85	5.79	5.72	5.64	5.55	5.46	5.36	5.25	5.13	4.99	4.83	4.64	4.41	4.11	3.70	3.03
	.01	7.27	7.20	7.13	7.05	6.96	6.87	6.77	6.66	6.54	6.41	6.26	6.08	5.88	5.63	5.32	4.89	4.21
16	.10	5.23	5.17	5.11	5.04	4.97	4.89	4.81	4.71	4.61	4.49	4.36	4.21	4.03	3.80	3.52	3.12	2.47
	.05	5.79	5.73	5.66	5.59	5.52	5.44	5.35	5.26	5.15	5.03	4.90	4.74	4.56	4.33	4.05	3.65	3.00
	.01	7.03	6.97	6.90	6.82	6.74	6.66	6.56	6.46	6.35	6.22	6.08	5.92	5.72	5.49	5.19	4.78	4.13
18	.10	5.16	5.10	5.04	4.98	4.91	4.83	4.75	4.66	4.55	4.44	4.31	4.16	3.98	3.77	3.49	3.10	2.45
	.05	5.69	5.63	5.57	5.50	5.43	5.35	5.27	5.17	5.07	4.96	4.82	4.67	4.49	4.28	4.00	3.61	2.97
	.01	6.85	6.79	6.73	6.65	6.58	6.50	6.41	6.31	6.20	6.08	5.94	5.79	5.60	5.38	5.09	4.70	4.07
20	.10	5.10	5.05	4.99	4.92	4.86	4.78	4.70	4.61	4.51	4.40	4.27	4.12	3.95	3.74	3.46	3.08	2.44
	.05	5.61	5.55	5.49	5.43	5.36	5.28	5.20	5.11	5.01	4.90	4.77	4.62	4.45	4.23	3.96	3.58	2.95
	.01	6.71	6.65	6.59	6.52	6.45	6.37	6.29	6.19	6.09	5.97	5.84	5.69	5.51	5.29	5.02	4.64	4.02
24	.10	5.02	4.97	4.91	4.85	4.78	4.71	4.63	4.54	4.45	4.34	4.21	4.07	3.90	3.69	3.42	3.05	2.42
	.05	5.49	5.44	5.38	5.32	5.25	5.18	5.1	5.01	4.92	4.81	4.68	4.54	4.37	4.17	3.9	3.53	2.92
	.01	6.51	6.45	6.39	6.33	6.26	6.19	6.11	6.02	5.92	5.81	5.69	5.54	5.37	5.17	4.91	4.54	3.96
30	.10	4.94	4.89	4.83	4.77	4.71	4.64	4.56	4.47	4.38	4.28	4.16	4.02	3.85	3.65	3.39	3.02	2.4
	.05	5.38	5.33	5.27	5.21	5.15	5.08	5	4.92	4.83	4.72	4.6	4.46	4.3	4.1	3.84	3.49	2.89
	.01	6.31	6.26	6.2	6.14	6.08	6.01	5.93	5.85	5.76	5.56	5.4	5.24	5.05	4.8	4.45	3.89	
40	.10	4.86	4.81	4.75	4.7	4.63	4.56	4.49	4.41	4.32	4.22	4.1	3.96	3.8	3.61	3.35	2.99	2.38
	.05	5.27	5.22	5.16	5.11	5.05	4.98	4.91	4.82	4.74	4.63	4.52	4.39	4.23	4.04	3.79	3.44	2.86
	.01	6.11	6.07	6.02	5.96	5.9	5.84	5.77	5.69	5.6	5.5	5.39	5.27	5.11	4.93	4.7	4.37	3.82
60	.10	4.78	4.73	4.68	4.62	4.56	4.49	4.42	4.34	4.26	4.16	4.04	3.91	3.76	3.56	3.31	2.96	2.36
	.05	5.15	5.11	5.06	5	4.94	4.88	4.81	4.73	4.65	4.55	4.44	4.31	4.16	3.98	3.74	3.4	2.83
	.01	5.93	5.89	5.84	5.79	5.73	5.67	5.6	5.53	5.45	5.36	5.25	5.13	4.99	4.82	4.6	4.28	3.76
120	.10	4.69	4.65	4.6	4.59	4.49	4.42	4.35	4.28	4.19	4.1	3.99	3.86	3.71	3.52	3.28	2.93	2.34
	.05	5.04	5	4.95	4.9	4.84	4.78	4.72	4.64	4.56	4.48	4.36	4.24	4.1	3.92	3.69	3.36	2.8
	.01	5.75	5.71	5.66	5.61	5.56	5.51	5.44	5.38	5.3	5.21	5.12	5.01	4.87	4.71	4.5	4.2	3.7

TABLE A.13: POWER OF ANOVA

Using Table A.13

The values in this table help you determine the optimal sample size for an analysis of variance given the anticipated effect size and α-level.

Example: Single-factor design

A researcher wishes to conduct a single-factor design with 3 levels of the independent variable. How many participants will the researcher require in each treatment condition to have power equal to $1 - \beta = .80$ when the effect size is moderate, $f = .25$ and $\alpha = .05$? In this example, $df_N = 2$. According to this table, $1 - \beta = .83$ when there are 55 participants in each treatment condition.

Example: Factorial design

A researcher designed a 3×4 factorial study. How many participants should the researcher use in each treatment condition to have power equal to $1 - \beta = .80$? Also assume that the effect size is moderate, $f = .25$.

First, determine the degrees of freedom for each effect in the ANOVA.

$$df_A = 2 = (3 - 1) \qquad j = \text{levels of Factor A}$$
$$df_B = 3 = (4 - 1) \qquad k = \text{levels of Factor B}$$
$$df_{AB} = 6 = (3 - 1)(4 - 1)$$

Next, adjust the degrees of freedom using the following equation. For this example, assume that the sample size is 10.

$$n'_{\text{effect}} = \frac{jk(n_{ij} - 1)}{df_{\text{effect}} + 1} + 1$$

	df_N		Adjusted sample size	Rounded* sample size	Estimated power
Factor A	2	$n' = \dfrac{12(10 - 1)}{2 + 1} + 1$	$n' = 37$	$n' = 40$	$1 - \beta \approx .68$
Factor B	3	$n' = \dfrac{12(10 - 1)}{3 + 1} + 1$	$n' = 28$	$n' = 30$	$1 - \beta \approx .61$
Factor AB	6	$n' = \dfrac{12(10 - 1)}{6 + 1} + 1$	$n' = 16.429$	$n' = 16$	$1 - \beta \approx .45$

*I rounded the adjusted sample size to conform to the values in the power tables.

Note

Effect size

Small $f = .10$ Medium $f = .25$ Large $f = .40$

TABLE A.13

		$\alpha = .05$		$df_N = 1$			$\alpha = .05$		$df_N = 2$			$\alpha = .05$		$df_N = 3$	
		Effect size, f					Effect size, f					Effect size, f			
n	F_c	.10	.25	.40	.55	F_c	.10	.25	.40	.55	F_c	.10	.25	.40	.55
10	4.414	.08	.19	.40	.65	3.354	.10	.22	.46	.72	2.866	.12	.26	.52	.79
11	4.351	.08	.21	.43	.70	3.316	.10	.24	.50	.77	2.839	.11	.27	.56	.83
12	4.301	.08	.22	.47	.74	3.285	.10	.25	.53	.81	2.816	.11	.29	.60	.87
13	4.260	.08	.23	.50	.78	3.259	.10	.27	.57	.85	2.798	.11	.31	.64	.90
14	4.225	.09	.25	.53	.81	3.238	.10	.28	.60	.88	2.783	.12	.32	.67	.92
15	4.196	.09	.26	.56	.84	3.220	.10	.30	.64	.90	2.769	.12	.34	.71	.94
16	4.171	.09	.28	.59	.87	3.204	.10	.32	.67	.92	2.758	.12	.36	.74	.96
17	4.149	.09	.29	.62	.89	3.191	.10	.33	.70	.94	2.748	.12	.38	.77	.97
18	4.130	.09	.30	.65	.91	3.179	.11	.35	.73	.95	2.739	.12	.39	.79	.98
19	4.113	.10	.32	.68	.92	3.168	.11	.36	.75	.96	2.732	.12	.41	.82	.98
20	4.098	.10	.33	.70	.94	3.159	.11	.38	.78	.97	2.725	.12	.43	.84	.99
21	4.085	.10	.35	.72	.95	3.150	.11	.40	.80	.98	2.719	.12	.45	.86	.99
22	4.073	.10	.36	.75	.96	3.143	.11	.41	.82	.98	2.713	.13	.47	.88	.99
23	4.062	.10	.37	.77	.97	3.136	.12	.43	.84	.99	2.708	.13	.49	.90	.99
24	4.052	.10	.39	.79	.97	3.130	.12	.44	.86	.99	2.704	.13	.50	.91	.99
25	4.043	.11	.40	.80	.98	3.124	.12	.46	.87	.99	2.699	.13	.52	.92	.99
26	4.034	.11	.42	.82	.98	3.119	.12	.48	.89	.99	2.696	.13	.54	.93	.99
27	4.027	.11	.43	.84	.99	3.114	.12	.49	.90	.99	2.692	.14	.56	.94	.99
28	4.020	.11	.44	.85	.99	3.109	.13	.51	.91	.99	2.689	.14	.57	.95	.99
29	4.013	.11	.46	.86	.99	3.105	.13	.52	.92	.99	2.686	.14	.59	.96	.99
30	4.007	.12	.47	.88	.99	3.101	.13	.54	.93	.99	2.683	.14	.61	.97	.99
31	4.001	.12	.48	.89	.99	3.098	.13	.55	.94	.99	2.680	.15	.62	.97	.99
32	3.996	.12	.50	.90	.99	3.094	.13	.57	.95	.99	2.678	.15	.64	.98	.99
33	3.991	.12	.51	.91	.99	3.091	.14	.58	.96	.99	2.675	.15	.65	.98	.99
34	3.986	.13	.52	.92	.99	3.088	.14	.60	.96	.99	2.673	.15	.67	.98	.99
35	3.982	.13	.54	.93	.99	3.085	.14	.61	.97	.99	2.671	.15	.68	.99	.99
36	3.978	.13	.55	.93	.99	3.083	.14	.62	.97	.99	2.669	.16	.70	.99	.99
37	3.974	.13	.56	.94	.99	3.080	.14	.64	.98	.99	2.667	.16	.71	.99	.99
38	3.970	.13	.57	.95	.99	3.078	.15	.65	.98	.99	2.666	.16	.72	.99	.99
39	3.967	.14	.59	.95	.99	3.076	.15	.66	.98	.99	2.664	.17	.74	.99	.99
40	3.963	.14	.60	.96	.99	3.074	.15	.68	.98	.99	2.663	.17	.75	.99	.99
45	3.949	.15	.65	.98	.99	3.065	.16	.73	.99	.99	2.656	.18	.81	.99	.99
50	3.938	.16	.70	.99	.99	3.058	.18	.78	.99	.99	2.651	.20	.85	.99	.99
55	3.929	.17	.75	.99	.99	3.052	.19	.83	.99	.99	2.646	.21	.89	.99	.99
60	3.921	.18	.79	.99	.99	3.047	.20	.86	.99	.99	2.643	.22	.92	.99	.99
70	3.910	.21	.85	.99	.99	3.040	.23	.92	.99	.99	2.637	.26	.96	.99	.99
80	3.901	.23	.90	.99	.99	3.034	.26	.95	.99	.99	2.633	.29	.98	.99	.99
90	3.894	.25	.93	.99	.99	3.030	.28	.97	.99	.99	2.630	.32	.99	.99	.99
100	3.889	.28	.96	.99	.99	3.026	.31	.99	.99	.99	2.627	.35	.99	.99	.99
110	3.884	.30	.97	.99	.99	3.023	.34	.99	.99	.99	2.625	.38	.99	.99	.99
120	3.881	.32	.98	.99	.99	3.021	.37	.99	.99	.99	2.624	.41	.99	.99	.99
130	3.878	.35	.99	.99	.99	3.019	.39	.99	.99	.99	2.622	.45	.99	.99	.99
140	3.875	.37	.99	.99	.99	3.017	.42	.99	.99	.99	2.621	.48	.99	.99	.99
150	3.873	.39	.99	.99	.99	3.016	.45	.99	.99	.99	2.620	.51	.99	.99	.99
160	3.871	.42	.99	.99	.99	3.015	.47	.99	.99	.99	2.619	.54	.99	.99	.99
170	3.869	.44	.99	.99	.99	3.014	.50	.99	.99	.99	2.618	.57	.99	.99	.99
180	3.868	.46	.99	.99	.99	3.013	.53	.99	.99	.99	2.617	.60	.99	.99	.99
190	3.866	.48	.99	.99	.99	3.012	.55	.99	.99	.99	2.617	.62	.99	.99	.99
200	3.865	.50	.99	.99	.99	3.011	.58	.99	.99	.99	2.616	.65	.99	.99	.99
300	3.857	.69	.99	.99	.99	3.006	.78	.99	.99	.99	2.612	.85	.99	.99	.99

(continued)

TABLE A.13 (*Cont'd.*)

		$\alpha = .05$	$df_N = 4$				$\alpha = .05$	$df_N = 5$				$\alpha = .05$	$df_N = 6$		
		Effect size, f					Effect size, f					Effect size, f			
n	F_c	.10	.25	.40	.55	F_c	.10	.25	.40	.55	F_c	.10	.25	.40	.55
10	2.579	.13	.29	.57	.83	2.386	.14	.32	.61	.87	2.246	.16	.34	.65	.89
11	2.557	.13	.31	.61	.87	2.368	.14	.33	.66	.90	2.231	.15	.36	.69	.93
12	2.540	.13	.32	.65	.91	2.354	.14	.35	.70	.93	2.219	.15	.38	.74	.95
13	2.525	.13	.34	.69	.93	2.342	.14	.37	.74	.95	2.209	.15	.40	.77	.97
14	2.513	.13	.36	.73	.95	2.332	.14	.39	.77	.97	2.200	.15	.42	.81	.98
15	2.503	.13	.38	.76	.96	2.323	.14	.42	.80	.98	2.193	.15	.45	.84	.99
16	2.494	.13	.40	.79	.97	2.316	.14	.44	.83	.99	2.186	.15	.47	.87	.99
17	2.486	.13	.42	.82	.98	2.309	.14	.46	.86	.99	2.181	.15	.49	.89	.99
18	2.479	.13	.44	.84	.99	2.303	.14	.48	.88	.99	2.176	.15	.51	.91	.99
19	2.473	.13	.46	.87	.99	2.298	.14	.50	.90	.99	2.171	.16	.54	.93	.99
20	2.467	.13	.48	.89	.99	2.294	.15	.52	.92	.99	2.167	.16	.56	.94	.99
21	2.463	.14	.50	.90	.99	2.290	.15	.54	.93	.99	2.164	.16	.58	.95	.99
22	2.458	.14	.52	.92	.99	2.286	.15	.56	.95	.99	2.161	.16	.60	.96	.99
23	2.454	.14	.54	.93	.99	2.283	.15	.58	.96	.99	2.158	.16	.62	.97	.99
24	2.451	.14	.56	.94	.99	2.280	.15	.60	.96	.99	2.155	.17	.65	.98	.99
25	2.447	.14	.58	.95	.99	2.277	.16	.62	.97	.99	2.153	.17	.67	.98	.99
26	2.444	.15	.59	.96	.99	2.274	.16	.64	.98	.99	2.151	.17	.69	.99	.99
27	2.441	.15	.61	.97	.99	2.272	.16	.66	.98	.99	2.149	.17	.70	.99	.99
28	2.439	.15	.63	.97	.99	2.270	.16	.68	.99	.99	2.147	.18	.72	.99	.99
29	2.436	.15	.65	.98	.99	2.268	.17	.70	.99	.99	2.145	.18	.74	.99	.99
30	2.434	.16	.66	.98	.99	2.266	.17	.72	.99	.99	2.143	.18	.76	.99	.99
31	2.432	.16	.68	.99	.99	2.264	.17	.73	.99	.99	2.142	.18	.77	.99	.99
32	2.430	.16	.70	.99	.99	2.263	.17	.75	.99	.99	2.141	.19	.79	.99	.99
33	2.428	.16	.71	.99	.99	2.261	.18	.76	.99	.99	2.139	.19	.80	.99	.99
34	2.426	.17	.73	.99	.99	2.260	.18	.78	.99	.99	2.138	.19	.82	.99	.99
35	2.425	.17	.74	.99	.99	2.258	.18	.79	.99	.99	2.137	.20	.83	.99	.99
36	2.423	.17	.76	.99	.99	2.257	.19	.80	.99	.99	2.136	.20	.84	.99	.99
37	2.422	.17	.77	.99	.99	2.256	.19	.82	.99	.99	2.135	.20	.85	.99	.99
38	2.420	.18	.78	.99	.99	2.255	.19	.83	.99	.99	2.134	.21	.87	.99	.99
39	2.419	.18	.80	.99	.99	2.254	.20	.84	.99	.99	2.133	.21	.88	.99	.99
40	2.418	.18	.81	.99	.99	2.253	.20	.85	.99	.99	2.132	.21	.89	.99	.99
45	2.413	.20	.86	.99	.99	2.248	.22	.90	.99	.99	2.128	.23	.93	.99	.99
50	2.408	.21	.90	.99	.99	2.245	.23	.93	.99	.99	2.125	.25	.95	.99	.99
55	2.405	.23	.93	.99	.99	2.242	.25	.96	.99	.99	2.123	.27	.97	.99	.99
60	2.402	.25	.95	.99	.99	2.239	.27	.97	.99	.99	2.121	.29	.98	.99	.99
70	2.398	.28	.98	.99	.99	2.236	.31	.99	.99	.99	2.117	.33	.99	.99	.99
80	2.395	.32	.99	.99	.99	2.233	.35	.99	.99	.99	2.115	.38	.99	.99	.99
90	2.392	.35	.99	.99	.99	2.231	.39	.99	.99	.99	2.113	.42	.99	.99	.99
100	2.390	.39	.99	.99	.99	2.229	.43	.99	.99	.99	2.112	.46	.99	.99	.99
110	2.388	.43	.99	.99	.99	2.228	.47	.99	.99	.99	2.110	.51	.99	.99	.99
120	2.387	.46	.99	.99	.99	2.227	.51	.99	.99	.99	2.109	.55	.99	.99	.99
130	2.386	.50	.99	.99	.99	2.226	.54	.99	.99	.99	2.109	.59	.99	.99	.99
140	2.385	.53	.99	.99	.99	2.225	.58	.99	.99	.99	2.108	.63	.99	.99	.99
150	2.384	.57	.99	.99	.99	2.224	.62	.99	.99	.99	2.107	.66	.99	.99	.99
160	2.383	.60	.99	.99	.99	2.223	.65	.99	.99	.99	2.107	.70	.99	.99	.99
170	2.382	.63	.99	.99	.99	2.223	.68	.99	.99	.99	2.106	.73	.99	.99	.99
180	2.382	.66	.99	.99	.99	2.222	.71	.99	.99	.99	2.106	.76	.99	.99	.99
190	2.381	.69	.99	.99	.99	2.222	.74	.99	.99	.99	2.105	.79	.99	.99	.99
200	2.381	.71	.99	.99	.99	2.222	.77	.99	.99	.99	2.105	.81	.99	.99	.99
300	2.378	.90	.99	.99	.99	2.219	.93	.99	.99	.99	2.103	.96	.99	.99	.99

TABLE A.13 (*Cont'd.*)

n	F_c	$\alpha=.01$ $df_N=1$ Effect size, f .10	.25	.40	.55	F_c	$\alpha=.01$ $df_N=2$ Effect size, f .10	.25	.40	.55	F_c	$\alpha=.01$ $df_N=3$ Effect size, f .10	.25	.40	.55
10	8.285	.02	.07	.19	.38	5.488	.03	.10	.25	.48	4.377	.04	.12	.30	.57
11	8.096	.02	.08	.21	.42	5.390	.03	.10	.27	.53	4.313	.04	.13	.34	.63
12	7.945	.02	.09	.23	.47	5.312	.03	.11	.30	.59	4.261	.04	.14	.37	.68
13	7.823	.03	.09	.26	.52	5.248	.03	.12	.33	.64	4.218	.04	.15	.41	.73
14	7.721	.03	.10	.28	.56	5.194	.03	.13	.36	.68	4.182	.04	.16	.44	.78
15	7.636	.03	.11	.31	.60	5.149	.03	.14	.39	.72	4.152	.04	.17	.48	.81
16	7.562	.03	.11	.33	.64	5.110	.03	.15	.42	.76	4.126	.04	.18	.51	.85
17	7.499	.03	.12	.36	.68	5.077	.03	.16	.45	.80	4.103	.04	.19	.55	.88
18	7.444	.03	.13	.38	.71	5.047	.04	.16	.49	.83	4.083	.04	.20	.58	.90
19	7.396	.03	.14	.41	.75	5.021	.04	.18	.52	.86	4.066	.04	.22	.61	.92
20	7.353	.03	.15	.43	.78	4.998	.04	.19	.54	.88	4.050	.04	.23	.64	.94
21	7.314	.03	.15	.46	.80	4.977	.04	.20	.57	.90	4.036	.04	.24	.67	.95
22	7.280	.03	.16	.48	.83	4.959	.04	.21	.60	.92	4.024	.04	.25	.70	.96
23	7.248	.03	.17	.51	.85	4.942	.04	.22	.63	.93	4.012	.05	.27	.73	.97
24	7.220	.03	.18	.53	.87	4.927	.04	.23	.66	.95	4.002	.05	.28	.75	.98
25	7.194	.03	.19	.56	.89	4.913	.04	.24	.68	.96	3.992	.05	.30	.78	.98
26	7.171	.03	.20	.58	.90	4.900	.04	.25	.70	.96	3.984	.05	.31	.80	.99
27	7.149	.03	.21	.60	.92	4.888	.04	.26	.73	.97	3.976	.05	.33	.82	.99
28	7.129	.04	.22	.62	.93	4.877	.04	.28	.75	.98	3.968	.05	.34	.84	.99
29	7.110	.04	.23	.65	.94	4.867	.04	.29	.77	.98	3.961	.05	.35	.86	1.00
30	7.093	.04	.24	.67	.95	4.858	.04	.30	.79	.99	3.955	.05	.37	.87	1.00
31	7.077	.04	.25	.69	.96	4.849	.04	.31	.81	.99	3.949	.05	.38	.89	1.00
32	7.062	.04	.26	.71	.96	4.841	.05	.33	.82	.99	3.944	.05	.40	.90	1.00
33	7.048	.04	.27	.72	.97	4.833	.05	.34	.84	.99	3.938	.05	.41	.91	1.00
34	7.035	.04	.28	.74	.97	4.826	.05	.35	.86	1.00	3.934	.05	.43	.92	1.00
35	7.023	.04	.29	.76	.98	4.819	.05	.36	.87	1.00	3.929	.06	.44	.93	1.00
36	7.011	.04	.30	.77	.98	4.813	.05	.38	.88	1.00	3.925	.06	.46	.94	1.00
37	7.000	.04	.31	.79	.98	4.807	.05	.39	.89	1.00	3.921	.06	.47	.95	1.00
38	6.990	.04	.32	.80	.99	4.802	.05	.40	.90	1.00	3.917	.06	.49	.96	1.00
39	6.981	.04	.33	.82	.99	4.796	.05	.42	.91	1.00	3.913	.06	.50	.96	1.00
40	6.971	.05	.34	.83	.99	4.791	.05	.43	.92	1.00	3.910	.06	.52	.97	1.00
45	6.932	.05	.39	.88	1.00	4.770	.06	.49	.96	1.00	3.895	.07	.59	.99	1.00
50	6.901	.06	.44	.92	1.00	4.753	.06	.55	.98	1.00	3.883	.07	.66	.99	1.00
55	6.876	.06	.49	.95	1.00	4.739	.07	.61	.99	1.00	3.874	.08	.72	1.00	1.00
60	6.855	.07	.54	.97	1.00	4.727	.08	.67	.99	1.00	3.866	.09	.77	1.00	1.00
70	6.822	.08	.63	.99	1.00	4.709	.09	.76	1.00	1.00	3.853	.11	.85	1.00	1.00
80	6.798	.09	.71	1.00	1.00	4.696	.10	.83	1.00	1.00	3.844	.12	.91	1.00	1.00
90	6.779	.10	.78	1.00	1.00	4.686	.12	.89	1.00	1.00	3.837	.14	.95	1.00	1.00
100	6.765	.11	.83	1.00	1.00	4.677	.14	.93	1.00	1.00	3.831	.16	.97	1.00	1.00
110	6.753	.13	.88	1.00	1.00	4.671	.15	.95	1.00	1.00	3.827	.18	.99	1.00	1.00
120	6.743	.14	.91	1.00	1.00	4.665	.17	.97	1.00	1.00	3.823	.21	.99	1.00	1.00
130	6.734	.15	.94	1.00	1.00	4.660	.19	.98	1.00	1.00	3.820	.23	1.00	1.00	1.00
140	6.727	.17	.96	1.00	1.00	4.656	.21	.99	1.00	1.00	3.817	.25	1.00	1.00	1.00
150	6.721	.18	.97	1.00	1.00	4.653	.23	.99	1.00	1.00	3.815	.28	1.00	1.00	1.00
160	6.715	.20	.98	1.00	1.00	4.650	.25	1.00	1.00	1.00	3.813	.30	1.00	1.00	1.00
170	6.710	.21	.99	1.00	1.00	4.647	.27	1.00	1.00	1.00	3.811	.33	1.00	1.00	1.00
180	6.706	.23	.99	1.00	1.00	4.645	.29	1.00	1.00	1.00	3.809	.35	1.00	1.00	1.00
190	6.702	.25	.99	1.00	1.00	4.643	.31	1.00	1.00	1.00	3.808	.38	1.00	1.00	1.00
200	6.699	.26	1.00	1.00	1.00	4.641	.33	1.00	1.00	1.00	3.806	.40	1.00	1.00	1.00
300	6.677	.43	1.00	1.00	1.00	4.629	.54	1.00	1.00	1.00	3.798	.65	1.00	1.00	1.00

(*continued*)

TABLE A.13 (*Cont'd.*)

n	F_c	$\alpha = .01$ $df_N = 4$ Effect size, f .10	.25	.40	.55	F_c	$\alpha = .01$ $df_N = 5$ Effect size, f .10	.25	.40	.55	F_c	$\alpha = .01$ $df_N = 6$ Effect size, f .10	.25	.40	.55
10	3.767	.05	.15	.36	.65	3.377	.06	.17	.41	.71	3.103	.07	.19	.45	.76
11	3.720	.05	.16	.40	.71	3.339	.06	.18	.45	.76	3.071	.07	.20	.50	.81
12	3.681	.05	.17	.43	.76	3.308	.06	.19	.49	.81	3.046	.07	.22	.54	.85
13	3.649	.05	.18	.47	.80	3.283	.06	.20	.53	.85	3.024	.07	.23	.58	.89
14	3.622	.05	.19	.51	.84	3.261	.06	.22	.57	.89	3.007	.07	.25	.62	.92
15	3.600	.05	.20	.55	.87	3.243	.06	.23	.61	.91	2.992	.07	.26	.67	.94
16	3.580	.05	.21	.59	.90	3.228	.06	.25	.65	.94	2.979	.07	.28	.70	.96
17	3.563	.05	.23	.62	.93	3.214	.06	.26	.69	.95	2.967	.06	.30	.74	.97
18	3.548	.05	.24	.66	.94	3.202	.06	.28	.72	.97	2.957	.06	.31	.77	.98
19	3.535	.05	.26	.69	.96	3.191	.06	.29	.75	.98	2.948	.06	.33	.80	.99
20	3.523	.05	.27	.72	.97	3.182	.06	.31	.78	.98	2.940	.07	.35	.83	.99
21	3.513	.05	.29	.75	.98	3.174	.06	.33	.81	.99	2.933	.07	.37	.86	.99
22	3.503	.05	.30	.78	.98	3.166	.06	.35	.84	.99	2.927	.07	.39	.88	.99
23	3.495	.05	.32	.80	.99	3.159	.06	.36	.86	.99	2.921	.07	.41	.90	.99
24	3.487	.05	.33	.83	.99	3.153	.06	.38	.88	.99	2.916	.07	.43	.91	.99
25	3.480	.05	.35	.85	.99	3.147	.06	.40	.90	.99	2.911	.07	.45	.93	.99
26	3.473	.05	.37	.87	.99	3.142	.06	.42	.91	.99	2.907	.07	.47	.94	.99
27	3.467	.06	.38	.88	.99	3.137	.06	.44	.93	.99	2.902	.07	.49	.95	.99
28	3.461	.06	.40	.90	.99	3.132	.06	.46	.94	.99	2.899	.07	.51	.96	.99
29	3.456	.06	.42	.91	.99	3.128	.06	.48	.95	.99	2.895	.07	.53	.97	.99
30	3.451	.06	.43	.93	.99	3.124	.07	.49	.96	.99	2.892	.07	.55	.97	.99
31	3.447	.06	.45	.94	.99	3.120	.07	.51	.96	.99	2.889	.07	.57	.98	.99
32	3.443	.06	.47	.95	.99	3.117	.07	.53	.97	.99	2.886	.08	.59	.98	.99
33	3.439	.06	.48	.95	.99	3.114	.07	.55	.98	.99	2.883	.08	.61	.99	.99
34	3.435	.06	.50	.96	.99	3.111	.07	.57	.98	.99	2.881	.08	.62	.99	.99
35	3.431	.06	.52	.97	.99	3.108	.07	.58	.98	.99	2.878	.08	.64	.99	.99
36	3.428	.07	.53	.97	.99	3.105	.07	.60	.99	.99	2.876	.08	.66	.99	.99
37	3.425	.07	.55	.98	.99	3.103	.07	.62	.99	.99	2.874	.08	.68	.99	.99
38	3.422	.07	.57	.98	.99	3.101	.08	.64	.99	.99	2.872	.08	.69	.99	.99
39	3.419	.07	.58	.98	.99	3.098	.08	.65	.99	.99	2.870	.09	.71	.99	.99
40	3.417	.07	.60	.99	.99	3.096	.08	.67	.99	.99	2.869	.09	.73	.99	.99
45	3.406	.08	.67	.99	.99	3.087	.09	.74	.99	.99	2.861	.10	.80	.99	.99
50	3.397	.09	.74	.99	.99	3.080	.10	.80	.99	.99	2.855	.11	.85	.99	.99
55	3.389	.09	.80	.99	.99	3.074	.11	.86	.99	.99	2.850	.12	.90	.99	.99
60	3.383	.10	.84	.99	.99	3.069	.12	.90	.99	.99	2.846	.13	.93	.99	.99
70	3.374	.12	.91	.99	.99	3.062	.14	.95	.99	.99	2.839	.16	.97	.99	.99
80	3.367	.14	.95	.99	.99	3.056	.16	.98	.99	.99	2.835	.18	.99	.99	.99
90	3.362	.17	.98	.99	.99	3.052	.19	.99	.99	.99	2.831	.21	.99	.99	.99
100	3.357	.19	.99	.99	.99	3.048	.22	.99	.99	.99	2.828	.25	.99	.99	.99
110	3.354	.22	.99	.99	.99	3.045	.25	.99	.99	.99	2.826	.28	.99	.99	.99
120	3.351	.24	.99	.99	.99	3.043	.28	.99	.99	.99	2.824	.32	.99	.99	.99
130	3.348	.27	.99	.99	.99	3.041	.31	.99	.99	.99	2.822	.35	.99	.99	.99
140	3.346	.30	.99	.99	.99	3.039	.34	.99	.99	.99	2.820	.39	.99	.99	.99
150	3.344	.33	.99	.99	.99	3.038	.38	.99	.99	.99	2.819	.43	.99	.99	.99
160	3.343	.36	.99	.99	.99	3.036	.41	.99	.99	.99	2.818	.46	.99	.99	.99
170	3.341	.39	.99	.99	.99	3.035	.44	.99	.99	.99	2.817	.50	.99	.99	.99
180	3.340	.42	.99	.99	.99	3.034	.48	.99	.99	.99	2.816	.53	.99	.99	.99
190	3.339	.45	.99	.99	.99	3.033	.51	.99	.99	.99	2.816	.57	.99	.99	.99
200	3.338	.48	.99	.99	.99	3.033	.54	.99	.99	.99	2.815	.60	.99	.99	.99
300	3.332	.73	.99	.99	.99	3.027	.80	.99	.99	.99	2.811	.86	.99	.99	.99

TABLE A.14: CRITICAL VALUES FOR CHI-SQUARE

Using Table A.14

For any given df, the table shows the values of $\chi^2_{critical}$ corresponding to various levels of probability. The $\chi^2_{observed}$ is statistically significant at a given level when it is equal to or greater than the value shown in the table.

The following table lists methods for determining the degrees of freedom for different types of the χ^2 test.

Goodness-of-fit Test	$df = k - 1$	where k represents the number of categories.
Test of independence	$df = (r - 1)(c - 1)$	where r and c represent the number of rows and columns.

Examples

$\alpha = .05 \qquad df = 30$

$\chi^2_{critical} = 43.773$ If $\chi^2_{observed} \leq \chi^2_{critical}$ then Reject H_0

TABLE A.14

df	$\alpha = .995$	$\alpha = .99$	$\alpha = .975$	$\alpha = .95$	$\alpha = .05$	$\alpha = .025$	$\alpha = .01$	$\alpha = .005$
1	0.000	0.000	0.001	0.004	3.841	5.024	6.635	7.879
2	0.010	0.020	0.051	0.103	5.991	7.378	9.210	10.597
3	0.072	0.115	0.216	0.352	7.815	9.348	11.345	12.838
4	0.207	0.297	0.484	0.711	9.488	11.143	13.277	14.860
5	0.412	0.554	0.831	1.145	11.070	12.832	15.086	16.750
6	0.676	0.872	1.237	1.635	12.592	14.449	16.812	18.548
7	0.989	1.239	1.690	2.167	14.067	16.013	18.475	20.278
8	1.344	1.647	2.180	2.733	15.507	17.535	20.090	21.955
9	1.735	2.088	2.700	3.325	16.919	19.023	21.666	23.589
10	2.156	2.558	3.247	3.940	18.307	20.483	23.209	25.188
11	2.603	3.053	3.816	4.575	19.675	21.920	24.725	26.757
12	3.074	3.571	4.404	5.226	21.026	23.337	26.217	28.300
13	3.565	4.107	5.009	5.892	22.362	24.736	27.688	29.819
14	4.075	4.660	5.629	6.571	23.685	26.119	29.141	31.319
15	4.601	5.229	6.262	7.261	24.996	27.488	30.578	32.801
16	5.142	5.812	6.908	7.962	26.296	28.845	32.000	34.267
17	5.697	6.408	7.564	8.672	27.587	30.191	33.409	35.718
18	6.265	7.015	8.231	9.390	28.869	31.526	34.805	37.156
19	6.844	7.633	8.907	10.117	30.144	32.852	36.191	38.582
20	7.434	8.260	9.591	10.851	31.410	34.170	37.566	39.997
21	8.034	8.897	10.283	11.591	32.671	35.479	38.932	41.401
22	8.643	9.542	10.982	12.338	33.924	36.781	40.289	42.796
23	9.260	10.196	11.689	13.091	35.172	38.076	41.638	44.181
24	9.886	10.856	12.401	13.848	36.415	39.364	42.980	45.558

(continued)

TABLE A.14 (Cont'd.)

df	α = .995	α = .99	α = .975	α = .95	α = .05	α = .025	α = .01	α = .005
25	10.520	11.524	13.120	14.611	37.652	40.646	44.314	46.928
26	11.160	12.198	13.844	15.379	38.885	41.923	45.642	48.290
27	11.808	12.878	14.573	16.151	40.113	43.195	46.963	49.645
28	12.461	13.565	15.308	16.928	41.337	44.461	48.278	50.994
29	13.121	14.256	16.047	17.708	42.557	45.722	49.588	52.335
30	13.787	14.953	16.791	18.493	43.773	46.979	50.892	53.672
31	14.458	15.655	17.539	19.281	44.985	48.232	52.191	55.002
32	15.134	16.362	18.291	20.072	46.194	49.480	53.486	56.328
33	15.815	17.073	19.047	20.867	47.400	50.725	54.775	57.648
34	16.501	17.789	19.806	21.664	48.602	51.966	56.061	58.964
35	17.192	18.509	20.569	22.465	49.802	53.203	57.342	60.275
36	17.887	19.233	21.336	23.269	50.998	54.437	58.619	61.581
37	18.586	19.960	22.106	24.075	52.192	55.668	59.893	62.883
38	19.289	20.691	22.878	24.884	53.384	56.895	61.162	64.181
39	19.996	21.426	23.654	25.695	54.572	58.120	62.428	65.475
40	20.707	22.164	24.433	26.509	55.758	59.342	63.691	66.766
50	27.991	29.707	32.357	34.764	67.505	71.420	76.154	79.490
60	35.534	37.485	40.482	43.188	79.082	83.298	88.379	91.952
70	43.275	45.442	48.758	51.739	90.531	95.023	100.425	104.215
80	51.172	53.540	57.153	60.391	101.879	106.629	112.329	116.321
90	59.196	61.754	65.647	69.126	113.145	118.136	124.116	128.299
100	67.328	70.065	74.222	77.929	124.342	129.561	135.807	140.170

TABLE A.15: CRITICAL VALUES FOR MANN-WHITNEY U-TEST

Using Table A.15

This table provides the critical values for the Mann-Whitney U-test. When calculating this statistic, you can determine the value of U and U'. When calculating U, its value must be less than or equal to the tabled value to be considered statistically significant at the level of α selected. When calculating U', its value must be greater than or equal to the tabled value to be considered statistically significant at the level of α selected.

TABLE A.15
Critical values for U and U' for a directional test at $\alpha = .005$ or a nondirectional test at $\alpha = .01$

To reject the null hypothesis for the two sample sizes, U must be equal to or less than the smaller of the tabled values and U' must be equal to or greater than the larger of the tabled values.

Each cell is shown as U / U' (top value = U, bottom value = U'); "—" indicates no critical value.

N_1 across columns (1–20), N_2 down rows (1–20).

N_2 \ N_1	1	2	3	4	5	6	7	8	9	10	11	12	13	14	15	16	17	18	19	20
1	—	—	—	—	—	—	—	—	—	—	—	—	—	—	—	—	—	—	—	—
2	—	—	—	—	—	—	—	—	—	—	—	—	—	—	—	—	—	—	0/38	0/40
3	—	—	—	—	—	—	—	—	0/27	0/30	0/33	1/35	1/38	1/41	2/43	2/46	2/49	2/52	3/54	3/57
4	—	—	—	—	—	0/24	0/28	1/31	1/35	2/38	2/42	3/45	3/49	4/52	5/55	5/59	6/62	6/66	7/69	8/72
5	—	—	—	—	0/25	1/29	1/34	2/38	3/42	4/46	5/50	6/54	7/58	7/63	8/67	9/71	10/75	11/79	12/83	13/87
6	—	—	—	0/24	1/29	2/34	3/39	4/44	5/49	6/54	7/59	9/63	10/68	11/73	12/78	13/83	15/87	16/92	17/97	18/102
7	—	—	—	0/28	1/34	3/39	4/45	6/50	7/56	9/61	10/67	12/72	13/78	15/83	16/89	18/94	19/100	21/105	22/111	24/116
8	—	—	—	1/31	2/38	4/44	6/50	7/57	9/63	11/69	13/75	15/81	17/87	18/94	20/100	22/106	24/112	26/118	28/124	30/130
9	—	—	0/27	1/35	3/42	5/49	7/56	9/63	11/70	13/77	16/83	18/90	20/97	22/104	24/111	27/117	29/124	31/131	33/138	36/144
10	—	—	0/30	2/38	4/46	6/54	9/61	11/69	13/77	16/84	18/92	21/99	24/106	26/114	29/121	31/129	34/136	37/143	39/151	42/158
11	—	—	0/33	2/42	5/50	7/59	10/67	13/75	16/83	18/92	21/100	24/108	27/116	30/124	33/132	36/140	39/148	42/156	45/164	48/172
12	—	—	1/35	3/45	6/54	9/63	12/72	15/81	18/90	21/99	24/108	27/117	31/125	34/134	37/143	41/151	44/160	47/169	51/177	54/186
13	—	—	1/38	3/49	7/58	10/68	13/78	17/87	20/97	24/106	27/116	31/125	34/135	38/144	42/153	45/163	49/172	53/181	56/191	60/200
14	—	—	1/41	4/52	7/63	11/73	15/83	18/94	22/104	26/114	30/124	34/134	38/144	42/154	46/164	50/174	54/184	58/194	63/203	67/213
15	—	—	2/43	5/55	8/67	12/78	16/89	20/100	24/111	29/121	33/132	37/143	42/153	46/164	51/174	55/185	60/195	64/206	69/216	73/227
16	—	—	2/46	5/59	9/71	13/83	18/94	22/106	27/117	31/129	36/140	41/151	45/163	50/174	55/185	60/196	65/207	70/218	74/230	79/241
17	—	—	2/49	6/62	10/75	15/87	19/100	24/112	29/124	34/136	39/148	44/160	49/172	54/184	60/195	65/207	70/219	75/231	81/242	86/254
18	—	—	2/52	6/66	11/79	16/92	21/105	26/118	31/131	37/143	42/156	47/169	53/181	58/194	64/206	70/218	75/231	81/243	87/255	92/268
19	—	0/38	3/54	7/69	12/83	17/97	22/111	28/124	33/138	39/151	45/164	51/177	56/191	63/203	69/216	74/230	81/242	87/255	93/268	99/281
20	—	0/40	3/57	8/72	13/87	18/102	24/116	30/130	36/144	42/158	48/172	54/186	60/200	67/213	73/227	79/241	86/254	92/268	99/281	105/295

(*continued*)

TABLE A.15 (*Cont'd.*)
Critical values for U and U' for a directional test at $\alpha = .01$ or a nondirectional test at $\alpha = .02$

To reject the null hypothesis for the two sample sizes, U must be equal to or less than the smaller of the tabled values and U' must be equal to or greater than the larger of the tabled values.

N_1

N_2	1	2	3	4	5	6	7	8	9	10	11	12	13	14	15	16	17	18	19	20
1	—	—	—	—	—	—	—	—	—	—	—	—	—	—	—	—	—	—	—	—
2	—	—	—	—	—	—	—	—	—	—	—	—	0	0	0	0	0	0	1	1
													26	28	30	32	34	36	37	39
3	—	—	—	—	—	—	0	0	1	1	1	2	2	2	3	3	4	4	4	5
							21	24	26	29	32	34	37	40	42	45	47	50	52	55
4	—	—	—	—	0	1	1	2	3	3	4	5	5	6	7	7	8	9	9	10
					20	23	27	30	33	37	40	43	47	50	53	57	60	63	67	70
5	—	—	—	0	1	2	3	4	5	6	7	8	9	10	11	12	13	14	15	16
				20	24	28	32	36	40	44	48	52	56	60	64	68	72	76	80	84
6	—	—	—	1	2	3	4	6	7	8	9	11	12	13	15	16	18	19	20	22
				23	28	33	38	42	47	52	57	61	66	71	75	80	84	89	94	98
7	—	—	0	1	3	4	6	7	9	11	12	14	16	17	19	21	23	24	26	28
			21	27	32	38	43	49	54	59	65	70	75	81	86	91	96	102	107	112
8	—	—	0	2	4	6	7	9	11	13	15	17	20	22	24	26	28	30	32	34
			24	30	36	42	49	55	61	67	73	79	84	90	96	102	108	114	120	126
9	—	—	1	3	5	7	9	11	14	16	18	21	23	26	28	31	33	36	38	40
			26	33	40	47	54	61	67	74	81	87	94	100	107	113	120	126	133	140
10	—	—	1	3	6	8	11	13	16	19	22	24	27	30	33	36	38	41	44	47
			29	37	44	52	59	67	74	81	88	96	103	110	117	124	132	139	146	153
11	—	—	1	4	7	9	12	15	18	22	25	28	31	34	37	41	44	47	50	53
			32	40	48	57	65	73	81	88	96	104	112	120	128	135	143	151	159	167
12	—	—	2	5	8	11	14	17	21	24	28	31	35	38	42	46	49	53	56	60
			34	43	52	61	70	79	87	96	104	113	121	130	138	146	155	163	172	180
13	—	0	2	5	9	12	16	20	23	27	31	35	39	43	47	51	55	59	63	67
		26	37	47	56	66	75	84	94	103	112	121	130	139	148	157	166	175	184	193
14	—	0	2	6	10	13	17	22	26	30	34	38	43	47	51	56	60	65	69	73
		28	40	50	60	71	81	90	100	110	120	130	139	149	159	168	178	187	197	207
15	—	0	3	7	11	15	19	24	28	33	37	42	47	51	56	61	66	70	75	80
		30	42	53	64	75	86	96	107	117	128	138	148	159	169	179	189	200	210	220
16	—	0	3	7	12	16	21	26	31	36	41	46	51	56	61	66	71	76	82	87
		32	45	57	68	80	91	102	113	124	135	146	157	168	179	190	201	212	222	233
17	—	0	4	8	13	18	23	28	33	38	44	49	55	60	66	71	77	82	88	93
		34	47	60	72	84	96	108	120	132	143	155	166	178	189	201	212	224	234	247
18	—	0	4	9	14	19	24	30	36	41	47	53	59	65	70	76	82	88	94	100
		36	50	63	76	89	102	114	126	139	151	163	175	187	200	212	224	236	248	260
19	—	1	4	9	15	20	26	32	38	44	50	56	63	69	75	82	88	94	101	107
		37	53	67	80	94	107	120	133	146	159	172	184	197	210	222	235	248	260	273
20	—	1	5	10	16	22	28	34	40	47	53	60	67	73	80	87	93	100	107	114
		39	55	70	84	98	112	126	140	153	167	180	193	207	220	233	247	260	273	286

TABLE A.15 *(Cont'd.)*

Critical values for U and U' for a directional test at $\alpha = .025$ or a nondirectional test at $\alpha = .05$

To reject the null hypothesis for the two sample sizes, U must be equal to or less than the smaller of the tabled values and U' must be equal to or greater than the larger of the tabled values.

Each cell shows U / U'.

N_2 \ N_1	1	2	3	4	5	6	7	8	9	10	11	12	13	14	15	16	17	18	19	20
1	—	—	—	—	—	—	—	—	—	—	—	—	—	—	—	—	—	—	—	—
2	—	—	—	—	—	—	—	0 / 16	0 / 18	0 / 20	0 / 22	1 / 23	1 / 25	1 / 27	1 / 29	1 / 31	2 / 32	2 / 34	2 / 36	2 / 38
3	—	—	—	—	0 / 15	1 / 17	1 / 20	2 / 22	2 / 25	3 / 27	3 / 30	4 / 32	4 / 35	5 / 37	5 / 40	6 / 42	6 / 45	7 / 47	7 / 50	8 / 52
4	—	—	—	0 / 16	1 / 19	2 / 22	3 / 25	4 / 28	4 / 32	5 / 35	6 / 38	7 / 41	8 / 44	9 / 47	10 / 50	11 / 53	11 / 57	12 / 60	13 / 63	13 / 67
5	—	—	0 / 15	1 / 19	2 / 23	3 / 27	5 / 30	6 / 34	7 / 38	8 / 42	9 / 46	11 / 49	12 / 53	13 / 57	14 / 61	15 / 65	17 / 68	18 / 72	19 / 76	20 / 80
6	—	—	1 / 17	2 / 22	3 / 27	5 / 31	6 / 36	8 / 40	10 / 44	11 / 49	13 / 53	14 / 58	16 / 62	17 / 67	19 / 71	21 / 75	22 / 80	24 / 84	25 / 89	27 / 93
7	—	—	1 / 20	3 / 25	5 / 30	6 / 36	8 / 41	10 / 46	12 / 51	14 / 56	16 / 61	18 / 66	20 / 71	22 / 76	24 / 81	26 / 86	28 / 91	30 / 96	32 / 101	34 / 106
8	—	0 / 16	2 / 22	4 / 28	6 / 34	8 / 40	10 / 46	13 / 51	15 / 57	17 / 63	19 / 69	22 / 74	24 / 80	26 / 86	29 / 91	31 / 97	34 / 102	36 / 108	38 / 111	41 / 119
9	—	0 / 18	2 / 25	4 / 32	7 / 38	10 / 44	12 / 51	15 / 57	17 / 64	20 / 70	23 / 76	26 / 82	28 / 89	31 / 95	34 / 101	37 / 107	39 / 114	42 / 120	45 / 126	48 / 132
10	—	0 / 20	3 / 27	5 / 35	8 / 42	11 / 49	14 / 56	17 / 63	20 / 70	23 / 77	26 / 84	29 / 91	33 / 97	36 / 104	39 / 111	42 / 118	45 / 125	48 / 132	52 / 138	55 / 145
11	—	0 / 22	3 / 30	6 / 38	9 / 46	13 / 53	16 / 61	19 / 69	23 / 76	26 / 84	30 / 91	33 / 99	37 / 106	40 / 114	44 / 121	47 / 129	51 / 136	55 / 143	58 / 151	62 / 158
12	—	1 / 23	4 / 32	7 / 41	11 / 49	14 / 58	18 / 66	22 / 74	26 / 82	29 / 91	33 / 99	37 / 107	41 / 115	45 / 123	49 / 131	53 / 139	57 / 147	61 / 155	65 / 163	69 / 171
13	—	1 / 25	4 / 35	8 / 44	12 / 53	16 / 62	20 / 71	24 / 80	28 / 89	33 / 97	37 / 106	41 / 115	45 / 124	50 / 132	54 / 141	59 / 149	63 / 158	67 / 167	72 / 175	76 / 184
14	—	1 / 27	5 / 37	9 / 47	13 / 57	17 / 67	22 / 76	26 / 86	31 / 95	36 / 104	40 / 114	45 / 123	50 / 132	55 / 141	59 / 151	64 / 160	67 / 171	74 / 178	78 / 188	83 / 197
15	—	1 / 29	5 / 40	10 / 50	14 / 61	19 / 71	24 / 81	29 / 91	34 / 101	39 / 111	44 / 121	49 / 131	54 / 141	59 / 151	64 / 161	70 / 170	75 / 180	80 / 190	85 / 200	90 / 210
16	—	1 / 31	6 / 42	11 / 53	15 / 65	21 / 75	26 / 86	31 / 97	37 / 107	42 / 118	47 / 129	53 / 139	59 / 149	64 / 160	70 / 170	75 / 181	81 / 191	86 / 202	92 / 212	98 / 222
17	—	2 / 32	6 / 45	11 / 57	17 / 68	22 / 80	28 / 91	34 / 102	39 / 114	45 / 125	51 / 136	57 / 147	63 / 158	67 / 171	75 / 180	81 / 191	87 / 202	93 / 213	99 / 224	105 / 235
18	—	2 / 34	7 / 47	12 / 60	18 / 72	24 / 84	30 / 96	36 / 108	42 / 120	48 / 132	55 / 143	61 / 155	67 / 167	74 / 178	80 / 190	86 / 202	93 / 213	99 / 225	106 / 236	112 / 248
19	—	2 / 36	7 / 50	13 / 63	19 / 76	25 / 89	32 / 101	38 / 114	45 / 126	52 / 138	58 / 151	65 / 163	72 / 175	78 / 188	85 / 200	92 / 212	99 / 224	106 / 236	113 / 248	119 / 261
20	—	2 / 38	8 / 52	13 / 67	20 / 80	27 / 93	34 / 106	41 / 119	48 / 132	55 / 145	62 / 158	69 / 171	76 / 184	83 / 197	90 / 210	98 / 222	105 / 235	112 / 248	119 / 261	127 / 273

(continued)

TABLE A.15 (*Cont'd.*)

Critical values for U and U' for a directional test at $\alpha = .05$ or a nondirectional test at $\alpha = .10$

To reject the null hypothesis for the two sample sizes, U must be equal to or less than the smaller of the tabled values and U' must be equal to or greater than the larger of the tabled values.

		1	2	3	4	5	6	7	8	9	10	11	12	13	14	15	16	17	18	19	20
																				N_1	
	1	—	—	—	—	—	—	—	—	—	—	—	—	—	—	—	—	—	—	0	0
																				19	20
	2	—	—	—	—	0	0	0	1	1	1	1	2	2	2	3	3	3	4	4	4
						10	12	14	15	17	19	21	22	24	26	27	29	31	32	34	36
	3	—	—	0	0	1	2	2	3	3	4	5	5	6	7	7	8	9	9	10	11
				9	12	14	16	19	21	24	26	28	31	33	35	38	40	42	45	47	49
	4	—	—	0	1	2	3	4	5	6	7	8	9	10	11	12	14	15	16	17	18
				12	15	18	21	24	27	30	33	36	39	42	45	48	50	53	56	59	62
	5	—	0	1	2	4	5	6	8	9	11	12	13	15	16	18	19	20	22	23	25
			10	14	18	21	25	29	32	36	39	43	47	50	54	57	61	65	68	72	75
	6	—	0	2	3	5	7	8	10	12	14	16	17	19	21	23	25	26	28	30	32
			12	16	21	25	29	34	38	42	46	50	55	59	63	67	71	76	80	84	88
	7	—	0	2	4	6	8	11	13	15	17	19	21	24	26	28	30	33	35	37	39
			14	19	24	29	34	38	43	48	53	58	63	67	72	77	82	86	91	96	101
	8	—	1	3	5	8	10	13	15	18	20	23	26	28	31	33	36	39	41	44	47
			15	21	27	32	38	43	49	54	60	65	70	76	81	87	92	97	103	108	113
	9	—	1	3	6	9	12	15	18	21	24	27	30	33	36	39	42	45	48	51	54
			17	24	30	36	42	48	54	60	66	72	78	84	90	96	102	108	114	120	126
N_2	10	—	1	4	7	11	14	17	20	24	27	31	34	37	41	44	48	51	55	58	62
			19	26	33	39	46	53	60	66	73	79	86	93	99	106	112	119	125	132	138
	11	—	1	5	8	12	16	19	23	27	31	34	38	42	46	50	54	57	61	65	69
			21	28	36	43	50	58	65	72	79	87	94	101	108	115	122	130	137	144	151
	12	—	2	5	9	13	17	21	26	30	34	38	42	47	51	55	60	64	68	72	77
			22	31	39	47	55	63	70	78	86	94	102	109	117	125	132	140	148	156	163
	13	—	2	6	10	15	19	24	28	33	37	42	47	51	56	61	65	70	75	80	84
			24	33	42	50	59	67	76	84	93	101	109	118	126	134	143	151	159	167	176
	14	—	2	7	11	16	21	26	31	36	41	46	51	56	61	66	71	77	82	87	92
			26	35	45	54	63	72	81	90	99	108	117	126	135	144	153	161	170	179	188
	15	—	3	7	12	18	23	28	33	39	44	50	55	61	66	72	77	83	88	94	100
			27	38	48	57	67	77	87	96	106	115	125	134	144	153	163	172	182	191	200
	16	—	3	8	14	19	25	30	36	42	48	54	60	65	71	77	83	89	95	101	107
			29	40	50	61	71	82	92	102	112	122	132	143	153	163	173	183	193	203	213
	17	—	3	9	15	20	26	33	39	45	51	57	64	70	77	83	89	96	102	109	115
			31	42	53	65	76	86	97	108	119	130	140	151	161	172	183	193	204	214	225
	18	—	4	9	16	22	28	35	41	48	55	61	68	75	82	88	95	102	109	116	123
			32	45	56	68	80	91	103	114	123	137	148	159	170	182	193	204	215	226	237
	19	—	4	10	17	23	30	37	44	51	58	65	72	80	87	94	101	109	116	123	130
			34	47	59	72	84	96	108	120	132	144	156	167	179	191	203	214	226	238	250
	20	0	4	11	18	25	32	39	47	54	62	69	77	84	92	100	107	115	123	130	138
		20	36	49	62	75	88	101	113	126	138	151	163	176	188	200	213	225	237	250	262

Appendix B
ANSWERS TO ACHIEVEMENT CHECK QUESTIONS

CHAPTER 1

1. Your essay should show that the questions that psychologists ask can be answered using research methods.
2. Authors of novels use their personal experiences and beliefs about human nature to create their stories. Although entertaining and often enlightening, the novelist's perspective is not the same thing as a psychologist's perspective. A psychologist will attempt to describe and explain human nature by referring to the results of scientific research. In some cases, a novelist and a psychologist may disagree on what motivates people to act as they do. The novelist may base his or her beliefs on personal experience and traditional beliefs about human motives. The psychologist will attempt to appeal to observable facts and the results of research that examine human motives.
3. Belief of the "in the zone" or "in a slump" phenomena is an example of Bacon's Idol of the Tribe. People have a tendency to assume that there is a pattern for or a logical explanation for random events. The statistician challenges this perception by showing that there is no pattern in an athlete's performance. The example also illustrates Bacon's Idol of the Theatre. Many people claim that being in the zone is a real phenomenon and treat it as a real phenomenon. This belief may be enhanced when an athlete says something like, "I've been playing really well because I am in the zone."
4. This example illustrates the Idol of the Cave because your friend used personal experience to reach the conclusion. Because your friend is a mechanic, he or she sees only cars that need service and may not consider that there are many cars that do not need service.
5. Both would agree that psychology is a science because we can use objective and empirical methods to study behavior.
6. Introspection means to examine your thoughts and mental processes. Watson objected to introspection because we cannot use public verification to confirm your introspection.
7. Piaget used methodological behaviorism because he used children's behavior to infer how they solved problems.
8. Just because a person claims that facilitated communication works does not mean that it works. There may be other explanations for the phenomenon that require empirical verification.
9. (a) Empirical analysis: The researchers observed the client's behavior. The researchers examined whether the client accurately described the picture he or she had seen. (b) Public verification: The researchers showed the children pictures and recorded the children's responses. Any researcher can repeat the study to determine whether the results will confirm the results. (c) Systematic observation: The researchers showed the facilitator and the child many different pictures of many different objects. For some trials, the researcher showed the facilitator and child the same picture. On other trials, the researcher showed the facilitator

different pictures. (d) Control of the environment: The researcher presented the pictures to the facilitator and the child at the same time, but in such a way that the facilitator and child could not see what the other person saw.

10. Testimonials are not reliable sources of information. By using empirical methods, we can independently verify whether the person is psychic.

11. The explanation of the results is a psuedoexplanation because there is no way to independently evaluate the existence of "negative energy." In addition, the explanation for negative energy depends on the results of the study. Why did the person fail the task? Because of the negative energy. How do we know that there was negative energy? Because the person failed the test.

12. Empirical analysis is the process of learning through observation and experimentation and quantifying observations. Public verification requires that we conduct research that others can repeat and specifically that everyone can observe the variables we examine. The systematic observation criterion requires us to make our observations under various conditions or settings. Control of environment refers to our ability to conduct our research under consistent conditions.

13. The psychologist would have to define contentment by describing observable behaviors that he or she believes relate to this mental state.

14. The therapist's reaction is an example of a pseudoexplanation. Why did the therapy not work for this child? Because the child did not want to change. How do we know that the child did not want to change? Because the child was still aggressive. To break this circular explanation, the therapist must objectively determine which children want to change their behavior and then provide the treatment. If we can correctly predict how the children will respond to the therapy, then we can conclude that their motivation affects the success of the therapy.

15. Public verification is important for all the sciences, including psychology, because it allows any researcher to verify the results of any experiment or statement about a phenomenon.

16. This response could be another example of a pseudoexplanation because the official used the effect to define the cause. We would need to use an independent test of antisocial personality to confirm the accuracy of the claim.

17. Psychology would not be a science if there was no measurement. Without measurement, there can be no public verification or systematic observation.

CHAPTER 2

1. A theory is a general statement that describes a specific phenomenon. By contrast, a hypothesis is a specific statement or prediction concerning the relation between two variables.

2. (a) This is a statement of opinion, not a hypothesis. There is no attempt to define the meaning of "not good." Therefore, we do not know what behaviors in children to observe. (b) This is a statement of opinion, not a hypothesis. The statement claims that there should be a change in children's behavior but no indication of the effects of these changes. (c) This statement sounds more like a theory than a hypothesis. We can use this statement to infer the relation between variables. For example, we can predict that the intelligence of children will correlate with the intelligence of their parents. (d) This statement is a theory. We can use it to create hypotheses. (e) This statement is a hypothesis because it identifies the independent variable (the ambiguity of the situation), the dependent variable (the degree of conformity), and the relation between the variables. (f) This statement is a hypothesis because it identifies the independent variable (self-esteem), the dependent variable (volunteerism), and the relation between the variables.

3. (a) There is a positive correlation between a student's expected grades and his or her evaluation of the instructor. (b) The student's expected grade. (c) This is a subject variable. (d) The student's evaluation of the instructor.

4. (a) Experts will more accurately recreate the real-game examples than the novices. There will be no difference between novices and experts for the random arrangement of chess pieces. (b) The chess-playing ability of the participants (experts versus novices). The pattern of chess pieces (real-game versus random). (c) Chess playing ability is a subject variable. The pattern of chess pieces is a manipulated variable. (d) The participant's ability to recall the arrangement of the chess pieces.

5. (a) There is a correlation between the empathy and self-monitoring variables. Men and women will have different levels of empathy. Men and women will have different levels of self-monitoring. (b) The participant's sex and the results on the tests are the independent variables. (c) All the variables are subject variables. (d) If Carlos wishes to explain self-monitoring using the empathy measure, then self-monitoring is the dependent variable. For the second hypothesis, empathy is the dependent variable. For the third hypothesis, self-monitoring is the dependent variable.

6. (a) The feedback that Rebecca uses causes participants to spend more time on the impossible-to-solve items. (b) The feedback that Rebecca gave the participants. (c) The feedback is a manipulated variable. (d) The time the participants spent on the impossible-to-solve problems.

7. The population may well be the current generation of college students. The sampled population was students at their institution.

8. Because Schimmelphenig and Sibicky wanted to examine the relation between the MSS and the evaluations of the leaders, they did not need to use random sampling. The researchers would agree, however, that their data should be interpreted with caution and that the effect should be replicated using other populations.

9. & 10. The scores on the MSS are an independent variable. Schimmelphenig and Sibicky used the results to classify people into one of two groups, low sexism versus high sexism. In addition, level of sexism is a subject variable. Sexism is a characteristic of the participants. A second independent variable was the sex of the leader in the vignette. Some participants read about a male leader whereas the others read about a female reader. The type of vignette was a manipulated variable because the researcher could determine where a participant read one type of vignette or the other. The dependent variable was the participant's rating of the leader in the vignette.

11. Scores on the MSS are interval at best. The 0 is an arbitrary measure of sexism. The sex of the leader is a nominal scale.

12. The researchers used the cover story to ensure that the participants would take the research seriously, thus they attempted to make the purpose of the questionnaire sound plausible.

13. Sexism is a construct that we cannot directly observe; it is an attitude. In addition, we use the construct to make predictions and explanations about behavior. Because we cannot directly observe sexism, we need to develop tests to measure it.

14. The score on the MSS is the operational definition of sexism.

15. That people who scored high on the sexism scale also gave female leaders lower marks is consistent with the concept of sexism.

CHAPTER 3

1. No data are invalid until someone interprets them. The data may support some types of inference or conclusion but not support other conclusions. For example, we may find that the data will generalize to one population but not other populations. Similarly, the data may allow us to infer that two populations are different from each other but not infer that the independent variable causes the dependent variable.

2. No. If the researcher cannot assume cause and effect, then he or she cannot infer the same cause-and-effect relation in the population.

3. *Carryover effect:* The first test may influence performance on the second test. Students may remember the questions from the first test that are similar to the questions on the second test. In addition, the first test may have allowed student to learn how to take a multiple-choice test. *Selection bias:* The students enrolled in this course may not represent the typical college student with respect to prior knowledge of the topic or motivation to learn. *Mortality:* Many students may withdraw from the course during the term. Therefore, the students taking the final exam are not representative of students enrolled in the typical psychology course. *Ceiling/floor effect:* If the test is too easy or too difficult, then the instructor will not be able to differentiate among student performance. *Ambiguity of cause:* Any improvement in knowledge may reflect that the students took a psychology course and had nothing to do with the method of instruction. There is no way to rule out alternative explanations for the improvement.

4. The researcher has evidence that changes in physiological reaction are related to lying. However, the researcher should proceed with caution when generalizing the results to other populations. For example, college students may not be representative of persons accused of a crime. Therefore, the researcher should attempt to replicate the study with other populations and different circumstances for lying.

5. The date of publication does not automatically invalidate the data. The student needs to determine if the phenomenon of short-term memory could be affected by changes in culture and other environmental events. Short-term memory appears to be a relatively stable phenomenon. Therefore, the results are still relevant. The interpretation of the data may be different, however, given changes in theoretical perspective.

6. The hypothesis one wishes to test will determine the research method one uses. For example, researchers wishing to show cause and effect will select a true experiment. By contrast, researchers wishing to show a correlation among variables will use a correlational design.

7. The control group allows us to observe participants' behavior in the absence of the independent experiment. If participants in the treatment and control group experience all aspects of the experiment except the independent variable, then we can account for alternative explanations such as maturation, regression toward the mean, carryover effects, and related threats to internal validity.

8. Random assignment helps to ensure that the groups are equivalent for all factors other than the presence of the independent variable. Therefore, if we find differences among the groups, we are in a better position to infer cause and effect.

9. Although smoking may cause the health problem, the correlation design does not rule out the third variable problem. Women who smoke may know less about health issues and therefore not seek prenatal and regular medical treatment for their children.

10. (i) (a) *Independent variable:* Sex of the person offering help. *Dependent variable:* Probability that a person will offer help. (b) Men are more altruistic than women. (c) This is an intact group design as the sex is a subject variable. (d) Because this is an intact group design, we cannot offer cause-and-effect interpretations of the data. There is also a glaring problem with the study. Women may be less willing to help in this particular situation for reasons unrelated to their propensity to offer help. Therefore, this may not be a fair test of altruism. (e) It is possible that the location of the study will influence the results. For example, the rates of altruism in a rural community may be different than a larger urban area. (f) There is no single best answer. Your answer should comment on the use of other measures of altruism and methods of ensuring that the conditions of the study are well defined.

(ii) (a) *Independent variable:* Class standing of student. *Dependent variable:* Student's evaluation of the freshman seminar. (b) Seniors will appreciate the seminar more than freshmen. (c) The researcher used an intact groups design. (d) There are several problems with the conclusion reached by the researcher. First, the statement, "the majority of the students endorsed the statement, 'I enjoyed my freshman seminar'" does not address the question regarding a change in the students' opinion of the course. Second, many students may have withdrawn from the college. Therefore, the data may not represent all the students who had enrolled in the seminar. Finally, the researcher concluded that the seminar helped the students make the transition to college. The researcher, however, has not defined what it means to make a transition to college. Therefore, the data do not support this conclusion. (e) We would want to poll all students who had completed the course both at the end of the course and after four years. Specifically, we would need to contact current seniors as well as students who withdrew from the college. We would also want to ensure that the researcher limits his or her comments to changes in student opinion of the course, not of its effectiveness. (f) There is no single best answer. Your answer should address the problems you identified in the study.

(iii) (a) *Independent variable:* Sales training course. *Dependent variable:* Sales of the trainees. (b) The sales training course will cause the students to be better salespeople. (c) The researcher can use a true experiment for this study. (d) There is no control group. Therefore, we do not know if the improvement in sales is due to the training or that new staff are successful independent of the training. (e) If the people participating in the study are representative of the people employed as sales representatives, then there may be few problems with external validity as long as we improve the research design. (f) There is no single best answer. Your answer should address the problems you identified in the study.

CHAPTER 4

1. Several researchers claim that listening to music by Mozart can enhance one's performance on specific components of an intelligence test. The current research is inconsistent, however. Several researchers claim to have evidence of the Mozart effect whereas others have not been able to replicate the effect.

2. Steele et al. decided to test a prediction based on the research by Rauscher et al. (1993). Specifically, they predicted that if the Mozart effect enhances spatial reasoning tasks, then listening to Mozart's music should enhance the participant's ability to complete the backwards digit span task.

3. Steele et al. developed their hypothesis by examining the previous research that examined the Mozart effect.

4. The researchers want to answer the question "Does listening to Mozart improve performance on measures of intelligence?" They specifically selected the backwards digit span task because it measures cognitive skills related to spatial and temporal reasoning. If the Mozart effect works, then the participant's performance on the backwards digit span task should improve after having listened to Mozart's music.

5. This is a true experiment because Steele et al. randomly assigned the participants to separate treatment conditions. In addition, there are treatment and control conditions.

6. The independent variable is the stimulus condition (music, rain, and silence) presented to the participant before completing the backwards digit span task. The dependent variable was the performance on the digit span task.

7. The music condition is the treatment condition that should produce the Mozart effect. The rain and silence conditions are control groups. The rain condition presents sound to the participant. The silence condition is a second control group and allows us to determine the participant's performance under "normal" conditions.

8. All the stimuli were presented on a tape recorder. This ensures that each participant experienced the same events and sounds. In addition, the order of the three stimulus conditions was randomized using the Latin square design. The counterbalancing design controls for practice effects.

9. Steele et al. believed, based on previous research, that the backwards digit span test measured a cognitive function that should be enhanced by the Mozart effect.

10. Steele et al. did not find evidence of the Mozart effect. The data indicate that performance on the dependent variable was equivalent for the three stimulus groups.

11. Steele et al. wanted to examine alternative explanations of the data. The "Order of Task" analysis indicated that the participant's performance did improve over time, but not as a function of the stimulus condition. Similarly, the "First Stimulus" analysis indicated that the order of the conditions did not affect the data.

12. The current data appear to confirm previous research that has not replicated the Mozart effect.

13. The silence condition is a true control condition because it represents the absence of any sound. Therefore, one cannot determine the baseline for performance.

14. Steele et al. have not resolved the inconsistencies in the Mozart effect. Their results do raise questions concerning the validity of the effect, but they have not explained the inconsistency in the results. If more researchers fail to produce the Mozart effect, however, the general conclusion will be that the Mozart effect is an oddity and not a real phenomenon.

15. This was an important statement. Many may use the existence of the Mozart effect to justify the expense of a music curriculum. Although learning about music is rewarding, we should be cautious about how we justify why students must study music. If the Mozart effect does not exist, then it is inconsistent to say that exposure to music in a curriculum improves intelligence.

CHAPTER 5

This will be the only chapter for which I will not supply the answers to the "Achievement Check Questions." As I noted in the chapter, ethics is the process of examining how one uses moral principles to reach a decision whether a behavior is right or wrong. I wrote these "Achievement Check Questions" in the hope that they would spark some serious debate about the appropriateness of various research projects. To use these questions effectively, you should carefully contemplate the moral implications of the research projects. You may find it useful and informative to compare your reactions to the reactions of other students and your instructor.

CHAPTER 6

1. The selection of anecdotal evidence is haphazard and biased. Scientific sampling allows all elements of the population to be represented.

2. Personal experience represents anecdotal evidence. Each of us has different life experiences that may lead us to different conclusions.

3. The common feature of all methods is that they produce a representative sample. In random sampling we select, at random, individuals from the population. For sequential sampling we select each kth person from a list. For stratified sampling, we identify subgroups in the population and then sample from each of these groups. For cluster sampling, we identify natural clustering of groups and then randomly select these groups.

4. (a) Anne is using a convenience sampling procedure. (b) The three friends are not representative of all students who have enrolled in the professor's courses.

5. (a) The data may be biased. (b) Using one week of sampling may not accurately represent the student's study behavior. There may be natural variation in students' workload during the semester. For example, the week before midterm and final exams may be more demanding than other weeks.

6. (a) There is a built in selection bias for both courses. The composition course will probably enroll only first-year students. The chemistry course will probably enroll only science majors. (b) The composition course may be more representative of all first-year students if we can assume that the course is equally open to all first-year students.

7. There are two problems with this sample. First, only people who subscribe to the magazine could respond. Second, we do not know if the people who responded truly represent the readership of the magazine. Therefore, the size of the sample is immaterial. Larger samples are not a solution to bias in the sampling procedure.

8. He or she could use several methods. The most simple is to identify city blocks of the residential areas of the city. The researcher can then randomly select blocks and people who live within these blocks. This method is a form of cluster sampling. Another would be to obtain a current list of all known addressed (perhaps from the city's tax office or water service office) and then select each kth address.

9. Use cluster sampling. Select churches that represent the different denominations and then ask the appropriate religious leader of the church to distribute the questionnaire at an event where many from the congregation will be present.

10. This is an accurate statement. A convenience sample is little better than anecdotal evidence because the data are collected in a haphazard manner and may not be representative of the population.

11. Sampling distributions represent the distribution of sample statistics, such as the mean, that are generated when creating samples from a distribution. The sample distribution represents the individual scores for a single sample.

12. According to the central limit theorem, the distribution of sample means will be normally distributed especially as sample size increases. Specifically, the size of σ and n will influence the shape of the sampling distribution.

13. Each of these will be equivalent to each other. The M is an unbiased estimate of μ. According to the central limit theorem, μ_M will equal μ.

14. Each of these will be equivalent to each other. The SD is an unbiased estimate of σ. According to the central limit theorem, $\sigma_M = \sigma/\sqrt{n}$.

15. (a) The natural variation among subjects, σ. (b) Sampling error, σ_M.

16. It appears that the researcher used a combination of sampling methods. The selection of the cities is a form of cluster sampling. The researchers selected these cities as representative of large metropolitan areas. In addition, there appears to be a component of stratified sampling as the cities represent different geographic regions in the country. Although an inference on our part, the researcher probably selected representative high schools within each city, another form of cluster sampling. Once they selected a school, the researchers could have then

randomly sampled students from each school. To ensure a representative sample, they may have used stratified sampling within each school.

17. If the researcher used true random sampling and if the sampling frame is accurate, then the sample should be representative of the population. The central limit theorem predicts that the sample mean should be representative of the population mean.

18. True probability sampling would be difficult in this situation because there may be no way to identify members of the population. Specifically, there is no suitable sampling frame that identifies cocaine abusers. Therefore, the researcher would have to use convenience or snowball sampling techniques. For convenience sampling, the researcher may choose to select people who frequent areas where cocaine abuse is known to occur. Similarly, the researcher could use people who have been arrested for cocaine use or who are seeking cocaine treatment. The researcher could also use snowball sampling by asking known cocaine uses to identify other users of the drug.

19. There may be several problems with the data. We do not know whether the alumni's records are accurate. The alumni office may have lost track of its less successful graduates and have accurate records of alumni who earn a large income. Even if the alumni records are accurate, many of the alumni may not have agreed to complete the questionnaire. Therefore, we may have reason to suspect that the data are biased.

20. Increasing sample size has no effect on the bias of the sampling procedure. Increasing sample size will only reduce the standard error of the mean.

Statistics Behind the Research: A Supplement

X_{a1}	z_{a1}	Percentile	X_{a2}	z_{a2}	Percentile
26	1.2	88.5	11	−1.2	11.5
23	0.6	72.6	29	0.6	72.6
17	−0.6	27.4	17	−0.6	27.4
29	1.8	96.4	41	1.8	96.4
22	0.4	65.5	27	0.4	65.5
19	−0.2	42.1	25	0.2	57.9
11	−1.8	3.6	5	−1.8	3.6
20	0.0	50.0	23	0.0	50.0
18	−0.4	34.5	19	−0.4	34.5
15	−1.0	15.9	33	1.0	84.1

(a) $\sum X_{a1} = 200$ $\sum X_{a2} = 230$

(b) $\sum X_{a1}^2 = 4,250$ $\sum X_{a2}^2 = 6,290$

(c) $\left(\sum X_{a1}\right)^2 = 40,000$ $\left(\sum X_{a2}\right)^2 = 52,900$

(d) $Mdn_{a1} = 19.5$ $Mdn_{a2} = 24$

(e) $M_{a1} = 20.0$ $M_{a2} = 23$

(f) $s_{a1}^2 = 25$ $s_{a2}^2 = 100$

(g) $s_{a1} = 5$ $s_{a2} = 10$

(h) $VAR_{a1} = 27.78$ $VAR_{a2} = 111.111$

(i) $SD_{a1} = 5.27$ $SD_{a2} = 10.54$

(j) See table

(k) See table

(l) $z = 1.28$. CI $= 20.0 \pm 1.28 \times (5.)$; CI $= 20.0 \pm 6.4$

(m) $z = 1.64$. CI $= 20.0 \pm 1.64 \times (5.)$; CI $= 20.0 \pm 8.2$

CHAPTER 7

1. Psychologists invent tests and measurements to help them understand the relation among variables. In some cases, the test may measure a "real" thing such as height, weight, or some other construct that is tangible. Many other constructs, such as personality or intelligence, are not tangible. The problem of reification occurs when we assume that any test measures a tangible construct when it does not.

2. "Mystique of quantity" means that people infer too much information from a few numbers. In many ways, the mystique of quantity is related to the reification problem.

3. Both constructs are related because they refer to conditions where people make inferences from measurements that cannot be supported.

4. Researchers use the terms "intelligence," "personality," and "anxiety" to help them explain the relation among several variables. We use these constructs to help us explain and predict different behavior. Therefore, these words are inventions that help us understand complex behavioral phenomena. By contrast, many people use these terms to describe enduring and tangible aspects of a person. For example, a person may claim that a friend has an extroverted personality. This use of the word suggests that there is a tangible part of the person that is introverted. By contrast, a researcher would say that the person's behaviors and attributions can be classified as extroverted for the purpose of predicting how a person will behave in a specific situation.

5. The goal of any science is to examine the relation among variables. For all empirical studies, the researcher uses some form of hypothesis that describes the predicted relation between the independent and the dependent variable. To test the accuracy of the hypothesis, the researcher must collect objective data. Without measurement there will be no data. Without data, the hypothesis will remain an untested speculation.

6. The goal of measurement is to collect data. We use measurement to determine what information to collect and to convert the bits of information into an objective and empirical form. All measurement is objective and standardized. Objective measurement implies that the data are not biased and that the data accurately represent the construct being measured. Standardized measurement implies that we use the same procedures consistently. As a consequence, we can directly compare different things measured with the same procedures.

7. Operational definitions are essential because they allow us to determine how we convert our observations to numbers.

8. An advantage of the personal interview is that the interviewer may be able to spend time with the participant to put him or her at ease and encourage them to answer honestly. The researcher can also ask follow-up questions to obtain more information about the person's views. The disadvantages of this technique is that it may be time consuming, and the person conducting the interview will have to be well trained to collect the data. A self-administered questionnaire may be easier and less time consuming to administer. The researcher will have to spend considerable time ensuring that the questions do not bias the participant's responses. Many people may lie about their attitudes. Therefore, the wording of the questions should be selected with care.

9. Both scales allow the researcher to assess the preference for various items. For the Likert format, we present the participants with one specific statement and then provide a format of potential responses. By contrast, for the Guttman format, we present a series of statements arranged in a meaningful sequence, and then ask the participants to endorse the statement with which they agree.

10. A face-to-face interview may allow the researcher to develop a rapport with the participant that may be more difficult to do over the telephone. At the same time, the reviewer can respond to facial cues and reword the question or ask follow-up questions. The telephone interview may

be for more cost effective because neither the researcher nor the participant must travel to complete the interview.

11. The researcher may get much data by posting the questionnaire on a web page, but there is no way to control who answers the questions. We would be suspicious of the representativeness of the data.

12. Pretesting allows you to ensure that the participants will understand the questions and response formats that you provide. In addition, the pretesting will allow you to determine if there are any objectionable questions that may reduce a participant's willingness to complete the questionnaire.

13. Yes, a researcher can use closed-response questions in a face-to-face interview. Nevertheless, this technique seems to miss the opportunity of allowing the participant to elaborate on his or her answer. Perhaps both could be used—a closed-ended question with the opportunity to elaborate.

14. The researcher could use a face-to-face interview, a mailed survey, or a survey administered to an identified group of people. The face-to-face interview and the identified group may produce higher levels of compliance with the request for information. The face-to-face interview may be expensive to conduct, and finding groups of people willing to complete a questionnaire may be difficult. The mailed survey is relatively inexpensive, but includes the risk of a low rate of compliance.

15. Closed-response questions are relatively easy to answer and score and do not require much time from the participant. There may be cases, however, when additional comments from the participant will be useful. Therefore, open-ended questions allow the participant to offer detailed comments that may produce useful information not captured by a closed-response question. Open-ended questions can be difficult to score, however, and many participants may not be willing to take the time to respond fully.

16. $\alpha = 0.02$; $z_\alpha = 2.326$; $n' = 3382$

	N	n'
(a)	1,000	772
(b)	5,000	2930
(c)	25,000	3027
(d)	50,000	3189

17. Dr. Blume needs to reassess how he trained the observers and how they go about making their judgments. It appears that there is considerable disagreement among the reviewers.

18. (a) You would probably select shows known to be popular among children. Therefore, one way to select the shows is to pick the shows most often watched by children. Another option would be to use cluster sampling and randomly select shows broadcast during the hours that children are most likely to watch television. (b) & (c) There is no single correct way to answer these questions. Your definition should be objective and allow you to quantify your observations. (d) Frequency would probably be the best technique for this case as you want to record the number of times the acts occur. In addition, both aggressive and altruistic acts do not require much time to complete.

19.

	Aggressive	Altruistic	Other	Totals
Aggressive	121	13	57	**191**
Altruistic	3	67	45	**115**
Other	12	10	93	**115**
Totals	**136**	**90**	**195**	**421**

$$P_A = \frac{\sum O_{ii}}{T} = \frac{121 + 67 + 93}{421} = \frac{281}{421} = .6675$$

$$P_C = \frac{\sum R_i C_i}{T^2} = \frac{(136 \times 191) + (90 \times 115) + (195 \times 115)}{421^2} = \frac{58751}{177241} = .3315$$

$$\kappa = \frac{P_A - P_C}{1 - P_C} = \frac{.6675 - .3315}{1 - .3315} = \frac{.3360}{.6685} = .5026$$

$$\kappa = .50$$

20. As we reviewed in the chapter on ethics, there are several ethical issues to consider including: (a) Informed consent—the participant must volunteer to participate and should be free to withdraw from the interview at any time. In addition, the participant should understand the nature of the questions before beginning the interview process. (b) Confidentiality—the researcher must ensure that the responses provided by the participant will remain confidential and anonymous. (c) Respect the dignity of the participant—we must ensure that the questions we ask do not harm the person and that there is a reasonable scientific merit to asking the questions.

21. If the behavior is in a clearly public space and the researcher does not interact with the individuals then there may be no need to inform the individuals that you are recording their behavior. If the recorded behavior occurs in a private area and if the researcher interacts with the participant, then the researcher will need to obtain the participant's consent to record the situation.

CHAPTER 8

1. The correlation coefficient converts the original scores to standardized or z-scores. Therefore, the coefficient converts the scores into the same scale before determining the relation between the variables.

2. The absolute value of the correlation coefficient indicates the strength of the relation between the two variables. An alternative method is to convert the correlation coefficient, r, to the coefficient of determination, r^2. The larger the coefficient of determination, the greater the relation between the two variables.

3. The only conclusion is that grades and study time are correlated. Because we cannot require a random group of students to study and another group to not study, we cannot rule out alternative explanations.

4. (a) Because of a small sample, she could have obtained a small correlation by chance. (b) The relation between the two variables is not well defined by a straight line. (c) It is possible that the sampling procedure produced a truncation in the range of potential scores. (d) There may be no meaningful relation between the two variables.

5. Devin has a problem with his sampling procedure. We can assume that only bright students are admitted to the college. Consequently, there is truncated range problem. Variance of test scores for these students will be much less than the full range of test scores of all high school graduates who take the test.

6. Weight is probably a far more stable characteristic than personality.

7. Both allow us to determine the degree to which two rates agree with each other.

8. The internal consistency of a test. Higher scores of coefficient alpha indicate greater agreement among the individual test items.

9. The items in this test do not measure the same construct. It is possible that the items measure different constructs.

10. Increase the length of the test and ensure that the items measure the same construct.

11. These forms of validity help us ensure that the test measures what it is supposed to measure (convergent validity) and does not measure different constructs (discriminant validity).

12. According to the regression to the mean phenomenon, we would expect that their scores would be lower the second time we tested them.

CHAPTER 9

1.

A. (a) *Independent variable:* Assertiveness counseling. *Dependent variable:* Participant's assertiveness as measured by the test. (b) Assertiveness counseling causes participants to become more assertive. (c) The researcher can use a true experiment for this study. (d) There is no control group. Therefore, we cannot infer cause and effect. For example, the researcher used only the people who scored low on the assertiveness test. Consequently, the improvements could represent regression toward the mean. Similarly, the improvements could represent maturation or a carryover effect. (e) We would need to know more information about the people included in the study to determine the types of inferences we can make to various populations. (f) There is no single best answer. Your answer should comment on the use of a control group and definition of the population to whom we wish the data to apply.

B. (a) *Independent variable:* Study technique. *Dependent variable:* Grades on the exam. (b) Elaborated rehearsal improves retention of academic material. (c) The researcher used a true experiment for this study. (d) There is a confounding variable. The amount of time a person studied is correlated with the type of studying they did. Specifically, the elaborated rehearsal requirement meant that the students spent more time thinking about the material. (e) If the students in the study are representative of college-age students, then there may be few problems with external validity as long as we improve the research design. (f) There is no single best answer. Your answer should address the problems you identified in the study. Specifically, the researcher needs to control the amount of time the students spend studying.

C. (a) *Independent variable:* The presence of lying. We would assume that research wants to determine the absence of presence of deception. *Dependent variable:* Performance of lie detector test. (b) The lie detector test allows one to detect deception. (c) There is no research design as the researcher used only one group. (d) There are many problems with this research, primarily that there is no control group in the study. The researcher needs to include a group of participants who did not receive the money. In addition, it appears that the researcher scored the lie detector tests. Therefore, we need to question his objectivity in evaluating the data. (e) We need to question whether the situation and the participants represent the situations experienced in situations where a lie detector is used to determine guilt. (f) There is no single best answer. Your answer should address the problems you identified in the study. Specifically, the researcher needs to include a control group as well as a double-blind procedure.

D. (a) *Independent variable:* The effects of a pornographic film. *Dependent variable:* Average length of electrical shocks given. (b) Watching pornography increases aggression. (c) There is no research design as the researcher used only one group. (d) There are many problems with this research, primarily that there is no control group in the study. The researcher needs to include a group of participants who did not watch the movie. The researcher could use control groups that had participants watch equal length films of different content to ensure that content of the pornographic film influenced the level of aggression. Finally, there is no clear rationale for using only men in the study. (e) The researcher needs to resolve the problems with internal validity before examining problems of external validity. In addition, the researcher needs to define the population to allow us to determine whether college men are representative of the population. (f) There is no single best answer. Your answer should address the problems you identified in the study. Specifically, the researcher needs to include sufficient control groups to examine the relation between the two variables.

2. Memory Recall Study

Men and women will differ in the number of positive memories recalled.

$$H_0: \quad \mu_M = \mu_W \qquad H_1: \quad \mu_M \neq \mu_W$$

Men and women will differ in the number of negative memories recalled.

$$H_0: \quad \mu_M = \mu_W \qquad H_1: \quad \mu_M \neq \mu_W$$

Men and women will differ in the average score of the Life Satisfaction Scale.

$$H_0: \quad \mu_M = \mu_W \qquad H_1: \quad \mu_M \neq \mu_W$$

Essay writing and attitudes

Writing an essay will change one's attitude about a 5% increase in tuition. Students in the control group will have a different attitude than students in the experimental group.

$$H_0: \quad \mu_C = \mu_E \qquad H_1: \quad \mu_C \neq \mu_E$$

3. Memory Recall Study

Positive Memories

$$d_2 = \frac{10.4667 - 8.4000}{\sqrt{\dfrac{4.5522 + 3.1142}{2}}}, \quad d_2 = \frac{2.0667}{1.9579}, \quad d_2 = 1.056$$

Negative Memories

$$d_2 = \frac{7.2000 - 5.5333}{\sqrt{\dfrac{4.1714 + 3.1237}{2}}}, \quad d_2 = \frac{1.6667}{1.9099}, \quad d_2 = 0.8727$$

Satisfaction with Life Scale

$$d_2 = \frac{6.1333 - 5.3333}{\sqrt{\dfrac{4.2667 + 4.0954}{2}}}, \quad d_2 = \frac{0.8000}{2.0448}, \quad d_2 = 0.3912$$

Essay writing and attitudes

$$d_2 = \frac{9.50 - 13.0}{\sqrt{\dfrac{5.17 + 4.66}{2}}}, \quad d_2 = \frac{-3.50}{4.915}, \quad d_2 = -0.712$$

4. For each data set, committing a Type I error means that we reject the null hypothesis when we should not. In the study examining the sex differences, we would assume that there is a difference between men and women when there is no such difference. By contrast, committing a Type II error means that we fail to reject the null hypothesis when we should reject it. For example, in the study examining the effects of essay writing, a Type II error would mean that we ignore the effect that writing has on attitude change.

One could argue that for all these studies, a Type II error is the greater problem in that the researcher wants to examine the relation between two variables. Ignoring this effect may mean that an important insight to human behavior will be missed. The consequence of a Type I error will be that the researcher is temporarily misled to believe that there is a meaningful relation among the variables. If the null hypothesis is correct, then the researcher and others will have a difficult time replicating the results.

CHAPTER 10

1. (a) The difference between the means will reflect the difference between the two populations, if any, and the effects of random sampling error. (b) The researcher cannot assume that the difference between the means represents anything more than random sampling error. The researcher needs to examine the standard error of the difference between means to evaluate the data. Using Student's t-ratio, the researcher can compare the difference between means to the standard error of the difference between means. If the t-ratio is sufficiently large, the researcher can reject the null hypothesis that the two population means are equivalent. (c) Decreases in the standard error will increase the absolute magnitude of the t-ratio. Increases in the standard error will decrease the absolute value of the t-ratio.

2. $H_0: \mu_1 \leq \mu_2$: No, the alternative hypothesis predicts that $H_1: \mu_1 > \mu_2$
   $H_0: \mu_1 \geq \mu_2$: Yes, if the t-ratio is sufficiently large. The alternative hypothesis predicts that $H_1: \mu_1 < \mu_2$

3. If the researcher wants to confirm a theory or a prediction, then he or she should make the prediction based on the theory, not a preliminary review of the data.

4. Researchers select inferential statistics based on the research design and research hypothesis they created and on the characteristics of the data.

5. Deciding whether to reject the null hypothesis is a value judgment and the researcher must consider the consequences of committing either a Type I or a Type II error. Rudner argued that these consequences should direct the criteria for rejecting the null hypothesis.

6. The researcher would have to show that the independent variable preceded the dependent variable and that all alternative explanations have been ruled out.

7. (a) *False.* Although the researcher may reject the null hypothesis, the decision was an inference. Therefore, there is always a probability that the null hypothesis is correct and the researcher made a Type I error. All the researcher can do is assume that there is reasonable evidence to tentatively reject the null hypothesis and accept the alternative hypothesis. (b) *False.* We have no way of objectively determining the probability that H_0 is true. (c) *False.* The only inference we can draw from p is that if the null hypothesis is a correct statement, then the probability of the outcome is $p < .01$. (d) *False.* The only inference we can draw from p is the probability of data is $p < .01$ if the null hypothesis is a correct statement. (e) *False.* This statement is an inference of power. We cannot use the size of p to determine the degree to which the results will be replicated with further research. (f) *True.*

8. (a) Because the probabilities are identical, we can infer that Mark's experiment had the greater power. He was able to detect a statistically significant effect with fewer participants. (b) The greater power may be due to the selection of levels of the independent variable, the reliability and accuracy of the measure used to quantify the dependent variable, the homogeneity of participants, or a combination of these factors.

9. $\alpha = .05 -$ two-tailed: $n = 400$ or 800 participants total.
   $\alpha = .05 -$ one-tailed: $n = 300$ or 600 participants total.

10. Khalil needs to determine if there are other levels of the independent variables that will increase the difference between the groups. He also needs to determine if there are better ways to measure the dependent variable that are more reliable and precise. For example, the researcher may be able to increase power by collecting more observations from each participant. Finally, Khalil should determine if there are ways to make the groups more homogeneous.

CHAPTER 11

1. There are a couple advantages. First, the F-ratio is a single test that simultaneously examines the differences among the groups. Therefore, the researcher avoids the problem associated with

an inflated Type I error rate created by multiple comparisons of sample means using the *t*-ratio. Second, the ANOVA allows the researcher to examine the relation that exists between the independent and dependent variables.

2. The researcher can assume a cause-and-effect relation if the researcher used random assignment to place participants into the treatment conditions, used a control group, and is able to discount or rule out alternative explanations.

3. The between-group variance represents the difference among the means of the groups. This variation represents the effect of the independent variable and the effect of random error. The treatment variance represents the specific effects of the independent variable.

4. The mean is 0 because we assume that the effects of error are random.

5. For a control group, $\alpha_j = 0$ because the research does not expose the participants to the independent variable.

6. *False.* The *F*-ratio is a comparison of the size of the between-groups variance to the within-groups variance. A large *F*-ratio only indicates the between-groups variance is larger than the within-groups variance.

7. *True.* As ε_{ij} increases the MS_{within} also increases. All else being equal, the *F*-ratio will increase as well.

8. *False.* No measure of variance can be less than 0.

9. *False.* We can never prove the null hypothesis to be a correct statement. The independent variable may influence the dependent variable; however, the low power of the research design failed to allow us to detect the effect.

10. *False.* In a true experiment the researcher controls the levels of the independent variable.

11. *True.* See answer 5.

12. *False.* This is false if the null hypothesis is a true statement.

13. The researcher will require approximately 18 participants per group.

14. All else being equal, any decrease in MS_{within} will result in a larger *F*-ratio.

15. The ANOVA is an omnibus test because it simultaneously compares the differences among all the group means.

16. Both tests compare the difference between means. The *t*-ratio compares the difference between two group means. The *F*-ratio compares the difference among two or more means.

CHAPTER 12

1.

	a_1	a_2	
b_1	$M_{11} = 2$	$M_{21} = 3$	$M_{b1} = 2.5$
b_2	$M_{12} = 3$	$M_{22} = 4$	$M_{b2} = 3.5$
	$M_{a1} = 2.5$	$M_{a2} = 3.5$	$\bar{M} = 3.0$

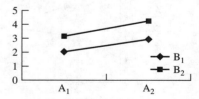

There appears to be main effects for Factors A and B, but no evidence of an interaction.

2.

	a_1	a_2	
b_1	$M_{11} = 4$	$M_{21} = 6$	$M_{b1} = 5$
b_2	$M_{12} = 5$	$M_{22} = 3$	$M_{b2} = 4$
	$M_{a1} = 4.5$	$M_{a2} = 4.5$	$\bar{M} = 4.5$

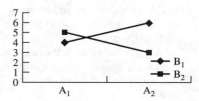

There appears to be a main effect for Factor B but not Factor A. In addition, there appears to be an interaction.

3.

	a_1	a_2	
b_1	$M_{11} = 4$	$M_{21} = 2$	$M_{b1} = 3$
b_2	$M_{12} = 2$	$M_{22} = 4$	$M_{b2} = 3$
	$M_{a1} = 3$	$M_{a2} = 3$	$\overline{M} = 3$

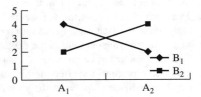

There are no main effects, but there is an interaction of the two factors.

4.

	a_1	a_2	
b_1	$M_{11} = 5$	$M_{21} = 9$	$M_{b1} = 7$
b_2	$M_{12} = 3$	$M_{22} = 5$	$M_{b2} = 4$
	$M_{a1} = 4$	$M_{a1} = 7$	$\overline{M} = 5.5$

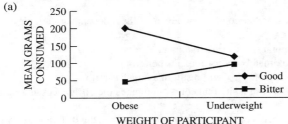

There appears to be significant main effects for both factors and the interaction.

5. (a)

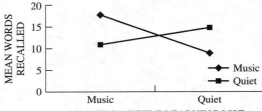

(b) There appears to be an interaction between the weight of the participant and the amount of ice cream consumed. Had the researchers not included the weight variable, then it would appear the people ate the same amount of good- and bitter-tasting ice cream. The data indicate that obese participants were greatly influenced by the taste of the ice cream.

6. (a)

(b) These data indicate an important interaction that could not be found using single-variable studies. The study indicates that people perform best when tested under the same conditions that they learned the material.

7. The SS_{total} would remain the same because the researcher is examining the same set of data. The SS_{within} would become smaller, however, because some of the variance will be subsumed within the effect of the newly identified independent variable and the interaction of the two variables.

8. The lack of a statistically significant main effect does not mean that the independent variable has no effect on the dependent variable. One must examine the interaction to determine whether there is an important interplay between the two independent variables used in the research.

9. The individual cell means represent the effects of the main effects as well as the interaction of the two independent variables.

10. The two-variable ANOVA may be more powerful because the researcher includes a second independent variable in the research design. The second variable, and its interaction with the other independent variable, may reduce the size of the within-groups variance.

CHAPTER 13

1. The matched groups and repeated measures designs are special forms of the correlated groups design. For both techniques, we identify a subject variable that can contribute to the total variability of the scores. Using matched groups design we group people together who share common features and then randomly assign them to different treatment conditions. This procedure ensures that the participants in the groups are highly correlated. Using the repeated measures design, we test the same participants under different treatment conditions or on several occasions. By identifying a significant source of variance related to the difference among the participants, we can reduce the size of the within group variance and more readily detect a difference among the group means.

2. In a matched-participants design, we group participants into similar levels based on a criterion measure and then assign the participants to the treatment conditions. In a repeated-measures design, we test the same participants under more than one condition.

3. Contrast: The participant reacts to the changes in the research conditions. Fatigue: The participants become bored or tired due to their participation in the study. Adaptation: The participants become used to the experiment and do not respond as they would if they were tested once. Learning: The participant's skill at the task increases. Pretest sensitization: The first measurement of the participant's behavior changes his or her perception of the purpose of the research.

4. There are several control conditions. The first control requires that we measure the participants' behavior on two occasions but not expose them to the treatment condition. This control allows us to examine how people's behavior will change over time if they do not experience the treatment. A second control condition requires us to expose the participants to the treatment and the follow-up measure, but use no pretest measure. This control allows us to examine the consequences of a treatment independent of any carryover effect. The last control group receives the posttest only. This control condition acts as the classic control group as the participants do not experience the effects of the treatment or the carryover effect.

5. Each person is his or her control because they will be tested in the control condition as well as the treatment condition. Therefore, we can use the ANOVA to determine how much of the change in the scores was due to the independent variable and how much was due to the differences among the participants.

6. A correlated groups ANOVA will increase power because the within-groups variance will be decreased by the variance due to the differences among the participants.

7. Researchers use these techniques when there is a significant threat of a carryover effect and the researcher wishes to use a repeated-measures design to increase power.

8. If the matching variable contributes to the within-groups variance, then this design along with the corresponding ANOVA will reduce estimates of random variance.

9. Both the matched-groups design and the yoked control design are similar in that we want to have a high correlation between the participants in the two groups. Indeed, both research

designs are special forms for the correlated groups design. The difference between the methods is how we create the groups. For the matched groups design we pretest our participants using a test and then pair participants who have similar scores. We then take each member of the pair and randomly assign them to either the treatment or control groups. For the yoked control condition we randomly assign pairs of participants to the experimental and control groups. We then arrange for the participant in the control group to have the same experiences as the participant in the experimental group.

10. For an independent-groups design, each participant's behavior is independent of other participants' behavior. The participant is tested only under one treatment condition. In a correlated groups design, the participant is tested under several situations (e.g., a repeated measures design) or the researcher uses a matched-groups design.

CHAPTER 14

1. The ABAB meets the requirements of a true experiment. The "A" phases of the design represent the control condition when the independent variable is absent. The "B" phase represents the presence of the independent variable. Therefore, the researcher can observe the relation between the independent and dependent variable by adding and removing the intervention. In addition, the researcher has direct control over the presentation of the intervention.

2. (a) In both cases, the researcher has control over the independent variable (the researcher can determine when the participants receive the treatment). Furthermore, the researcher includes a control condition that represents the absence of the critical variable. (b) Both researchers selected the participants from the same subject pool. Therefore, the concerns regarding the external validity about the generality of the findings are the same for the two studies.

3. In the conventional true experiment, we must withhold the treatment from all the participants in the control group. Depending on the length of the experiment, this may mean that the participants will suffer the depression while others are receiving what the researcher believes to be a useful treatment. By contrast, the multiple baseline procedures use a shorter baseline and ensure that all the participants receive the treatment.

4. The instructor could place all the students on a baseline (no homework) and routinely test their knowledge of the material. As the semester passes, the instructor would begin to ask some students to complete homework assignments. The data should indicate that knowledge of the material will increase once a student begins to complete the homework.

5. The primary difference between the two is the time frame used to study the changes in behavior. Longitudinal research designs tend to span long times measured in weeks, months, or years. Both are similar in that the researcher wants to examine how the passage of time influences changes in behavior.

6. The primary purpose of survival analysis is to examine the time it takes for a specific event to occur in a person's life. For example, a researcher may be interested in the risk of relapse of patients who have just completed a drug and alcohol rehabilitation program.

7. Both techniques include a baseline procedure and monitor behavior after the intervention begins. In both cases, the onset of the intervention can be staggered.

CHAPTER 15

1. The primary purpose of the statistic is to examine the difference between observed and expected scores. If the χ^2 statistic is sufficiently large, we can assume that the frequencies in the categories are not the result of chance factors. The goodness-of-fit test examines the

frequency of observations along one dimension. The test of independence examines the observations for two variables.

2. The data are not nominal. The number of bar presses is a ratio scale (there is an absolute 0). Consequently, the researcher needs to use a different statistical test such as the ANOVA.

3. Although the study is interesting, we must wonder whether the memories are independent of one another. For example, will a subject's memory of his or her father influence the memory of the mother? Because the memories may not be independent, the χ^2 test may not be valid.

4.

Goal	1965	1998	$\dfrac{(O_i - E_i)^2}{E_i}$
a	15	8	3.2667
b	53	48	0.4717
c	25	57	40.9600
d	27	47	14.8148
	120	160	59.5132

$$\chi^2(N = 280, 3) = 59.5132, p < .05$$

5.

Program	O	E	$\dfrac{(O_i - E_i)^2}{E_i}$
1	12	12.5714	0.0260
2	23	12.5714	8.6510
3	8	12.5714	1.6623
4	7	12.5714	2.4692
5	15	12.5714	0.4692
6	5	12.5714	4.5601
7	18	12.5714	2.3442
	88	88.0000	20.1818

$$\chi^2(N = 88, 7) = 20.1818, p < .05$$

6.

	Condition A	Condition B	Row total
Helped	$O_{11} = 75$	$O_{12} = 45$	$R_1 = 120$
	$E_{11} = \dfrac{115 \times 120}{240}$	$E_{12} = \dfrac{125 \times 120}{240}$	
	$E_{11} = 57.5$	$E_{12} = 62.5$	
No help	$O_{21} = 40$	$O_{22} = 80$	$R_2 = 120$
	$E_{21} = \dfrac{115 \times 120}{240}$	$E_{22} = \dfrac{125 \times 120}{240}$	
	$E_{21} = 57.5$	$E_{22} = 62.5$	
Column total	$C_1 = 115$	$C_2 = 125$	$T = 240$

$$\chi^2 = \frac{(75 - 57.5)^2}{57.5} + \frac{(45 - 62.5)^2}{62.5} + \frac{(40 - 57.5)^2}{57.5} + \frac{(80 - 62.5)^2}{62.5}$$

$$\chi^2 = 5.3261 + 4.9000 + 5.3261 + 4.9000$$

$$\chi^2(N = 240, 1) = 20.45, p < .05$$

7.

$$\chi^2 = \frac{(|25 - 30| - 1)^2}{25 + 30} = 0.2909 \qquad z = \sqrt{0.2909} = 0.5394$$

The differences are not statistically significant.

8.

	Male	Female	Row total
+	$O_{11} = 28$	$O_{12} = 30$	$R_1 = 58$
	$E_{11} = \dfrac{126 \times 58}{300}$	$E_{12} = \dfrac{174 \times 58}{300}$	
	$E_{11} = 24.36$	$E_{12} = 33.64$	
−	$O_{21} = 98$	$O_{22} = 144$	$R_2 = 242$
	$E_{21} = \dfrac{126 \times 242}{300}$	$E_{22} = \dfrac{174 \times 242}{300}$	
	$E_{21} = 101.64$	$E_{22} = 140.36$	
Column total	$C_1 = 126$	$C_2 = 174$	$T = 300$

$$\chi^2 = \frac{(28 - 24.36)^2}{24.36} + \frac{(98 - 101.64)^2}{101.64} + \frac{(30 - 33.64)^2}{33.64} + \frac{(144 - 140.36)^2}{140.36}$$

$$\chi^2(N = 240, \ 1) = 1.163, \ p > .05$$

According to these results we cannot reject the null hypothesis. Therefore, we must assume that we do not have data to indicate the there is a relation between one's sex and risk for binge drinking.

9.

	Letter	Phone call	Nothing	Row total
Compliance	$O_{11} = 44$	$O_{12} = 68$	$O_{13} = 21$	$R_1 = 133$
	$E_{11} = 44.33$	$E_{12} = 44.33$	$E_{12} = 44.33$	
	$\hat{e}_{11} = -0.08$	$\hat{e}_{12} = 5.84$	$\hat{e}_{13} = -5.73$	
No compliance	$O_{11} = 56$	$O_{12} = 32$	$O_{13} = 79$	$R_2 = 167$
	$E_{21} = 55.67$	$E_{22} = 55.67$	$E_{23} = 55.67$	
	$\hat{e}_{21} = 0.08$	$\hat{e}_{22} = -5.84$	$\hat{e}_{23} = 5.73$	
Column total	$C_1 = 100$	$C_2 = 100$	$C_3 = 100$	$T = 300$

$$\chi^2(N = 300, \ 2) = 44.762, \ p < .05$$

It is clear from the χ^2 test that there is a significant relation between presurvey contact and subsequent compliance. Examining the adjusted residuals, it is clear that the phone call had the greatest impact upon increasing compliance.

Appendix C
USEFUL INTERNET WEBSITES

DICTIONARIES

General Dictionaries

Merrill-Webster Dictionary and Thesaurus
- www.m-w.com/dictionary.htm

Psychology and General Science Dictionaries

A Lexicon and Concordance of Terms Used in Statistics and Empirical Research in Education
- www-iea.fmi.uni-sofia.bg/Lexicon/lex_main.htm
Gale Encyclopedia of Psychology
- www.findarticles.com/cf_0/g2699/mag.jhtml
PsyBox.Com
- www.psybox.com/web_dictionary/dictionaryWebindex.htm
Xrefer
- www.xrefer.com/search.jsp

ETHICS

American Psychological Association
- www.apa.org/ethics/code.html
Department of Health and Human Services: *Federal Policy for the Protection of Human Subjects*
- www.med.umich.edu/irbmed/FederalDocuments/hhs/HHS45CFR46.html
National Academy of Science
- www.nap.edu/readingroom/books/obas
National Institute of Health
- http://ohrp.osophs.dhhs.gov/humansubjects/guidance/ictips.htm
Office of Research Integrity
- http://ori.dhhs.gov
The Belmont Report
- http://ohrp.osophs.dhhs.gov/humansubjects/guidance/belmont.htm

GENERAL WEBSITES

Psychology Central
- www.psych-central.com

Research Methods
- http://trochim.human.cornell.edu/tutorial/TUTORIAL.HTM

The Skeptic
- www.skeptic.com

ONLINE RESEARCH

American Psychological Society
- http://psych.hanover.edu/APS/exponnet.html

The University of Mississippi
- http://psychexps.olemiss.edu

PSYCHOLOGICAL TESTS

Buros Institute
- www.unl.edu/buros

ERIC
- http://ericae.net/testcol.htm

PSYCHOLOGY ORGANIZATIONS

American Psychological Association
- www.apa.org

American Psychological Society
- www.psychologicalscience.org

APA Division 3: Experimental Psychology
- www.apa.org/about/division/div3.html

APA Division 5: Evaluation, Measurement, & Statistics
- www.apa.org/about/division/div5.html

Canadian Psychological Society
- www.cpa.ca

PsiChi
- www.psichi.com/content/home.asp

Psychonomic Society
- www.psychonomic.org/about.htm

RESEARCH REPORTS

General Reference

Classic Papers in Psychology
- http://psychclassics.yorku.ca/index.htm

Contemporary Full-Text Articles

- www.findarticles.com/Pl/index.jhtml

Government

Census
- www.census.gov
Centers for Disease Control and Prevention
- www.cdc.gov/publications.htm
Educational Resources Information Center
- www.eric.ed.gov
Government Accounting Office
- www.access.gpo.gov/su_docs/aces/aces160.shtml

STATISTICS

Power Calculator
- www.stat.uiowa.edu/~rlenth/Power/index.html
Statistics on the Web
- www.execpc.com/~helberg/statistics.html
Statistics Simulations
- www.ruf.rice.edu/~lane/rvls.html

REFERENCES

Chapter 1

Bacon, F. (1994). *Novum organum.* (P. Urbach & J. Gibson, Trans.). Chicago: Open Court. (Original work published 1620).

Baron, R. M., Graziano, W., & Stangor, C. (1991). Social perception and social cognition. In R. M. Baron & W. Graziano (Eds.), *Social psychology* (pp. 108–159). Fort Worth, TX: Holt, Rinehart and Winston.

Biklen, D. (1990). Communication unbound: Autism and praxis. *Harvard Educational Review, 60,* 291–315.

Dauber v. Merrell Dow Pharmaceuticals, Inc., 113 S. Ct. 2786 (1993).

Ebbinghaus, H. (1910). *A summary of psychology.* Leipzig: Veit.

Federal Judicial Center (1994). *Reference manual on scientific evidence.* Washington, DC: Author.

Garcia, J. (1980). Tilting at the paper mills of academe. *American Psychologist, 36,* 149–158.

Gould, S. J. (1999). *Rock of ages: Science and religion in the fullness of life.* New York: Ballantine.

Hudson, A., Melita, B., & Arnold, N. (1993). Assessing the validity of facilitated communication: A case study. *Journal of Autism and Developmental Disorders, 23,* 165–173.

Mazur, J. E. (1998). *Learning and behavior.* Upper Saddle River, NJ: Prentice-Hall.

Montee, B. B., Miltenberger, R. G., & Wittrock, D. (1995). An experimental analysis of facilitated communication. *Journal of Applied Behavior Analysis, 28,* 189–200.

Moore, S., Donovan, B., & Hudson, A. (1993). Facilitator-suggested conversational evaluation of facilitated communication. *Journal of Autism and Developmental Disorders, 23,* 451–551.

Murray, D. J. (1983). *A history of western psychology.* Englewood Cliffs, NJ: Prentice-Hall.

Nisbett, R. E., & Ross, L. (1980). *Human inference: Strategies and shortcomings of social judgment.* Englewood Cliffs, NJ: Prentice-Hall.

Ogles, B. M., Lambert, M. J., & Masters, K. S. (1996). *Assessing outcomes in clinical practice.* Boston: Allyn & Bacon.

Popper, K. (1963). *Science: Conjectures and refutations.* New York: Harper and Row.

Premack, D. (1959). Toward empirical behavioral laws: I. Positive reinforcement. *Psychological Review, 66,* 219–233.

Premack, D. (1965). Reinforcement theory. In D. Levine (Ed.), *Nebraska symposia on motivation* (pp. 123–180). Lincoln: University of Nebraska Press.

Rosnow, R. L., & Rosenthal, R. (1997). *People studying people: Artifacts and ethics in behavioral research.* New York: Freeman.

Scarr, S., Phillips, D., & McCartney, K. (1990). Facts, fantasies, and the future of child care in the United States. *Psychological Science, 1,* 255–264.

Timberlake, W., & Allison, J. (1974). Response deprivation: An empirical approach to instrumental performance. *Psychological Review, 81,* 146–164.

Watson, J. B. (1913). Psychology as the behaviorist views it. *Psychological Review, 20,* 158–177.

Wheeler, D. L., Jacobson, J. W., Paglieri, R. A., & Schwartz, A. A. (1993). An experimental assessment of facilitated communication. *Mental Retardation, 31,* 49–60.

Chapter 2

Bacon, F. (1994). *Novum organum.* (P. Urbach & J. Gibson, Trans.). Chicago: Open Court. (Original work published 1620).

Brief, A. P., Buttram, R. T., Elliott, J. D., Reizenstein, R. M., & McCline, R. L. (1995). Releasing the beast: A study of compliance with order to use race as a selection criterion. *Journal of Social Issues, 51,* 177–193.

Chase, W. G., & Simon, H. A. (1973). Perception in chess. *Cognitive Psychology, 4,* 55–81.

Hyde, J., & DeLamater, S. (1998). *Human Sexuality.* Boston: McGraw-Hill.

Kaplan, A. (1964). *The conduct of inquiry: Methodology for behavioral science.* San Francisco: Chandler.

Meeus, W. H. J., & Raaijmakers, Q. A. W. (1995). Obedience in modern society: The Utrecht studies. *Journal of Social Issues, 51,* 155–175.

Milgram, S. (1974). *Obedience to authority: An experimental view.* New York: Harper and Row.

Mills, J. S. (1986). *System of logic.* New York: Classworks (Original work published 1843).

Pavlov, I. P. (1927). *Conditioned reflexes: An investigation of the physiological activity of the cerebral cortex.* London: Oxford University.

Schimmelpfenig, D. W., & Sibicky, M. E. (1997, April). *Modern sexism and attitudes toward male and female leaders.* Poster session presented at the annual meeting of the Southeastern Psychological Association, Atlanta, GA.

Skinner, B. F. (1949). Are theories of learning necessary? *Psychological Review, 57,* 193–216.

Swim, J. K., Aikin, K. J., Hall, W. S., & Hunter, B. A. (1995). Sexism and racism: Old-fashioned and modern prejudices. *Journal of Personality and Social Psychology, 68,* 199–214.

Chapter 3

Anderson, C. A., & Bushman, B. J. (1997). External validity of "trivial" experiments: The case of laboratory aggression. *Review of General Psychology, 1,* 19–41.

Anne E. Casey Foundation (1999). *When teens have sex: Issues and trends.* Washington, DC: Author.

Brock, T. C., Green, M. C., & Reich, D. A. (1998). New evidence of flaws in the *Consumer Reports* study of psychotherapy. *American Psychologist, 53,* 62–63.

Brock, T. C., Green, M. C., Reich, D. A., & Evans, L. M. (1996). The *Consumer Reports* study of psychotherapy: Invalid is invalid. *American Psychologist, 51,* 1083.

Cook, T. D., & Campbell, D. T. (1979). *Quasi-experimentation: Design and analysis issues for field settings.* Chicago: Rand-McNally.

Freud, S., & Breuer, J. (1976). Studies in hysteria. In J. Strachey (Trans. and Ed.), *The complete psychological works* (vol. 2) (pp. 50–300). New York: Norton. (Original text published 1895).

Gardner, H. (1995). *Leading minds: An anatomy of leadership.* New York: Basic Books.

Glass, G. V. (1978). Integrating findings: The meta-analysis of research. *Review of Research in Education, 5,* 351–379.

Hyde, J. S., & Lynn, M. C. (1988). Gender differences in verbal ability. *Psychological Bulletin, 104,* 53–69.

Jacobson, N. S., & Christensen, A. (1996). Studying the effectiveness of psychotherapy: How well can clinical trials do the job? *American Psychologist, 51,* 1031–1039.

Kotkin, M., Daviet, C., & Gurin, J. (1996). The *Consumer Reports* mental health survey. *American Psychologist, 51,* 1080–1082.

Loftus, E., & Ketcham, K. (1994). *The myth of repressed memories: False memories and allegations of sexual abuse.* New York: St Martin's.

Maier, S. F., & Seligman, M. E. (1976). Learned helplessness: Theory and evidence. *Journal of Experimental Psychology: General, 105,* 3–46.

Mills, J. S. (1986). *System of logic.* New York: Classworks. (Original work published 1843).

Milner, B. (1966). Amnesia following operation on the temporal lobes. In C. W. M. Witty & O. L. Zangwill (Eds.), *Amnesia* (pp. 60–93). London: Buterworth.

Milner, B., Corkin, S., & Teuber, H. L. (1968). Further analysis of hippocampal syndrome: 14-year follow-up study of H. M. *Neuropsycholgia, 6,* 215–234.

Overmeier, J. B., & Seligman, M. E. (1967). Effect of inescapable shock upon subsequent escape and avoidance responding. *Journal of Comparative & Physiological Psychology, 63,* 28–33.

Premack, D. (1959). Toward empirical behavioral laws: I. Positive reinforcement. *Psychological Review, 66,* 219–233.

Premack, D. (1965). Reinforcement theory. In D. Levine (Ed.). *Nebraska symposia on motivation* (pp. 123–180). Lincoln: University of Nebraska Press.

Seligman, M. E. P. (1995). The effectiveness of psychotherapy: The *Consumer Reports* study. *American Psychologist, 50,* 965–974.

Seligman, M. E., & Maier, S. F. (1967). Failure to escape traumatic shock. *Journal of Experimental Psychology, 74,* 1–9.

Strupp, H. H. (1996). The tripartite model and the *Consumer Reports* study. *American Psychologist, 51,* 1017–1024.

Chapter 4

American Psychological Association (2001). *Thesaurus of psychological index terms* (9th ed.). Washington, DC: Author.

Brandt, D. S. (1996). Evaluating information on the Internet. *Computers in Libraries, 16,* 44–47.

Brandt, D. S. (1997). What flavor is your Internet search engine? *Computers in Libraries, 17,* 47–50.

Casper, R. C., & Jabine, L. N. (1996). An eight-year follow-up: Outcome from adolescent compared to adult onset anorexia nervosa. *Journal of Youth & Adolescence, 25,* 499–517.

Darley, J. M., & Latané, B. (1968). Bystander intervention in emergencies: Diffusion of responsibility. *Journal of Personality and Social Psychology, 10,* 202–214.

Latané, B., & Nida, S. A. (1981). Ten years of research on group size and helping. *Psychological Bulletin, 89,* 308–324.

Lerch, I. (1999, November). Reprint of letter to Dr. Richard McCarty. *Psychological Science Agenda, 12,* 2–3.

Myers, D. (2001). *Psychology* (6th ed.). New York: Worth.

Rauscher, F. H., Shaw, G. L., & Ky, K. N. (1993). Music and spatial task performance. *Nature, 365,* 611.

Rauscher, F. H., Shaw, G. L., & Ky, K. N. (1995). Listening to Mozart enhances spatial-temporal reasoning: Towards a neurophysiological basis. *Neuroscience Letters, 185,* 44–47.

Rideout, B. E., & Laubach, C. M. (1996). EEE correlates of enhanced spatial performance following exposure to music. *Perceptual & Motor Skills, 82,* 427–432.

Rind, B., Tromovitch, P., & Bauserman, R. (1998). A meta-analytic examination of assumed properties of child sexual abuse using college samples. *Psychological Bulletin, 124,* 22–53.

Steele, K. M., Ball, T. N., & Runk, R. (1997). Listening to Mozart does not enhance backwards digit span performance. *Perceptual and Motor Skills, 84,* 1179–1184.

Chapter 5

American Psychological Association (1992). Ethical principles of psychologists and code of conduct. *American Psychologist, 47,* 1597–1611.

Jones, J. (1982). *Bad blood*. New York: Free Press.

Kant, I. (1964). *Groundwork of the metaphysics of morals* (H. J. Paton, Trans.). New York: Harper & Row. (Original work published 1750).

Milgram, S. (1963). Behavioral study of obedience. *Journal of Abnormal and Social Behavior, 7,* 371–378.

Milgram, S. (1974). *Obedience to authority: An experimental view.* New York: Harper and Row.

National Bioethics Advisory Commission (1998). Research involving persons with mental disorders that may affect decision making capacity. Rockville, MD: Author.

Resnik, D. B. (1998). *The ethics of science: An introduction.* New York: Routledge.

Singer, P. (1990/1975). *Animal liberation* (Rev. ed.). New York: Avon.

Steinbock, B. (1978). Speciesism and the idea of equality. *Philosophy, 53,* 247–256.

Welsome, E. (1999). *The plutonium files: America's secret medical experiments in the cold war.* New York: Random House.

Chapter 6

American Psychiatric Association (1994). *Diagnostic and Statistical Manual of Mental Disorder* (4th ed.). Washington, DC: Author.

Babbie, E. (1998). *Survey Research Methods* (2nd ed.). Belmont, CA: Wadsworth.

Center for Disease Control (1999). Trends in HIV-related sexual risk behaviors among high school students—selected U.S. Cities, 1991–1997. *Morbidity and Mortality Weekly Review, 48,* 440–443.

Cochran, W. G. (1977). *Sampling techniques* (3rd ed.). New York: John Wiley & Sons.

Hooker, E. (1956). A preliminary analysis of group behavior of homosexuals. *Journal of Psychology, 42,* 217–225.

Hooker, E. (1957). The adjustment of the male overt homosexual. *Journal of Projective Techniques, 21,* 18–31.

Hooker, E. (1958). Male homosexuality in the Rorschach. *Journal of Projective Techniques, 21,* 18–31.

Pashley, P. J. (1993). On generating random sequences. In G. Keren & C. Lewis (Eds.). *A Handbook for data analysis in the behavioral sciences: Methodological issues* (pp. 395–418). Hillsdale, NJ: LEA.

Plous, S. (1993). *The psychology of judgment and decision making.* Boston: McGraw-Hill.

Rand Corporation (1955). *A million random digits with 100,000 normal deviates.* Glenco, IL: Free Press.

Salant, P., & Dillman, D. A. (1994). *How to conduct your own survey.* New York: John Wiley & Sons.

Ventura, S. J., Anderson, R. N., Martin, J. A., & Smith, B. L. (1998). Births and deaths: Preliminary data for 1997. *National Vital Statistics Reports, 47,* 4.

Wilkinson, L. (1999). Statistical methods in psychological journals: Guidelines and explanations. *American Psychologist, 54,* 594–604.

Chapter 7

Ainsworth, M. D. S., & Bell, S. M. (1970). Attachment, exploration, and separation: Illustrated by the behavior of one-year-olds in a strange situation. *Child Development, 41,* 49–67.

Ainsworth, M. D. S., Blehar, M. C., Waters, E., & Wall, S. (1978). *Patterns of attachment.* Hillsdale, NJ: Erlbaum.

Altman, D. G. (1991). *Practical statistics for medical research.* Boca Raton, FL: Chapman & Hall.

Altmann, J. (1974). Observational study of behavior: Sampling methods. *Behaviour, 49,* 227–267.

Barkhof, F., Filippi, M., van Waesberghe, J. H., Molyneux, P., Rovaris, M., Lycklama a' Nijeholt, G., Tubridy, N., Miller, D. H., Yousry, T. A., Radue, E. W., & Ader, H. J. (1997). Improving interobserver variation in reporting gadolinium-enhanced MRI lesion in multiple sclerosis. *Neurology, 49,* 1682–1688.

Barnette, J. J. (2000). Effects of stem and Likert response option reversals on survey internal consistency: If you feel the need, there is a better alternative to using those negatively worded stems. *Educational and Psychological Measurement, 60,* 361–370.

Chang, L. (1994). A psychometric evaluation of 4-point and 6-point Likert-type scales in relation reliability and validity. *Applied Psychological Measurement, 18,* 205–215.

Cialdini, R. B. (1984). *Influence: The psychology of persuasion.* New York: Quill.

Cochran, W. G. (1977). *Sampling techniques.* New York: Wiley.

Cronbach, L. J. (1950). Further evidence on response sets and test design. *Educational and Psychological Measurement, 10,* 3–31.

Davidson, J. W., & Lytle, M. H. (1992). *After the fact: The art of historical detection* (3rd. ed.). New York: McGraw-Hill.

DePaulo, B. M., & Kashy, D. A. (1998). Everyday lies in close and casual relationships. *Journal of Personality and Social Psychology, 74,* 63–79.

Dewdney, A. K. (1997). *Yes, we have no neutrons: An eye-opening tour through the twists and turns of bad science.* New York: John Wiley & Sons.

Dillman, D. A. (2000). *Mail and Internet surveys: The tailored design method* (2nd ed.). New York: John Wiley & Sons.

Fontana, A., & Frey, J. H. (1994). Interviewing: The art of science. In N. S. Denzin & Y. S. Lincoln (Eds.), *Handbook of qualitative research* (pp. 75–103). Thousand Oaks, CA: Sage.

Gould, S. J. (1981). *The mismeasure of man.* New York: W. W. Norton.

Humphreys, L. (1970). *Tearoom trade: Impersonal sex in public places.* Chicago: Aldine.

Kaplan, A. (1964). *The conduct of inquiry: Methodology for behavioral science.* San Francisco: Chandler.

Koss, M. P., & Oros, C. J. (1982). Sexual experiences survey: A research instrument investigating sexual aggression and victimization. *Journal of Consulting and Clinical Psychology, 50,* 455–457.

Lando, H. A. (1976). On being sane in insane places: A supplemental report. *Professional Psychology: Research & Practice, 7,* 47–52.

Larimer, M. E., Lydum, A. R., Anderson, B. K., & Turner, A. P. (1999). Male and female recipients of unwanted sexual contact in a college students sample: Prevalence rates, alcohol use, and depression symptoms. *Sex Roles, 40,* 295–308.

Miles-Tapping, C. (1996). Power wheelchairs and independent life styles. *Canadian Journal of Rehabilitation, 10,* 137–145.

Murphy, G., & Goodall, E. (1980). Measurement error in direct observation: A comparison of common recording methods. *Behaviour Research & Therapy, 18,* 147–150.

Pepler, D. J., & Craig, W. M. (1995). A peek behind the fence: Naturalistic observation of aggressive children with remote audiovisual recording. *Developmental Psychology, 31,* 548–553.

Preston, C. C., & Colman, A. M. (2000). Optimal number of response categories in rating scales: Reliability, validity, discriminating power, and respondent preferences. *Acta Psychologicia, 104,* 1–15.

Robinson, J. P., Shaver, P. R., & Wrightsman, L. S. (1991). *Measures of personality and social psychological attitudes: Volume 1 in measures of social psychological attitudes series.* San Diego: Academic Press.

Rosenberg, M. (1965). Society and the adolescent self-image. Princeton, NJ: Princeton University Press.

Rosenhan, D. L. (1973). On being sane in insane places. *Science, 179,* 250–258.

Rotter, J. B. (1966). Generalized expectancies for internal versus external control of reinforcement. *Psychological Monographs, 80* (1, Whole No. 609).

Salant, P., & Dillman, D. A. (1994). *How to conduct your own survey.* New York: John Wiley & Sons.

Swim, J. K., Aiken, K. J., Hall, W. S., & Hunter, B. A. (1995). Sexism and racism: Old-fashioned and modern prejudices. *Journal of Personality and Social Psychology, 68,* 199–214.

Thompson, H. (1985). *Hell's angles.* New York: Ballantine.

Tyler, S. (1979). Time-sampling: A matter of convention. *Animal Behaviour, 27,* 801–810.

Wilkinson, L. (1999). Statistical methods in psychological journals: Guidelines and explanations. *American Psychologist, 54,* 594–604.

Wood, M. D., Johnson, T. J., & Sher, K. J. (March, 1992). *Characteristics of frequent drinking game participants in college: An exploratory study.* Poster session presented at the annual meeting of the Research Society on Alcoholism, San Diego, CA.

Chapter 8

Campbell, D. T., & Fiske, D. W. (1959). Convergent and discriminant validation by the multitrait-multimethod matrix. *Psychological Bulletin, 56,* 81–105.

Cohen, J. (1988). *Statistical power analysis for the behavioral sciences* (2nd ed.). Hillsdale, NJ: LEA.

Cortina, J. M. (1993). What is coefficient alpha? An examination of theory and applications. *Journal of Applied Psychology, 78,* 98–104.

Cronbach, L. J. (1951). Coefficient alpha and the internal structure of tests. *Psychometrika, 16,* 297–334.

Cronbach, L. J. (1988). Five perspectives on the validity argument. In H. Wainer & H. I. Braun (Eds.), *Test validity* (pp. 63–79). Hillsdale, NJ: Erlbaum.

Galton, F. (1889). *Natural inheritance.* London: Macmillan.

Messick, S. (1980). Test validity and the ethics of assessment. *American Psychologist, 35,* 1012–1027.

Messick, S. (1988). The once and future issues of validity: Assessing the meaning and consequences of measurement. In H. Wainer & H. I. Braun (Eds.), *Test validity* (pp. 80–95). Hillsdale, NJ: Erlbaum.

Messick, S. (1989). Validity. In R. L. Linn (Ed.), *Educational measurement* (3rd ed.). New York: American Council on Education/Macmillan.

Schmitt, N. (1996). Uses and abuses of coefficient alpha. *Psychological Assessment, 8,* 350–353.

Searleman, A., & Hermann, D. (1994). *Memory from a broader perspective.* New York: McGraw-Hill.

Sternberg, S. (1966). High-speed scanning in human memory. *Science, 153,* 652–654.

Chapter 9

Bem, S. L. (1974). The measurement of psychological androgyny. *Journal of Consulting and Clinical Psychology, 42,* 155–162.

Bem, S. L. (1977). On the utility of alternate procedures for assessing psychological androgyny. *Journal of Consulting and Clinical Psychology, 45,* 196–205.

Bissonnette, V., Ickes, W., Bernstein, I. H., & Knowles, E. (1990). Personality moderating variables: A warning about statistical artifact and a comparison of analytic techniques. *Journal of Personality, 58,* 567–587.

Cohen, J. (1988). *Statistical power analysis for the behavioral sciences* (2nd ed.). Hillsdale, NJ: LEA.

Diener, E., Emmons, R. A., Larsen, R. A., & Griffin, S. (1985). The Satisfaction with Life Scale. *Journal of Personality Assessment, 49,* 71–75.

Garcia, J. (1980). Tilting at the paper mills of academe. *American Psychologist, 36,* 149–158.

Graziano, W. G., & Bryant, W. H. M. (1998). Self-monitoring and the self-attribution of positive emotions. *Journal of Personality and Social Psychology, 74,* 250–261.

Hyde, J. S. (1991). *Half the human experience: The psychology of women* (4th ed.). Lexington, MA: Heath.

Jones, L. V., & Tukey, J. W. (2000). A sensible formulation of the significance test. *Psychological Methods, 5,* 411–414.

Maxwell, S. E., & Delaney, H. D. (1993). Bivariate median splits and spurious statistical significance. *Psychological Bulletin, 113,* 181–190.

Parsons, H. M. (1974). What happened at Hawthorne? *Science, 183,* 922–932.

Rosenthal, R. (1994). Interpersonal expectancy effects: A 30-year perspective. *Current Directions in Psychological Science, 5,* 176–179.

Rosenthal, R., & Jacobson, L. (1968). *Pygmalion in the classroom.* New York: Holt, Reinhart & Winston.

Rosnow, R. L., & Rosenthal, R. (1997). *People studying people: Artifacts in behavioral research.* New York: Freeman.

Samuda, R. J. (1975). *Psychological testing of American minorities: Issues and consequences.* New York: Harper & Row.

Seidlitz, L., & Diener, E. (1998). Sex differences in the recall of affective experiences. *Journal of Personality and Social Psychology, 74,* 262–271.

Shakespeare, W. (1604). The Tragedy of *Hamlet, Prince of Denmark* Act 3, Scene 2. New York: Washington Square.

Stalder, D. R., & Baron, R. S. (1998). Attritional complexity as a moderator of dissonance-produced attitude change. *Journal of Personality and Social Psychology, 75,* 449–455.

Sundstorm, E., McIntyre, M., Halfhill, T., & Richards, H. (2000). Work groups from the Hawthorne studies to work teams of the 1990s and beyond. *Group Dynamics, 4,* 44–67.

Chapter 10

American Psychological Association (2001). *Publication manual of the American Psychological Association* (5th ed.). Washington, DC: Author.

Carver, R. P. (1978). The case against statistical significance testing. *Harvard Educational Review, 48,* 278–399.

Dixon, W. J., & Massey, F. J. (1951). *Introduction to statistical analysis.* New York: McGraw-Hill.

Moyé, L. A. (2000). *Statistical reasoning in medicine: The intuitive* p-*value primer.* New York: Springer.

Oakes, M. (1986). *Statistical inference: A commentary for the social and behavioral sciences.* New York: John Wiley & Sons.

Pedhazur, E. J. (1997). *Multiple regression in behavioral research: Explanation and prediction* (3rd ed.). Fort Worth, TX: Harcourt Brace.

Rudner, R. (1953). The scientist *qua* scientist makes value judgments. *Philosophy of Science, 20,* 349–380.

Seidlitz, L., & Diener, E. (1998). Sex differences in the recall of affective experiences. *Journal of Personality and Social Psychology, 74,* 262–271.

Shine, L. C. (1980). The fallacy of replacing an a priori significance level with an a posteriori significance level. *Educational and Psychological Measurement, 40,* 331–335.

Chapter 11

Abelson, R. P. (1985). A variance explanation paradox: When a little is a lot. *Psychological Bulletin, 97,* 129–133.

Cohen, J. (1988). *Statistical power analysis for the behavioral sciences* (2nd ed.). Hillsdale, NJ: LEA.

Ekman, P., & O'Sullivan, M. (1991). Who can catch a liar? *American Psychologist, 46,* 913–920.

Jaccard, J., Becker, M. A., & Wood, G. (1984). Pairwise multiple comparison procedures: A review. *Psychological Bulletin, 96,* 589–596.

Mueller, C. M., & Dweck, C. S. (1998). Praise for intelligence can undermine children's motivation and performance. *Journal of Personality and Social Psychology, 75,* 33–53.

Rotton, J., & Cohn, E. G. (2001). Temperature, routine activities, and domestic violence: A reanalysis. *Violence & Victims, 16,* 203–215.

Tukey, J. W. (1953). *The problem of multiple comparisons.* Princeton University, Mimeographed monograph.

Chapter 12

Chaiken, S., & Maheswaran, D. (1992). *Heuristic processing can bias systematic processing: The effect of source credibility, argument ambiguity, and task importance on attitude judgment.* Unpublished manuscript, New York University, New York, NY.

Cohen, D., Nisbett, R. E., Bowdle, B. F., & Schwarz, N. (1996). Insult, aggression, and the southern culture of honor: An "experimental ethnography." *Journal of Personality & Social Psychology, 70,* 945–960.

Cohen, J. (1988). *Statistical power analysis for the behavioral sciences* (2nd ed.). Hillsdale, NJ: LEA.

Eisenberger, R., & Armeli, S. (1997). Can salient reward increase creative performance without reducing intrinsic creative interest? *Journal of Personality & Social Psychology, 72,* 652–663.

Hayes, L. V. (1981). *Statistics.* New York: Holt, Rinehart, and Winston.

Kirk, R. E. (1982). *Experimental design* (2nd ed.). Monterey, CA: Brooks/Cole.

Rosenthal, R., & Rosnow, R. L. (1985). *Contrast analysis: Focused comparisons in the analysis of variance.* New York: Cambridge.

Tukey, J. W., Mosteller, F., & Hoaglin, D. G. (1991). Concepts and examples in analysis of variance. In D. G. Hoaglin, F. Mosteller, & J. W. Tukey (Eds.), *Fundamentals of exploratory analysis of variance* (pp. 13–33). New York: John Wiley & Sons.

Winer, B. J., Brown, D. R., & Michels, K. M. (1991). *Statistical principles in experimental design* (3rd ed.). New York: McGraw-Hill.

Zentall, S. S., & Shaw, J. H. (1980). Effects of classroom noise on performance and activity of second-grade hyperactive and control children. *Journal of Educational Psychology, 72,* 830–840.

Chapter 13

Brady, J. V. (1958). Ulcers in "executive" monkeys. *Scientific American, 199,* 95–104 .

Brady, J. V., Porter, R. W., Conrad, D. G., & Mason, J. W. (1958). Avoidance behavior and the development of gastroduodenal ulcers. *Journal of the Experimental Analysis of Behavior, 1,* 69–73.

Braver, M. C. W., & Braver, S. L. (1988). Statistical treatment of the Solomon four-group design: A meta-analytic approach. *Psychological Bulletin, 104,* 150–154.

Campbell, D. T., & Stanley, J. C. (1963). *Experimental and quasi-experimental designs for research.* Chicago: Rand McNally.

Crespi, L. P. (1942). Quantitative variation of incentive and performance in the white rat. *American Journal of Psychology, 55,* 467–517.

Eisenberger, R., & Leonard, J. M. (1980). Effects of conceptual task difficulty on generalized persistence. *American Journal of Psychology, 93,* 285–298.

Hayes, L. V. (1981). *Statistics.* New York: Holt, Rinehart, and Winston.

Kirk, R. E. (1982). *Experimental design* (2nd ed.). Monterey, CA: Brooks/Cole.

Solomon, R. L. (1949). An extension of control group design. *Psychological Bulletin, 46,* 137–150.

Walker, I., & Hulme, C. (1999). Concrete words are easier to recall than abstract words: Evidence for a semantic contribution to short-term serial recall. *Journal of Experimental Psychology: Learning, Memory, & Cognition, 25,* 1256–1271.

Weiss, J. M. (1971). Effects of coping behavior with and without a feedback signal on stress pathology in rats. *Journal of Comparative & Physiological Psychology, 77,* 22–30.

Wickens, D. D., Born, D. G., & Allen, C. K. (1963). Proactive inhibition and item similarity in short-term memory. *Journal of Verbal Learning and Verbal Behavior, 2,* 440–445.

Winer, B. J., Brown, D. R., & Michels, K. M. (1991). *Statistical principles in experimental design* (3rd ed.). New York: McGraw-Hill.

Chapter 14

Barlow, D. H., & Hersen, M. (1984). *Single case experimental designs: Strategies for studying behavior change* (2nd ed.). Boston: Allyn and Bacon.

Boring, E. G. (1957). *History of experimental psychology* (2nd ed.). New York: Appleton-Century-Crofts.

Campbell, D. T., & Stanley, J. C. (1966). *Experimental and quasi-experimental designs for research.* Chicago: Rand McNally.

Dermer, M. L., & Hoch, T. A. (1999). Improving descriptions of single-subject experiments in research texts written for undergraduates. *The Psychological Record, 49,* 49–66.

Ebbinghaus, H. (1913). *On memory: An investigation to experimental psychology* (H. A. Ruger & C. E. Bussenius, Trans.). New York: Columbia University Press. (Original work published 1885).

Ellis, M. V. (1999). Repeated measures designs. *The Counseling Psychologist, 27,* 552–578.

Fechner, G. (1966). *Elements of Psychophysics* (H. E. Adler, Trans.). New York: Holt, Rinehart, and Winston. (Original work published 1860).

Flynn, J. R. (1998). IQ gains over time: Toward finding the causes. In U. Neisser (Ed.), *The rising curve: Long-term gains in IQ and related measures* (pp. 25–66). Washington, DC: American Psychological Association.

Greenhouse, J. B., Stangl, D., & Bromberg, J. (1989). An introduction to survival analysis: Statistical methods for analysis of clinical trial data. *Journal of Consulting and Clinical Psychology, 57,* 536–544.

Gruber, F. A. (1999). Tutorial: Survival analysis—A statistic for clinical, efficacy, and theoretical applications. *Journal of Speech, Language, and Hearing Research, 42,* 432–447.

Hawton, K., Simkin, S., Deeks, J. J., O'Connor, S., Keen, A., Altman, D. G., Philo, G., & Bulstrode, C. (1999). Effects of a drug overdose in a television drama on presentations to hospital for self-poisoning: Time series and questionnaire study. *British Medical Journal, 318,* 972–977.

Koehler, M. J., & Levin, J. R. (1998). Regulated randomization: A potential sharper analytical tool for the multiple-baseline design. *Psychological Methods, 3,* 206–217.

Laberge, B., Gauthier, J. G., Côté, G., Plamondon, J., & Cormier, H. J. (1993). Cognitive-behavioral therapy of panic disorder with secondary major depression: A preliminary investigation. *Journal of Consulting and Clinical Psychology, 61,* 1028–1037.

Lewinsohn, P. M., Rohde, P., Seeley, J. R., & Fischer, S. A. (1993). Age-cohort changes in the lifetime occurrence of depression and other mental disorders. *Journal of Abnormal Psychology, 102,* 110–120.

Luke, D. A., & Homan, S. M. (1998). Time and change: Using survival analysis in clinical assessment and treatment evaluation. *Psychological Assessment, 10,* 360–378.

Morgan, D. L., & Morgan, R. K. (2001). Single-participant research design bringing science to managed care. *American Psychologist, 56,* 119–127.

Sidman, M. (1960). *Tactics of scientific research.* New York: Basic Books.

Singer, J. D., & Willett, J. B. (1991). Modeling the days of our lives: Using survival analysis when designing and analyzing longitudinal studies of duration and timing of events. *Psychological Bulletin, 110,* 268–290.

Skinner, B. F. (1953). Some contributions of an experimental analysis of behavior to psychology as a whole. *American Psychologist, 8,* 30–38.

Stice, E., Killen, J. D., Hayward, C., & Taylor, C. B. (1998). Age of onset for binge eating and purging during late adolescence: A 4-year analysis. *Journal of Abnormal Psychology, 4,* 671–675.

West, S. G., Biesanz, J. C., & Pitts, S. C. (2000). Causal inference and generalization in field settings. In H. T. Reis & C. M. Judd (Eds.), *Handbook of research methods in social and personality psychology* (pp. 40–84). Cambridge, UK: Cambridge University Press.

West, S. G., Hepworth, J. T., McCall, M. A., & Reich, J. W. (1989). An evaluation of Arizona's July 1982 drunk driving law: Effect on the city of Phoenix. *Journal of Applied Social Psychology, 19,* 1212–1237.

Willett, J. B., & Singer, J. D. (1993). Investigating onset, cessation, relapse, and recovery: Why you should, and how you can, use discrete-time survival analysis to examine event occurrence. *Journal of Consulting and Clinical Psychology, 61,* 952–965.

Chapter 15

American Psychiatric Association (1994). *Diagnostic and statistical manual of mental disorders* (4th ed.). Washington, DC: Author.

American Psychological Association (2001). *Publication mannual of the American Psychological Association* (5th ed.). Washington, DC: Author.

Cairns, R. B., Cairns, B. D., Neckerman, H. J., Ferguson, L. L., & et al. (1989). Growth and aggression: I. Childhood to early adolescence. *Developmental Psychology, 25,* 320–330.

Delucchi, K. L. (1993). On the use and misuse of the chi-square. In G. Keren & C. Lewis (Eds.), *A handbook for data analysis in the behavioral sciences: Statistical issues* (pp. 295–320). Hillsdale, NJ: LEA.

Gladstone, G., Parker, G., Wilhelm, K., Mitchell, P., & Austin, M. (1999). Characteristics of depressed patients who report childhood sexual abuse. *American Journal of Psychiatry, 156,* 431–437.

Good, I. J., Grover, T. N., & Mitchell, G. J. (1970). Exact distributions for chi-squared and for the likelihood-ratio statistic for the equiprobable multinomial distribution. *Journal of the American Statistical Association, 32,* 535–548.

Haberman, S. J. (1973). The analysis of residuals in cross-classified tables. *Biometrics, 29,* 205–220.

Mulder, R. T., Beautrais, A. L., Joyce, P. R., & Fergusson, D. M. (1998). Relationship between dissociation, childhood sexual abuse, childhood physical abuse, and mental illness in a general population sample. *American Journal of Psychiatry, 155,* 806–811.

Siegel, S., & Castellan, N. J. (1988). *Nonparametric statistics for the behavioral sciences* (2nd ed.). New York: McGraw-Hill.

Chapter 16

Allumbaugh, D. L., & Hoyt, W. T. (1999). Effectiveness of grief therapy: A meta-analysis. *Journal of Counseling Psychology, 46,* 370–380.

American Psychological Association (2001). *Publication manual of the American Psychological Association* (5th ed.). Washington, DC: Author.

Braver, M. C. W., & Braver, S. L. (1988). Statistical treatment of the Solomon four-group design: A meta-analytic approach. *Psychological Bulletin, 104,* 150–154.

Ehrenberg, A. S. C. (1977). Rudiments of numeracy. *Journal of the Royal Statistical Society A, 140* (Pt. 3), 277–297.

Eisenberger, R., & Armeli, S. (1997). Can salient reward increase creative performance without reducing intrinsic creative interest? *Journal of Personality and Social Psychology, 72,* 652–663.

Kohn, A. (1990). *You know that they say. . . .* New York: Harper Collins.

Kohn, A. (1993). Punished by rewards: *The trouble with gold stars, incentive plans, A's, praise, and other bribes.* Boston: Houghton Mifflin Co.

Kosslyn, S. M. (1994). *Elements of graph design.* New York: Freeman.

Runyon, R. P., Coleman, K. A., & Pittenger, D. J. (2000). *Fundamentals of behavioral statistics* (9th ed.). New York: McGraw-Hill.

Strunk, W., & White, E. B. (1979). *The elements of style* (3rd ed.). New York: Macmillan.

Tufte, E. R. (1983). *The visual display of quantitative information.* Cheshire, CT: Graphics Press.

Tufte, E. R. (1990). *Envisioning information.* Cheshire, CT: Graphics Press.

Twain, M. (1986/1876). *The adventures of Huckleberry Finn.* New York: Penguin.

Wainer, H. (1997). *Visual revelations: Graphical tales of fate and deception from Napoleon Bonaparte to Ross Perot.* New York: Springer-Verlag.

INDEX

Page numbers in **bold** refer to definitions.

Commonly Used Statistics and the Format for Presenting Them in the Text of the Results Section

Descriptive Statistics	Presentation in Text
Mean	$M = 25.67$
Median	$Mdn = 34.56$
Mode	$mode = 45.00$
Standard Deviation	$SD = 1.23$
Standard Error	$SE = 12.01$
Standard Error of Measurement	$SEM = 0.98$

Inferential Statistics	Presentation in Text
ANOVA	$F(2, 25) = 3.82, p = .036$
Chi-Square	$\chi^2(4, N = 55) = 12.02, p = .017$
Mann-Whitney U	$U(12, 15) = 5.67, p < .05$
Pearson's r	$r(98) = .872, p < .001$
Spearman's r	$r_s(74) = -.948, p < .001$
Student's t-ratio	$t(123) = 2.31, p = .023$

General notes regarding statistics in text

❏ The numbers within the parentheses represent the degrees of freedom for the statistic.
❏ Print the exact probability of the observed statistical test unless it is exceptionally small (e.g., $p < .001$) or you cannot determine the exact probability level.
❏ Italicize the letters representing the statistics and probability.
❏ In general, use only two to three numbers to the right of the decimal (e.g., 12.36 rather than 12.357431).

Examples for Formatting the Reference Section of an APA-style Research Report

Journal Articles

Single author:

Flora, S. R. (1990). Undermining intrinsic interest from the standpoint of a behaviorist. *Psychological Record, 40,* 323–346.

Zimmerman, B. J. (1985). The development of "intrinsic" motivation: A social learning analysis. *Annals of Child Development, 2,* 117–160.

Multiple authors:

Balsam, D. P., & Bondy, A. S. (1983). The negative side effects of reward. *Journal of Applied Behavior Analysis, 16,* 283–296.

Hatano, G., Sigler, R. S., Richards, D. D., Inagaki, K., Stavy, R., & Wax, N. (1993). The development of biological knowledge: A multi-national study. *Cognitive Development, 8,* 47–62.

Notes:
❏ Capitalize the first letter of the first word in the title of the article and of the first word following a colon.
❏ Capitalize the first letter of each major word in the name of the journal.
❏ Italicize the title of the journal, the volume number, and commas.
❏ Do not include the issue number unless the journal starts each issue with page 1.
❏ Use a nonbreaking hyphen for the page number to prevent the computer from splitting the numbers across two lines.
❏ If there are six or more authors, use the first author's name and "et al." in the text (e.g., "Hatano et al. (1993) examined . . .").